Praise for

Due Considerations

"Updike's first nonfiction collection in eight years displays breathtaking scope as well as the author's seeming inability to write badly."
—*The New York Times Book Review*

"The bulk of Updike's diligent work through the decades also allows for the extraction of a useful truth: such a quantity of quality is unusual—perhaps especially in book reviewing." —*Harper's Magazine*

"Extraordinary." —*The New York Observer*

"Elegant, imaginative . . . [a] crisp chronicle marvelously enlivened by creative description." —*Financial Times*

"Impossible to resist . . . [Updike] is certainly our greatest living essayist and critic." —*The Buffalo News*

"Sharp . . . graceful . . . elegant . . . [Updike] is a prolific, intelligent and generous critic. . . . For those of us who review books . . . *Due Considerations* is best taken as a master class. For anyone else who loves books, it's simply a treasure trove." —*St. Petersburg Times*

"[Updike] is a master of the arresting phrase and the illuminating definition, as adept at conveying the feel of a book as he is at summarizing its contents. . . . There is an openness to experience in his essays which liberates and exhilarates—especially in contrast to the styles of criticism which prevail elsewhere today." —*The New York Review of Books*

"One of our best novelists proves once again that he's one of our best writers." —*Kirkus Reviews* (starred review)

"[Updike] is perceptive and insightful. . . . This cornucopia of writing by a master will delight many readers." —*Bookpage*

Also by John Updike

POEMS

The Carpentered Hen (1958) • *Telephone Poles* (1963) • *Midpoint* (1969) • *Tossing and Turning* (1977) • *Facing Nature* (1985) • *Collected Poems* (1953–1993) • *Americana* (2001)

NOVELS

The Poorhouse Fair (1959) • *Rabbit, Run* (1960) • *The Centaur* (1963) • *Of the Farm* (1965) • *Couples* (1968) • *Rabbit Redux* (1971) • *A Month of Sundays* (1975) • *Marry Me* (1976) • *The Coup* (1978) • *Rabbit Is Rich* (1981) • *The Witches of Eastwick* (1984) • *Roger's Version* (1986) • *S.* (1988) • *Rabbit at Rest* (1990) • *Memories of the Ford Administration* (1992) • *Brazil* (1994) • *In the Beauty of the Lilies* (1996) • *Toward the End of Time* (1997) • *Gertrude and Claudius* (2000) • *Seek My Face* (2002) • *Villages* (2004) • *Terrorist* (2006)

SHORT STORIES

The Same Door (1959) • *Pigeon Feathers* (1962) • *Olinger Stories* (a selection, 1964) • *The Music School* (1966) • *Bech: A Book* (1970) • *Museums and Women* (1972) • *Problems and Other Stories* (1979) • *Too Far to Go* (a selection, 1979) • *Bech Is Back* (1982) • *Trust Me* (1987) • *The Afterlife* (1994) • *Bech at Bay* (1998) • *Licks of Love* (2000) • *The Complete Henry Bech* (2001) • *The Early Stories: 1953–1975* (2003)

ESSAYS AND CRITICISM

Assorted Prose (1965) • *Picked-Up Pieces* (1975) • *Hugging the Shore* (1983) • *Just Looking* (1989) • *Odd Jobs* (1991) • *Golf Dreams: Writings on Golf* (1996) • *More Matter* (1999) • *Still Looking* (2005)

PLAY

Buchanan Dying (1974)

MEMOIRS

Self-Consciousness (1989)

CHILDREN'S BOOKS

The Magic Flute (1962) • *The Ring* (1964) • *A Child's Calendar* (1965) • *Bottom's Dream* (1969) • *A Helpful Alphabet of Friendly Objects* (1996)

DUE CONSIDERATIONS

John Updike

DUE CONSIDERATIONS

ESSAYS AND CRITICISM

Ballantine Books
New York

2008 Ballantine Books Trade Paperback Edition

Published in the United States by Random House, an imprint of
The Random House Publishing Group, a division of
Random House, Inc., New York.

BALLANTINE and colophon are registered trademarks of
Random House, Inc.

Originally published in hardcover in the United States by
Alfred A. Knopf, a division of Random House, Inc., New York,
and in Canada by Random House of Canada Limited,
Toronto, in 2007.

Library of Congress Cataloging-in-Publication Data
Updike, John.
Due considerations: essays and criticism / by John Updike.
    p.   cm.
Includes index.
ISBN 978-0-345-49900-4
I. Title.
PS3571.P4D84 2007
814'.54—dc22
2007018665

Printed in the United States of America

www.ballantinebooks.com

246897531

Acknowledgments

Grateful acknowledgment is made to the following magazines and publishers, who first printed the pieces specified, sometimes under different titles and in slightly different form:

THE NEW YORKER: Sixty of the sixty-two book reviews, plus "Back from China," "A Sense of Change," "The Future of Faith," "Invisible Cathedral," "Late Works," "Early Employments and Inklings," "Magnum Opus," and Talk of the Town pieces on William Maxwell ("Maxwell's Touch"), John F. Kennedy, Jr., and the September 11, 2001, World Trade Center disaster.

THE NEW YORK REVIEW OF BOOKS: "A Tribute to Saul Steinberg," "Dürer's Passions," "The Thing Itself," "The Imaginary Builder," "On Literary Biography" (as "One Cheer for Literary Biography"), and introductions to *Seven Men, The Eighth Day, The Portrait of a Lady, The Blithedale Romance, The Golden West,* and *Is Sex Necessary?*

THE NEW YORK TIMES: "A Case for Books" (as "Books, Stay Yet a While"), "Looking Back to Now," "Ted Williams" (as "The Batter Who Mattered"), interview by Henry Bech (as "Questions of Character: There's No Wounded Ego like a Wounded Superego"), and "An Account of My Childhood Reading."

THE NEW YORK TIMES BOOK REVIEW: "Metropolitan Art."

LONDON TIMES: "Property and Presumption."

NEW YORK: "West 155th Street."

HOUGHTON MIFFLIN: Notes to three short stories chosen for a *Best* collection.

UNIVERSITY OF SOUTH CAROLINA PRESS: "On Literary Biography," as a small book printed in an edition of five hundred.

FORBES PUBLICATIONS: "The Tried and the Trēowe" and "Ten Epochal Moments in the American Libido."

NATURAL HISTORY: "A Layman's Scope."

OUTSIDE: "Hydrophobia."

LIFE: "My Life in Poker" and "Summer Love."

ARCHITECTURAL DIGEST: "My Life in Cars."

SÜDDEUTSCHE ZEITUNG: "William Shawn."

PUBLIC AFFAIRS: "The New Yorker" in *American Greats*, edited by Robert Wilson.

PROCEEDINGS OF THE AMERICAN ACADEMY OF ARTS AND LETTERS: "The Academy As It Was and Is" and the memorial tribute to Wright Morris.

YALE UNIVERSITY PRESS: "Ernest Hemingway," in *American Characters: Selections from the National Portrait Gallery, Accompanied by Literary Portraits*, edited by R.W.B. Lewis and Nancy Lewis.

THE OXFORD AMERICAN: Note on Eudora Welty.

BOSTON GLOBE: "11/22/63."

EVERYMAN'S LIBRARY: Preface to *The Mabinogion;* contribution to *There Are Kermodians*.

THE MODERN LIBRARY: Introduction to *The Blithedale Romance*.

PRINCETON UNIVERSITY PRESS: Introduction to *Walden*.

OXFORD UNIVERSITY PRESS: Introduction to *The Portrait of a Lady*.

HESPERUS PRESS LTD.: Forewords to *The Diary of Adam and Eve and Other Adamic Stories* and *The Rich Boy*.

HARPERCOLLINS: Introductions to new editions of *The Eighth Day, The Letters of E. B. White*, and *Is Sex Necessary?*

DAVID R. GODINE, PUBLISHER: Introduction to *The Golden West: Hollywood Stories*.

THE LIBRARY OF AMERICA: Introduction to *Karl Shapiro: Selected Poems*.

POMEGRANATE COMMUNICATIONS INC.: Introduction to *Elephant House, or, The Home of Edward Gorey*.

RANDOM HOUSE: Introduction to *Christmas at The New Yorker: Stories, Poems, Humor, and Art*.

BLACK DOG & LEVENTHAL: Introduction to the 1955–64 section of *The Complete Cartoons of The New Yorker*.

ABRAMS: "Thurber's Art," in *Cartoon America: Comic Art in the Library of Congress;* introduction to *Wolf Kahn's America*.

ARTISAN: Introduction to *The World of William Steig*.

LORD JOHN PRESS: "The Would-Be Animator" in *Lord John Film Festival;* foreword to *Humor in Fiction*.

FANTAGRAPHICS: Introduction to *Poor Arnold's Almanac*.

RIZZOLI: Introduction to *Chip Kidd: Book One: 1986–2006*.

MONTSERRAT COLLEGE OF ART: Foreword to *My Father's House*, catalogue of a show by Will Barnet.

HARVARD REVIEW: "A Reminiscence of Hyman Bloom."

MFA PUBLICATIONS: Foreword to their edition of *Just Looking*.

STACKPOLE BOOKS: Foreword to their edition of *Buchanan Dying*.

FRANKLIN LIBRARY: "Special Message" for their edition of *Gertrude and Claudius*.

PRE-TEXTOS: Preface to *Poemas 1953–1999*.

EASTON PRESS: Foreword to their edition of *Licks of Love*.

QUALITY PAPERBACK CLUB: Comment on "Your Lover Just Called," in the anthology *This Is My Best*.

INSIDE BORDERS: "Recurrent Characters."

OAK KNOLL PRESS: Foreword to my own bibliography.

YALE LITERARY MAGAZINE: "Who Have Been Your Masters?"

BOOK WORLD: Comment on Books that Serve as Comfort.

GQ: Comment on My Favorite Year.

ALLURE: "The Beautiful."

PHILADELPHIA: "My Philadelphia."

THE IMPROPER BOSTONIAN: "Why Do I Live in New England?"

THOMSON CUSTOM PUBLISHING: Statement for *There Is No Other Story: Ethics, Literature, and Theory*.

NATIONAL PUBLIC RADIO: "This I Believe."

Grateful acknowledgment is made to the following for permission to reprint previously published material:

ALASTAIR REID AND AGENCIA LITERARIA CARMEN BALCELLS: Excerpt from "A Street in Cordoba" ("En una calle de Córdoba") by Álvaro Mutis, translated by Alastair Reid (*World Literature Today*, vol. 77, July–September 2003, pages 12–22), copyright © 2003 by Alastair Reid. All rights reserved. Reprinted by permission of Alastair Reid and Agencia Literaria Carmen Balcells.

FARRAR, STRAUS & GIROUX, LLC: Excerpts from "Aubade," "Annus Mirabilis," "Explosion," "Faith Healing," "Grief," "Home Is So Sad," "Is It for Now or for Always," "The Mower," "The North Ship," "Pour Away That Youth," "This Be the Verse," "The Trees," and "The Whitsun Weddings" from *Collected Poems* by Philip Larkin (Farrar, Straus & Giroux, LLC, New York, 2004); excerpt from "Helen's Religion" from *Road Side Dog* by Czeslaw Milosz, copyright © 1998 by Czeslaw Milosz. Reprinted by permission of Farrar, Straus & Giroux, LLC.

HAROLD OBER ASSOCIATES: Excerpt from "The Irenicon" from *Poems* by Karl Shapiro, copyright © 1978 by Karl Shapiro; excerpt from "Bill Williams" from *The Old Horsefly* by Karl Shapiro, copyright © 1992 by Karl Shapiro; and excerpts from *The Younger Son* by Karl Shapiro, copyright © 1988 by Karl Shapiro. Reprinted by permission of Harold Ober Associates.

HARPERCOLLINS PUBLISHERS: Excerpt from "Natural History" from *Poems and Sketches* by E. B. White, copyright © 1929 by E. B. White. Reprinted by permission of HarperCollins Publishers.

THE MARVELL PRESS: Excerpts from "Absences," "Age," "At Grass," "Church Going," "Coming," "Deceptions," "Dry-Point," "Going," "If, My Darling," "Lines on a Young Lady's Photograph Album," "Maiden Name," "Next, Please," "No Road," "Places, Loved Ones," "Reasons for Attendance," "Skin," "Toads," "Triple Time," "Wants," and "Wedding-Wind" from *The Less Deceived* by Philip Larkin. Reprinted by permission of The Marvell Press, England and Australia.

RANDOM HOUSE, INC.: Excerpt from "Musée des Beaux Arts" from *Collected Poems* by W. H. Auden, copyright © 1940 and renewed 1968 by W. H. Auden. Reprinted by permission of Random House, Inc.

to DAVID REMNICK
and HENRY FINDER
who kept me in the game
into the late innings

Contents

TRIBUTES AND SHORT TAKES

Considering Books

INTRODUCTIONS

MONUMENTS

THURBER AND WHITE

AMERICAN FICTION

ENGLISH FICTION

IN ENGLISH BUT NOT ENGLISH

IN OTHER TONGUES

NON-FICTION

LITERARY BIOGRAPHY

ART

Personal Considerations

Preface

> What terrifies me now . . . is the whole question of catching & meeting & proceeding with the least tension (or emotion!) along docks, railway-platforms, ups or downs of any kind where being *due* at some moment plays a part.
>
> —HENRY JAMES, to Edith Wharton, 1912

BILLS COME DUE; dues must be paid. After eight years, I was due for another collection of non-fictional prose. I had hoped that, thanks to the dwindling powers of old age, the bulk would be significantly smaller than that of the two previous assemblages *Odd Jobs* (1991) and *More Matter* (1999). My hope, as I sorted and rooted through my deposits of old tearsheets and typescripts ("hard copies," we call them now), was slowly dashed. There was less, but not significantly less. There was no escaping the accumulated weight of my daily exertions.

The pieces gathered here, in my sixth such volume since *Assorted Prose* (1965), are end-products of an adolescent yearning to become a professional writer, or at least to enter in some guise into the mass of printed material that hung above the middle-browed middle class in the middle of the last century like a vast cloud gently raining ink. There were newspapers, both morning and afternoon, and magazines, printed on shiny paper like *Collier's* and *Life* or on duller stock like *Scribner's* or *Ellery Queen's Mystery Magazine*. As an office boy at the *Reading* (Pa.) *Eagle*, I saw how men in green eyeshades called down a clattering hail of brass matrices at their tall Linotype machines. I saw how comic strips arrived as bundled cardboard intaglios, of the same pulpy substance as egg cartons, which were flooded with hot lead and blended into curved plates clamped onto thunderously spinning rotary presses that hurled news and amusement to the far corners of diamond-shaped Berks County. Somewhere, in some manner, whether by wielding a pen precariously loaded with India ink or by pounding at keys that dented the inked ribbon of a typewriter, the boy I was sought to work his way into publication and a wider distribution than was afforded by what the scowling elders of his community called an "honest" job.

In that still-industrial era, there were tweedy exemplars, depicted in whiskey ads and on the cover of weekly journals like *The Saturday Review of Literature*, of The Professional Writer—Hemingway, Steinbeck, Thornton Wilder, Sinclair Lewis, Pearl Buck. There were genial exponents of the written word like Clifton Fadiman and Bennett Cerf, who as well as heading up Random House and editing volumes of the Modern Library assembled books of humorous anecdotes about celebrities and was himself one, ebulliently appearing on the early television show *What's My Line?* Television was soon to eclipse print's inky cloud with its magnetic flare of electrons, pulling millions from their reading chairs to the viewing couch. The older electric media, radio and the movies, coexisted more peaceably with the literary world. Movies were visited for a secluded two hours and then left behind with the empty Good & Plenty box, and the radio demanded only a corner of your attention—you could read a comic book as you listened. Robert Benchley for a time had his own radio show and was a sort of movie star. The Algonquin Round Table was an off-Broadway show in continual performance, it seemed. But by the time, in 1955, that I got to New York, with a professional perch on the eighteenth floor of 25 West Forty-third Street, and a steel desk and a daily replenished supply of sharp pencils, the Round Table was cultural history and Benchley had imbibed himself to death, his long-planned tome on the reign of Queen Anne never written. A particular party was over. As its celebrants were wearily bunching around the down elevator button, I panted up the stairs, résumé in hand, to audition for the roles of "humorist" or "professional writer."

In my naïve picture of the American economy, a writer developed certain verbal skills and produced certain saleable artifacts—"literary products," as my tax accountant annually states on the top line of Schedule C. The writer existed on an edge of his society from which its operations could be observed at his leisure, and he or she didn't stray beyond that edge into hostility, exile, and isolation. The dark side of modernism was just a rumor to me, though I had read *The Waste Land* in the Reading Public Library and dipped into the opening pages of *Ulysses*, much as one wades barefoot, in June, into the still-icy Atlantic and quickly retreats with aching ankles and a virtuous sense of initiation. The English department of Harvard College immersed me in an ocean of written classics, and when, six years after my graduation, I became a book reviewer, I was still wet behind the ears. Up to 1960, I had made my living selling short stories and light verse, for which there was a significant but fickle and possibly fading market. Reviewing books for *The New Yorker* was a way of maintaining a financial inflow, and getting into print, and keeping abreast, unsystematically, of what was happening in the fabled, embattled world of letters. There was something impure and even treacherous, I was warned, about a "creative" writer dealing in literary judgment and theory, but I brashly believed that I could protect the frail creator inside me from the bullying critic.

For nearly two years in the mid-Fifties I had worked cheerfully on *The New Yorker*'s Talk of the Town section, accepting the assignments that came down to me. To read a book and write about it was a task I could carry out far from the city, in exurban New England, where I had settled in hope of consorting with Americans more representative and relaxed than Manhattanites. A book review, in the spacious magazine that William Shawn edited back then, should be, he said, "something more"— an essay of sorts, with personal and humorous riffs allowed. He believed in assigning non-fiction books to non-experts in the concerned field, and I versatilely qualified as a non-expert in almost everything. Writing a book review felt physically close to writing a story—same blank paper inserted in the rubbery typewriter platen, same *rat-tat-tat* sound of impatient, inspired *x*-ing out. There was a similar need for a punchy beginning, a clinching ending, and a misty stretch in between that would connect the two. A review writer was generally safe—safe from rejection (though it could happen), and safe, as a judge himself, from judgment, though an occasional reader mailed in a correction or a complaint. The reviewer's services, in a world overwhelmed by books, loomed as patently necessary: to weed, to cull, to impose order upon profusion. The aim of art is to make a virtue of necessity. Two aesthetic impulses vividly experienced in my childhood go into a volume like this one: the collecting instinct, that delights in sets of things, and the wish to arrive, through small improvements, at a final form. The improvements are not all the author's: most of the texts collected here benefitted from the zealous scrutiny of *The New Yorker*'s checking department, and from the sensitive ear and grammatical scruples of editor Ann Goldstein. My editor at Knopf, Judith Jones, and copyeditor Terry Zaroff-Evans contributed their own refinements.

As I passed the sixty-two book reviews in this collection under my eyes again, I wondered if their customary geniality, almost effusive in the presence of a foreign writer or a factual topic, didn't somewhat sour when faced with a novel by a fellow-countryman. In the section "American Fiction," between the unfinished novel by Edmund Wilson and the recent E. L. Doctorow, there is little easy praise and much testy quibbling. I bristled at implausibilities that from an alien source wouldn't have raised an eyebrow. Why did I so humorlessly resist the cartoonish brio of Don DeLillo's Bruce Wayne–like protagonist's oft-interrupted limo ride westward on Forty-seventh Street? Why was I such a rudely squirming student in the classrooms of Denis Johnson's and Norman Rush's teacher-heroes, and sympathized so stingily with their romantic and spiritual dilemmas? Familiarity with American dilemmas and milieux bred, if not contempt, a possessive pickiness. Having begun my side career as a critic determined to model decent manners, I wound up as ill-tempered as the next. Never mind: a book reviewer must write what is felt at the time, when impressions are still warm and malleable, and leave second thoughts to prefaces.

A masochistic affection attaches to the reviews that worked me the hardest, in hoisting and in summarizing such thousand-page brutes as the complete works of Isaac Babel and Robert Alter's new translation of the Pentateuch. Ralph Waldo Emerson and Oz, indigenous inventions like the apple corer, were a comfort to handle. I had never intended to cope with the sinking of the *Lusitania* or Coco Chanel's unsinkable career, but am glad I did; out-of-the-way topics inject some revivifying new cells into the brain. And, complain though I do in this volume's opening essay about literary biography, I seem to have embraced happily enough the samples of the genre reviewed, from Byron to Iris Murdoch, and considered with extra affection the cautionary lives of Kierkegaard, Proust, and John O'Hara.

A critic, most gratefully regarded when he dismisses a new book from any obligation of ours to read it, performs a nobler social service in urging authors upon us. The baker's dozen of introductions that open the "Considering Books" section "anchor," as they say, this voluminous catchall. Giving Thoreau, Hawthorne, Mark Twain, and Henry James each their just deserts tests an American's mettle, and reacquaints him with what is best and most enduring in his native tradition. Thornton Wilder and Karl Shapiro, though not forgotten, have slipped in status, and it was with compensatory care that I recalled their virtues and mischievous quiddities. As the editor as well as the introducer of the Library of America edition of Shapiro's selected poems, I entered into the poet's corpus with the power to choose my favorites for a volume likely to stay in print for some duration; Shapiro's widow, Sophie Wilkins, an irrepressible letter-writer, encouraged me with facts, opinions, and gratitude before she herself died. Shapiro's poems spoke to me when few other twentieth-century poems did, and it was thrilling to put my hand, however lightly, to the work of their continued availability. The brash critic in me turns shy at the threshold of poetry; this book's only other venture into that hallowed precinct involves Philip Larkin, another singer of the mundane—of modest phenomena dignified by intent observation and strict metrics.

"Five Essays" gathers the few articles—as opposed to reviews or stories—published by *The New Yorker* in these eight years. "Back from China" was my idea, as a way of recovering some of my travel costs. "A Sense of Change" arose from the context of a special "Money" issue. "The Future of Faith" was proposed to me as a topic as the year 2000 approached. I resisted and even resented baring something as private and, however tenaciously held, as nebulous as a religious attitude; yet declining the assignment seemed a cop-out—a spurning of what, in Christian terms, might be construed as a "call." I fell short, I fear, for born-again and neo-orthodox readers, but did my level-headed best, dredging up more fin-de-siècle history than *The New Yorker* could use, and providing a personal epiphany from the depths of a wet night in Florence. My most enduring memory of the weeks when I carried the responsibility of this topic in my head is of the dreary, even hellish aspect the Venice Biennale presented in the light of old-time religions. Mockingly, monotonously, the various national pavilions taunted their visitors with absurdity and atheism. The giddy exuberance of Dada and the wooden humanism of Communist posters were no more, leaving the surly fury, the hostile irony, of deprived children. Science, assuming God to be dead, makes steady progress along the cleared ground, and Western governments benefit from a reduction of theocratic imperatives, but art, it appears, is inconsolable; it probes the God-shaped hole in the universe like a tongue compulsively seeking the soft-rimmed crater of an extraction. To shift the metaphor: it keeps rubbing our noses in it.

"Invisible Cathedral" was not, as you might think, a further discourse on spiritual matters but my response to an editorial invitation to inspect the freshly erected but as yet unopened new Museum of Modern Art. My impressions, meliorated by the jolly clatter of work in progress, were modified by later visits and find expression in an italic afterword. "Late Works" was my idea. It gave me a lot of trouble; there is no end of late works, and by the time I had emerged, scratched and muddy, from what Henry Finder, at *The New Yorker*, dryly called "the Shakespearean thicket," there was scarcely time to take up more than a few additional authors, and to draw a few shaky conclusions.

Even though my publisher has graciously and recently published a collection of my art reviews from *The New York Review of Books* (*Still Looking*, 2005), three more are included here—three which I felt could be adequately ornamented, as were some in *More Matter*, with black-and-white illustrations. The concluding section of *Due Considerations*, much as in its predecessor accumulations, preserves brief writings, autobiographical in tint, from an antic assortment of publications. More than one critic has complained of my including such trivia in collections with pretensions, on other pages, to gravity; but where else would I put them, in final form? A drop of truth, of lived experience, glistens in each. They underline the personal note that all essays and criticism, even those lacking a single first-person pronoun, contain. The joy of fiction, its liberation and challenge, comes with the author's standing aside from his own life and trying to create a freestanding image of other lives in action. The human event in non-fiction considerations like these is the exchange, implicit if not explicit, between reader and writer—one witness to the basic miracles of existence and consciousness offering his testimony to another such witness. Not only the Devil should be given his due.

J. U.

Everything Considered

ON LITERARY BIOGRAPHY

There never was a good biography of a good novelist. There couldn't be. He is too many people, if he's any good.
— F. SCOTT FITZGERALD, in his notebooks

Poets don't have biographies. Their work is their biography.
— OCTAVIO PAZ, "A Note to Himself"

THE MAIN QUESTION concerning literary biography is, surely, Why do we need it at all? When an author has devoted his life to expressing himself, and, if a poet or a writer of fiction, has used the sensations and critical events of his life as his basic material, what of significance can a biographer add to the record? Most writers lead quiet lives or, even if they don't, are of interest to us because of the words they set down in what had to have been quiet moments. Regardless of what fascinated his contemporaries, Byron interests us now because of *Don Juan* and those other poems that still sing, and, secondarily, because of his dashing, spirited letters. His physical beauty, his poignant limp, the scandalous collapse of his marriage and his flight from England as a social outcast, his picturesque European dissipations, his generous involvement in the cause of Greek independence, and his tragically youthful death at Missolonghi in 1824—all this sensational stuff would be buried in the mustiest archives of history did not Byron's literary achievement distinguish him from the scores of similarly vexed and dynamic men of this turbulent Romantic era. By his words he still lives, and they give the impetus to the

A talk given on November 13, 1998, at the University of South Carolina, in Columbia, in honor of the two hundredth volume produced by the *Dictionary of Literary Biography*. A less discursive version appeared in *The New York Review of Books*, January 21, 1999.

periodic biographies of which last year's, by Phyllis Grosskurth, will soon be followed, next year, by Benita Eisler's.*

I am not an especial devotee of literary biography. Indeed, I have my reasons to distrust it. Yet, looking back, I see that I have reviewed a fair amount of it, and, in addition, have read an amount on my own initiative, to satisfy my own curiosity. Although one rarely sees literary biography on the best-seller list,† a prodigious amount of it is produced, some of it at prodigious length. The estimable British biographer Michael Holroyd topped his two-volume biography of Lytton Strachey with a three-volume biography of George Bernard Shaw. Leon Edel's biography of Henry James took twenty-one years in the writing and occupies five volumes, of which the last is the bulkiest. In my barn I keep those books which, arriving free at the house, I deem too precious and potentially useful to give to the local church fair, and yet not so valuable as to win space on the packed shelves within my book-burdened domicile. Venturing out to my slapdash barn shelves, I note works of roughly five hundred pages on Edmund Wilson, Simone Weil, and Joyce Cary; six-hundred-page tomes on Oscar Wilde and Ivy Compton-Burnett; six hundred and fifty pages on Norman Mailer; seven hundred each on Jean Genet and Samuel Beckett; an eight-hundred-page work on Zola; and, the heavyweight champion in this vicinity, twelve hundred pages on the not notably prolific James Thurber. Length of life bears some relation to length of book; in the department of doomed poets, Sylvia Plath, dead at thirty, received three hundred fifty pages of attention, whereas Anne Sexton, who lived to be forty-six, one hundred more. However, Delmore Schwartz had the fifty-three years of his life compressed into a mere four hundred pages, as did the drink-raddled but surprisingly long-lived Dorothy Parker. And these are just the tenants in my barn.

My opening question—*Why do we need it at all?*—focuses us on the motives of the consumers, not the producers. Some literary biographies begin as Ph.D. theses; others as the personal accounts of a friend or acquaintance of the author. In general, people write books because they think they have some light to shed and because they aspire to the rewards and satisfactions of having written a book. We *read*, those of us who do, literary biographies for a variety of reasons, of which the first and perhaps the most worthy is the desire to prolong and extend our intimacy with the author—to partake again, from another angle, of the joys we have expe-

---

*See pp. 501–11.

†"They don't sell," my late friend the poet and book editor Peter Davison once flatly reassured me.

rienced within the author's oeuvre, in the presence of a voice and mind we have come to love.

An example of such a prolongation is George D. Painter's two-volume biography of Marcel Proust, which I read as a young man not long emerged from the full stretch of *Remembrance of Things Past*, intoxicated and thirsty for more. Painter's biography, unprecedented in its attempt to treat Proust's life with definitive completeness, allows us to enter the vast mansion of the novel by a back door, as it were, an approach that turns solid and hard and definite what in the novel was large and vague and inconsecutively arranged and beautifully charged with Proust's poetic sensibility. Painter must use research and investigation to build what Proust constructed out of his memory, but it is recognizably the same edifice, with some practical additions. Painter restores great omissions, such as the writer's younger brother Robert, and is frank and analytic where Proust was evasive, as in the matter of his narrator's sexual preference. The enchanted Combray, where little Marcel is fed a tea-soaked madeleine by his Aunt Léonie and waits with desperate longing for the bell on the garden gate to signify that Monsieur Swann has left and his mother is free to come upstairs and give her son a good-night kiss— Combray becomes Illiers, a town on the map, not far from Chartres, with a distinct history, cartography, and set of houses. Aunt Léonie, we are told, was based, almost without modification, on Proust's father's sister Elizabeth Amiot; her house still stands, and Painter describes little Marcel's bedroom with some of Proust's words but in an altogether more factual accent: "His bed was screened by high white curtains, and covered in the daytime with flowered quilts, embroidered counterpanes and cambric pillowcases which he had to remove and drape over a chair, 'where they consented to spend the night,' before he could go to bed. On a bedside table stood a blue glass tumbler and sugar-basin, with a water-jug to match, which his aunt always told Ernestine to empty on the day after his arrival, 'because the child might spill it.' On the mantelpiece was a clock muttering under a glass bell, so heavy that whenever the clock ran down they had to send for the clockmaker to wind it again; on the armchairs were little white antimacassars crocheted with roses, 'not without thorns,' since they stuck to him whenever he sat down . . ." and so on, in a strange but pleasing transposition of the Proustian world into our own. The schematic principle of the two "ways" whereby Proust organized his narrator's massive pilgrimage is sharply brought down to earth. Painter writes:

> To the child Marcel the two favourite walks of the family seemed to be in diametrically opposite directions, so that no two points in the world could

be so utterly separated as their never-reached destinations. Whether they left the house by the front door or by the garden-gate, they would turn one way for Méréglise and the other way for Saint-Eman. . . . In his novel Proust called Méréglise "Méséglise," for euphony; and as the way there went by the Pré Catalan, which he had transformed into Swann's park, he was able to say with truth that it was also Swann's Way.

The biography becomes, then, a way of re-experiencing the novel, with a closeness, and a delight in seeing imagined details conjured back into real ones, that only this particular writer and his vast autobiographical masterpiece could provide. Lovers of Proust will be inevitably drawn to Painter because it is more of the same, mirrored back into reality. Richard Ellmann's superb biography of James Joyce, though also dealing with a concentrated and highly personal oeuvre, cannot quite offer us such a mirroring, though its chapter epigraphs, ingeniously chosen quotations from Joyce, make glittering reflective shards. We read Ellmann not only to revisit Joyce's Dublin but to understand how Joyce, modernism's wonder-worker, did it—how did he produce from the drab facts of the provincial, sodden, priest-ridden Irish capital such rare and comprehensive art as is contained in *Dubliners*, *A Portrait of the Artist as a Young Man*, *Ulysses*, and *Finnegans Wake*? What I remember from my reading, years ago, in Ellmann's eight hundred pages is that *Ulysses* first came to Joyce as a short story, one more sketch of a Dubliner, and that during its seven-year composition, even to within a few weeks of its publication day, the author in his European exile pestered his relatives and friends back in Dublin for local details. He wrote his aunt Josephine Murray, concerning the Powells and the Dillons, models for Molly Bloom's family: "Get an ordinary sheet of foolscap and scribble any God damn drivel you may remember about these people." He asked her such relentlessly circumstantial questions as "Is it possible for an ordinary person to climb over the area railings of no 7 Eccles Street, either from the path or the steps, lower himself from the lowest part of the railings till his feet are within 2 feet or 3 of the ground and drop unhurt?" *Ulysses*, confronting the banality of modern life, compels quantities of drivel into a Thomistically schematic mold that parodies the incidents of the *Odyssey*; an excess of matter is heroically matched by an excess of form.

Perhaps only writers are interested in the details of craft, and how others manage the cunning dishevelment of composition. But of literary biographies I tend to remember curious methodological details: Ivy Compton-Burnett wrote sitting at one end of a sofa and stored the accumulating composition under a sofa cushion; Edith Wharton wrote in bed and threw her pages on the floor for a secretary to pick up and transcribe;

Joyce Cary worked at whatever scene of a novel came to him and trusted them to all tie up at the end; Hemingway wrote with freshly sharpened pencils while standing at a tall desk; Nabokov wrote on three-by-five index cards; John Keats would put on his best clothes before sitting down to write a poem; Henry James, after he suffered an attack of writer's cramp, began to dictate to a typist, and his later style was born in the dutiful transcription of his spoken longueurs, qualifications, and colloquialisms.

The question *How did he or she do it?* takes, in the case of William Shakespeare, the more drastic form *Did he do it?* A few years ago I went out and—always a reluctant move for a writer—purchased a book, Dennis Kay's 1992 biography of Shakespeare. I was interested to see what a modern scholar could assemble of evidence regarding the historical identity of the greatest writer in English. I was persuaded, as I had expected to be, that the son of a small-town burgess and high bailiff, an eldest son presumably educated in the strenuous Latin curriculum of the King's New School in Stratford, and evidently enlisted in a shotgun marriage at the tender age of eighteen, might go to London and become an actor and playwright and, in a career little more than twenty years long, write the greatest plays and some of the greatest poetry in the language. Unlike certain devotees of the nobility, I have never had any problem with the idea that a child of the middling provincial gentry (Shakespeare's mother was an Arden, a family of prosperous farmers) might enter the theatrical profession and spin a literary universe out of his dramatic flair, opportune learning, and country-bred street-smarts. Robert Greene's famous calumny, of "an upstart Crow, beautified with our feathers," who "supposes he is as well able to bombast out a blank verse as the best of you," fits the case perfectly. Shabby gentility has ever been the cradle of upstart writers. Nevertheless, there is a worrisome disproportion between the meagre verifiable biographical facts and the tremendous literary events associated with Shakespeare's name. Something of the same disproportion affects the case of Jane Austen, another exalted literary performer about whom we seem to know too little, so that the recent biography by Claire Tomalin must pad its substance with a wealth of detail about the historical period in which Austen lived.

Literary biography in all cases runs up against this limit of determinism: there is no clear reason why one secluded clergyman's daughter should have been a literary genius while hundreds of others were not. Certain generalizations might be made, in retrospect, about the flowering of, say, Elizabethan poetry or Greek drama or the Russian novel, but the appearance of a great individual remains an indeterminate matter of microcosmic luck and will. The cultural situation at the turn of the last century might be said to have been sickly; but Yeats and Proust and Joyce all took their beginnings in it. To quote an old couplet of my own:

> *Fin-de-siècle* sickliness became
> High-stepping Modernism, then went lame.

We read literary biography, often, in a diagnostic mood, as if dealing with a ward of sick men and women. Psychoanalytical theories of compensation and Edmund Wilson's moving essay "The Wound and the Bow" have alerted biographers to the relation of creative drive to human disabilities. Any biographer of Kafka must deal, for example, with the subject's insomnia, his unnatural awe of his father, his ambivalence toward his own Jewishness, and his inability, until fatally weakened by tuberculosis, to achieve a liaison with a woman—the entire psychological paralysis, in short, dramatized in Kafka's grave comedies of modern bafflement. Our mid-nineteenth-century giants Melville and Hawthorne, linked by an uneasy friendship, challenge any biographer with the mysteries of their affective lives. Melville's mental fragility, his homoerotic vein, his inadequacies as a husband and a father hardly fit with the humor and vigor of his best creations and the toughness that saw him through a longish life loaded with disappointments. And Hawthorne, who spent the years of his youth haunting Salem, writing in an attic, walking out mostly at dusk, chiefly consorting with an eccentrically shy mother and a strong-minded sister who was, it has been speculated, a virtual wife to him—how does this strangeness feed into the strangeness of his work, lending it a shadowy intensity and an evasive reliance upon whimsy and the play of fancy? The vocabularies of psychoanalysis and of literary analysis become increasingly entwined; though we must not forget that these invalids receive our attention because of the truth and poetry and entertainment to be found in their creations. A wound existed, but also a strong bow, and a target was struck.

From clinical examinations it is not a far step to those biographies, of which Lytton Strachey is the patron saint, that ridicule and denigrate their subjects. We read them, perhaps, in order to feel superior to well-known writers. Mark Schorer is supposed to have detested Sinclair Lewis by the time he finished his bulky biography of the man, and James Atlas could not have felt much more kindly toward Delmore Schwartz. I happened to review Jeffrey Meyers's 1994 biography of F. Scott Fitzgerald, and with your indulgence quote my review:

Before Mr. Meyers assembled his brief, we never knew quite how nasty a drunk Fitzgerald was. He repaid Gerald and Sara Murphy's elegant hospitality by "throwing Sara's gold-flecked Venetian wineglasses over the garden wall" and, when banned for this outrage, threw a can of garbage onto their patio while they were dining. As he and some friends were leaving the Casino at Juan-les-Pins, an old Frenchwoman held out a tray of nuts and candies, and Fitzgerald kicked the tray right out of her hands. He picked quarrels and started fistfights, which he usually got the worse of. A fierce malice and resentment emerged in the guise of pranks and teasing. He wrote in lipstick on the expensive dress of his friend John Peale Bishop's wife; dining with Hemingway and Edmund Wilson in New York, he turned the occasion into a revel of self-abasement. According to Wilson's journal: "Scott with his head down on the table between us like the dormouse at the Mad Tea Party—lay down on floor, went to can and puked—alternately made us hold his hand and asked us whether we liked him and insulted us."

Now, after reading such a summation, don't we feel released from ever having to take Scott Fitzgerald seriously again? But Mr. Meyers at least offers a medical excuse—Fitzgerald, like Poe, he asserts, suffered from hypoglycemia.* Michael Sheldon, in his 1995 biography of Graham Greene, offers no excuse for his subject, whom he indignantly portrays as an insincere Catholic, a faithless husband, a sexual masochist, a sadistic prankster, a burnt-out talent, and, in two veiled and hedged charges that mark some sort of sensationalist low point in literary biography, the actual murderer of a dismembered woman found in Brighton in 1930 and, in collaboration with his close friend Kim Philby, a traitor to England and the free world! Furthermore, Sheldon claims, Greene consorted with dictators and "rich men who enjoyed idle jests."

Such an assault, however, comes from a researcher who never met the subject, who in turn is safely dead, beyond personal hurt or recourse to lawsuit. Recent years in America have given rise to what we might call the Judas biography, in which a former spouse or friend of a living writer confides to print an intimate portrait less flattering than the subject might have hoped for. Claire Bloom, the ex-wife of Philip Roth, portrays him as having been, as their marriage rapidly unravelled, neurasthenic to the point of hospitalization, adulterous, callously selfish, and financially vindictive. Paul Theroux, finding himself snubbed by his friend and mentor of thirty years, recounts all he can remember about V. S. Naipaul, including a host of racist, misogynistic, cruel, and vain remarks made in their—Naipaul must have thought—private conversations. Joyce Maynard fascinatingly recalls, as part of her rather arduous self-development, her affair with J. D. Salinger and thus lifts the curtain on the most cele-

---

*A diagnosis not concurred in by Matthew Bruccoli, among other Fitzgerald experts.

brated privacy in America. Salinger is revealed as a food crank, a keen student of homeopathic medicine, a Reichian, a fan of old movies and present-day television, a man full of scornful opinions and rather creepily fond of very young girls. Maynard describes her inability to have genital sex with him and his insistence on her providing oral sex instead; she quotes, with more pertinence than perhaps she realizes, Salinger's saying, "It's a goddam embarrassment, publishing. The poor boob who lets himself in for it might as well walk down Madison Avenue with his pants down." Another cherished privacy, meanwhile, that of long-time *New Yorker* editor William Shawn, has been violated by Lillian Ross in her rapturous recounting of *their* affair. And, hot off the press, Rosemary Mahoney's *A Likely Story: One Summer with Lillian Hellman*, in a remarkable reprise of a teen-age housekeeper's casually harsh observations and easily wounded vanity, presents the septuagenarian Hellman as fearful, fussy, inconsiderate of her help, obsessed with food, hard-drinking, and physically hideous, with "the big beaky face of a sea turtle at rest on the ocean floor, dreaming and digesting, with one dyspeptic eye half open in a sluggish scan for predators and perhaps more food."

Insofar as we are consumers of such books, or of reviews of them, we are collaborators in their creation. As lovers of literature, we are lovers of truth, and regret the loss of, say, the letters and papers that Henry James and Walt Whitman burned as their ends approached; we would like to read the journals that Sylvia Plath kept in her darkest months and that her surviving spouse, the late Ted Hughes, apparently destroyed. Contrariwise, the reputation of Samuel Johnson would still be high had not Boswell spent so many informal hours with him; but drier, I dare say, without that close-up biography, and much less lively. Viewing the intimate underside of writers we have read is exciting. Even when the information has already been shaped into fiction, the revelations of another party, because less artful, seem more authentic. I raise the possibility that we resent a fiction writer's manipulation of his private life, including the private lives of those around him, and rejoice when he or she loses control of what is to be revealed.

In this art-wary age, it is the photograph we trust over the painting, and the more awkward and unposed the photograph the more trustworthy it appears. Which brings me to my own decided reluctance to be, were I ever invited, a subject of extended biographical treatment. A fiction writer's life is his treasure, his ore, his savings account, his jungle gym, and I marvel at the willingness of my friends William Styron and Joyce Carol Oates to coöperate in their recently published biographies. As long as I am alive, I don't want somebody else playing on my jungle gym—disturbing my children, quizzing my ex-wife, bugging my present wife, seeking for Judases among my friends, rummaging through yellow-ing old clippings, and quoting *in extenso* bad reviews I would rather see consigned to oblivion. I have even gone to the trouble, when there was a threat of a biography, of publishing, ten years ago, an autobiography of sorts, *Self-Consciousness*, describing in sometimes embarrassing detail what seemed to *me* significant or curious about my life, as it had been experienced from within. The book has been criticized as a parading of my wounds; but the wounds were mine to parade, and not some callow inquisitor's.

Someone else, in my limited experience, never gets things quite right. The exact socio-economic tone, the muddle and eddy of peculiar circum-stances are almost inevitably missed. For example, recently a man who has made a close study of my work, to the extent of preparing a so-called Updike Encyclopedia, showed me a brief biography he had prepared. I was astonished by the inaccuracies. He said, for instance, that I had been editor of my high-school mimeographed paper, *The Chatterbox*, and of our high-school class's yearbook, *Hi-Life*, but in fact I had been neither. He had been talking to some old classmates of mine, and their memory may have deceived them; or he had reasonably assumed that, since mine is the pre-eminent literary reputation to have thus far emerged from my high-school class, I naturally occupied these editorial eminences. But in truth, the wise faculty advisers felt my energy was better employed as a cartoonist and contributor. Two steady and able young women—Ann Weik and Frances Runge by name—were appointed to the respective editorships. Again, my maternal grandfather, John Hoyer, was identified as a minister, whereas it had been my *paternal* grandfather, my father's father, Hartley Updike, who had been a man of the cloth. The conflation of these two gentlemen does great violence to the subjective shape of my life, for Hartley Updike died before I was born and was to me a dim leg-end, alive only in certain reminiscences of my father, my mother, and my aunt, whereas John Hoyer, after whom I was named, loomed large to me, as the head of the household in which I took my place as an infant. He and I shared, with my grandmother, mother, and father, living quarters until I went off to college; he died at the age of ninety the same year I was married. He loved me, and I loved him. His creaking high-buttoned shoes, the eloquence of his slightly wheezy voice, the stoic set of his mouth beneath his grizzled mustache, the afterscent of his cigars were present to me, day after day, throughout my growing-up, and gave me the courage to write my first novel about old people, a novel in which he appears, caricatured, as John Hook. Whereas it took me forty years to try to imagine in print my other grandfather. Yet to a devoted Updike expert my grandfathers hazily merged.

Another conflation can occur between a writer's fiction and his facts; again and again I have corrected the assertion that my father was a science teacher. George Caldwell, in my novel *The Centaur*, taught science, for a variety of thematic reasons. My father, Wesley Updike, actually taught junior-high math, which included first-year algebra for ninth-graders. Fiction, even fiction with the appearance of autobiography, makes no claim to be factual. Compounded of memory and imagination, it at the very least tweaks and simplifies actual circumstances. *The Centaur* dramatizes my adolescent sense of public-school teaching as a martyrdom for my father, the vocational equivalent of the constant pain suffered by the centaur Chiron when struck by a poisoned arrow. In truth I wonder now if teaching didn't agree with him better than he admitted: it gave him, a clergyman's son, a prominent and respected role in the community; it utilized his considerable flair for self-dramatization; and it satisfied his craving for social contact. Of the several jobs he held before he came, in his mid-thirties, as a Depression recourse, to teaching, and of what his highest hopes for himself had been, my knowledge is hazy. Fiction writers build their ignorance—the shadows at the edge of their knowing—into the design. Our biographer, if thorough, will know many things we did not, or have forgotten. In fiction or poetry, a thing is true if the writer makes the reader feel it to be true. In biography, it is true if evidence bears it out. Otherwise, it—the merest and most plausible conjectural thought or conversation—should be left out, as probably inaccurate. Biography should not appropriate poetry's license to create truth.

To summarize, then, this rather cranky survey. Some literary biographies, the most gracious, extend a masterpiece and deliciously prolong our inhabitation of it. Some offer to explain how, whether by conscious method or unconscious compensatory maneuver, the author arrived at his effects. Still others seek to expose the writer in his or her fallible, or downright woeful, humanity, and thus demystify a process to which a certain mystique once attached. Even by such a nether route, however, the reader can be led back to the works themselves with heightened anticipation and sharpened understanding. The more or less meagre and ignoble and practical facts tie the author's balloon—his flotilla of balloons—to the earth, and tracing the connections tells us something of the nature of artistic creation. The life of a writer, which spins outside of itself a secondary life, offers an opportunity to study mind and body, or inside and outside, together, as one. Consider the many inventive yet judicious connections that Leon Edel makes between Henry James's evolving psyche and his accumulating corpus of work. The many people that James was (to use the phrasing of our epigraph from Scott Fitzgerald) to some extent unite. If literary biography enhances our access to literature, populating its annals with graspable, provocative personalities, then it does perform, I suppose, useful work; but in deflecting our attention from the work itself, the work in its necessary aloofness and autonomy, literary biography participates in the curious modern deconstructive neutering of art, which discredits its testimony and belittles its practitioners.

FIVE ESSAYS

Back from China

October 1998

"WHERE ARE THE PEOPLE?" my wife asked, looking around the Delta terminal at Kennedy Airport. We had disembarked from a thirteen-hour flight from Tokyo, after three weeks of a sightseeing tour in China organized by the Smithsonian Institution. We were so little used to handling our own luggage—we would set it outside the door of our hotel room at an appointed hour and it would magically reappear in our next hotel, in Wuhan or Chongqing, Shanghai or Guilin—that we had made a botch of getting it from the terminal containing Japan Airlines to the adjacent one, holding Delta, which would fly us to Boston. The two heaviest suitcases had wheels on them; we had dragged them outside into the fall-tinged American sunlight, an Occidental version of the Friday noon we had left behind a half-day ago in Japan, and set off up an empty and unpromising sidewalk. In the distance a sparkling wire fence apparently barred our progress. Cars and buses poured by, but there was not a soul to ask guidance of.

Improvising (after all, whose country was this?), we went down some steps to a lower roadway. Its sidewalk was scarcely two feet wide and shortly petered out in drifts of last winter's road sand. The wheels of our suitcases became mired; I seized their handles and struggled up an enigmatic asphalt hill, beyond which the Delta terminal loomed like a fortress without visible entrance. The pushbutton at a stoplight didn't function; tired of jabbing it, we jaywalked, with our unaccustomed burdens, and ascended to glass doors that said "First Class Passengers Only." We were strictly Business. We finally found a door we were permitted to use, secreted at an oblique angle in the towering façade. It yielded, surprisingly, to our pressure, and three diffident security personnel interrupted their chat in Spanish to give our bags a grudging pass through the X-ray machine. On the other side, in a large polished space with an off-center air of having just turned its back, not a single sign or a single other pedestrian offered to direct our steps. There were shops, but no one, shortly after noon, seemed to be in them; there were airline counters, but they were unmanned. I thought of Simone de Beauvoir's words on the Forbidden City: "This palace, in which not one dated memory is inscribed, strikes me as the unalterable seat of an unalterable institution and not the dwelling place of men who were one time alive." My wife asked me her question. I couldn't answer. The United States was a country with some amenities but inconveniently devoid of people.

Arriving at the Beijing airport over three weeks before, by way of the immaculate modernity of Japan Airlines, had been quite different. There were uneven linoleum floors, an earthy smell, an excited human clatter, a certain amount of physical horseplay. Jokes were being shouted; an exhilaration was being shared. Chinese laughter had a harsh boom to it, and the spoken language a certain bark. The qualities that the Chinese, in their global diaspora, project—intelligence, diligence, a concentrated quiet and canny reserve—did not, apparently, obtain on their native soil. In this first glimpse, they appeared to be what my father would have called "full of fun," as his own generation of raccoon-coated, Prohibition-mocking Americans had been. Chinese and Americans both, after all, enjoy the satisfactions of national largeness—one nation the most populous, the other the richest—and the benefits of a revolution that proclaimed all men equal. The Chinese seemed happy.

The captain of the boat, the SS *Splendid*, that for four days cruised us up the Yangtze, from Wuhan to Chongqing, seemed happy, as well he might have been, having begun his nautical career as a boy in 1945 and seen it continue through unimaginable national vicissitudes since. "*Ganbei!*" he shouted, meaning "Bottoms up!," as he made the rounds of the tables at our first dinner, toasting each one. He was drinking, we were told for our peace of mind, tea, and not the potent plum brandy we were served. Nevertheless, the enthusiasm he brought to this ceremonial duty, which he presumably performed at the beginning and end of every voyage, was infectious, and the speeches of welcome and farewell he delivered, in a voice that treated the microphone like a megaphone, must have been perfect of their kind. The passengers at his table asked, through a translator, questions about navigating the recently flooded Yangtze, which he answered efficiently; but the journey of his long career remained mysterious. Had there been cruises in 1947, with Civil War raging? In 1967, with the Cultural Revolution raging? Who, until the new China opened itself to us Western tourists, had been his passengers? We had to make do with the evident fact of his happiness. His female serving crew, entertaining us with the dances of some of China's fifty-three (or fifty-four, or fifty-five, depending on which guide you were listening to) ethnic minorities, were as slender as Paris models, whose deadpan, stalking manner they amusingly parodied in one number. Cherry, the very lovely cruise hostess, bravely wrestled with the English language, having especial difficulty (as I myself have) with "right" and "left." "Wish you a good health," the scale in our cabin said. On a railing at the bow was solicitously lettered "Aware Horn." It was some horn, sounded often in the mists of the Yangtze as we picked our way through the famous Three Gorges. The floods had subsided; the river was getting low. When the horn sounded, you tingled from the top of your skull down to the soles of your feet.

Kathy, the guide on our bus in Beijing, was also happy. Fluent, pretty, she was fond of teasing us with lessons in Chinese and riddles in English ("What was Beethoven doing in the cemetery? Decomposing!"). As the days went on, and we headed wearily back to dinner from the Forbidden City or the Summer Palace or the Temple of Heaven, she relaxed into accounts of her life: how she didn't date until she was twenty-three ("Late!" she admitted, with one of her sudden dazzling smiles) and how neighborhood watchdogs ("old people, retired") monitor behavior in their vicinities. When she was asked to contrast her own childhood with that of her adolescent daughter, she replied promptly, "The difference between Hell and Heaven." She had basically raised herself, on bread and water, while her grandparents, in those years of the Cultural Revolution, labored penitentially in the countryside and her parents, consigned to factory work, spent additional hours attending interminable Red Guard–led meetings of exhortation and self-criticism. Her daughter, one of China's many millions of only children, has all the electronic equipment a proper rock fan requires, and dismisses maternal complaints by saying, "You make the money, Mom, so I have to spend it!" Kathy, a former sales manager, makes enough yuan charming busloads of gray-headed English-speakers to own her own car. She allowed that many people still love Mao for the socialist levellings that ended the worst poverty, but you gathered that it was Deng Xiaoping's liberation into guarded capitalism that inspired her own affection, and that of the countless others able to breathe better and even thrive in the new China.

The great white mausoleum holding Mao's preserved body sits across

Tiananmen Square from the Forbidden City, on the same axial line that passes through the center of the moated imperial rectangle. Even the mole on the giant portrait of Mao that hangs on the other side of the square, above the Gate of Heavenly Peace, is centered. But Deng, in three-quarters view, smiles genially down from billboards. A two-god system: one to worship, one to obey. The bridge between them was built by such Party theorists as Yu Guangyuan, who, redefining the term "scientific socialism" in 1979, declared, in effect, that if it didn't work it wasn't scientific: pragmatism without the benefit of William James. Meanwhile, the long line to see the embalmed Mao moves quickly but reverently, two abreast and then dividing into single files, and out into an extensive souvenir shop. Newly married couples, we were told, often make this observance after the ceremony, the bride still in her Western-bourgeois white gown. Yet the Chinese we knew best, the local tour guides, rarely mentioned Mao, and then in a gingerly fashion, unlike our American lecturers, who gave the Chairman his due at such sympathetic length as to turn us, who had paid thousands for this education, into momentary Maoists. Radical land reform in their retrospect seemed an obvious humane and liberalizing move, like the WPA or the Emancipation Proclamation, and the fate of the displaced landlords and "rich peasants" became as abstract as the annihilated armies of the Warring States Period (403–221 B.C.).

The Cultural Revolution (1966–76 A.D.), lecturers and guides agreed, was a disaster. It formed the trauma that the present trend is fleeing. Executions and wrecked careers and smashed temples aside, it created a generation of ignorance, of Red Guards whose war on education has left them unemployable. A number of the other bus guides, mostly young males who were only a bit less engaging and confiding than Kathy, touched boldly upon the mistakes of the past. One even complained about his not being able to watch the English-language channels that we viewed in our hotels; he feared he would be reported if he did. Yet right on the bus listening to this complaint sat one of three young Party representatives, amiable "national guides," accompanying our tour, which was a large one of about one hundred twenty-five persons—three buses-full. These junior officials, wearing blue jeans and polo shirts, blended companionably with the three bilingual tour guides—one an American born in Taiwan, one a young Californian who had taken up the study of Mandarin as a college wager, and the third a Chinese national studying in Pittsburgh. They served, along with the tour manager from the Smithsonian, as our interface with this still imperfectly tourist-friendly society.

Things went smoothly. The authorities want tourism to work, Yangtze flooding or not. A side trip to the Yangtze cruise involved a ride through the gorges of the Shennongxi Stream on small, paddled boats, with old-style trackers—wiry, nearly naked, heavy-smoking men of the Tujia eth-nic minority—heaving and pushing us down the rapids. A mountain road on the way to the embarkation point had, in the summer's torrents, washed out for several hundred yards; we were taken as far as we could go on buses, led on foot through the staring phalanxes of the road-repair crew, and placed on a set of buses that had been brought from another province, a four-day journey. Such a feat of accommodation bespoke con-siderable governmental involvement, yet I detected none of the police-state emanations I remember from the Soviet Union in the Sixties: no hotel-room phones ringing a bed-check in the middle of the night, no hint of suppressed divulgence from our young Chinese guides. They wore freedom's manners lightly.

The science of government has been long pondered in China. Confu-cius, born in 551 B.C. in the feudal state of Lu, regretted the cruel ways of the lords toward their subjects, and the constant war they waged upon one another. He proposed a class of *junzi*, gentlemen, who would model principles of piety and harmony—*de*, *ren*, *yi*, *li*—derived from the patri-archal family, where children deferred to parents and women to men. His ideas made little headway in his lifetime, and his own failure to find high office led him to wander among neighboring states, seeking in vain an administrative post from which he might execute his reforms. His thought did not really catch on until the Han dynasty (206 B.C.–220 A.D.), which followed upon the unification of China under the extraordinary tyrant who named himself Qin Shihuangdi (*r.* 221–207 B.C.). Qin was not a Confucian but a Legalist, a proponent of the view that what people needed from above was not gentlemanly virtues but hard-and-fast laws. Having led his state of Qin (Ch'in in the old orthography) to victory over all the competing ones, thus ending the Warring States Period, he decreed standard weights and measures, imposed the Qin writing style, and introduced a style of coin (round with a square hole in the middle) that persisted until 1911. Notoriously, he burned all the non-Legalist books he could find, including much precious poetry and history, and buried some of the authors alive. He greatly extended canals and roads and linked the northern sections of various provincial defensive walls into one Great Wall—all this while conducting military campaigns in Central Asia and Vietnam. Having created China, he asked a great deal of it. Vio-lent rebellion followed hard upon his death; his was a one-man dynasty.

Our tour saw a number of Qin's mighty works, visiting not only a section of Great Wall, restored with German money, at Mutianyu, north of Beijing, but his stupendous grave sites outside Xian. The recently discovered buried army of terra-cotta warriors, each more than life-size and wearing a Mona Lisa smile, exists in three pits, to the number of some nine thousand, with many more still to be excavated and assembled. The clay figures, hollow but for their legs, were shattered when the wooden roof entombing them collapsed under its burden of earth. In the biggest pit, some archeological work was in progress, carried on in what seemed desultory fashion, with the dirt borne away basket by basket and then trundled in a two-wheeled cart up a plank ramp to be dumped—the labor of excavation a contemporary echo of the ant-labor whereby the massive project had been achieved. The terra-cotta army, in its ranks of muted pink and tan, makes, like so many monuments of ancient China, a timeless, weightless impression. The warriors are serene as angels, deployed in their underground batallions to await whatever demonic forces might threaten the posthumous security of Emperor Qin. They face east, where his enemies in his lifetime had their rival states. He was buried some distance off, in a mountainous burial mound containing, according to the account of the Grand Historian Sima Qian, a representation of the rivers of China in mercury, made to flow by machinery. By the same account, seven hundred thousand workmen labored on the tomb, and many of them were buried with the Emperor to keep its site secret. A month's digging in 1986 indicated extensive damage, most probably by grave robbers, and full excavation is being saved, by a patient administration, for the future.

In the perspective of such gargantuan evidences of effective authority, the American crisis in the White House rather dwindled. I had expected China to be the dark side of the moon, with an eclipse of American news, but the television sets in our hotel rooms all received CNN, so that, except for the days on the SS *Splendid*, we had hourly access to the latest twist in the saga of Monica and Bill, the latest dip in the stock market, and the latest feat in the home-run contest which saw Sosa pull even and then McGwire blast off into his super-Ruthian total of seventy. *China Daily*, the official English-language newspaper, usually printed the scandal developments on its back page, tersely, with as much dignity as it could muster. Several of our Chinese bus guides smilingly alluded to the visit of "your President" to this very site or city in June, but didn't pursue our nervous, tittering reaction to what in normal circumstances would have been a politic courtesy. Nor did we tourists, in my hearing, ever do more than dodge away from the topic with a jocular snort or shrug. Our embarrassed avoidance expressed perhaps a wish to avoid political arguments in a group signed up for three weeks' close company, or may have been a fair reflection of the national mood of baffled ambivalence and vicarious humiliation.

Through the emperors of old descended the Mandate of Heaven. On the one hand, Clinton would seem to have forfeited his mandate by besmirching the Presidency with "inappropriate" and mendacious behavior; on the other, the nation has fared well under him. The headlines in Asia are mostly economic; China, though for the time being spared the melt-down to its north in Russia and its south in capitalist Asia, is in the game now. Our boyish President, with his whiz-kid grasp of tedious details and his willingness to ease into a middle way, may be just the gamesman for a post-ideology world. So who is Ken Starr to take him from us?

That people need some kind of leader came clear during three weeks in a tour group. It's been a long time since I was so thoroughly immersed in a fixed sampling of Americans; like a high-school class or a set of suburban couples, we came to know each other all too well—who would be late for the bus, who would act up in the back, who would ask the guide the most pretentious questions, who would go to the hotel disco after a day with antiquity, who would need help up the steps to the pagoda. Without our Mandarin-speaking, string-pulling, bill-paying leaders, we would have been lost in an opaque teeming, wherein Communist doctrine has been replaced by a superheated mercantilism. To me, the least agreeable aspect of present-day China is the rampant entrepreneurism that lines the path to every notable sight, from the Great Wall down, with frantically aggressive vendors. They tend to vend the same things— bottled drinking water, silk scarves, chiming "healthy balls," carved jade, wind chimes, bamboo back scratchers, tiny lacquered boxes, and used and discarded copies of the once-sacred Little Red Book—for prices that, translated out of yuan, amount to little enough, but the clamor of beseechment drives all thought of purchase from the head of any but the most hardened shoppers. These salesmen, who push their wares right into your face, are, often, farmers who have rented a stall and its contents to earn a little extra income; the effect is of crazy duplication. In the cities, too, the little shops, dwarfed by the size of their spectacularly calligraphic signs, run on block after block. Who ever will buy the stuff, you wonder, with a concern you don't, somehow, bestow on the competing merchants of your own country. The "free" market we were walked through in the relatively small town of Yangshuo, on the Li River, presented a superabundance of perishable goods; bony men and sun-baked women squatted beside baskets of roots, beans, and live chickens amid an overriding stench that suggested the inside of a huge sardine can. Marketing in an advanced country occurs at an antiseptic distance, via print or television. Not so here. A little boy, four or so, outside the Reed Flute Cave, near Guilin, had been taught to say, "One yuan, one *yu*an," and as he held up his little green reed flute to be bought, the cry became a wail, with tears. In Beijing, waiting for our traffic-delayed bus, we were pinned amid parked cars and besieged, most memorably by a burn victim with a face like a pierced gourd, who held up to us, as if they were saleable artifacts, his poor clawlike, bent-back hands.

Generally, China's population presses lightly on a mere spectator, like the crowded details of a faded tapestry. Wherever you look in a city a person appears. One night in Beijing, our Taiwanese-born guide, irrepressibly in his element, led some of us, returning to our hotel from a restaurant, up an alley that grew narrower and narrower, lined as it was with people eating, cooking, sitting in their sliver of the open air. The city is lit at night, but as if by twenty-watt bulbs; the guide, sensing our unease as we crowded farther and farther into virtual living rooms, with children and old women needing only to lift a hand to touch us as we passed, announced reassuringly: "If I'm not sure a passageway comes out anywhere, I look for bicycle tracks." We strained our eyes to see some, but by then the narrow path had widened, and we were soon on a major thoroughfare, passing an eerie nighttime crowd of outdoor swing dancers—sexless shadows doing a stately, healthful Lindy to barely audible music from a source lodged in a doorway or an apartment window. One has trouble imagining the lives fitted into the endless apartment blocks, many to a room, like the brushstrokes that fill a square Mandarin character with a wealth of meanings. Our tour took us to cities—Wuhan, Chongqing—that we had scarcely heard of but which dwarfed Chicago and, depending on where the boundaries were drawn, even New York City. Shanghai looked like a New York where fresh skyscrapers were springing up in all five boroughs. But the abundance of population most vividly struck me when, as we tourists sat on the bow of the Yangtze cruise ship, somewhere after passing through the commotion of the great dam a-building, a pale cloud of settlement materialized at a bend of the river and kept growing before our eyes, rank on rank of apartment buildings and factories spread along the river for miles, a city without a name or a place on our schedule. Study of a map revealed the place to be called Wanxian, but it could have been one of hundreds of such cities, sewn as thickly on the map as poppyseeds on a roll.

One reason the gorges are so cherished in art and tourism alike must be that only here, where rivers have cut their way through the rumpled and upthrust limestone karst, are the slopes too steep and rocky to terrace, and the cliffs too sheer to inhabit. Pieces of pitted riverine rock, with their indecipherable hieroglyphs of erosion, adorn the classic Chinese garden, where humanity is implied by a precise formula of blessed absence. One has, in the most populous country in the world, unexpected glimpses of peace: the daily swarm of thousands of bicycles on the Beijing streets, noiseless, clashless, all gliding at the same sedate speed, as high-heeled career women merge with pedalling workmen bent low under brick-laden shoulder poles. Then there are, in the majestic new museum in Shanghai, the Shang bronze vessels, intricately cast in the second millennium before Christ, and the Tang celadon ceramics, shaped and fired during Europe's Dark Ages, waiting motionless behind glass for the next millennium's admiration.

The captain on his boat was happy, and Kathy on her bus was happy, and Premier Jiang Zemin seemed happy as he was shown in *China Daily* announcing his new and broadened human-rights policy or his new rules for family planning. And my wife was happy, beaming through every day in China. It was she who had wanted to go; she had read Pearl Buck as a girl, and two elderly great-aunts of hers had made the trip in the Thirties, a family adventure that had become legendary. She had taken courses and could tell the dynasties apart and learned to recognize through the bus window the characters for "China," "bank," and "agriculture."

To me, China was out of this world. Away from the mail and the news, away from the lawn chores and golf dates of September in New England, away from the self-centeredness and Eurocentricity of an aging American writer: that was how I pictured it. I had few boyhood associations beyond *Terry and the Pirates* and Fu Manchu. The Cold War years had implanted me with images unsuitable for a travel poster—waves of "volunteer" Chinese troops rolling our troops down the Korean Peninsula, nuclear-war scares over Quemoy and Matsu, dunce-capped professors and Little Red Book–brandishing crowds, Latin American guerrilla bands vying for ever purer allegiance to Maoist thought, the coy pop Maoism of art galleries and college dorms. China to me had been the Red Menace writ large, the global Other, intimately glimpsed in the American press only through the reports of Dutch or Australian journalists allowed into this forbidden land. Nixon and Kissinger, with a touch of Fu Manchu themselves, officially changed that in 1972, but for years afterward China remained a nation whose best international friends were Albania, North Korea, and the Khmer Rouge. To me, going there had an aspect of danger, of diving into a darkness on the other side of the globe.

But the journey had proved less far. Holiday Inn had prepared the way. Not just rice but Rice Krispies were offered. Most of the hotels were built around a great atrium, on whose floor a piano player, beginning at breakfast, rippled through Broadway tunes. CNN, ubiquitous, boasted of itself that it was "helping the world become a smaller place"; any smaller and the adventure of travel will dwindle to nothing. We had come to China, but China was coming to us with, it seemed, the speed of the earth's rotation. It was only back in my own bedroom, at last, that I felt estranged.

We had prolonged our sleep deprivation, picking through the mail, checking the house and garden, marvelling that after three weeks so little was changed in New England, even the color of the turning leaves. We fell asleep finally, with difficulty, and when I awoke the rug of the world had been pulled out from under me. The dark bedroom seemed perilously weird—alien and glimmering at the edges as if with ultraviolet flashers. All the habits and illusions that protect me from the fact that I am sixty-six and nearing death had fallen from me, me in my pajamas and skin, unable to calculate where the bathroom was, wondering why this great curved surface of dread lay beneath my bare feet. The room, once so familiar, felt immense, and, containing no other than my sleeping wife, devastatingly lonely. Perhaps I was missing the gang of one hundred twenty fellow-tourists, which had enclosed me like a bubble on my travels. Or perhaps it was the one point two billion Chinese that I missed. But cosmically bereft I was, and terrifyingly disoriented—out of this world.

A Sense of Change

March 1999

A FEW YEARS AGO, my stepson, still a college lad of modest means, handed me the stray change on his bureau top—perhaps two dollars' worth—because he did not like to have it jangling in his pocket. Gratefully, even greedily, I accepted the handful of pennies, nickels, dimes, and quarters. To me, once, these coins were huge in value, if not as huge as the fabled "cartwheels"—silver dollars—that now and then rolled as far east from the Western states as Pennsylvania. One of the advantages of having been a child in the Depression is that it takes very little money to gladden the heart. The Lincoln pennies we used to collect in piggy banks and glass ashtrays were not negligible: five would buy a Hershey bar, six a Tastykake, one a licorice stick, eleven (including a wartime tax) a child's ticket to the movies. Two hundred of them, dutifully accumulated over months and packaged in four paper wrappers holding fifty each, could be exchanged at the Whitner's Department Store book counter for an album of cartoons from *Collier's* magazine or an agreeably lightweight novel by Thorne Smith or P. G. Wodehouse. The wrappers were solemnly broken open and each penny respectfully counted by the saleswoman. Now spare pennies sit like a puddle of sludge in a dish on the counter of the post office and the convenience store, and sometimes a salesclerk, rather than bother counting out four cents in change, blithely hands you a nickel. I still stoop down to pick a penny up off the sidewalk, though.

Copper Lincoln cents—zinc-coated steel for a year of the war—figure in my earliest impressions of money. An old Indian Head, discontinued in 1909, would still turn up in Thirties change. Lincoln pennies are being minted ninety years later, the longest-lived of American coins and the first non-commemorative ones to bear a President's image. The other coins of my childhood have slowly ebbed from circulation: the Buffalo nickel (1913–38), crowded to the rim, obverse and reverse, with its heroic representations of Manifest Destiny's two victims, the defeated Indian and his all-but-exterminated pet prey; the Mercury dime (1916–45), so called because Miss Liberty wears an anomalous winged headdress atop her icy female profile, a profile that originally belonged, we children of Berks County did not realize, to Elsie Kachel Moll from Reading, who had married another local, the poet Wallace Stevens, and during their seven years in Manhattan had posed for not only the iconic head on the dime but the full-length Miss Liberty on the fifty-cent piece; and the Standing Liberty quarter (1916–30), whose figure (not Elsie Stevens's) was criticized for showing too much naked flesh and turned up more heavily draped in the second year of its issue. This coin, as it yielded to the Washington quarter (first minted in 1932), was treasured by small boys because the wings and head of the flying eagle on the reverse, turned upside down and partly covered with a knowing thumb, became striding legs and a penis. By the time the Walking Liberty half-dollar (1916–47), with its full-length sashaying lady about to put her foot on a rising sun, gave way to Ben Franklin and the Liberty Bell, I, at the age of fifteen, had ceased to hold money so close to my face and to count on it for erotic revelation. Half-dollars were less rare then than now—men accustomed to carrying pocket watches and pocket knives did not shun big coins—but a child seldom gained possession of one, unless it was to mark a holiday or birthday. Fifty cents was a lot of money. These metallic tokens projected a potent magic. My best friend, a lawyer's son, had a little tin box of money that, when I visited his home, he used to show me with an avid, ceremonial secrecy. My own, more meagre hoards resided in relatively frivolous piggy banks, the most important a grinning, red-tongued Mickey Mouse guarding a slotted treasure chest whose bottom could be opened with a key. I had won the bank in a third-grade spelling bee—the clinching word, I think, was "lonely"—and this quaint repository's disappearance, somewhere in the second half of the century, is one of the inconsolable losses of my life.

Money, which is now so preponderantly a matter of electronic notation, or else a breezy riffle of twenty-dollar bills thrust out by an ATM, was in those hard-up times an earthy outgrowth, like the sparkling diamonds that the dwarfs pile up in Disney's *Snow White*. My father's salary was received in cash in a small tan envelope, and was dumped into a red-and-white recipe box that sat on top of the icebox. To dip into it, I had to get a kitchen chair to stand on. My withdrawals were supervised; indeed, everyone's withdrawals from it were announced, like the stations on a train journey. When the box was empty, we were out of money.

My father, as a schoolteacher in charge of basketball admissions, used to bring home the cash receipts, and I often watched him count them at the dining-room table—the various denominations of coins mounting in slick stacks that were, when they reached a certain height, deftly slipped into a paper cylinder, which was then smartly tamped at both ends. When I tried it, the coins ran away, over the edge of the table onto the carpet and even beyond, a coin often ending upright on its edge in a floor crack way over in a corner. This willful, kinetic quality of metal money I notice now at the poker table, where a quarter tossed into the pot will unaccountably wobble to its feet, as it were, and travel clear across the table as if seeking another master.

The sensuous pleasure of handling money carries into the very thought of it. "Pennies from Heaven" was a song, and "We're in the Money" another. American millionaires—Ford and Rockefeller and, upholding Pennsylvania's honor, Andrew Carnegie and Andrew Mellon—were folk heroes, Paul Bunyans of cash. The millions who for a coin or two went to the movies did not seem to begrudge the tuxedoed personae of Charles Coburn and Eugene Pallette and Edward Arnold their pillared estates, their sound-stage lawns and swimming pools, their buffed and chauffeured English limousines, their beautiful giddy daughters in chiffon and pearls. To see such well-endowed lives projected in black and white on a big silver screen was itself pleasurable, like feeling coins swim through your fingers, or imagining—as in many a crime movie—a suitcase full of bundled bills. The American masses of the Depression had not quite lost the feudal ability to identify with an overlord's riches, alleviating their own poverty with vicarious enjoyment of an aristocracy's assets. The men and women who drudged their lives away in the local factories—most prominently, Wyomissing's Berkshire Knitting Mills, fondly known as "the Berkie"—shared in the pith of a great enterprise, though their share, Marxists and union leaders pointed out, was miserly. American society's refusal to crack beneath the dire load of the Depression owed something to a wealth of imagination that, via the movies, solaced the masses with debonair images of luxury. Images were in a way superior to the real thing, if we believed those Hollywood comedies in which the rich were often foolish and not infrequently miserable: they suffered from ulcers, financial reversals, and the discontents of excessive propriety; they were hostages to their fortunes, and prey to complications from which ordinary men were exempt. Our hearts went out to them, and their happy endings became ours. Movies, mediating between a silk-clad Myrna Loy and the twelve-dollar-a-week shopgirl, spun a web of trust, of sympathetic connection, like the bonds of patriotism and brand-name loyalty.

A coin, too, bespeaks trust, passing from hand to hand as an abstract signifier of value. Coins were once worth exactly their weight in silver or gold; opportunists clipped their edges and passed them on for the face amount. When the underpinning of real metallic worth was removed, the value inhered in nothing more than a general consent. A "pretend" level of wealth was invented, less substantial but also less perishable and cumbersome than food or clothing or jewelry. This airy immutability accounts for some of the fascination that money holds. As with words and feelings, money's value is impalpable. Yet money lasts, it doesn't flit by. Nor does it ask anything of its possessor. It melts, like ice cream, but very slowly, in the warmth of inflation. It has endurance and extension. These little disks and shallow sculptures enlist us in a conspiracy of users; a dime from a child's hand is worth just what it is from a grown-up's.

In that penny-proud world of my childhood, paper and cardboard play money carried the pretense to an even airier level. Whole afternoons went by in the counterfeit transactions of Monopoly. The war brought food tokens—little cardboard disks, red and blue—and stamps, and War Bonds, their purchase urged upon the public by movie stars and uniformed heroes and President Roosevelt. Before the Depression, my grandfather had invested in stocks and bonds and lost most of his investments; next thing, all of us, children included, were hustled by the wartime emergency back into an economy of credit and certificates, a coast-to coast trusting of the government to see us through and pay back its debt. My adulthood's slow divorce from hard cash was under way.

To one who has acquired his sense of money in the Depression, any payment, however modest—fifty-five dollars, say, for a poem, or a hundred for a reprint permission—seems impressive. My weekly allowance was thirty-five cents a week, my father's annual salary was twelve hundred dollars. Measured by these sustenance amounts, Nineties remunerations appear huge; I often must resist the impulse to send back checks to editors and lecture agencies on the grounds that I am being grossly overpaid. On the other hand, Nineties expenses are a constant outrage. Four hundred fifty dollars for one night in a hotel! Seventy-five dollars for a theatre ticket! Two million dollars for a condo on an airshaft! Thirty-three cents for a three-cent stamp! Eighty cents—can you believe it?—for a nickel candy bar! It is like going to Italy used to be, except that these are not lire but almighty American dollars. "The almighty dollar," "sound as a dollar," "another day, another dollar"—even the sayings from my childhood have been devalued by inflation. I simply cannot afford to live, it daily seems to me as I size up 1999 prices in the dollars of 1939. No, not the dollars; a Lilliputian in Brobdingnag, I still think in terms of 1939 quarters, dimes, nickels, and pennies. Or am I, hoisting up onto the counter a coin that feels as hefty as a millstone, the Brobdingnagian?

The Future of Faith

November 1999

FINS-DE-SIÈCLE have been rocky times for Christianity. By 1900, the great shocks of nineteenth-century science—Lyell's exposition of fossils and the vast extent of geologic time; Darwin's theory of evolution through natural selection; the so-called higher criticism of Biblical texts, which undermined their status as the direct word of God, plus the biographies of Jesus, by Strauss and Renan foremost, that presented Him as a mere historical mortal—had settled a commonplace atheism into the minds of the younger generations. Materialism had the cosmos firmly in hand; the gospels of Nietzsche and Marx embodied the new idealism. A. N. Wilson, in his brilliant, albeit somewhat saucy and jittery survey, *God's Funeral*, states, "The closing decades of the nineteenth century were the true era of 'the death of God.' " He quotes G. K. Chesterton's autobiography: "The background of all the world was not merely atheism, but atheist orthodoxy, and even atheist respectability. That was quite as common in Belgravia as in Bohemia. That was above all normal in Suburbia."

It was against this background of complacent suburban atheism that William James delivered, in 1900–1901, the Gifford Lectures on Natural Religion at the University of Edinburgh, which became his classic *The Varieties of Religious Experience;* that text's pluralistic pragmatism remains, Wilson maintains, the last best hope for religious faith in the twentieth century and, presumably, the twenty-first.

In 1800, Napoleon had begun to spread the anticlericalism of the Revolution across Europe, closing churches and monasteries and diverting their wealth to the coffers of freethinking republics. The bloodiest fury of the Revolution was past; thousands of priests and persons in holy orders died under the guillotine or gun between 1789 and 1800. At the height of its fervor, the Revolution reconsecrated the altar of Notre-Dame to the Goddess of Reason and began, in 1791, numbering the years afresh, doing away with Anni Domini. In 1801, Napoleon, a non-believer who shared Voltaire's belief that the ignorant masses still needed a religion, signed a concordat with Pope Pius VII, the more accommodating successor of Pius VI, whereby the church accepted subservience to the lay state, to the point of instituting a new catechism teaching children that "to honour and serve the Emperor is to honour and serve God himself," and that those who failed to do so would "render themselves worthy of eternal damnation." More than forty years later, in northern Italy, Charles Dickens observed the lasting effects of the Jacobin assault on the old Christian infrastructure: "Our walk through Mantua showed us, in almost every street, some suppressed church: now used for a warehouse, now for nothing at all." And on a recent trip to Italy I heard a guide in Arezzo make a point of informing us tourists that, among the depredations that weather and earlier restoration had worked on Piero della Francesca's masterly frescoes in the Church of San Francesco, there were, visible on several faces, slashes left by a French soldier's bayonet. Such hatred of a church, roused by real or perceived oppressions, is foreign to the experience of most Americans, though something of it can be felt in Hawthorne as he contemplated the moral tyranny of the little Puritan theocracies of New England. Where a church exerts worldly power, it will rouse worldly opposition.

Nor was the year 1000 a palmy period for the Christian faith, though we imagine Europe to have been full of fervent adherents. Geopolitically, they were pressed hard on the northern and western coasts by heathen Vikings, and on the south by Muslims, who occupied all of the Iberian Peninsula save for the embattled kingdoms of León and Navarre. The Magyar hordes had been defeated in 955, slowly becoming the Christian kingdom of Hungary, but beyond Russia all of Asia waited to release its next plague of infidel armies. There were comets and famines and here-sies to herald the possible coming of the Antichrist. According to Ralph Glaber, the Burgundian monk whose five-volume history provides the principal account of the first millennial fever, the passing of the year 1000 saw a revival of church-building, "as if the whole world were shaking itself free, shrugging off the burden of the past, and cladding itself every-where in a white mantle of churches." However, in 1014, as a war raged in England between Danish invaders and the forces of King Ethelred, Archbishop Wulfstan of York preached to his congregation:

> This world is in haste and is drawing ever closer to its end, and it always happens that the longer it lasts, the worse it becomes. . . . The devil has deceived this people too much, and there has been little faith among men, though they speak fair words, and too many crimes have gone unchecked in the land . . . and holy places are everywhere open to attack, and the houses of God are completely deprived of ancient rites, and stripped of all that is fitting; and religious orders have now for a long time been greatly despised . . . and, to speak most briefly, God's laws are hated and His com-mands despised.

As the year 2000 draws close, faith in America hangs on. The Christian right, with abortion and school prayer as its flagship issues, remains a vocal and intimidating political force, capable of getting evolution labelled a mere theory in Kansas, though not yet capable of legislating all the morality it thinks the nation needs. Our President, a proclaimed sorry sinner, speaks the language of the Bible Belt with a native accent. God and the afterlife still do well in polls, clocking affirmative ratings of around ninety percent for belief in God and eighty percent for the after-life. In fact, according to a 1999 study by Mark Chaves, a sociologist at the University of Arizona, belief in the afterlife is going up, even as church attendance drops. Attendance has been drifting lower ever since the baby boomers, joining churches as they began to generate families, started to wander away again. Though for decades polls have pegged the number of regular churchgoing Americans at around forty percent, Chaves claims that only twenty-eight percent of Roman Catholics attend Mass on a given weekend and fewer than·one in five Protestants are in church on Sunday morning. Home study and the Sunday-morning reli-gious shows on television are helping empty the pews. As part of the do-it-yourself trend, the sales of religious books have risen spectacularly, by fifty percent in the last ten years.

Yet those few who make it to worship service can testify that there is some liveliness within the churches. Ever younger, frequently female clergypersons have succeeded to the pulpits, and their tone, as they openly cope with such long-unspeakable issues as sexual prophylaxis and homosexual marriage rites, is, all in all, laid-back. A certain pleasantly faded flower-child, hug-your-neighbor sweetness has replaced the sterner old dispensations. Except for the Southern civil-rights movement led by the Reverend Martin Luther King, Jr., the widespread religious impulses of the Sixties in America occurred mainly outside the churches and, indeed, outside Christianity altogether; but the social gospel of love, with its outreach to the losers of the world, including endangered species, has come inside. Where else, in these "me" decades, can one hear it? The younger clergy strike me as resolutely liberal, cheerful, and fearless. Worldliness has no horrors to dismay them. They are bathed in the same blithe outpouring of televised mayhem and prurience as the unchurched. They are hard to shock. If a four-year-old child, welcomed now to the Episcopal altar rail to partake of the Host, makes a face and spits it out, no scandal attends; the sacrament, once attained through the scholarly coming-of-age process of confirmation, is taken to be profanation-proof. And there is much of the New Testament Jesus in this; the Gospels unite in describing Him as no prig.

Beyond the Christian precincts, all sorts of New Age mysticisms, from feng-shui and crystal-gazing to angelolatry and posthumous celebrity-spotting, thrive in spurts of publicity-driven fad. As William James asserted at the other end of the century, the human creature's religious instinct is as obdurate and resourceful as its sexual instinct, and as impervious to reason. Globally, Islamic fundamentalism demonstrates a creed's power to induce censorship and repression and to inspire solidarity and martyrdom; there is even, in India, a counterdefensive Hindu fundamentalism—the oldest living religion seeking in its plethora of deities the root revelation, the basic allegiance. Much of religious loyalty is, after all, a mode of defiance, insisting, *This is what I am.* One thinks of the Irish and the Polish rallying around their Roman Catholicism to spite their larger, colonizing neighbors. Now that the smothering mantle of Communism has been lifted from Eastern Europe, the churches are free to serve as more than foci of contrariety, and, after an immediate surge in attendance and attention, are facing indifference, in its way more deadly than hostility. "We are now past the era of euphoria," a Russian Orthodox Church spokesman has said. In the Czech Republic, four decades of official atheism successfully broke down the religious fabric over whose composition the seventeenth-century Czechs had spilled so much blood. The great Prague churches stand as gorgeous but empty monuments to the Counter-Reformation, and are used mostly to hold concerts for

Western tourists. An acquaintance of mine taking a Czech bride found his hopes of a church wedding in her village met with uncomprehending stares, as if some groom from New Guinea, wearing elaborate facial paint and a bone through his septum, were asking that the volcano god be propitiated with a blood sacrifice.

The welter of religious phenomena is not necessarily comforting to the professor of a specific faith; the very multiplicity and variety suggest that none of it is true, other than manifesting an undoubted human tendency. A Protestant Christian on the eve of the third millennium must struggle with the sensation that his sect is, like the universe itself in the latest cosmological news, winding down, growing thinner and thinner as entropy works an inevitable dimming upon the outspreading stars. There was a Big Bang, we know not why, and there will be no other, just a Big Fade-Out. No Big Crunch, and no Eternal Return, that cosmic reshuffle to whose celebration Nietzsche devoted his post-Christian hopes. As I travelled in Italy, trudging in a trance of jet lag from the Uffizi to the churchly sites of various delicately deteriorating and ingeniously restored frescoes and then on from Florence to damp Venice, the checkpoints of the Christian story as phrased by the Renaissance artists—Adam and Eve and the serpent, and then, in divine reversal of this Fall, the Annunciation, the Visitation, the Virgin's Adoration of the (usually oversized, rather superior and stern) God-Baby, the Adoration of the Wise Men, on up to the dénouement of the Crucifixion, Deposition from the Cross, Pietà, and (most thrillingly by Piero della Francesca on a wall in Sansepolcro) the Resurrection—began to seem opaque, inconsequent, a repetition like that of certain maddening television commercials, this ancient Christian story, this tale of cosmic anthropocentricity, which had provoked oceans of words and served a hundred generations of the faithful as a paradigm to live and die by, and whose details in hasty summary I profess assent to every time I attend church. How much more use can be squeezed from these darkened, crumbling images?

My wife at my side, I should say, never wearied. Each new Annunciation enchanted her with its difference from all the others: in some, Gabriel holds a lily, and in others a palm; the book Mary is traditionally reading can be in her hand, in her lap, or on a lectern; the mood of this amazing moment (imagine being a young Jewish girl informed that she is pregnant by and with God; imagine, for that matter, being a handsome heavenly messenger boy, youthful and androgynous and winged in rainbow colors, dispatched to deliver this incredible news) ranges with a wonderful freedom from aloof acceptance to gesticulating consternation.

Mary is variously alarmed, humble, demurely puzzled, regally pleased, and Gabriel gracefully kneeling, woodenly standing, or arriving in a breathless gust with both bare feet off the floor. In one Cinquecento example, at the Palazzo Grassi, in an exhibition devoted to the interaction between Venetian painting and Northern realism, a cat (symbolic perhaps of the Devil) leaps and bristles at the sudden announcement. My wife laughed in delight. And when we pressed our faces against the grille that rudely interferes with viewing the famous Deposition by Pontormo, in the Capponi Chapel in Florence's Santa Felicità, and, on the adjacent wall, an Annunciation that consists of two frescoed figures separated by a window and an ornate altarpiece, even I felt buoyed by the luminous floatingness Pontormo conveys in his electric, fruity colors—by the annulment of universal gravity proposed by the Christian comedy.

An Italian guide who took us to see the Pontormo Visitation that hangs in lonely grandeur in the parish church of San Michele, in Carmignano, seemed gratified at the idea, put forward by scholars of Renaissance art, that the apparent hollowness of the artist's figures, the doll-like blankness of their faces, and the refusal of their billowing robes to suggest bulk together confess an otherwise inexpressible emptying-out of belief: the mannerism of Pontormo—a man of considerable personal strangeness—anticipates postmodernism's irreverent mockeries.

At the end of two weeks of inspecting church walls and holy images, I thought to cleanse my palate, as it were, by visiting the Venice Biennale. My wife declined to waste her precious time on modern trash. Alone, a dazed and footsore pilgrim, I made my way from one pavilion to another, exposing myself to artificial fog and upside-down dandelions in the Belgian pavilion, unintelligible whispers and showers of magenta dust in the American, a room of electronic numbers in the Japanese, and in the Russian pavilion photographs taken by a chimpanzee and abstract paintings brushed by trained elephants. Everywhere, abrasive irony and nihilism. The Germans mounted huge videos of nothing much happening, and the Slovaks hundreds of tattoos, with an apparently sincere offer to needle any of the designs into a visitor's skin at appointed hours. A deafening, enraged roar of racing automobiles and stacks of painted tires filled the Danish pavilion; the French had actually dismantled the floor of their exhibit hall, a solid old structure dating back to 1912, and showed its fragments under a grate, ten feet down. The French also incorporated several utterly white rooms, along whose surfaces of blazing vacuity floated the specks of my aging vitreous humors. It was an innocent little nation—Uruguay, South Korea—that exhibited something, in used woods or nacreous sequins, that reminded one of art in the old sense, which prevailed until about 1965, of a physical object amenable to being housed and contemplated. The desire to shock the hardened art connoisseur into some kind of response had become veritably frantic; there was hardly an inch of the void, of disgust, of scorn left to expose, in this age of post-faith. Only the vegetation and the other spectators at the Biennale—generally young, drifting hand in hand from one calculated, not infrequently obscene affront to another—belonged to a world I wanted to be in, a world I could recognize to be continuous with the world of my childhood.

Faith is not so much a binary pole as a quantum state, which tends to vanish when closely examined. In the several New England suburbs where I have lived most of my adult life, there was no easy telling, from other signs, who was and who was not a churchgoer. Models of rectitude and conventionality turned out to scorn religious observance, to the point where even their funerals were held in the wild, a scattering of ashes leaving no trace. Other citizens of the suburbs, cheerfully dissolute on weekdays, appeared compulsively at early Sunday service under their cloud of hangover and carnal knowledge. We all know of the women who come to pray while their husbands lounge in front of *Face the Nation* or sit in the car reading the newspaper; but I have been struck by the number of unaccompanied men who show up in church, sitting, standing, and kneeling their way through this errand of habit or ancestral homage.* A differentiating factor of intelligence is not conspicuous. At the end of the millennium and of a century that has the Holocaust at its center, the reasons for doubt in God's existence are easily come by—His invisibility, His apparent indifference to the torrents of pain and cruelty that history books and the news media report, the persuasive explanations that science offers for almost all phenomena once thought mysterious. Church attendance must be taken, at least in the American Northeast, as a willful decision to evade atheist respectability.

To be sure, the church exists in the world. In its centuries of domi-

---

*There is also the phenomenon—I know several instances—of the faithful churchgoer who at the end spurns all the ecclesiastical consolation he would seem to have earned. The final depression sweeps aside all of faith's furniture. Samuel Beckett, reared in the Protestant Church of Ireland, is quoted in Deirdre Bair's biography as saying, "My mother and brother got no value from their religion when they died. At the moment of crisis it has no more depth than an old school tie." Church membership can be, among other things, an old school tie. In a review of me, come to think of it, Elizabeth Hardwick claims that by having my characters Piet Hanema and Rabbit Angstrom go to church (Rabbit erratically, at best) I am giving them "a sort of club handshake."

nance, it had the power to exclude and excommunicate; now, unlike most other organizations, it will take us in if we so much as show up. The weak, the misfit, the outcast are theoretically welcome. It is the last outpost of acceptance, the last resort of sociability. In many a town and neighborhood, the church still functions as a meeting place, and, in its charitable programs, a convivial place of good works. It is good for your health: a 1999 Duke University study shows that regular churchgoers were twenty-eight percent less likely to die in a given seven-year period than non-churchgoers. But a faith-based institution will not last long as merely a health club; other health clubs exist, and other, less demanding means for generating togetherness. The pith and poignance of a church lie in its being a company of believers.

It is difficult to imagine anyone shouldering the implausible complications of Christian doctrine—the Christian story, however pared-down since the days when Italians were painting it into walls of wet plaster—without some inheritance of positive prior involvement. I remember, for instance, taking collection with my father at Wednesday-night Lenten services, not long after we moved from a small town to the country, in southeastern Pennsylvania. Compared with the suburban church where my father had been a Sunday-school teacher and church-council member, the new church—a brown-steepled sandstone ark that my mother's father had helped build as a young man—drew on a sparse rural population. At these special Wednesday-night services, a scattering of the especially dutiful occupied the creaking Lutheran pews. The basement furnace audibly sighed and clunked as it chewed over the chilly Lenten air. I was fourteen or so, newly (and uncomfortably) confirmed; the dislocation to the country had unsettled me. I was experiencing my growth spurt, and, though never as tall as my father, I felt tall with him as we walked together down the aisle to receive the collection plates. I remember them as wooden and unexpectedly light in the hand, like model airplanes. There may have been a skeleton choir on Wednesday nights, but my memory is of silence as the plate was passed, skidding away down the pew and then returning heavier by a few bits of paper—dollar bills or Lenten-offering envelopes. Although my head at the time brimmed with worldly concerns (girls, cartoons, baseball), it was *nice*, I thought, of this church, where my father and I were still near-strangers, to cast the two of us in this responsible, even exalted, role.

My father to the day of his death more than twenty-five years later served that church, in various capacities, while I escaped to college and beyond. He was the son of a minister, but he felt his father had failed in the ministry, having lacked "the call" and, perhaps accordingly, the necessary devoted energy. Where many fathers—some of them described in late-Victorian novels—conveyed to their sons an oppressive faith that it was a joy to cast off, my father communicated to me, not with words but with his actions and his melancholy, a sense of the Christian religion as something weak and tenuous and in need of rescue. There *is* a way in which success disagrees with Christianity. Its proper venue is embattlement—a furtive hanging-on in the catacombs or at ill-attended services in dying rural and inner-city parishes. Its perilous, marginal, mocked existence serves as an image of our own, beneath whatever show of success can be momentarily mustered. At any rate, I had no Oedipal motive to discard it; at college and in New York City I found my way fitfully to Lutheran services, shunning deeper involvement but stealing away cleansed and lightened, and taking a certain contrarian pride in participating in ceremonies that, by the wisdom of the world, were profitless and irrational.

Against the terrific tide of rational disbelief must stand an inner sense of contact that is rather cumbersomely signified by terms like "witness" and "knowing Christ," or a sense, at least, of one's life being shaped, in its broadest eventualities, by transactions with the supernatural. My mother did not go to the small-town church my father taught Sunday school in; but in 1944, when she took it into her head to buy back the farm where she was born, she made some kind of inner bargain by whose terms she attended church for the rest of her life—forty-five years' worth of Sunday mornings. With such a family background, and with a consciousness of rare good fortune in my own life, I have found it psychologically convenient to maintain a Christian connection, which has wound through three Protestant denominations but left little trace, I fear, in the spiritual lives of my children. Some of my grandchildren are not even baptized, thus ending the dogged proprieties of Heaven knows how many generations of God-fearing Dutchmen—New Jersey Dutch on my father's side, Pennsylvania "Dutch" on my mother's. My consorts through the years have, I believe, found my going off to church, usually alone, an annoying affectation and not, as I felt it, a gallant donning of the armor in which a good citizen sallies forth: "Since we belong to the day," Paul wrote to the Thessalonians, "let us be sober, and put on the breastplate of faith and love, and for a helmet the hope of salvation."

The Berks County of my childhood was a region where everybody seemed to go to church, the presiding state-sponsored pieties went unquestioned, and the schools and town affairs were all run by Lutheran or Reformed Church deacons. It was not until I moved to New England that I saw people washing their cars on Sunday mornings—blasphemy in broad daylight! For me there has been no other contestant in the existential arena than the Christian creed, no other answer to the dread that one's mortal existence brings with it. "I am moved to terror," Pascal wrote, "like a man transported in his sleep to some terrifying desert island, who wakes up quite lost and with no means of escape." If this physical world is all, then it is a closed hell in which we are confined, as Pascal said elsewhere, like prisoners in chains, condemned to watch the other prisoners being slain—a hell where art-lovers must wander through the Venice Biennale, observing how art holds the mirror up to the grimacing post-human.

What might a faith of the future consist of? More of the same, most likely. Religions are conservative artifacts, made from scraps of others. Buddhism is a purification of Hinduism, and Christianity an offshoot of Judaism. Of the religions founded since Christianity, Islam, dating from the seventh century, rephrases Semitic monotheism, paying respect to its earlier embodiments. The Koran states, "God has ordained for you the religion he commended unto Noah and which we have revealed to thee and we commended unto Abraham and Moses and Jesus," and enjoins the faithful to say to "the People of the Book" (Jews and Christians), "Our God and your God are one." Whatever its present totalitarian tendencies, Islam began as non-exclusivist, and, for long eras, in many places, maintained a toleration of other faiths that Christianity could not match. Sikhism, founded in the late fifteenth century, numbers twenty million adherents, centered in the East Punjab, and combines Islamic and Hindu beliefs as formulated by its founder, Nanak, in a book of holy writings called the Guru Granth Sahib. Baha'ism emerged in nineteenth-century Persia out of the Shi'ite branch of Islam. A young man claimed to be the Bab, the "gate" of divine guidance, and was executed at the age of thirty. After his death, a disciple, Baha'u'llah, proclaimed himself one of a series of divine manifestations that also includes Jesus, Muhammad, Zoroaster, and the Buddha—a full deck. The six million Baha'is are scattered over the globe, most thickly in Iran, where they are persecuted.

Two Asian sects have recently troubled the governments of Japan and China, making headlines. Aum Shinrikyo, the Japanese cult indicted for planting poison gas in Tokyo subways, professes to practice a primitive or fundamental form of Buddhism, naming Lord Shiva, god of destruction and regeneration, as its highest god. Aum Shinrikyo's head, Shoko Asahara, a former acupuncturist now in jail, stresses "freedom from illness" in his teachings, and claims to be able to levitate as well as heal. Distinctly modern, perhaps, is the cult's attempt to bring on the apocalypse by killing subway riders with the nerve gas serin, and by such devout gadgetry as the Perfect Salvation cap, a piece of headgear, containing electrodes attached to a six-volt battery, designed to bring the wearer's brain waves into sync with Asahara's. His followers were also privileged, when he was at liberty, to kiss his big toe and to pay upwards of two hundred dollars for a drink of his used bathwater.

Beleaguered Aum numbers its membership merely in the thousands; Falun Gong, the Chinese movement so big that it has attracted a government ban, is estimated to have as many as seventy million followers. Meaning "Wheel of the Law," Falun Gong proposes a mystical wheel that rotates in the lower abdomen, curing disease and physical decay; its adherents perform outdoor exercises closely related to the ancient practice of *qi gong*, the use of breathing exercises to regulate the life force within the body. Harmless and venerable these practices might seem to be, but the government calls the sect subversive, alleging that it promulgates such disturbing ideas as "global doomsday" and "earth explosion," reducing some followers to insanity and suicide. Its founder, Li Hongzhi, lives in New York City exile, and exerts his sway via the Internet.

Ambitious novelists, too, are working at new religions: Tom Wolfe's *A Man in Full* portrays two characters' conversion to Epicurean Stoicism, including faith in a personal Zeus, and Don DeLillo's *Underworld* ends in a hymn to cyberspace. The notion that a new magical mode of being will emerge from cyberspace is widespread—I noticed it frequently in Italian television commercials—though what "cyberspace" might be, other than a digitized electronic grab-bag of everything already out there in ordinary space, including sales pitches, pornography, and rampant misspelling and misinformation, is not clear to at least this skeptic. Communism was no doubt a religion, with martyrs and a static future paradise, until its preachments were put into practice. Its collapse everywhere save for a few isolated holdouts and the ambivalent case of China has bred many weird maggots of belief, including a cult whose prophet is said to induce mass orgasms by mental telepathy. A Russian lawyer suing a Russian branch of Aum Shinrikyo put it that "the country has shared ideals and then, suddenly, they were gone. People need something new to believe in."

Yet the creation of new religions is circumscribed by the same dispassionate developments in science that wounded and weakened the old ones. Since Galileo, astronomy has had cosmology ever firmer in hand, and the present picture of the universe is dispiriting—a hugely prolonged, one-way, apparently accelerating expansion ending in an unthinkably diffuse dispersal of energy. Stars will cease forming, and eventually all will wink out. The black holes will evaporate, and in an ever thinner soup of subatomic particles individual positrons and electrons will seek to annihilate each other, forming inwardly spiralling mutual orbits over distances many times greater than the span of the present observable universe. According to Paul Davies's *The Last Three Minutes:*

> Their orbits would be many trillions of light-years in diameter! The particles would move so slowly that they would take a million years to travel a centimeter. So sluggish would the electrons and positrons have become that the spiral time works out at a staggering 10^{116} years. Nevertheless, the final fate of these positronium atoms is sealed from the moment they form.

A few scientists have tried to find cheer in even this titanically bleak scenario. In a 1979 paper, the physicist Freeman Dyson proposed that intelligent life of some futuristic sort could survive into this virtual eternity, by slowing its metabolism and rate of thought to match the environment, and conserving its energy with long periods of hibernation. A discussion of Dyson's proposals, by Lawrence M. Krauss and Glenn D. Starkman in the November 1999 issue of *Scientific American*, argues that the alarm clocks needed to time wake-up calls so widely spaced would run into the limits of quantum mechanics, and that the quality of life enjoyed by these hypothetical immortal organisms would be more hellish than heavenly: "All organisms would ever do is relive the past, having the same thoughts over and over again."

Frank Tipler, Professor of Mathematical Physics at Tulane University, goes Dyson one better. In his large, formula- and graph-ridden *The Physics of Immortality* (1993), he predicts, by what he insists is pure empirical deduction, an end-time when life will have "engulfed" the entire universe, milked the heat differential between various parts of it for "shear energy," and computerized everything. A God-like entity called the Omega Point will, for benevolent reasons that slipped by me, resurrect us all as computer simulations: "The dead will be resurrected when the computer capacity of the universe is so large that the amount of capacity required to store all possible human simulations is an insignificant fraction of the entire capacity." These ideas already figured in the last chapter of a book Tipler wrote with John D. Barrow, *The Anthropic Cosmological Principle* (1986). Our physical universe is, in a sense, highly unlikely; to be stable and long-lived enough to provide time for intelligent life to evolve, it required a number of long-odds happy coincidences among the physical constants, from the Big Bang's expansion rate to, subatomically, the fine-structure constant and the strength of the weak interaction. The "anthropic principle," in its strongest form, holds therefore that the universe was designed to produce us; it does not say why an omnipotent God would choose to create our species by such a lengthy, wasteful, and cruel method as evolution. Theistic exercises in science and logic, from Aristotle to Aquinas to Deism, may comfort believers but will rarely convert disbelievers. A God who could be proved would be an inescapable tyrant, an inert and imprisoning datum. No religion is apt to be founded on cold reason. Belief, like love, must be voluntary.

Or perhaps the religion of the future lies all about us, in the proliferating escapism and induced hysteria of electronic "entertainment." We are surrounded by entertainment more completely than medieval man was by the church and its propaganda. Feeling despondent and lonely? Turn on the television set. It is really hard to believe, after a while, that Tom Brokaw is not your friend—that he does not see you, and love you as you love him. To many an impoverished shut-in, the apparitions of television are realer than the priest and the social worker. People pray to Elvis; the Beatles were bigger than Jesus, as John Lennon pointed out before his celebrity brought martyrdom.

If the neural wiring that determines the religious instinct is "hard" and intrinsic, it is not surprising that religions have so strong a family resemblance. Buddhism, proposing a virtual atheism and an end to craving, sprouted idols and an elaborate afterlife. "Why are you all here?" the minister of a Congregational church asked me and the rest of his skimpy flock one Sunday morning. "Because you want to live forever!" Freud, in a paragraph of *Civilization and Its Discontents*, puts it all sternly in place. "Religion," he says,

> imposes equally on everyone its own path to the acquisition of happiness and protection from suffering. Its technique consists in depressing the value of life and distorting the picture of the real world in a delusional manner— which presupposes an intimidation of the intelligence. At this price, by forcibly fixing them in a state of psychical infantilism and by drawing them into a mass-delusion, religion succeeds in sparing many people an individual neurosis. But hardly anything more.

It surprised me, encountering this passage, that Freud did not think being spared neurosis was worth much. And that he saw religion as "depressing the value of life." William James—himself not much more of a believer than Freud—saw it as the enhancer of life: "Let Heaven smile upon the earth, and deities pay their visits; let faith and hope be the atmosphere which man breathes in;—and his days pass by with zest; they stir with prospects, they thrill with remoter values."

The Varieties of Religious Experience assembled a mass of testimony to give its readers what James called "the right to believe." Personal testimony is the empirical style of American religion, and it would be a shy essayist who came up with none. When half my present age, I was at a New England women's college to give a reading and judge a poetry contest, and was seized by terror. The nubile students' youth, innocence, and gentle appetite to know and be known struck me as amazing and monstrous, given that we were all poised above the chasm—suddenly quite present to me—of our eventual deaths. Numbly I went through my professorial performance, and in the dormitory bedroom to which I had been assigned prepared to pass the night with my terror. I had suffered such episodes before; it is as if one were suddenly flayed of the skin of habit and herd feeling that customarily enwraps and muffles our deep predicament. I once gave this experience to a fictional character, a Jewish character, though it may be a Christian-specific form of harrowing; Tolstoy describes it, and Unamuno. In the dorm room there was a small shelf of books, and one of the books, on the page I opened it to, directly addressed my sensations, offering, in plain and friendly language, various mental easements. It was, I suppose, self-help, with a pious flavor—not the sort of book I usually read. Ungratefully enough, I have forgotten the title and the author; nor did I have any desire to take the volume with me. The shamefulness of my impotent, grovelling anxiety attached to the book that allayed it. I slept after reading a number of pages. They got me through the night. The next day I was still scared, but in an achy, stiff-moving way, like muscles after too much exercise.

And a few weeks ago, in Florence, in a hotel room near the Duomo, I woke in the night, and felt, in the strange hotel room, fearful and adrift, near my life's end, a wide-awake mote in an alien, sleeping city. It had been the day of an atomic-plant disaster in Japan, and of Günter Grass's receiving the Nobel Prize. Part of my desolation, let me confess, was my having consented, against my better judgment, to write, as *The New Yorker*'s token Christian, this piece on the future of faith. The attempt felt dangerous; I feared it might empty out of me the last drops of what feeble faith had got me this far. To relieve my loneliness, I prayed, asking to be allowed to sleep, without much expecting the prayer to be answered.

But then, getting up to go to the bathroom, I became aware of noise, a rustling all around me, and then thunder's blanketing boom, repeated. I went to the window. The room had a diagonal view of the Duomo—Brunelleschi's engineering miracle, the hub of Florence, the crown of Santa Maria del Fiore, the fourth-largest church in Christendom. While I watched, the rain intensified, rattling on tile roofs near and far; it looked like rods of metal in the floodlight that illumined part of the great—the world's greatest, pre-steel—red-tiled dome. Lightning. Hectic gusts. The rain was furious. I was not alone in the universe. The rippling rods of rain drove down upon the vertical beam of light at the base of the Duomo as if to demolish it; but the pillar of light burned on, and the hulking old church crouched like a stoic mute dragon, and the thick tiles and gurgling gutters around me withstood the soaking, the thunder, the shuddering flashes. I was filled with a glad sense of exterior activity. My burden of being was being shared. God was at work—at ease, even, in this nocturnal Florentine commotion, this heavenly wrath and architectural defiance, this Jacobean wrestle. My wife woke up, admired the solemn tempest with me, and went back to bed. I lay down beside her and fell asleep amid the comforting, busy, self-careless drumming. All this felt like a transaction, a rescue, an answered prayer.

The future is not just an extension of the past; something new enters in. Judaism and Christianity are both religions of waiting—waiting in one case for the Messiah, in the other for the Messiah's Second Coming. This time that we occupy is an interim stretching much longer than the prophets and early saints expected. An event might enliven faith's future. Science might come up with a surprise—a loophole down among the quarks, or, as in Harry Mulisch's 1996 novel *The Discovery of Heaven*, a Heaven behind a pulsar. The dynamic of human nature, as it rolls past six billion living instances, might produce a qualitative change in the frame of faith or, to be accurate, of the world's tired, grotesque, irreplaceable faiths. What occurs won't be easily intelligible—the Gospels took most of a century to get written—but the yearning, the insistence that there be, to again quote William James, "something more," will persist. Our concepts of art and virtue and purpose are so tied up with the supernatural it is hard to foresee doing altogether without it.

Invisible Cathedral

(A Preview of the New Museum of Modern Art)

October 2004

TIMES SQUARE has been sanitized and skyscraperized; the subway cars are brightly lit inside and graffiti-free inside and out. New York is going pristine. It is not easy, while gingerly stepping over loose floorboards and extension cords as thick as boa constrictors, to picture the new Museum of Modern Art in every tidy and clean-swept detail, but enough was on view to persuade this visitor that the final effect will be immaculate, rectilinear, capacious, and chaste. Whether or not more could be asked of a museum, of a *modern* museum, I don't know. The white interiors, chamber upon chamber, some already hung with old friends from MoMA's priceless collection and some as bare as a freshly plastered storage closet, gave, a few weeks shy of their unveiling to the public, the impression of a condition delicately balanced between presence and absence. The architect, Yoshio Taniguchi, is Japanese, and a riddling Zen* reticence presided over the acres of white wall and white-oak floor, the panels of rare white bronze inset in aluminum door frames, the countless beady little halogen spotlights on discreetly recessed tracks, the sheets of light-filtering "fritted" glass with their tiny pale strips of baked-in ceramic, and the hushed escalators, whose oily works, not yet functional, were exposed to view and to the ministrations of workmen. Looking into these gears laid bare put me in mind, nostalgically, of the early Giacometti sculpture, *Woman with Her Throat Cut*, that used to lie on a low pedestal on the second floor, and of Arnaldo Pomodoro's great bronze ball, its polished skin partially flayed, that for a time sat in the old lobby.

Nothing in the new building is obtrusive, nothing is cheap. It feels breathless with unspared expense; it has the enchantment of a bank after hours, of a honeycomb emptied of honey and flooded with a soft glow. My guide, genial William J. Maloney, the project director, quoted the architect as saying to the museum trustees something like this: "Raise a lot of money for me, I'll give you good architecture. Raise even more money, I'll make the architecture disappear." And disappear, in a way, it has. The customary sensations that buildings give us—of secure enclosure, of masses of matter firmly supported—are diluted by a black gap, an inch and a quarter wide, that runs along the bottom and top of every interior wall, and even at the base of weight-bearing pillars, so that everything, subtly, floats. The gaps are useful for heat and air-conditioning, too, but their aesthetic accomplishment is to dematerialize the walls; the visitor moves through spaces demarcated as if by Japanese paper screens. As he moves, artfully arranged glimpses out into the city and across a dizzying, hundred-and-ten-foot-tall atrium orient him and vary his view. Maloney spoke again for the architect: "He didn't want a box that could be anywhere. He said, 'I want the people to know they are in New York

---

*There is a Zen term, *mu*, that seems applicable: it means "nothingness," as a spiritual and aesthetic concept, and in architecture approximates Mies van der Rohe's German term for the desired minimalism, *beinahe nichts*—"almost nothing." So now we have MuMA.

City.' " North-facing windows frame segments, like Hopper paintings, of the handsome brownstones along West Fifty-fourth Street. On the sixth, top floor, a wide skylight provides an alarming upward perspective of Cesar Pelli's fifty-two-story residential tower, which was erected in 1985 on museum land to one side of the existing museum and is now more or less in its center. "Can you imagine," Maloney asked, "we had to build this with *that* hanging over us?" He allowed that the tower's inhabitants had complained of a few jolts and shudders in the three years of construction beneath their feet. But no harm was done. Engineering miracles are a dime a dozen in Manhattan.

The museum has expanded a number of times since its opening on November 8, 1929, in a rented space on the twelfth floor of the Heckscher Building, at the corner of Fifth Avenue and Fifty-seventh Street. In spite of the stock-market crash in progress, the exhibit was so well attended that the building's other tenants complained of having to fight crowds at the elevators. The six improvised galleries showed four painters now classified as Post-Impressionist; the *Boston Transcript* sarcastically put it,

> Thursday the newly created Museum of Modern Art opened the doors of its temporary galleries and held a house-warming. The invited guests, besides the usual group of socially elect, were Cézanne, Gauguin, Seurat, and Van Gogh.

The fab four, in fact, attended in force—thirty-five Cézannes, twenty-six Gauguins, seventeen Seurats, and twenty-seven van Goghs. In 1932, the thriving museum moved to a five-story townhouse, owned by John D. Rockefeller, Jr., at 11 West Fifty-third Street, which is still its address. A boxy structure designed as a museum in the "International Style" by Philip L. Goodwin and Edward Durell Stone replaced it in 1939; this building was added on to in 1951, 1964, and 1984.

West Fifty-third and Fifty-fourth Streets were residential neighborhoods, with backyards and access alleys; therefore, museum expansion, except for the Abby Aldrich Rockefeller Sculpture Garden, worked sideways along Fifty-third Street, and the galleries were strung along a rather narrow and inflexible route. In 1996, the Dorset Hotel, fondly remembered for its exiguous lobby and dilatory elevators, plus several adjacent brownstones on Fifty-third and Fifty-fourth Streets, came up for sale; the museum acquired them, giving it a property stretching from Saint Thomas Church on Fifth Avenue to the Museum of American Folk Art a few doors up from the Avenue of the Americas. A thorough redesign was now possible, and it was entrusted to Taniguchi Associates, a Tokyo firm for whom this was the first international commission. The inkling, in the winter of 1928–29, shared by three well-to-do women (Mrs. John D. Rockefeller, Jr., Miss Lillie P. Bliss, and Mrs. Cornelius J. Sullivan), that New York should have a venue for the display of distinctly modern art had in seventy-five years bloomed into a cultural force able to commandeer swaths of midtown real estate and erect new buildings at a cost approaching a billion dollars. The goal for the capital campaign was set at eight hundred fifty-eight million dollars; more than seven hundred million has already been secured, with the Board of Trustees contributing a total of more than five hundred million. The project included the acquisition, as a temporary exhibition site and a permanent storage and study facility, of the old 160,000-square-foot staple factory now labeled MoMA Queens. The renovations and new construction at the midtown site alone came to four hundred twenty-five million.

A broad, slightly sloping lobby paved in green slate now connects Fifty-third and Fifty-fourth Streets and provides two entrances to the museum. On the eastern side, an eight-story Education and Research Building named for Lewis B. and Dorothy Cullman has arisen, and on the western side a thirteen-story tower for offices and galleries. In the middle, the lower seven floors of Pelli's high-rise have been incorporated into the museum itself. Outside on Fifty-third Street, the façades of the 1939 structure, with its piano-shaped canopy and square windows of translucent Thermolux, and of the 1964 addition by Philip Johnson, whose larger, milled-steel windows have rounded corners, are refurbished and preserved—a satisfying historical touch in an urban environment not given to many such. The accumulation, which endows the museum with a center-city presence to rival the Metropolitan's grand gracing of the Upper East Side, defers to its surroundings. Viewed from Fifty-third Street, through the dust and clamor of construction still in progress, the structure behind the medley of façades does not present an arresting silhouette, like Frank Lloyd Wright's top-shaped Guggenheim or Frank Gehry's titanium extravagance in Bilbao. The new MoMA is not that kind of showpiece. Rather, its six stories of reticent white chambers, tucked under Pelli's overbearing gray-and-brown glass tower, melt into the squared-off cityscape and form, with their treasures, an invisible cathedral.

It used to be said that airports were our new cathedrals, the Heaven-probing spires replaced by ascending and descending airplanes. But airports have become workaday and shabby, cluttered with the machinery of heightened security and menaced by airline bankruptcy—bus terminals on the brink, more like refuse-littered marketplaces than like places of worship. In their stead the art museums, once haunted by a few experts, students, and idlers, have become the thronged temples of the Ideal, of the *something else* that, if only for a peaceful moment, redeems our daily getting and spending; here resides a spirit beyond our quiet desperation, our animal urgencies. Leonardo scornfully spoke of men who do nothing in their time on earth but produce excrement. Art, in its traditional forms of painting, drawing, and sculpture, is a human by-product whose collection, in homes, galleries, and museums, lightens the load, as it were, of life. By its glow we bask in the promise of a brighter, more lasting realm reached by a favored few—Saint Vermeer, Saint Pollock, Saint Leonardo. In Paris and Florence, the tourists from Japan come by the busload, pose giggling for a photograph in front of the *Mona Lisa* or *The Birth of Venus*, and hurry back to the other side of the planet, obscurely blessed.

The old European museums tend to be converted palaces—the former residences of aristocrats whose duty to the masses was, by a curious clause in the social contract, conspicuous expenditure. Palatial, too, were their American equivalents, monuments to the Mellons and the Fricks and the Havemeyers; now the damask-covered walls and carved marble lintels compete, in a general outpouring of luxury, with the incalculably high-priced works on display. The frames themselves are princely and, once noticed, spectacular. But a fresh kind of opulence, submerged in a refined modesty, elaborately defers to the art itself. The seven-year-old Beyeler Museum on the outskirts of Basel was designed by Renzo Piano with the donor at his elbow urging (according to an informal talk that Beyeler, a handsome octogenarian, gave to a touring group of which I was a member) less architecture and more focus on his paintings. The art is accordingly lit with the latest louvered sunshades and mounted in a structure of noble simplicity, whose cost of more than forty million dollars is reflected mostly in the fine workmanship and elegant materials. The long, low building slips into the watery suburban landscape like a sword into a green sheath; the reddish porphyry of the walls tactfully echoes the local stone used to build the medieval Basel cathedral, now a Protestant church, with its cloisters and spectacular late-Gothic pulpit.

According to Russell Lynes's 1979 book, *Good Old Modern: An Intimate Portrait of the Museum of Modern Art*, at the time of MoMA's founding so-called modern art was ill regarded by most of the public. In 1921, a show of Impressionists and Post-Impressionists at the Metropolitan Museum of Art excited, eight years after the notorious Armory Show, outrage verging on the apoplectic; a four-page printed protest decreed, "This 'Modernistic' degenerate cult is simply the Bolshevic philosophy applied to art," and went on to claim:

> The real cult of "Modernism" began with a small group of neurotic Ego-Maniacs in Paris who styled themselves "Satanists"—worshipers of Satan—the God of Ugliness.

The Metropolitan did not venture to show modern art soon again, helping create the vacuum that the female founders of MoMA hoped to fill: the Museum of Modern Art has been called "the Metropolitan's worst mistake." In 1929, apropos of the infant MoMA's inaugural show, Jerome Klein wrote in the *Boston Transcript:*

> For a number of years the worthy trustees of America's greatest museum, the Metropolitan Museum of Art, have been subjected to considerable embarrassment; a great many people have had the bad taste to inquire in the public prints why the competent administrators of the museum have taken no cognizance of the emergence of art in the world of today. . . . The clamor grew and the trustees and their henchmen awoke one day to the horrible discovery that Cézanne and his upstarts had for years been taken up by the best society.

Now even the hoi polloi accept as obvious the beauty and power of the Post-Impressionists; long lines form at their megashows, and the museum stores do a busy trade in prints, posters, shopping bags, and notepads consecrated with their imagery. Fragile-appearing, jokey modernism—its little Cubist canvases, its yellowing collages and deadpan Dada pranks—grew and grew and eventually tore down the Dorset.

The new building inevitably incorporates modernism's problematical nature. When does modern art begin? Some say with Manet, and he did, with his individualized nudes in everyday settings, affront the bourgeoisie; but, then, so did Courbet, who nonetheless clearly belongs to the old dispensation. As to the Impressionists, they were revolutionaries, and the visual arts still inhabit their revolution. But modern? MoMA began, in late 1929, with the Post-Impressionists, and they make a good starting-point, around 1880. They have the theoretical, abstractifying bent typical of modernism, and its determined individuality of style, so that no mature artist can be confused with another, as a Monet might be with a Pissarro or a Sisley. Though the Post-Impressionists still portray the visible world, the reproduction of natural appearances is no longer the heart of the game. After centuries of shadowy, complex illusionism, they used bold colors and simplified shapes. We value them for the academic resistance they met, and they earn our love with their suffering—van Gogh in the insane asylum, Gauguin in the South Seas, Seurat dying young, Cézanne plodding to the easel day after day in eremitic isolation. All of them died before their immortality was widely acknowledged.

And when will modern art end? Robert Hughes, in his *The Shock of the New*, argues that it died around 1970, with Andy Warhol's anomic embrace of "business art" and the passing of the concept of the avant-garde. By the Seventies, a pervasive cultural permissiveness made a cutting edge hard to locate; suddenly, after Action Painting, Pop, Op, Color Field, and Minimalism, art ran out of nameable movements. There was no more "modern," there was just "contemporary." Glenn D. Lowry, MoMA's director since 1995, addresses, in a thoughtful ten-page essay, the museum's history and its situation—doubled attendance, proliferating collection—prior to Taniguchi's twenty-first-century expansion:

> A number of options were available, from ceasing to collect contemporary art all together—never a serious possibility—to establishing a separate museum for contemporary art, which, however, in establishing a division between the earliest and the most recent works in the collection, would have created more problems than it solved.

The new museum's layout is open-ended, with a double-height, column-free space set aside on the reinforced second floor for contemporary art—its sheets of warped steel, its mountains of bricks or tin cans or lavender teddy bears, its mazy installations and untidy ropeworks. Whatever contemporary art is not (pleasurable, say, or exquisite), it is *big*, and Taniguchi has created a giant room for it, stealing height from the floor above and providing a sliding door whereby oversize sculpture can be gantried in from the street. What is left of the third floor holds galleries for photographs, drawings, and architecture and design. The next floor up, the fourth, is intended for works, such as the large canvases of the Abstract Expressionists, from the postwar period to 1970, and the fifth, linked to it by a cantilevered staircase as well as by the escalators and elevators that connect every floor, will shelter the relatively small canvases and sculptures of classic modernism, from the end of the nineteenth century to 1945. The sixth floor is reserved for special exhibitions, and for the museum's opening its vast space will be devoted to two mural-sized pieces—the former billboard artist James Rosenquist's eighty-six-foot-wide *F-111*, and Ellsworth Kelly's playfully polychromatic *Sculpture for a Large Wall*.

The first floor will hold, besides the entry lobby and desks for admission and membership, the commercial enterprises increasingly conspicuous among a museum's attractions, the bookstore/shop and the restaurants. The largest restaurant, on the first floor, comes in three slices, fancy in direct proportion to their nearness to the Sculpture Garden. Farthest from it is the bar and the bar food, in a space fittingly named after the museum's fabled first director, Alfred H. Barr, Jr.; next, a café serving mostly grilled dishes; and then, with a proximate view of the garden and in season some outdoor tables, the *restaurant de résistance*, bluntly called the Modern and generaled by a name chef, Gabriel Kreuther, sprung from the Ritz-Carlton on Central Park South. All eating places (and there are more, on the second and fifth floors) will be operated by Danny Meyer's Union Square Hospital Group. The first-floor establishments can be entered by a kind of speakeasy entrance from noon until as late as eleven-thirty; one looks forward to a heist movie in which Robert De Niro and George Clooney sneak upstairs from their eleven-p.m. espresso and brandy to appropriate, as background music underlines the hair-raising suspense, some Picassos and Brancusis. The Sculpture Garden itself, longer and wider, and walled from Fifty-fourth Street not by the old brick construction but by severe granite slabs, has been born again with new young trees, replacing birches and weeping beeches that had been getting too big and shaggy anyway.

The cathedral stands ready for the faithful. Here they come: the sore-footed tourists, foreign and domestic; the suburban adventuresses in for lunch; the Brearley seniors with their flaxen tresses and spiral-bound sketchbooks; the East Village youths, two years out of Podunk, looking for an art fix even if it means sitting through Andy Warhol's static epic *Empire*. A few pilgrims, perhaps, will turn back from the counter when they are told that the admission fee is twenty dollars for adults and a mere twelve and sixteen respectively for students and sixty-five-and-overs who have the IDs to prove it. But a balcony seat at a failing Broadway musical costs three times that, and MoMA floor space has been increased by almost half again, from eighty-five thousand square feet to one hundred twenty-five thousand.

Is more truly more? MoMA, which I first visited in the late 1940s, was a relatively intimate collection of human-scale works in non-palatial rooms. Picasso's *Guernica*, on loan to keep it away from Franco, and Rousseau's *Sleeping Gypsy* were the biggest canvases in sight; Baziotes, Dubuffet, and Peter Blume were the latest things on the walls. You could hustle through it in an hour or two, on a one-way route. With the expansion of 1964, which added the splendid large Picasso-Matisse room, some choices for ambulation were offered; but the experience was still, on the second floor, a single one, with an entrance and an exit. Now four floors, plus soundproof galleries for video and media, beckon from all sides. One of the charms of the museum and of modern art was that there wasn't too much of it, just as a lifetime's worth of history isn't too much. After seventy-five years, a life is a stretch and a cathedral may have sprouted too many chapels. "*Nous verrons*," as Cézanne might remark, squinting toward Mont Sainte-Victoire. We shall see.

POSTSCRIPT: *A year after this favorable preview, several visits to MoMA in operation have left mixed impressions. The pristine walls showed scuff-marks. The floating look disappeared in rooms full of people. The Sculpture Garden had lost its charm along with the cozy old dimensions: the trees and accompanying ground cover appeared weedy, the zaftig Lachaise and Renoir sculptures no longer were present as relief from the angular steel abstractions, and the new wall on Fifty-fourth Street, even with the four Matisse backs back in place, was as dreary as Sheetrock. The chief architectural feature of the building, the great plunging atrium, did not serve, as promised, to orient gallerygoers; repeatedly my wife and I, one crowded day, became lost, our slight panic intensified by the aesthetic maze of overlapping art movements and of single artists, such as Matisse, who recur in different rooms. Worse, the atrium had an annoying acoustic effect, conveying crowd noise from floor to floor. The escalators intended to form the main vertical transportation seemed as hard to find as the boutique-scale lavatories. Despairing of the long lines and gross prices at the eateries inside, we went outside for hot dogs. The big rooms, one Arctic-white box after another, dwarfed and chilled the paintings produced before Abstract Expressionism upped canvas consumption, and we felt, for the first time in two lifetimes' worth of visits to MoMA, that there was too much to take in in one day's go. Half again as much space brought out half again as much second-rate modernism. The lower ceilings and humble utilitarian exhibits of the third-floor design section were a distinct relief, like a slice of MoMA perdu, or a friendly kitchenette tucked into a barny McMansion. Still, the joint was jumping, in many overheard languages, and it is a law of progress that new arrivals never know what they have missed.*

Late Works

December 2005–July 2006

LAST WORDS, recorded and treasured in the days when the deathbed was in the home, have fallen from fashion, perhaps because most people spend their last hours in the hospital, too drugged to make any sense. And only the night nurse hears them murmur. Yet, at least for this aging reader, works written late in a writer's life retain a fascination. They exist, as do last words, where life edges into death, and perhaps have something uncanny to tell us. In 1995, the critic, teacher, and journalist Edward W. Said, best known for his pro-Palestinian advocacy, taught at Columbia a popular course called "Last Works/Late Style." Up to his untimely death of leukemia, in 2003, he was working on a collection of essays and lectures gathered around the topic; this assemblage, edited and introduced by Michael Wood with the cooperation of Said's widow, has now been published by Pantheon under the title *On Late Style: Music and Literature Against the Grain*. Said's central idea, set forth in the first chapter, comes from the German philosopher Theodor Adorno (1903–1969), who wrote extensively, with an agitated profundity, on Beethoven's late works. Adorno found in the disharmonies and disjunctions of these works a refusal of bourgeois order, an "idea of surviving beyond what is acceptable and normal." In his own not easily understandable words, possibly clearer in the original German:

> Objective is the fractured landscape, subjective the light in which—alone— it glows into life. He [Beethoven] does not bring about their harmonious synthesis. As the power of disassociation, he tears them apart in time, in order perhaps, to preserve them for the eternal. In the history of art, late works are the catastrophes.

In Beethoven's case, the catastrophe was fruitful; what Said calls his "remorselessly alienated and obscure" late style "forecasts," Said's paraphrase of Adorno claims, "the totally authentic and *novel* art of Schoenberg," whose (in Adorno's translated words) "advanced music has no recourse but to insist on its own ossification without concession to that would-be humanitarianism which it sees through." Adorno writes from within a sardonically modern, anti-bourgeois mind-set that welcomes disassociation, catastrophe, and affronts to harmony and humanitarianism. Thus art, at least modern art, renews itself. Adorno decreed, "The power of subjectivity in the late works of art is the irascible gesture with which it takes leave of the works themselves."

The artists Said cites in *On Late Style* are predominantly composers and, in a chapter centered on Glenn Gould, performers. Said, an accomplished pianist and, among his other activities, music critic for *The Nation*, had an evidently insatiable appetite for musical performances and, though he disclaims a musicologist's competence, an extensive and technical grasp of music. Beethoven, Mozart, Richard Strauss, Bach:

among learned discussions of all these only a few writers are considered at any length, and they—the Sicilian aristocrat Giuseppe Tomasi di Lampedusa, the French criminal Jean Genet, the Greek Alexandrian poet Constantine Cavafy—are valued for their "against the grain" qualities of eccentricity and intransigence. A different list of literary performers would be needed for an inventory of late works that answer, perhaps, to what another literature professor, Barbara Herrnstein Smith, has termed the "senile sublime." Eve Kosofsky Sedgwich, in her book *Touching Feeling* (2003), uses the phrase to describe

> various more or less intelligible performances by old brilliant people, whether artists, scientists, or intellectuals, where the bare outlines of a creative idiom seem finally to emerge from what had been the obscuring puppy fat of personableness, timeliness, or sometimes even of coherent sense.

A sacrifice of, or impatience with, "coherent sense," as well as the requisite irascibility and what Said calls "highlighting and dramatizing . . . irreconcilabilities," can certainly be ascribed to the shimmering late works of Shakespeare, an artistic Titan on Beethoven's scale. Lateness came early to both, both dead in their fifties.

After the composition of Shakespeare's last tragedies—the opulent, spacious *Antony and Cleopatra* (1606–7), the cold, rhetorically contorted *Coriolanus* (1607–8), and the rough-hewn, one-note *Timon of Athens* (1607–8)—there is a slackening, as if something has snapped. *Timon of Athens*, apparently unfinished and unproduced, has been thought by some speculative scholars to mark a personal crisis for the writer; no less measured a source than the *Encyclopædia Britannica* perceived "a clear gulf" between it and the four plays that follow. These—*Pericles* (1607–8), *Cymbeline* (1609–10), *The Winter's Tale* (1610–11), and *The Tempest* (1611)—are commonly grouped together and called romances. Their form is a crowd-pleasing one, still in wide use: the audience, after witnessing many travails and perils, arrives at a happy, if implausible, ending: storms, terrors, and confusions give way to recognitions, reunions, forgiveness, and reconciliation. But a silvery chill blows through these late romances, a deliberate and at times brazen use of stage artifice.

Changes had overtaken Shakespeare's physical theatre—his company, now known as the King's Men, had succeeded in taking over the Blackfriars Theatre, and in 1609 began winter performances there, out of the weather and the democratic hubbub of the Globe. The Globe, erected by the Lord Chamberlain's Men in 1598, was one of the several London amphitheatres patterned on the inn courtyards where plays used to be staged, with little more scenery than what language could paint on the air. From its jutting platform stage, under the afternoon sky, the intricate verbal flights of Romeo and Juliet, Hamlet, and Lear were entrusted to the keen ears of illiterate groundlings. The cheapest admission was a penny, whereas the Blackfriars could charge sixpence, and stage for its more restricted audience more elaborate effects. Spectacle—which Aristotle's *Poetics* ranked, with Song, as the least of tragedy's necessary parts, behind Plot, Character, Diction, and Thought—grew in importance under James I; the Stuart court was more open to Continental divertissements than Elizabeth's had been. Masques, ornate interruptions of dramatic action invented in Italy and imported from France, enlisted such high English talents as Ben Jonson and Inigo Jones.

Shakespeare's plays became parades of wonders. *Pericles* brings the medieval poet John Gower onto stage to shepherd, in quaint tetrameters, its mythological hero back and forth across the Mediterranean. *Cymbeline*, whose plot was memorably characterized by Dr. Samuel Johnson as "unresisting imbecility" marked by "the impossibility of the events in any system of life," caps its absurdities with the rhyming apparition of the hero's dead parents and brothers and the descent of Jupiter "in thunder and lightning, sitting upon an eagle." *The Winter's Tale* subjects its protagonist, King Leontes of Sicilia, to an insane fit of jealousy at the beginning, and at the end has a statue of his wife, for sixteen years thought dead, dramatically come to life. Shakespeare, who was, after the early death of his son, Hamnet, the father of two daughters, inflicts upon his young romantic heroines, with their pretty names Marina, Perdita, and Imogen, no ordeal that they do not come shining through. As Stephen Orgel observes in his introduction to the Pelican *Pericles*, "death is acknowledged to be real" in a late tragedy like *Antony and Cleopatra*, but "that is what is denied in *Pericles*, as it is, though to a lesser extent, in *Cymbeline*, *The Winter's Tale*, and *The Tempest*."

However, the last of these, *The Tempest*, is one of Shakespeare's masterpieces—"one of the most beautiful literary objects ever made," Mark Van Doren wrote in his *Shakespeare*. The strained contrivances and righted wrongs of the previous romances—"Plot has always been the curse of serious drama," George Bernard Shaw said, discussing *Cymbeline*—fall simply into place, with the contriver in plain view, his motives and magical means established at the start. Prospero, the unjustly deposed Duke of Milan and a self-taught sorcerer, spins the plot before our eyes, beginning with the tempest that lands the cast of characters on his private island. The hero and the contriver merge into an omnipotent artificer. In the fourth act, having provided a suitor for his cloistered daughter, Miranda, he stages a masque, starring Iris, Juno, and Ceres, for Miranda and her swain, Prince Ferdinand. When an unpleasantness left over from earthy reality, the rebellion of his slave Caliban, disturbs the performers, so that, "to a strange, hollow, and confused noise, they heavily vanish," Prospero reassures his audience of two:

> These our actors,
> As I foretold you, were all spirits and
> Are melted into air, into thin air;
> And, like the baseless fabric of this vision,
> The cloud-capped towers, the gorgeous palaces,
> The solemn temples, the great globe itself,
> Yea, all which it inherit, shall dissolve,
> And, like this insubstantial pageant faded,
> Leave not a rack behind.

Tradition regards this stately valediction, this folding-up of the sorcerer's equipment, as not only Prospero's but Shakespeare's, bidding farewell to the Globe. In Prospero's self-descriptions, the word "art" reverberates. The romancer is a necromancer: "Graves at my command / Have waked their sleepers, oped, and let 'em forth / By my so potent art." His command is absolute; even sluggish, recalcitrant Caliban, the surly colonized lone native of the island, grumbles, "I must obey. His art is of such pow'r." Prospero reminds Ariel, "It was mine art . . . that made gape / The pine and let thee out." Ariel is beckoned by "Come with a thought!" and materializes saying, "Thy thoughts I cleave to." Only a writer with his quill poised over blank paper has thoughts leap into such instant effectuation, "to enact" his "present fancies." Prospero promises, "Deeper than did ever plummet sound, / I'll drown my book." Signs of an exceptional care exist in the text, which appears in the Folio of 1623 with almost none of the cruces common elsewhere, and with, we read in the complete works edited by George Lyman Kittredge, "unusually elaborate stage directions." The playwright was close enough to John Heminges and Henry Condell, his fellow-actors and his eventual editors, to bequeath them rings in his will—"xxvis viiid apiece to buy them rings." After his death, they assembled and edited the First Folio, without which half of his plays would not survive, and the other half only in very faulty quarto versions. He might have seen to it that they had a good text of his last farewell play, and even suggested to them they place it, in their contemplated collection, first. Their preface to the First Folio states, as if it had been a possibility, "It had bene a thing, we confesse, worthie to have bene wished, that the Author himselfe had liv'd to have set forth, and overseen his owne writings."

Why would Shakespeare say his farewell in a play written before he was fifty? He did not, we must make an effort to remember, have posterity's view of himself. The hectic rough-and-tumble of the Elizabethan theatre, like the television-script mills of today, did not promise high status or literary immortality. He arrived in London in the 1580s, it is thought, and found employment as an actor; within a few years, the player branched out to become a playwright. By 1592, he was already successful enough to attract bitter words from the dramatist Robert Greene, who famously wrote in *Greenes Groats-Worth of Witte*:

> ... there is an upstart Crow, beautified with our feathers, that with his Tygers hart wrapt in a Players hide, supposes he is as well able to bombast out a blanke verse as the best of you ... in his owne conceit the only Shakes-scene in a countrey.

In the next two decades Shakespeare wrote nearly two plays every year, besides composing the two long and popular narrative poems, *Venus and Adonis* and *The Rape of Lucrece*. These poems seem to be the only publications of his that he ever troubled to proofread. His sonnets were pirated and printed in a jumbled fashion. His duties as playwright and player are deplored as "public means" in Sonnet 111, a lament at Fortune, the "guilty goddess" who "did not better for my life provide / Than public means which public manners breeds" so that "my nature is subdued / To what it works in, like the dyer's hand."

Dirty work, in other words, though lucrative. For some time he had been making preparations for a gentleman's retirement from London to his native Stratford, completing his father's application for a coat of arms in 1596 and, the following year, acquiring New Place, one of the largest houses in the town. *The Tempest* ends with Prospero claiming his right to "retire me to my Milan, where / Every third thought shall be my grave." To Shakespeare's first biographer, Nicholas Rowe, nearly a century later, early retirement seemed natural enough:

> The latter part of his life was spent, as all Men of good Sense will wish theirs may be, in Ease, Retirement, and the Conversation of his Friends. He had the good Fortune to gather an Estate equal to his Occasion and, in that, to his Wish.

True, he was not quite done with London. In 1612, identified as "of Stratford-upon-Avon," he testified in a civil case involving some former London landlords of his. In 1613, he bought his first piece of London real estate, the gatehouse of the former Blackfriars Monastery, near the theatre. Evidence suggests that he did not get much use out of this pied-à-terre; he deviously listed as part owner three London associates who didn't put up a penny, and, in 1616, a tenant occupied it. Presumably, Shakespeare returned to town to collaborate with John Fletcher on three known plays: the lost *Cardenio*, based upon a story in *Don Quixote* and performed twice at court; *All Is True* or *Henry VIII*, a patriotic pageant centering upon Cardinal Wolsey's fall and the future Queen Elizabeth's birth; and *The Two Noble Kinsmen*, another surreal romance. Determined scholarship has sorted out the sections written by each man—Fletcher is less Metaphysical a poet, and his smoother diction requires fewer footnotes and rereading to get the sense. To Shakespeare is assigned this stoic valediction, spoken by Theseus in *The Two Noble Kinsmen*:

> O you heavenly charmers,
> What things you make of us! For what we lack
> We laugh, for what we have are sorry; still
> Are children in some kind. Let us be thankful
> For that which is, and with you leave dispute
> That are above our question. Let's go off,
> And bear us like the time.

These are likely the last words Shakespeare wrote for performance. *Henry VIII* involved a masque in which cannons were fired, and on June 29, 1613, a stray piece of ignited wadding landed on the Globe's thatch and burned it down. It was rebuilt within the year, but without Shakespeare as part owner. There is no mention in his will of any theatre shares.

The end of "the great Globe" seems to have ended Shakespeare's connection with the stage, three years short of his death. The causes of his death have been much speculated upon; syphilis and alcoholism are mentioned. The vicar of Stratford, around 1662, recorded in his diary that "Shakespeare, Drayton, and Ben Jonson, had a merie meeting, and itt seems drank too hard." Park Honan's biography argues for a case of springtime typhoid fever caught from the fetid stream that ran past New Place into the Avon. Our impression remains that *The Tempest* foretells Shakespeare's end. It is a lovingly composed late work, the roughness of its predecessor romances smoothed, their dissonances resolved in—as Said says in connection with the final compositions of Richard Strauss—a "recapitulatory and even backward-looking and abstracted quality."

* * *

Nathaniel Hawthorne's terminal illness came to pass in the clear light of nineteenth-century graphomania, but the two hundred fifty years of advances in medical science since Shakespeare's death leave the American romancer's diagnosis similarly vague. In early 1864, Hawthorne's wife, Sophia, wrote in alarm to his old friend Horatio Bridge,

> I have felt the wildest anxiety about him because he is a person who has been immaculately well all his life, and this illness has seemed to me an awful dream which could not be true. But he has wasted away very much and the suns in his eyes are collapsed, and he has no spirits, no appetite, and very little sleep.

Hawthorne had returned with his family to America in 1860, after seven years abroad—four as U.S. consul in Liverpool and three more as a sojourner in Italy and England—in outward good health, though within a year Sophia was confiding to his publisher, William Ticknor of Ticknor & Fields, that her husband was "low in tone and spirits. . . . He has lost the zest for life."

Settled in a spacious Concord house, the Wayside, with renovations that included a third-floor "tower room" to serve as a study, Hawthorne began to write the successor romance to *The Marble Faun* (1860), which had been, despite mixed reviews, a considerable commercial success. He began by picking up a tale, "The Ancestral Footprint," that he had begun and abandoned in 1858; it was based upon an anecdote he had heard at an English dinner party, of an indelible bloody footprint left on a flagstone at the bottom of a staircase in a Lancashire mansion. He attempted to merge this ominous detail with a vision of an American trying to claim an English inheritance. As James R. Mellow puts it in his biography of the writer, "They were, in fact, one theme—and a recurrent one in Hawthorne's fiction. A lost estate and an ancient crime—Eden and the Fall." Hawthornian though the materials were, he could not make the story go. He wrote in his journal,

> There seem to be things that I can almost get hold of, and think about; but when I am just on the point of seizing them, they start away, like slippery things.

He changed the title from "The Ancestral Footprint" to "Etherege" and then to "Grimshawe"; he shifted the action to a gloomy burial ground in Salem; he filled his margins with, as Edwin Haviland Miller puts it in another biography, "corrections, interpolations, exclamations of frustration, and unanswerable questions as to plot, characterization, and motivation." Always a stern self-critic, Hawthorne scribbled such cries of despair as "All this amounts to just nothing. I don't advance a step," and "I have not the least notion how to get on. . . . I never was in such a sad predicament before." Prompted by a story Thoreau told him, of a previous resident of the Wayside who had determined to live forever, he took up the theme of a magic elixir, which had already figured in his short story "Dr. Heidegger's Experiment." He placed his new romance in Concord, took as his hero a half-Indian seminary student undergoing a crisis of faith, and named him Septimius Felton, then Septimius Norton. Septimius, in an encounter that has strong homoerotic and narcissistic overtones, kills a British soldier and finds on his body the formula for eternal life. Hawthorne, wearily climbing the steep stairs to his tower room day after day, accumulated two manuscripts amounting to almost five hundred pages in the Centenary Edition of his works, and supplied three different endings for his hero—death by hanging, escape to the sea, and a successful career in the Continental Army—but finally gave up.

By 1863, the novelist presented a weakened appearance. "He looks gray and grand, with something very pathetic about him," Longfellow recorded in his journal. The Civil War was taking a toll; Hawthorne had always distrusted philanthropists, enthusiasts, and great causes, and his continued loyalty to his old Bowdoin classmate Franklin Pierce, an antebellum President actively expressing anti-Lincoln views to New Hampshire audiences, put him at odds with his abolitionist neighbors and in-laws—Emerson and Sophia's sister Elizabeth Peabody being especially militant. His block in regard to fiction did not keep him, however, from reshaping his English journals into articles for *The Atlantic Monthly;* they were collected into a book of British impressions, *Our Old Home* (1863). Though dismissed by Hawthorne himself as "not a good nor a weighty book," and freighted with a stubbornly, gallantly retained dedication to the unpopular Pierce, *Our Old Home* sold well enough to whet Ticknor & Fields's appetite for more Hawthorne.

In December, he showed Fields the first chapter of his final reworking of the elixir theme, now titled "The Dolliver Romance." In it, his imagination was back on the edge of the burial ground, and had conjured up a likable protagonist for his elixir theme, a very elderly guardian of a three-year-old great-granddaughter. Dr. Dolliver needs to live on for her benefit, rather than from any selfishness of his own; he wears—emblematic adornments characteristic of Hawthorne—an ancient dressing gown of many patches and, to shelter his tiny ward from the unnatural, elixir-fed gleam in his eyes, green spectacles. Fields pronounced the chapter "very fine" and, on the cover of the January 1864 issue of *The Atlantic Monthly,* advertised Hawthorne's forthcoming serialized novel. On February 25, the author wrote Fields a long and rather manic, self-mocking* letter about "the abortive Romance," stating:

> I shall never finish it. . . . I cannot finish it unless a great change comes over me; and if I make too great an effort to do so, it will be my death; not that I should care much for that, if I could fight the battle through and win it, thus ending a life of much smoulder and scanty fire in a blaze of glory.

The smoldering ceased twelve weeks later, when the author died in his sleep, not quite sixty years of age, on a trip north into New Hampshire with Pierce, who had hoped to revive his loyal old friend's body and spirits with a change of air. Hawthorne, who had a morbid aversion to being touched and handled, had refused to consult a doctor, but Sophia had persuaded Fields to obtain the opinion of Dr. Oliver Wendell Holmes. Holmes arranged a casual walk and chat in Boston, during which Hawthorne admitted to "boring pain, distention, difficult digestion" and the fear that his mind was going. Holmes reassured him about his mental health, but his overall verdict was summed up by Fields's sprightly young wife, Annie: "O.W.H. thinks the shark's tooth is upon him, but would not have this known."

Hawthorne's death seems as much a spiritual as a physical event. Like one of his blighted, poisoned, or irremediably stained characters, he wasted away, while personal demons balked his creative powers. Sophia, rarely at a loss for a phrase, wrote, "It seems to me that more and more delicate melodies are struck out from his mind at every revolution of the earth-ball, so that it gets to be a swan-song almost." As he stated in the preface to his first and best novel, *The Scarlet Letter* (1850), he had early determined to build his fiction on the moonlit "territory, somewhere between the real world and fairy-land, where the Actual and the Imaginary may meet, and each imbue itself with the nature of the other." This moonlit in-between ground supported many provocative and poetic short stories but really only one novel, the first; the rest, though rarely less than beautifully written, and shot through with shrewd rays of observation, are webs full of gaps the author was unable or disinclined to fill in. His journals show a sharp-eyed, amused realist, but his imagination,

---

*"Say to the Public what you think best, and as little as possible;—for example—
. . . 'Mr. Hawthorne's brain is addled at last, and, much to our satisfaction, he tells us that he cannot possibly go on with the Romance announced on the cover of the Jan[y] Magazine. We consider him finally shelved, and shall take early occasion to bury him under a heavy article, carefully summing up his merits (such as they were) and his demerits, what few of them can be touched upon in our limited space.' "

which ripened in the unnatural solitude of his young manhood in Salem, set itself feats of balance on the edge of the unreal that, as the real shadows closed in, he was unable to sustain. Longfellow, in his memorial poem "Hawthorne," wrote of his friend's "wand of magic power," as if he had been Prospero; but the summoned spirits in the end did not come. Shakespeare in his late romances had the coarse "public means" of stagecraft to solidify his death-denying fictions; Hawthorne, solitary in his Concord tower, had only secluded intuitions, and these darkened and dissolved. The writer depended upon a touch of spookiness, but the man did not believe in spooks. Death was real. As he put aside his second extended attempt to carry "The Ancestral Footprint" to completion, Hawthorne wrote of his protagonist:

> Some strange, vast, sombre, mysterious truth, which he seemed to have searched for long, appeared to be on the point of being revealed to him; a sense of something to come; something to happen that had been waiting long, long to happen; an opening of doors, a drawing away of veils, a lifting of heavy, magnificent curtains, whose dark folds hung before a spectacle of awe;—it was like the verge of the grave.

Herman Melville's *Billy Budd*, also published posthumously, and in a state of suspended revision, has fared better with posterity than Hawthorne's unfinished romances. This tale, less than novella-length, is the most studied and admired of Melville's works except for *Moby-Dick*—a globally ambitious novel greatly enriched by his acquaintance with Hawthorne and his elated discovery of the older writer's dark, symbol-laden short stories. Near the outset of *Billy Budd*, Melville invokes Hawthorne's name but in the next paragraph assures the reader that his story is "no romance." Far from evading death, he steers his narrative straight toward the hero's hanging. His frequent allusions to classical and Biblical myth and his excursions into British naval history decorate but do not divert the tale; like Faulkner at his most surging, he seems confident that the underlying story is simple and predetermined enough to survive any digression.

The setting is Melville's métier, shipboard, its planks reverberant and rolling underfoot. There are three essential characters, each with a tragic flaw—gloriously handsome Billy, with his stutter; staunch and sterling Captain Edward Vere, with "a queer streak of the pedantic running through him"; and master-at-arms John Claggart, with an unhealthily sallow complexion and a depraved antipathy to the sunny "moral phenomenon presented in Billy Budd." As in Hawthorne, there are themes of surrogate paternity and "natural" aristocracy and "elemental evil," but

Melville's arise within a firmly circumstantial setting—a sailing warship recalled in avid detail from within an age of steam—and a specific historical moment, the year 1797, when the ideas of the French Revolution had sparked the Great Mutiny and a harsh renewal of discipline within the British navy. Melville in the end deleted two paragraphs explaining this historical context; indeed, his stark story, told in many short segments, feels whittled down, as opposed to Hawthorne's desperately shifting accretion of "slippery things."

Melville's sentences, a little arthritic and desiccated decades after the headlong prose of his prime, and marked, the manuscript (at Harvard) reveals, by many hesitations and revisions, may sometimes grope, but his plot, the Christ-like martyrdom of his "fated boy," moves unflinchingly. Such a fated directness, driven by the yarning, reminiscing authorial voice, can be felt in other late works, such as Tolstoy's *Hadji Murad*, which, too, was published posthumously. "My vigor sensibly declines," Melville wrote in late 1889 to a Canadian admirer. "What little of it is left I husband for certain matters yet incomplete, and which, indeed, may never be completed." Melville was seventy at the time, and *Billy Budd* was almost certainly one of the matters; he had retired from the U.S. Customs Service in New York at the age of sixty-eight, and was seventy-two when he died. Not long before, Julian Hawthorne, Hawthorne's son, visited Melville in his near-total obscurity and found, in Julian's words, a "melancholy and pale wraith," fidgety and nervous, whose "words were vague and indeterminate." Yet this same man, initially undertaking to write a headnote to one of his poems—poetry had been, after the failure of three successive novels, his only literary exercise for more than thirty years—found vigor enough to crowd onto a naval incident from 1797 most of what he felt about male beauty, human justice, cosmic injustice, and the Christ myth.

Death, one would think, naturally haunts late works; yet perhaps it does not. A negation defies objectification; disappearance has no appearance. Adorno wrote, "Death is imposed on created beings, not on works of art, and thus it has appeared in art only in a refracted mode, as allegory." What does haunt late works are the author's previous works: he is burdensomely aware that he has been cast, unlike his ingénue self, as an author who writes in a certain way, with the inexorable consistency of his own handwriting. "I am tired of my own thoughts and fancies and my own mode of expressing them," Hawthorne wrote not many months before he died. Turning this way and that in his last creative torment, he kept meeting, with a shudder, his pet modes of imagining, chimeras on the fault line between the imaginary and the actual. Melville, no stranger to self-centered overcomplication, in old age found his way back to simplicity. Successful late works, shed of "obscuring puppy fat," often have a translucent thinness, wearisome complication dismissed.

In the twentieth century, James Joyce, when asked what he planned to write after the seventeen years' labor of *Finnegans Wake*, responded, "I think I'll write something very simple and very short." His actual last work, carried forward in the French village of Saint-Gérand-Le-Puy with the help of Paul Léon, was a list of more than a thousand misprints in *Finnegans Wake*—a significant task, given the unique letter-by-letter difficulty of the text and Joyce's near-blindness. A few weeks after escaping from Vichy France, early in 1941, he died in Zürich, following an operation for a perforated duodenal ulcer, at the age of fifty-eight. His last great work, whose punning title has Finnegan waking at his wake, could be said to deny the reality of an individual's death, lost as it is amid the great cycles of history and the tireless babble of humanity:

> Onetwo moremens more. So. Avelaval. My leaves have drifted from me. All. But one clings still. I'll bear it on me. To remind me of. Lff! So soft this morning, ours. Yes.

Few authors get to produce works as late in life as another expatriate Irishman, George Bernard Shaw. His last book brought together, with prefaces, the four-act play *Buoyant Billions*, six playlets titled *Farfetched Fables*, and the puppet play, mostly in blank verse, called *Shakes Versus Shav*; they were written when the author was, respectively, ninety-two, ninety-three, and ninety-four years old. We approach work by such an ancient with uneasiness, but the opening preface reassures us that we are in the hands of a masterly comedian, an irrepressible truth-teller, his faculties intact:

> At such an age I should apologize for perpetrating another play or presuming to pontificate in any fashion. I can hardly walk through my garden without a tumble or two; and it seems out of all reason to believe that a man who cannot do a simple thing like that can practice the craft of Shakespear. . . . Well, I grant all this; yet I cannot hold my tongue nor my pen. As long as I live I must write.

Writing, he cheerfully informs us, is no work at all. It is simply a matter of taking dictation: "When I take my pen or sit down to my typewriter, I am as much a medium as Browning's Mr Sludge or Dunglas Home, or as Job or John of Patmos. When I write a play I do not foresee nor intend a page of it from one end to the other: the play writes itself."

The claim is perhaps cagily ingenuous, by a writer often accused of being too cerebral and cool-hearted. With Shaw, whose fame didn't set in until his forties and whose *Saint Joan*, which in effect won him the Nobel Prize, was written in his sixty-seventh year, we have late works that display little loss of muscle, because his muscles were always concentrated in his head—his mischievous quick eyes, his agile tongue. He and Goethe and Victor Hugo show Americans what they have few native examples to learn from: writing can be a healthy, life-giving activity, sustainable—in Shaw's case with the help of teetotalism, vegetarianism, and bicycling—through a generous mortal span. His imminent death had no terrors for him—rather the reverse. In his brief but pithy preface to *Buoyant Billions*, Shaw writes of spiritualists, "They believe in personal immortality as far as any mortal can believe in an unimaginable horror." No such horror need apply for belief to this buoyant spirit; his *Farfetched Fables* grapple blithely with the atomic bomb and its threat of global annihilation, and his antic puppet play quotes Prospero's "great Globe itself" speech and caps it with the saucy lines

> Immortal William dead and turned to clay
> May stop a hole to keep the wind away.

Graham Greene, blessed with a longer life than his suicidal impulses, his hazardous travels, and his pessimistic novels would have presaged, saw his books shrink in size, from the respectable bulk of the best-selling *The Honorary Consul* (1973) and *The Human Factor* (1978) to such quirky bagatelles as *Doctor Fischer of Geneva; or The Bomb Party* (1980), *Monsignor Quixote* (1982), *J'Accuse—The Dark Side of Nice* (1982), *Getting to Know the General* (1984), and *The Captain and the Enemy* (1988). Greene's last book, edited and introduced by him but ushered into publication by Yvonne Cloetta, his mistress, in obedience to his deathbed request, is *A World of My Own: A Dream Diary* (1992), a selection of the dreams he habitually recorded in the last twenty-five years of his life. The dreams of this somewhat sinister writer (he chose for an epigraph to his entire oeuvre Browning's lines "Our interest's on the dangerous edge of things / The honest thief, the tender murderer") show his subconscious to have been, on the whole, a salubrious and well-lit site, full of books, public personalities, and a cheerful candor. The last dream finds Greene writing a verse on his own death "for a competition in a magazine called *Time and Tide*" ("My breath is folded up / like sheets in lavender. / The end for me / Arrives like nursery tea"), and the first reverts to an Edwardian childhood as he sees a train that "consisted of pretty carriages" and boards the next one:

I was much struck by the kindness and jollity of the passengers, who welcomed me and made room for me in a very packed carriage. They all wore strange clothes—Edwardian or Victorian—and I was fascinated by the stations we passed. On one wide platform children were playing with scarlet balloons; another station was built like a ruined Greek temple; at one point the track narrowed and the train went through a kind of tunnel made with mattresses.

I had never in my life felt such a sensation of happiness.

His dreams were for Greene a way of re-entering the past. Remembrance, always an element in the manipulated data of fiction, is often terminally fruitful in purer form, when living presences that once crowded and threatened the rebellious imagination have been rendered by the passage of time mistily distant and legally impotent. Not only Melville turned to the past; the familiar American careers of Hemingway and Faulkner end in reminiscence—of the innocent Paris of Hemingway's young manhood and artistic apprenticeship in *A Moveable Feast*, and of Yoknapatawpha County and Memphis as experienced by an eleven-year-old boy in Faulkner's *The Reivers: A Reminiscence*. The latter takes place in 1905, when an automobile was an oddity on the muddy roads of the South and lessons in love and honor were to be learned in a whorehouse and on a racetrack.

The past in one sense recedes but in another gains in interest as the writer ages and the stage of the present empties of decisive action. Henry James at the outset of the twentieth century brought to a triumphant climax his sustained practice of fiction with three stately novels that are marvels of prolonged design and nuanced sensibility—*The Wings of the Dove* (1902), *The Ambassadors* (1903), and *The Golden Bowl* (1904). He then, always an industrious critic and essayist, quite turned from fiction. He went back to America for the first time in twenty-five years and wrote of what he saw and what he remembered in *The American Scene* (1906). He revisited his creative, European past in the eighteen autobiographical prefaces to the twenty-four volumes of the New York edition of his selected works (1907–9). And he wrote two volumes of autobiography, *A Small Boy and Others* (1911) and *Notes of a Son and Brother* (1913).

However, in 1909 his stagestruck side, still smarting from the hooted failure of his play *Guy Domville* in 1895, was appealed to by a request from the Duke of York's Theatre that he contribute a play to a London repertory season organized by J. M. Barrie and the American producer Charles Frohman. He responded, intensely, by writing a play in the last weeks of 1909, called *The Outcry*, based upon a newsworthy incident wherein a public protest prevented the American plutocrat Henry Clay

Frick from buying a Holbein portrait from the Duke of Norfolk. In May of 1910, the death of Edward VII closed London's theatres, and James, who had not been well himself, responded to this latest theatrical frustration by turning the unproduced *Outcry* into a novel, using the play's dialogue little changed and nestling it in prose that closely resembles stage directions; the characters, announced by butlers, busily enter and exit. Reading it, one has a clear vision of a proscenium stage as it entertains quarrels and clinches in brisk succession. A jaunty curiosity not two hundred pages long, *The Outcry* is seldom pondered by contemporary Jamesians but at the time was something of a success, outselling *The Golden Bowl*. In its high-spoken mood of romp and rampant intellectuality, not to say the feminism forthrightly embodied by its conquering heroines, it might be a play by Shaw, who was also invited to contribute to the doomed repertory season. *The Outcry* survives as a novel, and is a light-hearted, quick-moving one, though the third-person voice emits plenty of the fluttering circumlocutions of the late James style. Ripe samples can be plucked from every page; here is an especially dense, velvet-skinned plum, giving us a taste of the principal lovers as they size each other up:

> They stood smiling at each other as in an exchange of sympathy already confessed—and even as if finding that their relation had grown during the lapse of contact, she recognizing the effect of what they had originally felt as bravely as he might name it. What the fine, slightly long oval of her essentially quiet face—quiet in spite of certain vague depths of reference to forces of the strong high order, forces involved and implanted, yet also rather spent in the process—kept in range from under her redundant black hat was the strength of expression, the directness of communications, that her guest appeared to borrow from the unframed and unattached nippers unceasingly perched, by their mere ground-glass rims, as she remembered, on the bony bridge of his indescribably authoritative (since it was at the same time decidedly inquisitive) young nose.

The cumbersome though finely painted charabanc of the late James style is pulled swaying along by a frisky pony of a plot, farcical and romantic, designed for stage-lit action. This most expatiatory and archly loquacious of novelists is obliged to hold the reins tight. The patter of his incongruous verbal felicities is invigorating; the style itself participates in the comedy. We feel on our faces—we, the reader and the sixty-seven-year-old author—the breeze of the senile sublime, a creativity liberated from its usual, anxiety-producing ambitions. The playful labor of this translation of drama into narrative was undertaken, Jean Strouse tells us in her introduction to the newest reprint of *The Outcry*, in the wake of "an acute depressive breakdown" brought on by the tepid reception of the New York ·edition, to which James had devoted heroic editorial effort, introducing and at times drastically revising his life's work.

Iris Murdoch's descent into the forgetfulness and incoherence of Alzheimer's disease was vividly described in the memoirs *Iris* and *Elegy for Iris* by her husband, John Bayley. The motion picture, starring Judi Dench, based on the memoirs shows the formerly prolific, consummately intelligent novelist pitifully struggling with the manuscript of the novel that was her last, *Jackson's Dilemma* (1995). The novel was received well enough by critics: the *San Francisco Examiner* called it "the kind of poetical feast that Shakespeare provided in *The Tempest*. . . . She has never written more lucidly or more lyrically"; Harold Bloom in the *New York Times Book Review* claimed that it demonstrated "Murdoch's particular mastery . . . in representing the maelstrom of falling in love, which is the characteristic activity of nearly all her men and women." I read *Jackson's Dilemma* fearing that the author—who didn't remember writing the book by the time she received finished copies from the publisher—had embarrassed herself, but the novel is not a steep falling-off. It has wispy, stylized, and casually irrational elements, but so do her major works. In *The Philosopher's Pupil* (1983), a flying saucer sends out a ray that blinds the novel's hero; the protagonist of *The Sea, the Sea* (1978) is miraculously rescued from a maelstrom by his cousin, an adept in yogic levitation. The membrane between our chaotic inner lives and external material reality is permeable in Murdoch—she writes of the UFO incident, "The inner is the outer, the outer is the inner: an old story, but who really understands it?" An early novel like *The Flight from the Enchanter* presents no fewer puzzles and implausibilities than the last. The most prominent weakness of *Jackson's Dilemma*, for me, lay with the eponymous Jackson; one of Murdoch's many spoiled priests, wistful for faith but not secure in it, he has no clear role (or dilemma) among the restless and self-indulgent English elite as they impulsively, wastefully shuttle from country home to London and back. We end in Jackson's head: "Is it all a *dream*, yes, perhaps a dream. . . . Death, its closeness . . . Was I in prison once? I cannot remember. At the end of what is necessary, I have come to a place where there is no road." Perhaps presumptuously, we imagine ourselves admitted to the mind of the author, as she feels her grip on the real world loosening. But her creative artistry lasted up to the verge of what Hawthorne called "a drawing away of veils, a lifting of heavy, magnificent curtains."

Hawthorne's inability to carry forth and complete "The Ancestral Footprint" was, in Adorno's term, a "catastrophe" for him personally. His struggles to find the key—the handle—demonstrate what a precarious feat it is to write a novel, organizing a host of inventions and polished details into a single movement toward resolution. Like sex, it is either easy or impossible. His failing physical health, his daughter Una's worsening mental health, his ambivalent and unfashionable feelings about the Civil War, the confinements of his happy marriage—he had his excuses, but there are always excuses not to do the job. He had no trouble, even as his block worsened, in turning his English journals into lively, sharp-eyed essays, while, in false loyalty perhaps to the attic-dwelling night-walker he had been in his youth, he tried to pen fiction by waning moonlight.

He drank excessively, it was rumored, and Henry Green—an aristocrat of a non-puritan sort—certainly did. There is a kind of gallantry, a Rimbaudesque flamboyance, in Green's premature embrace of silence; he produced the novel intended to be his last, *Concluding* (1948), when he was forty-three. He then let his creative instincts be seduced, by mid-life affairs with younger women, into two more novels, *Nothing* (1950) and *Doting* (1952), both dialogue-dominated and composed with an elegant economy; but their translucence feels slightly clouded by an air of corruption and defeat, especially *Doting*, with its madly bibulous ending.

A geriatric ebb of energy is bound to affect late works, not necessarily to their detriment. A *Billy Budd* produced in Melville's thirties might have been as full of bumptious bombast as *Mardi*. The later work's style, pedestrian and legalistic at intervals, at others slips into a metaphoric vein as primally strange as imagery from Hawthorne and *The Pilgrim's Progress*. Of the demonic Claggart:

> But upon any abrupt unforeseen encounter a red light would flash forth from his eye like a spark from an anvil in a dusk smithy. That quick, fierce light was a strange one, darted from orbs which in repose were of a color nearest approaching a deeper violet, the softest of shades.

Outer becomes inner; images take on a heated life of their own, freed from reality. "Late style," Said wrote in paraphrase of Adorno, "is what happens if art does not abdicate its rights in favor of reality." How real is death to those who still live? When the Shavian torrent dwindled to a trickle, it still twinkled; in his preface to *Buoyant Billions*, Shaw tells us that death is real, but in such a sprightly fashion that we do not believe it. Art arises, it may be, from the death-denying portion of the psyche, deeper than reason's reach. Repeatedly, Shakespeare's sonnets defy time:

> Yet do thy worst, old Time; despite thy wrong,
> My love shall in my verse ever live young.

The last four plays that can be assigned to Shakespeare's exclusive authorship, the romances, deny death the last word, though deaths occur: in *Cymbeline*, the odious Cloten dies; in *The Winter's Tale*, the staunch Antigonus, with the memorable stage direction "Exit, pursued by a bear," on the unreal seacoast of Bohemia. In all of them, the climactic events defy plausibility with wonderful returns from the dead or the lost. *The Tempest*, like Beethoven's late compositions, refuses, in Adorno's phrase, to "reconcile in a single image what is not reconciled." Said wrote, "What I find valuable in Adorno is this notion of tension, of highlighting and dramatizing what I call irreconcilabilities." *The Tempest* affirms Prospero's death-wish and retirement, and also Miranda's wonder, her naïve eagerness to live and to love. She has not yet come to the end of what is necessary. Father and daughter, far from irreconcilable, perform onstage together.

GENERAL CONSIDERATIONS

A Case for Books

EXPERTS—perhaps one should call them e-xperts—predict that the printed, paper-and-glue book will be rendered obsolete by electronic text-delivery systems, of which one, the Microsoft Reader, is already on the market, offering "books" on a Pocket PC manufactured by Hewlett-Packard. This is not an impossible prediction; already much of the written communication that used to be handled by letters, newspapers, and magazines has shifted over to PC screens and the vast digital library available over the Internet. If the worst comes true, and the paper book joins the papyrus scroll and parchment codex in extinction, we will miss, *I* predict, a number of things about it.

The book as furniture. Shelved rows of books warm and brighten the starkest room, and scattered single volumes reveal mental processes in progress—books in the act of consumption, abandoned but readily resumable, tomorrow or next year. By bedside and easy chair, books promise a cozy, swift, and silent release from this world into another, with no current involved but the free and scarcely detectable crackle of brain cells. For ease of access and storage, books are tough to beat.

The book as sensual pleasure. Smaller than a breadbox, bigger than a TV remote, the average book fits into the human hand with a seductive nestling, a kiss of texture, whether of cover cloth, glazed jacket, or flexible paperback. The weight can rest on the little finger of the right hand for hours without noticeable strain, while the thumb of that hand holds the pages open and fingers of the other hand turn them. The rectangular block of type, a product of five and a half centuries of printers' lore, yields

A *New York Times* Op-Ed piece, June 18, 2000.

to decipherment so gently that one is scarcely aware of the difference between daydreaming and reading.

In these last, troubled decades of the book's existence, the need to "present" impressively in bookstores has led to inflated volumes, with a page and type bigger than organically ideal, and with a painful strain on the above-mentioned little finger. The paper shortages of World War II rattled, it may be, the aesthetic confidence of book manufacturers; it is the books of the 1920s and '30s that are most inviting, with their handy size, generous margins, and sharp letterpress type. Still, even an indifferently designed book feels like a better companion in bed than a humming, wire-trailing laptop.

The book as souvenir. One's collection comes to symbolize the contents of one's mind. My mother's college texts, I remember, sat untouched in a corner of our country bookcase, radiating the glories of Renaissance poetry and Greek drama while being slowly hollowed by silverfish. The bulk of my own college books are still with me, rarely consulted but always there, reminders of moments, of stages, in a pilgrimage, while the decades since add their own drifts and strata of volumes read or half read or intended to be read. Books preserve, daintily, the redolence of their first reading—this beach, that apartment, that attack of croup, this flight to Indonesia. Without their physical evidence my life would be more phantasmal; as is, they are stacked around me, towering even over my head, as not only an extension into my past, sinking their foundations securely down to my accreted jejune marginal comments and reaching up into clouds of noble intention—books waiting to be read, as tempting as grapes unharvested and musky, years of dust to be blown off in a second of sudden plucking, their moment to be seized and absorbed come triumphantly round at last. Such books constitute a pledge of an infinite future, just as their brother books, already read but mostly forgotten, form an infinite resource of potential rereading, of new angles and insights on terrain where our footprints have all but vanished. Books externalize our brains, and turn our homes into thinking bodies.

Books as ballast. As movers and the moved both know, books are heavy freight, the weight of refrigerators and sofas broken up into cardboard boxes. They make us think twice about changing addresses. How many aging couples have decided to stay put because they can't imagine what to do with the books? How many divorces have been forestalled by love of the same jointly acquired library? Books hold our beams down; they act as counterweight to our fickle and flighty natures. In comparison, any electronic text-delivery device lacks substance. Further, speaking of obsolescence, it would be outdated in a year and within fifteen as inoperable as my formerly cutting-edge Wang word-processor from the mid-Eighties. Electronic equals (e-quals, if you will) immaterial, Ariel to our earthy Caliban. Without books, we might melt into the airwaves, and be just another set of blips.

Looking Back to Now

THE STUDENTS in my seminar "A Hundred Years Ago: The End of the Twentieth Century" find many of the details difficult to believe. That way back then all but the exceedingly impoverished owned a petroleum-consuming automobile, and that middle-class families commonly owned two or three, and that everyone from teen-agers to ninety-year-olds drove them here and there on the most trivial errands, throughout a North America extensively paved in asphalt for the convenience of these private vehicles, naturally strains the credulity of children raised in an environment where the rare personal change of location is achieved by means of underground methane-powered transportation tubes, and every square foot of precious soil not devoted to three-hundred-story housing projects is reserved for the cultivation of soybeans and other high-protein legumes. The amount of freedom, choice, and waste present in what is now known as the Late Capitalist Interval strikes them as fantastic and indecent.

Nothing titillates them more, or seems more grotesquely hilarious, than the random nature of copulation under the so-called free-enterprise system. The notion of couples achieving physical congress on no basis sounder than mutual desire and access (usually) to a walled room, and with no official permit and no government witness present to ensure that the terms of the permit are strictly observed, runs so astonishingly counter to their own experience that an instructor of history can be grateful for the multitude of novels and romantic films that document this implausible and genetically unsound behavior.

Students have trouble grasping the high value placed upon mobility even in the early decades of the Computer Revolution. "Why would any-one want to go anywhere else," they ask me, "when the same information-gathering terminals were present at every geographical point?" The primitive catch-phrases that permeated not only the twentieth century but earlier eras on the North American continent—"starting over,"

Another *Times* Op-Ed piece, December 22, 1999.

"heading west," "leaving it all behind," "fresh scenes," "new horizons"—
ring hollowly for those who have from birth let the world come to them,
in the form of computer-generated instruction, entertainment, and virtual experience. The need to "go out"—out to shop or to work or just to
walk around the block—seems as arcane and absurd to them as, say, Victorian family prayers or bloody Aztec sacrifices.

They ask me if the people weren't sickened and terrified by the unstable variety of their lives, the lack of officially prescribed order, the
dangerous waywardness of rubber-tired surface transportation, the multiplicity of casual social contacts, and—most clumsy and disgusting in
their view—the common need to deal in three real dimensions, rather
than in computer-generated simulacra which can be adjusted, erased, or
rerun at the pleasure of the keyboarder. Yes, one must answer, hands got
dirty, backs got strained, feet got tired; yet the people of the late twentieth century had always interacted with reality (discounting the meliora-
tive effect of certain so-called labor-saving devices) in this primitive,
coarse-grained way, and some of their poetry and autobiographical writings confide the satisfactions of what today's youth conceive as a totally
unnecessary and degrading physicality.

People of 1999, looking a century back from their own fin-de-siècle,
marvelled at the muddy filth of the horse-dominated and only partially
paved world of the 1890s; so we must marvel at the poisonous vapors and
noxious detritus with which the period's ponderous mechanisms flooded
the atmosphere and filled the junkyards. My students, in their form-
fitting plastic sheaths and osseo-supplemental ankle- and back-braces,
express horror that the free-roaming denizens of this befouled world
actually slaughtered other creatures and ate their cooked flesh; and that
soybeans shared the menu with a host of roots pulled from the heavily
chemicalized earth and with fruits ruthlessly pulled from trees, whose
keen vegetable pain was ignored not only by the logging interests but,
amazingly, by conservationists and botanists. These students find it
incredible that group conflicts (a difficult concept for them in any case)
led to forms of organized violence called, variously, war, police action,
revolution, labor strife, and political protest.

I must struggle to prove, in the face of their skepticism, that in the last
decade of the previous century the country then called the United States
of America enjoyed a singular global dominance. Not only, I point out,
did it possess an overwhelming edge in military weaponry, but no other
nation's film industry could come close to matching American cinema's
special effects, and no other national economy showed such relentless
upward drive. "What happened then?" the students understandably ask.

How did this fabulous, dynamic nation come to be so enfeebled, so scattered in its many states, that it gratefully accepted, in the critical year 2057, protectorate status within the Indo-Sino-Peruvian League of Sane and Benign Governance Providers? Some historians blame the hardening congressional habit of impeaching elected Presidents, to the extent that a standing House committee commenced proceedings on each Inauguration Day. Others blame the great shift of the aging American population to the Florida peninsula, which sank under the weight. Still others find a central cause in the PfizerLillySquibb Inc. Ultima Pill, one a week of which induced, with no deleterious side effects, the sensation of perfect contentment.

For whatever reason, the United States collectively ceased to "go out." As the last Secretary of State (and the first Native American to hold the post) put it: "I don't know—you go out there with your troops, and generate a little democracy, and three other places start to backslide. You get fed up." At first, the population stayed indoors, and then in the bedroom, and finally in bed, while less successful and prosperous nations mustered the energy to tame the last wild corners of the earth to soybean production and to impose a civilizing order upon the world's burgeoning billions. My students and I, of course, as we survey with shared alarm and distaste the anarchic, brutalizing past, are grateful for the impeccably regulated present, up to and including the appointed day when each of us is administered, by graceful Balinese nurses, the coup de grâce, the Ultima OD.

The Tried and the Trēowe

THE WRITER OF FICTION, a professional liar, is paradoxically obsessed with what is true—what feels true, what rings true in the fabrication being assembled on his desk. A career in writing begins with the sense that what has already been written, by others, has not been quite true enough; however revered, it lacks the latest information, the newest slant. For a while, the careerist confidently surfs near the curling crest of technological and cultural change; his generation *is* the new wave, and what he writes about himself and his peers is news. As he ages, the wave slips on, and he finds himself paddling in the foam-studded aftermath, indifferent to more and more fads and celebrities, failing to "get" more

A discourse on an elusive topic coaxed from me by *Forbes ASAP*, in the year 2000, a great year for such discourses.

and more cartoons in *The New Yorker.* Certainly, speech patterns and thought patterns and social habits, not to mention the physical accoutrements of daily existence, have greatly changed in the half-century or more since I received my basic impressions of life in America. Yet for truth I still have my humanity and the stretch of history my lengthening life includes. Art does not belong only to the young, far from it; what does belong to the young is the future, and with it the confidence that your instincts will be vindicated by future developments. You know what is true in your bones.

Untrue often means outmoded—the pieties of your fathers, foremost. These pieties may be a Presbyterian faith, or a socialist atheism, or a loyalty to this or the other established political party, or to labor unions or to *laissez-faire* economics or to the American flag or the planet Earth: to the bearer of the new truth the old issues are not even worth debating, they are beside the point. The new point is not easy to locate. Boredom and indifference are more readily felt than excitement. But excitement is the Geiger counter to the new true—for instance, the pleasure that youngsters effortlessly take in the manipulated digitized imagery of computer games and MTV videos. Millions find bliss of sorts in losing themselves in the vastness of the Internet, a phantom electronic creation which sublimates the bulky, dust-gathering contents of libraries and supermarkets into something impalpable and instantaneous. The Web is conjured like the genie of legend with a few strokes of the fingers, opening, with a phrase or two, a labyrinth littered with trash and pitted with chat rooms, wherein communication is antiseptically cleansed of all the germs and awkwardness of even the most mannerly transaction with another flesh-and-blood human being.

A mass retreat into a richly populated privacy has occurred before: in the acts of reading and of going to the movies. Excitement lay in both for my generation. Those of us who were young in the 1950s pored over the sacred, crabbed texts of Yeats and Eliot, Joyce and Pound, and of more ancient magi like Shakespeare, Donne, Milton, Pope, Keats, Dickens, and Browning. Their magic was to be extracted drop by drop and mixed with our own, still-unanalyzed elixirs. I have yet to be persuaded that the information revolution, so called, is anything but an exercise in reading and writing wherein evanescent and odorless PC screens take the place of durable, faintly fragrant paper and ink. As to the movies—who of my generation did not seek his inmost self within the glittering, surging world-picture that cinema presented to its rapt receivers in the semi-dark? What was worthwhile and true was somehow there, coded in Gary Cooper's pale-eyed deadpan and Esther Williams's underwater smile.

Forbes raises this question of the true at the terminus of a century whose first decades saw the theories of relativity and quantum mechanics undermine our intuitive sense of matter. The subatomic microcosm and the outer space populated by receding galaxies both defied plausibility, even as evidence relentlessly accumulated for the accuracy of the scientific world-picture. Materialism explains nearly everything now; only we, in our inner sense of ourselves, at the center of our ambitions and emotions, remain immaterial. Between preposterous cosmic immensities and madly multiple and elusive particles, human beings still seek to render their lives intelligible.

The unit of truth, at least for a fiction writer, is the human animal, belonging to a species, *Homo sapiens*, unchanged for at least a hundred thousand years. A Cro-Magnon man, properly shaved, dressed, and educated, could be the CEO of a cutting-edge computer-software company. He could be the man sharing your seat on the commuter train. He has our intelligence and physical appearance; the culture of Cro-Magnon times—its cave paintings and ritual mutilations and altars of aurochs skulls—catered to the same species as does contemporary culture, with its rock concerts and art museums and book reviews by Michiko Kakutani. Evolution moves more slowly than history, and much more slowly than the technology of recent centuries; surely sociobiology, surprisingly maligned in some scientific quarters, performs a useful service in investigating which traits are innate and which are acquired. What kind of cultural software can our evolved hard-wiring support? Fiction, in its groping way, is drawn to those moments of discomfort when society asks more than its individual member can, or cares to, provide. Friction on the page is what warms our hands and hearts as we write.

One of the casualties of the electronic age is, perhaps, a feel for history, in its cyclical repetitions and organically gradual progress. To minds conditioned by the rapid electronic reflexes of the computer and its allied entertainments, the end of the world is a flicker away, around the corner, and the significant past happened just yesterday. Compared with virtual reality, actual reality is sluggish. The patient virtues of the rural village make a hard sell even in the year of a Presidential campaign. But is every novelty around us really unprecedented and radically transformative? Was not bio-engineering, for instance, carried on by the prehistoric New World farmers who developed corn out of wild maize, and by the hunting and sheepherding tribesmen who tamed and split the wild wolf into an astonishing variety of canine breeds? Can family values, so called, and the morality of social interdependence be banished by a tap of the DELETE button, or do they sturdily spring from our basic biological makeup, which includes an instinctive, self-serving decency? Is our sense of the true foisted upon us by disintegrating tyrannies of the air, or does it spring from the ineluctable necessities of our creaturely selves? The root sense of the word, from the Old English *trēowe*, is not "not false" but "faithful." The fair maiden will be true to her knight; he will stay true to his vows. Amid so much electronic clutter and chatter in this dishevelled, oversupplied, desperately commercial world, the human organism compels us to remain true to it or else fall into ill health and spiritual discordancy. Freed from physical exercise, we re-embrace it for the body's sake; freed from religious fear, we still seek the peace, the relief from competitive striving, that religious acceptance brings.

Freud defined happiness as the relief of tension. To be human is to be in the tense condition of a death-foreseeing, vexedly libidinous animal. No other earthly creature suffers such a capacity for thought, such a complexity of envisioned but frustrated possibilities, such a troubling ability to question the tribal and biological imperatives. So conflicted and ingenious a creature makes an endlessly interesting focus for the meditations of fiction. It seems to me true that *Homo sapiens* will never settle into any utopia so complacently as to relax all its conflicts and erase all its perversity-generating neediness. It also seems, not quite incidentally, true that the human species is heading toward a planetary triumph as complete as that of corn in Iowa; the paved-over and wired-up earth will produce a single crop, people, plus what people eat, and there will be little left of non-human nature for contrast or enlivening metaphor. Monoculture of any sort is frightening. The banishment of natural balances invites a sinister triumph of the microscopic; already, microbes are outbreeding our pesticides. But even in the dire eventuality foreshadowed by the growing, crushing spread of our poisonous cities, nature will live on, in our own anatomy and biochemistry, a fortress and a touchstone, tried and true, amid whatever further illusions and distractions technology creates.

A Layman's Scope

BORN THREE YEARS before the old Hayden Planetarium was dedicated, I can remember when the Sunday supplements would carry articles speculating on what the inhabitants of the other planets looked like. We knew

---

For the celebration in *Natural History*, in February 2000, of the new Hayden Planetarium.

that Venus was hot, so the Venusians must be slim and flickering, like salamanders. We knew that Jupiter was a huge ball of gas, so its residents would be squat and splayfooted, like gravity-flattened camels treading the sand. When the imagination moved out to Neptune and Pluto, it became ghostly, conjuring up giant eyes to see in the dark, so far from the sun. Now, of course, the planets and their satellites have had the benefit of a Voyager fly-by or some other robotic close-up, and the stunning photographic images yield no sign of life. Mars is a desert, Europa a ball of ice, Io a giant pizza. The solar system has become more colorful and less companionable; the stars beyond, too, for all the efforts of cinematic science fiction to domesticate them, are more forbidding, for being more numerous, more violent, and more rapidly retreating than was thought sixty years ago. The universe refuses to be held to anything like human measure.

When the Milky Way arched over the nighttime desert like a powdery river and hovered above the Mediterranean as a slowly rotating disk of bright pinpricks, men sought intimacy with this unreachable reality by tracing and naming constellations; the planets, as these wanderers emerged from the dazzling mass, were given the names of deities. Humanity read itself into the heavens. The Christian religion supplanted the theologies of pagan Europe, and the stars were made to adorn the Virgin's crown, to stand watch over the divine Infant's manger, and to adhere to invisible spheres—as many as twenty-seven—that smoothly turned in concentric homage to God's glory.

The telescope roughened the picture: the moon had mountains, Saturn had rings, and moons rotated around Jupiter, puncturing the planet's hypothetical crystal sphere. The picture has widened and deepened ever since; fuzzy nebulae were revealed to be other galaxies, as full of stars as our own, and the chemistry of the stars yielded its statistics to spectro-analysis. A universal history was deduced, originated in a monstrous singularity, a Big Bang in which the vastness of all matter was for an iota of time contained in a volume smaller than a pea. As late as the early 1960s, I remember, the Big Bang had a hotly defended rival hypothesis, the steady-state universe, where hydrogen atoms emerged one by one to feed the observable expansion; but the discovery in 1965 of the Big Bang's radio-wave fossil, the $2.7°$ Kelvin background radiation uniformly spread in all directions of space, banished the rival to the same realm as the crystalline Ptolemaic spheres.

The earth's heavy elements, including the substance of our bodies, were forged in the cataclysms of dying stars: this is our connection with the starry empyrean, this and the mental ingenuity and persistence that chip away at the cosmic riddles, in which the physics of the inconceivably small merges with that of the inconceivably large. Perhaps the sky is no less comforting than it ever was. For billions of years into the future, barring an unlucky meteor, it will not intrude into our planetary privacy. Nor, it becomes increasingly clear, will we travel far into it; the speed of light is circumvented only in the impracticable overdrives, time warps, and quantum tunnels of light-fingered futuristic fantasy, and even at the speed of light all but a few of the stars are many human lifetimes away. What we see, looking up, is a glittering cage of impregnable distances. In the earth-years during which the Hayden Planetarium and I have been around, the universe has shed the cartoon face it wore in the Sunday supplements. It looms more and more as something utterly alien and unconscious, but for us, of its own blazing beauty and gargantuan extravagance. And yet it has a savor, when we look up, of benevolence.

Against Angelolatry

Cast: God
      The Archangel Gabriel
      The Archangel Michael
Scene: Heaven, a bare place with a few chairs

GOD: Uh, I've called you in today for a bit of a consult, a matter I suppose of public relations, though I hate the term. *(Pauses while the angels say nothing. Shows them a sheaf of papers.)* These polls—and I know you can only trust them up to a point, but still—show that among human beings, across the sectarian board, the popularity of angels is going up, while Mine seems to be going down. Now, how do you guys explain it?

GABRIEL: Sir, are You trying to make us feel guilty?

MICHAEL: It's not something we can control. Ever since You gave them free will—a step, I may remind you, that several of us warned against—they have been creatures of fads and whims. Angels are *in* right now, God knows why. Or I guess You don't, actually.

GABRIEL: If I venture a guess, sir, it relates to our greater accessibility, carrying all those messages back and forth, especially around Christmastime. We haven't let ourselves drift out of the loop.

Performed at the Loeb Drama Center's festival of one-minute plays, in Cambridge, Massachusetts, on June 1, 1998.

GOD: As *I* have, you're suggesting. Without Me, let Me remind you, there wouldn't *be* a loop. I said, *Let there be a loop*.

MICHAEL: My take on it, sir, is that with Your omnipotence people tend to blame You for their woe—for earthquakes and pestilence and war and so on. Also, we are easier to picture. White robes, golden sandals, our iridescent multi-colored wings, me in my armor, Gabe here with his lily—these have all been pretty vividly rendered, from the Sienese school on. Whereas You—no offense, sir—remain a bit cloudy. Except for that little crosspatch humpback, what's-his-name—Michelangelo, how could I forget!—no artist has quite dared to do You justice. The rest, they just take the easy way out and show You as a blur. People are increasingly visual. They only trust what they can see.

GOD: Can't they see Me in the waterfall? In the thunderhead? In Leviathan? In the rainbow? They used to.

GABRIEL: That was then, sir. This is now.

GOD: Are all these "sir"s meant to be sarcastic?

GABRIEL: Not a bit, s—

MICHAEL *(stepping forward shiningly in his armor)*: Trust us, this angel thing on Earth will blow over soon. You'll be right back at the top of the heap.

GOD: The top of the heap, huh? Tell Me—have either of you boys heard of redundancy? Of downsizing?

GABRIEL *(pondering his lily)*: Not in those words, exactly. We've heard talk of entropy and heat death, but the universe as I've known it has always been a pretty sound, expanding concern.

GOD: Well, boys, brace yourselves. I've been tinkering with a little merger. An archangel you may remember, Lucifer—

MICHAEL: An *awful* fellow—uppity, and given to anti-establishment oratory. We fixed his wagon, sir.

GOD: Well, he's been doing a fine job in his new location. *Thriv*ing. He didn't have much to go on at first, but he's made it work, and it's occurred to Me—to both of us, in fact—that the operation he's built up down there would dovetail very nicely with this one up here.

MICHAEL *(turning duller)*: Wow. That wouldn't leave many independent operators, would it? All under one management.

GOD: And, boys, he has a lot of angels on his staff. Fallen, but highly competent. *Hungry* angels.

GABRIEL *(lily wilting)*: Hungry.

GOD: Hungry, but not for publicity. No cutesy Christmas cards and angel calendars for Lucifer's crew. They do their work in the shadows, and never take a holiday. *So*. Think it over, and do give a little thought to significantly lowering your profile on My pet planet. Maybe stop answering prayers for a while. Stay off TV, for Chr—for My sake. You know Me, I'm no stickler for protocol, but I somehow do not appreciate being upstaged. What did I create you for, anyway?

BOTH ANGELS: To sing Your praises, sir.

GOD (*smiling, ripping up the poll sheets, and turning the fragments into cooing doves*): You've got it, guys. Go to it. I'm all ears.

Ten Epochal Moments in the American Libido

1. JAMESTOWN, VIRGINIA, 1608: The Indian maiden Pocahontas, daughter of Chief Powhatan, embraces the captured English colonist John Smith, whose head has been already placed on the sacrificial stone, and successfully begs that his life be spared. In the wake of her intervention, Smith is initiated into her tribe and she is converted to Christianity in Jamestown. She marries not Smith but John Rolfe, who has introduced tobacco cultivation to the area. With Rolfe she travels to England, is received at court, and becomes the hit of London society. However, while preparing for her return voyage she dies, in her early twenties. American themes: erotic charm of the dusky races; self-reckless teen-age crush on older (thickly bearded) man; death of a young woman (which Edgar Allan Poe thought the most poetic of topics); tobacco.

2. Plymouth, Massachusetts, c. 1623. *Mayflower* arriviste John Alden, paying court to Priscilla Mullins on behalf of his shy friend Myles Standish, is advised, "Speak for yourself, John." Alden and Priscilla swiftly marry; Alden goes on to serve for over forty years as assistant governor of the Plymouth colony, and to be the last *Mayflower* passenger to die, in 1687. Themes: New World, proto-feminist directiveness; clarified female role in mate-choice; health benefits of marriage to male partner.

3. A forest near Boston, c. 1650. Hester Prynne, seven years after secretly conceiving her illegitimate child, Pearl, by the venerated clergyman Arthur Dimmesdale, in his presence casts off her scarlet letter and lets down her hair. In the words of her chronicler, Nathaniel Hawthorne, "Down it fell upon her shoulders, dark and rich, with at once a shadow and a light in its abundance, and imparting the charm of softness to her features." She proposes to her former lover, who is tortured by his

---

For the tenth anniversary of *Forbes FYI*, at the behest of Christopher Buckley.

unconfessed sin, that the two of them, with their love child, either flee deeper into the forest or return to the Old World. At this prospect her vitality and beauty revive; she advises Dimmesdale to put behind him New England's "iron men, and their opinions." She tells him, "What we did had a consecration of its own," anticipating the pop-song lyric, "How can it be wrong, when it feels so right?" Themes: dismissal of Puritan morality; embrace of instinctual wilderness; greater erotic sophistication of Europe; superior natural courage and resilience of women.

4. New Bedford, Massachusetts, c. 1840. Ishmael, a Presbyterian sailor, finds himself obliged to share a bed at the Spouter Inn with Queequeg, a pagan South Seas harpooner with an alarmingly painted face. In the morning, according to Ishmael's report in *Moby-Dick*, "I found Queequeg's arm thrown over me in the most loving and affectionate manner. You had almost thought I had been his wife." In the course of the day and night following, spent "chatting and napping at short intervals," Ishmael, at first resistant to his companion's pipe-smoking, grows so fond of his barbaric companion that "I liked nothing better than to have Queequeg smoking by me, even in bed." He draws the moral, "Yet see how elastic our stiff prejudices grow when once love comes to bend them." Themes: tobacco; anti-Puritanism; charm of dusky races; relative ease and comfort of same-sex relations. Cf. *Huckleberry Finn, Butch Cassidy and the Sundance Kid.*

5. Brooklyn, New York, 1875. Henry Ward Beecher, the leading voice of Protestantism in his time, an advocate in his eloquent sermons of abolition, woman suffrage, evolution, and a mild Reconstruction, is sued for adultery by his former friend and protégé Theodore Tilton. The civil jury fails to reach agreement, but Beecher remains active and influential until his death in 1887. Themes: linkage of liberal politics, religiosity, and loose sexual behavior; "a consecration of its own"; societal allowances made for alpha male; hung jury; around-the-clock scandal coverage and the onset of infotainment.

6. New York, New York, 1906. Millionaire Harry K. Thaw shoots the distinguished architect Stanford White at the Madison Square Roof Garden, for offenses committed against Thaw's wife, the former showgirl and artists' model Florence Evelyn Nesbit, including persuading her to swing nude in a velvet swing hung in their love nest. Thaw says to the arresting officer, "He ruined my wife and then deserted the girl." The first jury cannot reach a verdict; the second finds Thaw not guilty by reason of insanity, and he is committed to an insane asylum. Nesbit suffers a career decline. American themes: female ruination; velvety, champagne-fuelled orgies among the rich; teen-age crushes on mustached men;

infotainment; the structural weaknesses of heavily corniced Beaux Arts architecture.

7. Hollywood, California, 1927. Clara Bow stars in the movie *It*, giving a word to what most everybody knew was there. Hollywood settles to three decades of aphrodisiac euphemism, never showing couples, married or not, in bed, not even Queequeg and Ishmael, censoring out the inside of a woman's thigh even if accidentally filmed as she is falling through the air. Yet rarely does the industry deviate from its faith that sex is what it's all about. Cagney pushing a grapefruit into Mae Clarke's face, Jane Russell pointing a pistol from beneath her filmy, *très décolleté* blouse—this was sex, too, and through Depression and world war the studios did not let America forget it. Themes: box office; id; casting couch; cutting-room floor.

8. Key West, Florida, c. 1934. Helen Gordon tells her husband, the fictional writer Richard Gordon, in the Hemingway novel *To Have and Have Not*, "Love was the greatest thing, wasn't it? Love was what we had that no one else had or could ever have? And you were a genius and I was your whole life. I was your partner and your little black flower. Slop. Love is just another dirty lie. Love is ergoapiol pills to make me come around because you were afraid to have a baby. Love is quinine and quinine and quinine until I'm deaf with it. Love is that dirty aborting horror that you took me to. Love is my insides all messed up. It's half catheters and half whirling douches. I know about love. Love always hangs up behind the bathroom door. It smells like lysol. To hell with love." American themes: disenchantment; realism; pregnancy avoidance; puritanism reconsidered. Cf. Rhett Butler, to Scarlett O'Hara, in the 1939 film *Gone with the Wind*: "Frankly, my dear, I don't give a damn."

9. Woodstock, New York, 1969. The news media photograph co-ed nudity in the course of a rain-drenched rock festival attended by four hundred thousand rapturous, not uncommonly stoned young people. Love is the opposite of war and can do no wrong. It reigns unchallenged until 1985, when Rock Hudson announces that he is dying of AIDS. Themes: optimism; pacifism; doing what comes naturally; liberal politics and sexuality; "How can it be wrong, when it feels so right?"

10. Washington, D.C., 1995. President William Jefferson Clinton submits to fellatio from a twenty-two-year-old female White House intern while shmoozing with a congressman over the telephone; on another occasion he relishes a cigar that has survived penetration of her vagina. Clinton is later impeached for the subsequent cover-up of these acts, but the Senate cannot summon the two-thirds vote needed to convict, and he continues, with high approval ratings, in office. Familiar

American themes: hung jury; crush on older man; pregnancy avoidance; dismissal of puritanism; casting couch; allowances for alpha male; female ruination; infotainment; disenchantment; sex and liberal politics and professed religiosity; pursuit of happiness; tobacco.

Five Great Novels About Loving

1. *Loving*, by Henry Green. An English estate in Ireland during World War II lyrically houses amorous doings among both masters and servants.

2. *Madame Bovary*, by Gustave Flaubert. A young bourgeois wife seeks spiritual and sexual fulfillment away from the marital bed and runs grievously into debt.

3. *The Princesse de Clèves*, by Madame de Lafayette. A long extramarital attraction is consummated by the heroine's announcement that the way to keep love alive is to not marry.

4. *Les Liaisons Dangereuses*, by Choderlos de Laclos. Polymorphous seduction and betrayal among terminally jaded eighteenth-century aristocrats: an epistolary novel.

5. *The Scarlet Letter*, by Nathaniel Hawthorne. Among the Puritan pioneers of Boston, a promising clergyman falls afoul of a dark-haired proto-feminist and her wizardly older husband.

A list compiled for the Salon.com *Reader's Guide to Contemporary Authors* (Penguin, 2000).

Hydrophobia

MY FEAR OF WATER began, I believe, when my father, treading water in a swimming pool, invited me to jump from the tile edge into his arms; I did, and slipped from his grasp, and sank, and inhaled water for a few seconds. It felt, when I gasped, as if a fist had been shoved into my throat; I saw bubbles rising in front of my face as I sank down into a blue-green darkness.

Then my father seized me and lifted me back into the air. I coughed up water for some minutes, and my mother was very angry with my father

---

One of a series of fears confessed by various timorous souls for a Santa Fe magazine called *Outside*.

for his mistake. Even then, it seems to me in the wavery warps of this memory, I took my father's side; he was, after all, trying to teach me to swim, a paternal duty, and it was just bad luck, a second's slip-up, that in fact he delayed my learning for several decades. Part of our problem, that traumatic summer day, was that we had little experience of swimming pools; not only did we have no pool ourselves, but no one in our neighborhood or circle of acquaintance did, in that blue-collar Depression world. We were not country-club people. It is a mystery to me how we found ourselves at that particular pool, in bathing suits. Nor do I know exactly how old I was—small enough to be trusting but big enough to surprise my father with my sudden weight.

Henceforth I knew what it was like to look through a chain-link fence at a public pool, its seethe of naked bodies in the sunshine, and inhale its sharp scent of chlorine, but not to swim there. At the local YMCA, the pool was a roofed-in monster whose chlorinated dragon-breath, amplified by the same acoustics that made voices echo, nearly asphyxiated me with fear. Aged twelve or thirteen by now, I tried to immerse my face in the water as the instructor directed, but it was like sticking my hand into fire; nothing could override my knowledge that water was not my element and would kill me if it could. At college five years later, where one had to pass a swimming test to graduate, I managed a froggy backstroke the length of the pool, my face straining upward out of the water, while a worried-looking instructor kept pace at poolside with a pole for me to grab in case I started to sink. I think I did sink, once or twice, but eventually passed the test, and stayed dry for years.

In the movies of my adolescence, Esther Williams smiled through the hateful element, using it to display her rotating body, but other movies, glorifying our wartime navy, showed sinking ships and sputtering submarines. One of my nightmares was of being trapped belowdecks and needing to force myself through liquid darkness toward air and light. My lungs felt flooded at the thought; my hydrophobia extended to a fear of choking, of breathlessness. Life seemed a tight passageway, a slippery path between volumes of unbreathable earth and water.

And yet, graduating from college, I took the *Coronia* to England, and contemplated the ocean calmly from the height of the deck, and slept behind a sealed porthole. Adulthood strives to right the imbalances of childhood, and to soothe its terrors. My fear of water eased as, in my mid-twenties, I moved with my wife and children to a seaside town. Paternity itself, with its vicarious dip into the amniotic fluids, made me braver, and the salty buoyance and shoreward push of seawater were marked improvements over perilously thin fresh water. We bought a house by a saltwater creek in the marshes, and that was better yet; I plunged into our private piece of creek as if I were one with the grasses, the muddy banks, the drifting current, the overhead vapory clouds—one with the water, my body mostly water. By middle age I had learned to swim and take pleasure in it, but still tended to float on my back, and to keep my face averted from the murky, suffocating depths beneath me. My crawl, with its rhythmic underwater exhalation, was a nervous one, and tended to end, a bit breathlessly, after a few strokes. Water had become my friend, but never one I could totally rely on.

My Life in Poker

MY TATTERED MAROON COPY of the 1950 *Registrar* for Harvard freshmen lists, next to my boyish but unsmiling image, "Poker, Chess, Cartooning" among my special interests. My interest in chess died when a fellow-frosh, Larry Wilde from Sonoma, California, played rings around me one evening in Hollis Hall and gave me and my king an unpleasant trapped feeling. My interest in cartooning persisted longer, into the pages of *The Harvard Lampoon*, but by graduation time I had come to the conclusion that concocting visual jokes wasn't the career for me. Poker, surprisingly, has stayed with me to this day, though I can only recall a few penny-ante games played in college and, in high school, a shy try at strip poker in someone's parents' attic, where one losing girl was reduced, having shed shoes, bobby socks, and barrettes, to groping into her sweater and fetching forth her bra.

It was a cold December afternoon, late in 1957, in the New England hamlet of Ipswich, Massachusetts, when a neighbor from across Essex Road telephoned and asked me, a newcomer to the town, if I would like to play poker that night. My startled wife gave a guarded blessing, and I went off into the dark to join the group, which was meeting for the first time. The same group, with many substitutions due to death, indifference, and Florida retirement, still gathers, every other Wednesday night. I and one other graybeard are the only founding members who still play. There have been changes over the years. In the 1960s, tired of counting out nickels and dimes, we made the minimum bet a quarter, with fifty cents on the last card, and no more than three raises per man per round: there the stakes have stayed ever since, inflation be damned. We no

___

Recollected for the chronically revived *Life*, issue of November 5, 2004.

longer play much five-card draw or two-card high-low or deuces wild; more ornate forms of stud and high-low number games like 5–15, 2–22, and 7–27 build bigger pots and sustain suspense longer. The last round once began at eleven and now it commences at nine-thirty; we used to run through two cases of beer, and now a pair of six-packs are plenty, with one of them a non-alcoholic brew; there is no longer a cloud of tobacco smoke over the table. In the almost five decades during which I have been a member, I have changed houses, church denominations, and wives. My publisher has been sold and resold. Only my children command a longer loyalty than this poker group. And I'm not even a good player.

I am careless, neglecting to count cards, preferring to sit there in a pleasant haze of bewilderment and anticipation. I am timid, tending to fold in the face of a relentless raiser. Yet I am also hopelessly optimistic, hanging in, feeding the pot quarters when only one card left in the deck can possibly help my hand. Poker's charm for me, beside which bridge seems fussy and gin rummy picayune, lies in its rapid renewals of opportunity—that, and the actual presence of money, visible and tangible, on the table, flowing into pots and back out again. My one short story about poker ended with the image of the players' aging hands, reaching, gathering in, relinquishing.

Poker is eminently human. Its strategy and parameters are based not merely on cards but on personalities, the tics and habits revealed over years of acquaintance. In my group, the Bad Loser growls and slams down his hand. The Bluffer blithely raises and, when called, fans out his cards in good-natured surrender, announcing "I've got shit." The Bottom Feeder taciturnly sticks around, hoping to sneak away with a piece of a cheap pot. Mr. By-the-Book, glancing down into a winner, raises and telegraphs his hand and everybody folds, except for the Long Sufferer, who says, "Well, it's only money," and yields up another dollar with a sigh.

Always being in character is a bad ploy. Never making a mistake is a mistake. A failed bluff may pay off a few hands down the road, when you really have the goods, and everyone, remembering the failed bluff, stays against you. Poker, like statecraft, tends to steer by the last miscalculation, trying to avoid it this time. Which can also be a mistake. Our group has given up, by and large, on poker faces; we know each other too well— how we fold, why we stay. We've given up, too, on insisting that a player call his hand correctly; we're getting senile, and let the cards speak. It's a comfortable group. Many the Wednesday evening, escaping from a domestic or professional crisis, I settled at the table as if my noisy buddies would protect me from life itself. In my one poker story, the hero has been just told he is fatally ill, and decides to go to poker anyway, and takes comfort by looking around and realizing that we all are dying—reaching out, gathering in, relinquishing. It was a story based on real life, though I didn't die; I was simply scared that I would some day.

Of course, there are other kinds of poker than the homey variety around a well-lit kitchen table, in casual clothes, with stakes that won't bend anybody's budget. There is the poker of the Western frontier, where men bet the ranch and draw guns. There is the high-seas, shipboard poker of the professional shark and the tender, often pickled, fish. There is, in recent years, Internet poker, pulling in three million dollars a day, with no faces and a computerized shuffle. There is televised poker, where the stakes are huge, the game is usually Texas Hold 'em, and cameras under the glass table show the hole cards to the viewer: one more spectator sport for couch potatoes. Since top-quality poker experts tend to be poker-faced nerds, there is celebrity poker, with mugging, chitchat, charity beneficiaries, and a high proportion of female players. There is even a Ladies' Night in the World Poker Tournament, where costumes are somewhat less scanty than those worn in women's beach volleyball. My own flexible group has, over the years, included an occasional wife or girlfriend, but in our limited experience she gets bored, feels bullied, and doesn't really get it—"it" being poker's unique mix of aggression and camaraderie, seriousness and comedy. Someone's accidentally spilling a beer all over the cards, for example, is a not infrequent highlight of our evening's fun.

Poker to me is bodies and cards. The electronic poker explosion is part of the dephysicalization of experience rampant in advanced countries. Do you trust a computer's shuffle to be truly random? I don't. Would you miss the slick feel of the cards and the coins as they slither through their dance of chance? I would. And the huge amounts of money with which TV poker tries to hold our attention seem to me, in this age of meaningless millions, vapid and curiously dampening. High-stakes, no-limit players, playing the odds, primly fold most of the time. In our friendly game, players hang around, tossing in their quarters, because folding is not belonging, and belonging is what poker's little democracy is all about.

My Life in Cars

T. S. ELIOT'S PRUFROCK says he has measured out his life in coffee spoons; Americans my age, thinking bigger, have measured out theirs in

---

For the Automotive Supplement, *Architectural Digest*, September 1999.

coupes, sedans, station wagons, and SUVs. I have owned more cars than I can count, though I am among the least automotive of men. Not for me the youthful mysteries of the Saturday disassembly, or the mature car-consumer's expertise as to rpm and mpg and cc's of cylinder volume. All I ask of an automobile is that it go when I press on the accelerator and stop when I stamp on the brake. Not all of my father's cars, somber Thirties models painted black and bought second-hand, did. Many the morning and evening we struggled with the dying chug of a starter that couldn't infect the engine with its spark. I lack, therefore, the true auto-aficionado's fondness for delicate antique makes; when a car gets temperamental on me, I get temperamental back and start thinking junkyard. Nevertheless, one lives in these machines, and loves them sometimes without knowing it.

My first car, acquired with the earnings from some free-lance magazine sales while I was being a graduate student in England, was a '55 four-door Waterfall Blue Ford sedan, bought new from my cousin Lew Kachel's agency on the Lancaster Pike. My parents negotiated it for me while I was across the ocean. It was the first new car in the family; we all helped give it its first bath. I was married by this time, with an infant daughter and a job in New York City. In New York I parked my car on the street, moving it back and forth on alternate days to avoid the no-parking interludes of the Upper West Side.

When we moved to Greenwich Village, where the squeeze was even tighter, I had to rent space in a parking lot, and in that lot, one sunny day, when men tarred the apartment-building roof next door, the pristine Waterfall Blue paint got spattered with drops of tar. Not large drops—it had been just a tar drizzle—but I no longer wanted to live in a city where such offhand vandalism could occur. So I moved, with my wife, my Ford, and my now two small children, to bucolic Massachusetts, where the car enjoyed a busy, hassle-free small-town life until its advancing age dictated that we trade it in. This loss, this betrayal, struck me so forcefully that I wrote a long short story about life, death, and automobiles; it sweepingly asserted: "We in America make love in our cars, and listen to ball games, and plot our wooing of the dollar: small wonder the landscape is sacrificed to these dreaming vehicles of our ideal and onrushing manhood."

The next dreaming vehicle was, I think, a navy-blue station wagon, a Ford Fairlane. As the family grew, and the scope of our consumerism expanded, the need for two cars became apparent. A sentimental fool for a pretty grille, I bought the old car back, from a carpenter who had ruined its upholstery by lugging lumber. In this battered jalopy, disgraced and redeemed, I felt free. When that car died a second time, I launched myself, in parallel with a succession of family station wagons, on a series of convertibles. I loved the bright wind battering at my head, and the trees whipping by as if fleeing a predator, and the sensation of trundling around town in a kind of bathtub, readily available for *plein-air* interviews. The first was a Ford, I believe, but then I defected to General Motors for a dear little dove-gray 1965 Corvair with a convertible top you pulled up by hand. It was Sixties do-it-yourself, tidy in its finlessness, and thrifty with fossil fuel, as ecological consciousness dawned. Its engine was in the rear, which made it dashing but skittish in handling. At least, my only two significant car accidents came in the Corvair: I skidded into a car that had abruptly backed out of a driveway, and later into a utility pole on a snowy night. To get back the deductible, I wrote a story about the latter mishap, called "The Taste of Metal." Here is the moment of bitter truth, as experienced by a protagonist with too many Stingers under his belt:

> Richard's responsive laugh was held in suspense as the car skidded on the curve. A dark upright shape had appeared in the center of the windshield, and he tried to remove it, but the automobile proved impervious to the steering wheel and instead drew closer, as if magnetized, to a telephone pole that rigidly insisted on its position in the center of the windshield. The pole enlarged. The little splinters pricked by the linemen's cleats leaped forward in the headlights, and there was a flat whack surprisingly unambiguous, considering how casually it had happened. Richard felt the sudden refusal of motion, the *No*, and knew, though his mind was deeply cushioned in cottony indifference, that an event had occurred which in another incarnation he would regret.

With no engine in it, the front acted a bit like an airbag; the hood was fearfully crumpled, the beams of the headlights now crossed, my passengers were stunned, and I became middle-aged on the spot.

We moved, two adults and four children from ages thirteen to eight, to London for a year (1968–69), and there I betrayed Detroit for the first time: I bought a green Citroën four-door sedan, in which we made many a stately family progress to the likes of Stonehenge and Salisbury Cathedral. That Citroën was a vehicle like no other, cushy with velour and engineered as if every mechanical question had to be addressed on revolutionary principles. When the engine started, the chassis rose up on cushions of air, and when the trip was over it sighed regretfully while subsiding back. It had a pointed piscine nose, and convex sleek sides afflicted with a couple of scrapes as I moved it in and out of our narrow Cumberland Terrace parking cubicle.

Back in the U.S.A.—one could still import Citroëns then—the car's eccentric Gallic flair, much admired at first in the neighborhood, began to wear thin. Under the hood it harbored a snake pit of tightly packed connections that only a very slender and determined contortionist could reach. The beautiful logic of its mechanical maze had little pragmatic tolerance in it; American mechanics threw up their hands. More and more I found myself at the nearest garage equipped to cope, a good hour away, an outpost of French thought in Watertown, where the head mechanic, with his beguiling accent, tried to teach me to regard my car as one would a profoundly troublesome, even perverse, but nevertheless magnificent woman. There was a secret Masonry, it turned out, of Citroën-lovers, and some of these emerged from their own tortured relationships to help me through a spat; impassioned hobbyists, they reached deep into my sulking car's innards, murmuring sweet nothings, and got her to go. But when, on the way to Watertown one day, my green-skinned inamorata began to cough like Camille and attempted to die in the middle of the Sumner Tunnel, the affair, for me, was over. She was last seen in a muddy front yard in Haverhill, in care of a gray-fingered young man who solemnly promised to love her as she deserved.

My marriage fell apart, too. Owning that Citroën had been the raciest thing my wife and I had done, automotively—our high-water mark as conspicuously licensed drivers. We went our separate ways, she to a boxy Volvo station wagon, for Swedish stability, and I to a lime-colored Mustang convertible, for American pizzazz. The blend was no Citroën substitute. My older son, now a legal motorist, passed the wheel of the Mustang to a girlfriend who adroitly ran the car through a row of concrete guard posts. His younger brother, coming into his license a little later, laid the Volvo sideways onto a stone wall. These were protest accidents, subconscious efforts to reverse a mid-Seventies domestic breakdown. And I, guiltily self-destructive, found myself buying, out of a front yard glimpsed from a train window, a little Karmann Ghia convertible previously owned by several bachelors each belonging to the Hundred Thousand Mile Club.

If the former convertibles had felt like bathtubs, this one was a bird's nest, in which I experienced an impulse to chirp as I watched the road skim by under my feet. Beside the distracting holes in the floor, it had a canvas top slashed by some inquisitive citizen of Boston, and a front right wheel that came off, with a gathering wobble and a banshee shriek, on Route 95. I put it back on the axle myself and drove on; the Karmann Ghia, a rakish shell with an air-cooled Volkswagen engine, made you a mechanic if you had as much as played with Tinker Toys. Shedding nuts and bolts like a fire engine in the old comic strip *Smokey Stover*, it tootled over Boston underpasses and fitted into many a tight parking spot. I have no memory of trading it in; perhaps it just dissolved, returning its elements one by one to Nature.

My second wife and I have recapitulated my first marriage's progression from Detroit models to foreign ones. My bride's blue Pinto station wagon and my red Maverick shared our first driveway. I had bought the Maverick second-hand because I liked the name and the pattern of ranch brands on the black leather seats. It proved to be my boyhood nightmare, a car that would not start. At first, it resisted on rainy mornings, then on misty ones; finally, even a tinge of humidity in the air seemed to smother its capacity for ignition. Luckily, we lived a block from the gas station, whose proprietor would trudge up the street and wave a few squirts of WD-40 in the direction of the carburetor. The car would start. When I tried the same trick, nothing happened; when I asked him what his secret was, he said, "Faith." A lot of cans of WD-40 were drained, on damp days, in demonstration of my lack of that Christian virtue.

As the marriage ripened, we felt substantial enough for a string of gray Audis—sleek machines whose German engineers had set themselves to solve the riddle of an asymmetrical, five-cylinder engine. If Audis had a weakness, it was in the pinion joints, whose replacement cost no less than eight hundred dollars every time, and at a service facility in a gritty old mill town whose public library I came to know well, as I logged days of Audi repair among its shelves. Also, those German engineers hadn't done much thinking about icy American driveways, and this became a severe deficiency when we moved to a house on a snow-capped hill. At the very last turn, the Audis kept sliding sideways, as hard to coax as a rogue elephant back on its heels. For our second car, I had reverted to my first loyalty, Ford, and owned a Taurus—or was it two, blending in memory into each another? The aerodrab period had arrived in the saga of automotive design, when all cars looked the same—the hood rounded and depressed to slide under the wind, and the trunk, on the same fuel-saving principles, raised perkily, like the rear end of a bitch in heat. The Taurus was front-wheel drive, and didn't exactly grab our icy driveway either.

Years ago, at the height of the crisis in which Japanese imports were devouring our domestic market like sharks at the belly of a whale, I had vowed never to buy a Japanese car. But my wife's sewing circle insisted that the only solution to our driveway problem was an all-wheel-drive Subaru. Every patriotic bone in my body screaming, I was dragged into the orbit of the rising sun. Our Subaru skimmed up the driveway just as my wife's consultants had said it would, but otherwise it was as glamorous as a breadbox. The propaganda about Japanese cars proved true: they rarely need repair. We replaced our third Audi with a Japanese version of (as dealers delicately put it) "near-luxury," an Infiniti; we have propped up the staggering Japanese economy and added several former Detroit assemblers to the welfare rolls. My fifty-year ride on rubber tires has become a guilt trip.

Looking back, I can pluck certain flowers of sensation from the blurred roadside. The ticking of the heater warming up in my father's '36 Buick, halfway to school, while the little glowing radio shared farm reports. The powerful notched feel of the floor shift of the lime-green Mustang, summoning RPMs from the vasty gearbox. The bobbing heads of my children and their cousins in the way-back of the Falcon station wagon, each eating a double-dip ice-cream cone that had to be, as its melting accelerated, jettisoned. The blasé sweep of the brilliantly engineered windshield wipers as I snugly drove my children, through a London downpour, to school in the Citroën, its pointy green hood imperviously beaded with raindrops. One of those elephantine Audis, its wheels spinning, gaining a foothold on a scattering of sand and making it up the last bit of driveway. The Waterfall Blue Ford sailing up the New Jersey Turnpike on a sunny October Monday while the radio broadcast Don Larson pitching his perfect World Series game.

There is a lot of radio in my memories, and a lot of rain, as the tires licked up the asphalt. There was a vivid illusion of privacy and motionless security. There was trust: a single jerk of my hand on the wheel could have brought death to everyone the car contained. Yet my hand did not twitch; we by and large live up to our empowerment—the balky, bulky, wasteful, wonderful mobility the auto has bestowed on this century. Heaven itself may not know, exactly, the number of miles my cars have carried me—back and forth, most of them, on forgettable errands that seemed important at the time. Not just "seemed"—*were* important, if a mundane life is important. I am proud of all my miles.

TRIBUTES AND SHORT TAKES

West 155th Street

TAXI DRIVERS don't want to go to West 155th Street. They don't want to be dragged so far uptown, with slim prospects of a fare back. If they bring you from the airport, they insist on trying to get there by the Harlem River Drive, discovering too late that the only way to get smoothly onto West 155th is to approach it from across the river, via the Yankee Stadium exit from the Deegan Expressway. Up this far, Broadway has a strong Hispanic accent and boasts a brisk trade in illegal drugs. Nevertheless, the long block of 155th between Broadway and Riverside Drive—one-way east—has idyllic qualities: it is broad enough for diagonal parking; cobbles peep through its asphalt; and on its southern side the greenery of Trinity Cemetery, lifted high on a succession of terraces, shades the stones and names of many a once-eminent citizen, including John James Audubon, John Jacob Astor, Mayor Fernando Wood (who wanted New York City to secede in 1861), Clement Clarke Moore (who wrote "A Visit from St. Nicholas"), and Charles Samuel Ruggles, the creator of Gramercy Park and Lexington Avenue, which he graciously declined to have named Ruggles Avenue.

On the northern side of West 155th Street, a succession of granite façades presents the back side of a noble plaza designated Audubon Terrace; planned in 1908, built on land once owned by the great painter of American birds, the Beaux Arts complex was intended as a cultural center. The National Museum of the American Indian has lately vacated its space here for a federal building in the Battery, but the American Numismatic Society and the Hispanic Society of America—with its Goyas and Velázquezes, a gloomy remainder of the plutocrat Archer Huntington's

---

In response to a request from *New York* magazine for a description of a favorite spot in New York City.

passion for Spain—hold on, as does, in the middle of the block, at number 633 West 155th, the American Academy of Arts and Letters. Beyond the heroically figured bronze doors, a sparsely visited interior, staffed by a crew of mostly female employees and bustling only during a few annual fêtes for its generally elderly membership, houses the apparatus of a self-elected artistic aristocracy. Sculptures by Paul Manship and paintings by Childe Hassam decorate the generous spaces, constructed in the early 1920s by the munificence of Huntington, himself a member. An auditorium added in 1930 turned out to have acoustical properties highly valued by today's recording companies. The library on the third floor, where dinners and meetings are held in sobering view of the cemetery across the street, is surely one of the loveliest, and emptiest, rooms in Manhattan.

But it is the street itself, which would be quite unknown to me but for this institution, that I wish to celebrate: it slopes down rather sharply toward the gliding Hudson, and a warm river wind brushes the faces of those marching down from Broadway to attend the Academy's mid-May ceremonial. Manhattan's claustrophobic closeness lifts in this vicinity; the buildings throw short shadows, and the neighborhood's stately elements—the terrace, the walled cemetery, the Episcopal church across Broadway—stand as a kind of pledge the past once made to the future. Some day, it is not unlikely, as population pressure extends the northern spread of gentrification, that taxi drivers will be less surprised to be directed here. Audubon Terrace was designated a New York City Historic District in 1979, and there was talk of renaming the 157th Street subway station in its honor. For now, pedestrian traffic is sparse and automobiles find curbside parking spaces. The metropolis is not all seethe; islands of antique aspiration and gracious scale persist. In my years of New York visitation this byway has served, with its slanting sidewalk and riverine vista, to remind me that a complete city includes pockets of quiet.

The Academy As It Was and Is

(A Talk, with Slides)

THE INSTITUTION whose splendid auditorium shelters us this afternoon* was born, a century ago, of a breath, a hint, on a porch in Saratoga, New York, to the effect that the American Social Science Association, which

---

*May 20, 1998.

dated back to 1856, might well contain, along with its other departments of human endeavor, one devoted to literature and the arts. The suggestion came from Dr. H. Holbrook Curtis, a throat specialist, and found the receptive ear of the president of the association, Judge Simeon Baldwin. Neither man was an artist, literary or otherwise, but Judge Baldwin submitted Curtis's proposal to the council of the Association in December, and it was approved, in 1898. Dr. Curtis and Mr. Charles Dudley Warner, an essayist and fiction writer who had collaborated with Mark Twain on *The Gilded Age*, were asked to oversee the selection of charter members of what was first called the National Institute of Art, Science, and Letters.

Curtis and Warner set about their assignment with admirable premodern dispatch: artists were consulted, scores of invitations were sent out, and most were accepted. On February 11, 1899, the new Institute had what was billed as its first annual meeting, at the Academy of Medicine on West Forty-third Street; Warner was made temporary president, and it was debated whether the fledgling organization should remain within the American Social Science Association or proclaim independence. In September of that year, the Association again met; the Institute did proclaim its independence, dropped the word "science" from its title, and announced the acceptances for its membership, to be limited to one hundred fifty. In the department of literature, the two names most lustrous now—not counting that of Theodore Roosevelt—are Mark Twain and Henry James. Still read or at least remembered are Hamlin Garland, Henry Adams, Joaquin Miller, Thomas Nelson Page, Thomas Bailey Aldrich, Thomas Wentworth Higginson, Charles Eliot Norton, Henry Cabot Lodge, and William Dean Howells, who presided over the Institute after the death of Warner in 1901.

The literature department from the first was much the largest; the charter art department included the sculptors Augustus Saint-Gaudens and Daniel Chester French, the architect Charles McKim, and a number of painters, foremost those American Impressionists—Childe Hassam, William Merritt Chase, John H. Twachtman, and J. Alden Weir—whose work continues to brighten museum walls. Winslow Homer, interestingly, was not elected until 1905, and Thomas Eakins until 1908, whereupon he declined membership. The music department, the smallest then and now, had fourteen members, of which the names of Edward MacDowell and Walter Damrosch still, as it were, resonate. The membership was primarily but not exclusively Eastern; it was certainly all white, all Gentile, and all male. Thomas Wentworth Higginson, the Boston editor, Civil War hero, and liberal activist, whose renown now depends upon his slight association with Emily Dickinson, declined membership because women were excluded; but his refusal was ignored and he is still carried on our lists as a founding member.

In its first years, the Institute did not so much thrive as persist. On the premises of other New York organizations, gatherings with a talk on a cultural topic were held four or so times a year, but were lightly attended; the attendance at one meeting in 1901 is listed as fourteen. The modest expenses were more than met; they averaged less than one hundred fifty dollars a year, and members were charged five dollars in dues. Still, there were complaints as to a lack of purpose, and some resignations. The Institute might have dwindled away, like similar high-minded, well-meant groups in the past, but for Robert Underwood Johnson, a poet and magazine editor and no doubt the most dedicated member in the institution's history. For some time he had been urging that the Institute should seek to raise an endowment, so it could offer prizes, publish papers, entertain foreign visitors, and, closest to Johnson's heart, erect a club-house, "a small beautiful classic building," that would serve Institute members as the Players Club did actors.

At a meeting called in 1904 to consider how to raise funds, the committee of three consisted of Johnson, MacDowell, and Edmund Clarence Stedman, a Wall Street broker turned poet and now best remembered as an anthologist and as one of the few literary men in New York who kept track of Herman Melville's whereabouts during the great mariner's long Manhattan obscurity. MacDowell suggested that the Institute could be divided into two classes, the choicer of which might have greater weight and influence with donors. Stedman proposed that the smaller body be called an academy. The proposal was put before a meeting of the Institute in April, in the Aldine Association on Fifth Avenue, twenty attending; the formation of the Academy was approved unanimously.

Thus began the institution's split-level existence and awkwardly compounded name. Johnson, already dominant in its proceedings, set in motion a complicated system of election whereby the first seven Academicians were chosen by ballot: they were, in order of votes received, Howells, Saint-Gaudens, Stedman, John La Farge, Mark Twain, John Hay, and MacDowell. Five of these seven, at the Academy's first meeting, in January of 1905, elected Henry James, Charles McKim, Henry Adams, Theodore Roosevelt, and four others. And so it went, the membership snowballing by fits and starts until the requisite thirty were elected. Besides Roosevelt and Hay, the former Secretary of the Interior Carl Schurz and Admiral Alfred Thayer Mahan, author of *The Influence of Sea Power upon History, 1660–1783*, gave public dignitaries a significant presence in the Academy. William James, elected in the final ten, declined, declaring in a letter that his decision was shaped "by the fact that my younger and shallower and vainer brother is already in the Academy, and that if I were there too, the other families might think the Jameses' influence too rank and strong."

In 1907, the end of the Institute's first decade, the "woman question" was diplomatically solved by the election of Julia Ward Howe; the eighty-eight-year-old author of "The Battle Hymn of the Republic" was not apt to dampen her colleagues' stag nights. At that same January meeting, it was voted to award a medal to one who "has rendered most distinguished service to any of the arts"; members were eligible. Johnson noted that these decisions "make the beginning of a policy of practical usefulness." Before the end of the year, the Academy voted to increase its membership to fifty, and the Institute voted to increase its own proportionally, to two hundred fifty.

Thus the Academy-Institute took the form it was to have for most of the twentieth century. In order to receive tax-exempt gifts, both institutions needed a national charter. Congress granted the Institute its in 1913, and yet balked at the Academy, claiming that no additional charter was needed, that the name was too similar to that of the American Academy of Arts and Sciences in Boston, and that the membership was too heavily drawn from the Atlantic seaboard. To counter the impression of a New York City club, meetings were held outside, with local dignitaries invited—in 1909 in Washington, in 1912 in Philadelphia, in 1913 in Chicago, in 1915 in Boston. Finally, in 1916, after four times passing in the Senate, the charter was approved by the House. Approval came in the nick of time, for already, by 1914, the extraordinary benefactions of Archer M. Huntington had begun.

(While the carousels are being changed, let me say that Betsey Feeley, of the Academy staff, selected and prepared these slides, and is doing the projecting.)

Archer Huntington, born illegitimately in 1870, became the adopted son of railroad millionaire Collis Potter Huntington after his mother, whom the elder Huntington had established as his mistress in a Fifth Avenue mansion, married her plutocratic lover in 1884. Young Archer, having thus sidled into a great American fortune, was shy and bookish, becoming a fervent student of things Spanish; on the strength of his writings on Spain he was elected to the Institute in 1911. By 1914, he was offering the Academy-Institute eight city lots on West 155th Street, with a hundred thousand dollars in endowment funds, provided they could raise sufficient additional funds to erect a building. In spite of Johnson's best efforts, no funds forthcame, and so Huntington himself provided two hundred thousand more for the erection of the administration building. Between 1921 and 1930, he further donated an estimated two million dollars—worth more than ten times that in today's dollars. In these benefactions he was accompanied by his mother. Born Belle Yarrington of Richmond, Virginia, she had changed her name to Arabella and, in 1913, widowed, had married her late husband's nephew, merging two Huntington fortunes into one. This auditorium, built in 1930, was, legend has it, financed by Archer Huntington with the sale of Rembrandt's *Aristotle Contemplating the Bust of Homer*, which he had inherited from his mother, for seven hundred thousand dollars. So well constructed that in a recent repainting its ornate ceiling showed not so much as a crack, this auditorium is thus built upon Rembrandt and, beneath that foundation, upon Belle Yarrington's charms.

It is not surprising that Huntington, for all his shyness and modesty, thought he might be entitled to some executive power. He had been elected a member of the Academy in 1919, and twenty years later there was a growing dissatisfaction in the Academy with the quality of the raffish, irreverent modern artists the Institute kept electing. For Robert Underwood Johnson, these buildings were a dream come true; at the cornerstone-laying of the administration building in 1921, performed by Marshal Foch of France with a silver trowel, Johnson's dedicatory sonnet began,

> If this be but a house, whose stone we place,
>> Better the prayer unbreathed, the music mute
>> Ere it be stifled in the rifted lute

and continued,

> No, 'tis a temple—where the mind may kneel
> And worship Beauty changeless and divine.

By 1933, he was writing in a letter, "It is now easier to get into the Institute than into the National Peanut Roasters Institute." He fought against the election of Robert Frost, Stephen Vincent Benét, Carl Sandburg, Robinson Jeffers, Sinclair Lewis, Theodore Dreiser, Ernest Hemingway, and H. L. Mencken—a virtual roll call of enduring interbellum reputations. In 1937, while losing a bitter battle against the election of Sinclair Lewis (already an Institute member and the first American winner of the Nobel Prize) to the Academy, Johnson died; but his words in a 1918 letter became prophetic. He had written, "If the Institute doesn't stand for standards and principles the Academy will be obliged to cut loose and choose its members from outside as well."

The final straw came in January of 1939, when five new members, among them William Faulkner and John Steinbeck, were elected to the Institute by declaration, ignoring the by-laws. At an Academy board meeting in October of 1939, Huntington introduced a resolution that would simply strike from its constitution the sentence "Only members of the National Institute of Arts and Letters shall be eligible for election to the Academy." This would have given the Academy the right to elect whomever it pleased. Rumors claimed that Huntington wished to install Black Jack Pershing, a World War I hero with no artistic qualifications, and that the Academy president, Nicholas Murray Butler, wanted to stack the ranks with professors from Columbia University, of which he was also president. Butler and three other directors concurred in Huntington's motion; only the eighty-seven-year-old Bostonian novelist Judge Robert Grant voted against it. But Grant was soon joined in resistance by the Institute president, Walter Damrosch—also an Academy member—and by the majority of the Academy.

The upshot of the so-called Row was that the Academy board was reshuffled by insurgent candidates; Huntington resigned with a vow, which he kept, never to set foot in the building again; and the long-time secretary of the Academy, Grace Vanamee, and her faithful companion, Colonel Frank P. Crasto, fled to Florida with substantial pensions. Damrosch, the new Academy president, and Arthur P. Train, the new head of the Institute, took charge of the shaken organizations. Damrosch wrote, "It seems that an enormous office force has occupied that building for many, many years, virtually almost only twirling their thumbs, and their salaries and upkeep of the building swallowing our entire income." The staff, which had included doormen in livery, was cut from nineteen to eight, and a new emphasis was placed upon the granting of artistic prizes to non-members. The first public ceremonial was held at Carnegie Hall in 1941, and every May thereafter a ceremonial has been held here.

Enough of the Academy as it was; what of it now? In 1976, the Academy and Institute were financially amalgamated; as of 1993, they together became simply the Academy, and all two hundred and fifty members Academicians. They are still predominantly, but no longer exclusively, white, male, and Eastern. They no longer profess to worship "Beauty changeless and divine." Any organization formally devoted to honoring the arts runs the risk of overvaluing yesterday's values and styles, but if we do so it is not for lack of trying to do otherwise. We welcome—we must welcome—new blood, and we welcome today new members, prize-winners young and old, and you of this audience to our hundredth-birthday party.

The Centennial Committee, of which I have had the pleasure of being chairman, includes or has included Will Barnet, Jack Beeson, John Guare, Elizabeth Hardwick, Ada Louise Huxtable, Jacob Lawrence, Jack Levine, Richard Lippold, Cynthia Ozick, Ned Rorem, Harrison Salisbury, Robert Venturi, and Hugo Weisgall. Our collective effort to mark this happy occasion took the form, first, of a number of needful repairs and renovations and improvements to the building undertaken under the presidency of Kevin Roche, who has contributed generously of his time and wisdom. Academy hats, bearing the silvery emblem of Pegasus, have appeared, in both billed and floppy styles. A book has been produced, entitled *A Century of Arts and Letters*, handsomely published by Columbia University Press and written by eleven members, who each took a decade of this institution's history and wrote a chapter about it. My talk has lifted its facts from its colorful narrative. Members of the art department, with contributions from members in music and literature as well, donated fifty prints, limited to editions of a hundred, collected in a centennial portfolio and to be displayed this fall both here and in a midtown gallery. We thank you all for being with us today. Though none of us, alas, will be here in the year 2098, we trust and hope that the American Academy of Arts and Letters will be.

The New Yorker

GREATNESS did not come immediately to *The New Yorker*, which was founded in February of 1925. But the magazine had going for it the zeal and enthusiasm of its founder and first editor, Harold Ross; the financial indulgence of his principal backer, Raoul Fleischmann; and the elegance of its first cover, displaying the Knickerbocker dandy drawn by Rea Irvin and later dubbed Eustace Tilley. Its cover was the best thing about the first issue—"The magazine *stank*," Fleischmann is supposed to have pronounced—and until the reign of Tina Brown as editor (1992–98), the same cover, unchanged but for the slowly rising price of the magazine (the first issue cost fifteen cents), ran on every anniversary issue, in the third week of February.

The first year was perilous; by its fourth month of publication, *The New Yorker*'s circulation had sunk to four thousand (from an initial fifteen thousand) and there were only three or four pages of advertising in each

A tribute composed for a posh book called *American Greats*, edited by Robert Wilson, published by PublicAffairs (New York, 1999), and underwritten by American Airlines.

issue. Fleischmann narrowly agreed to keep things running through the summer, and by fall the magazine was finding its own tone. The liveliness of the times helped. New York was at its gaudiest in these Prohibition years, a magnetic marketplace for writing and graphic art and musical comedy, and before long a host of bright young talents was attracted to the pages of this hopeful little weekly. Some, like Robert Benchley and Ralph Barton, already had established names; others, like E. B. White, came in from the cold of advertising work (in 1926). White brought James Thurber after him. The cartoonists Peter Arno and Helen Hokinson became regulars that first year, as did Janet Flanner, who contributed her letters from Paris under the pseudonym "Genêt." Katharine Angell, later to become White's wife, came aboard as editor, and her Bryn Mawr-educated taste proved an important complement to Ross's newspaperish idea, both rowdy and prim, of a magazine. As well as getting funnier, *The New Yorker* in its fiction and reporting and poetry got more serious. It flourished during the Depression—so much so that Ross and Fleischmann, who wanted to keep their pet in bounds, actively discouraged new subscriptions.

Greatness, perhaps, arrived in the years of World War II, which was extensively covered by such correspondents as A. J. Liebling and Daniel Lang. A stripped-down overseas "pony" edition introduced the magazine to GIs, thousands of whom became subscribers after the war. The devotion, in 1946, of an entire issue to John Hersey's sober account, from six perspectives, of the dropping of an atomic bomb on Hiroshima, demonstrated to all that *The New Yorker* was no longer a merely funny magazine. William Shawn, the non-fiction editor who persuaded Ross to make this striking gesture—the issue omitted cartoons and The Talk of the Town—succeeded to the editorship of the magazine upon Ross's untimely death of cancer in 1951.

Shawn's long reign, from 1951 to 1987, saw a financial heyday and then a decline in advertising revenue; Peter Fleischmann, Raoul's son, sold the magazine to Condé Nast Publications in 1985. Shawn was, against his will, eased out two years later; the short reign of Robert Gottlieb ended in 1992; Tina Brown shook up the format and the traditional understated demeanor; and now David Remnick, a thirty-nine-year-old writer when he took charge, a Princeton *summa cum laude* graduate fluent in the languages of Russia and boxing, calmly leads the venerable weekly, its fifth editor, into the future.

The New Yorker as I first knew it, from my early acquaintance with its pages as a child of eleven, and then as a contributor from the age of twenty-two, seemed unique—not only the best general magazine in

America, but perhaps the best that America ever produced. What was great about it, from a reader's point of view, was the variety and intelligence of its written contents, the beauty and energy of its cartoons, the rigorous factual and typographical accuracy, and the enclosing decorum and decency of it all. The writer's name appeared at the end, there were no bothersome, cute editor-manufactured subheads to "hook" the reader, and for a long time there was not even a table of contents, the product was so austerely pure. Everything in the magazine was trusted to speak for itself. Take it or leave it, the pages implied: Shawn claimed that the editors merely published what they found interesting, and gave no thought to pleasing an imagined or projected readership.

From a contributor's standpoint, these external virtues were matched by an incomparably solicitous editing process, one that sometimes irked with its thoroughness but saved a writer from many a slip and prodded him to many an improvement. The old editors—in my dealings, Mrs. White, William Maxwell, G. S. Lobrano, Howard Moss, Shawn himself—radiated gratitude for what they considered a worthy contribution. They had uncanny ears for a false note; they sometimes surprised you by accepting a daring or experimental piece; they manifested a cloistered virtue, in a fallen, hustling world, that made appearing anywhere else feel like a dangerous trespass. To be sure, there were quirks of editorial taste and a prudery that became anachronistic; still, your words looked better in *The New Yorker* than anywhere else. As the poet William Stafford once said to me, a poem in *The New Yorker* was like a letter to your friends. For a fledgling short-story writer, appearing there readily opened the doors of publishing houses.

The magazine's towering integrity rested on a handful of personalities, those of Ross and Shawn foremost. Through week after week of words and images, it set a standard that still haunts the national literary awareness. Without *The New Yorker* in this century, every literate person's sights would have been lowered.

William Shawn

THE SEVENTY-FIFTH BIRTHDAY of *The New Yorker* has been greeted, in the United States, with a number of books and memoirs, not all of them worshipful, as well as with the publication of two hefty anthologies of

---

Written for *Süddeutsche Zeitung*, February 2000.

writings, selected by the present editor, David Remnick, from the magazine. An excellent, equable, thorough history of the magazine by Ben
Yagoda has been overshadowed, in terms of publicity, by a curiously sour,
and in spots vindictive, memoir by Renata Adler, who contributed to the
magazine, off and on, for twenty-five years. She focuses on the long reign
of William Shawn, with whom she enjoyed a favored status, based primarily upon her brilliance as a writer but also tinged, she tells us in a startling aside, with love. What she means by "love" appears to be Platonic
and paternal-filial; not so in the case of fellow-contributor Lillian Ross,
whose book of two years ago, *Here But Not Here* (the positional title
oddly consonant with Ms. Adler's, *Gone*), described in sometimes steamy
terms a sexual love affair that she enjoyed with Shawn from 1952 to
Shawn's death in 1992. To Ross, Shawn was a passionate lover and a selfless saint giving up his life for an insatiably demanding magazine. To
Adler, he was an elusive and sometimes maddening father-figure who in
the end naïvely led *The New Yorker* to the wolves of Condé Nast. To Ved
Mehta, whose *Remembering Mr. Shawn's New Yorker* came out the same
year as Ross's book, Shawn was an infinitely wise guide and protector
who published Mr. Mehta's prose in whatever lavish quantity it was supplied. In Brendan Gill's bouncy and blithe *Here at The New Yorker*, published when the magazine enjoyed its fiftieth anniversary, Shawn figures
as a somewhat sinister figure, a shy, soft-voiced man who nevertheless
"always got his whispery way."

This spate of mixed reports has been fascinating to me, to whom
Shawn was an ineffable eminence who held my literary fate in his hands
and did not let it drop. I had admired the magazine as a boy, mostly for its
humor and cartoons. I was in college when Harold Ross, the first editor,
died at the young age of fifty-nine, in 1951. Though unknown to the general public, Shawn's right to succession was clear to the magazine's inner
circle, in which E. B. White was the most admired writer and his wife,
Katharine, the most significant editor. By the time, in 1954, that I had a
few poems and a short story accepted by the magazine, Shawn was firmly
in charge, and it was he, in the following year, who interviewed me for a
job and who gave me one, at what seemed the princely wage of one hundred dollars a week. Driving to the interview from Pennsylvania, with my
mother along for the ride, I had become lost in a traffic jam under the
Pulaski Skyway in New Jersey; it was my humiliating task to find a phone
booth and call him to say, while trucks roared overhead, that I would be
hopelessly late. It was the first time I had heard his faint, quavery, yet
clear and definite voice; he expressed much sympathy and told me he
would wait for me to show up, however long it took, a courteous and for-

giving offer I declined, making another appointment and managing to keep that one.

I was hired to be a reporter for Talk of the Town, the opening section of the magazine, containing, then, local stories of seven or eight hundred words each. I turned out to have a knack for them; I worked in the office for twenty happy months, but the city itself was no place in which to raise a family or hatch novels. When I told Shawn that I wanted to leave New York to become a free-lance writer, he offered to find me a better apartment—my failure to find a new one that my wife liked had been one of the precipitating causes of my defection.

I moved away, yet kept his good will, and never stopped thinking of myself as, in some extended sense, a part of *The New Yorker*. Courtesy and generosity were the hallmarks of his management; busy and shy, he kept his distance, but I felt his benign if feathery touch in every acceptance and check. That he had a personal life, and doubts and torments, surprises me as much as would the same revelation about a revered headmaster. His sense of honor, his sometimes venturesome taste, his wish to make every issue a thing of beauty permeated the magazine; if he did, as is now said, stay at the helm too long, and did employ deception in his personal and editorial life, he remains, for me, a model of acumen and kindness, with something truly otherworldly in his dedication to exalted, disinterested standards within the easily sullied, and increasingly crass, world of the printed word.

William Maxwell

WILLIAM MAXWELL was born in 1908 in Lincoln, Illinois, whose houses and inhabitants still vitally figured in his fiction after fifty years of Eastern residence. His mother, with the lovely name of Blossom, died of the flu epidemic of 1918. Receiving the Gold Medal for Fiction from the American Academy of Arts and Letters in 1995, Maxwell said, "The novelist works with what life has given him. It was no small gift that I was allowed to lead my boyhood in a small town in Illinois where the elm trees cast a mixture of light and shade over the pavements. And also that, at a fairly early age, I was made aware of the fragility of human happiness." He commemorated his mother's early and sudden death a number of times in

---

Published in *The New Yorker*'s Talk of the Town under the title "Maxwell's Touch."

his work, nowhere more movingly than in his second novel, *They Came like Swallows*. He accepted with his customary grace his own contrary fate of living on and on, nearly to the age of ninety-two. He died last Monday—July 31, 2000—in his Manhattan apartment, eight days after the death of his wife of fifty-five years' duration, Emily; it was as if, having long sustained the frailties of advanced old age, he gave himself at last permission to leave. Beneath his soft-spoken manner and invariable gentleness, he had a strong will, an artist's will.

After an education at the Urbana campus of the University of Illinois and at Harvard, he came to work for *The New Yorker* in 1936, as an assistant to Katharine White. The magazine offered its staff of young people a variety of odd jobs. Maxwell described sitting in on Harold Ross's art meetings as "the easiest thing in the world. You sat there looking at a lot of unfunny roughs, and when a funny one came up, everybody laughed." It was at the suggestion of Wolcott Gibbs that he became a fiction editor. Until 1976, he gave *The New Yorker* three days a week as an editor and gave himself and his own writing the remaining four. To those he edited he gave a tenderness and an acuity of attention that could not but enhance their sense of vocation. His writers included John Cheever, Eudora Welty, Vladimir Nabokov, Frank O'Connor, Sylvia Townsend Warner, and Mavis Gallant; he tamed the irascible John O'Hara and nursed into flower such younger talents as Elizabeth Cullinan and Larry Woiwode. His editing had the warm touch of a man who himself wrote beautifully; it also had the firm touch of a man who guarded the gates of *The New Yorker* against anything, to his taste, unworthy. His taste merged with the taste of the magazine, and significantly helped make it, in those four decades of his employment, the fine and surprising journal it was.

After retiring, he did not return to haunt, as many fondly regarded departed were encouraged to do, the corridors. He said it was easier to stay home in his pajamas and write, and he did—stories, book reviews, and wonderful letters, fresh, frank, droll, and encouraging. His last letter to me made light of a fall and a broken arm ("I did much more damage to myself when I was two and fell down the stairs") and of "ocular degeneration, which I suspected from the fact that color seemed to be departing from the flowers." He went on to observe, "Worse things happened to, for instance, King Lear. After so much good fortune it would be small-minded to complain and I try not to, though I seem to be doing it right this minute." His disapproval sought no stronger terms than "small-minded." He was himself so large-minded, so selflessly in love with the best the world could offer, that he enlarged and relaxed all those who knew him. His was a rare, brave spirit, early annealed in terrible loss. He had a gift for affection, and another—or was it the same gift?—for paying attention. With both he graced this magazine.

Wright Morris

MY OWN LITERARY LIFE and that of Wright Morris crossed, as best I can remember, three times. In 1959, at the height of his reputation and prestige, he gave my first novel what is called in the trade a puff, which then appeared on its jacket. I do not know how this kind endorsement was solicited, since Morris and I had no connection—we did not even share a publisher—but I knew, young as I was, that his gesture was a generous and atypical one; the years since have hardened my early suspicions that, for writers with any claim to the term "established," no importunity is more frequent and fruitless than the plea for a puff. Next, in editing the so-called *Best American Short Stories of 1984*, I was happy to make one of my twenty picks a story by him, "Glimpse into Another Country"—a casually surreal evocation of the confusions and trepidations of aging. More years went by, and one day an unsolicited manuscript arrived in the mail. It was from Wright Morris, who in an accompanying letter explained that this short novel had met resistance from his usual editors and he appealed to me for my own opinion; what was wrong with it? Opening himself to my verdict like this, like bestowing his quotable praise on my novel decades before, was a more direct and innocent gesture than one expects in the literary jungle. I read it, and felt constrained to tell him that, though the prose showed the usual Morris economy and whirling liveliness, it didn't in the end add up, or quite make sense. It pained me to express this opinion, but he wrote back swiftly a cordial letter of thanks, saying that it was as he had suspected, and that I had helped him. The novel, which might have been his last, never appeared.

I have the strong impression that, amid these purely literary contacts—achieved coast to coast, since I lived north of Boston and he north of San Francisco—I somewhere met him, shook his hand, and put a seal, so to speak, on our intermittent association. But I cannot place the encounter, and it may be simply a hallucination induced by his later dust jackets, which show a rather truculently handsome man with beetling black eyebrows and a whitening mustache and thick, wavy, straight-back

---

A memorial tribute delivered at the American Academy of Arts and Letters, April 3, 2001.

hair: the flamboyant hair of an orchestra conductor, or of a tugboat captain facing into the wind. He was elected to the National Institute of Arts and Letters in 1970, but excused himself from attending his inauguration—he did not like to fly, he said—and indeed visited these premises only once, in 1972. Had he been more of a presence in cosmopolitan literary circles, he might have won more notice, but then he would have been less of what he proudly was, a writer of the America west of the Mississippi.

He was born in Central City, Nebraska, in 1910, and died in Mill Valley, California, in 1998. Six days after his birth, his mother died, and he became, in his phrase, "half an orphan." His father's attempts to provide him with a stepmother and to make a living in the chicken-and-egg business were at best half successful, and in 1925, when Wright was fifteen, they moved from the Platte Valley to Chicago. In this motherlessness and adolescent migration to Chicago he resembles another of our commemorees today, William Maxwell; Maxwell became a Manhattanite, but both men in their writing consistently reverted to their Midwestern boyhoods, the terrain of the essential enchantment and sorrow.

Morris is sometimes spoken of as a Nebraska writer, much as Faulkner is a Mississippi writer and Steinbeck a California writer; but in fact his fiction often takes place elsewhere. His most celebrated novel, *The Field of Vision* of 1956, takes place at a Mexican bullfight and has as its epigraph Milton's "The mind is its own place, and in itself / Can make a Heav'n of Hell, a Hell of Heav'n." In his fiction the Great Plains appear in a rather withering, desolating light. Whatever happened there—Indians, pioneers, farming—happened long ago, leaving dusty relics. In *The Field of Vision*, Tom Scanlon, who came west with a wagon train, lies in his bed in an otherwise deserted hotel in the ghost town of Lone Tree, waiting to die, looking out the window with failing eyes at a view

> every bit as wide and as empty as a view of the sea. . . . The hotel faced the plain, once called a square, where . . . it was believed that the town would appear like the orchards in the seed catalogues. . . . There was nothing to see, but perhaps that was what he liked about it. . . . The truth was, he didn't know he was so blind until they came for him. In Lone Tree, where nothing had changed, he saw things in their places without the need to look at them.

In the 1971 novel *Fire Sermon*, another ancient survivor, Floyd Warner, achieves an epic drive in an antiquated Maxwell from California to his Nebraska home town of Chapman, where his dead sister's house and barn, unchanged since his boyhood, are crammed with artifacts of the old days—oil lamps, buggy harness, oak iceboxes, corn shellers and grinders, "numerous machines supplied with cranks"—that were bequeathed to her by neighbors as they died off. Morris's small towns possess not the boosterish bustle of Sinclair Lewis's Main Street but the dreaming torpor of Sherwood Anderson's Winesburg: a psychiatrist in *Field of Vision*, Lehmann, reflects on

> small towns . . . where the lights burned over empty corners, the houses dark with the dreams they would ask Lehmann to analyze. . . . They left, but never got away. Trailing along behind them, like clouds of glory, were the umbilical cords. On his mind's eye Lehmann saw them like the road lines on a map. Thousands stretched to reach Chicago. Millions stretched to reach New York.

With an unmatched particularity and itemizing patience Morris renders the professional tics and private cogitations of small-town men like *Field of Vision*'s McKee, who lead "a simple frame-house sort of life with an upstairs and a downstairs, and a kitchen where he lived, a parlor where he didn't, a stove where the children could dress on winter mornings, a porch where time could be passed summer evenings, an attic for the preservation of the past, a basement for tinkering with the future, and a bedroom for making such connections as the nature of the house would stand."

Beginning in the Depression, Morris photographed the houses and furniture, the musty interiors and stark exteriors, of America, producing frontal images of an uncanny quiet, which were bound into experimental hybrid books like *The Inhabitants* and *The Home Place*; some of his photographs are in the collection of the Museum of Modern Art. Only Eudora Welty, to my knowledge, used the typewriter and the camera with such dual distinction; her photographs, however, are of human beings, whereas Morris's are by and large still lifes, haunted rather than inhabited by humanity. Though he can be merry—his comedy comes in novels like *Love Among the Cannibals* and short stories like "Since When Do They Charge Admission?"—his voice has a pawky dislocated tone, a stoic facticity like the conversation of a farmer who has known his share of drought, which perhaps prevented a larger public from warming to it.

The Field of Vision won the National Book Award in 1957, and *Plains Song*, Morris's unsentimental tribute to the women of the male-dominated prairie, won the 1981 American Book Award. He taught in a range of colleges from the early Fifties on, and published a number of lilting, opinionated books of criticism, and three wry volumes of autobiography. Of his writing he told an interviewer, "Writing has made me rich—not in money, but in a couple of hundred characters out there, whose pursuits and anguish and triumphs I've shared." He took the American character as he found it, with its dry and bleak stretches, its nagging air of hopeful dissatisfaction, its enigmatic blend of bluntness and reserve, and the sometimes colorful complexity bred by psychological isolation. Morris said of himself, "I'm a spokesman for people who don't want to be spoken for and who don't particularly want to read about themselves." In his life he was always leaving Nebraska, but in his writing he kept the quizzical, wary, far-seeing eye of a plainsman.

Eudora Welty

I CANNOT CLAIM to have known Eudora Welty except through her amazing work. We met a few times, and she was, of course, gracious and, slyly, willing to be amused. Her sociability was inseparable from her creativity and in her last decades came to replace it. A slight personal connection between us arose when I discovered that she and I were among the few American writers on record as greatly admiring the English novelist Henry Green; when I sought to put him up for foreign membership in the American Academy of Arts and Letters (he didn't make it), Miss Welty seconded the nomination that I had persuaded W. H. Auden to write. I was grateful for that seconding, and for the phrase, coined in her review of E. B. White's *Charlotte's Web*, "the good backbone of succinctness that only the most highly imaginative stories seem to grow." She and I shared an editor at *The New Yorker*, William Maxwell, and it was he who told me, with fond wonder in his voice, that when Eudora Welty composed a story, she pinned the sheets of paper together! I therefore have a fixed image of this angular author with pins bristling from her mouth as, like a dressmaker working from a paper pattern, she tacked her frill-free paragraphs into a seamless narrative, patiently tailoring the prose to fit her one-of-a-kind reality.

Ernest Hemingway

I. *On Receipt of the 1999 Ernest Hemingway Literary Light Award, Annually Bestowed at the Hemingway International Festival on Sanibel Island:*

Published in *Oxford American* the year, 2001, of her death.

To win this award is certainly a fine way for me to end the century. Of the classic American writers of the twentieth century, Hemingway is the one with whom I have the longest and most animated relationship. It began sometime in my preteens, when I took it into my childish head to read, off the shelves of the local public library, its copy of *Death in the Afternoon*—not the usual place to begin Hemingway studies. But the photographs of matadors and, as I read, the saucy interludes of authorial dialogue with a mysterious little old lady pulled me into a cruel but stylish world, presented in a stringent, striking voice. The first novel I read, strange to say, was *To Have and Have Not*, with its uncharacteristic sorties into female points of view—we are told what it is like to make love to a one-armed man (he has a kind of flipper) and what a woman thinks as she masturbates. I came much later to the better-known novels, *A Farewell to Arms*, with its devastating ending ("It's just a dirty trick," Catherine says), and *The Sun Also Rises*, which made his name and named a generation. *For Whom the Bell Tolls* I read within recent memory, though I long ago had seen the movie with Cooper and Bergman. With millions of others I devoured *The Old Man and the Sea* when it came out entire in *Life*—an overlap of popular and highbrow culture that won't soon recur. And the priceless short stories: travelling behind the Iron Curtain as a cultural ambassador in 1964, I carried with me a paperback of *In Our Time* to remind me, in the hotel rooms at night, of what it was to be an American writer.

When I became a book reviewer, the posthumous books fell to me— *Islands in the Stream*, *The Garden of Eden*. They weren't purely from the master's hand, and he couldn't get it quite together those last writing years, but there was a magical touch or two on every page. I even read through, with pleasure and admiration, *The Selected Letters, 1917–1961*, all nine hundred–plus pages of them, and the Penguin book *By-Line: Ernest Hemingway*, and hunted up a copy of *The Torrents of Spring*, and have read a number of times his remarkable introduction to the anthology of *Men at War*. Hemingway's seems to me a sensibility worth following into every nook where it expressed itself; he had a fierce will to be exquisite, to be honest, to cut the crap of "literature" in the interests of literature. He was both a man of action and a bookish man; to some extent all writers are both, but not so extremely. He gave those of us who would write in this century lessons in dialogue, in blunt and elliptical verity, in gallows humor, in risk as a kind of corporeal poetry, in the pencil-wielder's daily patience. Even those of us who may seem to have slept through all his lessons write better because of him, and think better of our craft and vocation.

II. *The entry for Ernest Hemingway in* American Characters: Selections from the National Portrait Gallery, Accompanied by Literary Portraits, *edited by R. W. B. Lewis and Nancy Lewis (Yale University Press, 1999):*

He projected not just a literary style but a style of life. For several generations, American men carried themselves with a laconic stoicism and consoled themselves with an elemental hedonism of sensation and beverage and place because Hemingway had done so. He brought word of the remaining good places the overused world still held—Spain and Upper Michigan and Africa and Cuba and the Paris of young and impoverished bohemians. His style needed a certain luxuriously austere diet of landscape and adventure to be so blunt and luminous. In 1924, he wrote to Gertrude Stein of his Michigan story "Big Two-Hearted River," "I'm trying to do the country like Cézanne and having a hell of a time and sometimes getting it a little bit."

I came to him when still a boy by way of lesser works—*Death in the Afternoon*, an intent study, with grimly antic interludes, of his era's bullfighters, and *To Have and Have Not*, a muddled and squalid novel of Depression Florida. Strong stuff, it told me that the world was a brutal, burnt-out place with a shimmer of beauty. He had nearly died at age eighteen of an exploding shell in Italy, and hunting and killing was one way of keeping alive the authenticity of that experience. After celebrity and alcohol softened him up he became easy to mock, as his style was easy to parody, but up to and including his ending his own life with a shotgun he kept a larger-than-life dignity, the stark Greek dignity of those who challenge the gods.

Ted Williams

TED took his time leaving this world, and he's not quite out of it yet. He is cryonically frozen in Arizona, drained of blood and upside down but pretty much intact,* waiting for whatever resurrection technology can eventually produce. This bizarre turn in the Williams saga, which two of his three children claim to be by his own wish, does accord with a general

---

For the *New York Times Magazine*, in a round-up of those who died in 2002.

*It's worse than I thought: his head has been severed and is preserved. His body? Who knows? The engineer of the remains' disposal, Williams's only son, the unfortunate John-Henry, himself died in 2004, of leukemia, at the age of thirty-five.

perception among his admirers that there was something very precious about him, worth preserving if at all possible. To those of us who saw him at the plate, he seemed the concentrated essence of baseball: a tall, long-necked man wringing the bat handle and snapping the slender implement of Kentucky ash back and forth, back and forth in his impatience to hit the ball, to win the battle of wits and eye-hand coördination that, inning after inning, pits the solitary batter against the nine opposing men on the field.

For most of two decades—1939 to 1960, with time out for service in two wars—he was the main reason that people went to Red Sox games in Boston. In those decades he made the American League all-star team eighteen times and had the highest overall batting average, .344. The decades since his retirement, abounding in careers uninterrupted by national service and bolstered by a livelier ball and new techniques of physical conditioning, have seen him slip lower in the record lists; his home-run total of 521, third behind Babe Ruth and Jimmy Foxx in 1960, is now tied for twelfth, with Willie McCovey. Just last season, the phenomenal Barry Bonds broke one of Williams's still-standing records—his on-base percentage of .551, set in 1941. Bonds also, in each of his last two years, exceeded by a good margin a total in which Williams for many years had ranked second only to Ruth, that of walks drawn in a single season.

One Williams statistic, however, gathers luster rather than dust as the years go by—his season average, in 1941, of .406. For over sixty years he has remained the last of the .400 hitters, his .406 nailed down in a double-header in Philadelphia that he could have sat out; he was batting .39955, which rounds up to .400, but he elected to play and went six-for-eight in the two games. In fact, he hit .400 in three seasons, counting the truncated bits of 1952 and '53, when he was drafted into the Korean War: four hits in ten appearances before he reported for duty, and thirty-seven in ninety-one when he came back the following year. In 1957, he hit .388, including four home runs in as many official at-bats when a bout of flu had reduced him to a pinch-hitter. That year, and then the next, he became the oldest man ever to win a batting title. In the two preceding seasons he had the highest average in the league, but injuries and illness kept him from getting four hundred at-bats. These latter seasons, when he was playing for indifferent teams with an accumulated, underpublicized burden of aches and pains, cemented his claim to be called the greatest hitter of his era, an era that included Joe DiMaggio and Stan Musial.

Yet, when an athlete or opera singer or exhilarating personality dies, it is the live performance we remember, the unduplicable presence, the shimmer and sparkle and poignance, perceived from however far back a seat in the audience. The swing—the coiled wait, the popped hip, the long and graceful follow-through that left his body yearning toward first base—was a grand motion, never a lunge or a hasty fending or a mini-malist Ruthian swat; it took up a lot of space and seemed fully serious in its sweep. At six foot three, he was one of the taller men on the field, and we in the crowd brought with us an awareness, like the layer of cigarette smoke that used to hover under the lights, of his dangerous rage to excel—of his on-field temper tantrums, his spats with the press, his struggles with marriage, and his failure, as the years ground on, to make it back to a World Series and redeem his weak performance in 1946. We knew he never tipped his hat to the crowd when he hit a home run, and many of us loved him more for it, not less. He was focusing on the assigned task. Success and failure in baseball are right out there for all to see; his body language declared that he wanted to be the best, that this was more than a game or a livelihood for him. He was paid, toward the end of his career, a record (believe it or not) $125,000 a season, and after his worst season, his only sub-.300 season, in 1959, he asked management for a pay cut.

In the long stretch after 1946, as the excellent Sox teams of the Forties yielded to the mediocre Fifties teams, Ted kept up the show. The inten-sity, the handsome lankiness, the electric hum as the line-up worked around to his appearance were summer constants. Fenway Park, in those days, was not always full; the advance-ticket crowds from Maine and New Hampshire hadn't yet materialized in that thinner era, which took its baseball as a homely staple, without luxury boxes. On an impulse, I bought in for a few dollars to his last game, and the park was two-thirds empty. He hit a home run at his last at-bat, an event I wrote about, in part because his departure, taking with it the heart of Boston baseball, had been so meagerly witnessed.

With retirement, slowly, he became what William Butler Yeats called a "smiling public man." The stern, temperamental baseball perfectionist dropped his concentrated air of work-in-progress and joined us on the sidelines. He managed a team, the Washington Senators, with a middle-aged patience. He faithfully showed up at Red Sox spring training and was generous—in a voice bellicosely loud in part because flying jets in Korea had half-deafened him—with advice and praise, to friend and foe alike. He fished with the same obsessive passion with which he had ana-lyzed the geometry of the strike zone. He continued to serve as the sym-bol of the Jimmy Fund, which he had animated with a thousand personal encouragements of cancer-stricken children. He used his Baseball Hall of Fame acceptance speech to plead for the admission of the great players of the old Negro leagues; in a bygone era when the majors brimmed with unreconstructed rednecks, he had welcomed baseball's integration and befriended the Red Sox's belated black recruits.

He drew closer to his three children, and the public drew closer to him. The new journalism generated interviews in which his language, long held to the locker room, was revealed as bumptiously obscene and youthfully enthusiastic. Compared now with DiMaggio, he appeared more open, less wary, with nothing to hide and everything to share, as the darkness of failing eyesight, the helplessness of strokes and daily dialysis and the desperate operations that the wealthy and famous must endure closed in. On two occasions his aging body was hauled to Boston and he made a show of tipping his cap to the crowd; but we didn't need that. The crowd and Ted had always shared what was important, a belief that this boys' game terrifically mattered.

November 22, 1963

I WAS SITTING in Brookline, in the dental offices of Dr. Frank Eich, who was working on some crowns for my sadly deteriorated teeth, when the soothing "easy listening" music on the radio was interrupted, around one o'clock, with a bulletin stating that shots had been heard in the vicinity of the Presidential cavalcade in Dallas, Texas. The music resumed, only to be interrupted a few minutes later by word that President Kennedy had been hit. Within the hour, without benefit of any more easy listening, we were informed that he had been shot in the head, rushed to the hospital, and pronounced dead.

Dr. Eich and I were shocked, but our appointment dutifully continued. My reaction, if memory serves, was that this was a pretty stupid country where a handsome, brash, witty, and gallant young President could be exterminated like a rat at the dump. Before present revelations as to his ill health and reckless sexual behavior, we—Democrats, at least—thought of JFK as an exemplary politician, who after the long reigns of Truman and Eisenhower was returning government to the relatively young; he felt, when I was in my thirties, like one of us. He had brought us through the Cuban missile crisis still intact; his domestic intentions all seemed good.

In retrospect, there has been much speculation as to whether or not he

---

A memory, forty years later, of the day of John F. Kennedy's assassination, for the *Boston Globe*, November 22, 2003.

would have eased us out of Vietnam, with a persuasive grace Lyndon Johnson could not muster; but in 1963 our involvement still seemed minor. The debonair young chief executive's abrupt death (at the hands, it turned out, of a pathetic left-wing drifter—not a Texas neo-fascist, as one instinctively first thought) stuck in the throat. I left the Brookline office, stepping into a bright and strangely still fall day, conscious of my smooth new crowns and of the fact that weird and terrible things can happen, in a land that would never seem as safe, secure, and righteous again.

JFK, Jr.

THE NATION never forgot the little boy in shorts and pale-blue topcoat saluting the casket of his father as it passed on a sunny Washington street; but, as he later said, that was our memory, not his. John F. Kennedy, Jr., had turned three that very day, and what stayed with him was the absence of a father. He did have a memory, he told persistent interviewers, of the Presidential desk, probably from underneath, where he had been more than once photographed playing, while a smiling John F. Kennedy, Sr., attempted to lead the free world overhead. We bought those images, contrived or not: young President, young family, a fresh breath of verve and hope come into the White House with the new decade. The President, at ease on television like no President before him, never seemed more genuinely warm and glad than when greeting his two scrambling tots as he disembarked from an airplane, or as he acted, at apparent leisure, the part of their father on the beach or lawn at Hyannis. The public was charmed to be a vicarious part of that handsome family, the father so jaunty and self-assured, the mother so young, lovely, shy, cultivated, and gracious.

It was a long time ago, but vivid enough to those alive and impressionable then. Tawdry revelations and revisionist history concerning JFK's thousand days in office cannot finally tarnish the shining moment, nor can the plague of scandals and griefs that have subsequently dogged the hard-living, high-aspiring Kennedy clan. Now America's tormented romance with this one family, just as it seemed at last outgrown, has been subjected to another stunning twist, another tragic surprise, with the

For The Talk of the Town, July 1999.

death by airplane, thirty-six years later, of that three-year-old innocent bystander, John F. Kennedy, Jr., and of his wife and sister-in-law.

Clips of his unforgettable salute, broadcast countless times this past week, show the black-veiled mother leaning down a moment before, whispering in her son's ear, and the obedient child wheeling and facing outward, toward the funeral cortege, his hand bravely to his brow. Jacqueline Kennedy was to coach him for life. Kennedy was his name and the name of his fame, but in dark Bouvier looks and soft-spoken demeanor he was her child. For most of his life, she was Mrs. Onassis. She raised him away from the Kennedy compound, its Cape clambakes and macho derring-do. He spoke with a touch of his father's calm drone but without the hard Massachusetts "a"s and dropped "r"; he spoke cogently, even wittily, but without snap or an undercurrent of aggression. His sister, Caroline, can be recognized as one of the toothy, sad-eyed tribe of Jack and Bobby and Eunice and Ted, but John, as he became a man, seemed to have arisen purely from a *Cosmo* girl's dreambook of ideal male beauty.

His phenomenal handsomeness, like his being a President's son and then losing his father to the Presidency, was something visited upon him; apart from these fascinating gifts of fate, he came on as a regular guy who just wanted to be allowed to do his thing. He had thought, in college, of an acting career—a sensible use of good looks and an indeterminate personality—but his mother had talked him into law school, the broad beaten path into American politics. For him it proved a detour into the public humiliation of flunking the bar exam twice. By the time she died, he had left the law; he became, as she had been, an editor. He founded a light-hearted political magazine, as if there could be such a thing. Politics as celebrity: who knew more about it than he? He was the pure political celebrity, one with no apparent political ambition—though he was, of course, still young. The ordeal of running for public office still lay, if he wished, before him. He left behind rather few anecdotes for the obituary writers, but Joseph Nye, dean of the Kennedy School, remembered asking him, as they stood together in a White House reception line, "Do you remember this place?" The answer came, "Only vaguely." Nye asked, "Do you want to come back?" John Kennedy, Jr., smiled and repeated, "Only vaguely."

He had learned to dodge his fame with grace and skill, and he took as wife a woman as elegantly elusive as he. His wedding, on a hard-to-reach Georgia island once owned by the Carnegie family, was a dashing coup of publicity avoidance. Rollerblading in a knit cap through the streets of Manhattan was another appealing feint. He turned his celebrity into a poster for his impudent magazine and, business aside, he put the great city on its mettle and dared it to let him alone. The grandeur of his celebrity was not noticeable until his nighttime disappearance swept aside a full Saturday's programming on all the networks. The funereal aftermath has dominated the airwaves in the week since with mythy images: the underwater search, the retrieval of Icarus from the depths, the famous kin hidden in the white wedding tent converted to sorrowing Masses, the corpulent uncle bowed once again in the rites of grief, the great gray destroyer bodying forth the sympathy of the living President, the impromptu shrines, the ashes scattered in a site no more local than the sea, beyond the reach of any Dianaesque cult of celebrity.

The media, in making so very much of this particular bad news, imposed their own love for the newsworthy Kennedys upon the public. After all, slightly more than half the voting electorate, in 1960, voted against our first Roman Catholic President; nor is the public necessarily admiring of how Joseph Kennedy, Sr., accumulated his fortune and enriched his descendants. Their bottomlessly monied world is a fantasy to most Americans. The news frenzy's object might have smiled one of his light, practiced smiles of forbearance at seeing his privacy definitively invaded in one wrap-up after another, and such a tide of eulogy whipped up for a man whose life, but for that gallant child's moment in 1963, could be described as glamorous preamble. Our romance with the Kennedys is partly with their griefs—with the way this particular extensive family straddles, more visibly than others, the line between life and death, as if the living and the dead are striving together toward a single objective.

This most recent misfortune was brought about, it seems sadly certain, by pilot error, an insouciance and inexperience that ended three lives; reckless misadventures, sometimes fatal to others, dot the annals of the clan, whose worthiest trait is a call to public service rather than a cultivation of their wealth. John had not yet developed the clan's political drive. We have seen more of him on television these last days than in all the years before. The softness of his speech, in this hardmouthed age, disarms us. The sleepiness in his light-brown eyes defends him against the lifelong spotlight. Being born to fame is not like earning it: you have to create your own worth in other coin, you have to escape history's shadow and get, as they say, a life. To his credit, he was trying, and seemed to be succeeding.

September 11, 2001

SUDDENLY SUMMONED to witness something immense and terrible, we keep fighting not to reduce it to our own smallness. From the viewpoint of a tenth-floor apartment in Brooklyn Heights, where I happened to be visiting some kin, the destruction of the World Trade Center Twin Towers had the false intimacy of television, on a day of perfect reception. A four-year-old girl and her babysitter called from the library and pointed out through the window the smoking top of the north tower, not a mile away. It seemed, at that first glance, more curious than horrendous: smoke speckled with bits of paper curled into the cloudless sky, and strange inky rivulets ran down the giant structure's vertically corrugated surface. The WTC had formed a pale background to our Brooklyn view of lower Manhattan, not beloved like the stony, spired midtown skyscrapers it had displaced as the city's tallest, but, with its pre-postmodern combination of unignorable immensity and architectural reticence, in some lights beautiful. As we saw the second tower burst into ballooning flame (an intervening building had hidden the approach of the second airplane), there persisted the notion that, as on television, this was not quite real; it could be adjusted; the technocracy the towers symbolized would find a way to put out the fire and reverse the damage.

And then, within an hour, as my wife and I watched from the Brooklyn building's roof, the south tower dropped from the screen of our viewing; it fell straight down like an elevator, with a tinkling shiver and a groan of concussion distinct across the mile of air. We knew we had just witnessed many deaths; we clung to each other as if we ourselves were falling. Amid the glittering impassivity of the office buildings across the East River, an empty spot had appeared as if by electronic command beneath the sky that, but for the sulfurous cloud streaming south toward the ocean, was pure blue, rendered uncannily pristine by the absence of jet trails. A swiftly expanding burst of smoke and dust enveloped the rest of lower Manhattan. We saw the collapse of the second tower only on television, where the footage of hellbent airplane, exploding jet fuel, and imploding tower was played and replayed, much-rehearsed moments from a nightmare ballet.

The nightmare is still on. The bodies are beneath the rubble, the last-minute phone calls—remarkably calm and loving, many of them—are

---

For The Talk of the Town, September 2001.

still being reported, the sound of an airplane overhead still bears an unfamiliar menace, the thought of boarding an airplane with our old blasé blitheness keeps receding into the past. Determined men who have inwardly transposed their own lives to a martyr's afterlife can still inflict an amount of destruction that defies belief. War is conducted with a fury that requires abstraction—that turns a planeful of peaceful passengers, children included, into a missile the faceless enemy deserves. The other side has the abstractions; we have only the mundane duties of survivors—to pick up the pieces, to bury the dead, to take more precautions, to go on living.

American freedom of motion, one of our prides, has taken a hit. Can we afford the openness that lets future kamikaze pilots, say, enroll in Florida flight schools? A Florida neighbor of Mohamed Atta remembers him telling her he didn't like the United States: "He said it was too lax. He said, 'I can go anywhere I want to, and they can't stop me.' " It was a strange complaint, a begging perhaps to be stopped. Strange, too, the silence of the heavens these days, as flying has ceased across America. But fly again we must; risk is a price of freedom, and walking around Brooklyn Heights that afternoon, as ash drifted from the sky and moving cars were few and voluble open-air luncheons continued as usual on Montague Street, renewed the impression that this is a country worth fighting for. Freedom, reflected in the street's diversity and quotidian ease, felt palpable. It is mankind's elixir, even if a few turn it to poison.

The next morning, I went back to the open vantage from which we had watched the tower so dreadfully slip from sight. The fresh sun shone on the eastward façades. A few boats tentatively moved in the river. The ruins were still sending out smoke, but Manhattan looked glorious. The day was offering itself as if nothing had changed.

Considering Books

INTRODUCTIONS

To the Everyman's Library edition of The Mabinogion

THE INTRODUCTION by Gwyn Jones, who with Thomas Jones translated this version in 1948, gives *The Mabinogion*'s provenance and history of prior translation, and enthusiastically expounds the eleven tales' differing merits as examples of Welsh language and literature. An American inexpert in medieval studies can only ask, by way of a preface, what claim these archaic texts can possibly exert, in this brand-new millennium, upon the general reader and the contemporary writer. Imagine a reader confronted with a collection of modern short stories seven or eight hundred years from now. Beyond the solvable puzzles posed by terminology and machinery and usages long obsolete, there would loom the larger difficulty of appropriate readerly reaction. In our unmediated evocations of twentieth-century happenstance, dealing with sexual relations and career disappointments and social embarrassments, heavy with dialogue and the revelations of childhood and ending with epiphanic moments of self-knowledge or of terse spoken farewell, all lightly larded with descriptions of nature the characters pass through or furniture they sit on or television shows they half-heartedly watch—in all this, what was meant, the future reader must ask himself, to be surprising, to be in its small surprise amusing, to deviate interestingly from normal expectation, to be, in brief, *news*, telling the vanished inhabitant of today's long-settled dust what he did not quite know before, broadening and enlightening his sensibility with the delicate shocks of art?

The narrative art depends upon an interplay with a cultured audience saturated in certain presumptions and previous artistic experiences. The sexual explicitness, for instance, so liberating and enlightening as it limned heroines from Joyce's Molly Bloom to Nabokov's Lolita, is now, I believe, a little baffling to younger readers—the flash of boldness has lost

its background of repression and reticence. The cleansing verbal directness and starkness of Hemingway, or for that matter of Eliot and Imagism, needed, for their tonic effect to be felt, a setting of lusher and less
abrupt styles habitually accepted by a readership comfortable with more
padding; and this effect is more readily felt than the differences among
the various later minimalisms practiced by, say, Raymond Carver, Donald
Barthelme, Angela Carter, and Kurt Vonnegut. These writers wrote out
of a certain late-twentieth-century mood of burn-out, of humorous anti-
romanticism; how much "point" will be left when that mood has evapo-
rated?

All of which is to say that we feel, reading *The Mabinogion*, as if we are
dancing with a partner who hears a distinctly different music. The speed
of the telling leaves us frequently stumbling. The incidents come toward
us like the thirteen Irish ships at the beginning of "Branwen Daughter of
Llyr"—"with an easy swift motion." In this particular story, which is singled out by Gwyn Jones for "that effect of illumination and extension of
time and space which lies beyond the reach of all save the world's greatest
writers," marvel succeeds marvel and cruelty is heaped on cruelty at a
pace that seems, to a contemporary inner ear, heedless. Where a modern
author would make much of, say, Branwen's (at the least) conflicted feelings as she is unceremoniously pledged to the Irish visitor Matholwch
and bedded by him, we are given, instead, data of kinship and the surprising aside that Bendigeidfran, the King of the Island of the Mighty, is so
large that he has "never been contained within a house." It falls to the villain, Efnisien, to defend his sister's honor, as he perceives it, by mutilat-
ing the horses of their Irish guests, cutting off their lips and ears and even
eyelids—an insult that is repaired by a lavish bestowal of replacement
horses and other gifts, which include a magic cauldron that can restore a
corpse to life, with all powers but that of speech.

Branwen is happy in Ireland, and bears Matholwch a child, Gwern. But
rumors of the insult done Matholwch when abroad circulate and cause an
uprising "till there was no peace for him unless he avenge the disgrace."
Unaccountably, Branwen, an innocent bystander to her brother's wicked
deed, is condemned to the castle's kitchen and boxed on the ear every day
by the butcher. A magical bird smuggles word back to her kinsmen of her
plight; they arrive in Ireland by using the body of their huge king as a
bridge across the river Llinon. Efnisien, at a parlay which seems to be
going well, commits another atrocity by thrusting Gwern, named as the
new King of Ireland, into the fire. The narrator grants Efnisien the gift of
anticipatory remorse: before roasting Gwern he reflects, "By my confession to God an enormity the household would not think might be committed is the enormity I shall now commit." When the Irish are using the

magic cauldron to revive their army (hidden in sacks that Efnisien has presciently crushed with his hands), the fitfully Christian mischief-maker says in his heart, "Alas, God, woe is me that I should be the cause of this heap of the men of the Island of the Mighty," and gets himself tossed into the cauldron, which he bursts. The havoc is near total: Branwen, though blameless, cries, "Woe is me that ever I was born: two good islands have been laid waste because of me," and heaves a great sigh, and lets her heart break. The giant Bendigeidfran bids his surviving troop of seven men to cut off his head and bury it in London with its face toward France. On their way, however, the men are beguiled for seven years by the singing of three birds, and then for eighty years more they tarry in a palace where all memory of sorrow is erased. At last they open a door which has been sealed, and memory of their sorrows floods upon them, and they complete their errand, burying the head on White Mount, where it guards the Island against plague.

What freight did such a caravan of marvels and barbarities carry for its auditors? They inhabited a world where the naming of places was still in progress; psychology had not yet replaced geography as an orienting science. What we are is, to an extent, *where* we are, and what links of loyalty, to political entities embodied in kings and chieftains, hold us in place. In a world without technological change, history is genealogy; the tale of Branwen ends with the Irish race reduced to five pregnant women, who bear sons who mate, when mature, "one by one with the other's mother," and thus repopulate an island still divided, commemoratively, into five provinces. Courtesy, here, is for ceremonial occasions; beyond the roaring hearth and loaded table of formal hospitality and truce there reigns a continual carnage, as mechanical and innocent as the chirrupping mayhem of a video game. We can recognize from comic books consumed in childhood the rigid lineaments of a superhero like the hero of "Peredur the Son of Efrawg," who as he hits his stride throws men in batches of a hundred to the ground, and scorns the assistance of a loyal hundred, lest "I would have no more fame than any one of you," in slaying the fearful Worm. As *The Mabinogion* progresses from the mythic to the merely fabulous, the Middle Ages of tourneys and fair maidens replaces the Dark Ages of genocidal tribal battle and sturdy queens treated like serving wenches. The warrior society dons the plumes of courtly love; the sociable arts are cultivated—"there was not a fault at court so great as their being men so poor at conversation"—and roll calls and heraldic specifics clutter an Arthurian elaboration like "The Dream of Rhonabwy."

Dreams, irrepressibly erotic in content, are, with place-names and heroic genealogies, a possible means of orientation for the dwellers in the world of these tales. "The Dream of Macsen Wledig" depicts a maiden sitting in a chair of red gold, who rises and embraces the dreaming Emperor, and has him sit with her in a chair that, dreamily, is "no straiter for them both than for the maiden alone"—as elastic as a vagina. Like tumescences during sleep are the visions the heroes have of their destined ladies; when Owein beholds the Lady of the Fountain, "he was fired with love of her, till each part of him was filled therewith." Math, son of Math-onwy, conjures a woman out of flowers, as if of sheer velvety and odorous sensation, and she, thus conjured, is herself susceptible; when she first sights Gwydion, "there was no part of her that was not filled with love of him. . . . Nor did they delay longer than that night ere they embraced each other." Such instant mutual gratifications extend into romance the unceremonious beddings of older, gruffer tales; the audiences, like perusers of modern magazine advertisements, received from their min-strels images to aspire to—images of a superior existence, of elaborately colored costumes and resplendent armor, of travels and gallantry, of visions, blurring into the sleeping part of life, that lifted their attention away from the squalor, fear, and brutality common around them.

Fiction seeks to concoct imaginary lives more patently significant than our own. The elements of fantasy and symbolism that arouse interest are less prominent in classic novels than in these bardic tales, but neverthe-less give those novels, and much popular fiction still, an educational and communal motive lacking in the current fiction whose sole excuse for being is the implicit claim that this is how things are. We should know, of course, how things are—how else can we appraise and negotiate reality?—but the singers or authors of the fables gathered as *The Mabino-gion* were concerned with how things *were*, in that pre-time when names were bestowed and giants engendered races, a pre-time still present in our own fibers. Legend blends with reality's live underside of dream and wish-fulfillment. Here, wishes *are* horses and beggars *do* ride. The old tales drink from the spring wherein fact has not yet been filtered from fancy, and remind us that any narrator begins by believing that he has something marvellous to tell. An appetite for the marvellous comes with our first childish comprehensions, as a mode of acclimatization to the marvel of being alive.

To The Blithedale Romance, *by Nathaniel Hawthorne*

HAWTHORNE lived in the socialistic community of Brook Farm, in West Roxbury, eight or nine miles to the southwest of Boston, from April to

November of 1841, with some weeks away in September. That so reclusive and skeptical a spirit might make his home in an idealistic farming commune seems in retrospect an unlikely hope; but he was thirty-seven, stalled in his writing career, newly quit of his job as a measurer of salt and coal at the Boston Custom House, engaged to Sophia Peabody (an engagement still secret from his mother in Salem), and casting about for a way to set up housekeeping and revive his literary efforts. In the previous year, 1840, he had sat for the smolderingly handsome, faintly agitated portrait by Charles Osgood that still hangs in Salem's Peabody Essex Museum. He was a prize among the eccentrics who settled on Brook Farm's two hundred acres by the meandering Charles, with its isolated farmhouse on the Dedham-Watertown Road. "He is our prince," wrote the wife of George Ripley, the disaffected Unitarian clergyman who founded the community, "—our prince in everything—yet despising no labour and very athletic and able-bodied in the barnyard and field." Hawthorne was initially enthusiastic, writing to Sophia, "I feel the original Adam reviving within me." He had invested the considerable sum of fifteen hundred dollars in the joint-stock company, and even as his doubts about Brook Farm grew he was elected, in September, a trustee and chairman of the Committee of Finance. He assured Sophia, "Beloved, my accession to these august offices does not at all decide the question of my remaining here permanently." Yet he was reluctant to make the break, not resigning until October of 1842, nearly a year after his stay there ended, and only in 1845 suing (unsuccessfully) for the return of his investment. Brook Farm had but a few years to go, taking a fatal blow in March of 1846, when its new central building, called the Phalanstery in honor of the French social theorist Charles Fourier, burned to the ground the very night its completion was being celebrated.

In the summer of 1851, two years after the property had been auctioned off and George Ripley had found gainful employment as literary critic for Horace Greeley's *New York Tribune*, Hawthorne began to contemplate the novel that became *The Blithedale Romance*. On July 24 he wrote a friend, "When I write another romance, I shall take the Community for a subject, and shall give some of my experiences and observations at Brook Farm." By this time the author had published *The Scarlet Letter*, *The House of the Seven Gables*, and *Mosses from an Old Manse*; his fame if not his fortune was secure. After sojourns in Concord, Salem, and Lenox, in western Massachusetts, he and Sophia, now the parents of three children, resettled in a rented house in West Newton; once settled, in November, Hawthorne warned a magazine editor that he was about to "engage in a longer work." Early in May of the following year, he sent the completed "huge bundle of scribble" to the critic Edwin Whipple, saying that "Nobody has yet read it, except my wife; and her sympathy, though very gratifying, is a little too unreserved to afford me the advantages of criticism." With the startling speed of nineteenth-century publishing, the book was on its way to print by the middle of the month and in the bookstores by the middle of July. There was a second impression in August, but sales rapidly fell off; among the critics, Whipple (already enlisted in the text's service) called it "the most perfect in execution of any of Hawthorne's works, and as a work of art, hardly equalled by anything else which the country has produced."

The romance tells of, as the third chapter is titled, "A Knot of Dreamers"—a square knot, consisting of four principals. Miles Coverdale, a New England poet of lesser reputation than Hawthorne, arrives at Blithedale on a wintry April night to be greeted by Zenobia, a wealthy Boston woman who is a benefactress as well as a dominant resident of the dreamers' community. That same snowy night, Hollingsworth, a virile blacksmith turned to philanthropy and reform of the penal system, arrives with Priscilla, a pale little seamstress entrusted to his care by a cringing drifter, Moodie. In a swirl of attachments worthy of Iris Murdoch, Zenobia loves Hollingsworth, but he favors Priscilla, who turns out to be Zenobia's poor half-sister. Between Coverdale and Hollingsworth, too, exists a tormented affection, born when the blacksmith nurses the poet through a severe fever contracted early in his stay, and given a fatal blow when Coverdale, recovered, declines to be his "brother" in his "great scheme of good," even though Hollingsworth pleads, "There is not a man in this wide world, whom I can love as I could you. Do not forsake me!" At the same time, additional entanglements are introduced by the sinister figure of Westervelt, a mesmerist who has used Priscilla as a stage foil called the Veiled Lady, and who claims an intimate prior acquaintance with Zenobia, perhaps (this is never made quite clear) as her husband. The knot flies apart when Zenobia, rejected by Hollingsworth in favor of Priscilla, drowns herself in the Charles, leaving Hollingsworth a man broken by his guilt and Coverdale a man rather aimlessly restored to the outer world.

Critics less friendly than Whipple complained that Zenobia's suicide was implausible, that the author had been too hard on philanthropists, that he had been too easy on socialist experiments and their "dreams of world reform." James Fields, of Hawthorne's publisher, Ticknor, Reed & Fields, wrote in a letter to London, "I hope Hawthorne will give us no more Blithedales." Nor was the book pleasing to former tenants of Brook Farm; one of them, Georgiana Kirby, later remembered of Hawthorne:

No one could have been more out of place than he. . . . He was morbidly shy and reserved, needing to be sheltered from his fellows, and obtaining the fruits of observation at second-hand. He was therefore not amenable to the democratic influences of the Community which enriched the others, and made them declare, in after years, that the years or months spent there had been the most valuable ones in their lives.

Hawthorne's description of Miles Coverdale does not contradict this impression. Coverdale is Hawthorne's most extended self-portrait, an alter ego to whom he denies his own fruitful marriage and energetic authorship, leaving a detached introvert, a languid dandy cripplingly aloof from illusions both erotic and idealistic. Such a man is apt to miss out: in the "unsatisfied retrospect" of his final chapter, "Miles Coverdale's Confession," the narrator, in the same terrain of ripe middle age as Hawthorne himself, looks back upon a "colorless life," and confesses it has come to "an idle pass with me." Idly he yearns for a cause to which he might sacrifice his life, with the wry quibble that "the effort did not involve an unreasonable amount of trouble." Even ten years earlier, conversing with the Blithedale community's adopted waif, Priscilla, Coverdale pronounced his past life a "tiresome one enough," and told her, in this colony dedicated to a better future for mankind,

we may be very sure, for one thing, that the good we aim at will not be attained. People never do get just the good they seek. If it come at all, it is something else, which they never dreamed of, and did not particularly want.

These aphorisms hold the true accent of the author, who sampled but in the end disdained the enthusiasms of his enthusiastic age—the Kantian yea-saying of Emerson and Margaret Fuller, the religious fervor of Shakers and evangelical revivalists, the reforming zeal of philanthropy, the political passion of the abolitionists, and even the militant righteousness of the Union cause in the Civil War, which he thought should not be fought, the Southern secession left unresisted.

Zenobia accuses Coverdale of a lack of seriousness, of commitment, of involvement: "I have long recognized you as a sort of transcendental Yankee, with all the native propensity of your countrymen to investigate matters that come within their range, but rendered almost poetical, in your case, by the refined methods which you adopt for its gratification." From their first encounter, by the roaring fire that greets his arrival at Blithedale in a snowstorm, to their last, when he discovers her desolated by Hollingsworth's rejection and she rallies by accusing him of "turning this whole affair into a ballad," Zenobia has taunted him with his poems as a toying on the edge of the human adventure, a non-participant's cool sport. This was Hawthorne's fear for himself, his distrust of his own temperament. For ten years he had led a shadow-life in Salem, living with a mother frozen in mourning and two spinster sisters, concocting for magazines his graceful trifles of antiquarian curiosity and moral allegory, his wispy version of the once vigorous and tyrannical Puritan faith. In 1837, he confessed to Longfellow, "I have seen so little of the world, that I have nothing but thin air to concoct my stories of, and it is not easy to give a lifelike semblance to such shadowy stuff." Hawthorne presents himself, in the ghostly, penetrating world of his fanciful sketches and stories, as "Monsieur du Miroir"—"a wanderer from the spiritual world, with nothing human, except his illusive garment of visibility"—or as "M. de l'Aubépine," the fictional author of "Rappaccini's Daughter," to whom Hawthorne devotes a mischievous, mordant paragraph:

> As a writer, he seems to occupy an unfortunate position between the Transcendentalists . . . and the great body of pen-and-ink men who address the intellect and sympathies of the multitude. If not too refined, at all events too remote, too shadowy and unsubstantial in his modes of development, to suit the taste of the latter class, and yet too popular to satisfy the spiritual or metaphysical requisitions of the former, he must necessarily find himself without an audience. . . . His writings, to do them justice, are not altogether destitute of fancy and originality; they might have won him great reputation but for an inveterate love of allegory, which is apt to invest his plots and characters with the aspect of scenery and people in the clouds, and to steal away the human warmth out of his conceptions.

It is in a burst of warmth, by a fresh-laid log fire, that Zenobia first confronts Miles Coverdale; her physical vitality is such that he seems to behold "her fine, perfectly developed figure" naked, "in Eve's earliest garment." Naked in his imagination, she comes at him with her conversational sword flashing—welcoming, flirting, challenging him in ornate and charged thrusts of eloquence. She has the voice of Hester Prynne in the forest, transposed into a nineteenth-century United States where social and feminist issues are as common as fresh-baked pies. Those who are quick to identify Zenobia with Margaret Fuller should take pause from Hawthorne's aversion to transcendentalism's loquacious queen: in one of his first letters to Sophia from Brook Farm, he warns her away from Fuller's Boston circle, which he terms a "Babel of talkers," expressing the wish that "Miss Margaret Fuller might lose her tongue!—or my Dove her ears, and so be left wholly to her husband's golden silence." As Henry James puts it in his unsurpassable little book on Hawthorne, "It is safe to assume that Hawthorne could not, on the whole, have had a high relish for the very positive personality of this accomplished and argumentative woman, in whose intellect high noon seemed ever to reign, as twilight did in his own." And Zenobia is above all a beauty, whereas Fuller was marked by, in the phrase of the sympathetic Emerson, an "exceeding plainness." Further, Fuller, though a moral supporter of the experiment, was rarely on Brook Farm's premises, whereas other considerable, possibly memorable women were: the cultured and favorably impressed Mrs. Ripley, for one, and, as mentioned in James R. Mellow's biography of Hawthorne, "Almira Barlow, a vivacious young matron recently separated from her husband."

What Margaret Fuller did lend her fictional sister was force, a force of personal presentation and intellect that Miles Coverdale construes as the displayed vivacity of an actress: "Her poor little stories and tracts never half did justice to her intellect; it was only the lack of a fitter avenue that drove her to seek development in literature. . . . I recognized no severe culture in Zenobia; her mind was full of weeds. . . . The stage would have been her proper sphere." He resents, in fact, the intrusion of her intellect upon her "instinctive sense of where the life lies . . . the relation between the sexes." Yet from his side of this particular relation Coverdale quite fails to rise to so magnificent a bait, as she more than once chastises him:

> "Mr. Coverdale, I have been exposed to a great deal of eye-shot in the few years of my mixing in the world, but never, I think, to precisely such glances as you are in the habit of favoring me with. I seem to interest you very much; and yet—or else a woman's instinct is for once deceived—I cannot reckon you as an admirer."

She is a Gorgon before whom Coverdale stands transfixed and fascinated. In her persona Hawthorne has conjured, blending Fuller's repulsive dynamism with softer memories and impressions, the Actual, to borrow a term from his favorite dualism (as expressed in the foreword to *The Scarlet Letter* and elsewhere) of the Actual and the Imaginary. She is uniquely vivid. Henry James calls Zenobia "his only very definite attempt at the representation of character."

She lives in her bantering wit (not an attribute of Fuller's recorded outpourings) and half-angry animation, and the novel lives from one confrontation between her and Coverdale to the next; they are really the only two characters in it. Hollingsworth is a thickset and blackened embodiment of Hawthorne's deep distrust of any philanthropy or any proclaimed altruism, and Priscilla is one of his cherished spectres hovering, like a transparent dragonfly, on the boundary between the Actual and the Imaginary. She was based on a "little sempstress from Boston, about seventeen years old," who, he wrote Sophia at the time, visited Brook Farm for a week, long enough for Hawthorne to perceive that "she is not a little girl, but really a little woman, with all the prerogatives and liabilities of a woman." To these unspecified gender liabilities is added a touch of lower-class vulgarity; worse, "her intellect is very ordinary, and she never says anything worth hearing, or even laughing at, in itself." Priscilla is faithful to her original; she is virtually mute, though credited with a stage presence as the Veiled Lady. Coverdale's concluding profession of love is scarcely to be believed, even in the volatile, shape-shifting netherworld of a Hawthorne romance.

If a vital character is one that draws upon an author's energy at a source beyond or below his conscious intentions, then the enigmatic Devil-figure of Westervelt, with his coal-black hair and eyes, his dandyish garb, and his brilliant false teeth, can claim a more than schematic existence; he has drawn forth something involuntary and unpremeditated from the narrator—"the naked exposure of something that ought not to be left prominent." Westervelt manages a successful theatrical enterprise and always talks to the point, albeit with "cold skepticism." Coverdale admits, "A part of my own nature showed itself responsive to him." The "calm observer" in Coverdale is cousin to the Devil: something of Puritan self-accusation scorches this recognition.

Though not his greatest, *The Blithedale Romance* is the most "actual" of Hawthorne's novels, the one most responsive to the author's contemporary world. We enjoy, in the direct way of lively reportage, the details of the farm with its presiding agriculturalist, the lumpish and practical Silas Foster, and Coverdale's shrewd observations of the commune, many of which ring true for the social experiments of the 1960s:

> While inclining us to the soft affections of the Golden Age, it seemed to authorize any individual, of either sex, to fall in love with any other, regardless of what would elsewhere be judged suitable and prudent. Accordingly, the tender passion was very rife among us.

We enjoy the romance's images of homely country life undertaken by excessively refined sensibilities: the vivacious doomed pigs; the oxen who, though given a Sunday freedom from the yoke, keep close in tandem while browsing; the quintessentially Hawthornian image of "Good Mrs. Foster" falling asleep while knitting and "still keeping her needles in brisk movement, and, to the best of my observation, absolutely footing a stocking out of the texture of a dream."

A different environment is bracingly entered when Coverdale leaves for Boston and partakes of city life, with its coal fires and ringing bells, its flights of stairs and rows of lit windows, images that draw upon the author's several pre–Brook Farm years of Boston employment and residence in rented rooms at Somerset Place and Pinckney Street. Zenobia takes on another aspect, transferred to the equivalent of Beacon Hill, where her wealth and status give her embodiment of the Actual an intimidating glitter. The reader has been told of her wealth, but the sight of her "costly robes" and "exceedingly rich" furniture lifts it to a palpable plane. The hothouse flower she so implausibly wears in her hair in their rural retreat has become a piece of jewelry, and she in alliance with Westervelt shows a brisk ruthlessness, imperiously bundling Priscilla back into her theatrical captivity. This drawing-room scene makes one aware of how few such fine rooms exist in Hawthorne's fiction, and how relatively sparse is his evocation of the antebellum American civilization in which he did, after all, participate as editor, magazine writer, and wharf official before his Bowdoin classmate Franklin Pierce, newly elected President, granted him, in 1853, a political post that transported him to England and the European scenes of *The Marble Faun*.

Hawthorne's sense of art required always the fanciful, half-real touch—Zenobia's far-fetched flower, Hester's "A" written in the sky, Donatello's elusive faun's ears in *The Marble Faun*. He had to begin with images; in that, though not (unlike Emerson, Thoreau, and Melville) a versifier, he was, like Coverdale, a poet. Those who wish to see the novelist's acute if diffident sensibility operating in relative freedom from his compulsive symbolism, having taken its start from a recollected experience still fresh in his mind and having as its theme revolutionary engagement with current concerns, should consult, after the journals, this novel. Hawthorne's twilit imagination never admitted more local American daylight than in *The Blithedale Romance*.

To Walden, *by Henry David Thoreau: 150th Anniversary Edition*

A CENTURY AND A HALF after its initial publication, *Walden* has become such a totem of the back-to-nature, preservationist, anti-business, civil-disobedience mind-set, and Thoreau so vivid a protester, so perfect a crank and hermit saint, that the book itself risks being as revered and unread as the Bible. Of the American classics densely arisen in the middle of the nineteenth century—Hawthorne's *Scarlet Letter* (1850), Melville's *Moby Dick* (1851), Whitman's *Leaves of Grass* (1855), to which we might add Harriet Beecher Stowe's *Uncle Tom's Cabin* (1852) as a nation-stirring best-seller and Emerson's essays as an indispensable preparation of the ground—*Walden* has contributed most to America's present sense of itself. In a time of informational overload, of clamorously inane and ubiquitous electronic entertainment, and of a fraught, globally challenged, ever more demanding workplace, the urge to build a cabin in the woods and thus reform, simplify, and cleanse one's life—"to front," in Thoreau's ringing verb, "only the essential facts of life"—remains strong. The vacation industry, so called, thrives on it, and camper sales, and the weekend recourse to second homes in the Northern forests or the Western mountains, where the pollutions of industry and commerce are relatively light. "Simplify, simplify," *Walden* advises, and we try, even though in the twenty-first century the attainment of a rustic, elemental simplicity entails further complications of budget and transport.

Thoreau would not scorn contemporary efforts to effect his gospel and follow his example; *Walden* aims at conversion, and polemical purpose gives it the energy and drive missing in the meanders of the sole other book he saw into publication during his short lifetime, *A Week on the Concord and Merrimack Rivers* (1849). Like *A Week*, *Walden* is farraginous, and was subject to Thoreau's habit of constant revision and expansion—begun in his two years, 1845–47, in his lakeside cabin, it went through eight known drafts—but an imagined debate with his neighbors, defending his eccentric reclusion, generates a vigorous, humorous tone at the outset:

> I should not obtrude my affairs so much on the notice of my readers if very particular inquiries had not been made by my townsmen concerning my mode of life, which some would call impertinent, though they did not appear to me at all impertinent, but, considering the circumstances, very natural and pertinent.

The circumstances, the malaise of drudgery and petty distraction in the society around him, are described, and his general "wish to live deliberately, to front only the essential facts of life, and see if I could not learn what it had to teach, and not, when I came to die, discover that I had not lived," but he underemphasizes a very practical motive: he wanted to be a writer and, like many another of like ambition, needed privacy, quiet, and a "broad margin" where his mind could roam.

In his two years by Walden Pond, living in a single-room house he built on his mentor Emerson's land, more than a mile south of Concord Village, he completed *A Week on the Concord and Merrimack Rivers*, which he had been working on since 1839, the year in which he and his brother John had taken the canoe trip described, as well as composed the first draft of *Walden* and a long essay on Thomas Carlyle, part of which he gave as a lecture at the Concord Lyceum in 1846. Also in 1846, he refused to pay his accumulated town poll taxes, on the grounds that the national government condoned and protected slavery, and spent a night in jail, thus laying the basis for his celebrated essay "On the Duty of Civil Disobedience." Thoreau was twenty-seven when he took up residence in the cabin by Walden Pond; he had graduated from Harvard in the middle of his class of about fifty, tried teaching with small success, helped his father in the family pencil business, did local odd jobs for a dollar a day, and lived with the Emersons for two years as handyman and gardener. He travelled to Long Island and, after a brief spell of tutoring and testing the literary market, left it, and, despite Emerson's sponsorship and a few poems and essays in the transcendentalist quarterly *The Dial*, had made no mark. He emerged from the cabin in 1847 as essentially the Thoreau known to literary history.

His appearance was sufficiently arresting to have attracted a number of descriptions. The fastidious but not unfriendly Hawthorne, a sometime resident of Concord, described him in 1842 as "a young man with much of wild original nature still remaining in him. . . . He is as ugly as sin, long-nosed, queer-mouthed, and with uncouth and somewhat rustic, although courteous manners. [He] seems inclined to lead a sort of Indian life among civilized men—an Indian life, I mean, as respects the absences of any systematic effort for a livelihood." James Kendall Hosmer recalled how an older Thoreau "stood in the doorway with hair which looked as if it had been dressed with a pine-cone, inattentive gray eyes, hazy with far-away musings, an emphatic nose and disheveled attire that bore signs of tramps in woods and swamps." His New Bedford disciple Daniel Ricketson recalled, as phrased by Thoreau's biographer Walter Harding, "the gentleness, humanity, and intelligence of Thoreau's blue eyes" and noted that, "though his arms were long, his legs short, his hands and feet large, and his shoulders markedly sloping, he was strong and vigorous in his walk." His voice was impressive, even toward the end, when weakened by tuberculosis. On his last journey, a rather desperate excursion to Minnesota for the possibly healing effects of its supposedly drier climate, the minister upon whom he called in Chicago, the Unitarian Robert Collyer, remembered:

> His words also were as distinct and true to the ear as those of a great singer. . . . He would hesitate for an instant now and then, waiting for the right word, or would pause with a pathetic patience to master the trouble in his chest, but when he was through the sentence was perfect and entire,

lacking nothing, and the word was so purely one with the man that when I
read his books now and then I do not hear my own voice within my reading
but the voice I heard that day.

How did Thoreau achieve his literary voice, which has worn better, to a
modern ear, than Emerson's more fluent, worldly, and—to be expected
from a former clergyman—oratorical one? The very agility with which
Emerson's pithy, exhortative sentences dance to keep the listener's attention wearies the reader now; we feel the audience before him, basking as
he beams epigrams and encouragements into their faces. The mood of
Thoreau is more interior; the eye is not on an audience but on a multitudinous world of sensation, seen and named with precision. Take, at
random, these sentences from near the beginning of *A Week:*

> We glided noiselessly down the stream, occasionally driving a pickerel or a
> bream from the covert of the pads, and the smaller bittern now and then
> sailed away on sluggish wings from some recess in the shore, or the large
> lifted itself out of the long grass at our approach, and carried its precious
> legs away to deposit them in a place of safety. The tortoises also rapidly
> dropped into the water, as our boat ruffled the surface amid the willows,
> breaking the reflections of the trees. The banks had passed the height of
> their beauty, and some of the brighter flowers showed by their faded tints
> that the season was verging toward the afternoon of the year; but this som-
> bre tinge enhanced their sincerity, and in the still unabated heats they
> seemed like the mossy brink of some cool well.

All is limpid fact, gliding from one bittern to another, until the startling
remark that fading color enhanced the flowers' "sincerity," as if they have
been pressing a case. The long paragraph goes on to enumerate, with the
Latin names, the flowers of the Concord meadows, and ends with reminiscence of the mornings when the writer, on the water before sunrise,
witnessed the sudden opening of water lilies to the touch of dawn sun,
when "whole fields of white blossoms seemed to flash open before me, as
I floated along, like the unfolding of a banner." This is not exactly
"nature writing," though it holds the freshness of a continent still being
explored and catalogued, as by a Humboldt or an Audubon; it is a live,
particularized demonstration of Emerson's hopeful boast, set forward in
its most theological form in his slim first book, *Nature*, that "every natural fact is a symbol of some spiritual fact." Nature is at bottom Spirit, and
"Spirit alters, moulds, makes it."

Emerson approvingly quoted Swedenborg's "The visible world and the
relation of its parts, is the dial plate of the invisible," and asserted, "The
axioms of physics translate the laws of ethics." Imbibing Idealism from

Emerson, Thoreau soaked himself in Nature's great metaphor, and became a scientist of sorts—"a mystic, a transcendentalist, and a natural philosopher to boot," he later called himself—and an autobiographer. He gathered, and transferred to journals amounting in the end to two million words, rare moments and observations of increasing refinement and subtlety, harvested where he would. Emerson, like other respectable citizens of Concord, was skeptical of so vague a project, confiding to his journal, "Thoreau wants a little ambition in his mixture. . . . Instead of being the head of American engineers, he is captain of a huckleberry party." Thoreau's taste for figurative huckleberry-gathering took him far afield, walking Cape Cod's wave-beaten coast and ascending to the stony summit of Maine's Mount Ktaadn, but he always returned to the little wildernesses of Concord, a microcosm that was cosmos enough.

F. O. Mattheissen, in his *American Renaissance*, points out how much the great writers of that renaissance owed to the English writers of the seventeenth century—Donne and Herbert, Marvell and Browne—with their belief in correspondences between the little and the large, the inner world of the self and the outer world of Nature. "The Heart of Man," John Donne wrote, "Is an epitome of God's great book / Of creatures, and men need no further look." George Herbert put it, "Man is one world, and hath / Another to attend him," thus extending Nature into the unseen realms of heavenly solicitude. By a great leap of kinship, the Metaphysicals of the seventeenth century ignited in the spiritual descendants of seventeenth-century Puritans a blaze of introspectively charged particulars.

Walden lives in its particulars. The long opening chapter, "Economy," joyously details just how to build a house—"a tight shingled and plastered house, ten feet wide by fifteen long, and eight-feet posts, with a garret and a closet, a large window on each side, two trap doors, one door at the end, and a brick fireplace opposite"—down to a list of expenses totalling $28.12. Briskly marketing to the world his program of austerity and self-reliance, Thoreau itemizes the few foodstuffs he paid for and the profits he obtained from his seven miles of bean rows. He tells us how to make his unleavened bread of rye and Indian meal, and "a very good molasses either of pumpkin or beets." In another experiment, he eats a woodchuck, enjoying it "notwithstanding its musky flavor," though he doubts it will become an item for the village butcher. He shares the details of his housekeeping with us:

Housework was a pleasant pastime. When my floor was dirty, I rose early, and, setting all my furniture out of doors on the grass, bed and bedstead making but one budget, dashed water on the floor, and sprinkled white sand from the pond on it, and then with a broom scrubbed it clean and white.

Further—and this is a stroke of his sensitive, pawky genius—he contemplates his momentarily displaced furniture and its air of enchanting strangeness:

> It was pleasant to see my whole household effects out on the grass, making a little pile like a gypsy's pack, and my three-legged table, from which I did not remove the books and pen and ink, standing amid the pines and hickories. . . . It was worth the while to see the sun shine on these things, and hear the free wind blow on them; so much more interesting most familiar objects look out of the doors than in the house.

Many things, in Thoreau's liberated state, are worth the while to see— the feeding manners of chickadees, the trickles of spring thaw along the railroad cut, "resembling, as you look down on them, the laciniated lobed and imbricated thalluses of some lichens." At the same moment he is "cheered by the music of a thousand tinkling rills and rivulets whose veins are filled with the blood of winter which they are bearing off"; at other times he eavesdrops on "the faint wiry peep" of the baby woodcock being led by their mother through the swamp. In *Walden*'s most bravura chapter, "Sounds," he hears not only the cries and rustles of myriad creatures but, with surprising approval, the whistle and racket of the Fitchburg Railroad train as it makes its way, a hundred rods off, along the edge of Walden Pond:

> Commerce is unexpectedly confident and serene, alert, adventurous, and unwearied. It is very natural in its methods withal, far more so than many fantastic enterprises and sentimental experiments. . . . I am refreshed and expanded when the freight train rattles past me, and I smell the stores which go dispensing their odors all the way from Long Wharf to Lake Champlain.

His admiration of Nature is not selective; it includes the "iron steed" that thrusts its noisy way into his woods, earning several pages of paean capped by perhaps his best-known poem, beginning, "What's the railroad to me? / I never go to see / Where it ends."

The Concord of the 1840s, where, in Thoreau's perception, men "lead lives of quiet desperation," slave-drivers of themselves with "no time to be any thing but a machine," was by our lights a bucolic world, the steam engine being the technological ultimate and the main labor farm labor. It is the farmer, according to Thoreau, whose "poor immortal soul" is "well nigh crushed and smothered under its load, creeping down the road of life, pushing before it a barn seventy-five feet by forty, its Augean stables never cleansed"; it is a farmer he encounters in the middle of the night, driving his livestock to a dawn appointment in Boston, while the disencumbered hermit returns to sleep in his cozy cabin. Thoreau was the scion of a small industrialist, John Thoreau the pencil-manufacturer. In the local social scale he was something of a gentleman, and he asserts a gentleman's prerogative in pursuing his unprofitable hobbies. We slightly wince, on behalf of those more tightly bound to laborious necessity, when we read that "to maintain one's self on this earth is not hardship but a pastime, if we will live simply and wisely" and that "by working about six weeks in a year, I could meet all the expenses of living." Not everyone is offered free land to squat on for a personal experiment or can draw so freely on the society of a nearby village. Thoreau makes light of most men's need to work, and ignores the wave of industrial toil that is breaking upon New England. In his trip up the Merrimack he takes small note of the factories that made this river the New World's first industrial zone, whose raw exploitations Melville sought to dramatize in his short story "The Tartarus of Maids."

Thoreau's protest centers on the end-product of industry, the consumerism that urges us to buy its products. His proposed remedy is to do without: "A man is rich in proportion to the number of things which he can afford to let alone." This includes doing without sex ("The generative energy, which, when we are loose, dissipates and makes us unclean, when we are continent invigorates and inspires us"), and would carry with it, as Hawthorne sensed, an end to most of the interactions that form civilization, a return to "Indian life" and beyond—to a degree of individual independence that no human society, least of all a tribal one, could tolerate. His retreat to the cabin was a luxury financed by the surplus that an interwoven, slave-driving economy generated. Even so staunch a Thoreauvian as E. B. White (whose own withdrawal to the Maine coast was financed by the advertising revenues of a New York magazine), in writing a tribute for Walden's hundredth anniversary fifty years ago, admitted that "the plodding economist will . . . have rough going if he hopes to emerge from the book with a clear system of economic thought," and that Thoreau sometimes wrote as if "all his readers were male, unmarried, and well-connected." But if it cannot be swallowed as a cure-all, *Walden* can be relished as a condiment, a flavoring, a head-clearing spice. White, remembering how the book heartened him when he read it in his youth, saw *Walden* as "an invitation to life's dance, assuring the troubled recipient that . . . the music is played for him, too, if he will but listen and move his feet." "Love your life," Thoreau wrote, "poor as it is."

Walden can be taken as an antidote to apathy and anxiety. With its high spirits and sharp pictures for the senses, it fortifies. Its time of writing was a troubled time for Thoreau, young but old enough to have accomplished more, and for the nation, laboring under the cloud of the slavery issue and the coming Civil War. If Thoreau did not make much of the industrial revolution, he felt the crisis in belief whereby even near-creedless Unitarianism demanded too much faith. His nature studies pointed to naturalism, to philosophical materialism. "Darwin, the naturalist," is cited early in *Walden*, as witness to those "inhabitants of Tierra del Fuego" who went "naked with impunity, while the European shivers in his clothes"—model citizens of Thoreau's Utopia of doing without. Harding's biography tells us that the ailing Thoreau lived to read, in 1860, Darwin's *Origin of Species*, and "took six pages of notes on it in one of his commonplace books, and . . . liked the book very much." But the theological furor over the book did not engage him, or affect his own thinking. He had once experienced, *Walden* confides, "a slight insanity in my mood" whereby Nature seemed unfriendly, a mood quickly cancelled by a sense, in a gentle rain, of "an infinite and unaccountable friendliness all at once like an atmosphere sustaining me." He avowed, "There can be no very black melancholy to him who lives in the midst of Nature and has his senses still."

Thoreau resembled Darwin in his careful observations and Benjamin Franklin in his inventive practicality. Unlike most transcendentalists, Thoreau could *do* things—tend garden and make home repairs for Emerson, or actualize with real carpentry Bronson Alcott's fanciful vision of a summerhouse. "I have as many trades as fingers," he says in *Walden*. He figures in Henry Petroski's technological history of the pencil (*The Pencil*, 1990) as the inventor, not long after his graduation from Harvard, of a seven-foot-high grinding machine that captured only the particles of graphite fine enough to rise highest into the air; for a time, accordingly, Thoreau pencils were the best—the least gritty—in America. We trust the narrator of *Walden* and his spiritual aspirations better because of repeated examples of his practical know-how. A call to "ethereal life" begins with a trick of fitting an ax tight to its handle:

> One day, when my axe had come off and I had cut a green hickory for a wedge, driving it with a stone, and had placed the whole to soak in a pond hole in order to swell the wood, I saw a striped snake run into the water, and he lay on the bottom, apparently without inconvenience, as long as I staid there, or more than a quarter of an hour; perhaps because he had not yet fairly come out of the torpid state. It appeared to me that for a like reason men remain in their present low and primitive condition; but if they should

feel the influence of the spring of springs arousing them, they would of necessity rise to a higher and more ethereal life.

Surviving in the woods, he becomes a student of physical process. Water swells wood; dead leaves absorb the sun's heat: "The elements . . . abetted me in making a path through the deepest snow in the woods, for when I had once gone through the wind blew the oak leaves into my tracks, where they lodged, and by absorbing the rays of the sun melted the snow, and so not only made a dry bed for my feet, but in the night their dark line was my guide." The pond covered with winter ice moves him to especially close observation; as he had anatomized the spring thaw, so the winter freezing prompts his minute inspection of bubbles, "narrow oblong perpendicular bubbles about half an inch long, sharp cones with the apex upward." In a warm spell, they expand and run together, "often like silvery coins poured from a bag, one overlapping another"; at the end of the passage he lifts his almost microscopic examination of "the infinite number of minute bubbles" into the resounding open: "These are the little air-guns which contribute to make the ice crack and whoop." He veers close to the secret of microörganisms when he asks, "Why is it that a bucket of water soon becomes putrid, but frozen remains sweet forever?" The question dissolves, however, in the dry witticism "It is commonly said that this is the difference between the affections and the intellect."

Much as the railroad cuts exposed new geology, the commercial ice-cutting in the winter of 1846–47 gave Thoreau new opportunities for examining ice, remarking distinctions in tint with the same devout precision that the contemporary landscapist Frederick Edwin Church brought to his oil studies of icebergs. Early in 1846, Thoreau seized the opportunity of a frozen Walden to perform the chief technical labor of his years there. "With compass and chain and sounding line," cutting holes in straight lines in several directions, he sounded the pond, presenting the reader with a drawn map, forty rods to an inch, and a scale profile of the bottom. The pond had been long rumored to be bottomless: "It is remarkable how long men will believe in the bottomlessness of a pond without taking the trouble to sound it." The surveyor is proud to announce, "But I can assure my readers that Walden has a reasonably tight bottom at a not unreasonable, though at an unusual depth." Ponds are shallower than we imagine: "Most ponds, emptied, would leave a meadow no more hollow than we frequently see." Most mysteries, by the same token, yield to the emptying action of patient scientific examination. Readers new to *Walden* may be surprised at the high proportion of its energy given to empirical exploration and demonstration. Thoreau's purpose is to reconcile us, after centuries of hazy anthropocentrism, to Nature as it is, relentless and remorseless. We need to be called out from the shared comforts and illusions of village life.

> We need the tonic of wildness. . . . We can never have enough of Nature. We must be refreshed by the sight of inexhaustible vigor, vast and Titanic features. . . . We need to witness our own limits transgressed, and some life pasturing freely where we never wander. We are cheered when we observe the vulture feeding on the carrion which disgusts and disheartens us and deriving health and strength from the repast.

On the path to his little cabin, he relates, there was a dead horse, whose aroma repulsed him but heartened him with "the assurance it gave me of the strong appetite and inviolable health of Nature." The vision of "Nature, red in tooth and claw," which desolated Tennyson and other Victorians, is embraced by Thoreau:

> I love to see that Nature is so rife with life that myriads can be afforded to be sacrificed and suffered to prey on one another; that tender organizations can be so serenely squashed out of existence like pulp—tadpoles which herons gobble up, and tortoises and toads run over in the road; and that sometimes it has rained flesh and blood! With the liability to accident, we must see how little account is to be made of it. The impression made on a wise man is that of universal innocence. . . . Compassion is a very untenable ground.

He sounds, as it were, the fatal bottom of our organic existence, and yet claims not merely to accept the universe, as another Transcendentalist, Margaret Fuller, put it, but to rejoice in it.

He met his own death, at forty-four, of consumption, with a serenity admired by his Concord acquaintances. "One world at a time," he famously told those seeking to prepare him for the next. He did not quite renounce personal immortality; a number of his phrases tease the possibility, and not far from the passages above he evokes the "wild river valley and the woods . . . bathed in so pure and bright a light as would have waked the dead," concluding, "There needs no stronger proof of immortality. All things must live in such a light." Yet the meaning is unclear, a fillip of animal optimism after a book-length, clear-eyed exaltation of Nature as a chemical and molecular and mathematical construct— Nature seized in the tightening grip of science, stripped of the pathetic fallacy even in the sophisticated form in which Emerson's neo-Platonism couched it. No more Idealism, no more Platonic forms, no shimmering archetypes having an existence somehow independent of individual things. "No ideas but in things," William Carlos Williams said, giving modernism a motto. The poetry of Williams and Eliot and Pound demonstrated that things, assembled even as enigmatic fragments, as images without spelled-out emotional and logical connectives, give life back to the language and immediacy to the communication between writer and reader. It is the thinginess of Thoreau's prose that still excites us—the athleticism with which he springs from detail to detail, image to image, while still toting something of transcendentalism's metaphysical burden. Without that burden, which considerably lightens in the later explorations posthumously collected as *The Maine Wood* and *Cape Cod*, he comes close to being merely an attentive and eloquent travel-writer. Even so, the chaotic, mist-swept top of Mount Ktaadn—"the raw materials of a planet dropped from an unseen quarry"—and the wrecks and wind-stunted apple trees of Cape Cod afford us the metaphysical shudder of a man confronting in inscrutable Nature an image of something scouringly bleak within him.

His later years, as the preachments of abolitionists and slaveholders reached their shrill adumbration of bloody war, were marked, even made notorious, by his fiery championing of John Brown, whom he had briefly met in Concord, finding him "a man of great common sense, deliberate and practical," endowed with "tact and prudence" and the Spartan habits and spare diet of a soldier. The peaceable Thoreau extols this grim killer for a practical reason: Brown has taken action, violent action, against the sanctioned violence of the slavery-protecting state:

> It was his peculiar doctrine that a man has a perfect right to interfere by force with the slaveholder, in order to rescue the slave. I agree with him. . . . I do not wish to kill nor to be killed, but I can foresee circumstances in which both these things would be by me unavoidable. We preserve the so-called "peace" of our community by deeds of petty violence every day.

Thoreau's recognitions endeared him to the revolutionaries of the Sixties: he perceived the violence behind the established order, the enslaving nature of private property, and the media's substitution of "the news" for private reality: "Shams and delusions are esteemed for soundest truths, while reality is fabulous." The word "reality" rings through *Walden:*

> Let us settle ourselves, and work and wedge our feet downward through the mud and slush of opinion, and prejudice, and tradition, and delusion, and appearance . . . till we come to a hard bottom and rocks in place, which we can call reality. . . . Be it life or death, we crave only reality. If we are really dying, let us hear the rattle in our throats and feel cold in the extremities; if we are alive, let us go about our business.

To the dark immensity of material Nature's indifference we can oppose only the brief light, like a lamp in a cabin, of our consciousness; the invigorating benison of *Walden* is to make us feel that the match is equal, and fair.

The United States of 1850, at twenty-three millions, was small enough to be addressed as a single congregation. Though famous as the man who lived alone in the woods, as Melville was as "the man who had lived among cannibals," Thoreau was in his gingerly fashion gregarious. Visiting his friends the Loomises in Cambridge, he was once handed, in 1856, and for an awkward moment held upside down the newborn Mabel Loomis, who was to achieve fame as the first editor of Emily Dickinson's poetry and, in the twentieth century, as a leading instance, in Peter Gay's social history *The Tender Passion*, of the sexually fulfilled and unrepressed Victorian female. In 1852, Thoreau, already acquainted with most of New England's writers, visited Walt Whitman in Brooklyn, in the bedroom where Whitman lived in slovenly style with his feeble-minded brother. Although they differed in their estimate of the common man, so that Whitman later diagnosed the Yankee as having "a very aggravated case of superciliousness," and Thoreau pronounced some of the New Yorker's poems as "disagreeable to say the least, simply sensual . . . as if the beasts spoke," both were left with favorable impressions. "He is a great fellow," Thoreau wrote of Whitman in a letter, and of his book of poems, "On the whole it sounds to me very brave & American after whatever deductions. I do not believe that all the sermons so called that have been preached in this land put together are equal to it for preaching." *Leaves of Grass* and *Walden* have emerged over time as the two great testaments of American individualism, assuring the New World man, in the absence of the old corporate reassurances, of the value and power of the unfettered self.

To The Portrait of a Lady, *by Henry James*

WITH SOME BOOKS, the reading of them leaves an impression as vivid as their contents. I first read *The Portrait of a Lady* as a young man of twenty-three in New York City, in the very World's Classic edition which I am invited, forty-three years later, to introduce. Back then, because the book was physically small, and James one of the great names of literature that my formal education had but nominally included, I would slip the handy volume, with its pleasingly severe blue cover, in my coat pocket before leaving the modest, triangular apartment I shared with my wife and infant daughter on Riverside Drive near Eighty-fifth Street; I would walk over to Broadway, catch the subway at Eighty-sixth Street, and stare into the closely printed pages for the seven stops and twenty minutes it took to arrive at Times Square. And so, in reverse, on the way back. During those rush hours I usually had to stand, swaying, jostled, gripping a porcelain loop while I buried my head, ostrichlike, in the accreting sands of James's tale as it made its leisurely way from England to Paris to Florence and Rome and back to England, to betranced and lovely Gardencourt, the home of successive invalids. There was a certain swank, it certainly occurred to the vain youth I was, in dulling the indignities of my twice-daily passage with a fiction so refined, so aloof in its voice and milieux from the underground congestion of the American metropolis. But the method of such short, distracted doses may, possibly, have weakened my overall impression of the book, for most of what I remembered was the tea party at the beginning and the kiss like lightning at the end.

In preparation for this present task of introduction, I took the same nostalgic volume with me to China, where, on the all-but-endless trans-Pacific flight and in brief bedtime snatches at the weary end of many a sightseeing day, I made my way through it again. This second time around, I lacked a young man's exultant sense of a practically infinite life ahead of him, with time in which to read and write any number of books. Instead, a much older man took a certain sour comfort in the likelihood that he would not be setting himself to read this particular masterpiece a third time. The novel's beginning felt unnecessarily arch and the ending unnecessarily frustrating. Between beginning and end, of course, there was marvellous writing, as James lovingly drew the filaments of his rather thin and Gothic tale into momentary marvels of witty metaphor and particular sensation:

> It was not that his spirits were visibly high—he would never, in the concert of pleasure, touch the big drum by so much as a knuckle.

> Time had breathed upon his heart and, without chilling it, given it a relieved sense of having taken the air.

> To cease utterly, to give it all up and not know anything more—this idea was as sweet as the vision of a cool bath in a marble tank, in a darkened chamber, in a hot land.

James does not begrudge Gilbert Osmond, otherwise deprived of sympathetic traits, the author's own gift for adroit simile: Osmond, taking a perverse liking to Caspar Goodwood, imagines marriage to him as "like living under some tall belfry which would strike all the hours"; extending the trope, he adds that to have conversation with him "you had to climb up an interminable steep staircase, up to the top of the tower; but when you got there you had a big view and felt a little fresh breeze."

In the years, 1880–81, when James was composing *The Portrait of a Lady*, supplying monthly installments simultaneously to Boston's *Atlantic Monthly* and London's *Macmillan's Magazine*, he turned thirty-eight and enjoyed his sixth consecutive year of residence abroad. After attempts, in the 1870s, to live in New England and New York, he settled in the Old World, with London as his base and Paris and Italy as his spas for spiritual refreshment. *Portrait* is not only his longest and most variously populated novel up to this time but his most geographically expansive; no mere snapshot acquaintance deepens the brilliant verbs in these swift watercolors of Rome's most visited sites:

> The sun had begun to sink, the air was a golden haze, and the long shadows of broken column and vague pedestal leaned across the field of ruin.

> . . . the first time she found herself beneath the far-arching dome [of Saint Peter's] and saw the light drizzle down through the air thickened with incense and with the reflections of marble and gilt, of mosaic and bronze, her conception of greatness rose and dizzily rose.

We are seeing the light drizzle and the shadows lean through the eyes of Isabel Archer, the epitome of the young American female, a type to whom James had given some celebrity in his short novel *Daisy Miller*, of 1878. Daisy, "an inscrutable combination of audacity and innocence," dies young, as had James's loved cousin, Minny Temple. Minny had died helplessly of tuberculosis, and Daisy of a recklessly courted malaria; Isabel is reckless in another regard, marring with an ill marital choice what looks to be a long life. Recast as Milly Theale in *The Wings of the Dove*, one of the three ample novels with which James rounded out his career, the pliant wraith of Minny Temple both dies and is betrayed by a female friend, who shares with Isabel's friend an ornithological name of sinister hue: Croy / crow and Merle / blackbird. When James's cousin died at the age of twenty-four, James was not quite twenty-seven; he wrote to his brother William, "She *represented*, in a manner, in my life several of the elements or phases of life at large—her own sex, to begin with, but even more *Youth*, with which owing to my invalidism, I always felt in rather indirect relation." He wrote his mother of Minny, "Twenty years hence, what a pure eloquent vision she will be." And in memoirs composed late in life he recalled her as "the very figure and image of a felt interest in life ... the supreme case of a taste for life as life, as personal living, of an endlessly active and yet somehow a careless, an illusionless, a sublimely forewarned curiosity about it."

Graham Greene, in his warm introduction to the Oxford edition that I read in that subway of long ago, does eloquent justice to the large sentimental intention that underlies the portrait of Isabel Archer.

> When we remember how patiently and faithfully throughout his life he drew the portrait of one young woman who died, one wonders whether it was just simply a death that opened his eyes to the inherent disappointment of existence, the betrayal of hope.

It remains for me to wonder how fully James realized his wish to embody something as abstract and noble as "a taste for life as life" within the lineaments of this particular heroine. She comes clear visually—"undeniably spare, and ponderably light, and proveably tall. . . . Her hair, which was dark even to blackness, had been an object of envy to many women; her light grey eyes, a little too firm perhaps in her graver moments, had an enchanting range of concession"—but this promising outline does not effortlessly fill in. As the installments of *Portrait* arrived at *The Atlantic Monthly*, William Dean Howells, its editor and a loyal champion of James, suggested that Isabel was being overanalyzed; James replied that he "intended to make a young woman about whom there should be a great deal to tell and as to whom such telling should be interesting."

But in truth we are assured of Isabel's superb qualities more than we are permitted to see her demonstrate them. Her life abroad is one of reaction, usually negative; there remains something comically schematic in the ready way in which two suitors, each a paragon in his fashion, press marriage upon her, and a third admirer, handicapped by his own fragile health, must content himself with brooding upon her image and arranging that she inherit a fortune. Though James assures us that "her imagination was . . . remarkably active," the Countess Gemini late in the novel has occasion to marvel, to Isabel's face, at all "the things, all around you, that you've appeared to succeed in not knowing." The Countess, Madame Merle, Mrs. Touchett, and even the broadly brushed Henrietta Stackpole (not to mention Catherine Sloper, the touchingly lumpish and limited heroine of James's preceding novel, *Washington Square*) outdo Isabel in palpable vitality. It is not until the later stages of *Portrait*, as dark revelations gather, that she acquires an edged voice, a speaking personality—suggesting the surely unintended moral that a woman needs a bad marriage to become interesting.

But an introducer must leave the plot between the reader and the author. James was very proud of the shapeliness of this plot, "a structure reared with an 'architectural' competence, as Turgenieff would have said," while admitting, with that disarming and intricate frankness that makes his prefaces like no other author's, a danger of "thinness" in this "ado about Isabel Archer," a thinness he intended to forestall with his "cultivation of the lively." As, among the present hordes and ancient wonders of China, I maneuvered through this studied ado, I tried to picture those magazine readers of over a century ago, who, with no disciplinary incentive bred of James's now unchallengeable status as an American classic, followed the monthly installments as they were published. What sparked and maintained their interest? The spectacle of a young woman struggling for her soul, in a male world which heavily favors those who would dominate, exploit, and numb her, of course interests female readers and men who wish to be privy to female lives. Jane Austen's novels, Hawthorne's *Scarlet Letter*, Flaubert's *Madame Bovary*, and—especially present, I think, to James's mind as an exemplar to be reckoned with— George Eliot's *Middlemarch* preceded this particular "ado" over a "frail vessel." To this day females write fiction and read it with what seems greater facility than men, as if their more sensitive and sociable natures find fiction's reports more urgent. James's insight into femininity—into his own feminine side, it might be said—and his mature preference for female protagonists conjure up few American parallels; one thinks of Hawthorne in a few soaring passages and of a writer in point of literary refinement and social experience far removed from James, Theodore Dreiser. The readers of *The Atlantic Monthly* of the early 1880s would have recognized human truth, I imagine, in this wry sentence concerning two old lovers:

> They stood there knowing each other well and each on the whole willing to accept the satisfaction of knowing as a compensation for the inconvenience—whatever it might be—of being known.

Those readers, too, would have been flattered by their entry, via James's early novels, into the exotic and rarefied world of Americans living, more or less richly, in Europe. "There's nothing for a gentleman in America," says little Ned Rosier, one of the set of Parisian Americans whose portrait is surprisingly acid, for James was after all one of these expatriates, and exploration of their corruptible innocence was his stock in trade. Though Henry James, Sr., had traded in his Scots Presbyterianism for the more expansive doctrines of Swedenborg, and his son Henry was less orthodox still, there is something of the lost and damned about these escapees from their vast young land, what Isabel calls "the great country stretching away beyond the rivers and across the prairie, blooming and smiling and spreading till it stops at the green Pacific!" In their exile they don't do anything, by and large, except live on inherited money, and to a hard-working professional like Henry James this was something of a scandal. The villains of his "ado" here, Gilbert Osmond and Madame Merle, are both failed artists, he a watercolorist and she a pianist of considerable but unmarketable accomplishment, both subsisting bitterly on barely adequate incomes amid the borrowed elegancies of European culture. There was a mercenary reason for the humming expatriate colonies that the United States established in Europe: the Gilded Age dollar went further here than at home, and a life of some luxury could be afforded by those who might find, as did the young Henry James in 1875, New York City too expensive. Money is what the tall vaults of James's novels, with their portentous intimate betrayals and conspiracies cloaked in the velvet language of politeness, rest upon. His grand tone veils an ignoble scramble for money among people incapable of earning any. The bare facts glint through, now and then; beneath the exquisite frescoes that James executed on European models lies a coat of plain Puritan whitewash.

The attenuation of James's expatriate scene, with its glamour like that of a threadbare theatre company, manifests itself as comedy. The comedy of names, for instance: a century before "wood" became known as porn-film slang for an erection, James coined the name "Caspar Goodwood" for the personification of "hard manhood," whose "stiff insistence" Isabel flees from even as it obscurely delights her. Is there a funnier line in the annals of courtship than Lord Warburton's expressed fear that it is not he she finds unacceptable but his castle: "Some people don't like a moat, you know"? This demur finds echo, in its startling concreteness, much later when to the rejected lord Isabel upholds her husband by affirming, "He has a genius for upholstery." James, too, had a genius for upholstery, which leads us to forget the underlying spareness of his stories. There is no ignoring, however, the abrupt and unsatisfactory ending in which the heroine is, as Greene said, "deserted even by her creator," a creator who has so meticulously supplied her with all the tools and supplies she needs to make her escape. The last paragraph is a study in deflation, each clause of which leads us and the faithful Mr. Goodwood lower into hopelessness:

> On which he looked up at her—but only to guess, from her face, with a revulsion, that she simply meant he was young. She stood shining at him with that cheap comfort, and it added, on the spot, thirty years to his life. She walked him away with her, however, as if she had given him now the key to patience.

Its elaborations were grafted, in the course of James's revisions for the New York Edition (1908), upon a concluding sentence (in the Houghton, Mifflin edition of 1881) of singular starkness: "On which he looked up at her." Stark, but with an implication of action in its rhythm. His kiss of a page before was elaborated, for the New York Edition, into intimations of enduring penetration—intimations then deliberately dashed. Sex existed for James mostly as a rumor, a hidden center of ado, and some impatience attends his treatment of it. Age strengthened in him his propensity, whether born of rueful observation or submerged animus, to let his most ambitious and appealing female characters—Isabel, Kate Croy, Charlotte Stant, Madame de Cintré in *The American*, Madame de Vionnet in *The Ambassadors*—stew, as it were, in their own juices.

The reader, then—a subscriber to an 1880s magazine or to a 1990s tour of China—runs the risk of clipped wings and dashed hopes in submitting to the endlessly productive but resolutely pessimistic sensibility of Henry James. His sense of life comes down to denial and limitation. His 1908 preface states:

> The question comes back thus, obviously, to the kind and the degree of the artist's prime sensibility, which is the soil out of which his subject springs. The quality and capacity of that soil, its ability to 'grow' with due freshness and straightness any vision of life, represents, strongly or weakly, the projected morality.

In locating the morality of art with such narrow squareness upon its creator's sensibility, rather than upon any corroborating interchange with an audience's social needs and expectations, James sounded, with superb intelligence, the clarion egoistic note of modern art. The creator owes his public nothing but himself (or herself, needless to say). If the finished designs, in James's case, seem somewhat vengefully confining, the designer's ease, the joy and pride felt in each phrase of the fashioning, make a liberating air still delicious to breathe. No other American novelist thought so well of his craft, or thought so well *on* it, or gave the novelist at large such a generous mandate.

To The Diary of Adam and Eve and Other Adamic Stories, *by Mark Twain*

MOST NINETEENTH-CENTURY AMERICANS, even if not conventionally churchgoing, grew up with the sayings and stories of the Bible. The Missourian Samuel Clemens, who became the writer Mark Twain, was no exception; but where a literal interpretation of the Bible spelled comfort, if vaguely, to most listeners, to Mark Twain it increasingly offered a purchase on the absurdity of the Christian religion and the cruelty of the alleged Creator. Like the atheist evangel Robert Ingersoll, he sharply turned the Bible against itself. To burlesque its myths took merely a plain retelling in a down-to-earth American voice. With Adam, the primal man and first human victim of God's whimsical tyranny, Clemens enjoyed a natural identification: he saw his own life in terms of lost paradises*—the lost paradise of the Hannibal, Missouri, of his childhood and, later, of his family life in Hartford, Connecticut, from 1875 to 1891, where he wrote, among much else, his two masterpieces, *Huckleberry Finn* and *Life on the Mississippi*. After 1891, he fell, as it were, into a wilderness of business failure, bankruptcy, family illness, celebrity, travel, loneliness, and increasingly dark views of God and humankind.

His inspirations were ever wayward; no great writer more haphazardly courted greatness. "Extracts from Adam's Diary" existed in some form before 1893, when Clemens received a request for a humorous piece on Niagara Falls, to be part of a souvenir book for the 1893 World's Fair in Buffalo, New York. At first he declined, but then saw that "Adam's Diary" might be relocated to an Eden that contained Niagara Falls. This insouciant transposition served its purpose; *The Niagara Book* published his contribution, though the author only received five hundred dollars of the promised thousand. In 1905, a request came from *Harper's Magazine* for a contribution to their Christmas issue, and Clemens complied with a diary for Eve that led him to consider Adam's anew. Hoping for *Harper's* to publish the two diaries together, he cut seven hundred words from Adam's and wrote some new pages in Adam's voice which he inserted, italicized, into Eve's diary. To the editor of *Harper's* he pronounced the result "dam good—sixty times as good as it was." The magazine published only "Eve's Diary," however, and the two were not published together, as they appear here, until 1931.

At least five posthumously published pieces—"That Day in Eden," "Eve Speaks," "Adam's Soliloquy," "Papers from the Adam Family," and "Eve's Autobiography"—extend Mark Twain's animation of Adam and Eve. "Eve Speaks," for instance, dated at around 1900, begins with her bewildered questioning of God and His angelic agents ("They drove us

---

*This insight, and much of the bibliographic information here, come from *A Reader's Guide to the Short Stories of Mark Twain*, by James D. Wilson (Boston: G. K. Hall & Co., 1987).

from the Garden with their swords of flame, the fierce cherubim. And what had we done? We meant no harm. We were ignorant, and did as any other children might do"), proceeds to describe her pathetic misapprehension that her slain son Abel is merely sleeping, and ends with this brief entry from Satan's Diary:

> Death has entered the world, the creatures are perishing; one of The Family is fallen; the product of the Moral Sense is complete. The Family think ill of death—they will change their minds.

As Mark Twain became, with the death of his wife and his favorite daughter, Suzie, increasingly isolated and lonely, he identified more and more with the first, singular man. He came to see himself as "*the* American," and even "*the* man." His quarrel with God became more savage in the wake of his financial miseries and family tragedies, which eventually carried off another daughter, Jean. His Adamic diaries are one of the many modes with which, in the last decade of his life, the author sought to confront ultimate questions and the great Christian fraud, in writings whose blasphemous and nihilistic nature by and large precluded publication. *The Mysterious Stranger* and *Letters from the Earth* are the most extensive, vehement examples.

"The Diary of Adam and Eve," as published here, is a more agreeable work, toying with Genesis in a mood less of indignation than of affection, taking the myth as a paradigm of the relations between the sexes. Adam is a typical male, into whose solitude a talkative, inquisitive, organizing, long-haired creature has abruptly intruded. He is slow to recognize her as being closer to him than to the other animals, and the revelation of her gender brings no accompaniment of desire: "What she is were nothing to me if she would but go by herself and not talk." She spoils his fun, whose main ingredient is going over Niagara Falls, in a barrel or without. When Eve produces children, he has no idea where they came from, and is very slow to see that they resemble, in miniature, him. Boyishly, he stands outside all social processes; he attempts to recover his pristine solitude outside of Eden, where she follows him and feeds him the forbidden apples. Eating them is against his principles, but he finds—in the voice of Mark Twain the immoralist—"that principles have no real force except when one is well fed."

Eve, on the other hand, is, in the feminist term of fashion, "relational" to a fault. Like Adam, she takes her mate for a mere animal at first. She resents this animal's interest in resting ("It would tire me to rest so much"), but when it speaks, she begins to fall in love: "For I love to talk; I talk, all day, and in my sleep, too, and I am very interesting, but if I had another to talk to I could be twice as interesting, and would never stop, if desired." Eve is embodied activity; she talks all day, gives things their names, discovers fire, befriends animals, and perpetrates a wifely love beyond all limit and reason. Her attempt to plumb her love for Adam reaches into female masochism, in this age when Freud and Havelock Ellis were anatomizing Eros:

> Then why is it that I love him? *Merely because he is masculine*, I think.
> At bottom he is good, and I love him for that, but I could love him without it. If he should beat me and abuse me, I should go on loving him. I know it, it is a matter of sex, I think.

"Eve's Diary" makes a bold foray into female sexuality, a territory that Bernard De Voto thought presented a conspicuous gap in Mark Twain's world: "None of Mark Twain's nubile girls, young women, or young matrons are believable." Yet Clemens, a product of the trafficked Mississippi and the Wild West, who did not marry until he was thirty-five, was no prude; in *Letters from the Earth* he dared complain about the lack of copulation in Heaven: "From youth to middle age all men and all women prize copulation above all other pleasures combined," brief as its "overwhelming climax" is, compared with the "supremest ecstacies unbroken and without withdrawal for centuries" that angels enjoy. Eve's indiscriminate subjection to the masculine principle has something in it of Victorian hysteria and something of biological truth, the hot truth. Mark Twain is at his hottest, his least guarded, in these sweeping avowals of Eve's. Her diary concludes with Adam's saying at her grave that, "wheresoever she was, there was Eden": a lightly disguised tribute to Clemens's recently deceased wife, Olivia. Adam and Eve, half mocked, yet gave him a path into intimate feelings unapproached by the beguiling, brusquely fantastic, altogether masculine yarns that dominate his oeuvre.

Introduction to Seven Men, *by Max Beerbohm*

THE MATHEMATICALLY ADEPT READER, counting the names of the men listed in the table of contents, will notice that there are only six. The seventh is the author, Max Beerbohm himself, who from story to story is seen interacting with his half-dozen heroes; in his elegant fashion he was as specialized and fantastical a specimen of late-Imperial English manhood as any of these fictional creations. Born in 1872, he early developed a preternatural poise and grace as a writer and a caricaturist. While still an undergraduate at Oxford he became a contributor to *The Yellow Book;* Oxford became the magical milieu of his only novel, the blithe love farce *Zuleika Dobson*, an extravagant collegiate *hommage*. Beerbohm retained into old age an undergraduate playfulness, spending much of his later years ornamenting with illustration, collage, and marginalia his own books and the books of others. His life was bookish, but the bookishness was sunny, skimming the essence, in marvellous parodies, from his more earnest and ponderous contemporaries, and penning essays collected in volumes whose titles themselves signal a refusal to take his enterprise altogether seriously: the first was *The Works of Max Beerbohm*, followed by *More, Yet Again*, and *And Even Now*. As a young man he cut a dandyish figure about London; George Bernard Shaw, whom he replaced as theatre critic of *The Saturday Review* in 1898, dubbed him "the incomparable Max." In 1910, the maturing dandy married Florence Kahn, an American actress renowned for her portrayals of Ibsen heroines, and the couple took up residence, interrupted only by the two world wars, in Rapallo, on the Italian Riviera. Keenly appreciated but not widely bought during his prime, he achieved geriatric celebrity with his reminiscing broadcasts over the BBC, beginning in 1935, and with the postwar biographical attentions of J. M. Rewald and S. N. Behrman. By his death in 1956, at the age of eighty-four, he seemed a carefully self-preserved souvenir of a spatted, straw-hatted era long absorbed into history.

Always, even when in the thick of London literary life, Beerbohm projected the isolating aura of a man dancing to his own tune, who would not be deflected from his private bent by the competitive examples of others. The willful exquisitism of Wilde and Beardsley stayed with him after these hothouse flowers had met their dooms, taking the French perfumes of fin-de-siècle decadence with them; the heartily prolific late Victorians and Edwardians who were his contemporaries—Shaw, Wells, Chesterton, Belloc, Bennett, Galsworthy—inspired him not to energetic emulation but to the scrupulous, devastating imitations collected in *A Christmas Garland*, the finest book of prose parodies in the English language. His brief preface to it arrestingly states an educational fact true for generations of British stylists:

> I had had some sort of aptitude for Latin prose and Latin verse. I wondered often whether those two things, essential though they were (and are) to the making of a decent style in English prose, sufficed for the making of a style more than decent. I felt that I must have other models. And thus I acquired the habit of aping, now and again, quite sedulously, this or that live writer— sometimes, it must be admitted, in the hope of learning rather what to avoid.

Henry James and Conrad earned, it would seem, his warmest admiration, and only Kipling, with his sometimes callous jingoism, a real animosity. But the ambition of these men, their willingness to extend their gifts into laughable exertions, was alien to the incomparable Max. In "James Pethel," the most earnest of the stories collected in *Seven Men*, the somewhat Conradian hero, James Pethel, says to the narrator, who has been admiring Pethel's nerve and sang-froid while gambling, "Ah, but you despise us all the same!" Us—the gamblers, the doers of the world. Pethel adds "that he has always envied men who had resources within themselves." Beerbohm, by his account, in answer "laughed lightly, to imply that it *was* very pleasant to have such resources, but that I didn't want to boast." A few pages later in the evening of this encounter, Pethel, who has described himself as a "very great admirer" of Beerbohm's work,

> asked what I was writing now, and said that he looked to me to "do something big, one of these days," and that he was sure I had it "in" me. This remark (though of course I pretended to be pleased by it) irritated me very much.

The story containing this delicately confessional exchange is the only one that has no element of formal parody and that shows, in driving home its moral, some strain: Beerbohm's antipathy to ruthless gamblers exceeds, by a shade, the reader's.

Pethel, with no interior artistic resources, must keep testing himself, and those he loves, against high-stakes risk; the heroes of the other four tales are captive to imaginations more distinctly literary. A. V. Laider's "limpness of demeanor" is marked only by an incongruous shock of white hair that gives him a touch of the charlatan; behind his bland reticence he is revealed to be a compulsive story-spinner, a wildly inventive bard. The tortuous shifts and obsessive pains of literary rivalry are displayed with a fiendish animation in "Hilary Maltby and Stephen Braxton," a distinguished specimen of the raft of ghost stories which Victorian religiosity trailed after it. The moment when poor Maltby is, while attending church service, encased within the phantom body of his rival—"All I knew was a sudden black blotting-out of things; an infinite and impenetrable darkness. . . . I calculate that as we sat there my eyes were just beneath the roof of his mouth. Horrible!"—transcends comedy, funny as it is, and touches a chord, worthy of an earthier author, deep within the human body, where Beerbohm did not usually choose to go.

Maltby's nightmare, given a placid dénouement in Italy's Lucca, and " 'Savonarola' Brown" both date from 1917, when Beerbohm, having taken shelter from the First World War in a cottage on the English farm of his friend the painter Will Rothenstein, found further shelter in recollection of the literary London of his youth. Brown, first met at school and remet fifteen years later, is a "second nighter"—a more passionate devotee of the stage than the showy first-nighters. "He did not seem to know much, or to wish to know more, about life. Books and plays, first editions and second nights, were what he cared for." The derivative tragedy, concerning the Florentine monk Savonarola, upon which Brown has been effortfully laboring, turns out, when he dies, to be one act short of five, and in its maladroit blank verse and mob of Renaissance characters a travesty of Shakespeare. Max was a versifier of dainty skill, and the comic effects, to be savored line by line, hinge on fine points, such as contractions run riot to fit the meter, unhappy coinages like "friskfulness," clanging iambs, and drooping enjambments. Yet there is something wild and dishevelled about the piece overall, especially the last three pages, where Beerbohm asserts his own presence; Bardolatry is possibly so big and so well armored it has splayed his pen.

"Enoch Soames" is the first and oldest of these sketches, and to me the most moving. The littérateur who has everything—dedication, ego, bohemian flair, an adequate private income—except talent is an apparition too sadly plausible for any writer to contemplate without unease. The narrator's tone, especially intimate and insistent, urges our sober attention, yet with a lovely urbane lightness carries off even the shopworn presence of the Devil, in a fondly described vanished restaurant. Soames's visit, purchased at the price of his soul, to the British Museum of a hundred years hence is heartbreaking—a visit to his own nonexistence, in the one realm that matters to him. He finds his three slender volumes in the card catalogue but no reference amid posterity's critical writings save a brief mention of Beerbohm's story "Enoch Soames"!

Were the wraith of Beerbohm himself to make a similar pilgrimage, he would be greeted by more structural changes—including an overarching glass roof—in the venerable research facility than his tale predicts, and would find in the fabled catalogue (computer-accessed by now) not only his modest list of titles but enough bibliographical attention to flatter a major artist. Minor artistry became in him a determination, a boast; like Ronald Firbank and Nathanael West, he remains readable while many mightier oeuvres gather dust. The filigree is fine, but of the purest gold.

To The Rich Boy, *a small volume containing three stories by F. Scott Fitzgerald: "The Rich Boy," "The Bridal Party," "The Last of the Belles"*

"THE RICH BOY," one of Fitzgerald's more ambitious and deeply felt short stories, contains a sentence that occasioned a tiff between the author and his formidable friend and rival, Ernest Hemingway. In August of 1936, after Fitzgerald had confessed in print the low ebb of his fortunes and mental condition, *Esquire* published a Hemingway story, "The Snows of Kilimanjaro," containing this passage from the autobiographical hero's thought-stream:

> The rich were dull and they drank too much or they played too much backgammon. They were dull and they were repetitious. He remembered poor Scott Fitzgerald and his romantic awe of them and how he had started a story once that began, "The rich are different from you and me." And how someone had said to Scott, Yes, they have more money. But that was not humorous to Scott. He thought they were a special glamorous race and when he found they weren't it wrecked him just as much as any other thing that wrecked him.

Fitzgerald, living at the time in Asheville, North Carolina, was quick to respond, in a letter as gracious as it was blunt:

> Dear Ernest:
> Please lay off me in print. If I choose to write de profundis sometimes it doesn't mean I want friends praying aloud over my corpse. No doubt you meant it kindly but it cost me a night's sleep. And when you incorporate it (the story) in a book would you mind cutting my name?

When the story appeared in a Hemingway collection, the name had been changed to "Julian." This was at the insistence of Maxwell Perkins, the editor at Scribner's of both men, according to the scholar Matthew Bruccoli, in a long footnote in his *F. Scott Fitzgerald: A Life in Letters*. Bruccoli claims that the object of the put-down had been not Fitzgerald but Hemingway himself, bragging, "I am getting to know the rich," at a luncheon with Perkins and the critic Mary Colum, who had then said, "The only difference between the rich and other people is that the rich have more money."

In any case, it is not much of a put-down, and Hemingway's self-serving account ignores the next sentence in "The Rich Boy," which begins to explain the difference:

They possess and enjoy early, and it does something to them, makes them soft where we are hard, and cynical where we are trustful, in a way that, unless you were born rich, it is very difficult to understand.

It was important to Fitzgerald to try to understand. Literary pilgrims to Saint Paul can still see the modest houses that his struggling, shabby-genteel parents rented in the vicinity of (but rarely on) Summit Avenue, the street of the local rich. His father, a delicate man whom he physically resembled, was descended from Maryland aristocracy, including Francis Scott Key, the writer of "The Star-Spangled Banner," but Edward Fitzgerald lacked the drive and vitality to be a successful businessman. Scott's mother, born Molly McQuillan, brought a fierce Irish Catholicism and some money—inherited from her immigrant father, a grocer—to the marriage, but only enough to cling to the edges of respectability, and to send her son to private school and Princeton. At Princeton, Fitzgerald associated with the sons of the rich, and afterwards his short stories for *The Saturday Evening Post* made him, for a time, wealthy. However, he and his reckless wife, Zelda, had no gift for accumulating money; in 1924, he wrote for the *Post* a comic essay, "How to Live on $36,000 a Year," when this was a fortune. Financial security eluded him just as his glamorous heroines elude his heroes. Jay Gatsby does not know, but the reader can see, that Daisy will always choose, over her old suitor's quixotic devotion and flashy, shady semblance of wealth, the secure protection of her brutish husband, who is truly rich.

The other aphorism on the first page of "The Rich Boy" is: "Begin with an individual, and before you know it you find that you have created a type; begin with a type, and you find that you have created—nothing." Yet, though Fitzgerald closely based Anson Hunter on his hard-drinking Princeton friend Ludlow Fowler—"It is in a large measure the story of your life," he ingenuously wrote Fowler in 1925, "toned down here and there and simplified"—the rich boy retains something of the rotundity and vagueness of a type. Increasingly plump because of his drinking, he becomes, out of the wreck of his two main romances, a womanizer compulsively seeking the flattery his sense of inherent superiority demands. That sense, presumably, makes him incapable of popping the question to Paula Legendre, preferring to keep her as a legend of lost love, or of consummating his romance with the more sporty, less idealized Dolly Karger. Anson has, in his privileged vanity, a sterilizing touch, killing the harmless affair between his Aunt Edna and a young man much like himself but without the clout of his money.

Fitzgerald was a considerable student of how money functioned.

Anson, at first a dynamic and bluff and shrewd performer in the broker-age house he joins, acquires, touchingly, the "fussy pessimism of a man of forty," and is urged by his firm to take a vacation, since "on every trans-action in which he was involved he acted as a drag and a strain." "The Bridal Party" portrays, in the person of Hamilton Rutherford, a more buoyant and successful type, who no sooner goes broke in a stock-market downturn than he is offered a fifty-thousand-dollar-a-year job: "He hap-pens to have it—that young man. . . . In another year he'll be back with the millionaires." Also, he carries off the girl. To Fitzgerald, money sig-nals animal vitality; sexual success is part of its romance. But, by his own inner lights, sexual success wasn't worth celebrating; it had something coarse about it. His rejection by the cold-blooded Ginevra King inspired more fiction than his acceptance by the impetuous Zelda Sayre.

His typical heroes mourn the loss of their true loves, usually met in the heady Southern atmosphere of magnolias and moonlight evoked in "The Last of the Belles." In his own life he *did* get the girl—spectacular, beau-tiful Zelda from Montgomery, Alabama—and for a spell they were the ultimate Jazz Age couple. But she became a mentally troubled liability, and the difficulties and disappointments of possessing the love object defied Fitzgerald's graceful powers of description. *Tender Is the Night* tries to encompass his predicament, and cannot, for all its labor of polish, be called a successful novel; it does not master its own matter, as *The Great Gatsby*, through the agency of its bystander narrator, so satisfacto-rily does. "The Rich Boy" was one of the few works to come out of the hectic year and a half, from April of 1925 to December of 1926, that Scott and Zelda spent in Paris after *Gatsby*'s completion. We can feel in the story, for all its earnest, ruminative care, how difficult it was becom-ing for Fitzgerald, once so fabulously fluent, to write—to bring his sus-ceptibility to romantic inertia and illusion into harmony with his clear-eyed, large-minded realism.

To The Eighth Day, *by Thornton Wilder*

THE EIGHTH DAY was published in late March of 1967, three weeks before Thornton Wilder's seventieth birthday. Reviews were mixed, from Edmund Wilson's calling it "the best thing he ever wrote" to Edith Oliver's judgment, in *The New Yorker,* that "none of the characters, major or minor, is essentially credible to the reader" and Stanley Kauffmann's, in *The New Republic*, that "we have—from a man who has always meant well—a book that means nothing." Nevertheless, Wilder's first novel in nearly twenty years had Book-of-the-Month Club endorsement, spent twenty-six weeks on the best-seller list, and won the 1968 National Book Award. I was one of the judges, much the youngest; the other two were Granville Hicks and Josephine Herbst. Hicks and I wanted the award to go to Wilder; Herbst politely acceded, and my two senior colleagues asked me to write the citation. On the spot I scratched it off:

> Through the lens of a turn-of-the-century murder mystery, Mr. Wilder surveys a world that is both vanished and coming to birth; in a clean gay prose sharp with aphoristic wit and the sense and scent of Midwestern America and Andean Chile, he takes us on a chase of Providence and delivers us, exhilarated and edified, into the care of an ambiguous conclusion.

Having just reread, thirty-five years later, *The Eighth Day*, I am only slightly disposed to quarrel with this rash summary. The "coming to birth" and "chase of Providence" seemed muted the second time around, with a louder emphasis on the misery and muddle of the human condition. "Clean gay" are not the adjectives with which I would now characterize the prose, though there is considerable gaiety in the narration's swift onward flow, its sudden pools of rumination and opinionizing, its pleasure in its own inventions, the impish leaps in time that telegraph crucial plot developments so quickly we can scarcely believe our eyes, and the globe-spanning nimbleness and cosmic liftoff of it all.

Wilder was the product of a pious (though progressive and cultured) Protestant household and Christian educational institutions; he kept religion's bias—its basic gaiety—while leaving the dogmas behind. His comedies skate on the skin of the void. If not a theist like Teilhard de Chardin and Kierkegaard, both of whom he admired and drew upon, he declined to write off the universe as a bad job. His Caesar in *The Ides of March* (1948) writes a friend that he is not certain "that in no corner of my being there lingers the recognition that there is a possibility of a mind in and behind the universe which influences our minds and shapes our actions"; in a later letter Caesar confesses, "Yet even in my last bitterness I cannot disavow the memory of bliss. Life, life has this mystery that we dare not say the last word about it, that it is good or bad, that it is senseless, or that it is ordered." In Wilder's personal journal, on August 14, 1955, he chastised himself for his unexpungeable religiosity:

> I must emerge from this dibble-dabble in religious subject-matter; I must shake my whole self and learn what I do and do not believe, or else eschew such themes altogether. I am ashamed of this lukewarm imitative dilettante religiosity. Pfui!

As late as 1968, he had not made up his mind: he wrote to an inquirer who had asked what his philosophy was, "I'm optimist and pessimist and religious and non-religious. I try 'em out for size. I'm tossed from pole to pole. I'm an awful wobbler." Wobbling may be the way most people get through life, but it doesn't win intellectual friends; literary critics who could accept Roman Catholicism and High Anglicanism and Communism as counters in a desperate game of twentieth-century commitment had little patience for Wilder's God-tinged semi-optimism. He was dismissed as sentimental when he was only being realistic, in the skeptical yet hopeful American style.

The Eighth Day revisits and extends the small-town world of *Our Town* (1938), the stark and dreamy drama that has turned out to be one of the most enduring and beloved of American plays. The play and the novel share a provincial location (southern New Hampshire, southern Illinois), a brace of households with romantically entwined offspring (George Gibbs and Emily Webb in the play; Roger Ashley and Felicity Lansing, late in the novel), an intervening village explainer (the Stage Manager, the nameless narrator), and a brooding sense of cosmic import within ordinary human events. The Stage Manager states:

> We all know that *something* is eternal. And it ain't houses and it ain't names, and it ain't earth, and it ain't even the stars. . . . Everybody knows in their bones that *something* is eternal, and that something has to do with human beings. . . . There's something way down deep that's eternal about every human being.

Both works are located in turn-of-the-century, pre-automobile America, when Wilder was a very small child; the young people of these dramas are almost a generation older than he. Nor did he experience a settled small-town upbringing. Born in Madison, Wisconsin, where his father, Amos Wilder, ran a financially challenged newspaper, he was moved before his ninth birthday to Hong Kong; his father had managed, through his Yale friend William Howard Taft, to secure President Theodore Roosevelt's appointment as consul general there. Before the year was out, Isabella Wilder took her four children back to the United States—to Berkeley, California, where they lived until late 1910, when they again sailed across the Pacific to rejoin the head of the household, who had been promoted to the consulship in Shanghai. Thornton was placed in the China Inland Mission Boys and Girls School, four hundred fifty miles to the north. There the boy learned Latin and loneliness and the look of human misery; China was in the throes of Sun Yat-sen's revolution.

More dispersals followed: Mrs. Wilder, now the mother of five, took the two youngest children, both daughters, to join her sister in Florence, and at the age of fifteen Thornton joined his older brother, Amos, at the Thacher School in California's Ojai Valley. There, in the school's sporty, outdoor atmosphere, he first experienced the pleasures of participating in organized theatrics, though his father forbade him from taking the female role of Lady Bracknell in *The Importance of Being Earnest*. His mother returned from Italy, and Thornton was enrolled in Berkeley High School, from which he graduated in 1915, going on to two years at Oberlin and then to Yale, from which, after brief wartime service in the Coast Guard Artillery Corps, he graduated in 1920. He proceeded to a year at the American Academy in Rome, studying Latin and archeology and gathering the impressions for his first novel, *The Cabala* (1926). So scattered an upbringing provided the model, we can conjecture, not only for *The Eighth Day*'s Ashley family—its father absentee and its mother withdrawn and two of its three children early fled to metropolises—but for the peripatetic life that the adult Wilder, once he was affluent and widely acquainted, pursued, lugging his manuscripts and fitful inspirations from one hotel room to another.

He was a gregarious man, fond of talk and drink and late hours, with a rapacious and whimsical intellectual curiosity. He devoted hundreds of hours to his exegesis of *Finnegans Wake* and his dating of the hundreds of plays by the Spaniard Lope de Vega. Of the American writers his age, a formidable group including Hemingway, Faulkner, Fitzgerald, and Dos Passos, he was much the most erudite and academically inclined, teaching French at the Lawrenceville School from 1921 to 1928 and English at the University of Chicago from 1930 to 1936. In 1950, he undertook to deliver the Norton Lectures, a series of six, at Harvard, and found himself so enmeshed in other duties, academic and social, that he broke down in March and never did complete the series, though he had flooded his journals with enough vigorous thoughts on the American classics to fill out twenty lectures. A play called *The Emporium* similarly stalled. Another, long in the works, titled *The Alcestiad*, conspicuously flopped in Edinburgh. Much socializing, many honors, unrealized operatic projects, relentless travel: at the age of sixty-five, recognizing that he was in danger of frittering his talent away in mere busy-ness, Wilder announced a retreat to the Southwest, where, he told an Associated Press reporter in Germany, he would live "without neckties, without shoelaces and without cultivated conversation." His car broke down in Douglas, Arizona, and there he stayed, first in a hotel and then in a bachelor apartment. In nine months he wrote his sister Isabel that he had ninety pages of a novel—a long family saga, an adventure story, "as though *Little Women* were being mulled over by Dostoevsky." It was tentatively called

Anthracite, and then *Make Straight in the Desert*, after a quote from Isaiah, and finally *The Eighth Day*.

He left Arizona with the novel unfinished. His labors on it were sandwiched into many trips—to Nice and Cannes, to the Netherlands Antilles, to the White House to accept the first National Medal for Literature, to Casablanca, Gibraltar, and Italy on the *Leonardo da Vinci*, and so on; in late 1965, he wrote his sister, "All I need is a hotel room. . . . It looks as tho' I may be able to finish the book by January—but not the last finicky touches." One can suspect that it might have been a more unified book if he had stayed at his desk in Connecticut, but writing on the run had often been Wilder's way; distraction and stimulation were closely linked in his nervous system. As a child he had been chastised for "jumpiness," and as a well-off bachelor at ease in the major languages of Europe he confessed to "a mania for constant change."

Composed in many locales, the novel offers a succession of persuasively realized settings: aside from Coaltown, there are Chicago, Hoboken, Andean Chile, the Caribbean island of Saint Kitts, with quick trips to Iowa, New Orleans, Russia, and upstate New York. Wilder, who in *The Bridge of San Luis Rey* (1927) had invented a persuasive Peru from whole cloth, played upon the world's map as on the keyboard of a clavier. His evocation of Coaltown, set forth in the prologue with the firmness of a hand that has penned many stage directions, is memorably emblematic: a town built between two tall bluffs, so it never sees a dawn or a sunset, a town darkened by the dust of its coal mines, strung out along "an unhappy stream, the Kangaheela," with the two notable homes, the Ashleys' and the Lansings', at either end.

In the plot's throng of incidents and images, some stand out as especially poetic and moving—written, as it were, in warmer ink. The first chapter, "The Elms," reminiscent of *Little Women*, tells how Sophie and then her sisters and mother are roused, after their father has been wrongly convicted of murder, to create a boarding house on the ruins of their fortune and reputation. The chapter combines, as the isolated family's tiny triumphs mount, the chirpiness and speed of stage action with the stomach-gnawing reality of social humiliation and economic peril; Wilder must have dipped back into his childhood memories of insecurity, as his family fled debt for the strangeness of China. The heroic Sophie, a mere fourteen, and destined for her own breakdown, alone of the Ashleys seems fully human, without the rather cool imperviousness of the others. The savage dialogue, late in the book, of the ailing Breckinridge Lansing with his long-suffering wife, also bares a warm vein, of intimacy both cruel and weary; we can taste the unhappiness of this marriage.

Wilder usually, even in the sketchy *Our Town*, places his venues on a geological base, the earth apprehended in its dwarfing antiquity and grudging usefulness. The mines of *The Eighth Day* function as magnificent images of human endeavor pitted against dark and adamant matter, exposed to view when the abandoned mines collapse after heavy rains:

> The townspeople would drive out to peer into these earthworks. They seemed more to resemble the ruins of some past greatness than the prisons where so many had labored twenty hours—later, ten hours—a day and where so many had coughed and spat their lungs away. Even small boys were hushed by the view of those long galleries and arcades, rotundas and throne rooms.

Throne rooms! The gods are there, underground. "By the following year squawbush and wild vines were covering the entrances to the underworld. The population of bats increased, emerging at first in whirling clouds above the valley."

Wilder, called "tirelessly eclectic" by one critic, wove a number of borrowed ideas into *The Eighth Day*. The idea behind the title, that we are entering a new week of Creation, though expressed by Coaltown's omniscient Dr. Gillies, was taken from the French priest and philosopher of science Teilhard de Chardin. Quiet, unobtrusive John Ashley, "odd through a very lack of striking characteristics," was meant to represent Kierkegaard's "knight of faith," of whom the Danish philosopher wrote in *Fear and Trembling*, "No heavenly glance or any other token of the incommensurable betrays him; if one did not know him, it would be impossible to distinguish him from the rest of the congregation."* Though it might be doubted that John Ashley's tranquil demeanor and kindly acts sufficiently distinguish him, the notion of a hidden elect—a cabal, a saving remnant, a secret masonry of virtue whose members recognize one another—was more than a notion to Wilder; it was an *idée fixe*. In his first novel, the ancient gods struggle on, and in his superb third, *Heaven's My Destination* (1935), the knight of faith, twenty-three-year-old George Brush, affronts Depression-era America with his naïve Christianity; when his faith and health fail, he is saved by a sign—the bequest of a spoon, with its apostolic associations—from another of the world's rare believers, Father Pasziewski of Kansas City. In *The Eighth Day*, the fugitive John Ashley encounters a succession of women—Mrs. Hodge, María Icaza, Mrs. Wickersham—who intuitively protect him

---

*Wilder read *Fear and Trembling*; if he read *Concluding Unscientific Postscript*, he would have come across: "Is not his incognito this, that there is nothing whatever to be noticed, nothing at all that could arouse suspicion of the hidden inwardness?"

and pass him on. As he parts from the last, the narrator tells us, "The leave-takings of the children of faith are like first recognitions."

Children of faith, poets and saints, dot the cruel world, and give Wilder's novels a reticular tension, the suspense of a hidden design about to emerge—"the unfoldment of God's plan for the world," as John Ashley remembers his grandmother saying in prayer. In *The Eighth Day*, however, the traces of Providence are subsumed in a tracery of heritage, as the genealogies of the Ashleys and the Lansings are displayed, illustrative pieces of "that enormous tapestry" which is human history. As with the Wilder family, two common threads are celebrity and eccentricity—though the Wilders, as far as I know, did not share the Ashleys' tendency to big feet and prominent ears, or the rich racial mix and mismatched eyes that Eustacia Sims brought to the blond Iowa Lansings. Fame and distinction come readily to these children of Coaltown when they leave their narrow sunless valley—heights of journalism, singing, acting, and social activism are quickly scaled. As he approaches seventy, the author can scarcely imagine a life not crowned by honors and high regard, such as a funeral "with military bands and statesmen in silk hats" or a birthday celebration to which the Emperor of Japan sends a flower and a poem.

But among these fictional children George Lansing is half crazy and Sophie suffers early breakdown. Their fragility seems an amplification of Wilder's own restless, jittery, nervous streak. His mind was not just active but hyperactive; browsing through his journals, with their extravagant wealth of large ideas, is giddying. Aborted and frivolous projects litter his curriculum vitae; the concentration, economy, and solid calm of his best work were achieved, we feel, by a man determinedly holding himself fast to the earth. Like John Ashley in his own son's eyes, he was "high, high up"—he gravitated to the elevated view, portraying the human adventure as a planetary incident. *The Skin of Our Teeth* (1942) wears this cosmic scope as a comic confusion; *The Eighth Day*—his one real novel, he more than once said, and much his longest—opens itself to the digression, the sermonette, the stray inspiration that might capture the simultaneous largeness and smallness of the human adventure. Untidily, self-delightingly, it brims with wonder and wisdom, and aspires to prophecy. We marvel at a novel of such spiritual ambition and benign flamboyance.

To The Golden West: Hollywood Stories, *by Daniel Fuchs*

WHEN FILMS CEASED TO BE SILENT, a migration of Eastern writers, playwrights, and wits swarmed to the Golden State, to write scripts for the studios. Though it wasn't exactly the Donner Party, its annals are not happy ones. One thinks of Fitzgerald and his quixotic, dashed hopes of bringing his brand of literary refinement and glamour to film; of Faulkner sneaking back to Mississippi as soon as one of his raids on the studio coffers had yielded its loot; of Dorothy Parker complaining that Hollywood money melted like snow and embracing Communism, perhaps in protest. Novels from Nathanael West's *The Day of the Locust* (1939) to Bruce Wagner's *Force Majeure* (1991) and *I'm Losing You* (1996) portray a nearly apocalyptic community of grotesque losers—schemers and dreamers driven mad by the wealth and fame apparently to be had all around them. The insider's view, as painted by Hollywood offspring Budd Schulberg and Leslie Epstein, is scarcely rosier. Even as benign a visitor as Ludwig Bemelmans struck off a novel, *Dirty Eddie* (1947), despairing of the screenwriter's lucrative but thankless lot.

What can we make, then, of long-term Hollywood denizen Daniel Fuchs, who in 1937 left behind a schoolteacher's job in Brooklyn, three quite brilliant novels produced in his twenties, and a career of frequent acceptances of his short fiction by *The New Yorker, The Saturday Evening Post,* and *Collier's,* to become one of RKO's scribbling minions, and who never looked back with regret? In "The Earthquake of 1971," Fuchs extols southern California as he found it in 1937, "still undeveloped . . . fresh and brimming and unawakened, at the beginning . . . everything in this new land wonderfully solitary, burning, and kind." For him at the time, "The studios exude an excitement, a sense of life, a reach and hope, to an extent hard to describe." With delight he wanders the studio backlots, their elaborate fabrications of Western streets and bygone fishing villages, and watches "the studio bravos in their costumes at their perpetual play, folk coming from backgrounds unknown to me, people with a smiling, generous style." He relishes, as the years go by, the uncanny cleanliness and health of his growing, tanned children. Looking back on thirty-four years of residence, he thanks the gods of filmdom

> for the boon of work, for the joy of leisure, the happy, lazy days; for the castles and drowsy back-lots; for the stalwarts I've come to know, John and Bob and Sam; for the parties at Barney's, the times at Phil's, the flowers, the sycamores, the blessings of the sun.

No sour grapes on these vines. In his long story "Triplicate," Fuchs lets a character assert with admitted exaggeration but without contradiction,

> "What people don't understand about this place is that the whole idea is not to make great pictures but to enjoy life in the sun. They keep asking for works of art, but the picture-making from the beginning was secondary,

starting with the Fairbanks-Pickford days when they entertained visiting royalty and statesmen. That's why the pictures had their worldwide success. They were made without strain by happy, unneurotic people who were busy having a good time and who worked naturally out of their instincts, and audiences everywhere were intelligent enough to perceive this and treasure it. It's the climate, the desert. It comes with the locality."

Fuchs's fiction tells a somewhat more complicated and qualified story, of feverish rises and falls, rousing successes and creeping failures, of neurosis and frustration amid the sunshine and bougainvillea. The three stories he wrote in the 1930s, soon after his arrival, are Kafkaesque, showing the screenwriter's Hollywood as a nightmare of aborted projects and inscrutable higher powers. But the longest of them, "Florida" (originally titled "Toilers of the Screen"), ends with a decision to stay in this "screwy, heartbreaking" place, and Fuchs remains a rarity, a literary Easterner who never opted out or badmouthed the Tinseltown hands that fed him. The equanimity, the pervasive amused sympathy, with which he regarded the waifs and gangsters of Brooklyn's tough Williamsburg section and of New York's racing crowd—*Low Company*, one of his novels is titled—extended to the movie crowd, whose brand of flamboyance and voiced desperation fills to overflowing the party scenes of "Triplicate" and "The Golden West." Fuchs resembles Bellow in his admiration of energy, however ill expended. He anticipated Bellow's rapid easy tumble of imagery and dialogue, with its sometimes breathtakingly fresh adjectives: "this world of celebrity, of fast movement and shiny living"; "the larceny in his eyes, as he devoted himself to the girl, wooing her and getting her rosy." There is the same acceptance, both offhand and tender, of people as the messy, troublesome spirits they are. Bellow, however, sometimes takes positions, presses a point—Herzog writing all those querulous letters to the mighty—where Fuchs maintains an unblemished dispassion, an unblinking, unblaming candor, and, with all his street smarts, an innocence.

His alter ego Rosengarten, the detached writer-witness of "Triplicate," explains that "what was of most importance in a piece of writing was a certain exhilaration, a life, a liveliness, a sense of well-being arising from the scene and the people, hard for him to describe or even to understand clearly, and yet the thing that gave him a sinking terror when it was missing, when he knew it wasn't there." Farther down the page, he falls into self-exhortation:

"Make something that didn't exist before," he said to himself, "a thing, a fact, your own, absolute, unassailable. Do something with it. Don't let it just stand there. Make something happen—an elation, a joy."

* * *

The first words by Daniel Fuchs I ever read were a paragraph typed and posted on the bulletin board of William Maxwell, a fiction editor at *The New Yorker*, when I worked in the magazine's offices in the mid-1950s. Maxwell, Fuchs's editor, had loved this paragraph—something about clowns and balloons, in my fading memory—enough to type it up and pin it up as an epitome of elation and joy in prose. (It was Maxwell, I believe, to whom Fuchs was referring, in the introduction to his collection *The Apathetic Bookie Joint*, as "the most urbane and kindliest man I have ever known.") The copyright credits for *The Apathetic Bookie Joint* list a number of *New Yorker* short stories after 1937, but they stop in 1942, to resume, briefly, with four titles, in 1953–54. Brendan Gill, in my hearing, exclaimed of this resumption, "Boy, didn't he come out of the West with his six-guns blazing!" They all, including "The Golden West" in this volume, were dazzling stories. Fuchs's demonstration, after a decade's silence, of so much vitality, subtlety, clairvoyance, and edginess in the short-story form made him something of a legend in Eastern literary circles. How could the writer of such fiction be content with the drudgery, the compromises, the abasement of screenwriting?

In his 1989 Letter from Hollywood, published in *Commentary* as "Strictly Movie," he himself wrote:

> Critics and bystanders who concern themselves with the plight of the Hollywood screenwriter don't know the real grief that goes with the job. The worst is the dreariness in the dead sunny afternoons when you consider the misses, the scripts you've labored on and had high hopes for and that wind up on the shelf, when you think of the mountains of failed screenplays on the shelf at the different movie companies; in all my time at the studios, I managed to get my name on a little more than a dozen pictures, most unmemorable, one a major success.

Little more than a dozen pictures, most with shared credits, in all those decades seems a bleak harvest. The "major success," for which Fuchs received an Academy Award, was *Love Me or Leave Me*. Fuchs credits its success to Joe Pasternak's getting James Cagney to act the part of the crippled thug Moe Snyder; he doesn't mention the sensation of the picture, what the crowds paid to see—Doris Day's playing a tough girl, the singer Ruth Etting, smoking and drinking and getting knocked around and standing spread-legged in a spangly little flapper dress and singing, "Come on, Big Boy—ten cents a dance!" Fuchs follows his description of the screenwriter's sorrows with the demur "It's the same when you write for publication, on your own. . . . Of course, the difference is that in the

movies you get paid when you fail and there is that to carry you over."
This ignores the likelihood that the print-writer, if he possesses Fuchs's
distinction and contacts, will wind up with a published book, a work all
his own, warped by no actor or director or producer or studio head, available for years to come in libraries if not in bookstores, a virtually everlasting personal testament.

In fact, Fuchs was dissatisfied with writing for print before Hollywood
beckoned. His three novels had received some good notices but didn't
sell, and would have sold less if his fellow-schoolteachers hadn't loyally
bought a number. He accepted an ill-fated invitation from the Broadway
producer Jed Harris (who appears in "Triplicate" as the provocative, self-
destructive Rogers Hammet) to adopt his novel *Homage to Blenholt*, and
the experience, though nothing finally came of it, left Fuchs with an
appetite for outscale, show-biz personalities: "He put on a continuous
show. It had been a revelation, all new to me—the recklessness, his commitment to his star, the fierce expenditure of energy and the turbulence
he created around him." This quotation comes from a remarkably full
account of himself that Fuchs wrote in 1987 for Gale's *Contemporary
Authors Autobiography Series*. In the same piece he describes his growing
distrust of his own writing, its humor, its comedy: "The brave jollity—it
increasingly seemed to me—was an evasion; it dodged and skidded
around the truth and would not meet it fairly. . . . I was, in the end, in the
peculiar position of a writer whose forte was a quality he secretly disliked
and wanted to lean on less and less and not at all, and who, on the other
hand, had no other special talent or great idea to offer in its place."

Fuchs found refuge, it would seem, in the collaborative craft of movie-
making. Like few other veterans of the script mills, he unfailingly communicates respect for the industrial process, the many-sided group effort.
His 1962 Letter from Hollywood, published in *Commentary* under the
title "Writing for the Movies," compellingly describes an early assignment, trying to save a film, already in rough cut, from the stubbornly
unsuitable acting of the lead, a thinly disguised George Raft. In this salvage operation the youthful, awe-struck Fuchs had as his collaborator a
writer "who was no less than one of perhaps the ten most important literary figures in the world"—William Faulkner. The two can't communicate, the task seems impossible, and yet, at last, "abruptly, miraculously,
everything was calm. The fever was over. Everything that needed to be
done was done. . . . The wonder was the picture. It was whole now,
sound—the myriad nerve-lines of continuity in working order, the
conglomeration of effects artfully re-juggled, brisk and full of urgent
meaning."

Fuchs saw no shame in shaping a product for a mass audience; rather, he saw wizardry, and a special kind of truth:

> It had to be a truth that was worthy and could legitimately engage an audience. It had to have an opulence; or an urbanity; or a gaiety; a strength and assurance; a sense of life with its illimitable reach and promise. As a matter of fact, it didn't even have to be the truth.

He managed to have good words to say about tyrants of the industry like Louis B. Mayer and Harry Cohn, men who, however misguided, lived for the movies, who demanded *the work*. "It was always surprising how underneath the outcries and confusion the work steadily went on. They never slackened; fighting the *malach-ha-movess* [the Hebrew Angel of Death] and the dingy seepage of time, they beat away to the limits of their strength and endowments, striving to get it right, to run down the answers, to realize and secure the picture." Twenty-seven years later, in his 1989 Letter from Hollywood, he still praised the work:

> You get absorbed in the picture-making itself. It's a large-scale, generous art or occupation, and you're grateful to be part of it. . . . What impressed me about the people on the set as I looked on was the intensity with which they worked. . . . They were artists or talented people—the photographers, set designers, editors, and others whose names you see on the credit lists. They worked with the assiduity and worry of artists, putting in the effort to secure the effect needed by the story, to go further than that and enhance the story, and not mar it.

The fiction writer works as a solitary, to please himself and, usually, a modest audience; the "large-scale, generous" corporate enterprise of motion-picture-making touched, amid all the scuffling of egos, an idealistic chord within Fuchs, a yearning for absorption in something bigger, something mass-oriented. In an ideological decade, with fascism and Communism both urging the sublimation of individual identity, Fuchs's renunciation of New York–style fiction for the Hollywood mills was a political act, a vote for the everymen and everywomen who filled the seats of the movie theatres. At the same time, it provided him with bourgeois comfort in an idyllic climate and exposed to his admiration the vivacity, intensity, and fantasy of Hollywood's immigrants from the East and Europe. There were "shenanigans and excesses" on the studio lots; there were the endless, free-form weekend parties that figure in his fiction as Chekhovian orgies of lamentation and comically confessed folly.

The longest piece of fiction here, the short novel *West of the Rockies*, concerns one of the technical problems that arise in the industry and threaten to impair the work—the star breakdown, the overload of narcissistic anxiety and self-medication that short-circuits the Marilyn Monroes and Judy Garlands of the film world and stops production. Adele Hogue, overwhelmed by "the clamor in her," has fled the set and holed up in Palm Springs. Fuchs, both tender and impatient with his heroine, limns her humble beginnings and fierce scramble into celebrity, her "fanatic energy" and "the fury in her, the rage of disbelief and bewilderment, now that all this which she had fought for so desperately was so soon to be taken away from her." She is aging, fattening: her body is guilty of "the widening at the waist—that thickening which, it had been surveyed and studied in the business, the young people in the movie houses spotted and resented, perhaps without even knowing what they resented, which from their vantage point and youth they found repellent and wouldn't accept." Yet she still "was a big name, one of the handful who really brought people into the movie house." A jaded talent agent, a former athlete and her sometime lover, Burt Claris, sees her as worth rescuing, and at the novel's end she silently mouths, "I love you, I love you, I love you," at him as they announce their engagement to the press. The author closes by musing on how "we are each of us precious to ourselves and wouldn't exchange ourselves, the being in us, with any other."

The novel, published when Fuchs was in his sixties, feels hurried, written in uncharacteristic run-on sentences, and the author's manner of glimmering diffidence verges on boredom when the plot arrives at its well-prepared climactic scenes; and yet this tale of deals forged out of weaknesses is his most limpid attempt to plumb movie magic—its human essence, the sway stars hold over an audience when mounted in a sufficiently well-engineered story, one lubricated with what Fuchs calls (in a passing homage to the obstreperous Harry Cohn) "those secret elixirs, hideously slippery and intangible, that make a work of the imagination go." The word "elixir" recurs in a brief fit of literary introspection in 1989: "What is the secret elixir that we must look for, the thing that gives a story life? . . . It's the melodic line—when it all comes together, when it sings." Fuchs in his modesty and optimism construed his tortuous Hollywood labors, with their mere dozen credited scripts, as an attempt to sing.

To Karl Shapiro: Selected Poems

KARL JAY SHAPIRO was born in Baltimore in 1913; when he was drafted into the peacetime army, in March of 1941, he was no teenage conscript but a twenty-seven-year-old man whose poetic vocation was already well developed. His poems were appearing in *Poetry* and *Partisan Review*, and on the eve of his shipping out to Australia in 1942 (on the *Queen Mary* painted gray as a troopship), he had arranged with Reynal & Hitchcock for his first commercially published collection, *Person, Place and Thing*. This was not his first appearance between hard covers. In 1935, his father and uncle had arranged, through a medical-textbook company, for a volume, *Poems*, to be privately printed by The Waverly Press in Baltimore— an event sardonically recalled in "Recapitulations," number V. In 1941, twenty-one of his poems, under the laconic overall title "Noun," represented him in *Five Young American Poets*, the second of a New Directions series. *Person, Place and Thing* appeared in 1942, though a year was to pass before he saw a copy; it won warm reviews* and *Poetry*'s Levinson Prize. While stationed in Australia, he became the friend and lover of Cecily Crozier, the editor of the literary magazine *A Comment;* his lively memoir of his youth, *The Younger Son*, disguised her as "Bonamy Quorn." She published for him, in 1942, in Melbourne, a new collection, *The Place of Love*, containing poems of his and fragments of the letters they exchanged when his military duties separated them. He was in the Medical Corps, and saw most of his action in New Guinea. In his three years overseas, under what his introduction called "the peculiarly enlivening circumstances of soldiering," he composed most of the contents of *V-Letter and Other Poems* (1944) and all of the 2,030-line verse *Essay on Rime* (1945). *V-Letter*, edited and arranged by his agent and future first wife, Evalyn Katz, won the 1945 Pulitzer Prize for Poetry.

While still a soldier, Shapiro had already achieved some celebrity back in the States as "a kind of phenomenon, a poet in the Battle Zone." Honors awaited him in peacetime America. He served in 1946–47 as the Consultant in Poetry at the Library of Congress, a post now dignified as Poet Laureate. In 1947 he was named an associate professor at Johns Hopkins, though his own forays into higher education had never quite earned him a college degree. He left that job in 1950 to edit *Poetry* in Chicago; in 1956 he became professor at the University of Nebraska and the editor of *Prairie Schooner.* From 1966 to 1968 he taught at the Circle Campus of the University of Illinois in Chicago, and from 1968 to 1985 at the University of California at Davis.

His reputation, to some extent, went west with him; Robert Lowell and Elizabeth Bishop became the favored poets of his generation, and

---

*"His is on all grounds the finest young American talent to appear in many seasons"— Louise Bogan in *The New Yorker.* "A book which everyone interested in modern poetry ought to read"—Delmore Schwartz in *The Nation.*

though Shapiro won the Bollingen Prize in 1968, the award was shared with John Berryman. Impolitically, he published criticism of his peers, beginning with *Essay on Rime*. "Nothing is more perilous to a poet's reputation than indulgence in criticism," he wrote in *The Younger Son*, but "he* didn't see any point in keeping mum about anything so important as his opinion." His publication, in 1964, of *The Bourgeois Poet*, consisting entirely of untitled, aggressively personal, and frequently sardonic prose-poems, seemed almost an abdication, alienating readers who had admired his mastery and variety of metrical form. In later verse he wryly noted that "My Fame's Not Feeling Well" and registered his irritation at such a slight as his being dropped from the 1976 edition of *The Oxford Book of American Verse*, having been well represented in the 1950 edition ("On Being Yanked from a Favorite Anthology").† With his third wife, the translator Sophie Wilkins,‡ Shapiro returned to the Eastern United States in 1994, and he lived on New York City's Upper West Side until his death in the year 2000.

His habits of mind were restless and contrarian. The originality, charm, and power of his early poems lie in their eagerness to render aspects of American experience never before given the dignity of a high rhetoric. Shapiro came to poetry in the wake of his more academically gifted older brother, Irvin; he grew up overhearing Irvin's conversations with his intellectual friends and prowling through the large number of books that came into the house by way of overflow from his father's moving-and-storage business, which included appropriation of unclaimed lots. The younger son read Poe, Baltimore's own in his last years, and Whitman, and late Victorians like Coventry Patmore and Charles Algernon Swinburne, whose long lines haunted Karl Shapiro's verse into his maturity; he was perhaps the last significant poet with an appetite and a flair for anapestic meter. The poems in his first, privately published volume include quaintly crabbed love sonnets, Shakespearean rather than Petrarchan in form; a rondeau, a triolet, a villanelle; verses of an antiquarian quaintness ("Gladdith! thy flag aflaunt / Thou lusty Troyno-

---

*Writing in the 1980s, Shapiro follows Norman Mailer's example and speaks of himself in the third person, as "the poet."

†The 1950 edition was edited by F. O. Matthiessen, to whom Shapiro dedicated a collection and addressed a heroic poem on the anniversary of the critic's suicide; the 1976 edition was edited by the critic and Joyce biographer Richard Ellmann, who in "On Being Yanked . . ." appears as an "antisemitic Jew," a "text-louse, pilpulistic Joycean cockroach," and a "whore."

‡His second wife, Teri Kovach, whom he had married in the year, 1967, of his divorce from Evalyn Katz, died in 1982. Shapiro remarried in 1985.

vaunt!"); and then, after this elaborate Georgian eclecticism, spare free verse skinny and clipped on the page, imitating E. E. Cummings and William Carlos Williams.

Williams was his first living exemplar; he sent the Rutherford doctor a copy of *Poems* and Williams responded with "a long reply, a warm, friendly, encouraging greeting that said nothing about the quality of the poems." Shapiro, in *The Younger Son*, praises Williams as his favorite American poet, though he cannot be, he says, a Williams disciple. The doctor-poet, in his Rutherford domain, functioned as "an authority and a savior and a cop, a force in the little town," and his minimal, direct, joyful poems on "an apple on the porch rail or a cat putting his foot into the jam pot" required, Shapiro felt, "a sense of propriety": "Williams was an owner, and the young poet could never own Baltimore." Baltimore was owned by others—the rich old Catholic families and "the richer blue-eyed Protestants" and even the Sephardic and Germanic Jews. An offspring of Russian Jews living "on a modest car-lined street where the almost-rich Jews lived" would have to settle for being "a spy or at least a watcher."

Williams, with his direct embrace of American facts, gave Shapiro his attitude. Auden gave him his voice, "the natural modern diction and the use of words that had never appeared in poetry, textbook words, newspaper words, the convoluted syntax, the mixture of economics and love, the brilliance and the gloom." Baltimore, especially Jewish Baltimore, was a center of Communist activity; Shapiro discovered Auden in a British magazine in a Communist bookstore, and was inspired by the "long Auden historical-prophetic sweep" to write the most ambitious of his juvenile poems, a tortuous meditation on Marxism called "Irenicon," clotted with words like "trepid," "connate," and "guerdon." It is rough chewing, but at least Shapiro had taken a bite of the real city around him:

> If squirrels were rats, how ugly they would be—
> And passing the dumps, these men seem rats enough,
> In fire-silt trudging the bitterness of trash. . . .

A frequent streetcar ride carried the poet past an extensive cemetery, and, as he relates in *The Younger Son*,

> he began to think of a poem about this great city of the dead, which when he wrote it would have a slightly Marxist tone of indignation, touching on the class distinctions of the cemetery world. . . . It would be his first authentic poem, as he thought of it in afteryears, and for the poetics he could thank Auden, at least for the diction of the epithets.

The poem was "Necropolis," and my selection begins with it. "Necropolis," together with "University," "Midnight Show," and "Love Poem," made up the first batch of his poems accepted by *Poetry*, in August of 1940; he tells of how he read the blue note of acceptance at the trolley stop, waved the trolley past, ran back to his apartment, phoned to inform his employer (Sears, Roebuck) that he would not be in that day, and "sat back and read holes in the blue notice." "Auto Wreck" is another early poem whose inspiration he recalled. Leaving an evening of lovemaking with a perfume salesgirl whose sexuality receives his memoir's highest rating, he encountered, while walking the three miles back home through the summer night, a spectacular, sickening auto wreck. For more than a page he dwells upon the prosody of the poem, its iambs and spondees, and Donne's and Herbert's and Milton's exemplary metrics, and then explains

> To leave her in the peace of the night and walk home in sleeping streets among sleepers, straight into this nightmare, was like the world just now, seemingly quietly going about its business but walking straight into the nightmare that nobody could stop.

The future soldier-poet was already moving toward the coming nightmare, "for the world was now wound to the utmost tightness in spite of the last détente." His anticipatory mood reached a climax in the surreal, jangling "Scyros," which was also influenced by seventeenth-century diction, its stanza based on that of Milton's "Nativity Ode." It is a poem Shapiro included in all his self-anthologies, though it is untypical— Auden at his most unconscionably jaunty—and not easy to make sense of, even when we know that Scyros is where Rupert Brooke died and that the odd epigraph "snuffle and sniff and handkerchief" is from a poem by him. Some other poems, too, are clarified by what Shapiro remembers about their inspirations: the snide tone of "University" derived from a snub delivered to him on the campus of the University of Virginia ("unequals blankly pass"), not by a Gentile but by two German Jews who had been friendly acquaintances in Baltimore. Shapiro's mother came from Virginia, his family lived there for a time, and he thought of himself as something of a Southerner. Emporia was the Virginia town where his maternal grandfather had a dry-goods store, a modest "Emporium." On the troopship taking him to Australia, Shapiro used some of his time translating Baudelaire's poem "Giantess." "Glass Poem" arose from a "big one-room apartment" in Australia, "full of reflections and distracting glimmers"; the poem capped his seduction of the room's inhabitant. "Phenomenon," he tells us in a note, "refers to the world of the Nazis," and the sonnet "Carte Postale" is easier to grasp under its final title, "French Postcard."

In general Shapiro's poems are accessible without private clues—perhaps, for New Critical tastes, too accessible. Randall Jarrell, in phrasing whose subtle hostility did not prevent Shapiro from quoting it, described the poems as "fresh and young and rash and live; their hard clear outline, their flat bold colors create a world like that of a knowing and skillful neo-primitive painting, without any of the confusion or profundity of atmosphere." Shapiro recalled of his beloved perfume salesgirl that "she was, like him, one of those born with the happiness gene," and his models, Whitman and Williams and Auden, were happy poets, busily turning the world into words. Even amid "the necessary futility of war," the poet-soldier "would not go so far as to say he was happy, but he wasn't the opposite, either; his writing saw to that." His mind-set is opposed to that of Eliot and Lowell, for whom the world is invincibly tainted and in some distasteful way alien. Of himself Shapiro said, "To write poetry out of commonplaceness is to love or accept the common, and in fact he did." In such poems as "Auto Wreck," "Drug Store," "Buick," "Haircut," and "Honkytonk," an urban, commercialized, industrial environment is illumined and cherished in a prosody ranging from rolling, raucous anapests to packed iambic pentameter, a formal virtuosity learned from Auden and from autodidactic study of classic English poetry. The poet's tone is breezy, surly, rapturous as the mood rapidly shifts. The last lines often stub our toe and invite us to reread. The concreteness can seem defiant, in-your-face. The reader does not forget a line like the first of "The Fly": "O hideous little bat, the size of snot."

"No ideas but in things," William Carlos Williams had said. Shapiro follows the dictum but in a more ornate style than the fragmentary Imagism and free-floating voices of those moderns influenced by Ezra Pound. A late poem, "Bill Williams," pays tribute to the

> Hard-working slum doc and fulltime poet
> Whose poems were prescriptions,
> Who tried to get the monkey Ezra off his back
> And never quite kicked the habit.

Shapiro thought a great deal about the politics of poetics and probably wrote more poems about other poets, living and dead, than any other poet of his stature. His book-length *Essay on Rime* is an earnest, methodical tour de force, an extended schoolbook exercise represented herein with a few excerpts, if only to illustrate the severe seriousness with which poetry was taken by the generation of which this one member, without research materials but, as the company clerk, in control of a typewriter, pounded out this *summa poetica* at the rate of thirty lines a day in the heat of embattled New Guinea.

The poems of *V-Letter* are somewhat looser than those of *Person, Place and Thing*, and less studious in avoiding clichés. Shapiro's tenderness and candor make them the foremost verse monument to that war's daily reality. This was American soldiering, from the receipt of V-Mail on the first page ("Aside") to the sending of it on the last. In between, there were an amputation, camp movies, the fear of bombs falling under a full moon, and a self-inflicted death whose commemoration accepts the perhaps inevitable rhyming of "in pain" with "not died in vain." His introduction stated, "I try to write freely, one day as a Christian, the next as a Jew, the next as a soldier who sees the gigantic slapstick of modern war." Shapiro knew he was fortunate in that the Army cast him—on no more basis, his memoir speculates, than his coming from the hospital town of Baltimore—as a healer rather than a killer; he wondered how well he would have done as an infantryman. As a medical corpsman, he won four bronze stars, achieved the rank of sergeant, survived air raids and landings under bombardment, witnessed much suffering, and did an impressive amount of writing and tomcatting.

His poems do not wave the flag, nor do they mock it. Like most young males of the time, he accepted the call to arms without protest: "the poet, for all his elbow-rubbing with Socialists, Communists, Trotskyites, believed in—Virginia." He recalled with distaste the phony medical discharge that a fellow-student from Baltimore arranged for himself. Some stress overseas seems indicated by his flirtation, in New Guinea, with conversion to Catholicism; an attractive fellow-student at the Pratt Library School had urged her religion on him, but the chaplain brushed him off. Traces of this Christian by-blow remain in his poems ("The Convert," "The Missal," number X of "Recapitulations," and the last of "Six Religious Lyrics"). His lower-case catholicity goes with his wish to contain, like Whitman, contradictions, to cover all bets—an anti-Communist who consorts with Communists, an atheist who says his prayers. Like Bellow and Mailer, he is interested in his Jewishness, and does not deny it, but is more interested in the general enterprise of being American.

From the 1942 Australian volume *The Place of Love*, the impetuous and dishevelled issue of a love affair, I have taken a brief prose-poem, "My Hair," which Shapiro never reprinted, as well as the sonnet "The Tongue." Both these small poems give us a tactile intimacy not always allowed by the young poet's grave and pugnacious artifice. A selection from Shapiro's full poetic output should include enough of the early poems that form his reputation's base without stinting the venturesome, often rakish later work. His first truly postwar collection was *Trial of a Poet* (1947), and I have taken forty lines from the long title poem to illustrate the Jewish poet's magnanimous attempt to dramatize and understand the foremost literary scandal of the decade, Ezra Pound's trial for treason, with its Solomonic decision to confine him not as a traitor but as a madman. The Pound drama involved Shapiro personally, since, after being initially seduced by Eliot's personal appeal, he ended up opposing the 1948 Bollingen Prize to Pound; as the Library of Congress's former Consultant in Poetry, Shapiro had a vote in the matter. Pound won anyway, but his strident anti-Semitism did not pass without editorial protest: in an article in *The Partisan Review*, Shapiro wrote, "I voted against Pound in the belief that the poet's political and moral philosophy ultimately vitiates his poetry." Characteristically, a few years later, in *Poetry*, he repeated this assertion but added, "Otherwise I can only say that the book the *Pisan Cantos* was the best book of verse of that year, and of many years."

Most of the poems in the collection *Poems of a Jew* (1958) had been published in earlier books; his introduction served as a pledge of allegiance to his Jewishness, complex and elusive yet insistent as it was:

> The Jewish Question, whatever that might be, is not my concern. Nor is Judaism. Nor is Jewry. Nor is Israel. . . . I am one of those who views with disgust and disappointment . . . the backsliding of artists and intellectuals toward religion. . . . These poems, in any case, are not religious poems but the poems of a Jew. No one has been able to define *Jew*, and in essence this defiance of definition is the central meaning of Jewish consciousness. . . . As a third-generation American I grew up with the obsessive idea of personal liberty which engrosses all Americans except the oldest and richest families. As a Jew I grew up in an atmosphere of mysterious pride and sensitivity, an atmosphere in which even the greatest achievement was touched by a sense of the comic.

In spite of himself Shapiro was a ground-breaker, in a country whose literature had been predominantly Protestant since the Puritans. The only American Jewish poet he had read as a young man was the pseudo-Biblical, now forgotten James Oppenheimer. In academic English departments, there were Lionel Trilling at Columbia and Harry Levin at Harvard and precious few others. As Shapiro wrote to Lee Bartlett, his bibliographer, "I was the second Jew to be hired at Johns Hopkins, and a good friend of mine was the first Jew to get a Ph.D. at Hopkins. This is recent history! But now of course the Jews practically run the place." He once thought of changing his name to the Waspish "Karl Camden," but settled for "Karl," a more Germanic, and hence higher-class, spelling than the original "Carl." Even without formal Jewish affiliations, he responded to the founding of Israel with the stirring "Israel," read at a mass meeting in Baltimore, and composed long poems on Adam and Eve, David and Bathsheba, and Moses.

The title of *The Bourgeois Poet* (1964) came from the mouth of another poet, Shapiro told his assiduous bibliographer. After a reading in Seattle, the drunken Theodore Roethke greeted his entry at a party with, "Well, here comes the bourgeois poet!" Thence Shapiro resolved, "I was going to accept the fact that I am a bourgeois poet. . . . I wanted to say, 'Yeah, I do like living in split-level houses, and so on.' " It seems odd that Shapiro would thus be singled out, since postwar academic appointments for poets and "creative" writers had generated a large tribe of housebroken penmen and, later, penwomen, habituated to steady wages, the adoration of students, and residence in green and pleasant college communities. Nevertheless, he did feel a difficulty in "being a poet and a bourgeois American at the same time," and his upbringing among the Marxists of Baltimore perhaps lent a special sting to the epithet. The original text of the book was much longer and was edited down by the poet and his long-time editor, Albert Erskine; but, he confided to Bartlett, "I've always felt I should have re-edited it, making it less jerky and less obscure."

The published version consisted of ninety-six untitled pieces of prose ranging in length from six lines to ten pages. When some of these took their place in his *Selected Poems* (1968), they were titled with their opening words, but in *Collected Poems 1940–1978*, they were given short titles, which I have adopted here. One poem not in the 1978 volume I have titled myself ("War Movies"). That Shapiro had an appetite for writing prose is evident in his numerous reviews, his several books of essays,* his two volumes of autobiography,† his messy but vigorous and scabrous lone

---

Beyond Criticism (1953); *In Defense of Ignorance* (1960); *To Abolish Children and Other Essays* (1968); *The Poetry Wreck: Selected Essays 1950–1970* (1975).

†The second volume, *Reports of My Death*, came out in 1990, two years after *The Younger Son*. It is relatively diffuse and dispirited as it sketches the literary and academic life experienced after 1945 by the returned soldier-poet. In the first volume, poetry is his *princesse lointaine*; in the second, he has married her. His offhand, rather truculent prose picks up in the last two chapters. The depression and attempted suicide of his second wife weirdly metamorphose into false journalistic reports of his own suicide, which depress him. Teri's swift death by cancer is soon followed by the advent of Shapiro's third wife, Sophie; the last chapter describes a visit he and she, a native Austrian, paid to the tomb of his hero, Auden, and the poem that resulted.

novel, *Edsel*, and in his prose-poems, which he produced early, after the examples of Baudelaire, Rimbaud, and Eliot. During his Library of Congress appointment he showed a copy of *The Place of Love* to the French Nobel Laureate Saint-John Perse, who "said that I should write in the style of 'The Dirty Word'; in other words, the prose poem."

White-Haired Lover (1968), a volume of dainty slenderness, composed of sanserif apostrophes, mostly sonnets, to his second wife; *Adult Bookstore* (1976), whose venues have moved from Nebraska and Chicago to California and whose title was also that of a movie that Shapiro made but was "too hot" to distribute; and *The Old Horsefly* (1992), dedicated to his third wife in the Latin of Horace and crotchety-magisterial in tone: these volumes returned the bourgeois prose-poet to the conventional look of verse on the page. There is little trace of Auden's metrical acrobatics and deft hand with great issues, though the presumptions of Sixties militant radicals do lead Shapiro to compose a sestina parodying the vocabulary of the counter-culture. He became conservative, or perhaps had always been, growing up skeptical among Baltimore's Communists. He writes in *The Old Horsefly* of what has always concerned him most, poetry and poets—Whitman and Williams, Ovid and Hopkins, Joyce and Stevens, and Eliot and Pound, who functioned not only as his *bêtes noires* but his *points de départ*, the inescapable modernists. With his untiring eye for American facts he writes about Kleenex; New York City; the plague of Creative Writing, "stronger than gonorrhea"; and "Fucking," of which he disarmingly confesses, "I never got the hang of it, really."

In his lifetime Shapiro published, aside from *Poems of a Jew*, five selections of his own work: *Poems 1940–1953*, *Selected Poems* (1968), *Collected Poems 1940–1978*, *Love & War, Art & God: The Poems of Karl Shapiro* (1984), and *New & Selected Poems 1940–1986*. This last distillation is just over a hundred pages long; any poem in it that was shunned in my own selection I reread attentively, hoping to like it better. I have partaken sparingly of Shapiro the balladeer and deviser of historical tableaux—Beethoven dying, Admiral Peary seeking admission to Japan. He has a mood of lofty apostrophe which can become overbearing, and which makes his smaller, airier lyrics appealing to an anthologist. My choices are arranged in roughly chronological order, in line with known magazine-publication dates, his own accountings, and the move into wartime and back. I have kept, after omitting a number, the poems from *V-Letter* in the sequence devised by his loving agent.

When a poet makes a selection of himself, there are elements of suppression, of reshaping his work in line with the ongoing creativity. Perspectives change again with an artist's death. He becomes an inhabitant of history, an index to certain global moments. And we treasure, more than he did, revelations of the man, the personality, with his soft spots for war and Christmas and tough plebeian streets, his habits of contention and sentiment, his "American slouch," as he explained in *The Younger Son:*

> The poet must wear his uniform lightly, and unlike the General's it is not part of his skin. . . . He must wear his America lightly like a civilian, he must glow with it and not flaunt it. It was part of his luck, his ease, part of the American slouch.

He aimed to be what the Germans called a *Dinge Dichter,* a thing poet. He wrote of himself: "The substantive [*Person, Place and Thing; Noun*] fascinated him, as something to fix upon and hold on to." His feet planted on the substantive, he could be modest and casual but also bold, with the boldness of truth personally verified. Though he is best remembered, still, as the poet in khaki, Shapiro devoted his long peacetime life to the modernist battle, a fight for the specific and pressingly contemporary, a rescue of language from poetic conventions, easy assumptions, usages worn smooth, polite palaver, rhetoric:

> That was the enemy, rhetoric, and always had been. Leave patriotic and antipatriotic to John Philip Sousa. Poets had tastier fish to fry—what soldiering was like, what it did to the man, the soul, the poetry, and the artifacts everywhere, the Buicks, the university, the grandmothers, the flies, oh the flies, American flies in Petersburg, Virginia.

To Elephant House, or, The Home of Edward Gorey,
photographs and text by Kevin McDermott

EDWARD GOREY was, artistically speaking, a thin man who cast a fat shadow. His books, all of them slender and most of them distinctly whimsical, inspired an enthusiasm and loyalty disproportionate to their size. Edmund Wilson, no less, became a Gorey fan and collector, and in a lengthy *New Yorker* review admired how Gorey "has created a whole little personal world, equally amusing and somber, nostalgic and claustrophobic, at the same time poetic and poisoned."

Gorey came to my own attention when I entered Harvard in the fall of 1950: the Registration Issue of *The Harvard Advocate,* the college literary magazine, sported a cover drawn by "Edward St. J. Gorey" that showed, startlingly, two browless, mustachioed, long-footed, high-collared, seemingly Edwardian gentlemen tossing sticks at two smiling though disembodied jesters' heads. The previous term's Commencement Issue, also made available to incoming freshmen, displayed a virtually identical pair of bizarrely profiled male persons, this time waving "L'adieu," with white handkerchiefs and akimbo feet, to what appeared to be an Arctic sun. The style was eccentric but consummately mature; it hardly changed in the next fifty years, as I followed it on Anchor Books (the pioneering quality-paperback line, with many covers drawn and lettered by Gorey), through a hail of playbills and precious chapbooks, to its belated arrival in the pages of *The New Yorker* and its superb animated version in the opening titles of WGBH's *Mystery!* television program.

An artist and writer who rarely strayed from his curious corner of Anglophile nostalgia, he wound up widely on view. Like another Edward, Lear, he was a cheerfully morbid bachelor uncle who declined to follow the example of Saint Paul and put away childish things. His hobbies, from the ballet of Balanchine to antique-store gleanings, were pursued with a vocational thoroughness—indeed, his life was virtually *all* hobby. Kevin McDermott's photographs of his home, taken a week after Gorey's sudden death at the age of seventy-five, show a master collector, an acquisitor of appealing oddments who in his solitude filled room after room with inanimate friends—dolls and stones and tomes and metal frogs and tinted glass and lead sinkers and marble eggs and TV tapes and simulacra of elephants. Then there were the living cats, occasionally dabbling in wet ink as Gorey labored at his tiny worktable, and the big old wooden house itself; New Englanders will recognize the peeling sills, the loosening panes, the pine floorboards, the comfortable sense of partial abandonment.

Wood deteriorates but can always be renewed and replaced; such houses prompt a spirit of improvisation, and this spirit lingers here, embodied in an endless collection of cherished things. McDermott's photographs bring us closer to Gorey than his art, in a way; the art evoked a unique bygone world he and we could escape to, where patient crosshatching deepened wistful shadows and the shy personae never looked us in the eye. Gorey the householder feels like a happier man, who threw nothing out, and kept the pleasure in everything. The odd miniature worlds of his books were ones he somehow wanted to inhabit; here is the world, equally personal and creative, that he *did* inhabit.

To Christmas at The New Yorker: Stories, Poems, Humor, and Art

NEW YORK CITY is the capital of the American Christmas. The Puritan settlements to the north banned the holiday as Popish and pagan; and so it was, descended from the ancient Roman solstitial Saturnalia. But mercantile, diverse Nieuw Amsterdam—not just Dutch fur-traders but French-speaking Protestant Walloons; arrivals from Ireland, Spain, Portugal, and Poland; African slaves; twenty-three Sephardic Jews (as of 1654); a Danish sea-captain, Jonas Bronck, whose farm "the Broncks" gave its name to a borough; and, in the alarmed words of Peter Stuyvesant's adviser the Calvinist minister Johannes Megapolensis, "Papists, Mennonites, and Lutherans among the Dutch"—celebrated two separate winter occasions with gift-giving. Saint Nicholas Day, on December 6th, involved Santa Claus and goodies left in good children's wooden shoes; New Year's Day was the traditional Dutch day for adult presents and ceremonial calls.

When the English took over in 1664, they brought with them an Anglican toleration of customs frowned upon by the stricter Reformed churches. Saint Nicholas survived the eighteenth century and by the early nineteenth his day had merged with the English Christmas. In 1823, a New Yorker, the Bible scholar Clement Clarke Moore (who also donated the land on which the General Theological Seminary of the Episcopal Church stands), published the poem, beginning "'Twas the night before Christmas," that gave Christmas its American mythos. The most famous American short story about the holiday, O. Henry's "The Gift of the Magi," was composed by an adopted New Yorker and concerns two humble, striving, big-hearted members of the city's then population of four million; it appeared in the *New York World* in 1905, and in the author's 1906 collection *The Four Million*. The best-known American Christmas movie, *Miracle on 34th Street* (1947), takes place in and around Macy's, and was partly shot on location. In the Yuletide season, which now begins before Halloween and extends through many a worried January review of consumer shopping performance, Manhattan becomes one big bauble—a towering mass of glowing boxes, a cascade of elaborate window displays, an island gaily tied with ribbons called, north-south, avenues and, east-west, streets. The Empire State Building glows red and green; Saint Patrick's Cathedral gazes toward Rockefeller Center's giant Christmas tree while rubbing its left shoulder against Saks Fifth Avenue, one of the enduring venues of spectacular Christmas windows. Throughout America, Main Street has run to the suburbs and hidden in the malls, but New York still wears Christmas on its sleeve. Here Salvation Army bell-ringers still tend charity's tripodded pot and chestnuts roast on street vendors' grills. Here Santa Claus sports, behind his white beard, many a sub-Arctic complexion.

So it is no wonder that *The New Yorker*, a publication devoted since 1925 to the gala spirit of its eponymous metropolis, has generously partaken, year after year, of Christmas cheer. The writer of this preface, when a boy, intimately associated the magazine with the season, since his list for Santa usually included one of the *New Yorker* cartoon anthologies that, in the early decades of the magazine's existence, were regularly offered to book-buyers. The glossy paper of these droll and sophisticated albums gathered sheen from the snow (or hopes of snow) outside the living-room windows; the scent of the fresh binding glue mingled with the resin of the family Christmas tree; the elegance of the drawings glittered like the paper star topping the tree. Those big slim volumes, either devoted to an individual cartoonist—Arno, Addams, Cobean, Robert Day, George Price, Carl Rose—or culled from a few years of the magazine's run, endure on my shelves, sixty years later, as still-precious remembrances of otherwise irrecoverable Christmases past.

But the book in your hands contains more than cartoons. It samples *The New Yorker*'s breadth of offerings—covers, fiction, poetry, humor, reminiscence, Talk of the Town, even spot drawings and newsbreaks—as it basked in the Christmas glow from 1925 (Rea Irvin, depicting a maharaja receiving an elaborately presented necktie) to 2002 (Roz Chast, showing Santa Claus being nagged by his elves). The editors have sifted assiduously, retrieving the tiniest bright bit of tinsel along with paper chains, cranberry festoons, papier-mâché angels, and hand-painted glass balls the size of emu eggs. Here you will find James Thurber rewriting Clement Moore's poem in the voice of Hemingway (1927); S. J. Perelman putting Santa's workshop onstage in the manner of Clifford Odets (1936); William Cox redoing "The Gift of the Magi" for hippies (1967); Max Hill remembering a not totally unmerry Christmas in a Japanese prison (1942); and Alice Munro evoking, more fondly still, a season of girlhood spent gutting Christmas turkeys in Ontario (1980). Here are poems by Karl Shapiro and Phyllis McGinley, Adrienne Rich and Ogden Nash, James Dickey and Calvin Trillin and others, in mood reverent or ir-, in form rhymed or un-, in import pro-Christmas or anti-. "Greetings, Friends!," of which four rollicking examples are included, is, of course, the annual seasonal salute, in rhymed couplets of festive breeziness, that *The New Yorker* has traditionally addressed to its friends and selected celebrities of the day; the first was composed by Frank Sullivan in 1932 and his last in 1974; from 1976 until recently the custom has been carried on, in kindred metrics and jubilo, by Roger Angell.

Younger readers who know the opening paragraphs of The Talk of the Town, called "Notes and Comment," only as political editorials of a pondered weight, should be aware that this section began and long continued as a grab-bag of humorous oddments, a short-winded gallimaufry of mild, resolutely apolitical jests and grimaces. It was, above all, E. B. White who broadened and deepened the department; no one has ever been better at infusing a light, even facetious tone with graver notes from the inner man and the larger world. His Notes and Comment of Christmas 1944 is a wartime threnody; dozens of battles and thousands of deaths are wrapped into a central conceit, the conquered terrains of global war as Christmas presents to us, the American people. The Norman coast, Saipan, Guam, Leghorn, the Alban Hills, a forest south of Aachen, and many other hard-won territories come "not wrapped as gifts (there was no time to wrap them), but you will find them under the lighted tree with the other presents."

The magazine's covers ring the first chime and get our holiday juices flowing. Butlers, those anachronistic representatives of well-financed domestic order, figure in some of the most memorable—in 1940, Helen E. Hokinson's servitor lends a dignified finger to his harried mistress's ribbon-tying; that same December, Robert Day's man, in white hair and muffler, smartly brings a blazing plum pudding to an English bomb shelter; eight years later, Peter Arno's monumental old retainer ignites his plum-pudding brandy with a cigarette lighter. Santas—Santa being dressed by his valet, Santa punching a time clock, Santa sitting alone and rueful in a cafeteria or sitting sleek and dapper at a corporation desk where the Naughty stack towers above the Nice—recur, forming a jigsaw puzzle here and a dog's uncomfortable costume there and, in a subway car, a veritable mob of masquerading misfits, caught red-suited by George Price's scratchy pen. Curiously, this was Price's only cover, though his raffish cartoons were legion; two other prolific artists, Ralph Barton and Edward Gorey, also seized the occasion of Christmas for their solo New Yorker covers. Whereas Charles Addams, both as cover artist and as cartoonist, couldn't get enough of the holiday, unveiling a sinister side to it usually suppressed.

Suicides, notoriously, rise in the Christmas season; its call for rejoicing and universal good will stresses the human psyche in ways faithfully recorded by the seismograph of fiction. "Christmas is a kids' gag," one of John McNulty's barflies tells another in a vignette of 1944. For the characters in Sally Benson's "Spirit of Christmas" and Peter De Vries's "Flesh and the Devil," the holiday stirs up romantic sparks and marital awkwardness. For those in Emily Hahn's "No Santa Claus" and Richard Ford's "Crèche," the celebrative muddle borders on the noir. Frank O'Connor's "Christmas Morning" ends with this grim realization by the young hero:

> I knew there was no Santa Claus flying over the rooftops with his reindeer and his red coat—there was only my mother trying to scrape together a few pence from the housekeeping money that my father gave her. I knew that he was mean and common and a drunkard, and that she had been relying on me to study and rescue her from the misery which threatened to engulf her.

At the other extreme, John Cheever's "Christmas Is a Sad Season for the Poor" argues that the city's lower echelons, beginning with elevator operators, are overwhelmed by a surfeit of gifts, rich and poor all "bound, one to another, in licentious benevolence." Licentious benevolence!

Christmas can cast a harsh, cold light. But in William Maxwell's "Homecoming" and Vladimir Nabokov's "Christmas" it shines in two death-scarred households, as, respectively, an electrical connection is mended and an old cocoon gives birth. Ken Kesey and H. L. Mencken see a measure of cheer brought to Skid Row. In Patrick Chamoiseau's Martinique, a cherished pig becomes gifts for many; in J. F. Powers's Minnesota, a peripatetic priest finds "Christmas as it was celebrated nowadays still pretty much to his liking" and compares the season's agile, hard-breathing merchants to the tumbler who performed acrobatics as an offering to Our Lady. In the Pennsylvania of John O'Hara and Linda Grace Hoyer, poetry and memory shed grace on a rather obligatory social whirl. To get through the year's shortest, darkest days, we grasp at straws. The holiday offers little resistance to the secular; its hustle blends, in New York, with the all-year hustle. There is something in the Christmas story for everyone—the baby in the manger for innocents, the sheep and the oxen for animal lovers, Joseph for natural bystanders, the Magi for diversity and high fashion, the Star for astrophysicists. The whole panorama sprouted from rather few Biblical verses: the Virgin Birth and the wise men appear in Matthew, the Annunciation and shepherds and angels and the manger in Luke. If crèches, halos, and bended knees have been phased out of department-store windows, that still leaves Frosty the Snowman and Rudolph the Red-Nosed Reindeer, Tiny Tim and sleigh riders from the fabled Knickerbocker days, with top hats and ermine muffs. The tree with pagan roots continues to accept grafts.

The art and prose and poetry assembled here range widely in setting and tone, but for this sentimental reader it kept coming home to an older, gentler, more credulous New York, a pre–Lever House city of brick and granite, a pre-television city that lived for parties, a city where a wreath on an apartment door and a tree in a brownstone window came and went as naturally as jonquils in the spring and yellow gingko leaves in the fall. The oldest poem here reports from 1926:

> When bankers quote the Golden Rule,
> And visitors enjoyment seek,
> And lads and maids are home from school,
> New York's engulfed in Christmas week.

A city, in short, *drenched* in Christmas, which is the way I think of New York in December, and the way it exists—rejoice!—in these pages.

To the German catalogue of an exhibit of photographs by Ulrich Mack of the Ipswich marshes

AS THE WORLD grows ever more cluttered with the works of Man, virgin spaces become fewer and more precious. Deserts, mountaintops, tundra, ice fields, the dwindling forests—adventurers resort to them, and the less adventurous of us rest our eyes and mind in contemplation of their images and of the holy, inhuman silence they suggest. Relatively open places lie closer to hand, in city parks and cemeteries, in golf courses and hiking trails, but among the purest and most proximate gifts of space are salt marshes. These natural meadows, largely impervious to agriculture and human development, are created and interpenetrated by the tidal motions of the ocean; they are, one could say, the sea's little offspring, meekly holding the mother's vastness and volatility in stretches of grass, mud, and cloud-mirroring channels of water. The marshes can be navigated, but with many turns and a danger of scraping bottom; they can be walked, but with a danger of a misstep into a ditch or hole. Wildlife loves them, and painters and photographers also. The mid-nineteenth-century painter Martin Johnson Heade devoted much of his oeuvre to the portrayal, on horizontal canvases, of the great marshes of the Northeastern United States, in his day the scene of summer harvests of the usefully weed-free salt hay. The German photographer Ulrich Mack, early in this twenty-first century, has made a harvest of photographic beauty in the salt marshes of Ipswich, Massachusetts, an especially spectacular stretch north of Boston, reaching from Rowley and Newbury on the north to Essex on the south.

As one who lived in Ipswich for seventeen years, and some of those years in a house on a tidal creek, I remember how, as I drove on Argilla Road toward the beach, a view of the marshes opened up at a certain turn of the road like a view from space of an alien but not hostile new planet, with blue veins and green drumlins and a distant white edge of sand dunes. I remember the warm autumnal tints of the marsh grasses, between brown and orange in intensity, and the tousled, nearly dead color of the grass as it emerged from beneath its winter load of ice-cakes, created by the cold and piled up by the tide. I remember the intimacy of the tidal channels as they snaked their way, between tall mud banks, toward the narrow terminus where the faithful push of the tide gives out, and the chill of the water that buoyed a swimmer up with the saline density of the ocean, without the ocean's waves and rocky bottom. I have known children, children of my own, who lived by the marsh and treated it as a giant toy, a planetary machine whose regular influx of water brought in fresh driftwood and empty bottles and brightly painted lobster buoys torn loose from their moorings and at rest in the wrack of high tide. I have known pink-cheeked elderly sailors whose last craft was a wide-bottomed catboat for threading the marshes, with never a foray into the open, white-crested water beyond.

The marshes are alive. Their mud bubbles with the respiration of clams and crabs; their grass hides nesting birds. They change, as mud banks erode and tidal currents find new patterns. The tides sweep through twice a day, hissing and percolating, and thus this terrain between water and land is forever clean, forever fresh. Ulrich Mack has caught this freshness, this untamed innocence, in these marvellously serene and spacious photographs of a gentle wilderness little changed since the time of Puritan duck-hunters and Native American spear-fishermen.

MONUMENTS

The Great I Am

THE FIVE BOOKS OF MOSES: *A Translation with Commentary*, by Robert Alter.
1,064 pp. Norton, 2004.

In this age of widespread education and flagging creativity, new translations abound. The old standbys who nurtured our youth—Constance
Garnett rendering the Russians, C. K. Scott Moncrieff putting his spin
on Proust, the Muirs translating Kafka, H. T. Lowe-Porter doing
Thomas Mann—are all being retired, with condescending remarks
about their slips and elisions, by successors whose more modern versions
infallibly miss, it seems to this possibly crotchety scanner, the tone, the
voice, the *presence* of the text that we first read. In general—if it's generalizations you want—the closer the translator is in time to the translated,
the more closely shared their vision and style will be. The Modern
Library chose to reprint the 1700–1703 translation of *Don Quixote* by
Peter Motteux; after that peppery stew of italicized names and apostro-
phe-bedeck'd past tenses, every other *Quixote* feels watered down.

Of all translations into English, the one most read and admired is, of
course, the King James Bible (1611), our language's lone masterpiece
produced by committee, at least until this year's *The 9/11 Commission
Report*. Nevertheless, new translations of the Bible—the world's best-
seller, long out of copyright—tumble forth, for the reasons, if any are
offered, that contemporary scholarship presents a superior understanding of ancient Hebrew and that Renaissance English is increasingly,
inconveniently archaic. The Hebrew scholar and literary critic Robert
Alter, in introducing his thousand-page version, with copious commentary, of the first five books of the Bible—commonly called the Pentateuch or Torah—under the title *The Five Books of Moses*, writes:

Broadly speaking, one may say that in the case of the modern versions, the problem is a shaky sense of English and in the case of the King James Version, a shaky sense of Hebrew. The present translation is an experiment in re-presenting the Bible—and, above all, biblical narrative prose—in a language that conveys with some precision the semantic nuances and the lively orchestration of literary effects of the Hebrew and at the same time has stylistic and rhythmic integrity as literary English.

Professor Alter, whose earlier works include *Fielding and the Nature of the Novel* (1968) and *A Lion for Love: A Critical Biography of Stendhal* (1979), has been tilling the Biblical fields ever since *The Art of Biblical Narrative* (1981) and *The Art of Biblical Poetry* (1985). As his footnotes, which take up at least half of all but a few pages, make clear, Alter is profoundly steeped not just in the linguistic details of Hebrew but in the nigh-overwhelming amount of previous commentary, including the Midrash of rabbinical interpreters going back to the early centuries of the Christian era. At the same time he has, as his oeuvre shows, an appetite for literary theory—*Motives for Fiction* (1984), *Partial Magic: The Novel as Self-Conscious Genre* (1975)—and, as the passage quoted above indicates, a resolute sense of the Biblical style to be achieved.

He sees Biblical Hebrew as a "conventionally delimited language, roughly analogous in this respect to the French of the neoclassical theatre," and significantly though indeterminately distinct from the vanished vernacular of three thousand years ago. (The vernacular vocabulary, according to the Spanish Hebrew scholar Angel Sáenz-Badillos, must have exceeded the Bible's, a lexicon "so restricted that it is hard to believe it could have served all the purposes of quotidian existence in a highly developed society.") Alter has set himself to create a corresponding English—"stylized, decorous, dignified, and readily identified by its audiences as a language of literature," with a "slight strangeness," "beautiful rhythms," and other qualities (suppleness, precision, concreteness) that "by and large have been given short shrift by translators with their eyes on other goals." Why should not Alter's version, its program so richly contemplated and persuasively outlined, become the definitive one, replacing on the shelf not only the King James but the plethora of its revised, uninspired, and "accessible" versions?

Several reasons why not, in the course of my reading through this massive tome (sold sturdily boxed, as if to support its weight), emerged. The sheer amount of accompanying commentary and philological footnotes is one of them. The fifty-four churchmen and scholars empowered at a conference at Hampton Court in January of 1604 to provide an authoritative English Bible had a clear charge: to supply English readers with a self-explanatory text. When they encountered a crux, they took their best guess and worked on; many of the guesses can be improved upon now, but no suggestion of an unclear and imperfect original was allowed to trouble the Word of God. Alter's more academic and literary commission allows him to luxuriate in the forked possibilities of the Hebrew text, in its oldest forms written entirely in consonants, and without punctuation. Sample footnotes, taken at random from Deuteronomy:

> Some recent scholars have accepted Jacob Milgrom's proposal that here the verb *q-r-b* ("approach") is used in a political extension of its cultic meaning, "to encroach upon," though there is no compelling necessity to see that sense of the word in this verse.

> The second of the two Hebrew words here, *we'oyvenu pelilim*, is a notorious crux, evidently already a source of puzzlement to the ancient Greek translators. . . . If one notes that *pelilim* rhymes richly with *'elilim*, "idols," and if one recalls this poet's verbal inventiveness in coining designations for the nonentity of the pagan gods, "would-be gods" is a distinct possibility.

It is difficult for the reader, given the overload of elucidation imposed upon the basic text, to maintain much momentum, and, indeed, one finds welcome refuge from the tedium and harshness of some Biblical passages in the companionable contemporary voice of the learned commentator. However, in his very zeal to communicate the nuances of the underlying Hebrew, Alter falls into the error of Vladimir Nabokov's translation of *Eugene Onegin:* in his effort to achieve absolute fidelity, he settles on some distinctly odd English.

Take Alter's version, for starters, of the opening verses of Genesis:

> When God began to create heaven and earth, and the earth then was welter and waste and darkness over the deep and God's breath hovering over the waters, God said, "Let there be light." And there was light.

The King James has it thus:

> In the beginning God created the heaven and the earth.
> And the earth was without form, and void; and darkness was upon the face of the deep. And the Spirit of God moved upon the face of the waters.
> And God said, Let there be light: and there was light.

Alter is the more concise, and is not above duplicating certain phrases of the King James, much as the royal committee drew upon the translation by Tyndale. But Alter's syntax goes off the rails when "God's breath hovering over the waters" is tacked onto a series of non-parallel nouns; by comparison, "And the Spirit of God moved upon the face of the waters" is clearer narrative and great poetry. It may stray minutely from the Hebrew but it is theologically intelligible.

Both translations can be usefully compared with that of Everett Fox, also titled *The Five Books of Moses* and published in 1995. Alter cites Fox as the outstanding exception to the general trend of a blandly readable English Bible—an extremist in the style of Martin Buber and Franz Rosenzweig, whose German Bible "flaunts Hebrew etymologies, preserves nearly all repetitions of Hebrew terms, and invents German words." Fox's version, set in lines like poetry, reads:

> At the beginning of God's creating of the heavens and the earth,
> when the earth was wild and waste,
> darkness over the face of Ocean,
> rushing-spirit of God hovering over the face of the waters—
> God said: Let there be light! And there was light.

This is a relatively tame specimen; elsewhere, Fox liberally coins compound adjectives like "heavy-with-stubbornness" and verbs like "adulter"—the Seventh Commandment becomes "You are not to adulter."

Alter is less extreme, but he does keep the ubiquitous sentence-beginning "and" derived from the Hebrew particle *waw;* he retains emphatic repetitions, as in "she, she, too" and "this red red stuff." He strives to preserve ambiguities and puns in the original. He conspicuously bends colloquial English in such renderings as: "Pharaoh will lift up your head from upon you"; "the land in the seven years of plenty made gatherings"; "A lion's whelp is Judah, / from the prey, O my son, you mount"; "Israel saw the great hand that the LORD had performed against Egypt"; "Moses would speak, and God would answer him with voice"; "Whether a son it gore or a daughter it gore, according to this practice it shall be done to him"; "and a man lie with her in seed-coupling"; "in the hand of the priest shall be the bitter besetting water"; "And it happened that there were men who were defiled by human corpse"; " 'Let us put up a head and return to Egypt.' "; "And the LORD said to me, saying, 'Long enough you have swung round this high country.' " Alter has an annoying trick, no doubt in deference to the Hebrew, of putting a comma where we expect an article or preposition: "it was evening and it was morning, second day"; "the tree of knowledge, good and evil." In translating Exodus, he persists in using, in reference to Pharaoh's heart, the verb "toughened" where the usual translation uses "hardened" ("And Pharaoh's heart toughened"; "And the LORD toughened Pharaoh's heart"). He tests our knowledge of livestock terminology by employing "get" as a noun, as in Deuteronomy 28:4: "Blessed the fruit of your womb and the fruit of your soil and the fruit of your beasts, the get of your herds and the offspring of your flock."

A reader, however, should not shy from the rare but exact word, and none of Alter's eccentricities of diction substantially undermines his attempt to deliver a strongly rhythmic and ruggedly direct equivalent of the Hebrew. But who will read it? Fanciers of sheer literature will be put off by its bulk and its pedantic cross-weave, and the millions of believers, Christian and Jewish, already have their versions, with cherished, trusted phrasings. The Bible in its centuries of recitation and memorization has generated a host of familiar images that turn out to be mistranslations. Jacob's ladder is really, it seems, Jacob's "ramp," the Hebrew word occurring only in this one instance and suggestive, to experts steeped in the ancient Mideast, of a Mesopotamian ziggurat. Nor did Jacob, dreaming his dream of angels ascending and descending, have his head pillowed on a stone: "Rashi, followed by some modern scholars, proposes that the stone is not placed under Jacob's head but alongside it, as a kind of protective barrier." Joseph's coat of many colors has been altered to a mere "ornamented tunic." Onan, it turns out, was not guilty of onanism but, more likely, of prudent *coitus interruptus* with his brother's widow. Michelangelo was wrong: Moses did not come down from the mountain with the second edition of the Ten Commandments having sprouted horns, as recorded in the Vulgate and Aquila's translation into the Greek. His face merely glowed, from its recent exposure to the Divinity.

Reading through this book, or five books, is a wearying, disorienting, and at times revelatory experience. Our interest trends downhill. Of Genesis, Alter writes, "If this were the work of a single writer, one would say he begins at the top of his form." The Creation, the Garden, the Fall, the Flood, the Tower of Babel, and the patriarchal saga of Abraham, Isaac, Jacob, and Joseph make a more or less continuous story. Rereading it awakened certain sensations from my Sunday-school education, more than sixty years ago, when I seemed to stand on the edge of a brink gazing down at polychrome miniatures of abasement and terror, betrayal and reconciliation. Jacob deceiving blind Isaac with patches of animal hair on the backs of his hands, Joseph being stripped of his gaudy coat and left in a pit by his brothers, little Benjamin being fetched years later by these same treacherous brothers into the imperious presence of a mysterious stranger invested with all Pharaoh's authority—these glimpses into a world ancestral to our own, a robed and sandaled world of origins and crude conflict and direct discourse with God, came to me via flimsy leaflets illustrating that week's lesson, and were mediated by the mild-mannered commentary of the Sunday-school teacher, a humorless embodiment of small-town respectability passing on conventional Christianity by rote. Nevertheless, I was stirred and disturbed, feeling exposed to the perilous basis underneath the surface of daily routine—of practical schooling and family interchange and peer pressure and popular culture.

The curious, heated familial closeness of the Biblical narrative distinguishes it from other compilations of legend. Erich Auerbach, in the first chapter of his masterly *Mimesis* (1946), compares Abraham's near-sacrifice of Isaac with an incident in the *Odyssey*, and exclaims of the Biblical characters, "How much wider is the pendulum swing of their lives than that of the Homeric heroes!" He explains:

> For they are bearers of the divine will, and yet they are fallible, subject to misfortune and humiliation. . . . There is hardly one of them who does not, like Adam, undergo the deepest humiliation—and hardly one who is not deemed worthy of God's personal intervention and inspiration.

Leaving God out of it, Auerbach claims that the Biblical protagonists give

> a more concrete, direct, and historical impression than the figures of the Homeric world—not because they are better described in terms of sense (the contrary is the case) but because the confused, contradictory multiplicity of events, the psychological and factual cross-purposes, which true history reveals, have not disappeared in the representation but still remain clearly perceptible.

In Exodus, dominated by Moses, the narrative begins to sour; the warmth and humanity of Genesis drain away. Moses is Israel's foremost prophet, but he is not a patriarch, and lacks the charm that ancestors possess. The intimate family scale of Genesis yields to something cooler and more mechanical; Alter in his introduction speaks of a "new wide-angle lens" and "the distancing of the central character and the distancing of the figure of God." Not that God is silent; He has more to say than before or since. Moses is His mouthpiece and, like any lawyer with a demanding client, Moses sometimes loses his temper. The long negotiation with Pharaoh over the release of the Jews from captivity (chapters 7 to 14) is especially aggravating, as God sends plague after plague upon Egypt, only to "toughen" Pharaoh's heart, each time, just as a deal seems cinched. The plea, in the King James version, "Let my people go," has become in Alter the more businesslike, almost side-of-the-mouth, "Send off My people." God directs Moses to "tell in the hearing of your son and your son's son how I toyed with Egypt"; the King James has "what things

I have wrought in Egypt," but Alter's "toyed" better catches the mood of mounting sadism and vengefulness, up to God's killing "every firstborn in the land of Egypt from the firstborn of man to the firstborn of beast." Jahweh vows, "From all the gods of Egypt I will exact retribution."

In the vaulted, newly fashioned skies over Genesis, God, as Auerbach notes, "was not fixed in form and content, and was alone." In the more crowded and pluralistic world of Exodus, God appears to forget that He is the object of a monotheistic cult. He competes with Pharaoh as an equal. His First Commandment declares him to be a jealous god. A footnote to "Who is like You among the gods, O LORD" admits, "Hebrew writers had no difficulty in conceding the existence of other deities, though always stipulating, as here, their absolute inferiority to the God of Israel." Not only does primitive polytheism haunt Exodus's long sojourn in the wilderness, but there is a flavor of stage magic: pillars of smoke and flame, rocks that gush water, manna from Heaven, finger-writing in stone, and elaborate specifications for the Ark containing the tablets of the Covenant and the tent enclosing the Ark. The magic of equivalence roughly shapes justice: "You shall pay a life for a life, an eye for an eye, a tooth for a tooth, a hand for a hand, a foot for a foot, a burn for a burn, a wound for a wound, a bruise for a bruise."

Strictures and specifications continue in Leviticus; indeed, Leviticus contains little else, and reads like an instruction manual for the emergent priestly class and their Levite assistants. Multitudinous avoidances of impurity define the solidifying Israelite identity. Unclean are: carcasses; menstruating women; men who have just had a seminal emission; the meat of reptiles, amphibians, birds of prey, pigs, bats, rats, animals that bring up the cud but lack hooves, and animals that go on four paws. (From the injunction "You shall not boil a kid in its mother's milk," presumably a pagan delicacy, was derived the Judaic prohibition of any combination of meat and dairy products.) A relentless prophylaxis regulates every bodily activity and constantly reminds the Israelites of their responsibility: they must be kept pure, unique, chosen. An offender shall be "cut off from his kin." Amid these relentless pages of exclusionary rules, it is a salutary shock to find the inclusive injunction "And you shall love your fellow man as yourself."

The Book of Numbers extends the ritual of enumeration with a proud toting-up of the Israelite tribes, reckoned to include more than six hundred thousand adult males, and an account of conquests that prepares us, Alter states, "for the defining moment of the crossing of the Jordan, with Joshua in command." The bound galleys of *The Five Books of Moses*, by printer's error or editorial intention, placed Numbers fifth, so that it would lead into the Book of Joshua, but the finished edition restores Deuteronomy to its traditional fifth position. In it Moses delivers a lengthy, highly rhetorical valedictory to the Israelites as they prepare to cross the Jordan into the Promised Land. He rehearses their forty years of wandering; he repeats laws enunciated in Exodus and Leviticus; he threatens his audience with an outpour of curses. Consumption and jaundice, madness and blindness, hemorrhoids and drought: "All these curses will come upon you and pursue you and overtake you until you are destroyed." Moses recites two long and obscure poems that, dating back perhaps to the eleventh century B.C., the time of the Judges, are among the oldest texts in the Bible. The historical events, if any, behind the stories in Exodus are dated to the thirteenth century B.C., and the passionate rhetoric of Deuteronomy was meant, according to Alter, "to persuade audiences of the late First Commonwealth and exilic period of the palpable and authoritative reality of an event that never occurred, or at any rate surely did not occur as it is represented in this text." The definitive collection and composition, by priestly writers, of much of the Old Testament belongs to the sixth and fifth centuries B.C., in the Babylonian exile, after the descendants of Abraham had seen, God's promises to the contrary, Jerusalem conquered and the Temple destroyed. The gathering fierceness and severity of the Torah are those of an embattled people and an embattled priesthood.

In the course of the Pentateuch, God's personality deteriorates. The deity of Genesis—Who with His own hands fashions Adam from dust ("humus" in one of Alter's less happy improvements upon the King James text) and Who strolls in the evening cool of Eden, teases Sarah into geriatric childbearing, and wrestles the night away with her grandson Jacob—becomes, after His implacable hail of plagues upon Pharaoh's land in Exodus, dismayingly cruel. More than once He urges Moses' followers to put opposing nations "under the ban"—that is, to massacre them, to wreak genocide upon them. "He will cast off many nations from before you," Moses promises in Deuteronomy.

> "And the LORD your God will give them before you and you shall strike them down. You shall surely put them under the ban. You shall not seal a covenant with them and shall show them no mercy."

In a footnote, Alter uneasily explains that one commentator calls the emphasis on *herem* ("the ban") "utopian" and "wishful thinking." He adds, "There is, thankfully, no archeological evidence that this program of annihilation was ever implemented." God advocates *herem* not just for Canaanite foes but for Israelite cities that have backslid into pagan practices: "You shall surely strike down the inhabitants of that town by the edge of the sword, putting it under the ban, it and everything in it, and its beasts, by the edge of the sword." Again, Alter pleads utopian thinking. Utopian also must be stoning to death "a man or a woman who does evil in the eyes of the LORD," or cutting off the offending hand of a woman who, in trying "to rescue her man from the hand of the one striking him," inadvertently seizes his genitals. Such punishments persist in parts of the Middle East, though the Koran, a thousand years younger than the Pentateuch, is relatively lenient.

The Lord's striking dead a number of hungry Israelites who have begun to eat some sun-dried quail—"The meat was still between their teeth, it had not yet been chewed, when the LORD's wrath flared against the people"—seems savage, as does the burial alive, in Numbers 16, of Korah, Datham, and Abiram, the leaders of a few Levite grumblers, along with their "wives and their sons and their little ones." It is swiftly followed by the fiery extermination of two hundred fifty others. In embarrassment, before their consumption in God's wrathful fire, Moses tells them, "The Lord has sent me to do all these deeds. . . . It was not from my own heart." Alter in a footnote also seems embarrassed: "This justice by cataclysmic portent is pitiless, and scarcely accords with the discrimination of guilty agents elsewhere in the Mosaic Code."

And God's treatment of Moses, his servant and spokesman through forty years of trial, puzzles the modern reader: Moses is sentenced to die on Mount Abarim, in sight of the Promised Land, because he and his brother Aaron, in God's words, "betrayed Me in the midst of the Israelites through the waters of Meribah-Kadesh in the Wilderness of Zin." Beg Your pardon? Zin is Sinai, and Kadesh is the way-stop where Miriam died and Moses, as his people clamored of thirst, was instructed by the Lord to take his staff and assemble the community and lead them to a certain rock: "You shall speak to the rock before their eyes, and it will yield its water, and I shall bring forth water for them." Instead of merely speaking, Moses, whether out of impatience or anxiety the account does not say, struck the rock twice with his staff. "Abundant water came out," but the Lord was offended, admonishing Moses, "Inasmuch as you did not trust Me to sanctify Me before the eyes of the Israelites, even so you shall not bring this assembly to the land that I have given to them." The divine complaint of an insufficiently absolute trust is repeatedly registered. Earlier, in Numbers 13 and 14, a scouting party comes back and claims that the Canaanites are too big to attack; the alarmed Israelites wonder if it might be better to go back to Egypt. For these qualms all the scouts but two, Caleb and Joshua, are slain by God, and the wandering multitude is condemned to forty years of the wilderness. The exasperated Lord indignantly asks Moses, "How long will this people despise Me, and how long will they not trust Me, with all the signs that I have done in their midst?," and decrees, "By the number of days that you scouted the land, forty days, a day for a year, a day for a year, you will bear your crimes forty years, and you will know what it is to thwart Me."

The ferocity of this tribal God measures the ferocity of tribal existence. In Exodus 3:14, when Moses asks God his name, the answer in Hebrew, 'Ehyeh-'Asher-'Ehyeh, has been commonly rendered I-AM-THAT-I-AM but could be, Alter reports, simply I-AM-I-AM. An impression grew upon me, as I made my way through these obdurate old texts, that to the ancient Hebrews "God" was simply a word for what was: a universe often beautiful and gracious but also implacable and unfathomable. In this encompassing semi-darkness, the figures in the Bible pursue difficulties oddly similar (contrasted with those of Greek gods and aristocrats) to those in our own problematic, mostly domestic lives, and in this they are the patriarchs and matriarchs of modern fiction, which also strives to illuminate the human predicament. The miracle of the Pentateuch is that the Jews and their God, unlike the numerous other tribes and gods that vitally figure in it, have survived three millennia. The Israelites' effort to claim and maintain their Promised Land fuels a contemporary crisis and occupies today's painful headlines. It is still cruelly true that, as we read in the Alter version of Numbers:

> And if you do not dispossess the inhabitants of the land from before you, it will come about that those of them you leave will become stings in your eyes and thorns in your sides, and they will be foes to you on the land in which you dwell.

Big Dead White Male

A YEAR WITH EMERSON: *A Daybook*, selected and edited by Richard Grossman, with engravings by Barry Moser. 204 pp. David R. Godine, 2003.

UNDERSTANDING EMERSON: *"The American Scholar" and His Struggle for Self-Reliance*, by Kenneth S. Sacks. 199 pp. Princeton University Press, 2003.

EMERSON, by Lawrence Buell. 397 pp. Harvard University Press, 2003.

The observances this year of the two hundredth anniversary of Ralph Waldo Emerson's birth in 1803 have been measured but widespread:

conferences were scheduled in the great man's adopted home town of Concord, Massachusetts, and, this fall, in Beijing and Rome. The year's issue of the *Journal of Unitarian Universalist History* is devoted to Emerson. A bicentennial exhibition ran at Harvard's Houghton Library from March to June, and in his birth month of May it was possible in Concord to mingle with actors playing the roles of such friends as Henry David Thoreau and the Alcott sisters and such significant relatives as his eldest daughter, Ellen, and his redoubtable aunt, Mary Moody Emerson. There were many newspaper editorials, including one in the *New York Times* that credited Emerson with formulating the "pernicious, and currently thriving, philosophy of American individualism run amok—call it American self-absorption." The Republican tax cut, tilted toward the rich, and the administration's us-first, go-it-alone foreign policy, not to mention the financial rapacity of Enron and Tyco executives and Wall Street misadvisers, were all traced by the *Times* to Emerson's gospel of self-reliance.

In the world of books—the world that preserves Emerson's memory and message, now that his hypnotic baritone voice and reassuring platform presence are no more—the celebration has been restrained. The Boston firm of David R. Godine has issued a pleasing anthology, *A Year with Emerson*, edited by Richard Grossman and with typically fine engravings by Barry Moser. Emerson, a disbeliever in "foolish consistency" who customarily assembled his lectures from thoughts and sentences written in journals that he began keeping as a Harvard undergraduate, has always lent himself well to being excerpted. His published essays—refined and expanded versions of the lectures—can seem unduly long and, once read, slippery in the mind. The three hundred sixty-five items assembled in this "daybook" are drawn from letters and poems as well as from the canonized prose; though it is hard to imagine even the most devout Emersonian undertaking the pious discipline of a daily reading, Grossman's arranged and annotated progress through the year hops about in lively fashion and often surprises us. Surprise was an aesthetic effect Emerson cherished, as we read in the journal entry titled "Good Writing":

> All writing should be selection in order to drop every dead word. Why do you not save out of your speech or thinking only the vital things—the spirited mot which amused or warmed you when you spoke it—because of its luck & newness. I have just been reading, in this careful book of a most intelligent & learned man, a number of flat conventional words & sentences. If a man would learn to read his own manuscript severely—becoming really a third person, & search only for what interested him, he would blot to purpose—& how every page would gain! Then all the words will be sprightly, & every sentence a surprise.

The passage sets out, in small, Emerson's priorities—spontaneity over convention, vitality over formality, luck and newness over system. Out with what is dead! But keep, along with the spirited *mot*, a third-person detachment. Though he averred, "I would write on the lintels of the door-post, *Whim*," he was a scrupulous and patient reviser, who extensively reworked most of his lectures for their appearance in print.

Also this spring, the Princeton University Press has issued a slim volume, Kenneth S. Sacks's *Understanding Emerson: "The American Scholar" and His Struggle for Self-Reliance*. Sacks, a professor of history at Brown, describes the heated intellectual context in which Emerson delivered, on August 31, 1837, the annual address before the Phi Beta Kappa Society at Harvard, a speech afterward titled "The American Scholar" and destined to become, according to Sacks, "the most famous in American academic history." It, and Emerson's address to the senior class of the Harvard Divinity School the following July, staked out his turf and made his name. Both addresses were, beneath their flowers of rhetoric, inflammatorily hostile to the host institution, from which Emerson had graduated in 1821, thirtieth in a class of fifty-nine. Harvard, in Professor Sacks's analysis, was a bastion of Unitarianism, which had become the religion of the ruling elite of Boston; its members tended to have Harvard degrees. Unitarianism, which in 1819 was called "the half-way house to infidelity" by a professor at the rival Andover Theological Seminary, and is now seen, with its sister the Universalist Church, as the ultimate in liberal Protestantism, by 1837 had acquired an aristocratic and conservative bias that disdained populist revivalism and, closer to home, so-called transcendentalism, an intellectual movement derived from the mystic streak in Goethe, Wordsworth, Coleridge, and Carlyle. Emerson praised these writers for being "blood-warm" and for perceiving "the worth of the vulgar"; these were fighting words, as was his insistence on the great value of the individual person's subjectivity. According to Sacks,

> Harvard-Unitarian culture found spiritual and intellectual confirmation in empirical proof, scientific progress, and material success. Emerson acknowledged understanding derived from observation of external phenomena, but believed that the more important truths are eternal and intuitive, emerging from within. Ostensibly a struggle between the schools of Locke and Kant, after 2200 years it still pretty much came down to Aristotle versus Plato. But Emerson's scholar wasn't the elite Guardian of Plato's *Republic*; it was instead Socrates, son of a stone mason.

European Romanticism, rephrased for the American democracy, posed a revolutionary threat to a rationalist elite. At the same time, it upset

Christian orthodoxy, even the attenuated Unitarian form. Emerson's
Divinity School Address, amid its offenses, reduced Jesus to a sublimely
typical man, one who was "true to what is in you and me," alive to the
"daily miracle" of "man's life," and manifesting not miracles and an
impossible sanctity but "a sweet, natural goodness, a goodness like thine
and mine, and that so invites thine and mine to be and to grow." To the
future ministers, Emerson, having vividly sketched the dismal state of the
contemporary church—"It has lost its grasp on the affection of the good,
and the fear of the bad"—said, "Cast behind you all conformity, and
acquaint men at first hand with Deity." He admonished them "to go
alone; to refuse the good models, even those which are sacred in the
imagination of men, and dare to love God without mediator or veil."
That the terrain to which his auditors are released is dauntingly featureless did not curb Emerson's own delight in solitary freedom. His father, a
dry, conforming Unitarian clergyman, had died early, leaving little legacy
of affection in his seven-year-old son's memory, and Emerson had liberated himself from a parish minister's duties, including the personally distasteful one of administering the Lord's Supper, before the age of thirty.
Yet he continued to supply preaching throughout the 1830s, and called
his public lectures "lay sermons." His two aggressively sweeping Harvard
addresses advanced his burgeoning career as a lyceum speaker, a free-
ranging secular prophet.

Proper Boston resisted his message. Attending a Harvard ceremony
not long after giving the Divinity School Address, he noted in his journal,
"The young people & the mature hint at odium, & aversion of faces to be
presently encountered in society. I say no: I fear it not." Sacks quotes
Convers Francis, who, taking tea with a "family belonging to the straitest
sect of Boston conservatism," found that his hosts "abhor & abominate
R. W. Emerson as a sort of mad dog: & when I defended that pure and
angelic spirit . . . they laughed at me with amazement." By this light,
Emerson's transcendentalism, with its claims in these two addresses that
"all men have sublime thoughts," that "the active soul" is something
"every man is entitled to," and that, "if the single man plant himself
indomitably on his instincts, and there abide, the huge world will come
round to him," formed part of the Jacksonian revolution whereby the
democracy's yeomen sought to wrest power and responsibility from an
aristocracy of merchants and planters.

The weightiest bicentennial volume thus far has been *Emerson*, by the
Harvard professor Lawrence Buell. A three-hundred-and-thirty-four-
page rumination in seven chapters, the book has the relaxed, sometimes

personal air of a graduate-student seminar rather than the clarion tones of a lecture in an undergraduate survey course. We are assumed to know something about Emerson already. The biographical facts are swiftly sketched and subjected to skeptical inquiry; the patriotic "jingoism" of his stirring ceremonial hymn beginning "By the rude bridge that arched the flood," for example, is minimized in Buell's conclusion that "Emerson's own concern was with values that stand the test of time and unite the world." Buell's repeatedly solicitous, corrective slant has the unintended effect of showing how thoroughly Emerson, who spoke to wake up the democratic masses to the powers within them, is now captive to the contentious, incestuous circles of academia. An endorsement on the back of the jacket, by Sacvan Bercovitch, the author of *The Puritan Origins of the American Self*, salutes Buell's book as "the harvest of the past half-century of Emersonian revaluations and the harbinger, guide, and provocation for the next generations of Emerson scholars and critics"; Emerson scholars and critics, in their generations, are evidently world enough. Buell rarely pitches his voice above classroom level. Saving type at the price of obscurity, he identifies many key quotations by their page numbers in "CW," specified on page xi as *The Complete Works of Ralph Waldo Emerson*, 12 vols., Ed. Edward Waldo Emerson. Boston: Houghton-Mifflin, 1903–1904," leaving those who happen to lack that twelve-volume set from the outset of the last century to guess, often, what essay is being quoted. Such ill-equipped readers must guess, too, at the shadowy content of scholarly disputes that are second nature to the sixty-four-year-old Buell, who in his preface confides that he has been mulling Emerson over since he was twenty-six.

He makes an extensive case against "a present-day literary-Americanist standpoint" that, in his view, takes too seriously the concluding peroration of "The American Scholar" ("We have listened too long to the courtly muses of Europe. . . . We will walk on our own feet; we will work with our own hands; we will speak our own minds. . . . A nation of men will for the first time exist, because each believes himself inspired by the Divine Soul which also inspires all men") and not seriously enough Emerson as a global intellectual shaped by European and Asian (Hindu, Buddhist, Persian Sufi) influences and, in turn, influential abroad, with declared admirers ranging from Matthew Arnold and Friedrich Nietzsche to such outriggers as the Cuban poet-revolutionary José Martí, the Australian Charles Harpur, the Jewish Indian poet Nissim Ezekiel, and — a great catch — Marcel Proust. But who is arguing? To someone of Emerson's generation, European thought and writing was almost all there was; Puritan sermons, Benjamin Franklin's blithe compositions, the Founding Fathers' chiselled eloquence, Washington Irving's sketches, and James

Fenimore Cooper's Leatherstocking Tales—all were easily overlookable by a serious American aspirant to high thought and poetry in the early nineteenth century. To Emerson, Poe, his only peer as a homegrown critical and creative mind, was "the jingle man."

In the heavily politicized world of contemporary American academic studies, nuances of emphasis loom with the menace of frontal assaults. Buell frequently sounds defensive, admitting that "Emerson's significance as a force in U.S. literary history has shrunk since the ethnic renaissances of the twentieth century, the late-century expansion of the American canon, and increasing disenchantment with the whole idea of literary canonicity." The category of "canonicity," of practical concern mostly to textbook manufacturers, has interfered, supposedly, with individual aesthetic reactions and evaluations. The "so-called new Americanist criticism of the last two decades," we read, "tends to see the tensions between margin and center (in particular of race, ethnicity, gender, class, and sexuality) as more central to U.S. cultural history than any supposed aesthetic mainstream. . . . No longer does it seem so self-evident that Emerson and Transcendentalism were the gateway to U.S. literary emergence." When *was* it self-evident? It wasn't so to Melville and Hawthorne, who both took a satiric and suspect view of Emerson's soul-talk. "This Plato who talks thro' his nose," Melville called him, adding, "To one who has weathered Cape Horn as a common sailor what stuff all this is."

Professor Buell, while trying to lend Emerson the benefit of his forty years of close and fond attention, gives evidence of having weathered too many storms of political correctness. He seems, within his discourse, distracted by hectoring students and fractious fellow-faculty. Of Emerson's reluctance to join the militant abolitionists, it has to be explained that he had "initial scruples about joining what today seems a far more self-evidently righteous cause than it did to the great majority of nineteenth-century northern whites in the 1840s and 1850s." Buell pleads that "overall, Emerson's racism was certainly no greater than that of most northern white abolitionists, and far less than the average northern white." Again, Buell allows, "Nor, despite his awareness of and support for American diversity, did he cease to think of Englishness as the dominant ethnic influence in the making of America and especially of New England"—as if in 1850 any other view were possible. Bows are awkwardly made to severer theorists:

Myra Jehlen argues that Emerson's vision of man coming into his godship through the conquest of nature reads suspiciously like an apology for westward expansion. Christopher Newfield argues that Emerson's appeal to transpersonal authorities like aboriginal self and the "orphic poet" who says the last words in *Nature* implies a forfeiture of individualism and acquiescence to dominant cultural forces that make for a parallel between Emerson's life course and the rise of corporatism in nineteenth-century America.

Buell's account of Emerson's responsiveness to intellectual women like Margaret Fuller, who believed that his "model of personal transformation" opened "the door to female liberation," is accompanied by the gratuitous disclaimer "though admiration was apt to be tinged with lingering misogynistic judgmentalism." On the matter of theistic belief, Buell smilingly enlists in a collegial infidelity, with a frown for today's zealots: Emerson's frequent mention of God "is hardly calculated to appeal to the majority of university researchers who presently dominate Emerson studies. For the most part, we are a thoroughly secularized lot, all the more skeptical of God-talk given the rise of fervid evangelical power blocks at home and abroad."

A hundred years after Emerson's centennial was declared a school holiday in Concord and marked by an oration by William James and a public prayer that the spirit of Emerson inspire all present, he is put forward gingerly, apologetically, as a devalued stock on which we might still want to take a flyer. Buell, interviewed by the *Boston Globe* (which reviewed his book as "scholarly natterings"), is quoted as saying, "If you're looking for strong guidance, look elsewhere. But if you're looking for the courage to maintain sanity and resolution when the rest of society seems to have gone mad, Emerson may be your man." The endorsement seems excessively hedged, linking the sage's value to a presumed madness in society. Emerson was too much a realist, I think, to dismiss the workings of a society as mad, even a society like his own, passionately riven antebellum America. He pitched his palace of the Ideal on the particularities and rationale of what existed. One of Buell's few wholehearted sentences exclaims, "How many of the great essays end by propelling the reader out into the world!" Yes; Emerson wanted to encourage us, to make us fit for the world.

So *is* there anything left to say, outside the classroom, about the Sage of Concord? Some of his disciples do still excite non-academic interest: Whitman, who credited Emerson with bringing him to a boil, and who received from him a handsome endorsement, triumphantly survives, as a revolutionary versifier and unabashed celebrant of his American self. Thoreau is still read without being assigned, and lives as a patron saint of ecology. Though Emerson extolled Nature, centering his youthful testament, *Nature*, on its manifestations and opening his Divinity School Address with a lyrical evocation of the summer in progress, he was not a naturalist. He wrote about people, people in their stressed psychic anatomies, and, as he aged, people in history and society. These later, more worldly writings better suit our modern taste—more concrete, less high-flown. Mark Van Doren, in assembling the Viking *Portable Emerson* back in 1946, leaned heavily upon *English Traits* and the short biographies and omitted many of the relatively youthful philosophical essays. "For he was at his best," Van Doren wrote, "not when he was basic, not when he was trying to understand the man he was, but when he was being that man, when he was applying the ideas which that man had furnished him. He needed matter to illuminate."

Yet the later, more material and genially circumstantial Emerson is not the one whose bicentennial we celebrate. Were his surviving writings confined to those after, say, 1850, they would be remembered the way Washington Irving's travel and historical writings are, and Emerson as another Unitarian clergyman turned literary intellectual, like George Ripley. Emerson won his high place in American esteem as the founder and proponent of a religion, one of many offshoots and modifications of Christianity—Mormonism, Shakerism, the Millerites—that flourished in the first half of the nineteenth century while Calvinism, with its baleful predestinarian God, lost its hold. Emerson's inspiriting stroke of genius was to rephrase and re-emphasize the dualism of Christianity in palatable terms adapted from German philosophy and European Romanticism. On the second page of his first book, *Nature*, first published in 1836 and based, Buell tells us, on ideas in an early sermon, we read:

> Philosophically considered, the universe is composed of Nature and the Soul. Strictly speaking, therefore, all that is separate from us, all which Philosophy distinguishes as the NOT ME, that is, both nature and art, all other men and my own body, must be ranked under this name, NATURE.

A year later, in "The American Scholar," the "not me" becomes the "other me," and a relation between the two entities is drawn: "The world,—this shadow of the soul, or *other me*, lies wide around. Its attractions are the keys which unlock my thoughts and make me acquainted with myself." In *Nature*'s seventh chapter, titled "Spirit," an intermediary element had appeared, on both sides of the cleavage: "The noblest ministry of nature is to stand as the apparition of God. It is the organ through which the universal spirit speaks to the individual, and strives to lead back the individual to it." The universal spirit, that striver, would seem to be God, clad in transparent robes of Kantian idealism: "Idealism saith: matter is a phenomenon, not a substance. . . . Yet, if it only deny the existence of matter, it does not satisfy the demands of the spirit. It leaves God out of me." The word "spirit" bounces from the me to the not-me and back again, yet amid this legerdemain Emerson formulates a profound and primitive fact about the human condition—"the total disparity between the evidence of our own being, and the evidence of the world's being." Consciousness creates duality. We exist, to ourselves, non-phenomenally. Our subjective existence is absolute, though indescribable. "The soul *is*," Emerson says in the essay "Compensation." "Under all this running sea of circumstance, whose waters ebb and flow with perfect balance, lies the aboriginal abyss of real Being. Essence, or God, is not a relation, or a part, but the whole. Being is the vast affirmative, excluding negation, self-balanced, and swallowing up all relations, parts and times within itself."

From the absoluteness of the "me" a great deal of religious consolation can be spun. The self is pitted against the vast physical universe as if the two were equal. From "Compensation": "The soul refuses limits, and always affirms an Optimism, never a Pessimism. . . . In the nature of the soul is the compensation for the inequalities of condition." The doctrine is tailor-made for Americans. Emerson's America was also Hawthorne's, which Henry James famously described in a cascade of negatives: "No sovereign, no court, no personal loyalty, no aristocracy, no church, no clergy, no army . . . no country gentlemen, no palaces, no castles, nor manors," etc. In a New World so bare and barren, and faced with an overweening Nature such as the species has not encountered since pre-historic migrations, what does a person have? A self. And that is plenty, Emerson assures us. "In all my lectures," he stated in his journals, "I have taught one doctrine, the infinitude of the private man." Possessing his own infinity, a man has nothing to fear, not even (though Emerson treads light on the thin ice of personal immortality) death itself.

In essay after essay, waving aside evil as "merely privative," Emerson justifies optimism and declares a holiday for the hard-pressed American soul. Like most faiths, his makes light of the world and its usual trials. His most pessimistic essay, "Experience"—that in which he declares, "I have set my heart on honesty"—proclaims the transience and shallowness of grief and love: "The great and crescive self, rooted in absolute nature, supplants all relative existence, and ruins the kingdom of mortal friendship and love. . . . We believe in ourselves, as we do not believe in others. We permit all things to ourselves, and that which we call sin in others, is experiment for us." Elsewhere he expresses a brusque impatience with charity and the clamor of worthy causes. "I must be myself," he tells us. "I cannot break myself any longer for you, or you." This very well suits our native bent. In this country, the self is not dissolved in Oriental group-think, or subordinated within medieval hierarchy. Our spiritual essence, it may be, is selfishness; certainly our art, from Whitman to the Abstract Expressionists, flaunts the naked self with a boldness rarely seen in other national cultures. On this score Emerson is matched only by his hero Montaigne, who confessed, "The world always looks outward, I turn my gaze inward; there I fix it, and there I keep it busy. Everyone looks before him; I look within. I have no business but with myself."

A country imposed on a wilderness needs strong selves. Whether American self-assertiveness fits into today's crammed and touchy world can be doubted. But Emerson, with a cobbled-together mythology, in melodious accents that sincerely feigned the old Christian reassurances, sought to instill confidence and courage in his democratic audience, and it is for this, rather than for his mellowed powers of observation and wit, that he is honored, if honored more than read. His relative neglect, a decline from a heyday of gilt-edged uniform editions and soul-stirring fireside perusal, he would have regarded philosophically. He knew how the world moves on, after eating at our attention and essential solitude. "Experience" ends:

> We dress our garden, eat our dinners, discuss the household with our wives, and these things make no impression, are forgotten next week; but in the solitude to which every man is always returning, he has a sanity and revela-tions, which in his passage into new worlds he will carry with him. Never mind the ridicule, never mind the defeat: up again, old heart!

Down the River

THE ANNOTATED UNCLE TOM'S CABIN, edited with an introduction and notes by Henry Louis Gates, Jr., and Hollis Robbins. 480 pp. W. W. Norton, 2007.

The best-selling American novel of the nineteenth century, *Uncle Tom's Cabin*, by Harriet Beecher Stowe, does not quite go away, much as many Americans, from black militants to white aesthetes, might wish it. Within a year of its publication, in March of 1852, it had sold three hun-dred thousand copies in a country one-thirteenth its present size and—in a surprising show of Victorian globalization—more than two million in the rest of the world. Ten years later, in 1862, Abraham Lincoln allegedly greeted its diminutive author in the White House with the words "So you're the little woman who wrote the book that started this great war!"

The President's subsequent abolition of slavery and the Union's hard-won victory in the Civil War would seem to have taken the wind out of Stowe's fiercely abolitionist narrative, but its melodramatic images—the Kentucky slave Eliza's flight across the ice-choked Ohio River, pursued by bloodhounds, with her son in her arms; the Louisiana slave-holder Simon Legree's boastful villainy; fair-haired little Eva's saintly death and the snaggle-headed black orphan Topsy's reluctant reformation—persisted, though travestied, in popular plays, shows, films, figurines, and cartoons.

American readership did slowly decline, to the extent that only second-hand copies were available when, in 1948, Modern Library reprinted the text, but *Uncle Tom's Cabin* continued to be read in Europe, especially in Russia, and by Anglophone men of letters. George Orwell cited it as the "supreme example" of a " 'good bad' book": "It is an unintentionally ludicrous book, full of preposterous melodramatic incidents; it is also deeply moving and essentially true." Edmund Wilson and Alfred Kazin gave it their critical attention; Kazin noted Henry James's recollection of his childhood reading—"one lived and moved at the time, with great intensity, in Mrs. Stowe's novel"—and his curious judgment that no other book "probably ever reached its mark, the mark of exciting interest, without having at least groped for that goal *as* a book or by the exposure of some literary side." In postwar academia, the novel excited interest as a female production during an "American renaissance" of masculine masterpieces canonized by such male critics as Lewis Mumford and F. O. Matthiessen. Stowe's biographer Joan D. Hedrick blames her subject's fall from critical grace on "the removal of literature from the parlor to institutions to which women had limited access: men's clubs, high-culture journals, and prestigious universities." Now a prominent African-American scholar, Harvard professor Henry Louis Gates, Jr., has edited, with Hollis Robbins of Johns Hopkins University, *The Annotated Uncle Tom's Cabin*, the latest in a select series that began with Martin Gardner's *The Annotated Alice* and has continued with oversize annotated editions of *The Wizard of Oz*, *Huckleberry Finn*, Dickens's *A Christmas Carol*, and the tales of Sherlock Holmes.

In such iconic company, *Uncle Tom* seems uneasy. The annotations by Gates and Robbins do not overflow the margins like those, say, by Michael Patrick Hearn as he gleefully spills all there is to know about Oz and its creator, L. Frank Baum, or exult in arcane erudition as Gardner does in exploring Lewis Carroll's pedantically loaded Wonderland. The editors at hand provide, beyond an introduction preoccupied with James Baldwin and Richard Wright, some historical background on the slave trade and the cotton industry, the chapter and verse for Stowe's numerous Biblical quotations, and a wealth of illustrations that the novel received in the course of its many editions—reproduced at too small a scale, sometimes, to bear out the racist nuances described in the captions. The least suspect illustrations, by the great Mexican caricaturist Miguel Covarrubias, adorned a 1938 edition; the others tend to whiten sympathetic black characters and to desexualize Uncle Tom, who, as the father of very young children, must possess a virility belied by his presentation as an avuncular oldster. The bound galleys, interestingly, sported on their cover an incongruously jubilant bevy of minstrel-show darkies; the jacket of the finished book has demurely substituted the ivy-clad log cabin limned for the first edition by Hammatt Billings.

The voice of the annotations fluctuates between "we" and a first-person singular that can sound downright petulant:

> Without good looks or interesting verbiage to keep us interested, I am close to turning the page. Perhaps Stowe has learned too well from Jane Austen, whose long monologues of Miss Bates (in *Emma*) bore us silly.

Not infrequently the notes, printed in red, seem an irritable sniping from the sidelines: "There is no way to completely explain away the narrator's ugly tone here"; "Another instance of racist thought: Eliza's face is black *but* comely"; "This description serves little real purpose . . . but it pleased Stowe greatly to write"; "We didn't really need more evidence of Haley's hard-heartedness, but Stowe has provided it anyway"; "Clearly Stowe is pandering to her older female readership here"; "One of many hints to Stowe's readers that Eva is not long for this world"; "The episode is plodding. I confess that my eyes glaze over"; "George is a bit too talky in this scene"; "Where, one asks again, are the things that remind him of Chloe?"

Indeed, this reader, with a hundred pages to go, switched from the wide-format, double-focused annotated version to the text as presented by the Library of America, where the feverish and nakedly exhortative climax is allowed to work its spell without editorial heckling. I found Stowe's fervor infectious. Her political aim—to provide a panorama, with a range of specimen slaves and masters, that would show black slavery in the United States to be an odious institution, poisoning all that it touches—is achieved several times over, and is not a unique achievement; the passing of the Fugitive Slave Act, as part of the Compromise of 1850, made all Americans legally obligated to help recapture escaped slaves, and spurred an upwelling of abolitionist eloquence. Stowe emphasizes, in her protest novel, the slaves' complete lack of human rights, including those of self-defense and of offering court testimony; what attachments and families they created were destroyed at whim by their owners, whose human property could be sold down the river, pursued through every state and territory, and, in the case of young females, exploited as a harem.

Stowe was born in Connecticut, the seventh child and fourth daughter of Lyman Beecher, later the president of Lane Theological Seminary, and the sister of the prominent and eventually notorious preacher Henry Ward Beecher. When she was twenty-one, she moved with her family to Cincinnati, across the Ohio River from Kentucky and a prime stop on the "underground railroad" that smuggled escaped slaves into Canada. For her novel, she relied on reports in the Cincinnati press, published slave narratives, personal acquaintance with freed and refugee slaves, and a single visit, in 1834, to Kentucky. In 1850, she moved, with her husband, Calvin Stowe, and their five children, back to New England, where her husband had accepted a position as Professor of Natural and Revealed Religion at Bowdoin College. As she undertook, that same year, the writing of *Uncle Tom's Cabin*, the Cincinnati years gave concreteness and warmth to her imaginings, and help account for her confident, spirited use of Southern idiom, both the "linguistic capering of Sam and Andy," bantering black characters, and the "barroom conviviality" of racist whites. Gates and Robbins compliment Stowe's dialogue among blacks as "very contemporary sounding and surprisingly accurate."

Coming to read *Uncle Tom's Cabin* for the first time, I was unprepared for its bursts of humor. Its most famous episode, Eliza's crossing to freedom on the ice cakes, is rendered twice, once as harrowing subjective sensation—

> In that dizzy moment her feet to her scarce seemed to touch the ground, and a moment brought her to the water's edge. Right on behind they [hounds and a posse of slavers] came; and, nerved with strength such as God gives only to the desperate, with one wild cry and flying leap, she vaulted sheer over the turbid current by the shore, on to the raft of ice beyond. . . . The huge green fragment of ice on which she alighted pitched and creaked as her weight come on it, but she staid there not a moment. With wild cries and desperate energy she leaped to another and still another cake;—stumbling—leaping—slipping—springing upwards again! Her shoes are gone—her stockings cut from her feet—while blood marked every step; but she saw nothing, felt nothing, till dimly, as in a dream, she saw the Ohio side, and a man helping her up the bank . . .

—and then, some pages on, through the telling of a black pursuer, as physical comedy:

"We come right behind her, and I thought my soul he'd got her sure enough,—when she gin sich a screech as I never hearn, and thar she was, clar over t' other side the current, on the ice, and then on she went, a screeching and a jumpin',—the ice went crack! c'wallop! cracking! chunk! and she a boundin' like a buck! Lord, the spring that ar gal's got in her an't common, I'm o' 'pinion."

Stowe read Dickens aloud to her children, and must have learned from him, and from Shakespeare, how to leaven a grim story with comic relief; even Legree's hellish plantation has on it two clowns, the brutish black henchmen Sambo and Quimbo, who finally leave off villainy to become Christian converts.

James Baldwin, the stepson of a Harlem preacher who, Baldwin wrote, "having taken his own conversion too literally never, at bottom, forgave the white world . . . for having saddled him with a Christ in whom, to judge at least from their treatment of him, they themselves no longer believed," inveighed, in the overwrought indictment titled "Everybody's Protest Novel," against the religiosity of Stowe's book:

> Here, black equates with evil and white with grace; if, being mindful of the necessity of good works, she could not cast out the blacks—a wretched, huddled mass, apparently, claiming, like an obsession, her inner eye—she could not embrace them either without purifying them of sin. She must cover their intimidating nakedness, robe them in white, the garments of salvation.

There can be no denying that *Uncle Tom's Cabin* insistently presents Christianity as the main means of black integration—the path to respectability, the call to liberty, the antidote to despair (though Stowe, like Baldwin, concludes that anti-black racism is so ingrained in the United States that a black man would do better living elsewhere, be it Europe or Liberia). Christianity in Dickens or Trollope is just a lick and a promise compared with Christianity for Stowe. The daughter, sister, and wife of theologians, she repeatedly confronts the most accessible argument for atheism, God's apparent silence and indifference to human suffering. She herself, in 1849, had lost an infant son to cholera, and the novel's most eloquent atheist, Legree's concubine, the ladylike quadroon Cassy, has killed her infant son with laudanum rather than let him live as a slave. She tells Tom, the novel's central embodiment of submissive faith, after Legree has given him a savage beating:

> "There's no use calling on the Lord—he never hears . . . ; there isn't any God, I believe; or, if there is, he's taken sides against us. All goes against us, heaven and earth. Everything is pushing us into hell. Why shouldn't we go?"

Similarly, Dinah, a hapless servant in the household of a decent but acquiescent and whimsical slaveholder and his unconscionably selfish wife, has earlier described to Tom how "Missis tuck sick" and forced her to neglect her infant in caring for her: "She made me sleep in her room; and I had to put it away off in a little kind o' garret, and thar it cried itself to death, one night. It did; and I tuck to drinkin', to keep its crying out of my ears!" Tom tries to comfort her:

> "O, ye poor crittur," said Tom, "han't nobody never telled ye how the Lord Jesus loved ye, and died for ye? Han't they telled ye that he'll help ye, and ye can go to heaven, and have rest, at last?"

Debating with the more sophisticated and hardened Cassy, Tom nearly crumples:

> Tom folded his hands; all was darkness and horror.
> "O Jesus! Lord Jesus! have you quite forgot us poor critturs?" burst forth, at last;—"help, Lord, I perish!"

Yet this dark night of Tom's soul is followed by a fresh religious resolve. His answer to the problem of suffering is the traditional, creedal one: God incarnate suffered, too. "Wan't he allays poor?" Tom pleads with Cassy, "and have we, any on us, yet come so low as he come?" Newly settled in his faith, Tom in imitation of Christ embarks upon a path of quiet defiance that will take him to a martyr's death. Legree, who shows an unexpected taste for debate on high matters ("This yer religion is all a mess of lying trumpery, Tom. I know all about it. Ye'd better hold to me; I'm somebody, and can do something!"), can no longer touch Tom where he lives. The novel's huge success stemmed, it may be, as much from its vivid religious affirmations as from its attack on slavery. Stowe, who experienced a religious rebirth at the age of thirty-one, had dwelt longer and more deeply with Christianity than with abolitionism. The two in any case were entwined; the nation's compact with slavery was to provoke, in the minimally religious Abraham Lincoln, his Second Inaugural's grave reflections on divine punishment:

> If God wills that [the war] continue until all the wealth piled by the bonds-man's two hundred and fifty years of unrequited toil shall be sunk, and until every drop of blood drawn with the lash shall be paid by another drawn with the sword, as was said three thousand years ago, so still it must be said "the judgments of the Lord are true and righteous altogether."

Uncle Tom's Cabin, long relegated to the archives of another century's headlines, popped back into critical favor in 1996, when the novelist Jane Smiley wrote in a *Harper's* article of her rereading, while laid up with a broken leg, Mark Twain's *Adventures of Huckleberry Finn* for the first time since junior-high school and finding herself "stunned . . . by the notion that . . . this is a great novel, that this is even a serious novel." Having surveyed *Huck*'s shortcomings as a treatment of black-white relations, even in the 1840s, she subjected it to invidious comparison with Stowe's uncanonized best-seller:

> Ernest Hemingway, thinking of himself, as always, once said that all American literature grew out of *Huck Finn*. It undoubtedly would have been better for American literature, and American culture, if our literature had grown out of one of the best-selling novels of all time, another American work of the nineteenth century, *Uncle Tom's Cabin*, which for its portrayal of an array of thoughtful, autonomous, and passionate black characters leaves *Huck Finn* far behind.

As Smiley could have foreseen, a host of professors and critics, mostly male, rose to defend *Huck*, already under heavy siege from black parents and school authorities offended by the book's anarchic spirit and liberal employment of the word "nigger." Yet it is impossible, for at least this reader, to dip into the first half of the book without being seduced by the informal beauty of the boy narrator's voice and the natural, easy density of the realism. Religion, in Huck's mouth, melts to a joke, and nature, heedless and carefree, takes over the canvas. America has never looked as broad, fresh, and majestic as the Mississippi does from Huck and Jim's raft. No wonder Hemingway, who was always looking for the secret of keeping prose honest, went overboard.

But in the second half, beginning with the Grangerford-Shepherdson feud, and more decidedly with the introduction of the Duke and the Dauphin, the novel's idyll curdles. Mark Twain's foolery and misogyny swamp the raft; his fascination with a storybook Middle Ages inspires quixotic divagations. It is painful to follow the improbable ins and outs of the plot that Tom Sawyer contrives to rescue Jim from Southern capture. When Tom appears in the book, Huck—the wiser, truly experienced boy—fades. The author makes a grave miscalculation when he reveals that Tom knew all along that Jim had been already freed by his mistress's will. It's as if Mark Twain forgot what slavery is—the constriction of it, the helplessness of it, all suspended while Tom Sawyer toys with a tediously extended, bookish prank. Jim, in a plot strand that could have come from *Uncle Tom's Cabin*,* has a wife and two children, one of them

---

*The two novels hail from recognizably the same world: the going prices for Tom and Jim are both given as around a thousand dollars. The theme of breaking up slave families, so central to Stowe's protest, forcefully arises in the twenty-seventh chapter of *Huckleberry*

deaf, whom he hopes to buy into freedom; he is a responsible person, with hopes and plans. For his time on the raft, when he is allowed a free man's resourcefulness and time for reflection, he projects a warmer, more three-dimensional presence than any of Stowe's many black characters, all of whom exist in her pages to make a point, to illustrate an aspect of a problem. It seems too much to say, as Smiley does, that "The power of *Uncle Tom's Cabin* is the power of brilliant analysis married to great wisdom of feeling." Its power is that, crude and manipulative as parts of it are, it never makes light of slavery and its attendant vast misery.

Oz Is Us

THE ANNOTATED WIZARD OF OZ, by L. Frank Baum, annotated and edited by Michael Patrick Hearn. 396 pp. Norton, 2000.

A hundred years ago, *The Wonderful Wizard of Oz*, by L. Frank Baum, was published, by the soon-to-be-defunct Chicago-based firm of George M. Hill. The Library of Congress is hosting a commemorative exhibition, and Norton has brought out a centennial edition of *The Annotated Wizard of Oz*, edited and annotated by Michael Patrick Hearn. Hearn, we learn from a preface by Martin Gardner, became a Baum expert while an English major at Bard College, and put an annotated *Wizard* forward when only twenty years old. Gardner, the polymathic compiler of *The Annotated Alice* (1960) and *More Annotated Alice* (1990), had been invited to do the same, in 1970, for Baum's fable; disclaiming competence, he recommended the young Bard Baumist to Clarkson & Potter, who published Hearn's tome in 1973. In the years since, Hearn has produced annotated versions of Charles Dickens's *Christmas Carol* and Mark Twain's *Huckleberry Finn*, added to the vast tracts of Baum scholarship, co-authored a biography of W. W. Denslow, *The Wizard*'s illustrator, and

---

Finn, when the fraudulent appropriators of Peter Wilks's estate quickly sell the dead man's slaves off to traders, "and away they went, the two sons up the river to Memphis, and their mother down the river to Orleans." Huck tells us: "I thought them poor girls [the rightful heirs] and them niggers would break their hearts for grief; they cried around each other, and took on so it most made me down sick to see it. The girls said they hadn't ever dreamed of seeing the family separated or sold away from the town." The damage is swiftly undone as the mischief unravels, but in any case the incident is part of a basically nostalgic picture of the antebellum South whose basis in slavery Stowe is out to expose and destroy.

labored at a still-unpublished "definitive biography" of Baum. Presumably he and Norton have been patiently waiting, with their slews of fresh annotation and illustration, for the centennial (also that of Dreiser's *Sister Carrie*, Conrad's *Lord Jim*, Colette's first Claudine novel, and Freud's *Interpretation of Dreams*) to roll around.

It is not hard to imagine why Gardner ducked the original assignment. The two "Alice" books are more literate, intricate, and modernist than Baum's *Wonderful Wizard*, and Lewis Carroll's mind, laden with mathematical lore, chess moves, semantic puzzles, and the riddles of Victorian religion, was more susceptible to explication, at least by the like-minded Gardner. But Baum, Hearn shows in his introduction, was a complicated character, too—a Theosophist, an expert on poultry, a stagestruck actor and singer, a fine amateur photographer, an inventive household tinkerer, a travelling china-salesman, and, only by a final shift, a children's writer. He was forty-four when *The Wonderful Wizard of Oz* was published. His prior bibliography included a directory of stamp dealers, a treatise on the mating and management of Hamburg chickens, a definitive work entitled *The Art of Decorating Dry Goods Windows and Interiors*—also celebrating its centennial—and a few small volumes for children. Baum's life (1856–1919) reflects the economic and ideological adventurism of his America. Hearn tells us that his father, Benjamin Ward Baum, "followed nearly as many careers as his son would. He was building a barrel factory in Chittenango [New York] when the boy was born, but made a fortune in the infant Pennsylvania oil industry only a few years later." Lyman Frank, one of nine children, of whom five survived into adulthood, was raised on a luxurious estate in Syracuse and educated by English tutors. He was a dreamy reader as a boy. He lasted only two years at Peekskill Military School, and went on to Syracuse Classical School, without, apparently, graduating. He married the twenty-year-old Maud Gage when he was twenty-six and, grown into a lanky man with a large mustache, was touring as the star of a musical melodrama, *The Maid of Arran*, which he had written—book, lyrics, and music. His mother-in-law, Matilda Joslyn Gage, was a prominent feminist and a keen Theosophist; she had not wanted her daughter to leave Cornell to marry an actor. But Maud did anyway, and when she became pregnant Frank left the theatre. With his uncle, Adam Baum, he established Baum's Castorine Company, marketing an axle grease invented by his brother Benjamin and still, in this slippery world, being manufactured.

Maud's sisters and brother had all settled in the Dakota Territory; in 1888 Frank moved with his family to Aberdeen, South Dakota, where he opened a variety store, Baum's Bazaar. Drought and depression caused the store to fail; in 1890 Baum took over a weekly newspaper, calling it the *Saturday Pioneer*, and by 1891 it, too, was failing. He found employment in Chicago, first as a reporter and then as a travelling salesman with the wholesale china-and-glassware firm of Pitkin & Brooks. The two-and-a-half-year Dakota interval gave him, however, the Plains flavor crucial to the myth of Dorothy and the Wizard; gray desolation and hardscrabble rural survival compose the negative of which Oz is the colorful print. In Baum's Kansas, "even the grass was not green, for the sun had burned the tops of the long blades until they were the same gray color to be seen everywhere." Chicago's spectacular White City, built of plaster and cement for the 1893 World's Columbian Exposition on the lakeside marshes, gave both Baum and his illustrator the glitz and scale, but not the tint, of Oz's Emerald City. A contemporary writer, Frances Hodgson Burnett, likened the White City to the City Beautiful in Bunyan's *Pilgrim's Progress*, and wrote,

> Endless chains of jewels seemed strung and wound about it. The Palace of Flowers held up a great crystal of light glowing against the dark blue of the sky, towers and domes were crowned and diademed, thousands of jewels hung among the masses of leaves, or reflected themselves, sparkling in the darkness of the lagoons, fountains of molten jewels sprung up, and flamed and changed.

Woven of electric illusion (newly feasible, thanks to the Wizard of Menlo Park) and quickly an abandoned ruin, the White City fed into Baum's book a melancholy undertone of insubstantiality. A Bobbs-Merrill press release in 1903 claimed that the name Oz came from the "O–Z" drawer of the author's filing cabinet, but the name resonates with a Shelley poem known to most Victorians:

> And on the pedestal these words appear:
> "My name is Ozymandias,* king of kings:
> Look on my works, ye Mighty, and despair!"
> Nothing beside remains.

A note of hollowness, of dazzling fraud, of frontier fustian and quackery taints the Wizard in the first of the many Oz books, before a plethora of wonders turns him into a real sorcerer. In the M-G-M movie, the seekers along the Yellow Brick Road rapturously sing, "The Wizard of Oz is one

---

*The name, in classical times, for the Egyptian Pharaoh and mighty monument-builder Ramses II (1304–1237 B.C.), possibly derived from his ancient Egyptian name, User-maat-Re. Shelley wrote his poem after visiting the British Museum and viewing a statue of Ramses housed there; he never saw the colossal statues at Abu Simbel and elsewhere along the Nile, of which many in fact do remain.

because / . . . because of the wonderful things he does"; then it turns out that what he does is concoct visual hokum with a crank and escape in a mismanaged hot-air balloon.

But Baum, who turned to editing and writing as a way of spending more time with his four young sons, proved to be an authentic wizard as a children's author. He had made the acquaintance of William Wallace Denslow, a footloose artist from Philadelphia who had come to Chicago for the Exposition; the two had definite and ambitious ideas about what children's books should look like, and paid for the color plates of their first collaboration, a book of Baum's verses called *Father Goose, His Book*. The book attracted praise from Mark Twain, William Dean Howells, and Admiral George Dewey and, Hearn says, "became the best-selling picture book of 1900." That year saw the publication of no fewer than five titles by Baum, of which the *Wizard* was the last. Hill was overwhelmed by orders, and went back to press four times, for a total of ninety thousand copies. The *Minneapolis Journal* called it, in November, "the best children's story-book of the century"—high praise if the nineteenth century was meant, more modest if the nascent twentieth was denoted.

In 1902, the George M. Hill Company went bankrupt in spite of Baum's success, and the rights in *The Wizard* were placed in the crasser hands of Bobbs-Merrill; meanwhile, Baum and Denslow parted, each taking the Oz characters with him, since their contract provided for separate ownership of text and illustrations. That same year saw the opening, at Chicago's Grand Opera House, of *The Wizard of Oz*, a "musical extravaganza" created by Julian Mitchell, who was later to mastermind *The Ziegfeld Follies*. Mitchell had scrawled "NO GOOD" across Baum's script for a five-act operetta closely based on his tale, and substituted a vaudevillian hodgepodge that capped its Chicago success with a year-and-a-half run on Broadway and a road career that lasted, off and on, until 1911. The extravaganza increased Baum's wealth, but it also encouraged his tropism toward the theatrical. His first sequel to *The Wizard*, *The Marvelous Land of Oz* in 1904, was designed to be the basis of another extravaganza, featuring the vaudeville performers David C. Montgomery and Fred A. Stone, who had played the Tin Woodman and the Scarecrow in the Mitchell production. The book was dedicated to them and loaded with patter and puns suitable to their routines. It sold as a book, but failed as a musical called *The Woggle-Bug*, with lyrics by Baum and without, in the end, Montgomery and Stone. Anticipating the piggyback publicity system perfected by Walt Disney, Baum promoted this unfortunate production with a "Woggle-Bug Contest" in a Sunday comic page drawn by Walt McDougall and titled *Queer Visitors from the Marvelous Land of Oz*.

Despite frail health (angina, gallstones, inflamed appendix), Baum was a whirlwind of activity until his death at the age of sixty-two. Along with thirteen Oz sequels, he wrote a teen-oriented *Aunt Jane's Nieces* series under the name of Edith Van Dyne, young people's books under four other pseudonyms, an adult novel published anonymously, and many unpublished plays. Splendidly dressed in a white frock coat with silk lapels, he toured with film-and-slide presentations called *The Fairylogue and Radio-Plays*. A reviewer in the *Chicago Tribune* wrote that "his ability to hold a large audience's attention during two hours of tenuous entertainment was amply demonstrated." These early electronic productions were expensive, however, and by 1911 had helped bankrupt him. Thriftily moving his California winter residence from the Hotel del Coronado to a "handsome bungalow he christened Ozcot" in Hollywood, Baum found himself surrounded by the burgeoning movie industry without finding a way to tap into it profitably. The Oz Film Manufacturing Company, with Baum as president, produced some silent films, beginning with *The Patchwork Girl of Oz* in 1914, but, dismissed as "kiddie shows," they fell short at the box office. In 1925, six years after Baum's death in 1919, a movie of *The Wizard of Oz* was released; according to Hearn in one of his sterner moods, it was "totally lacking the magic of Baum's book" (though a Laurel-less Oliver Hardy played the Tin Woodman) and "had a dreadful script, written in part by the author's son Frank J. Baum." It was M-G-M's 1939 adaptation, of course, that hit the jackpot: the three-million-dollar film showed no profit on its original release, but it became a staple of postwar television. A hundred years after *The Wizard*'s publication, the movie is the main road into Oz.

Oz had very quickly become zoned for commercial activity. There is something depressing about the chronicle of its exploitation, a chronicle that Hearn caps with a compendious footnote that takes us up through the all-black *Wiz* (stage 1975, movie 1978) and the dead-on-arrival Disney *Return to Oz* (1985). And then there is the upcoming television series *Lost in Oz*. It is hard to read Baum's later Oz books without feeling the exploitation in progress, by a writer who only dimly understands his own masterpiece. After his death the series was extended by Ruth Plumly Thompson, who between 1921 and 1939 added nineteen titles; then, briefly, by John R. Neill, whose spidery, often insipid drawings illustrate all the Oz books but the first; by Jack Snow, a "minor science fiction writer"; by Rachel Cosgrove; by Eloise Jarvis McGraw and Lauren McGraw Wagner; and even by Baum's son, who legally battled his mother for the precious trademark "Oz." And, Hearn indefatigably tells us, "of late there has grown up a peculiar literary sub-genre of adult novels drawing on the Oz mythology," such as Geoff Ryman's *Was* (1992) and Gregory Maguire's *Wicked: The Life and Times of the Wicked Witch of the West* (1995)—the products, presumably, of Oz-besotted children now aged into postmodern creators freed from fear of copyright infringement.

The potent images of *The Wizard* do cry out for extension and elaboration. The M-G-M motion picture improves upon the book in a number of ways. It eliminates, for example, the all-too-Aesopian (and, prior to computer graphics, probably unfilmable) episode wherein the Queen of the mice and her many minions transport the Cowardly Lion out of the poppy bed where they have fallen asleep; instead, it retrieves from the 1902 musical the effective stage business that had a sudden snowstorm annul the spell of the poppies. The movie weeds out a number of extravagant beasts and the especially artificial episode of "the Dainty China Country" quaintly planted on the path to the witch's lair. The scenario amplifies the role of the Wicked Witch of the West, showing her as the source of all the obstacles in the pilgrims' path, as she watches them on the early television of her crystal ball. In the book, she is a relatively passive presence, easily doused ("I never thought a little girl like you would ever be able to melt me and end my wicked deeds. Look out—here I go!"), compared with the cackling green-faced film presence of Margaret Hamilton, who dies mourning her "beautiful wickedness!" Once she is dead, the film picks up speed; after the Wizard's unmasking and his unplanned departure, it is virtually over, whereas Baum's tale dillydallies through further complications on the way to the Good Witch of the South, involving fresh humanoid gadgetry like Fighting Trees and armless Hammer-Heads and a mechanical plot dependency upon the Golden Cap and its three-wish control of the Winged Monkeys. As a writer, Baum rarely knew when to quit, unfurling marvel after marvel while the human content—a content shaped by non-magical limitations—leaked away. He did not grasp that *The Wizard* concerns our ability to survive disillusion; miracles are humbug.

The Hollywood film begins with the human, gray Kansas and, unlike the book, plants on that drab land all the actors who will dominate Oz—the three farmhands, the wicked Almira Gulch on her bicycle, Professor Marvel in his flimsy van. They are there, and Dorothy returns to them. Hearn calls it "unforgivable" that the M-G-M movie cast Oz as a dream; but Dorothy on awakening protests, "It wasn't a dream." It was an alternative reality, an inner depiction of how we grow. As Jerome Charyn observes in his unsung but wonderful *Movieland: Hollywood and the Great American Dream Culture* (1989), "The whole film was about metamorphosis." Judy Garland, who was sixteen and noticeably buxom in the role of Baum's prepubescent Dorothy, was "a woman who seemed to flower from an ordinary little girl."* Growth is metamorphosis, and self-understanding is growth. The Scarecrow already has brains, the Tin Woodman is sentimental to a fault, the Lion has courage enough, but until the Wizard bestows external evidences (in the movie, more wittily than in the book) they feel deficient. Dorothy, capable and clear-sighted from the start, needs only to accept the grayness of home as a precious color, and to wish to return as ardently as she wished to escape "Over the Rainbow"—the movie's grand theme song, nearly removed from the final cut.

Like Charyn and Salman Rushdie (who has extolled *The Wizard* as "a parable of the migrant condition"), I belong to the generation more affected by the movie than by the book. For the testimony of one who read all the Oz books with adolescent credulity and delight, Gore Vidal's long essay of 1977, printed in two parts in *The New York Review of Books*, is impressive and peppery. He sees Baum as a protester against the violence of the rising American empire and "the iron Puritan order." It is true that an undercurrent of dissidence in the Oz books seems to have antagonized some librarians and critics; the director of the Detroit Library System, Ralph Ulveling, in 1957 pronounced them guilty of "negativism" and "a cowardly approach to life." Baum, in his introduction to *The Wizard*, strikes a challenging note; he deplores the "horrible and blood-curdling" incidents contained in "the old-time fairy tale" and promises his readers "a modernized fairy tale, in which the wonderment and joy are retained and the heart-aches and nightmares are left out." American Theosophy, to which Baum had been introduced by his formidable mother-in-law, mixed spiritualism and Buddhist and Hindu beliefs with a meliorism that rejected the darker, Devil-acknowledging side of Christianity. "God is Nature, and Nature God," Baum said; yet he also professed an animistic vision in which

> every bit of wood, every drop of liquid, every grain of sand or portion of rock has its myriads of inhabitants. . . . These invisible and vapory beings are known as Elementals. . . . They are soulless, but immortal; frequently possessed of extraordinary intelligence, and again remarkably stupid.

Madame H. P. Blavatsky, the founder of the Theosophical Society, in her *Isis Unveiled* (1877) wrote of these Elementals as "the creatures evolved in the four kingdoms of earth, air, fire, and water, and called by the kabalists gnomes, sylphs, salamanders, and undines." This giddying, virtually

---

*As Charyn puts it earlier in *Movieland*, "Judy Garland, a chubby child with tits. One of the pleasures of *The Wizard of Oz* is watching Judy grow within the film from a Kansas girl with baby fat into some kind of woman."

bacterial multitudinousness came to characterize Oz as its sequels multi-plied its regions and its strange and magical tribes; but *The Wizard* itself presents an uncluttered cosmogony, drawn in bright tints. According to Theosophy, our astral bodies come in distinct colors; so do the regions of Oz, with their inhabitants. As Vidal points out, Oz exists in orderly patches like the extensive gardens that Baum remembered from his child-hood home, and which he re-created in the geometrical plots of his gar-den at Ozcot.

The evils of capitalism, whose rewards proved so fickle for Baum, are absent from his alternative world: socialism-averse readers find in *The Emerald City* this much-quoted passage:

> There were no poor people . . . because there was no such thing as money, and all property of every sort belonged to the Ruler. The people were her children, and she [Princess Ozma] cared for them. Each person was given freely by his neighbors whatever he required for his use, which is as much as anyone may reasonably desire.

But the proletariat does not rule; rather, it is ruled in a mock-medieval manner by benevolent tyrants more often than not female, in keeping, perhaps, with the feminist tendencies of Theosophy and Matilda Gage's militant suffragism. Baum's rulers have a parental absolutism: Glinda is the ideal, ever-resourceful mother and the Wizard a typically bumbling father in Oz's sit-com as Baum first conceived it. Though he supported the pop-ulist William Jennings Bryan in 1896 and 1900, and the literature of the late nineteenth century abounds in literary Utopias, Oz is too unearthly to carry much political punch. It is constructed not of revolutionary intent but of wishful thinking. What earthiness *The Wizard* does have derives in considerable part from Denslow's sturdy, antic illustrations. Denslow, we learn in Hearn's *Annotated Wizard*, sometimes operated independently of the text: he drew a bear where Baum mentions a tiger, crowns the Lion before the author does, dresses Dorothy in her old gingham frock when Baum still has her in her Emerald City silks, and consistently omits (as does the movie) the "round, shining mark" that the Good Witch of the North plants, as protection, on her forehead with a kiss.

A centennial is a time for praise, but this reader is inclined to accept the invitation to argue with Hearn when he states, "Arguably there have been three great classic quests in American literature, Herman Melville's *Moby Dick; or The Whale* (1851), Mark Twain's *Adventures of Huckleberry Finn* (1883), and L. Frank Baum's *The Wonderful Wizard of Oz* (1900)." What-ever their flaws of carelessness or aesthetic miscalculation, the first two titles were gloriously *written*, in the ambition of telling all the truth, "heart-aches and nightmares" included. *The Wizard* is relatively a lucky gem, composed in the flat clear style of a man giving dictation. Hearn has been too long peering through the magnifying glass of *The Baum Bugle*, the triquarterly publication of the International Wizard of Oz Club, "founded in 1957 by thirteen-year-old Justin G. Schiller." In the course of his devotedly researched footnotes he sometimes nods into critical banality: the Cowardly Lion, it is said, "proves Ernest Hemingway's dictum that courage is grace under pressure." A juster analogy, drawn by Hearn more than once, is with *The Pilgrim's Progress*, another few-frills picaresque search story by an author in his forties with a habit of public performance (Bunyan was a preacher). *The Wizard* is a *Pilgrim's Progress* emptied of religion, except for the Theosophist inkling that there are many universes. At a time when children's literature was still drenched in what Hearn calls "the putrid Puritan morality of the Sunday schools," Baum produced a refreshingly agnostic fantasy. The witches are too comically wicked to be evil. The humbug Wizard, accused by Dorothy of being "a very bad man," protests, "I'm really a very good man; but I'm a very bad Wizard, I must admit." In another bold stroke of American simplification, Baum invented escapism without escape. Dorothy opts to forsake Oz; gray, windswept Kansas is reinstated (less thumpingly than in the movie) as the seat of lasting, familial happiness. Indeed, as a practical matter it is easier to color with contentment the place where we are than to find a Technicolor paradise. Denslow's last drawing shows the return with more exuberance than Baum's prose manages. In her hurry, chubby little Dorothy runs so hard that her silver shoes, Baum's less photogenic original of M-G-M's glistening ruby slippers, are flying off; we feel her rounding the bases (Scarecrow, Tin Woodman, Cowardly Lion) to home plate.

Hide and Seek

THE COMPLETE WORKS OF ISAAC BABEL, edited by Nathalie Babel, translated by Peter Constantine. 1072 pp., boxed. W. W. Norton, 2001.

Isaac Babel was born in the Moldavanka, a poor and raffish district of Odessa, in 1894, and died, it has been established only within the last ten years, in Moscow's Lubyanka Prison early in the morning on January 27, 1940. He was shot by a firing squad after a twenty-minute trial held the day before in the private chambers of Lavrenti Beria, the infamous head of the NKVD, the KGB's predecessor. Babel was convicted of "active participation in an anti-Soviet Trotskyite organization" and of "being a member of a terrorist conspiracy, as well as spying for the French and Austrian governments." He had confessed, during the previous eight months of imprisonment and interrogation, to charges of espionage, but his last recorded statement protested, "I am innocent. I have never been a spy. I never allowed any action against the Soviet Union. . . . I am asking for only one thing—let me finish my work."

This miserable end befell a writer whom Maxim Gorky had described to André Malraux in 1926 as "the best Russia has to offer." A quarter of a century later, Babel's contemporary Konstantin Paustovsky wrote in his reminiscences, "He was, for us, the first really Soviet writer." Babel was a Jew who embraced the Bolshevik Revolution of 1917 as a deliverance from (among other things) the anti-Semitic restrictions and sanctioned pogroms of the Czarist regime; to an extent, he embraced the violence of the era in which he came to manhood. His terse, polished short stories make heroes of the Moldavanka's murderous Jewish gangsters and of the brutal Cossacks with whom he rode as a war correspondent and Party propagandist during the Red Army's ill-fated invasion of Poland in the summer of 1920. His artistic star rose under the protection of Gorky, shone brightest with the publication of the collection *Red Cavalry* in 1926, and glimmered out as Stalin's rule, beginning in 1924 with Lenin's death, suffocated freedom of expression and imposed terror. Babel and the poet Osip Mandelstam, who died in 1938 in a concentration camp, were Stalin's most distinguished literary victims.

Ilya Ehrenburg, a fellow-Jew and a journalist with survival skills superior to the provocative Babel's, first mentions his old friend in his memoirs in a passage on games that writers play: "Isaak Babel used to hide from everybody, not because people would disturb his work but because he loved the game of hide-and-seek." Babel was, indeed, a man of many habitations, many styles, several pseudonyms, eight or so languages; he had three children by three different women, and for many years kept his common-law household in Moscow a secret from his legal wife, whom he married in 1919 and who lived in France from 1925 on. The daughter of that marriage, Nathalie, born in 1929, survived with her mother in Occupied France and eventually immigrated to the United States in 1961, four years after her mother died. A varied academic career brought Nathalie Babel around, through English and French and Latin American literature, to Slavic studies and the work of her elusive father, whom she met when she was a small child, during two visits he made to Paris in the 1930s. In the 1960s she edited a book of his letters and a book of lesser-known short stories; early in that decade she had met her Russian half-sister, Lidya, and Lidya's mother, Antonina, an impressive woman who had been the first construction engineer of her sex to work on the Moscow subway system and who at the age of eighty co-edited the most nearly complete edition, in two volumes, of Babel's works in Russian. Now Nathalie Babel, at the age of seventy-two, has edited a still fuller edition, translated into English by Peter Constantine. His oeuvre— stories, journals, journalistic reports, suppressed plays, film scripts produced and unproduced—can no longer play hide and seek; it is gathered here, a thousand pages strong.

The son of a dealer in agricultural machinery, Babel was well educated as a child, studying English, French, and German. The stories of Maupassant especially impressed him; his own first stories were written in literary French. His first published story, "Old Shloyme," written in Russian, appeared when he was eighteen and concerned the controversial matter of coerced Christian conversions under Czarist laws: its eighty-six-year-old hero commits suicide rather than change his religion to avoid eviction. Babel wrote about Jews with a brisk, at times scornful knowingness; he seemed prouder of being an Odessan, a child of this southerly Black Sea port equipped (the sketch "Odessa" tells us) with "sweet and oppressive spring evenings, the spicy aroma of acacias, and a moon filled with an unwavering, irresistible light shining over a dark sea." It is, he affirms, "the only Russian town where there is a good chance that our very own, sorely needed, homegrown Maupassant might be born." He asks, "If you think about it, doesn't it strike you that in Russian literature there haven't been so far any real, clear, cheerful descriptions of the sun?" His youthful stories supply this lack: "The sun hung from the sky like the pink tongue of a thirsty dog" ("Lyubka the Cossack"); "The sun . . . poured into the clouds like the blood of a gouged boar" and "The sun soared up into the sky and spun like a red bowl on the tip of a spear" ("Sunset"); "The orange sun is rolling across the sky like a severed head" ("Crossing the River Zbrucz").

The violence of these metaphors owes something to the Russian Symbolists, Aleksandr Blok and Andrei Bely foremost, whose poetry and prose place Russian under a pressure of metaphoric extravagance that English, since the age of Shakespeare, has rarely been asked to bear (unless by Gerard Manley Hopkins and Hart Crane). Babel's far-fetched tropes, in Peter Constantine's hard-working translation, explode off the page: "The stars scattered in front of the window like urinating soldiers" and "The velvet tablecloths knocked his eyes right off their feet" ("Sunset"); "I sat to the side, dozed, dreams pouncing around me like kittens" ("Italian Sun"); "A sour odor rose from the ground, as from a soldier's wife at dawn" ("Sashka Christ"); "The skies above me open up like a many-buttoned concertina" ("The Life of Matvey Rodionovich Pavlichenko"); "The silence of the sunset turned the grass around the castle blue. The moon rose green as a lizard above the pond" ("Berestechko"). In the relatively few stories written after those of *Red Cavalry*, many of them in a voice of boyhood reminiscence, the Symbolist skyrockets are fewer, though there are flares like "Caught between these two men, I watched the hoops of other people's happiness roll past me" ("Di Grasso") and this burst of imagery: "The night was lilac and heavy, like a bright mountain crystal. Veins of frozen rivulets lay across it. A star sank into a well of black clouds" ("Kolyvushka"). The solitary star is a frequent image in Babel, and his artistic pilgrimage feels like a lonely one, in an increasingly cold climate. The stories in *Red Cavalry*—so close to the journalism he was simultaneously producing—incautiously named a number of commanders, not always in a flattering context, and two of them, Semyon Budyonny and Kliment Voroshilov, rose in Stalin's hierarchy. In 1928, a Soviet critic chastised Babel for his low production, his "silence," but, travelling in 1929–30, "in search of new material," he witnessed the brutal collectivization and famine in the Ukraine, and there was little he dared say. "Revolution indeed! It's disappeared!" he is reported to have confided to Yuri Annenkov, a Russian artist and Paris expatriate. "It's the Central Committees that are pushing forward—they'll be more effective. They don't need wheels—they have machine guns instead. All the rest is clear and needs no further commentary, as they say in polite society." Yet he passed up opportunities to stay in Paris. Rather than be a French taxi driver, he always returned to the straitened and perilous vocation of a writer in Russia.

Paustovsky's memoir illuminates Babel's aesthetic: "Writers, he said, should write in Kipling's iron-clad prose; authors should have the clearest possible notion of what was to come out of their pens. A short story must have the precision of a military communiqué or a bank check." He describes him at work:

> Babel would go up to his desk and stroke his manuscript cautiously as though it were a wild creature which had still not been properly domesticated. Often he would get up during the night and reread three or four pages by the light of an oil lamp. . . . He would always find a few unnecessary words and throw them out with malicious glee. He used to say, "Your language becomes clear and strong, not when you can no longer add a sentence, but when you can no longer take away from it."

One thinks of Hemingway in Paris, honing language to a fresh starkness, and Hemingway had read Babel, as he stated in a 1936 letter to Ivan Kashkin: "Babel I know ever since his first stories were translated in French and the Red Calvary came out. I like his writing very much." But Hemingway included no Babel in his thousand-page anthology, *Men at War* (1942). *Red Cavalry* contains little war in the sense of clearly delineated military encounters; it is not even very clear that the Poles defeated the invading Red Army, including the Cossack cavalry. One of Babel's political offenses with the book was, as an editorial headnote states, giving lasting publicity to this "disastrous campaign," the Bolshevik regime's rash "first venture at bringing Communism to the world." Another offense was to describe, with an inarguable terseness, the atrocities incidental to the military action — prisoners shot, women raped, children and elders slain and mutilated, churches and synagogues desecrated, even beehives torched.

Although the thirty-four stories of *Red Cavalry*, some of them not much longer than the italic vignettes of war that Hemingway inserted in his collection *In Our Time*, are told from several points of view, including that of a hardened soldier, the predominant impression is of a noncombatant's struggle to trail the military action while hungry, sleep-deprived, and billeted among Galician civilians as confused and helpless as he. Shtetls abounded in the border region of western Ukraine and eastern Poland, and the story cycle traces not only a bookish young Jew's attempt to learn war — to "fathom the soul of a fighter," to "understand life, to see what it actually is" — but Babel's homecoming, by way of witnessed Jewish suffering, to his own Jewishness. This progress, as well as the progress of the campaign, is more easily followed in the journal Babel kept in that summer of 1920 than in the stories, where the varied viewpoints and rigorous literary economy create a somewhat enigmatic and decontextualized effect, as of scenes lit by a fitful barrage. The journal has a constant, increasingly disillusioned hero, who gravitates toward the Jewish bystanders of this invasion: "Discussions with Jews, my people, they think I'm Russian, and my soul opens up to them." "An old Jew—I love talking with our people—they understand me." "I roam about the shtetl, there is pitiful, powerful, undying life inside the Jewish hovels." Of a synagogue: "Everything is white and plain to the point of asceticism, everything is incorporeal and bloodless to a monstrous degree, to grasp it fully you have to have the soul of a Jew. But what does this soul consist of? Is it not bound to be our century in which they will perish?" The Jews suffered looting and raping from Polish and Soviet armies alternately. Babel takes note as he trots by: "A terrible, uncanny shtetl, Jews stand at their doors like corpses, I wonder about them: what more are you going to have to go through?" In the wake of a bloody Polish pogrom in the town of Komarow, Babel observes his own army "going around indifferently, looting where they can, ripping the clothes off the butchered people."

The so-called Odessa stories, written and published in periodicals somewhat before the stories of *Red Cavalry*, also trace disillusion with the Bolshevik Revolution. Benya Krik, the dashingly ruthless crime boss at the center of the stories, in his confident heyday jests of the Jewish situation in Russia:

> "Didn't God Himself make a mistake when he settled the Jews in Russia so they could be tormented as if they were in hell? Wouldn't it have been better to have the Jews living in Switzerland, where they would've been surrounded by first-class lakes, mountain air, and Frenchmen galore?"

These gangsters' attempt to make a congenial environment for themselves in Odessa, however, runs afoul of the new regime; when the Cheka arrests and executes the criminals, their patriarch, old one-eyed Froim Grach, goes to the chairman of the Cheka, a bureaucrat from Moscow named Vladislav Simen, and pleads, "You're killing off all the lions! And you know what you'll be left with if you keep it up? You'll be left with shit!" Simen offers Froim Grach cognac but arranges to have him unceremoniously shot by two Red Army men, who afterward boast of how many bullets it took to kill him; one of them explains, "If you don't butcher an old man like that, he'll live forever." When a native Odessan protests, telling Simen that he "can't understand what the old man represented," the out-of-towner asks, "What use would that man have been to the society we are building?" The answer reluctantly comes: "I suppose no use at all." Babel never published the story, "Froim Grach," in Russia; it first appeared in a New York Russian-language journal, in 1963.

The tale "How Things Were Done in Odessa" begins with an invitation, "Let's talk about Benya Krik. Let's talk about his lightning-quick beginning and his terrible end." But it was only in a screenplay for a silent movie entitled *Benya Krik* that Babel revealed the terrible end. The archcriminal, who "got his way . . . because he was passionate, and passion holds sway over the universe," is double-crossed by the Red Army while hijacking a boxcar full of watermelons, and is shot from behind:

> The back of Benya's shaved neck. A spot appears on it, a gaping wound with blood spurting in all directions.
> FADEOUT

Babel's compressed, imagistic style and taste for grotesquerie consorted well with the genius of silent films. The five surviving scripts (three for silents, one for a talkie, and one a fragment of two scenes) conjure up a twitchy, fast-moving world of long shadows, raking lights, sinister freaks, and Eisensteinian close-ups. The script for *Roaming Stars* begins:

> The edge of a double bed. Night. The broad back of old Ratkovich, the rich man of the shtetl. He is asleep. Somebody's bare arm slithers over his pillow. Old Ratkovich rolls over, and in his sleep traps the thief's hand, moves again, the hand frees itself, snatches a bundle of keys from under the pillow, and disappears.

Toward the end:

> Rogdai's hand clutching Kalnischker's false teeth. The bullet pierces the dead man's hand and the fingers unclench, dropping the false teeth. The hanging man's body turns its back to the viewer. Cut.

The alleged comedy among the screenplays, *The Chinese Mill* (*An Attempted Mobilization*) is a fairly inscrutable joke on misplaced Komsomol—Young Communist League—zeal, and the talkie, *Number 4 Staraya Square*, also gingerly undertakes political satire; its heroine, a stalwart aeronautical engineer, may be derived from Babel's common-law wife, the pioneering Antonina. The scripts and his two plays—*Sunset*, performed at the Moscow Art Theatre in 1928 but criticized for its ambivalent attitude toward the bourgeoisie and dropped from the theatre's repertoire, and *Maria*, published in 1935 but cancelled during rehearsals and causing Babel's patron Gorky to decry his "Baudelairean predilection for rotting meat"—suggest that after *Red Cavalry* Babel was seeking coöperative art forms in which to hide or mute his potentially fatal honesty.

"I have no imagination," he told Paustovsky. "I can't invent. I have to know everything down to the last vein, otherwise I can't write a thing. My motto is *authenticity*." His late short stories retreated to the relatively safe area of his boyhood in Czarist times, in Odessa and the town of Nikolayev. Some of these, like "The Story of My Dovecote," describing his grandfather's death in a pogrom, and "The Awakening," about his failure to become the violin prodigy that Jewish parents in Odessa hoped for, are among his best-known. They are more accessible and anthologizable than his aggressively gaudy earlier stories. Even so, the frankly sexual "My First Fee," recounting how the young author traded a spoken tale for sex with a prostitute, went unpublished. (Prostitution is a favorite theme, and Babel's Communism is nowhere more enthusiastic than in this diary entry on the women in the Red Army: "They gallop ahead with hitched-up skirts, dust-covered, fat-breasted, all of them whores, but comrades too, and whores because they are comrades, that's the most important thing, they serve in every way they can, these heroines.") A passing utterance from the heroine of "My First Fee" might serve as the motto for much of his proclamatory fiction and reportage:

> "The things men do," Vera whispered, without turning around. "My God, the things men do!"

Cynthia Ozick, in an elegant introduction—offered along with a preface by Nathalie Babel and a foreword by the translator—makes the case that the time has come "to set Babel beside Kafka." Each "was an acutely conscious Jew," she says. "Each invented a type of literary modernism." The two of them "can be said to be the twentieth century's European coordinates." Both, she need hardly point out, died in their forties and left behind a fragmentary, truncated body of work; they are wounded authors. But, for all Babel's unblinking witness and electric, heroically wrought prose, of which a final measure of music and slangy pungency must inevitably be left behind in the Russian, it is hard to feel him Kafka's equal. Kafka *could* invent, and the forces that oppressed him were enough interior to be converted into giant fables, comic representations of modern man's cosmic unease. Babel's oppressors were exterior—the philistine censors and paranoid enforcers of the increasingly totalitarian revolution he initially supported and, to the end, sought to accommodate. But no imaginative conversion, and not even silence, once his talent had announced itself, could evade or placate those enforcers. Babel's art flourished in Lenin's false dawn. As Stalin's darkness fell, he became his talent's warder; his vitality became his enemy.

THURBER AND WHITE

Introduction to the Perennial Edition of Is Sex Necessary?

FOR SOME YEARS, including the months of 1929 when they jointly composed *Is Sex Necessary?*, James Thurber and E. B. White shared, during office hours, a small room at *The New Yorker*. White had already become the darling of the magazine's editor, Harold Ross; it was through White's suggestion, in 1927, that Ross had hired Thurber, who at the age of thirty-two was still a struggling writer from Columbus, Ohio, with little to show for several journalistic stints and aspiring sojourns in Manhattan and Paris. While they shared their close quarters, White tutored Thurber in the art of writing for Talk of the Town, and Thurber gradually became the chief Talk writer and rewrite man. When Thurber died in 1961, White remembered the period fondly:

> It was a fine thing to be young and at work in New York for a new magazine when Thurber was young and at work, and I will always be glad that this happened to me.
>
> It was fortunate that we got on well; the office we shared was the size of a hall bedroom. There was just room enough for two men, two typewriters, and a stack of copy paper. The copy paper disappeared at a scandalous rate—not because our production was high (although it was) but because Thurber used copy paper as the natural receptacle for discarded sorrows, immediate joys, stale dreams, golden prophecies, and messages of good cheer to the outside world and to fellow-workers. His mind was never at rest, and his pencil was connected to his mind by the best conductive tissue I have ever seen in action.

Is Sex Necessary? was published in November of 1929, enjoying warm reviews and healthy sales—eleven printings totalling forty-five thousand copies in the first five months. Scott Elledge's biography of White asserts that "Eight months earlier the authors had begun to think about collaborating on a parody of some of the works on sex produced by 'heavy writers' (doctors, psychiatrists, and 'other students of misbehavior') with which the market had recently been flooded." Robert Emmet Long's biography of Thurber puts it rather differently: "One day in the late 1920s, Thurber and White discovered that they had each begun parodies of the same subject—the current rash of books that, with pseudoscientific nomenclature, explained sex and psychological adjustment to the layman." In a list of the unsuccessful works that Thurber had accumulated by 1927, Long mentions "an elaborate, unpublished parody of current best-sellers, 'Why We Behave Like Microbe Hunters.' " Certainly Thurber's chapters in *Is Sex Necessary?*—the odd-numbered ones, the glossary, and the preface by "Lt. Col. H.R.L. Le Boutellier, C.I.E."— show the greater enthusiasm for the parodistic premise of the book, which is that the authors are specialists following in the footsteps of the fictional doctors Karl Zaner and Walter Tithridge, "the deans of American sex." Thurber had a keener interest than White in specifically psychological predicaments; he was the more consciously troubled, with his non-starting literary career, his compromised eyesight (he had lost an eye to a brother's arrow in a childhood accident, and the other eye was succumbing to "sympathetic ophthalmia"), and his marriage to Althea née Adams, a tall, ambitious former campus beauty queen at Ohio State University in Columbus. Their union early encountered sexual disarray; Thurber told a friend that "sleeping with Althea is like sleeping with the Statue of Liberty," and she is believed to have inspired the menacing female figure in so many of his drawings.

White's contributions to *Is Sex Necessary?*—the even-numbered chapters, the foreword, "Answers to Hard Questions," and "A Note on the Drawings in This Book"—seem relatively diffident and innocent. Beginning in Chapter II with a bumbling, Benchleyesque embarrassment over distinguishing love from passion, White does work up a certain comedic enthusiasm in Chapter IV over *Schmalhausen* trouble, specific to "girls who have taken a small apartment (*schmalhausen*) and are reading the behaviorism essays of Samuel D. Schmalhausen," and ends in Chapter VIII by invoking the minnesingers and the medieval tradition of romantic love, anticipating by ten years Denis de Rougemont's *Love in the Western World*. Chapter VIII is the only one jointly composed: Long credits White with "the first and final parts," leaving the hilarious yet heartfelt account of the frigid male's "recessive knee" to Thurber:

> Simply stated, the knee phenomenon is this: occasions arise sometimes when a girl presses her knee, ever so gently, against the knee of the young man she is out with. . . . Often the topic of conversation has something to

do with it: the young people, talking along pleasantly, will suddenly experience a sensation of compatibility, or of friendliness, or of pity, or of community-of-interests. One of them will make a remark singularly agreeable to the other person—a chance word or phrase that seems to establish a bond between them. Such a remark can cause the knee of the girl to be placed against the knee of the young man. Or, if the two people are in a cab, the turning of a sharp corner will do it. In canoes, the wash from a larger vessel will bring it about. In restaurants and dining-rooms it often takes place under the table, as though by accident. On divans, sofas, settees, couches, davenports, and the like, the slight twist of the young lady's body incident to receiving a light for her cigarette will cause it. . . . Now, a normal male in whom there are no traces of frigidity will allow his knee to retain its original position, sometimes even exerting a very slight counter-pressure. A frigid male, however, will move his knee away at the first suggestion of contact, denying himself the electric stimulus of love's first stirring.

Parts of this exposition, especially a passage that describes "the merest touch of knee to knee, light as the brush of a falling blossom against one's cheek, and just as lovely," sound more like White than Thurber; but Chapter V, "The Lilies-and-Bluebird Delusion," is pure Thurber:

I have in mind the case of a young lady whose silly mother had taught her to believe that she would have a little son, three years old, named Ronald, as soon as her husband brought a pair of bluebirds into a room filled with lilies-of-the-valley. The young man (to say nothing of the young woman) was thus made the victim of one of the extremest cases of Bird and Flowers Fixation which has ever come to my attention. I shall transcribe, from Dr. Tithridge's note, the first dialogue on the subject that took place between the young couple. . . . On the evening of the 25th of June, when the couple were married, the young husband entered their hotel suite to find it literally a garden of lilies-of-the-valley. He was profoundly touched, but baffled, and asked his wife who was dead.

"Where are the bluebirds?" she replied, coyly.

"What bluebirds?" he demanded.

"*The* bluebirds," she said, blushing.

Both men had reason for sexual perplexity as 1929 wound down. Thurber felt simultaneously trapped and spurned in his six-year-old marriage to Althea, which had become an erratically "open" one of separate residences and overlooked affairs. A "boxed-in feeling," we read in Chapter VII, can lead to "delusions of persecution [that] may attain astounding proportions." Thurber's inner life, hyperactive since his boyhood, when his natural frailty was intensified by his ophthalmological impairment, could indeed achieve astounding proportions; the convenient diagnosis "nervous breakdown" entered his medical history a number of times, and there were, as he aged, increasingly frequent explosions of wild and rageful drunken behavior. White, at the time of co-authoring *Is Sex Necessary?*, was involved with an older woman, a divorcée with two children, a woman so seductively intelligent and beautifully understanding as to overwhelm the evasive tactics that had kept him a bachelor during his footloose twenties. As a free creative spirit, he had travelled across the country in a Model T Ford when the Western roads were rudimentary, and had shipped out of the country on a one-way boat ticket to Alaska. Harold Ross, who wanted him steadfast on the editorial bridge of the good ship *New Yorker*, pressed another sort of suit, which White dodged by such maneuvers as taking refuge in a Canadian boys' camp and threatening to become a camp counsellor. But Ross and, on the romantic front, Ross's right-hand woman, Katharine Angell, proved too much for the rising writer's vision of an ideal freedom. White and Katharine abruptly married a few days after *Is Sex Necessary?* was published, occasioning this item in Walter Winchell's gossip column:

> News that couldn't wait until Monday: E. B. White, of *The New Yorker*'s comical department and one of the better wits in the town, and Katharine Angell, the managing editor of *The New Yorker*, eloped Tuesday and were sealed up-state.
>
> The groom recently co-authored a book titled (heh-heh): "Is Sex Necessary?"

The wedding was performed in Bedford Village, in a Presbyterian church after the couple failed to find a justice of the peace, and the bride's dog, Daisy (a gift from the Thurbers), got into a fight with the minister's police dog. White later remembered, "It was a very nice wedding—nobody threw anything, and there was a dog fight." The marriage, of which Katharine had told a friend at the time, "If it lasts only a year, it will be worth it," lasted until she died in 1977, and was by all signs a happy and mutually supportive one.

In *Is Sex Necessary?*, it may have been Thurber who wrote, in the climactic eighth chapter, "Life, as we know, is very insistent; almost daily people become involved with other people," but it was White who observed, in the penultimate paragraph, "An imagined kiss is more easily controlled, more thoroughly enjoyed, and less cluttery than an actual kiss." The danger of entrapment in reality (e.g., women) is a theme common to both writers, both of them nervous, wary men who at this tender point in their lives could not foresee their future renown or the lasting success of the magazine that had given them professional shelter. Their joint answer to the question the title of their book poses would seem to be "Maybe, but we'd rather it weren't." Seldom has a book with the word "sex" in the title had so little good to say for it.

The two men never collaborated on another book, and their office-sharing ended in 1930. Thurber was five years older and yet the more extravagant in his behavior and art. He was a natural show-off, given, like his mother, to amateur theatrics and antic monologues. In his near-blindness he found it entertaining to hoax his friends with uncannily imitated voices over the telephone. Fame held no terrors for him. In 1960, a Broadway revue based on his work, titled *A Thurber Carnival*, was faltering at the box office; he stepped in and played himself, delivering a monologue each night from a chair whisked to the center of the stage on a conveyor belt. Elliott Nugent, his old friend and the co-author of their play *The Male Animal*, commented, "That S.O.B. has been trying to get on the stage for forty years, to my certain knowledge." White, in contrast, never spoke in public and appeared onstage only for the mute acceptance of some honorary degrees. Still, as Elledge points out:

> In background and experience the two men had much in common. Their parents had not gone to college. Each had been given as a middle name the name of a Protestant minister. The middle-class culture of Mount Vernon, New York, was not much different from that of Columbus, Ohio. Both had been editors of university newspapers. . . . Both had written scripts for campus musicals. Neither had shown much ability to write fiction; both admired the great American paragraphers.

Both, he could have gone on, became the biological father of one child—Rosemary Thurber, Joel White—and stayed young by writing elegant and, in White's case, classic books for children. Both achieved high literary status without ever publishing a novel for adults. Both were, it is almost unnecessary to say, white, Protestant males when to be anything else was to enjoy, in the United States, minority status. In White's chapter "The Sexual Revolution: Being a Rather Complete Survey of the Entire Sexual Scene," a generic figure called "Man"—of two illustrative drawings by Thurber, one has Thurber's mustache and spectacles and the other White's furrowed brow and central hair-parting—"had come to know enough about permutations and combinations to realize that with millions of Caucasian females to choose from, the chances of his choosing the ideal mate were almost zero." Damsels of African, Asian, or Jewish blood evidently needed not apply.

Rereading *Is Sex Necessary?* seventy-five years after its creation, one is more conscious than its good-humored, liberal-minded authors could have been of its phallocratic assumptions and misogynistic tendencies. Thurber, in the chapter "Claustrophobia, or What Every Young Wife Should Know," amusingly relates the case of a husband (born, like Thurber, in 1894) who is heedlessly painted into the bathroom while shaving and then is told by his wife, "You'll simply have to stay in there till the paint dries." He traces, in an increasingly urgent tone, how the difficulties a husband experiences with guest towels and such enigmatic household details lead to "the inception of a Persecution Complex and the slow deterioration of mind and spirit incident upon claustrophobia," and he concludes by decrying the "heavy toll of male minds as the result of the carelessness or stupidity of wives." White ends the next chapter on an equally harsh and abrupt note: "So you see, frigidity in men has many aspects, many angles. To me it is vastly more engrossing than frigidity in women, which is such a simple phenomenon you wonder anybody bothers about it at all." *The Vagina Monologues* lay well in the future.

White and Thurber, though agnostic as adults, were raised as Christians early in the last century, when the Puritan heritage was still vitally felt in the respectable middle class. Both families were shocked and offended by their sons' chastely racy spoof. White overheard his father say to his mother, "Well, I don't know what *you* think about it, but *I'm* ashamed of it." Thurber's loyal father back in Columbus told an inquirer, "That name sort of bothered me at first. I spent plenty of time dodging the young woman [the librarian] every time I visited the public library." The two writers' voices harmonize in a distrust of sex and resentment of the contortions and submissions that sex exacts from men. The early-twenty-first-century reader, amid the furor over gay marriage and in the wake of the Pill, the free-loving counterculture of the Sixties, the women's liberation of the Seventies, and the outing of AIDS in the Eighties, must make an effort to feel how sweetly daring it was for these two non-Casanovas to put their modest experience and considerable qualms at the service of this spoof, which for all its flimsiness and signs of carefree haste says much that is honest and true about human sexual discomfort.

The drawings, of course, keep the text from ever too heavily touching the ground. As White explains in his note on the drawings, it was he, in the offices of the young *New Yorker*, who noticed them, retrieved them from the wastebasket, inked them in, and presented them to Harper and Brothers as the finished illustrations. It was a stroke of critical genius on White's part, and it launched Thurber's career as an artist: after *Is Sex Necessary?* appeared, Ross began to run Thurber's cartoons in the magazine. They became, along with those of Peter Arno and Helen Hokinson and Charles Addams, signature adornments of its pages.

With White's marriage, the collaborative fever between the two Talk writers cooled, and, as the magazine prospered and expanded, the office the size of a hall bedroom no longer needed to be shared. But the names of Thurber and White were linked for good, and the Whites never quite surrendered their old friendship to Thurber's later provocations and fractious egotism. *Is Sex Necessary?*, breezy and slight and overextended as it is, has never been out of print. It stands as a rare conjunction of singular talents, a fusion bred of close professional quarters. Its jests cast shadows; melancholy and anxiety underlie its high spirits. *Sex isn't everything*, the book seems to say, *but, then, what is?*

Thurber's Art

JAMES THURBER once told a newspaper interviewer, "I'm not an artist. I'm a painstaking writer who doodles for relaxation." Yet the drawings rival his writings in their fame and lasting appeal. By the mid-1930s, his cartoons had become staples in *The New Yorker*, where Thurber had been publishing Talk of the Town pieces and signed humor since 1927. Until blindness overtook him, he illustrated his books—his comic masterpiece, *My Life and Hard Times* (1933), and his insouciant *Fables for Our Time* (1940), and his ardent, 430-word, pre-war "parable in pictures," *The Last Flower* (1939). The author as his own more or less naïve illustrator had twentieth-century precedents in Clarence Day, Max Beerbohm, and Hilaire Belloc. Nineteenth-century writer/artists like Goethe, Thackeray, Victor Hugo, and Oscar Wilde date from an age when drawing lessons were an intrinsic part of a gentleman's education. Thurber surely drew as a Columbus, Ohio, schoolboy; but an accident at the age of eight led to the loss of one eye and to limited, deteriorating vision in the other, and his development as a picture-maker was arrested at a lively, winsome primitivism. Some of his best-known cartoons, indeed, were the product of a carefree ineptitude: the one captioned "All right, have it your way— you heard a seal bark" originated, by his own testimony, when an attempt to draw a seal on a rock came out looking more like a seal on the headboard of a bed. A similar improvisation titled "That's my first wife up there, and this is the *present* Mrs. Harris" turned a woman crouching at

A contribution to *Cartoon America: Comic Art in the Library of Congress* (2006).

"All Right, Have It Your Way—You Heard a Seal Bark!"

the head of a badly drawn staircase into one crouched, or stuffed and mounted, on a bookcase. And in the cartoon captioned "You're not my patient, you're my meat, Mrs. Quist!" there seems no reason why the mustachioed medico leering down at the alarmed bed-ridden woman should be standing on a chair except that Thurber—who after White stopped inking-in for him drew directly in pen and ink on the paper—had neglected to make him tall enough for his feet to reach the floor.

"Well, What's Come Over *You* Suddenly?"

In his 1950 preface to his first cartoon collection, originally published in 1932, Thurber recounts how White, discovering him working at such refinements as crosshatching, exclaimed, "Good God, don't do that! If you ever became good you'd be mediocre." Yet one should not underestimate Thurber's conventional skills: in the drawing captioned "Well, what's come over *you* suddenly?" he took care to darken the other woman's shoe to show that the husband has been transfixed by a game of under-the-table footsie. Some of his captionless spots for *The New Yorker*, and his illustrations for his 1945 children's book *The White Deer*, carried out in Conté crayon when his failing sight no longer permitted pen and ink, show a care and balance considerably removed from the scratchy slapdash of his captioned cartoons.

Many of the captions provoke hilarity only because Thurber drew the picture: imagine *"Touché!"* by any other artist, or "What have you done with Dr. Millmoss?" Nor would his many treatments of what he called, in one droll yet ominous sequence, "The War Between Men and Women," be funny if the interchangeable men and women—"with the outer semblance," Dorothy Parker said, "of unbaked cookies"—were any more finely formed. The utterances so breezily illustrated savor of his sexually

"Touché!"

"What have you done with Dr. Millmoss?"

vexed first marriage to the stately Ohio beauty Althea Adams, and of its boozy dishevelment: "When I realize that I once actually *loved* you I go cold all over"; "Everybody noticed it. You gawked at her all evening"; "This gentleman was kind enough to see me home, darling"; "With you I have known peace, Lida, and now you say you're going crazy"; "I'm helping Mr. Gorley with his novel, darling"; "Your wife seems terribly smart, Mr. Bruce"; "Your husband has talked about nothing but you, Mrs. Miller"; "You keep your wife's name out of this, Ashby!"; "That martyred look won't get you anywhere with me!"; "Have you fordotten our ittle suicide pact?"; "Have you seen my pistol, Honey-bun?"; "If you can keep a secret, I'll tell you how my husband died"; "Which you am I talking to now?"

Thurber's childish drawings served up advanced adult fare; his men and women were libidinous to an extent that pressed *The New Yorker's* youthful prudery to its limit. The Library of Congress is in possession of an exuberant pencil drawing, on lined paper, that didn't make it into mass circulation—the impending copulation of unbaked cookies. Thurber's head buzzed with not only sex but literature, especially the Victorian sort memorized in the Columbus, Ohio, of his youth. Nineteenth-century chestnuts like Longfellow's "Excelsior," Sir Walter Scott's "Lochinvar," Tennyson's "Locksley Hall," and Whittier's "Barbara Frietchie" became weirdly endearing, with unexpected pockets of pathos, when he illustrated them, as did such literary cartoon captions as "I come from haunts of coot and hern!" and "I said the hounds of Spring are on Winter's traces—but let it pass, let it pass!"

Thurber's drawing feels unstoppable, like the speech of a man who does not know a foreign language very well but compensates by speaking it very fast. His technically challenged style delivered a shock amid the opulently finished, subtly washed, anatomically correct *New Yorker* cartoons of mostly, in those days, art-school graduates; his more crudely amateurish successors in contemporary minimalism demonstrate by contrast how dynamic and expressive, how oddly tender, Thurber's art was— a personal art that captured in ingenuous scrawls a modern man's bitter experience and nervous excess.

Magnum Opus

TOWARD THE END of her not long but certainly brave, sensible, inventive, and distinguished life, the heroine of E. B. White's *Charlotte's Web* responds to a question from her friend and protégé Wilbur the pig. He has noticed that she has painstakingly made, in a high corner of his pen, a round fuzzy object, and asks, "Is it a plaything?" She responds:

> "Plaything? I should say not. It is my egg sac, my *magnum opus*."
> "I don't know what a magnum opus is," said Wilbur.
> "That's Latin," explained Charlotte. "It means 'great work.' This egg sac is my great work—the finest thing I have ever made."

Her egg sac, in the fullness of time, releases five hundred fourteen tiny spiders, all but three of whom float away on balloons of silk let loose from their spinnerets, to add to the world's arachnid population; White's book, in the fullness of time, has sold over ten million copies and been translated into more than twenty languages. Scott Elledge's 1984 biography of White states, "For the last twenty years in America, *Charlotte's Web* has outsold *Winnie the Pooh*, any single Mary Poppins book, *The Wind in the Willows*, *The Little Prince*, and *Alice in Wonderland*." A 1976 *Publishers Weekly* poll, of teachers and librarians and other word-folk, to determine the ten best children's books written in America since 1776, placed *Charlotte's Web* first. A century after White's birth, it would seem to be the book, of his fifteen or so, most certain to carry his reputation, via the tenacious strands of renewed readership, into the next millennium.

Who would have predicted this in 1952, when his tale of talking barnyard animals was first published? White at the time was fifty-three, widely esteemed as a poetic humorist, an incomparably graceful and pungent essayist, and the mainstay of *The New Yorker*—the pure yet sober,

---

Penned for the centenary of White's birth, in 1999.

light yet piercing voice sounding above all its other gathered weekly voices. As far back as 1926, Harold Ross had recognized that voice as the one his new magazine needed; Ross clung with all the devices at an editor's command (money, love, guilt-inducement) to his sometimes wriggling prize. Ralph Ingersoll, the managing editor in *The New Yorker*'s early years, once said, "I can't remember a piece by anyone but E. B. White that Ross ever really thought just right. White was the exception to prove his lack of faith in everyone else." Yet the young writer was prone to absenting himself from the offices where he was the indispensable editorialist (in Notes and Comment) and "newsbreaks" commentator, as well as contributor of "casuals" (humorous pieces and fiction), versifier, cartoon-caption fine-tuner, and general inspirator. In 1929, having left New York City for Camp Otter, in Ontario, where he had worked for two happy summers, in 1920 and 1921, he wrote Ross,

> next to yourself and maybe one or two others, I probably have as tender a feeling for your magazine as anybody. For me it isn't a complete life, though, and that's one reason why returning to this place . . . has been such a satisfying experience. . . . The fellow that I first came here with is now running the camp, and we're working on a plan for going in business together.

This same truant summer, another *New Yorker* mainstay, editor Katharine Sergeant Angell, was in Reno getting a divorce. Entertaining some prospects of marrying White, she wrote him, as woman and editor, a letter of remarkable acumen and seductiveness, which read in part:

> You say you're a failure at the writing racket and that you could be contented in your present job if you didn't mind being just a hack. . . . You feel that in thirty years you haven't produced a really important book, poem or piece of prose—Most people haven't by then. It seems to me, though, that you are pre-eminently a writer—everything you do has a certain perfection that is rare. . . . For you to give up writing now would be like a violinist so good that he could always be the Concert Master of one of the four or five leading orchestras of the world, giving up fiddling because he couldn't be Heifetz. Perhaps you'll never be a Heifetz, perhaps you will. . . . But it doesn't seem sensible for a concert master to throw over music, the thing he most loved in the world, because he can't be Heifetz.

In the event, White returned to the magazine, married Mrs. Angell, and continued in concertmaster harness, though with periodic restlessness and chafing. He moved her, himself, and their son, Joel, to Maine in the Thirties, came back to New York in the Forties, and went to Maine for good in the Fifties, twice throwing a spanner into her career as editor.

While still contributing to *The New Yorker*, and ennobling the modest newsbreaks with his genius, he had a tricky way of doing some of his best and freest work away from the magazine's Ross-run pages: the essays of *One Man's Meat* appeared, but for a few, as a monthly column in *Harper's* from 1938 to 1943, and the perennially fresh tribute "Here Is New York" was done for *Holiday* in 1948.

He was both a natural and a reluctant writer. A letter to his brother Stanley in 1947 says, "I can remember, really quite distinctly, looking a sheet of paper square in the eyes when I was seven or eight years old and thinking 'This is where I belong, this is it.' " To a college student he confided in 1963, "I was a writing fool when I was eleven years old and have been tapering off ever since." In 1945, in a note to Ross, he claimed, "I am not as sure of myself as I used to be, and write rather timidly, staring at each word as it comes out, and wondering what is wrong with *it*." In a 1949 Notes and Comment he wrote:

> The thought of writing hangs over our mind like an ugly cloud, making us apprehensive and depressed, as before a summer storm, so that we begin the day by subsiding after breakfast, or by going away, often to seedy and inconclusive destinations: the nearest zoo, or a branch post office to buy a few stamped envelopes. Our professional life has been a long, shameless exercise in avoidance. . . . Yet the record is there. Not even lying down and closing the blinds stops us from writing; not even our family, and our preoccupation with same, stops us. We have never counted the words, but we estimated them once and the estimate was staggering.

He had high standards, fretful health, dazzling success at magazine work, and a hankering for a vague but majestic magnum opus. In 1937, he attempted to take time off, not only from *The New Yorker* but from his wife and son, to write a long poem; what came of it was his longest and strangest piece of self-description, "Zoo Revisited: Or the Life and Death of Olie Hackstaff." The poem, which imitates *The Waste Land* in its refrains, chantlike short lines, and pervasive anomie, waited seventeen years before White published it, in *The Second Tree from the Corner*, whose title story is another rendering of a nibbling, disorienting, unshakable unease: "the dizziness in the streets, the constricting pain in the back of the neck, the apprehensions, the tightness of the scalp, the inability to concentrate, the despondency and the melancholy times, the feeling of pressure and tension, the anger at not being able to work, the anxiety over work not done, the gas on the stomach." The same collection holds "The Door," a piece of humor that skids off into dread: its central image is of rats that "the Professor had driven crazy by forcing them to deal with problems which were beyond the scope of rats, the insoluble problems." For a while, various doors marked with symbols of religion, commerce, and sex open when the ratlike hero jumps at them, but then they suddenly refuse to give, and the ache in the head is so great that the solution seems to be surgical removal of the prefrontal lobe, which

> only means a whiff of ether, a few deft strokes, and the higher animal becomes a little easier in his mind and more like the lower one. From now on, you see, that's the way it will be, the ones with the small prefrontal lobes will win because the other ones are hurt too much by this incessant bumping.

The ease of being a simple animal powerfully attracted White. His idyllic (as he recalled it) boyhood was rich in pets and vacations among wildlife; when he transplanted himself to Maine, he filled the barn with domestic animals. From the civilized discontent of being a humanoid tortured rat it was a short hop to being a footloose humanoid mouse—Stuart Little. In the late Twenties, while sleeping in a Pullman upper berth, White had dreamed of "a small character who had the features of a mouse, was nicely dressed, courageous, and questing." To entertain his eighteen nephews and nieces, he made up episodes about this plucky little dream-mouse and wrote them down; in 1938, having tried and failed to find a publisher, he took his "rejected child" to Maine. Returning to New York seven years later, in the winter of 1944–45, he was, by his account, "almost sure I was about to die, my head felt so queer." In order "to ease the lot of my poor widow," he completed *Stuart Little* with relative swiftness, before going to San Francisco to witness the birth of the United Nations, in his new role as editorialist for world government. Harper and Brothers published *Stuart Little* in 1945. The gynecological horror of a woman (Mrs. Frederick C. Little) giving birth to a mouse appalled some librarians and teachers, and White was compelled to fudge the freak by maintaining that Stuart is just "a small guy who *looks* very much like a mouse." Stuart meets the challenge of his smallness with a verve and bonhomie that have enchanted children nevertheless. The mouse-boy-guy character and his adventures emerge from a dreamy nest of sublimations—White had described his ailments of this period as "mice in the subconscious and spurs in the cervical spine"—and there is something fey and disconnected about the series of episodes that prevent it, for all its charm and oblique autobiography, from being the desired magnum opus. But White had found the one way, apparently, in which he could write a novel: by writing it as a children's book.

Charlotte's Web was honored, in 1994, with *The Annotated Charlotte's Web*, a wide-format edition in which the text, studded by green footnotes, is accompanied by many elucidatory comments in the same leafy tint by

Peter F. Neumeyer, teacher, critic, and children's-book author. Neumeyer included, as appendices, testimony by Garth Williams, the story's excellent illustrator, and samples of White's considerable research on spiders, and selections from relevant letters and writings, and, most valuably, an accounting, with quotations and reproduced pages, of the eight (at least) drafts whereby White revised *Charlotte's Web* into its consummate final state.

The book first entered White's correspondence in October of 1949, when he told Cass Canfield, the head of Harper and Brothers, "My next book is in sight. I look at it every day. I keep it in a carton as you would a kitten." That summer he had written his most fervent literary essay, a strikingly empathetic foreword for Don Marquis's *archy and mehitabel*—vers libre by the "unsatisfied" and "gloomy" newspaper columnist Marquis featuring a raffish cat who is "toujours gai" and a cockroach who writes by diving headfirst onto a typewriter keyboard, one key at a time. Shades of the head-bumping rat, and of a tiny literate critter to come! Another of White's finest short works, the essay "Death of a Pig," had been composed the previous year. That pig, unnamed but vividly personified, had been killed by disease before the autumn butchering scheduled for it. White was troubled, he wrote in the brief essay "Pigs and Spiders," by the "double-dealing" of pig husbandry: "The theme of *Charlotte's Web* is that a pig shall be saved, and I have an idea that somewhere deep inside me there was a wish to that effect." To one of the book's many readers he wrote:

> The idea . . . came to me one day when I was on my way down through the orchard carrying a pail of slops to my pig. I had made up my mind to write a children's book about animals, and I needed a way to save a pig's life, and I had been watching a large spider in the backhouse, and what with one thing and another, the idea came to me.

He finished a draft in January of 1951, but on the first of March he wrote Harper's children's-book editor, Ursula Nordstrom, "I've recently finished another children's book, but have put it away for a while to ripen (let the body heat go out of it). It doesn't satisfy me the way it is and I think eventually I shall rewrite it pretty much, in order to shift the emphasis and make other reforms." He spelled out those reforms when he donated the manuscripts to Cornell in 1961:

> I added five chapters, starting the narrative with the birth of the pig on the John Arable farm and giving the little girl a more important place in the story. The book was published during the following year, 1952.

"From the evidence," White later wrote, "I had as much trouble getting off the ground as did the Wright Brothers." His first starts had a flavor of the faux-naïve: "Charlotte was a big gray spider"; "I shall speak first of Wilbur"; "The best part of Zuckerman's barn was the part underneath where the cows were on the south side." The narrative, centered on the home base of his happiness, the Maine farm, had tendencies toward the rapturous which White's revisions sought to curb with concreteness and specificity. He began again: "At midnight, John Arable pulled his boots on, lit a lantern, and walked out through the woods to the hog house." Having introduced a human character ahead of the pig, spider, or barn, he finally arrived at the riveting first sentence:

"Where's Papa going with that ax?" said Fern to her mother as they were setting the table for breakfast.

The four Arables manifest themselves in a rapid tumble of dialogue. Eight-year-old Fern rises against her father, who is on his way to slay the runt pig of a new litter, with the cry "The pig couldn't help being born small, could it? If *I* had been very small at birth, would you have killed *me*?" Mr. Arable tries to explain the difference between human beings and animals, but it doesn't wash, with Fern or with us readers, and we are off on a barnyard saga where not only do animals talk but a spider lectures in polysyllables and spells out words in her web. The first chapter also brings us Garth Williams's gorgeous drawing of Fern nursing the tiny pig. After the second chapter ("Fern loved Wilbur more than anything," it begins), the reader is ready to be told, at the beginning of chapter III, "The barn was very large. It was very old. It smelled of hay and it smelled of manure," and to enter into White's paean to natural reality, death and manure and all. To a reader he avowed, "All that I hope to say in books, all that I ever hope to say, is that I love the world."

The master stroke of the final revision—the perfectionist's delay of 1951—was to mediate this love through a female child. Fern is not just the initiator of the tale of Wilbur and Charlotte; she is its witness and, in a sense, its imaginer. Neumeyer points out that, though she reports the barnyard animals' conversations to her mother, she never takes part in them, sitting silently on her milk stool in the barn cellar. Her human consciousness somehow enables the drama which the animals live out, even though they live it to a conclusion after her attention has wandered toward boys, in the person of Henry Fussy, and the world beyond the barn, represented by the bright lights and the Ferris wheel of the County Fair. White is present twice in this book: as Fern, the interested witness, and as Charlotte, the persistent, ingenious, heroic, mortal writer. He is also present, in his most innocent and world-loving form, as the id-pig Wilbur, who finds in a gray spider a mother who will arrange for him not to die.* White had achieved the connection he defined in a letter of 1956: "The whole problem is to establish communication with one's self."

A boy intermediary would not have done, as we can see from the boisterous, loutish behavior of Fern's brother, Avery. Olie Hackstaff, in that would-be magnum opus "Zoo Revisited," is sullied by sexual curiosity and harried by the puritanical admonition, "*Don't put your mouth on that dirty old rail!*" *Charlotte's Web* was White's way of putting his mouth on that dirty old rail, the rural fence rail and the knotty, splintery rail of life. Charlotte, in her valedictory to Wilbur, says, "After all, what's a life, anyway? We're born, we live a little while, we die. A spider's life can't help being something of a mess, with all this trapping and eating flies." The novel is not just about death, which ends our contact with "this lovely world, these precious days," but about the messy nexus of living and killing and eating which sustains us and all creatures in our "sweet, sweet, sweet interlude."

Food in its disgusting deliciousness is repeatedly anatomized. One of Wilbur's meals is specified as "skim milk, wheat middlings, leftover pancakes, half a doughnut, the rind of a summer squash, two pieces of stale toast, a third of a gingersnap, a fish tail, one orange peel, several noodles from a noodle soup, the scum off a cup of cocoa, an ancient jelly roll, a strip of paper from the lining of the garbage pail, and a spoonful of raspberry jello." When the rat Templeton, the plot's sneering, amoral factotum, has to be persuaded to come to the County Fair, it is with visions of edible trash. An eloquent old sheep assures him:

> "In the trampled grass of the infield you will find old discarded lunch boxes containing the foul remains of peanut butter sandwiches, hard-boiled eggs, cracker crumbs, bits of doughnuts, and particles of cheese. In the hard-packed dirt of the midway, after the glaring lights are out and the people have gone home to bed, you will find a veritable treasure of popcorn fragments, frozen custard dribblings, candied apples abandoned by tired children, sugar fluff crystals, salted almonds, popsicles, partially gnawed ice cream cones, and the wooden sticks of lollypops. Everywhere is loot for a rat—in tents, in booths, in haylofts—why, a fair has enough disgusting leftover food to satisfy a whole army of rats."

---

*There is, in a tale that presents the Arables as churchgoers, a religious resonance: Wilbur is the holy infant who is saved from the slaughter of his peers, and Charlotte, hovering above him like—in Matthew's description of Christ's baptism—"the Spirit of God descending like a dove," is the Holy Ghost, whose pronouncement "This is my beloved Son, in whom I am well pleased" (Matthew 3:17) is an early version of "Some pig."

The catalogue is Joycean in its exhaustiveness, its willingness to stand as metaphor for the whole foul, disgusting, overstocked world. The worried, frustrated rat of "The Door" has become the triumphantly replete, stoical Templeton, who, when asked to help Charlotte save Wilbur's life, snarls, "Let him die. I should worry," and, when warned by an old sheep that he is gorging himself to death, sneers, "Who wants to live forever?" The anxious, exquisite paragrapher and contriver of "casuals" becomes, for the 184 pages of *Charlotte's Web*, a Heifetz of easy, fearless compass— a master of country truths, singer of the harsh and beautiful nature that is.

With some few omissions. We do not meet the father of the five hundred and fourteen baby spiders, nor does the mother discuss him. And one of Neumeyer's sidelights concerns the illustration of Charlotte herself, in which White, who had a good graphic sense, took an active hand. Originally, Garth Williams attempted to give her a face, the face of a woman, and she was (in White's words) "horrible and would have wrecked the book." He advised Williams, through the Harper editors, "Spiders don't have much of any face—in fact they have hardly any head," and suggested that the eight long, many-jointed legs "offer a great chance for ballet treatment." When Williams drew Charlotte thinking, head-down, White himself, according to the artist, "put two dots on the edge of her face" (for eyes) and "put 3 strokes to suggest hair on the top of her head." A real spider has eight eyes and two big fangs, as a number of illustrations consulted by White and included in the appendix repulsively show. Murder and manure could make it into the *Charlotte's Web*'s Nature, but not merciless sideways fangs. Also, Neumeyer brings us among his annotations one that caused him, he confesses, "amazement." The magnum opus's last words— "It is not often that someone comes along who is a true friend and a good writer. Charlotte was both"—were closely anticipated in a letter that Katharine White wrote, in 1943, to a woman who had attacked White in a letter to the *New York Times:* "They are not words that should be applied to anyone who is an honest man and an honest writer. Andy is both." What can one make of this convergence? A subconscious echo? A joint approach to a Jungian archetype of phraseology? Or a sly and fond marital in-joke? I lean toward the last, in which White, ever modest, transferred his wife's homage to his good gray heroine—transferred it but kept it, for in a poem, "Natural History," addressed to Katharine from Toronto in 1929, he had already identified himself as a spider:

> Thus I, gone forth, as spiders do,
> In spider's web a truth discerning,
> Attach one silken strand to you
> For my returning.

Introduction to a New Edition of
The Letters of E. B. White

THE PROSE OF E. B. WHITE, as manifested in his letters, lopes along sensibly and informatively, like many other writer's, until it delivers an unexpected poetic punch. Looking at just the hitherto unpublished letters in this revised collection, we find, apropos of his packing and dispatching the papers of his recently deceased wife:

> The labor has been time-consuming and exhausting as well as melancholy:
> I now wander about this old house staring into empty shelves and fighting
> back my memories.

"Fighting back"—the sensation, familiar to all who have grieved, is caught with a rare bluntness and resonance. Some months later, White turns his eye on a dog's loneliness: "One day while I was away he found a wool shirt of mine in the livingroom and proceeded to take it all to pieces, whether from anger or from uneasiness I do not know." Uneasiness was, in old age and youth, White's element. His writing career began, according to a thinly fictionalized portrait of a "Mr. Volente," when a waitress in a Childs Restaurant spilled a glass of buttermilk on him: "Mr. Volente had written an account of the catastrophe at the time and sold it to a young and inexperienced magazine, thus making for himself the enormously important discovery that the world would pay a man for setting down a simple, legible account of his own misfortunes." At the opposite end of White's career, the misfortunes of old age are echoed in the fall of a tree:

> I spent hundreds of dollars trying to save my elm, but it didn't work. The
> tree landed on the lawn with a tremendous thuddd. Now they want me to
> spend a lot of money trying to save my retinas, but that isn't going to work,
> either.

This painfully sensitive and clear-sighted man found the world of artistic enterprise also productive of thuds, as when his children's classic *Charlotte's Web* was made into an animated movie: "After listening to Wilbur sing 'I Can Talk, I Can Talk,' in the Hanna Barbera picture, I can take anything. I wanted to run on my sword but couldn't find it."

Much of White's correspondence in the last years of his life was directed, with an asperity softened by affection, to Scott Elledge as this Cornell professor labored on White's biography. Patiently White corrected errors, provided facts, delivered droll demurs:

I feel that the manuscript, even with the cutting you have done, is too long. The horrid truth is, my life is not all that interesting. I kept falling asleep over it, even though it was my life.

When the manuscript had become a book, its subject expressed "misgivings about the jacket blurb":

The blurb calls me "America's most beloved writer." That is not only open to question, it isn't a good pulling idea anyway. I'm an old advertising man, and I know that people would rather buy a book about a writer everybody hates the guts of.

Some months later, he rather shockingly describes the biography to its author as "your book about the American author who never quite made it into the big time." Two years earlier in their collaboration, White both bowed out and bowed in, telling Elledge:

I would think twice about describing "the vigorous part" I played in your final revisions lest you give readers the idea that I've been breathing down your neck and writing my own story. It is, after all, unusual to have the subject of a biography still alive and kicking, and I have felt uneasy in this role and uncertain just how to behave. I have been torn between the strong desire to keep out of it and the equally strong desire to help clarify it.

White's collaboration with Dorothy Lobrano Guth, his goddaughter, in the 1976 publication of nearly seven hundred pages of his letters also engendered unease. The invasion of his own privacy, and to an extent that of his correspondents, went against his grain, and probably would not have occurred had not Katharine White's long and expensive illnesses made it appear necessary. The note he attached to that volume said as much, with typical bounce and reticence:

Ideally, a book of letters should be published posthumously. The advantages are obvious: the editor enjoys a free hand, and the author enjoys a perfect hiding place—the grave, where he is impervious to embarrassments and beyond the reach of libel. I have failed to cooperate with this ideal arrangement. Through some typical bit of mismanagement, I am still alive, and the book has had to adjust to that awkward fact.

Living long enough to be a reluctantly coöperative party to his biography and his collected letters was a bother, even something of a plague, for him, but a boon to the multitudes of White-lovers, in the many corrections and felicitous refinements he lent to the two tasks. *Letters of E. B. White* is by far his longest book, and by many measures his most autobiographical. It opens with ten lovely pages, in italics, that he supplied on the subject of his happy childhood in the New York suburb of Mount Vernon. The first letter published, to his brother Albert, was composed when he was nine and shows a flash or two of the compression, crystal clarity, and lightly worn melancholy which would become characteristic:

It isn't a very nice day and I've got a cold so I didn't go to school. Mamma brought me a tennis ball and if I be [note the artful subjunctive] very careful can I use your racket? I just heard now while I'm writing this letter that Philis Goodwin [a neighbor's child] died. They wouldn't have a doctor and so you see.

His brothers, especially Stanley, were to become the correspondents that elicited the young White's freest self-expression. With rapidly developing literary flourishes, his letters take him through early love and some automotive vagabondage to Cornell, and thence to an advertising job in New York, to which he commuted from his parents' home in Mount Vernon. In 1925, he moved to the city, sharing an apartment on West Thirteenth Street with three other Cornellians, and tried free-lancing, finding acceptance in Franklin P. Adams's influential newspaper column "The Conning Tower" and the fledgling *New Yorker* magazine. Harold Ross, the perfectionistic if dishevelled editor of the magazine, invited him to join the staff and assigned him the lowliest editorial job: "the newsbreak job—editing the little fillers from other papers and writing punchlines for them." White proved so good at this, so deft and fancy-free in his touches, that he won Ross's heart; fifty-six years later, he was still at the anonymous newsbreaks job, resigning finally in April of 1982 because of his deteriorating eyesight. At *The New Yorker* he found his livelihood, his lifelong podium, and his wife, the editor Katharine Sergeant Angell, who greeted him at his first appearance in the office: "I noted," he remembered long afterward, "that she had a lot of back hair [a bun] and the knack of making a young contributor feel at ease. I sat there peacefully gazing at the classic features of my future wife without, as usual, knowing what I was doing." His letters in the fat middle of this collection trace, with unfailing grace and good humor, his relation with the magazine, its readers, and his fellow-contributors, including his volatile and uproarious office mate, James Thurber. Along with grace and good humor, his letters hold a restless unease—a desire to look beyond Harold Ross's magazine, where he enjoyed a singular and cosseted but confining eminence. Nervously he nursed, behind an epistolary manner of humorous diffidence, a steely ambition, confessing in 1981 to Eugene Kinkead, a fellow-veteran at *The New Yorker*:

As I recall it, I sometimes signed a pseudonym when I found a piece wanting in merit, or virtue. I wanted the name "E. B. White" to be associated with excellence—literary splendor. It is possible that I once sent in a piece to the NYer signed with a phony name to see if I could get a rejection instead of an acceptance, but I have no clear recollection of having done that. I wouldn't put it past me, though. I was a fidgety young man, worried about all sorts of real and imaginary failings.

He hovered between a love for New York and a love for Maine; in 1938, he escaped the city to a saltwater farm in North Brooklin, Maine, recording his life there in monthly columns for *Harper's* that, in the end, added up to—if one must be named—his very best adult book, *One Man's Meat*. In a foreword written forty years after its initial publication in 1942, White recollected:

> Once in everyone's life there is apt to be a period when he is fully awake, instead of half asleep. I think of those five years in Maine as the time when this happened to me. . . . I was suddenly seeing, feeling, and listening as a child sees, feels, and listens. It was one of those rare interludes that can never be repeated, a time of enchantment. I am fortunate indeed to have had the chance to get some of it down on paper.

In the years afterward, he ventured into a variety of genres: with Katharine he edited *A Subtreasury of American Humor;* his contributions to the generally apolitical Notes and Comment section of *The New Yorker* began to plead, as World War II wound down, for a trans-national entity that would enforce peace, and he attended the founding of the UN in San Francisco as a reporter; he edited the grammar handbook of his old Cornell professor William Strunk into a best-selling guide to English composition; at the request of his stepson, Roger Angell, he wrote an imperishable evocation of New York City for *Holiday* magazine; he produced his three remarkable novels for children. He busied himself all the while, on his farm, with non-literary projects—nursing animals, shingling roofs, working with his hands. The manual work whereby he made his living, at his manual typewriter, was pursued with relative wariness. He did not consider himself much of a letter-writer, telling Stanley, "I avoid writing letters—it resembles too closely writing itself, and gives me a headache."

In truth, his shrewd head and aspiring spirit were fragile, prey to migraines and what he describes, in a letter of October 28, 1943, as "a nervous crack-up." In 1945, he reassured Stanley,

> Don't worry about my health—I am a lot better and plenty good enough for my purposes. I had two things the matter with me—mice in the subconscious and spurs in the cervical spine. Of the two the spine trouble was less bothersome. It took me eighteen months to find out how you get rid of mice. . . . Anyway, here I am, in the clear again and damned thankful to be

there. I can work without falling all apart, and can sleep—which is quite refreshing after a year and a half.

His unease had become a malaise, treated with a psychiatric therapy delicately reflected in his short stories "The Second Tree from the Corner" and "The Door." In the long list of advisements provided to his persistent biographer in May of 1982, there is this: "My panic fear, as near as I can make out, is not of death. It is an amorphous fear, lacking in form." This fear, objectified in such exhilarating yet ominous essays as "Death of a Pig" and "Once More to the Lake," was his deepest topic.

Now that a sheaf of communications from his last, spunky years have been added, under his granddaughter's editorial direction, to his collected letters, the full curve of a sterling career, as traced in these entertaining and at times beautiful by-products, can be seen—a career pursued against the resistance of a crass world, imperfect health, and a certain fastidious modesty. His voice had the natural self-deprecating trick of a humorist, but, unlike Benchley and Perelman and Frank Sullivan, White did not remain purely a humorist; he won for himself the right to be taken seriously, as a major American stylist and a celebrant of life in its full range of moods and aspects. Beginning as (his term) "a 'short' writer" of squibs and poems, he persisted in enlarging and purifying his talent, while avoiding the larger forms. His fragmentary "Zoo Revisited; or, The Life and Death of Olie Hackstaff" shows the intent to write a major poem; he even took one of his extended holidays to write it, in mid-1937, explaining to his possibly surprised wife, "A person afflicted with poetic longings of one sort or another searches for a kind of intellectual and spiritual privacy [and] *does* have to forswear certain easy rituals, such as earning a living and running the world's errands." He apparently never attempted a novel for adults. His letters give us, though, what a novel scarcely can: the dailiness of a life, its wearing parade of duties and decencies, its endless-seeming fending (though it does end); its accumulating pyramid of, amid errands, carelessly or alertly experienced hours; and the frequent if rarely stated discriminations whereby an artist picks his path.

AMERICAN FICTION

These Trashy Years

THE HIGHER JAZZ, by Edmund Wilson, edited by Neale Reinitz. 239 pp. University of Iowa Press, 1998.

After Edmund Wilson, there have been journalistic critics, like John Leonard, and academic critics, like Denis Donoghue, but none who combine zest and authority, an opinionated voice and a scholarly thoroughness in quite the resonant, one might say statesmanlike Wilsonian style. A keenly interactive man with an above-average appetite for sex, liquor, and conversation, he did not think of himself as primarily a critic—a journalist, rather, and a poet, playwright, and fiction writer. His facility with ideas and texts and languages tended to push his fiction to one side of his general literary enterprise, but he managed to produce an intermittently lively, if strenuously schematic, valentine to the Greenwich Village of the Twenties, *I Thought of Daisy* (1929), and a best-seller, *Memoirs of Hecate County* (1946), which possesses a certain saturnine majesty and passages of ground-breaking sexual realism. He was too much an old-fashioned patrician to soften the truth in his telling of it. This gave his criticism its energy and weight, but may have handicapped his fiction: it has frequent, often word-for-word recourse to the journals he faithfully kept throughout his life. His fiction is lumpy, as it were, with transcribed journal entries where an airier penman would have been making things up. Nevertheless, his distinction of mind was such that a reader would think that an uncompleted novel by him, begun and abandoned between the two published ones, would have seen print sooner than twenty-six years after his death, in 1972, and courtesy of a publisher more mainstream than the University of Iowa Press.

The press and the editor, Neale Reinitz, have done an excellent job with this little volume, *The Higher Jazz*, which is produced in the compact, sensible format that Wilson asked his publishers to give his books, beginning with *Europe Without Baedeker* in 1947. Reinitz, a professor emeritus of English at Colorado College, has taken the title from an essay Wilson published in *The New Republic* in 1926 and included in *The American Earthquake* (1958) as "The Problem of the Higher Jazz." In considering recently performed music by Louis Gruenberg, Arthur Honegger, George Gershwin, Aaron Copland, Paul Whiteman, and Deems Taylor, the *New Republic* essay tackled the problem of "conveying the excitement, the emotion, of the time, which has its popular expression in jazz, in a distinguished musical form." Except for the Copland, Wilson found the attempts too tame. The hero of his novel, which began as one segment of an ambitious narrative, *The Story of the Three Wishes*, is a German-American businessman and aspiring composer from Pittsburgh, Fritz Dietrich, who diffidently worries at the rather abstract issue of the higher jazz between drunken parties and bouts of unease with his sexy wife, Caroline. Professor Reinitz relates with admirable clarity and care the short, inconclusive novel's incidents and characters to those in Wilson's life and the rest of his oeuvre. If a text which a writer opted to put aside is posthumously published, it should be done, as here, with scholarly honors, rather than with the, say, minimal editorial apparatus that has accompanied the numerous fragments culled from Hemingway's muddled leavings, encouraging in book-buyers the illusion of a live master hand still at work.

The critic can scarcely find fault with a work the writer himself disowned; like a burglar breaking into a house, one is obliged to search for precious things. It is not hard to imagine why this project finally defeated Wilson: its characters, who are resolutely dissipated and silly, make scarcely a move toward dramatizing the author's grand theme of popular energy versus high art. The novel abruptly ends, if not exactly concludes, with some gnomic Yankee pronouncements by Edgar Rockland, a late-arriving character based on Charles Ives, who *has* managed to compose the higher jazz, full of modern dissonance and tunes, in New Hampshire isolation. In contrast, Fritz fitfully doodles at the piano, and permits a few thoughts of Wilsonian cogency to enter his brain; but his main occupation is keeping up with the social set, or awkwardly overlapping sets, in which he and Caroline find their fledgling marriage enmeshed. She is a version of Wilson's second wife, Margaret Canby, who was to die of a fall in 1932 and who appears in *Hecate County* as the "Western girl" Jo Gates. As that book winds down, the hero is apprehensively contemplating the question of "whether or not I ought, finally, to marry Jo." She has children by a troublesome former husband, is something of a philistine, and has "become more and more addicted to a migratory cocktail set who were mostly far too rich for me and by the [nineteen-]thirties had come to disgust me." In *The Higher Jazz*, Fritz succumbs to Caroline's "cunning, little thick body" and marries her. He confides in her his hope that they will together give "damn interesting parties—the kind of parties that almost nobody is giving." Yet the parties they give are dishevelled and inharmonious, thanks in part to the sodden intrusions of her former husband and the tireless juvenile frivolity of Fritz's Yale classmate Nick Carter, Nick's platonic playmate Kay Burke, and Kay's idle young lover Bill Shippen, the three of whom incessantly impersonate members of an imaginary family called the Ratsbys.

There is literary history here: Nick is closely based on Robert Benchley, and Kay on Dorothy Parker. Wilson's Twenties journals record that he found the celebrated Algonquin Round Table crowd a "rather tiresome" collection of provincial and suburban mentalities playing at "New York sophistication," but his fictionalization of Parker, especially, shows a considerable interest. He endeavors to dramatize her romantic turmoil and a suicide attempt, which took an effort of imagination on Wilson's part, since, though he and Parker had been colleagues at *Vanity Fair*, he was not an intimate. His portrait of the Algonquin wits here stands as a corrective to their glamorization and as a case study of a peculiar form of social morbidity—an extended jest whose obsessed perpetrators "tend to lose the sense of reality" and "shut out the rest of the world and become incapable of coöperating with it." A sense of wasted talent broods over the parties, which run on into one another blearily, and Wilson, having labored on this slight, distracted tale for some of 1941 and 1942, accumulating two hundred seven pages of handwritten yellow legal-size lined paper, evidently decided it would be a waste of his own talent to continue. He abandoned his alter ego, who seems neither very German nor very musical, and turned to writing the six episodes of *Hecate County* from the viewpoint of a different alter ago, an art critic who is both more direct and more detached than Fritz, embodying the self, as we read in *Hecate County*'s final pages, "for which I really lived and which kept up its austere virtue, the self which had survived through these trashy years."

That self speaks in *The Higher Jazz* in the general tone, bemused but not resigned to bemusement, and in images, many lifted from the journals, of clarity and instinctive affection. The most glowing chapter is the first, "A Weekend at the Shore," taking Fritz and Caroline to a hotel in Sea Bright, a northern–New Jersey resort town adjacent to Wilson's native Red Bank. In this plebeian but deeply familiar setting, the hero enjoys the sea, sex, and booze in shifting proportions, and unprogrammatically records how

> we were let into a fine corner room that looked out two ways on the ocean
> and that had twin white iron beds, furniture with that slightly bleached look
> that everything gets beside the sea, and a glass pitcher with inverted tumblers sitting on a glass tray.

With this transparent moment—"that slightly bleached look"—the dour narrative perspective lets in bare reality and, somehow, emotion with it: we glimpse as through blowing curtains the lyric spirit of his friend Scott Fitzgerald. How aggravating it must have been for Wilson, in his generous reconnaissance of literature, to perceive that his wastrel, alcoholic, relatively ignorant classmate from Princeton possessed, in his fiction, a liveliness, concision, and flashing beauty beyond any his own, superior mind could muster. *The Higher Jazz* gives us a Fitzgerald that wasn't, from a Wilson that formidably was.

Coming Home

Don't the Moon Look Lonesome: *A Novel in Blues and Swing*, by Stanley Crouch. 546 pp. Pantheon, 2000.

In Stanley Crouch's ambitious first novel, the heroine, a white jazz singer from South Dakota named Carla Hamsun, loves Maxwell Davis, a black tenor-saxophonist from Texas. For five hundred forty-six pages, she keeps on loving him through a hurricane of talk, much of it in italic flashback. This is a big jam session of a novel, in which every character stands up and blows, and if some of the riffs remind us of Stanley Crouch's essays, well, welcome to his particular universe. The overall topic is black and white in America, and the issue is, Can a nice black-white couple, sharing venturesome, industrious temperaments, an interest in jazz, and errant sisters, form a more perfect union in an environment not infrequently hostile from both directions? Black women sashay up to Maxwell saying things like "You brothers need to come home," and it's getting to him, Carla senses. A visit to his old home in Houston is reassuring—his parents both take to her—and fills the first half of the book, but the next half returns the duo to New York City, whence Maxwell hits the road and where rueful Carla puts in one of the longest days in literature since Leopold Bloom perambulated Dublin on June 16, 1904.

What makes the days and the pages go by slowly is their irrepressible burden of what Crouch himself labels "blah-blah" and "Jabberwocky." The lead offender, among many logorrheic candidates, is Leeann, a tall black model from South Carolina whose "very swanky" life of first-class jet tickets and limos with one-way windows has not dulled her gift for such "blowtorch humor" as:

> I feel a grass hut over my head this evening. I hear me some drums. I'm getting ancestral. I feel the slave ship swaying across the mighty Atlantic Ocean. Seem just like yesterday. I feel the cries of the crammed and the damned. I smell the toe jam. I'm all the way back to the bushwack. I feel a cotton sack on my tired black back. I'm feeling a feeling this evening. I'm talking about Daddy. Papa De-Dada. Dada. Dahomey. Home, down home with my homeys is what I'm talking about.

Or, in a less nostalgic mood:

> All right. Here's the niggergram delivered right to your door, Mr. Bandstand Caliban. About all this black studies, or coon studies or whatever the fuck they are, you must lift every voice, Maxwell, my brother. You got to get the dickhead niggers in charge to tell the kids the white man don't *want* you to know about this.

Not that Maxwell is among the tongue-tied; he can expatiate by the paragraph on topics as diverse as New York City weather and the racial politics of Sylvester Stallone's *Rocky* movies. Carla laps up his japes—"*Mighty white of you, he joked, and she smiled, her entire personality caught up in that curve of lips and teeth*"—perhaps because they remind her of her father, a history teacher who was "always trying to frame the world he was in" with strenuous soliloquies. In his own tireless voice Crouch writes a loosely buttoned and highly figurative English that is meant, I think, to remind us of the unwindings of jazz and the blues:

> When she was with Bobo, his unapologetic tenderness had the power to reduce every last bit of her to a translucent sigh and a startling, reluctant squeal, something like an anger at the fact of loneliness itself, a rage that spanked the flank of her orgasm as it ran free.

> There was more to Maxwell's mom than the Negro earth mother white women like herself were so frequently seeking to complement their own mothers, to provide folk insights, humor, and tales of bewildering disasters limited in their effect by an immutable stoicism rinsed in the blues and shaped up as the gospel bird of rhythm that rose up from the frying pan of hard times and flapped heavenward, headless and featherless but dripping buckets of greasy soul.

On the other hand, Carla's white-racist sister, Ramona, is "hugging the thorn bush of the past so that the pain stayed alive." Yearning has "unsullied" Carla's soul "and was right inside the pocket of the groove you were always after on the bandstand." Contemplation of Carla's insides turns the prose semi-liquid: we read of "every drop of the swampy goo inside her own soul," and of the way her "heart became the twin of a hot fudge brownie fresh from the oven when Maxwell nodded at Dad." How can you not go soft on a man whose "face took on a stonewall assurance mooshed up with humor and erotic underplay"?

What is Crouch's preachment in this mooshy romance? A cultivated, jazz-crazy man of color, he is against tribalisms that would divide Americans one from another, and black from white especially. Not all the diatribes his characters deliver can be taken as his own point of view, but among the targets vigorously attacked are black studies, separate black tables and dormitories, and social pressures that would discourage men and women of unlike color from falling in love. He is an integrationist, as indicated by his dedication of this novel to Albert Murray, Ralph Ellison, and Saul Bellow—"mentors all." He (through Maxwell) expresses distaste for today's popular black music—"gangster rappers," purveying "anger and disruption . . . not to mention the exceedingly low level of the musicianship"—and (through Carla) wonders, "How long, oh, Lord, how long . . . would it be before Americans and Europeans and everybody else who became civilized understood that continually vitalizing the middle class was the issue, not hiding in costumes and bad behavior?" The Houston section makes real, in its portrait of middle-class black life, what the white bourgeois novel has lost: the sense of hazard from underneath, from the greedy agents of degradation, and the triumph of will and endeavor that decent respectability represents. In the novel's longest set piece, thirty-five pages are devoted to a church service, every word of the prayers and sermon, with a bona-fide resurrection from the dead thrown in for good measure.

Crouch's case for miscegenation would be stronger if Carla did not appear to be a black in whiteface. The author does well enough with her Dakota prairie, her girlhood on ice and in snow, her cheerleading, classbeauty days, and her good-natured Lutheran parents, but when Maxwell and Crouch draw close to Carla her salient and most appreciated feature is her steatopygous bottom. It is the first thing we learn about her:

> The slippery nature of life had landed her on the abundant curve of buttocks that made this white woman . . . an anatomical anomaly. . . . Maxwell used to nickname her "Tailback" or "Back in Action" or "Black Bottom" or

phone her from the road and ask, "How are those Viking grandes dames doing?" . . . An older drummer friend of his . . . said to Maxwell . . . "Boy, now ain't *you* a bitch? You got a blonde with a black ass."

She has a long neck, too, another African beauty mark, and her great achievement, after tutorship by a trio of black-musician lovers, is to sing on the same wavelength as Billie Holiday and Dinah Washington. The reader can only wish Crouch and Maxwell joy of their "two-apple-assed" "Viking Hottentot," but as, in the New York section, one long scene of black palaver—diatribal, expository, campy—follows another, Carla has little to do but listen. The discussants fitfully remind themselves that she is white—the meek lone ofay in the room—but when the reader tries to picture her, it is hard to come up with anyone paler than Lena Horne or Dorothy Dandridge.

Since Maxwell and Carla are warriors in a cause that Crouch believes in, they have a muralistic largeness, an idealized perfection that excludes the fallibility which generates suspense in both real and fictional narratives. Their musicianship must be consummate, "releasing their personalities through the order and shape of musical logic," and receives the benefit of Crouch's passionate expertise—every song in the sets Carla sings is named, and we hear "how using triplet eighths and other subdivisions *within* quarter-note triplets allowed her to swing completely different kinds of rhythms while *right inside* four/four." Not only does she sing great; she beats a bunch of rich white guys at poker and, but for a high-school accident, might have skated in the Olympics. Her love for her man, likewise, has no flaw, nor his for her, but for the intruding sour note of segregationist politics. So the novel becomes less an action than a disquisition, a wordy, wide-ranging array of voiced opinions, to which we settle like bleary customers in a late-night jazz club: the musicians are playing for themselves on the stand, there is a lot of excited, apparently hilarious talk at the surrounding tables, it is past time to go to bed, but, baby, it's cold outside, and a stupefied kind of happiness comes with just being here.

Tote That Ephemera

JOHN HENRY DAYS, by Colson Whitehead. 389 pp. Doubleday, 2001.

The young African-American writer to watch may well be a thirty-one-year-old Harvard graduate with the catchy name of Colson Whitehead. His first novel, *The Intuitionist*, came out in 1999 and won a flock of fledgling honors: *Esquire* named it the best first novel of the year, *GQ* anointed it nothing less than one of the best books of the millennium, the Quality Paperback Book Club gave it the New Voices Award. It was a strikingly original and polished debut, concerning the travails of Lila Mae Watson, the first black woman elevator inspector in a city that was not quite New York, in the way that Batman's Gotham isn't quite either. The novel seizes upon an unsung wonder in our midst, the elevator, and sings its history, its technology, its romance, adding to the novelist's solid research a scintillating pinch of sci-fi fantasy.

The extensive guild of metropolitan elevator inspectors is split, it would seem, between the Empiricists, who plod through their inspections one material criterion at a time, and the Intuitionists, who take a more mystical, gestalt approach to the detection of safety flaws. The latter are disciples of James Fulton, the author of *Theoretical Elevators* and other advanced works in liftology; he turns out, in the novel's cheerful convolutions, to have been a black man, and his search for the perfect, shaftless elevator had something to do, it seems allegorically evident, with rising clear of racist America's obstructive structures. Whitehead's raddled undercity unfolds with the terse poetry and numinous dignity of the early Malamud. The prose is a gas, bubbly, clean, often funny in its bursts of mock-mandarin social exposition:

> The spa failed after newer spas opened in the weatherless regions of the Southwest. Weatherlessness is much more amenable to those in search of succor for bodily complaint, evoking timelessness and immortality, and soon the rich neurasthenic women from the Northeast's larger cities boarded planes to be free of the seasons and the proximity of their braying families, the cause of their disrepair.

Whitehead can try too hard ("Thick black mustaches shrub beneath their nostrils, intrepid vegetation on petrous faces") but generally his writing does what writing should do: it refreshes our sense of the world, as when the hissing of steam heat is described as "sonic adipose" and a pedestrian's eyes greet "the steel-eyed cop on the corner with the sun in his buttons."

This blithely gifted writer's second novel, *John Henry Days*, is longer and more various, and also slacker and more diffuse. His hip wit sits on the narrative now less as delicious icing than as a nervous burden; self-consciousness threatens to block every simple feeling. In his dense weave of cultural reference he mentions a successful first-novelist whose "second novel, recapitulating some of the first's themes, [is] somehow lacking—emboldened by success he tries to tackle too much." Whitehead's own first novel comes up for a parodic allusion: "It's about two warring groups of chiropodists. One group does it the natural way, looking for fungus and corns, and the other—" With the serial ingenuity of *Ulysses*, a medley of voices and short scenes in a virtuosic variety of styles seeks to encompass a mighty but elusive subject. The author's instinct for the epic has led him to the mythic black hero John Henry, who in the novel's central event is being honored, on the weekend of July 12, 1996, with a three-day celebration in Talcott, West Virginia. Talcott is the site of the Big Bend Tunnel, a railroad tunnel where, purportedly, around 1870, the fabulously strong steel-driver challenged a steam drill to a race and won, though his heart gave out afterwards. John Henry and three other American legends—Paul Bunyan, Mighty Casey, and Pecos Bill—are being recognized with an ethnically balanced quartet of Folk Heroes stamps issued by the United States Postal Service, and our novel's hero, J. (a mystery initial) Sutter, a roving black journalist and writer on pop culture, has come to the little mountain town on a junket. He is engaged in a feat of his own: he is attempting to break the record of a fabled earlier junketeer, Bobby Figgis, who attended publicity parties continuously for nine months before disappearing, "devoured by pop." J. is on his third month, "a three-month junket jag he is too unwilling or too scared to break."

The guild of freeloading, ephemera-writing junketeers lacks the municipal muscle and dark plunge-potential of the elevator-inspector crowd, but it has its rites and solidarity. Present for the festivities in Talcott are the veteran Dave Brown, whose "byline is a roach whose gradual infestation of the world's print media can only be sketchily documented"; One Eye, who lost his other orb to some gesturing fingers while thirstily lunging at the open bar of a Manhattan venue; Frenchie, a fashion expert with a stalled book ("If he wanted sympathy he should have never written those Talk of the Towns for the *New Yorker*, a sure friendship-killer in the freelance world"); J.; and Tiny, a leviathan grown great on gratis hors d'oeuvres:

At three hundred pounds, the man is hunger, gorging and grazing at the free spreads of life. If any person deserves to be on the List, it is Tiny, a creature who has evolved into the perfect mooching machine, leaving no glass undrained or napkin unstained by chicken skewer residue. He sucks up freebies in a banquet room like a baleen whale inhaling colonies of hapless plankton, swooping primeval and perfect, eyelids blinking slowly in the unlit fathoms of media. The dirigible prowls the food and travel magazine circuit; as a party trick he has been known to throw darts at a map of the world and name a princely dish native to that region, belching up its flavor on command, an archival gust from deep in his belly.

Also present is Pamela Street, whose father collected John Henry memorabilia and created a sorely neglected John Henry Museum in Harlem. Now that he is dead, the town of Talcott has offered to buy the collection, and she is checking the place out. Like J., she is black, and their guarded attraction to each other furnishes the novel's romantic interest and its main, rather meagrely fuelled engine of suspense. A catastrophe during the John Henry Days is early foretold and hovers promisingly in the reader's mind, but the narrative supplies so many foci, so many momentary scenes and diversionary points of interest, that attention skids and stalls. In *The Intuitionist*, Whitehead employed a trick of jumping back and forth in the time sequence, but the plot never wandered far from Lila Mae and the theme of elevators. In this novel, the John Henry theme, though attacked from every angle, refuses to yield a unifying principle that would include J. Sutter and his very contemporary predicament, that of a talent lost in "the brittle domain of irony" and selling itself short by cranking out promotion pieces.

The brief scenes bodying forth the epic black laborer and his tunnelling cohorts are tours de force; the extensive treatment of J. Sutter's demimonde of publicity jaunts on the culture beat has considerable satiric energy; and the several imaginings of the legend of John Henry as it touched past lives (at the turn of the century, a young Jewish songplugger decides to launch himself as a composer with his version of the ballad; decades later, an itinerant black bluesman called Moses records his version in Chicago, in a session that pays forty dollars a side; in the Thirties, two academic folklorists, one white and one black, search the vicinity of Talcott for living witnesses to the contest of 1870; in 1940, Paul Robeson struggles through the failing musical *John Henry*, based on a 1931 novel by Roark Bradford; just after World War II, a small girl whom we take to be J. Sutter's mother, a child of the middle class on Strivers Row in Harlem, encounters the ballad's sheet music and is scolded for playing it on the piano, her mother calling it music for "good-for-nothing niggers who don't care about making a better life for themselves") are all caringly worked. These diverse episodes, however, seem beads on a string or, more aptly, cars in a long train dragging its length up a mountain slope.

The book takes its name from John Henry, epitome of black strength and heartbreak, but its central character, the disgusted junketeer J. Sutter, need not be black at all. His discontent might just as well be that of a young white or Asian-American of literary bent. J.'s educational advantages and his relatively race-blind milieu of pop culture deprive him of the claim that black characters, from the slave narratives on, traditionally exert upon the American conscience: the heroism that persecution and disadvantage impose. With comfortable assurance Whitehead evokes the particulars of past racial oppression: John Henry, not ten years after Emancipation, working like a slave for white contractors; the singer Moses making his wary, hungover way to the white man's recording studio; Guy, the black academic, being rebuffed by his surprised white correspondent when he appears in person—"I don't know where you got that, but I don't have nothing to say about that letter, boy." J. himself, venturing south with Mississippi in his mind and apprehensively mixing in the small-town scene, encounters no overt racial slights and finds "More black people than he expected; he's doing a lot of the old afro-nod, the hello you give to folks when you get out of the city and into friendlier climes."

For the J. Sutters of the republic, the prophetic thunders and righteous wrath of Frederick Douglass and W. E. B. Du Bois and Richard Wright and James Baldwin have dwindled to the mumbling ambivalences of freedom in a money-driven, morally numbed consumer society. A metropolitan book party throngs into J.'s memory, and its panorama of up-to-date types includes this vignette: "The biracial who adopted a superficial militancy to overcompensate for light skin discussed the perfidy of ice people with the gangster rapper ashamed of a placid upbringing in a middle-class suburb." As assimilation and integration achieve their dilutions and ironies, what remains worth fighting for? How does a black man save his soul? Fortunate black citizens are now privileged to share the moral inconsequence of the entire society; this is progress of a sort, but not necessarily aesthetic progress. In *John Henry Days* the sepia mood has produced an ambitious, animated work frustratingly vague in its resolution. At the end, the novel falls into the jackhammer prose of old newsreel voiceovers, and delivers what is either the best-disguised happy ending or the most muted tragic note of the publishing season. J. stands there "as if choices are possible" but says nothing. Well, if choices aren't possible, why is he taking up space in the middle of a work of fiction? The novel's nominal hero decided to battle a machine and won, losing his life in the process. J. has his qualities, but he's no John Henry.

Dog's Tears

THE NAME OF THE WORLD, by Denis Johnson. 129 pp. HarperCollins, 2000.

There is a kind of radiant prose, sparking in short circuits, that can be achieved only through a point of view that is youthful and stoned:

I stood outside the motel hitchhiking, dressed up in a hurry, shirtless under my jacket, with the wind crying through my earring. A bus came. I climbed aboard and sat on the plastic seat while the things of our city turned in the windows like the images in a slot machine.

It was a Polish neighborhood somewhere or other. The Polish neighborhoods have that snow. They have that fruit with the light on it, they have that music you can't find. We ended up in a laundromat, where the guy took off his shirt and put it in a washer.

The sky was a bruised red shot with black, almost exactly the colors of a tattoo. Sunset had two minutes left to live.

These quotations are from Denis Johnson's *Jesus' Son*, a 1992 collection of short stories that was recently made into a motion picture. Though the book is short, it offers a definitive description of a certain world, a drug-user's 1970s world, remembered in an agreeable haze. It calls to mind Jayne Anne Phillips's youthful *Black Tickets*, and the short stories of Thom Jones and Raymond Carver, though Jones's heroes are more muscular and Carver's less airily down-and-out than Johnson's, being drunks in various stages of desperation and reform rather than heroin addicts. We are reminded, further, of the gleaming economy and aggressive minimalism of early Hemingway, the Hemingway of *In Our Time*, with its paragraph-long prose-poems sandwiched between stories distinguished by their beautifully bleak language and dialogues of non-connection. Like Hemingway at eighteen, the typical Johnson hero has known death, been in and out of his body, and seen life by an X-raying black light. "Catty-corner from me," a narrator in *Jesus' Son* relates, "sat a dear little black child maybe sixteen, all messed up on skag. She couldn't keep her head up. She couldn't stay out of her dreams. She knew: shit, we might as well have been drinking a dog's tears. Nothing mattered except that we were alive."

Johnson's new novel, *The Name of the World*, also carries the translucent taste of dog's tears, but its hero, Mike Reed, is fifty-three, "baby faced . . . with cheery blue eyes," and ensconced in academe. Shakily and marginally ensconced, it is true, as an Adjunct Associate Professor of History, a post that seems to involve little besides a few "small seminars," rather like Writer-in-Residence; he is nevertheless tamed by an establishment and subject to its politics. Four years ago, Reed's thirty-four-year-old wife and four-year-old daughter were killed in an auto accident, having accepted a ride from a senile neighbor in the aftermath of an ice storm. Since then, the widower, "virtually dead," has gone through the motions of living, finding obscure consolation in watching the students skate around and around on the pond of his Midwestern university and in pondering the "sorrowful concentricity" of an anonymous slave's drawing in the art museum. "Man is but a reed," Pascal wrote, "the weakest in nature, but he is a thinking reed." Though Mike Reed is not "Jesus' son" (a quote from Lou Reed's song "Heroin"), Johnson's eerie clarity of description, with its subtly askew precision, remains:

> This day of my visit to the Swan's Grove Campus the weather felt new. Winter's edges had been pushed back, the sidewalks were clear and the roads were dry. The deep snow in the fields had collapsed into dimples that had become, at last, here and there, craters with soaked gray pasture at their bottoms.

Yet the world of a middle-aged academic simply does not yield the numinous dishevelment, the shimmer of blithe violence, common in the surreal milieu of a young addict and odd-jobber. Abrupt and casual auto accidents, a frequent feature of *Jesus' Son*, have taken on a weight of consequence. After four years of not having a car, Reed gets into a BMW and floors the pedal, but his courtship of a fatal accident ends when, having "worn myself out going too fast," he pulls over, calms down, drives safely home, and parks the car in his garage. The events of this academic novel flirt with predictability: the faculty scheming, the learned freeloading, the abruptly terminated position, the professor's sexual attraction to a graduate student. The student here, bearing the symbolically double-barrelled name of Flower Cannon, pops up variously in Mike Reed's life—as a tipsy, white-shouldered cellist at a faculty dinner party; as an art-department performance artist publicly shaving her pubic hair; as a college caterer's waitress; as the naked winner of an off-campus dive's Friday dance contest; as a participant in the Sing Night of the Anabaptist Friesland Fellowship; and finally, in the short novel's longest scene, as a friendly and fey, if elusive, conquest. It is Mike Reed, actually, who does the eluding, fleeing Flower's compliant presence when the memory of his wife and daughter short-circuits his desire.

The narrator, increasingly authorial and confiding as the book goes on, tells us, "Looking over the pages of this reminiscence, I see I've misled. I've created the impression that what I've been aiming at is the account of a one-night stand, and that the item pending most crucially between Flower and me was my loss of a kind of late-life virginity." O.K., but if not that, what? Johnson loses us in the later pages, which look back upon his university days from a curious paradise he has found as a journalist during the 1991 Gulf War. Flower, though lovingly sculpted, in touch after touch, as the book builds toward a culminating intimacy, melts away, and is retrospectively dismissed in a rude voice: "As for Flower Cannon, I have no idea what's become of her, but if I ever track her down I'm sure she'll be up to something quite shocking and also absolutely no surprise." Like the feckless scattered heroes of *Jesus' Son*, where women are generally bedraggled and ill used, and like the buzz-brained principals in Johnson's lengthy, witty, and wild exercise in California noir, *Already Dead*, Mike Reed is too advanced in the school of life to be transformed by a sexual encounter. He is looking for something more, something unnameable. When Flower asks for a phrase in his handwriting, to add to a collection of such phrases she keeps in a wooden box, he pens, "*The name of the world.*" It gives the novel a title but not, for me, a meaning.

The hero's sense of meaning emerges in his nostalgia for a drug trip's benignly pointless, potentially revelatory confusion. The fondly evoked dives of *Jesus' Son* have a tame equivalent in a basement tavern in the new novel's university town: "Here I've let my memory veer down the stairs and float alongside the bar and hover in the light of the jukebox, when actually there's no point. Nothing worth telling about happened down there. Or up in the world, for that matter." Point arrives in the poetic coinages such venues stimulate in Johnson: of a habituée he writes, "Eloise laughed and hacked. She had the smashed sinuses of an English bulldog." The simile is smashing, and Mike Reed comes closest to pleasure in the presence of things being smashed: at the novel's end, the Gulf War has him flying "through black smoke overclouding a world pocked by burning oil wells like flickering signals of distress, of helplessness," and praising this, in an oddly prim phrase, as "a life I believe to be utterly remarkable."

There is religion in Johnson, a memory of visions. Like Allen Ginsberg's "angelheaded hipsters burning for the ancient heavenly connection to the starry dynamo in the machinery of night," Mike Reed has glimpsed at the world's core a kind of glowing jelly. Formal religious structures and creeds don't hold this jelly but constitute a memorial to it, a vacated tabernacle. The novel's spiritual climax shows Reed following Flower to Friesland Sing Night, where the singing is transcendental: "They sang in multiple harmony, in a fullness and with a competence that didn't seem studied, but perfectly natural, innate, all talent. I heard none of the usual bad voices." In the midst of this music, it comes to our thinking Reed that there is no God:

> I didn't think often about that which people called God, but for some time now I'd certainly hated it, this killer, this perpetrator, in whose blank silver eyes nobody was too insignificant, too unremarkable, too innocent and small to be overlooked in the parceling out of tragedy. I'd felt this all-

powerful thing as a darkness and weight. Now it had vanished. A tight winding of chains had burst. Someone had unstuck my eyes. A huge ringing in my head had stopped. This is what the grand and lovely multitude of singers did to me.

The moment seems psychologically clear: Reed absolves the depersonalized universe of blame for the deaths of his wife and daughter. He feels his heart "going up and up into an endless interval with nothing to get in the way. All my happy liberated soul came out of my throat." The remaining forty pages, including his long-anticipated tryst with Flower Cannon, are a relative muddle, full of effortful enigmas and presumably pregnant pauses. She comes toward him "carrying her message from a vanished god," and he says (he thinks), "I still can't feel anything," a by now rather tired post-Romantic boast that elicits "no response from Flower. Maybe she didn't hear." Non-response is followed by non-coition; Mike Reed achieves closure by assaulting a car full of teen-age youths, fleeing town, and, as an existential Foreign Legionnaire, heading toward Iraq.

Like the Bible, *The Name of the World* ends on an apocalyptic note:

> Our century has torn its way out of its chrysalis and become too beautiful to be examined, too alive to be debated and exploited by played-out intellectuals. The important thing is no longer to predict in what way its grand convulsions might next shake us. Now the important thing is to ride it into the sky.

To hope that limited, tactical struggles like the Gulf War are big enough to ride into the sky seems optimistic. Fireworks aren't a spaceship launch. Explosions don't last, and Denis Johnson's radioactive wine holds up best in small bottles, before the decay of rhetoric sets in. This novel about anomic grief thirsts for tears; the hero winds up crying into a bathtub, "a tiny flood of my own tears, enough to fill a shot glass." He then supplements the tears by turning on the faucet, and bathes "until my bath was cold." Through a possible short circuit of my own, this bathos left me cold.

One-Way Street

COSMOPOLIS, by Don DeLillo. 209 pp. Scribner, 2003.

In a land of chunky, garish, anxious-to-please books, Don DeLillo's thirteenth novel, *Cosmopolis*, is physically cool, as sleek and silver-touched and palely pure as a white stretch limo, which is in fact the action's main venue. On the front of the book jacket we see the limo from the front, and on the back from the back, and in between stretch a tad more than two hundred tall, generous-margined pages of metafiction. Eric Packer, a twenty-eight-year-old billionaire manager of other people's money, rises after a sleepless night in April of the year 2000, in his forty-eight-room, $104-million triplex (w/ shark tank, borzoi pen, lap pool, gym) at the top of an eighty-nine-story apartment building on First Avenue, and tells his chief of security, "bald and no-necked" Torval, that he wants to get a haircut at the other end of Forty-seventh Street. Their exchange illustrates the terse, deflective, somewhat lobotomized quality of the novel's dialogue:

> "I want a haircut."
> "The president's in town."
> "We don't care. We need a haircut. We need to go crosstown."
> "You will hit traffic that speaks in quarter inches."
> "Just so I know. Which president are we talking about?"
> "United States. Barriers will be set up," he said. "Entire streets deleted from the map."
> "Show me my car," he told the man.

The crosstown epic begins. In its oft-interrupted course, Packer follows, via his limo's bank of electronic screens—"all the flowing symbols and alpine charts, the polychrome numbers pulsing"—the stubborn rise of the yen, on whose fall he has bet heavily. He takes in details of city life ("A man in women's clothing walked seven elegant dogs") and notices that on the limo's spycam his image makes a gesture a second or two before he makes it in reality. This temporal dislocation recurs, indicating an underlying shift in the past-future paradigm. Packer's "chief of theory," Vija Kinski, explains it thus:

> "Computer power eliminates doubt. All doubt rises from past experience.
> But the past is disappearing. We used to know the past but not the future.
> This is changing."

DeLillo's post-Christian search for "an order at some deep level" has brought him to global computerization: "the zero-oneness of the world, the digital imperative that defined every breath of the planet's living billions."

The limo, floored in Carrara marble, in its stop-and-go progress admits a coming and going of other passengers, including two advisers who advise Packer to bail out of the yen before he is ruined. Instead, the financier bails out of the limo for a number of quick trysts. After spotting her in a passing taxi, he has breakfast with "his wife of twenty-two days, Elise Shifrin, a poet who had right of blood to the fabulous Shifrin banking fortune of Europe"; soon thereafter he copulates with an old acquaintance, an art dealer, and a newer one, a bodyguard, who pop up along his route. On the West Side, where Broadway and Seventh Avenue intersect, Packer runs into a violent demonstration against world capitalism, inspired, it seems, by the line from Zbigniew Herbert, "a rat became the unit of currency," that DeLillo uses as an epigraph for *Cosmopolis*. The demonstrators rock the limo, spray-paint it, urinate on it, and hurl a trash can at the rear window. Nevertheless, Packer aloofly reflects within the tormented vehicle that

> there was something theatrical about the protest, ingratiating even. . . . There was a shadow of transaction between the demonstrators and the state. The protest was a form of systemic hygiene, purging and lubricating. It attested again, for the ten thousandth time, to the market culture's innovative brilliance, its ability to shape itself to its own flexible ends, absorbing everything around it.

Vija Kinski, the third expert adviser the limo takes aboard—"a small woman in a button-down business shirt, an old embroidered vest and a long pleated skirt of a thousand launderings"—tends to agree, and says of the yen, "To pull back now would not be authentic."

This farce of extravagant wealth and electronic mysticism might feel more authentic from the pen of Kurt Vonnegut or that of Paul Auster, to whom *Cosmopolis* is dedicated. *Nouveau roman* meets Manhattan geography, under sci-fi moonlight. Vonnegut and Auster, however, keep on their fantastic plane undeviatingly, as if there is no other, whereas DeLillo gives signs of wanting to drop us down into the quotidian mundane, where we can be wounded. Though always a concept-driven writer, whose characters spout smart, swift essays at one another, he has shown himself—in large parts of *Underworld*, in almost all of *White Noise*—capable of realism's patient surfaces and saturation in personally verified detail. His visionary side, fed by the bleak implausibilities of modern technology and tabloidized popular culture, has often enough enjoyed a counterweight of domestic emotion and common decency. In *White Noise*, the surreal supermarkets are the real thing, hilariously familiar, and Jack Gladney's paeans to family life, from within his nest of impudently precocious children and spooky ex-wives, are not ironic. In *Cosmopolis*, implausibility reigns unchecked, mounting to a phantasmagoric funeral parade down Ninth Avenue for the Sufi rapper Brutha Fez; on parade are "the mayor and police commissioner in sober profile," a dozen congressmen, "faces from film and TV," foreign dignitaries, "figures of world religion in their robes, cowls, kimonos, sandals and soutanes," break dancers, nuns in full habit, and whirling dervishes.

Now, a reader undertaking a novel grants the writer a generous initial draft of suspended disbelief. DeLillo spends this advance payment as recklessly as his hero overinvests in loans against the yen. Falling in love, in life and in novels, is an unpredictable business, but what about while you're hunched over having a digital prostate examination in a limo parked in front of the Mercantile Library and at your other end consulting with your chief of finance, lean Jane Melman, sweaty from a jog on her day off? As never before, she and her boss are closely face to face:

> Her mouth was open, showing large gapped teeth. Something passed between them, deeply, a sympathy beyond the standard meanings that also encompassed these meanings, pity, affinity, tenderness, the whole physiology of neural maneuver, of heartbeat and secretion, some vast sexus of arousal drawing him toward her, complicatedly, with [Dr.] Ingram's finger up his ass.

DeLillo's fervent intelligence and his fastidious, edgy prose, buzzing with expressions like "wave arrays of information," weave halos of import around every event, however far-fetched and random. But the trouble with a tale where anything can happen is that somehow nothing happens. How much should we care about the threatened assassination of a hero as unsympathetic and bizarre as Eric Packer? DeLillo has a fearless reach of empathy; in *Mao II* he tells us just what it's like to be a Moonie, and how the homeless talk. But for what it's like to be a young Master of the Universe, read Tom Wolfe instead. DeLillo's sympathies are so much with the poor that his rich man seems a madman. In one of Packer's most outrageous acts of diffident destruction, the money manipulator, responding to his wife's generous offer to help him out of his difficulties with her own fortune, contrives, on a wristwatch computer, to break into her assets and lose them all for her. He even sneers at the amount: "The total in U.S. dollars was seven hundred and thirty-five million. The number seemed puny, a lottery jackpot shared by seventeen postal workers. . . . He tried to be ashamed on her behalf." When he later confesses to her what he has done, she playfully laughs and makes love. She evidently doesn't care, and the reader feels foolish for having cared on her behalf.

Packer, I suppose we should keep in mind, is working through a crisis in self-confidence. His first sexual partner of this busy April day, the art dealer Didi Fancher, tells him, "You're beginning to think it's more interesting to doubt than to act." His would-be murderer, in a conversation so

companionable and mutually attuned that murder seems a form of suicide, likens him to "Icarus falling" and tells him, "You did it to yourself."
On reflection, Packer has to wonder, "What did he want that was not
posthumous?" Death has become his thing.

His Pharaonic limo ride to an underground garage on the far West
Side does, however, have a few stops in the world of the living, of the substantially felt. The very notion of a day-long push along Forty-seventh
Street is funny and metaphoric—a soul's slow-motion hurtle from the
UN's posh environs to the desolation of Hell's Kitchen, with the diamond block between Fifth and Sixth Avenues providing a splash of noon-
tide sparkle. And the notion of a wife wears some shred of the sacred for
Packer and DeLillo both; Elise and Eric, though they were estranged
from the start, keep meeting, in a series of coincidences that must be
fated, and maximize their rapport while lying naked, as movie extras, on
the tar surface of Eleventh Avenue. Eric "felt the textural variation of
slubs of chewing gum compressed by decades of traffic. He smelled the
ground fumes, the oil leaks and rubbery skids, summers of hot tar": the
billionaire, "his body . . . a pearly froth of animal fat in some industrial
waste," comes home to basic materials.

And he comes home to, it is tempting to reveal, the barber shop of his
childhood, where clipped, elliptical DeLillo-diction sounds just right:

> "But how come you're such a stranger lately?"
> "Hello, Anthony."
> "Long time."
> "Long time. I need a haircut."
> "You look like what. Get in here so I can look at you. . . . I never seen
> such ratty hair on a human."

Lulled by the barber shop, its archaic scents and voices, Eric Packer,
whose father grew up in a tenement across the street, relaxes his day's
work of frenetic self-assertion and falls, for a few blessed moments,
asleep. The novel, relaxing likewise, gives us at last a venue in which we
can repose belief.

Red Loves Rex, Alas

THE GREEN HOUR, by Frederic Tuten. 265 pp. Norton, 2002.

Once upon a time—in 1971, if you must know—I read a slender book
that seemed to me original, droll, and mysteriously precious. Wrapped in

its posterish Roy Lichtenstein dust jacket, and set in narrow-measure boldface sanserif, Frederic Tuten's *The Adventures of Mao on the Long March* was a deadpan amalgam of quotation, parody, history, and fanciful fiction whose central image is that of Mao Tse-tung as a keen fan of Godard films and Minimal art, a Pateresque aesthete with a billion people on his hands. In an age when Mao posters adorned college dorms and Donald Barthelme ruled the *nouvelle vague* of fiction, the book made more sense than you might think; crediting a totalitarian icon with a thoroughly hip American mentality was wishful thinking of a merciful sort during the grim dénouement of our intervention in Vietnam. *The Adventures of Mao* had Barthelme's bold surrealism without his personal quality, his short stories' effect of being coded private reports from the front lines of city and, specifically, Village life. With all its bland absurdity, Tuten's book took a lofty tone; it was a collage of his soul's contents, where militant socialism and languid aestheticism coexisted in peaceful stalemate.

When I recently tried to find the volume, in the safe niche within my diffuse and uncatalogued holdings where I imagined I had cached it, it had vanished. Perhaps this is fitting, since after 1971 the author, too, rather vanished. Where has he been? Earning a living, of course, with Guggenheim grants and teaching stints—a number of years in Paris, countless years as director of the Graduate Program in Literature and Creative Writing at City College in New York. A loyal band of fellow-Manhattanites (Susan Sontag, Joseph McElroy, Jerome Charyn, Walter Mosley) provided warm endorsements for the three titles that Tuten turned out in three decades: *Tallien: A Brief Romance* (1988), *Tintin in the New World: A Romance* (1993), and *Van Gogh's Bad Café: A Love Story* (1997). All are pastiches of a sort. The first, addressed to the author's dead father, a "renegade Baptist and radical," tells, in accents both orotund and colloquial, the true story of Jean-Lambert Tallien, a French revolutionary who led the attack on Robespierre and survived the Terror, dying miserably in 1820. The second, in an irresistibly comic diction imitating, one assumes, the French, followed the adolescent detective Tintin, with his faithful dog Snowy and his crusty sidekick Captain Haddock, to Peru, where the major characters from Thomas Mann's *The Magic Mountain* have assembled. The third is a short but turgid pipe dream conflating the narrator's seedy, soggy times in the East Village with van Gogh's crazy last days in Auvers-sur-Oise; the painter's favorite dive, the Bad Café, translates as Mousey's Bar on Avenue C. Tuten's protagonists fall in love, which weakens their altruistic vocations. Political idealism, wistful aestheticism, counterproductive obsessive love, Francophilia, red hair, gemlike flames, a borrowed voice: all these ingredients are present, though more lugubriously, in his new novel, *The Green Hour.*

The book is his most conventional. It features a heroine with the upscale name of Dominique, who moves through clouds of academic, New Lefty glamour. She is an art historian, teaching at a New York City university; she has survived one bout of cancer and its treatment but is permanently afflicted with love for a high-minded drifter called Rex. Rex, as it happens, is the name Tuten gave his father in *Tallien*, and, like that Rex, this one dabbles in social activism, intermittently organizing the world's laborers into unions and strikes. His main activity, though, seems to be tormenting Dominique by reappearing in her life when it suits him and disappearing whenever she settles into a contented dependency. Their most sustained cohabitation comes in the working-class Paris suburb of Saint-Denis, where they live above a café whose green illumination gives the apartment the tint of the novel's title:

> "The green hour," she said, *"l'heure verte,* called so because in the early evening everyone in Paris went to the cafés to drown themselves in milky green absinthe. Did you know that, Rex?"
> "Sort of, Red."

That's the way he talks. He calls her Red, though he has red hair also. He is not very giving, but she loves him. It is easier to fathom why Marcel adores Albertine and Hans Castorp pines for Clavdia Chauchat than to wrap one's mind around this particular overestimation of the love object. They are not alone in the blissful green interval; Rex has a son, Kenji, the fruit of a brief entanglement with a rich Japanese radical who is not into, as they used to say, motherhood. Meanwhile, Dominique, whom no man can resist, is keeping on her string a super-rich American, Eric, which is also the name, in *Tallien*, of a Bronx Communist so devoted that he asphyxiates himself when Khrushchev denounces Stalin. Go figure. The newer-model Eric is an avid capitalist and far from suicidal, though his patient courtship of Dominique while she moons, year after year, over the mostly absentee Rex does smack of masochism. As she approaches fifty, she shifts her mooning to Kenji, who has evidently been kidnapped by his indifferent mother's powerful family. The child, at the age of five, shows a gift for sententious utterance as allegedly enchanting as his father's—"pronouncements saved from the oracular and pompous by the unassuming manner of his delivery." As one of his babysitters puts it, *"Il est très philosophe."* A sample Kenjiism: "The world is the world," he explains, in declining the facetious offer of a newspaper. When he and his mother visit the Louvre and view the paintings by her pet, Poussin, they enjoy this exchange:

"They are beautiful, Mama," he said. Adding, "But I do not like them."
"Really," she said. "And why, my little wise man?"
"*Elles sont tellement mortes*, Mama," he said. "They are really dead."

Tuten in his other novels showed a flair for an adopted voice, especially in the stately but festive rhythms of *Tintin in the New World*. But in *The Green Hour* his style has a stilted, airless quality, as if he were parodying something without quite realizing it. He does realize it, at moments, but pushes on anyway:

> They drank champagne, she and Claude, as lovers were supposed to do; they screwed on the bed and on the floor, they walked along gray beach and looked out on gray sea—as had other couples in every middling French movie—while the November mists chilled them and returned them to bed. He actually said, "O là là" when he came.

Cinema underlies Red's romantic life—"He always liked it when she did the hardboiled routine; very American, like the noir movies he loved, where the waitress called the police detective 'bub' or just plain 'mister.' " Hemingway sponsors a lusty string of "and"s: "Their being healthy and sexy and smart and in Paris in the spring and in the park reading and knowing they would eventually go back to the hotel and to their soft white wide bed." At the same time, a quaint and solemn diction of sentiment drains the tale of hard-boiled fun:

> He had held back cautiously for three years and not only from professional scruples or even from his knowing that she was already and deeply absorbed in another person but from the fear that he would spoil their ever deepening friendship and ruin his—their—chances for love.

Wallow where you will: on a single page we get "love's dramas and screams which were born in the deepest tissue of the self" and "She was the wet material that had fallen from the archaic sky in an explosion of atoms crashing and merging in the silent blackness." Tuten's vocabulary, coolly equal to ironic occasions, is tugged awry by the stresses of his love story: the heroine submits to intercourse with her "hinds" (hindquarters?) "in the air" and takes satisfaction in the "surety" (sureness? certainty?) "of her feelings"; an admirer wears "an expression so tender of [sic] her that she impulsively kissed his cheek"—a prepositional vagary as startling as "too many asides into the deeper realm of her feelings." Pseudo-nouns ("Kenji's vanishment," "a day of museuming") vie with bizarrely stretched verbs as in "leaves did not molt the page" (molt onto?) and the suddenly agronomic "Didn't she realize that modern capitalism was the new socialism, limed with fresh thoughts and new hopes?" Not that Tuten or any other writer with a slant to share need knuckle under to every copyeditors' quibble; but this prose feels floridly and hastily translated from another language—the language of film.

It is in the movies that obsessed and doomed love still, with a brave little smile, reigns, and the super-rich—a bottomless reservoir of improbabilities—finance abductions and underwrite, for unrequited love of a lady, such quixotic ventures as Rex's manufacture of one-of-a-kind, tailored-for-you bicycles. Dominique treats Eric like an unaudited expense account: "Now that she had returned, however temporarily, to his orbit, [he] facilitated her eventual repatriation—shipping, storage, plane tickets, and taxi to her apartment included." Not just she but the novel's world seems exempted from earthy consequences, suspended in a cocoon woven entirely of cultural allusions. Though it would be extreme to suggest that Tuten has no taste for life unless it is mediated by culture, his art is freed into its natural gaiety and nimbleness by the intercession of figments—Mao, Tintin, van Gogh, characters from *The Magic Mountain*, the stylized participants in the French Revolution. *The Green Hour* contains no such figment, though it is haunted by dead painters and the traditional gestures of glamour. As in an old-time Hollywood, or contemporary French, movie, there is a lot of reckless smoking, with careful brand identification: Lucky Strikes, "Delicados, the sweetish Mexican cigarettes which he smoked one after the other in the darkness of their bed," Gitanes and "Gauloise yellow," and back home to Camels, all on screen without a placement fee. As in a movie, every site the lovers visit is photogenic, from "Tangiers, where they stayed at the floppy old Hôtel Villa de France, in the room where—it was said—Matisse had lived, painting the trees and archway to the market beneath his window," to Rex's last crash pad, "a drab room with wonderfully rich bookcases" in New Mexico, where "a huge bouquet of dried red peppers hung from a beam above the table" competes visually with "a large and deep stone fireplace flanked by windows almost the room's height and facing mountains and sky." The word "elegant" occurs on page one and keeps recurring. Marxist aesthetes, or aesthetic Marxists, know how to pose for *Architectural Digest*, however unhappily in love or perennially out of work. Radical chic still works in the movies—something about its high cheekbones—but in novels it begins to look callow. There, we expect illusions to be, however half-heartedly, penetrated. Tuten's invincibly attractive, though cancerous, heroine does penetrate to as far as a recognition of herself as poor faithful Echo in the Poussin painting of Echo and Narcissus (reproduced as a frontispiece in the novel), and claims to be "exhausted with herself": "the hotel was tired with its stale tradition and tired carpets, and she was tired of her own story and its chronic repetitions." But this reader could not quite believe her final haven—a Montauk castle and cave like something out of *Dr. No*, with classier wall candy—or quite forgive her for putting us, apropos of Rex, through two hundred and fifty pages of vacillating, unconsciously arrogant infatuation.

Angel-Tits and Hellmouth

MORTALS, by Norman Rush. 715 pp. Knopf, 2003.

Ray Finch, the hero of Norman Rush's lengthy new novel, finds many things annoying. A teacher of English at an Episcopal school in the southern-African nation of Botswana, he harbors frustrated literary ambitions and sardonically reflects, concerning a huge opus sent to him from San Francisco by his younger brother, Rex, that he is "on the point of being dragged into collaborating with someone seeking the lowest form of literary immortality as established and pioneered by the annoying James Joyce, who thought it would be such a good idea to create puzzle palaces for thousands of specialists to wander around in forever." A contract CIA agent, Ray lets slip that "the sixties annoyed him," explaining,

> The sixties said that if you knocked down certain well-meaning but imperfect institutions you would get something altogether more beautiful and wonderful flowering up to replace them. People never appreciated how touch and go it had been with the Russians at certain points.

A keen Africanophile and linguist, he nevertheless finds it "fucking annoying and unnecessary, the multiplicity of mutually uncomprehending cultures." His brother, who is gay and was his mother's favorite, and who has become a moderately successful Bay Area columnist and has taken to regaling Ray's wife, Iris, with long letters designed, Ray thinks, to lure her away from Africa, deeply annoys him. So does his superior in the CIA, "chief of station" Chester Boyle, who in his stuffy secret consulting room displays a multitude of annoying mannerisms; even more annoying is the new arrival in town, Davis Morel, a pale-black American doctor who has a messianic scheme to rid Africa of Christianity and "credulism" and who, on a more practical level, is curing Iris of her hypoadrenia and cystitis. Iris and Ray have been married for seventeen years, and she gives signs of having the seventeen-year itch. This is less surprising to the reader than to Ray, who is perhaps the most annoying hero this reviewer has ever spent seven hundred pages with.

Ray is a control freak, a fussbudget, a tireless ruminator and annoyance-nurser, and most of his overflowing mental energy goes into an anxious gloating over his happy marriage. He is crazy about his wife, we are reassured over and over: "The fact was that without her the world would be unintelligible to him." Or:

> They were bone to bone, almost. If only his love could travel into her mind physically, by pure resonance in some way, straight in, so she would feel it and know it. Her hair was perfect. Her body was heaven to him, the pastures of heaven, perfection.

All right, all right. Happy marriages in real life should be encouraged and celebrated, as basic constituents of a sound society; but in fiction they rapidly tend to cloy. *Mortals* provides many pages of marital discourse, its mutual satisfactions only slightly tinged by intimations of disquiet.

> "I adore you," she said as he got back into bed.
> "Thanks."
> "I do, Ray. And you're gorgeous."
> "I am. Hm. May I call you angel-tits, then?"
> "Stop that. But listen to this, before you begin. This is wonderful. The other day when we were talking about why we're so attracted to each other . . ."

There was much of this smothering pillow talk—self-consciousness squared—in Rush's previous, prize-winning novel, *Mating*, but there the point of view was that of the nameless female protagonist, a thirty-two-year-old anthropologist engaged in a courtship pursuit of an older, married Utopian activist, and this male reader, through whatever kink in his gendered nature, was comfortable with it. (The hero and heroine of *Mating*, now Mr. and Mrs. Nelson Denoon, return in this novel, he fifteen years the worse for wear but she equipped, for the first time, with a name, Karen Ann, née Dooley, which became Hoyt before it became Denoon. She is still "a sturdy specimen, athletic," without makeup but with a "fine, bold face" and a good figure—rather like Iris, in fact. Ray "liked her type.")

In his obsessive dithering over the exact state and direction of his wife's affections, Ray abuses his CIA powers, focusing all his attention on his perceived rival, Morel, while ignoring, against Boyle's orders, a benign agricultural theorist, the Scots-educated Botswana native Samuel Kerekang, who turns out to be the real disturber of the national order. Ray has even hired, at the expense of American taxpayers, a spy to sit in at Morel's anti-credulism lectures: "Sending in a live asset had been rational, granted that he had been in an irrational state himself over Morel."

Ray, frantic with love-worry, heads north, with a driver, into the Kalahari, where trouble has brewed. Just as *Mating*'s most vivid section was the heroine's trek across that desert, *Mortals* takes on spaciousness and breathing room with Iris left behind. She is ever in Ray's thoughts, though, and the viscid complications of his awareness contrive to slow, with insertions of remembered poetry, song, and details of childhood, the persuasively rendered action. A gun battle, on the roof of a splendid abandoned resort hotel, between Kerekang's motley band of rebels and a better-armed group of South African mercenaries who have been summoned, it turns out, by the CIA, is a believable hell as opposed to the hyperbolic one weighing on Ray's mind: "Hell was another man's cock going into your beloved's cunt." But the reality of these battle scenes is considerably sapped by Ray's bizarre, presumably semi-delirious behavior, involving total nudity and his brother's bulky manuscript duct-taped to his body like a suicide bomb. Scene after scene tests the reader's own credulism with fantastic juxtapositions—torture and song, fury and innocence—under an African sky of burning sun and blazing stars. The concept of hell, of Hellmouth as an eruption of the world's evil, recurs; Ray, in his English-literature phase, is a specialist in Milton, and Rush's three books (his first, *Whites*, is a collection of short stories) all have on their covers pictorial details from Hieronymus Bosch. Boschian grotesqueries energetically cram the canvas of *Mortals*, to an effect of comic, rageful tangle. There is a truculent edge to Rush's style; he omitted quotation marks (annoyingly) in *Mating*, and employs them here, but with so many unclosed sets, in prolonged speeches broken into paragraph, that it takes constant vigilance to know who is talking.

It is annoying, one could say, that a novel demonstrating so acute, well stocked, and witty a sensibility is such a trial to read. Individual passages flare up with a visionary economy:

> He walked in a circle around the dying fire. He was still enclosed in the quasi-tent [of netting], carrying it with him like a fool of some kind. He needed to list the options he had for interpreting what she had done to him, putting *Madame Bovary* in his hands. But fire interrupted him, a bloom of flame declaring itself around him, dragging the breath out of his lungs. The netting had gone up. He had dragged it across an ember. He pitched the burning mass away. He was all right. He was trembling. His hair had gotten singed in back, was all. He had made a spectacle.

In other passages, the story feels impeded by a joyless exactitude. A lecture site:

> A small table and a chair had been set to the left of the lectern, and a chrome steel utility cart had been pushed up against it on the right. The cart bore a

display of bouquets obviously recycled from the hospital wards. The center-piece was a protea in a pot, drooping in a gold foil calyx. A gooseneck microphone was mounted on the lectern, needlessly, considering the dimensions of the room.

An abundance of expository quotation (Rex's gabby, sardonic letters; his epigrammatic, disjointed manuscript; Morel's anti-religion lectures, with counterarguments by Kerekang) suggests an overflow from some other, less fictional book. As the plot heats up, two characters issue applicable criticisms: Morel explosively tells Ray, "You never shut up, is the problem," and Iris, rejecting Ray's notion that she should have revealed her every impulse, says that "it would have led to a talk opera."

A talk opera is just what Ray likes, and what *Mortals* at bottom is. Even more than love's paradise and Africa's hell, words are what the novelist cares about. In the midst of breaking down a prison wall, Ray coins the word "crackage" and complains, "The working vocabulary of Americans is half what it was in 1950. That's horrifying." His avid marital discourse with Iris is peppered with such questions as "why there was a single term in English for affirmative head movements but for the negative you were forced to use three words . . . why there was no one-word antonym of nod." Iris speaks of "Kleenices" as the plural of "Kleenex" and tells him loftily, "You don't need to convince me you're concupiscent." Ray muses to himself, "Celerity was another one of those perfectly good words destined for the bone pile." In the midst of mayhem on the roof, he finds time to mourn the obsolescence of the word "affray": "Affray was one of those words that was vanishing from the language. The makers of the English language would be appalled, whoever they had been." A little later, he reflects:

> There should be an Académie Anglaise. He wouldn't mind working for that kind of body. He was going to need a job. It would be a job that would let him elevate some of his brother's coinages like *to harbinge* into the dictionary, some dictionary.

Lines of poetry bubble up in Ray's mind at crisis moments (though the only Milton that comes to him is Satan's "Evil, be thou my good"), and the most sympathetic character in the novel, Kerekang, is another poetry buff, favoring the Victorians. "Literature is humanity talking to itself, Ray thought."

Are CIA novels literature? I haven't read many, but Rush seems to have the lingo down pretty well, and the little subterfugal tricks. However, Ray's apologetic, I-hate-myself attitude about involvement with the agency seems, after September 2001, rather dated: instead of being considered too meddlesome and sinisterly omnipotent, the CIA appears to have been, with other national watchdogs, sound asleep at the switch. The events in *Mortals* take place in 1992–93, with the Soviet Union newly collapsed and white rule slowly surrendering in South Africa. Norman Rush, we learn from the note on the author, "with his wife, Elsa . . . lived and worked in Africa from 1978 to 1983," as a member of the Peace Corps. One wonders if, with two novels that total twelve hundred pages, he hasn't gotten most of what he is going to get out of Botswana. It may be time for Rush to bring his logomania and global perspective back to the United States; his take on cultural developments in the West, as they are forwarded by the American correspondents of our overseas couple, is mordant and lively. Ray sums up the recent history of female unhappiness:

> What was happening was that the general unhappiness of women was turning into a force and developing institutions and mandibles whereas before it had been a kind of background condition like the temperature, as he had thought, something that rose and fell within certain stable limits. . . . What they wanted, he gathered, feeling pleased with himself, was for their own personal rational deliberation to replace what? . . . to replace tradition and custom and instinct, what men called instinct, in arriving at the nine or ten major decisions life presents us with. . . . It was immense, of course, because the only kind of societies the human race had ever been able to build were ones in which half the population was being very accommodating to the other half.

Such a bold, droll, inclusive anthropology must have needed an African sojourn for its maturation; still, I would be happy to see a Stateside sequel, no longer than, say, *Candide* or *The Great Gatsby*, to this (quoting Rush in another context) "unhelpful olla podrida" of a somewhat Miltonian epic.

Mind/Body Problems—I

THE CONFESSIONS OF MAX TIVOLI, by Andrew Sean Greer. 271 pp. Farrar, Straus and Giroux, 2004.

We look to fiction for images of reality—real life rendered as vicarious experience, with a circumstantial intimacy that more factual, explanatory accounts cannot quite supply. Yet the freedom to invent tempts the fiction writer to fantasy. Already, his manipulation of time, speeding it up and slowing it down according to the needs of his story, and his scanting of the routine and banality that make up most of life's substance take unrealistic liberties. John Hawkes, a conspicuous avant-garde libertarian, once announced, to the astonishment of a writing class in which I was enrolled, "When I want a character to fly, I just write, 'He flew.' " In its dizzying freedom, fiction holds an opportunity to dramatize certain existential questions that mark the beginnings of philosophy in a child. Why am I—my consciousness, my mind—in this body and not another? Why do I exist now instead of in the past or the future? Why does time only move forward? What would it be like to live life backwards, from old age to infancy?

This last question, lent some weight by the remaining puzzles in the biology of aging and by actual, pathological instances of premature senility in the very young, has an American literary pedigree. F. Scott Fitzgerald published a story, "The Curious Case of Benjamin Button," on the theme in 1922; including it in his collection *Tales of the Jazz Age*, he noted in a foreword:

> This story was inspired by a remark of Mark Twain's to the effect that it was a pity that the best part of life came at the beginning and the worst part at the end. By trying the experiment upon only one man in a perfectly normal world I have scarcely given his idea a fair trial. Several weeks after completing it, I discovered an almost identical plot in Samuel Butler's "Note-books."

It perhaps says something about Fitzgerald's psychology that the story's opening sections, with Button as an old man, come across as coarse and brittle farce, whereas the end, in which the hero regresses into infancy, feels seductively real:

> Through the noons and nights he breathed and over him there were soft mumblings and murmurings that he scarcely heard, and faintly differentiated smells, and light and darkness.
>
> Then it was all dark, and his white crib and the dim faces that moved above him, and the warm sweet aroma of the milk, faded out altogether from his mind.

Though not one of Fitzgerald's best, the story was reprised eighty years later by Gabriel Brownstein, in his story collection *The Curious Case of Benjamin Button, Apt. 3W* (2002). The title story, a fantastic riff upon a fantasy, almost duplicates Fitzgerald's for a few sentences but goes off weirdly in its own directions. Button, born ancient in 1912, masquerades in "shtetl drag" as a jazz pianist "known variously as the Hey-Hey Hebrew, the Jitterbug Jew, and the Kokomotion Kike" during the late

Twenties, and reappears in the Seventies as a barefoot hippie living, with his aged mother, in the same West Side apartment building occupied by the adolescent narrator and his rascally pals. Benjamin Button's parents are a Southern woman and a "merchant banker" who is trying to suppress his Jewish, East Side origins, as the grandson of a rabbi. A great deal of new baggage is thus loaded upon the tenuous figure of Button, and he sinks beneath it, as Fitzgerald's ending returns in starker, more structuralist terms:

> Soon, he could not tell day from night, pain from want, and finally presence from absence. Long after he ceased to feel the movement of time, he faded completely from its progress.

Two years later in this succession, an entire novel, resplendently poetic and loftily sorrowing, has appeared. The name Benjamin Button has been retired, but the thought-experiment remains. This time, the man at the end of his life is born in 1871, in San Francisco, of a Southern woman and a self-invented entrepreneur, not Jewish but Danish, who has changed his name from Asgar Van Daler to Tivoli, in honor of the Copenhagen park he remembers. Young-old Max's early memories are richly entwined with the animal wonders of San Francisco's Woodward's Gardens, one of the many lost local sights that Greer revives, with an eerie sensory omniscience, from the dry pages of research. He is one of the numerous young-old contemporary fiction-writers—Mark Helprin, Thomas Mallon, Caleb Carr, Alice Munro, Andrea Barrett, with E. L. Doctorow as godfather—to whom time past is an open book, a theme park in which they wander with a child's delight in the gaudiness and violence. What Henry James, himself now part of the past and available as a theme-park exhibit, breathlessly called the "palpable present *intimate* that throbs responsive" is pointedly neglected in favor of what he called "mere *escamotage* . . . the little facts that can be got from pictures and documents, relics and prints." All fiction, insofar as it draws upon the writer's memories, is historical in a sense; but a reader who has hearkened to Henry James enters guardedly reconstructed worlds that ceased to exist before the author was born. A circumstantiality assembled of little documentary facts can feel flimsy, offering less resistance to enchantment than the unsifted environment clumsily pressing all around us.

That said, *The Confessions of Max Tivoli* is enchanting, in the perfumed, dandified style of disenchantment brought to grandeur by Proust and Nabokov. "Love . . . ever unsatisfied, lives always in the moment that is about to come," runs the novel's epigraph, from Proust, and Greer's opening sentence reads, "We are each the love of someone's life." The general fate of misdirected, unarrived love, then, merges with the singular case of Max Tivoli, who begins with the innocent mind of a child in an old man's body, and, after a brief and blissful intersection, in 1906, of his inner age with his physical age, ends with a man's mournful wisdom in a child's body. Max differs from Benjamin Button in that Button begins with a fully stocked old brain and ends with a newborn's *tabula rasa;* whereas Max learns as he goes, as do all those of us not condemned to age in reverse. Sex, for example, comes upon him when he has the able body of a fifty-three-year-old and the inexperience of an exceptionally chaste seventeen-year-old. His lover, the downstairs tenant Mrs. Levy, is ardent enough for two, crooning to him as they copulate in a bed of phlox, "You're a good man, Max, don't worry, you haven't touched a woman in a while, have you? Max, you good, good man." However, it is not the mother Max loves, but the daughter, fourteen-year-old Alice, upon whom he spies with the ornate prurience of Humbert Humbert yearning for Lolita. Max (whose memoirs are written for Alice eventually to read) glimpses her one night looking for something in their shared back garden:

> I could see through the neck of your loose cotton chemise a pink landscape
> of skin. You turned and writhed in your cloud and I turned and writhed in
> mine. I saw your legs stretching and tensing as you hunted and jerked your
> body in hope; women's pantaloons were devious things in those days, split
> down the crotch with overlapping fabric, and once you shifted just care-
> lessly enough to allow the veil to part and I glimpsed the vulnerable blue
> veins of your thighs. . . . I hope you'll find it flattering, now that you are old
> as well, to think of me in bed, staring at my memory like a French postcard,
> watching the starlight trickle into the darkness of your clothes.

The passage illustrates the author's remarkably confident acquaintance with female clothes of the era 1880–1930, as well as, in the epithet "trickle," the gemmy sparkle of his prose. Elsewhere, he writes of "a face unlatched with longing" and a beloved older woman's "sky-gray hair" and a deer's "moon-iced antlers." With no evident effort, he works into his intricately unfolding narrative such startling bygone details as "a newspaper still warm from the butler's iron" and "a saloon owner with a gold cane and vulcanized rubber fillings in his smile" and "the latest Paris fashion: a live beetle, iridescently winged, attached to her dress with a golden chain." A great love for a vanished San Francisco, the pre-earthquake "old San Francisco of gilt-edged gas lamps and velvet walls," breathes through these pages, whose sepia background of luxury and brutality almost swallows the central characters and their schematically star-crossed affections. Even as young Max ogles the ineffable Alice, her attention fastens upon his one and only friend, Hughie, faithful Hughie, who has played with the senescent little freak as if he were a normal boy, and who keeps their friendship through fifty eventful years, while he himself harbors, beneath the surface life of a respectable married lawyer . . . Never mind. Save Hughie's cathexis for the end of the book. Rest assured, patient reader, that *The Confessions of Max Tivoli* is long on longing and short on lasting satisfactions, as full of broken hearts as it is of dazzling local, time-specific color. "We each have an awful bargain in our lives" is one of Greer's aphorisms; on the next page another boasts, "It is a brave and stupid thing, a beautiful thing, to waste one's life for love." In one of the fine if faintly preening stories collected in Greer's *How It Was for Me*, "Blame It on My Youth," an aphoristic surge suggests how the author might have been drawn to the reversed life-story:

> Love works backward in time, like all secrets. It colors memory and first impressions, dull evenings and late sleepless nights. It makes them glow with heat, like coals taken for dead.

The huge technical challenge of framing a life lived backwards is cunningly, handsomely met. Max, who supposedly indicts these confessions in the year 1930, having lodged himself in a small household containing an irksome and insulting boy roughly his apparent age and a kindly if preoccupied mother approaching sixty, has survived a number of the young century's crises. He and his wife are thrown together in the great earthquake of 1906, and feverishly separate in a siege of flu in 1917; the Great War provides a convenient theatre in which Max, enlisting, can bury his grief. The advents of electricity and the automobile are woven into his ever more youthful life's fabric. He and Hughie, on a footloose auto journey slyly echoing the highway wanderings in *Lolita*, rig their Chrysler with a radio and, while Max turns too boyish to drive, the scattered, staticky programs of the late Twenties crackle from the depths of the past, with not just the names—Baby Snooks, the Fat Man—but the contents:

> "Yowsah yowsah yowsah," the maestro Ben Bernie used to whisper to us, and "Au revoir, pleasant dreams." And advertisements, of course, an interesting insight into the obsessions of the middle class: "If you want your teeth to shine like pearls, buy Dr. Straaska's Toothpaste." I admit it; I bought some.

Terrifyingly, during this trip Max is overtaken by childhood: "In the last few years, I had noticed a definite shift in things; my muscles lost their form, my shoes became too big, and, most astonishing of all, the world began to rise around me. . . . It was never going to be safe in my body again." This feels believable; we shrink toward the end. At the other end, Greer does all he can to distract us from the initial blow to the reader's suspension of disbelief, the anatomical grotesquerie of a woman giving birth to a full-sized old man. Fitzgerald and Brownstein bluster it through with noisy hospital scenes, summoning up outraged doctors and nurses and bearded ancients crammed into cribs and bassinets, whereas Greer fudges the newborn's size, and the Danish father cheerfully gives the "wrinkled, palsied" apparition the friendly status of a Nordic legend, a fabled gnome:

> "He is a *Nisse*! He is lucky, darling." He leaned down to kiss her forehead
> and then my own, which was falsely lined with decades of worry. He smiled
> at his wife and then spoke sternly to the midwife: "He is ours, we will not let
> him go."

As Max matures, his maladjustments are not far off the beaten track. Normal men, too, can feel too young for sex, and too old for the world's rough-and-tumble, and out of sync with their love objects, and prey to unstoppable bodily changes. For Max, the added effort of coördinating his inner age with the world's expectations of his outer shell gives his life-passage a heightened focus and alertness; whatever his woes, he is spared the boredom of settling into an allotted spot and growing old in it. Growing against the grain of time, he feels time densely; the terror of transience and the tragedy of life's limits permeate this novel in a way that make *Lolita* seem, relatively, a merry book, sporting an immigrant's amusement at America and his connivance in its vulgar freedoms. Like Proust, Greer presents life as essentially a solitude, an ever-renewed exile from the present, a shifting set of gorgeous mirages that nothing but descriptive genius can hold fast. Max writes, "Life is short, and full of sorrows, and I loved it." His poignantly awry existence, set out with such a wealth of verbal flourishes and gilded touches, serves as a heightened version of the strangeness, the muffled disharmony, of being human.

Mixed Messages

EXTREMELY LOUD & INCREDIBLY CLOSE, by Jonathan Safran Foer. 350 pp. Houghton Mifflin, 2005.

Jonathan Safran Foer, born in 1977, came out swinging in 2002, with the publication of his astounding, clownish, tender, intricately and extravagantly plotted novel *Everything Is Illuminated*. From the hilarious overreacher's English of the Ukrainian tour guide Alexander Perchov to the passionately fanciful evocation of a Polish-Jewish shtetl from 1791 to 1942, the prose kept jolting the reader into the heightened awareness that comes with writing whose exact like hasn't been seen before. Foer's second novel, *Extremely Loud & Incredibly Close*, continues on a high plane of inventiveness and emotional urgency, but takes place on the thoroughly explored turf of New York City and centers on the aftermath of that most familiar of recent catastrophes, the 2001 World Trade Center blitz. The hero, a nine-year-old boy called Oskar Schell, has lost his father, Thomas, in the collapse of one of the Twin Towers. Further, he is the only person to have heard the five decreasingly sanguine messages that Thomas, trapped in a morning meeting at Windows on the World, left on the family answering machine. A year later, Oskar has many symptoms of distress: insomnia, fear of elevators and Arabs, a sense of being "in the middle of a huge black ocean." This reader's heart slightly sank when he realized he was going to spend over three hundred pages in the company of an unhappy, partially wised-up nine-year-old. The novel, traditionally a mirror held up to the Western bourgeoisie, to teach them how to shave, dress, and behave, has focused on adult moral choices and their consequences. With some brilliant exceptions like Dickens and Mark Twain and Henry James, novelists have not taken children seriously enough to make them protagonists. However sensitive and observant, the ordinary child lacks property and the capacity for sexual engagement; he exists, therefore, on the margins of the social contract— a rider, as it were, on the imperatives and compromises of others. Yet in recent years a number of young novelists—Stephen Millhauser and Jonathan Lethem, for two—have devoted their most ambitious and energetic efforts to detailing the fervent hobbies and the intoxicating overdoses on popular culture, the estrangement and the dependence that characterize contemporary American childhood. Childhood's new viability as novelistic ground may signal a shift in the very nature of being a human being, considered anthropologically as a receiver and continuer of tribal myths, beliefs, and strictures. Older novels, and novelists up through Joyce, Proust, and Hemingway, portrayed the pained shedding of this traditional baggage. The newer novelists, having inherited almost no set beliefs from their liberal, distracted middle-class parents, see childhood as the place where one invents the baggage—totems, rituals, lessons to live by—of a solitary one-person tribe.

Foer's protagonist, a nine-year-old atheist whose immediate family consists of a dog called Buckminster, an unusually permissive and remote working mother, a loving grandmother who lives across the street and talks to him through a baby monitor, and a grandfather whom the trauma of the Dresden firebombing has robbed of the gift of speech, has few acculturated antibodies to heal the wound of his father's abrupt death. While the twenty-year-old hero of *Everything Is Illuminated* has distinctly Jewish ancestors, full of folkloric shtetl vitality, as a cornerstone of his self, little Oskar has only a tambourine, a scrapbook titled *Stuff That Happened to Me*, and a psychiatrist who thinks he should be hospitalized, lest in his unassuaged grief and shock he harm himself. His family seems oddly deracinated; his paternal grandparents spoke German, but they are not Jewish, since they were moving about freely in Dresden at the time of the Allied incendiary raid of February 1945, and indeed his grandmother's family was hiding a Jew. Nor do they give any evidence of being Christian, though Grandma is said to believe in God. Oskar's mother is a busy lawyer, and his father reluctantly ran a jewelry business founded by his speechless father, who wanted to be a sculptor, but Foer's Schells basically exist in the same West Side economic zone as J. D. Salinger's Glass family: there is enough money to sustain their wordy absorption in one another and their wounded pasts.

The grandparents, who met in a Broadway bakery, impulsively married as a mutual rescue. Actually, they had met before, as young people in Dresden, Grandma being the younger sister of a girl that the grandfather had loved, impregnated, and lost in Dresden's firebombing. The couple create a low-sex marriage of silence and strictly observed zones of Nothing and Something in their apartment. The grandfather flees back to Dresden in 1963, when he learns that his wife—breaking one of their rules—is pregnant. She leaves New York forty years later. From their places of retreat they shower letters upon those callously left behind— Grandma upon Oskar, and the elder Thomas Schell upon his son, also Thomas, whom he never sees and who died on September 11, 2001, at the age of forty. Each letter-writer possesses an eccentric style, recognizable at a glance. Grandma's letters have short, flush-left paragraphs and extra spaces between sentences. The senior Thomas Schell writes in one big paragraph when he is not, as a means of carrying on a conversation, writing out single sentences. These responses are published one on a page, making for a real page-turner of a novel, a kind of serial fortune cookie:

I'm sorry, this is the smallest I've got
Start spreading the news . . .
The regular, please
Thank you, but I'm about to burst
I'm not sure, but it's late

Help
Ha ha ha!
Please marry me

The junior Thomas Schell, among the habits and skills intensely endearing to his son, always read with a red pen in hand, encircling mistakes. He makes his mark on the pages of Foer's novel in the form of many red (truly red; this is a four-color print job) encirclings of the text of one letter that, in April of 1978, happened, apparently, to reach him. The picto-typographical antics don't end there; the text is interrupted by photographs, of stars and jewels and keys and Manhattan windows and fingerprints and the backs of heads and an elephant's eye and turtles mating and Stephen Hawking appearing on television and Sir Laurence Olivier playing Hamlet and, lifted from a Portuguese site on the Internet, a blurred body falling from one of the World Trade Center towers. Oskar thinks it could be his father; all the photographs show things in his mind. Again, the longest of the grandfather's letters, in illustration of his sensation that "there won't be enough pages in this book for me to tell you what I need to tell you," exploits the possibilities of computerized typesetting by slowly squeezing, page by page, the lines and the words within the lines until the pages become illegible and, finally, almost as solidly black as an Ad Reinhardt canvas. Earlier in this remarkable missive, Thomas tells of tapping out words by means of the telephone keypad and gives us two and a half pages of numerals that an ideal reader (not I) could, with patience and a keypad, decipher. There are also three blank pages in the middle of the book, illustrating a mishap whereby Grandma settled at a typewriter to write the story of her life and did so to the tune of *a thousand pages* only to learn that there had been no ribbon in the machine. How come she didn't notice? She has, she is always saying, "crummy eyes." Even as a magic-realist parable of non-communication, her blind persistence boggles the mind.

This reader's mind was boggled, too, by a nine-year-old boy's being allowed to roam, every weekend, all over the five boroughs, inquiring, in alphabetical order, at the two hundred sixteen different addresses listed under the name "Black," which was written on an envelope containing a key found within a blue vase on a high shelf of his father's closet. He goes on foot at first, continually shaking his tambourine, "because it helped me to remember that even though I was going through different neighborhoods, I was still me." This heroic ordeal is his way of drawing near to his dead father; he draws near to his live mother by zipping up the back of her dress as she prepares to go out.

In the apartment above them, it happens, there is a hundred-and-three-year-old man called Black—Mr. Black, to be exact. Though he hasn't left his apartment for twenty-four years, he agrees to accompany Oskar on his search. Foer has a flair for the list, the inventive inventory, and his ramble through the Blacks has its vivid moments: Abby Black lives in the narrowest house in New York, formerly occupied by Edna Saint Vincent Millay, and is an epidemiologist; she chats with Oskar about elephants' memories and tears while an unseen man shouts for her attention in the next room; Abe Black lives in Coney Island and takes Oskar for a ride on the Cyclone; Ada Black owns two Picassos, has an African-American maid called Gail, and seems to know suspiciously much about Oskar; Fo Black, in Chinatown, has "I ♥ NY" posters everywhere because *ny* means "you" in Chinese; Georgia Black, in Staten Island, has established a museum of her husband's life in her living room, and he has created one for her in the next room. I don't doubt that Foer is resourceful enough to take us all the way through the alphabet with amiable freaks, but I was grateful that he didn't; playful inventiveness can come down with a case of the cutes. After a while, Foer allows us to forget Oskar's tambourine, and his use of the expression "zipping up the sleeping bag of myself" for emotional withdrawal and "wearing heavy boots" for depression. As to Oskar's inventions—a teakettle whose spout becomes a mouth that "could whistle pretty melodies, or do Shakespeare"; little microphones that, once swallowed, would play the sounds of our hearts for all to hear; a biodegradable car; safety nets everywhere—they measure, I suppose, his desire to improve an implacable world, and serve to placate a child's seething impotence.

The book's graphic embellishments reach a climax in the last pages, when the flip-the-pages device present in some children's books answers Oskar's yearning that everything unfortunate be run backward—a fall is turned into an ascent. It is one of the more curious happy endings ever contrived, and strangely moving. But, overall, the book's hyperactive visual surface covers up a certain hollow monotony in its human drama. An anomie and a disaffection afflict the Schells which no description of the Dresden firebombing or Hiroshima (it's in here, too, for good measure) can quite excuse. There is a disproportion not felt with the Nazi atrocities that haunt the grandfathers in *Everything Is Illuminated*. The later novel, on its local ground, seems thinner, overextended, and sentimentally watery, compared with its Old World predecessor. Grandfather Schell's abandoning his newly pregnant wife never feels explained, it is just chewed over. Grandma recounts his departure to Oskar:

Why are you leaving me?
He wrote, I do not know how to live.

I do not know either, but I am trying.
I do not know how to try.

To explain her own narrow and static life, she proposes: "That's been my problem. I miss what I already have, and I surround myself with things that are missing." The voices of both grandparents protest too much, crying, "I love you, I love you!" while receding. It's as if the author wants to give his characters his own warm heart, but intimacy disagrees with them: "I love you so much it hurts me," Grandma writes Oskar. In this family, everybody keeps saying, "I'm sorry," but nobody acts sorry.

Oskar's mother, it turns out, is watching over him more closely than it appears, but the child has to deduce this on his own. His prose style, interestingly, is to run dialogue together in paragraphs, except, sometimes, when he and his mother talk; then he runs their laconic exchanges down the page as thin as the mouse's tail in that pioneering study of childhood, *Alice in Wonderland*. In similar minimalist, straggling fashion, Grandma's last letter expresses what seems to be the novel's preachment, Oskar's lesson to live by. She remembers sleeping as a girl next to her sister, her husband's true love, Anna:

> The hairs of our arms touched.
> It was late, and we were tired.
> We assumed there would be other nights. . . .
> I said, I want to tell you something.
> She said, You can tell me tomorrow.
> I had never told her how much I loved her. . . .
> I thought about waking her.
> But it was unnecessary.
> There would be other nights.
> And how can you say I love you to someone you love?
> I rolled onto my side and fell asleep next to her.
> Here is the point of everything I have been trying to tell you, Oskar.
> It's always necessary.

This is magnificent in its quiet way, but possibly assigns too much importance to verbalization, as children do. Adults know more than they are told. They know when they are loved, and did even in eras when "love" was not the obligatory catchword it has become. As no less aloof an eminence than T. S. Eliot wrote:

> There's no vocabulary
> For love within a family, love that's lived in
> But not looked at, love within the light of which
> All else is seen, the love within which

All other love finds speech.
This love is silent.

We must trust our parents, our children, to hear us even in silence, in an age that fears silence. Muzak, TV, and their computerized counterparts fill the few crannies left by traffic noise. Foer is, I would say, a naturally noisy writer—a natural parodist, a jokester, full of ideas and special effects, keen to keep us off-balance and entertained. The very title, *Extremely Loud & Incredibly Close*, suggests the kind of impact he wants to make on the reader. But a little more silence, a few fewer messages, and less graphic apparatus might let Foer's excellent empathy, imagination, and good will sound out all the louder.

The Great Game Gone

LEGENDS: *A Novel of Dissimulation*, by Robert Littell. 395 pp. Overlook, 2005.

The spy thriller still pines for the Soviet Union. No post–Iron Curtain intrigue, no replay of the British Empire's Great Game in Afghanistan or its intrusions into the Middle East, no elaborate "security measures," no double-double cross in the murk of CIA-FBI rivalry, can match, for heart-stoppingly high geopolitical stakes, the good old days when, in terms of John le Carré's fiction, MI6's Smiley matched wits with the KGB's Karla on the global chessboard. There was an intelligibility if not a friendly intimacy in the old contest, one between two large, idealistic, rough-mannered nations seeking to maintain their spheres of influence short of tripping into nuclear war. As one hardened undercover functionary cozily tells another in Robert Littell's new book, *Legends: A Novel of Dissimulation*, "We all came of age in the cold war. We all fought the good fight. I'm sure we can work something out." The so-called war on terror has no such surety; "working something out" is just what the other side, or sides, doesn't want. Littell conscientiously covers the new ground—the post-Soviet Russia of the oligarchs; the potential for financial shenanigans opened up by worldwide computerization; the stagnant antipathy between Israel and its neighbors; Bosnia; Chechnya; and (news to me) an international smugglers' cove where the borders of Paraguay, Brazil, and Argentina meet and whores dance sleepily in one another's arms—but he remains most excited by, and most at home with, occupants of the old U.S.S.R. as they strike up fresh relations with capitalism and the CIA.

Littell, a former *Newsweek* reporter now resident in southern France, began his career as a fictional spymaster with *The Defection of A. J. Lewinter: A Novel of Duplicity* (1973), a deft and light-hearted performance on the edge of parody, and capped it, a dozen books later, with the best-selling magnum opus *The Company: A Novel of the CIA* (2002), a nostalgic recapitulation, in nearly nine hundred pages, of the Cold War intelligence marathon from 1950 to 1995. Littell is not the only author to scent an epic here; Norman Mailer's giant, possibly ongoing saga, *Harlot's Ghost*, deals also with this secretive struggle and the striking historical figure of gaunt, erudite, borderline-paranoid James Jesus Angleton, for some twenty years head of CIA counterintelligence. *Legends*, though falling short of Tolstoyan, or Maileresque, amplitude, does not scant, expertly roaming the continents and offering a psychological puzzle to go with an abundance of deception and violence.

Martin Odum, to give the novel's confusing hero his most-often-used name, is an ex–CIA operative who has, he feels, lost his real identity in the shuffle of "legends"—false identities, with carefully worked-out histories and trade skills, assumed for a particular piece of espionage. Odum has paid a personal price for doing his devious patriotic duty: he suffers from migraine headaches; his occasional lover finds her side of their relationship "like sleepwalking through a string of one-night stands that were physically satisfying but emotionally frustrating"; he plans to spend the rest of his life, he confesses to her, "boring himself to death." The CIA retired him, after his psychoanalysis at the taxpayers' expense was abruptly terminated. His diagnosis was MPD, multiple-personality disorder. Along with his well-remembered roles of Dante Pippen, an IRA explosives expert training Hezbollah jihadists in Lebanon, and Lincoln Dittman, a Civil War buff doubling as an arms dealer in Brazil, there are hints of a "legend," an alter ego, beyond his memory's reach. These impersonations having served their dangerous purpose, and Odum having outlived his usefulness to the CIA, he makes ends meet as a private detective in the Crown Heights section of Brooklyn, using two pool tables as his office furniture. Well, one day in walks this dame called Stella, wearing a long raincoat and on her lips a ghost of a smile. . . .

It's a long story, and Littell should be allowed to tell it, twist after twist after twist. This reviewer put up some initial resistance against the plot's ruthless manipulations of chronological sequence, the arch chapter titles ("1997: Oskar Alexandrovich Kastner Discovers the Weight of a Cigarette"), the excessively vivid verbs ("The jetliner elbowed through the towering clouds"; "He heard Stella's voice breasting the static"), the occasional fusillade of clichés ("He must have been off his rocker to think he could trace a husband who had jumped ship. Finding a needle in a haystack would be child's play by comparison"), the clammy, overcooked atmospherics ("eyes burning with excitement"; "the muscles on her face contorting with heartache"), and the heavy-breathing ruminations about identity, that hackneyed modern problem. Almost all the characters, including stray taxi-drivers and hookers (maybe *especially* hookers, adepts at dissimulation and undercover work), are pretending to be somebody else, under another name. In a "nightmarish world," we are left to conclude, "people who are broken have several selves." Why does this theme feel tired? Is it just those Jason Bourne movies, starring Matt Damon?

But, as I rounded page 300 and headed into the book's last quarter, the pieces of the puzzle began to click together and I felt myself sinking into an earlier assumed identity: I became a fourteen-year-old boy lying on a red caneback sofa in Pennsylvania eating peanut-butter-and-raisin sandwiches (a site-specific ethnic treat) and reading one mystery novel after another. Not just mysteries—Ellery Queen, Agatha Christie, John Dickson Carr, Ngaio Marsh, Erle Stanley Gardner—but an occasional international thriller, like Eric Ambler's *A Coffin for Demetrios* and Graham Greene's *The Third Man*. The idea of reading a non-genre novel, with its stodgy domestic realism and sissy fuss over female heartbreak, repelled me then, but I could lose myself all morning and afternoon in narratives of skulduggery, detection, and eventual triumphant justice. And so, to judge from the best-seller lists, can millions still. Thrillers, as we shall call them, offer the reader a firm contract: there will be violent events; we will go places our parents don't take us; the protagonist will conquer and survive; and social order will, however temporarily, be restored. The reader's essential safety, as he reclines on his red sofa, will not be breached. The world around him and the world he reads about remain distinct; the partition between them is not undermined by any connection to depths within himself. At this same age, I remember, I looked into Joyce's *Ulysses* and Orwell's *1984* and was badly shaken by the unmistakable impression that these suffocating, inescapable worlds could be the very one I lived in.

To complain of thrillers, or romances, that they are less than real is to invite several countercharges. It could be said that a book like *Legends* consummately achieves the Novel's basic purpose, implicit in its name, of bearing news. Littell, a former reporter, is generous in the amount of data he provides about not just guns, explosives, and the procedures of terrorism (how to plant a bomb in a dead dog), the Battle of Fredericksburg, the Civil War nursing career of Walt (known to his soldier friends as Walter) Whitman, chess, Lithuanian history, Russian as spoken with a Polish accent, and so on; he persuasively conjures up a desolate ruined island in the sadly depleted Aral Sea, top-secret conference rooms in Washington and Tel Aviv, and a medically vivid simulacrum of Osama bin Laden. Facts, fascinating facts, are the bones of his fable, and who doubts that the CIA really exists and that describing how nations and corporate entities relate to one another brings more important news than describing the relations of mere individuals? On the other hand, it could be argued that all fiction is escapist: by its means we escape our own heads and lives and enter into other heads and lives. Whether the head belongs to a Hobbit in Tolkien or to one of Virginia Woolf's sensitive, externally unadventurous women does not change the nature of the escape: what gives relief and pleasure in fiction is its otherness. It can hardly help being other, no two sets of experience being identical. An American, for example, finds in English fiction a different slant and social atmosphere, and a realistic Victorian novel like *Middlemarch* develops, as decades pass and electricity and automobiles overtake reality, a refreshing strangeness.

The slippery difference between a thriller and a non-thriller would hardly be worth groping for did not the thriller-writers themselves seem to be restive—chafing to escape, yearning for a less restrictive contract with the reader. They write longer than they used to, with more flourishes. Nothing in Agatha Christie's brilliantly compact, stylized, and efficient mysteries suggests that larger ambitions would have served her; the genre in its lean classic English form fit her like a cat burglar's thin black glove. But Littell and le Carré and the estimable P. D. James give signs of wanting to be "real" novelists, free to follow character where it takes them and to display their knowledge of the world without the obligation to provide what William Dean Howells disapprovingly called "a complicated plot, spiced with perils, surprises, and suspenses." The hero of *Legends* at times shows sympathetic depths but in the end turns into a killing machine as remorseless as the novel's savage opening vignette. The heroine never comes clearer than that ghost of a smile and the three shirt buttons she tends to leave undone. The villainess, Bondishly named Crystal Quest, chews ice, literally—cold-blooded, eh? The amorous dialogue, the little there is of it, feels painfully awkward, if not at bottom hostile, and the rest creaks like an ox cart under its burden of conveying data. A random sample:

> "In the early nineteen-eighties," Kastner explained, "Ugor-Zhilov was a small-time hoodlum in a small pond—he ran a used-car dealership in Yerevan, the capital of Armenia. He had a KGB record: He'd been arrested in the early seventies for bribery and black market activities and sent to a gulag

in the Kolyma Mountains for eight years" [and so on, for sixteen more lines of type].

"You seem to know an awful lot about Tzvetan Ugor-Zhilov," Martin observed.

"I was the conducting officer in charge of the investigation into the *Oligarkh*'s affairs."

Martin saw where the story was going. "I'll take a wild guess—he paid off the Sixth Directorate."

Legends patiently details the patient, detail-centered labor of espionage; in turn, the reading of it can feel like a labor. Various checkpoints of the intricate plot are repeated almost in toto, lest the reader carefreely lose track and, like a scholar in springtime, gaze out the window at the birds and trees of the non-espionage world. Espionage, this novel implies, borders on the tragic, hollowing out a man so that he no longer feels real to himself. The games the CIA would play with the world take on, in the plot's developments, a megalomaniacal hubris. Littell, and history with him, has come a long way since 1973, when *The Defection of A. J. Lewinter* marked his debut. That novel is airy and comic, speedy and understated; it shares many grim ingredients with *Legends*, including a CIA whose presumptuous meddling destroys lives, but has a warmth in its portraits of Russia and individual Russians that extends to the American heroine and her romantic involvement with the machinations of the state. The passage of time, too, as with *Middlemarch*, has added a nostalgic patina. More than thirty years later, the MIRVs and missile defense at the heart of the intrigues around Lewinter have faded from the foreground of our anxieties. The Cold War, surprisingly, did come to an end, and the U.S.-U.S.S.R. rivalry did not produce a nuclear holocaust. Now we fear not missiles sent forth by an organized state playing at brinkmanship but loosely sponsored suicide missions turning passenger jets into missiles. An opaque seethe of religious animus and insatiable grievance has replaced the hidden counsels of the Kremlin, whose inhabitants, in softening retrospect, became over time fellow-conspirators of a sort, enemies whose fears and aspirations mirrored our own.

A Cloud of Dust

THE MARCH, by E. L. Doctorow, 366 pp. Random House, 2005.

A number of readers, including this one, had a problem with E. L. Doctorow's best-known and best-selling novel, *Ragtime* (1975). Brilliantly written in a ricky-ticky ragtime prose, the book not only mingled the American celebrities of 1902 (Harry Houdini, J. P. Morgan) with the typical and the obscure (the narrator's upper-middle-class New Rochelle family, the tenement-dwelling Jewish artist Tateh and his daughter) but had the historical figures do things and achieve conjunctions that never transpired—the rich killer Harry Thaw stripping naked and banging his penis between the bars of his cell at the Tombs while Houdini watches, radical Emma Goldman relieving scandalous Evelyn Nesbit of her corset and giving her a loving oil massage. It smacked of playing with helpless dead puppets, and turned the historical novel into a gravity-free, faintly sadistic game.* Doctorow is a stranger writer than he at first seems; his fiction, though generous with the conventional pleasures of dramatic plot, colorful characters, and information-rich prose, yet challenges the reader with a puckish truculence. His novels and short stories generally seek the shelter of a bygone period in which to take root; when they are set in the present, like *City of God* (2000), an imp of modernist experimentation and fantasy takes over. Even his tenderest, most autobiographical, and least souped-up work, *The World's Fair* (1986), builds to a climactic scene in which naked women underwater, holding their breaths as prolongedly as mermaids, are molested by Oscar the Amorous Octopus. His recent collection, *Sweet Land Stories* (2004), held five stories that, like his novella *The Waterworks* (1994) and the prize-winning novel *Billy Bathgate* (1989), tingle with their injections of the murderous and the macabre.

His splendid new novel, *The March*, pretty well cures my Doctorow problem. A many-faceted recounting of General William Tecumseh Sherman's famous, and in some quarters still infamous, march of sixty-two thousand Union soldiers, in 1864–65, through Georgia and then the Carolinas, it combines the author's saturnine strengths with an elegiac compassion and prose of a glittering, swift-moving economy. The novel shares with *Ragtime* a texture of terse episodes and dialogue shorn, in avant-garde fashion, of quotation marks, but has little of the older book's distancing jazz, its impudent, mocking shuffle of facts; it celebrates its

---

*In an interview with Janet Maslin in the *New York Times* of September 27, 2005, Doctorow remembered his contrarian mood at the time of writing: " 'The feeling of *Ragtime* was a rebellious feeling,' he said. Three decades ago nonfiction was attracting a lot of attention, and it filled him with what he now calls impertinence. 'My feeling was "if they want facts, I'll give 'em facts like they've never had before," ' he said." He confided that many of the apparent facts in *The March*, including authentic-sounding letters and persuasive Sherman adjutants, were similarly invented.

epic war with the stirring music of a brass marching band heard from afar, then loud and up close, and finally receding over the horizon.* Reading historical fiction, we often itch, our curiosity piqued, to consult a book of straight history, to get to the facts without the fiction. But *The March* stimulates little such itch; it offers an illumination, fitful and flickering, of an historic upheaval which only fiction could provide. Doctorow here appears not so much a reconstructor of history as a visionary who seeks in time past occasions for poetry. At the novel's outset, black slaves in Georgia see a brown tint in the sky, "as if the world was turned upside down":

> And, as they watched, the brown cloud took on a reddish cast. It moved forward, thin as a hatchet blade in front and then widening like the furrow from the plow. . . . When the sound of this cloud reached them, it was like nothing they had ever heard in their lives. It was not fearsomely heaven-made, like thunder or lightning or howling wind, but something felt through their feet, a resonance, as if the earth was humming. Then, carried on a gust of wind, the sound became for moments a rhythmic tromp that relieved them as the human reason for the great cloud of dust.

Sherman's march is conjured up as a human entity as large as the weather, a "floating world" that destroys as it goes and carries along some living fragments. It is a revolution in motion—"On the march is the new way to live. . . . The world was remade, everything become something else"—bringing in its wake a crowd of freed slaves that reaches twenty-five thousand in number. It picks up a pair of Confederate soldiers, Will Kirkland and Arly Wilcox, who were waiting in prison to be tried, respectively, for desertion and for sleeping on picket duty, and who, released to fight in a battle, change into Union uniforms and are in turn captured by the Confederates and, in the fog of war, let loose again. Two respectable Southern women, Mattie Jameson and Emily Thompson, their homes invaded and abandoned, join the march and find employment and protection in the staff of an army surgeon, Colonel Wrede Sartorius, a German-born "neatly put-together man who seemed inviolate in the carnage around him," and whom Doctorow readers have previously met as the embodiment of cold-blooded science in *The Water-*

---

*Or, in Doctorow's own evocation, through the eyes and ears of Pearl, in *The March:* "What mighty music this was, the drums spattering . . . and the brass horns shooting out the rays of the sun like to their blare, and flutes and piccolos peeping from the top of the music like birds lighting on it, and the big tubas pumping away under it, and at the very back the two big bass drums announcing the appearance of the blocks of bluecoats in dress parade behind them."

works. Among the black followers of the march are Emily's housemaid Wilma Jones, who is saved from drowning by a handsome banjo-playing enlistee in the Negro construction-working "pioneers"; his name is Coalhouse Walker, and he will be the father of Coalhouse Walker Jr., the noblest figure in *Ragtime.*

Mattie Jameson's husband, John, has fathered a child by a female slave, and the child, called Pearl, looks white, and passes for a time as a Union drummer boy. She acquires literacy and nursing skills on the march, plus the love of an Irish-American New Yorker, Stephen Walsh, who of all this horde of characters seems closest to Doctorow's own point of view—an illusionless skeptic, yet capable of romantic courage and love. Walsh and Pearl head into the future, but part of their future's relative brightness rests on her apparent whiteness, a moral conundrum that afflicts her with a grave case of that twentieth-century ailment, liberal guilt. Her name borrowed from the elfin child in Hawthorne's masterpiece, her presence dusted with the magic realism of a Toni Morrison novel, Pearl is hard to picture, though we are assured that she becomes beautiful. She also becomes almost superhuman; in the aftermath of a battle she reunites Mattie, by now a widow, with her only surviving son, while briskly lecturing both of them on their past sins under the slave system.

Pearl is the most sympathetic character in *The March,* the one we root for, but her ability to do everything right opens the author to the charge of sentimentality, to which white writers on the evils of slavery are understandably prone. There is not an unkind or unwise black character in the book. One old plantation-owner is allowed a speech, harsh with self-righteous paternalism, of some eloquence, but John Jameson personifies the slave system's inhuman brutality: as the march approaches, he sells off a dozen field hands with the vow "No buck nigger of mine will wear a Federal uniform, I'll promise you that," and he turns out the docile and elderly Roscoe with the explanation that he'd "got the best out of Roscoe and what was left wasn't worth providing for." Doctorow offers, through the mind of Stephen Walsh, a dystopian vision of a South where the institution was perpetuated indefinitely:

> In this strange country down here, after generations of its hideous ways, slaves were no longer simply black, they were degrees of white. Yes, he thought, if the South were to prevail, theoretically there could be a time when whiteness alone would not guarantee the identity of a free man. Anyone might be indentured and shackled and sold on an auction block, the color black having been a temporary expedient, the idea of a slave class itself being the underlying premise.

The march also collects, to round out this partial roll call, a black child, David, who flees the plantation mansion to attach himself to an English journalist and reluctant foster father, Hugh Pryce; and a black photographer, Calvin Harper, who is partially blinded in saving General Sherman's life, a deed for which he receives no thanks and is nearly executed. Sherman himself, the directing brain behind the great plow-shaped cloud of dust, makes an unprepossessing first appearance, on a horse too small for him, "so that his feet practically touched the ground. He was not at all military-looking, with his tunic covered with dust and half unbuttoned, and a handkerchief tied at his neck, an old beaten-up cap, and a cigar stub in his mouth, and a red beard with streaks of gray." Doctorow's leftish anti-establishmentarianism does not, as *The March* moves from the realm of freed slaves and disenfranchised women up into the councils of the powerful, indict the leaders of the Union. Sherman is portrayed as an insomniac brandy-tippler with an odd fondness for a soldier's Spartan life, but his fire of purpose and his strategic intelligence are admirable. He sheds a deflected paternal love on little Pearl when she is masquerading as a drummer boy, gallantly receives his enemy General Joe Johnston as a fellow-member of the West Point aristocracy, and shows a theatrical literary streak that is endearing. He is openly emotional, telling Pearl, "Sometimes I want to cry, too." When, toward the end of the novel, Sherman and Grant and Lincoln have a shipboard conference on the James River, the effect is as gentle as an old salted-paper print, and the conversations are scarcely more than a murmur.

Seen through the eyes of Wrede Sartorius, who is present, Grant is "rather short, stocky, brown beard of a thick texture, a quiet man clearly not interested in making any kind of impression, unlike Sherman, who didn't seem to be able to stop talking," and Lincoln is "someone eaten away by life, with eyes pained and a physiognomy almost sepulchral." The doctor professionally observes that "Grant's color was good, and his eyes only slightly bloodshot," and Lincoln, who wears a shawl and "the weak, hopeful smile of the sick," may have "some sort of hereditary condition, a syndrome of overdeveloped extremities and rude features." It measures the book's largeness of sympathy that, unsparingly and repetitively as it details the carnage of the Civil War—"war at its purest, a mindless mass rage severed from any cause, ideal or moral principle"; a "monumentality of human disaster"—it spares respect and even affection for those whose decisions and relentless sense of purpose carry the ordeal onward. An especially poignant glimpse of leadership in action comes early in the book, and involves "boys from the Georgia Military Institute who had been given the honor of bearing the brunt of an attack":

Over on the other side the terrain was less swampy, and in the mossy glades Milledgeville cadets lay dead or wounded behind their logs and mounds of earth. Boys without a scratch on them wandered in a daze. Some were crying. Cadet officers went among them, pushing them back to their positions, slapping them to make them obey.

Doctorow, at ease in the nineteenth century, demonstrates an impressive familiarity with military logistics and tactics prior to fully mechanized warfare, including the grim fate of horses, who not only suffer battle wounds but are slain by the armies to make way for newer ones. Arly explains, "An army works its animals near to death so on a re'glar basis it rids itself of its consumed-up animals." The smell of their many bloated corpses on the banks of the Cape Fear River in Fayetteville is terrible. The floating world of the march, with its sixty thousand unbathing men and all their excrement, can be smelled at a distance. Emily, setting out to become a camp follower, "knew the direction the armies had taken. You just followed the roads that were beaten down, and before long you would hear a sound not natural to the countryside. And then you would smell them." Medical procedures of the time are rendered with special, well-researched fidelity, and they include not only the lightning-fast amputations of the field tent but a delicate, truly clinical detail unique in my reading of sex scenes: virgin Emily, about to give herself, after long infatuation, to Wrede Sartorius, "heard him open his instrument case. To spare you pain, he said, standing above her, I will do this small procedure. You will feel only a slight sting. And she felt his fingers dilating her, and then it was just as he said, and there was no blood to speak of."

The writing, solid and swift in the modern manner, is subtly tinged with older usages. Sherman reflects upon "our civil war, the devastating manufacture of the bones of our sons." Grant observes that the President "can only wait on our news, sitting in Washington without the hell-may-care that comes from a good battle." One battle carries into "the declivitous patch in sight of the plantation house." Birds sing "softer, twittier songs, like the birds knew full well what a fearful war was around them." Asked by Arly, "Are you for religion, young Will?," Will answers, as naturally as you please, "I never did countenance it." Victorian fancywork inflects the narrative voice: "The city of Fayetteville was of a dark blue aspect, as if the abstract color had found an organic vestiture for itself." The voice of the black South, which comes on heavy in Pearl's early appearances ("Nobody doan never have touch Porhl! When I little, de brudder try. Oh yeah. I raise up dis bony knee hard in his what he got dere, and dat were dat and nobody since!"), is lightly caught in such a piece of dialogue as Wilma's saying, "Judge Thompson's who I was bound to." Arly, who turns out to be demented as well as highly verbal, sports the rhetoric of the courtly South as he expostulates to innocent Will on the joys of copulation:

> "And when we go inside them, plum into their beings, and they cry out in our ear and we feel there is nothing softer, warmer, or more honeyed up in God's world than what embraces our stiff tool, and we are made by God to shiver into them the issue of our loins, well, boy, don't talk to me about what you don't know."

Poetry enters prose in such a simple surreal touch as Emily noticing, of her dead father's face, "With the eyes closed, the nose seemed to grow," and in such a simple description of physical desolation as "She had turned into the spacious yards of a manse that had seen some fire. The front was scorched, the roof shingles half torn away, and tree vines out front hanging black and limp like dead snakes." *The March* carries us through all its moments of wonder and pity, terror and comedy, toward the triumph of Southern surrender and the sudden tragedy of Lincoln's assassination. Sherman's march is large enough, American myth enough, to pull even a laggard recruit along. Doctorow's impertinent imagination holds fast to the reality of history even as he paints it in heightened colors.

ENGLISH FICTION

Property and Presumption

DEATH IN SUMMER, by William Trevor. 214 pp. Viking, 1998.

To say that William Trevor's novels do not make as strong an impression as his short stories is a mild complaint, since he has become, with the death of V. S. Pritchett, the best short-story writer in England if not in the English language. His breadth of empathy, his deeply humane ruefulness, and his patient love for the sound of demotic English in all its inflections of class and geography give his short stories the timbre of novels. At novel length, however, his gifts of concision and implication produce a certain feeling of disjointedness and overload; in *Death in Summer*, two hundred fourteen pages hold enough characters to populate a narrative twice that length. The prose at spots feels dry and crabbed, detail after detail set down with the obligatory tight fit of tile-setting. A detective who makes a momentary appearance "is a bulky dishevelled man, not in uniform, the frayed part of his tie half hidden in its knot. The tie is red and green, held in place with a tiepin. There's a trace of cigarette ash on the brown of his jacket." He is unnamed at first, but this is later corrected: "His name is Baker, christened Henry Nevil, but known as Dusty among his friends and colleagues." No figure in Trevor's fiction is too marginal to be particularized; the protagonists can easily get lost in a crowd so evenly animated.

And so, up to a point, does Thaddeus Davenant, our hero. He is something of a blank, even to himself—"a spare, handsome man in his midforties, with pale brown eyes beneath hair that almost matches them." He is defined mostly by negatives: the "inheritor of a property set in the flatlands of Essex," he has no profession, other than selling "the produce of his garden"; he is undemonstrative and reticent, even in his love affairs; he does not love his wife, Letitia, though she is an epitome of goodness and has brought him the money that enabled him to repair his inheritance, a Victorian house and property that are his main source of gratification, or were until the birth of his daughter, Georgina. His mother-in-law, the unsympathetic Mrs. Iveson, considers him "shoddy goods." To warm up this cold fish to normal human temperature it takes, under Trevor's dispensations, a plot of mystery-novel complexity and three deaths, in an otherwise cloudless summer.

The genteel numbness of Quincunx House—built in 1896 and named after the five cherry trees planted in the walled garden, four in the corners and one in the center—meets the aching memories of another house, the Morning Star, a London establishment, now a condemned empty building, where orphan children were raised and, apparently, prostituted to Sunday visitors called "uncles." One runaway from this squalid milieu, the girl Pettie, "just into her twenties but seeming younger," applies to Quincunx House for the position of Georgina's nanny. Though she doesn't get the job, she remains fascinated by the place and by Thaddeus, as she tells her friend and protector, Albert. He ran away with her and supports himself by cleaning up Underground graffiti and doing favors for elderly invalids—a man with elephantiasis, and the bed-ridden Mrs. Biddle. The height of Albert's ambition is to join the Salvation Army; his attempts to protect Pettie from her own thieving, romantic instincts are saintly but futile. Such limited, faintly sinister types as these are dear to Trevor's imagination. His attempt to illumine Pettie from within—her underfurnished delusions and twisted passions, her way of passing time in the Soft Rock Café and of making little butterflies out of cigarette-pack cellophane—is, if not entirely effortless, persuasive enough to give the novel its pathos and, as the dénouement gathers momentum, its Graham Greene–ish horror.

Trevor spins out the events with a little too much fancy scene-shifting and flashbacking. The author's sense of social justice leads him to animate, to no clear purpose, Maidment and Zenobia, the hired couple who take care of Quincunx and its few inhabitants. Many pages are devoted to a Mrs. Ferry, a garish hotel receptionist with whom Thaddeus, among many others, once had a fling; his reunion with her, now that she is ailing and alone and drinking heavily, forms one of the novel's two great set pieces. The other is Albert's long, tangled attempt—a blundering version of a detective story's terminal explanations—to set things right with the inhabitants of Quincunx. Both encounters, their dialogue so tenderly recorded in its comic agony of the awkwardly said and the downright unsayable, measure the distances of class in England. Thaddeus is, whatever his lacks, a man of property, and Mrs. Iveson, however elderly and distraught, a woman of wealth; they are oblivious of the exigencies that dominate lives lower in the social scale.

In a sense, *Death in Summer* traces Pettie's revenge for being unfeelingly dismissed; she insists, crazily, on being taken into account. And Albert, shambling out to Essex from his homely London depths (the good news is that he has attained his Salvation Army uniform; the bad news is that it gets drenched by country rain), arrives to demonstrate how little we all comprehend of one another's worlds. One world invades another:

> Darkened by rainfall, the drawing-room is invaded by other people and another place, by the faces of children, black and white and Indian; by dank downstairs passages, Cardinal polish on concrete floors, a mangle forgotten in a corner; by window-panes painted white, bare stairway treads, rust marks on mattresses.

"We're not concerned with these people," Mrs. Iveson protests. "We don't understand what all this is about," says Thaddeus, as close to rudeness as he can come. A foundling-home girl has presumed to fall in love with him and, more presumptuous still, left flowers on his unloved wife's grave. In these spaces of non-comprehension, Trevor's wide social reach attains a Dickensian majesty, illustrating the moral of *Bleak House*, that social barriers are permeable and a slum child can shake a mighty house. Fiction needs to keep reminding England of this truth. No man can cultivate his garden, pursue his hobby, nurture his fortune or his daughter in isolation. It is not in the nature of people to let one another alone. With elegant craftsmanship Trevor insists on a gritty democracy of feelings, feelings which fumblingly seek to form connections.

A Same-Sex Idyll

THE SPELL, by Alan Hollinghurst. 257 pp. Viking, 1999.

The novels of the English writer Alan Hollinghurst take some getting used to; they are relentlessly gay in their personnel, and after a while you begin to long for the chirp and swing and civilizing animation of a female character. Save for the briefly and reluctantly glimpsed sister or mother, there are none.* Not that the fair sex doesn't cast an ominous shadow. In

---

*Well, in *The Folding Star* there are several, minor in significance but given distinguishing characteristics and some notice from the narrator. Edward Manners, the narrator, has an English female buddy, Edie ("she wasn't a fag-hag . . . it was I who was a hag-fag"), and a Flemish colleague, Helene; he remembers his literary Auntie Tina and his parents' friend

the first, and fullest, of Hollinghurst's three novels, *The Swimming-Pool Library*, one main character gingerly asks the other if he likes girls, and upon being falsely answered in the positive volunteers, "There are chaps who don't care for them, you know. . . . Can't stand the sight of them, their titties and their big sit-upons, even the smell of them." Much later in the book, the two repose in the assurance that "men don't really want women around much." In the third, new novel, *The Spell*, Danny, the youngest of the four main characters, thinks, "Really, hetero life was so archaic and mad," and emits "a quiet chuckle of relief at his own good fortune." Hollinghurst does not merely write, like Ronald Firbank or Manuel Puig, from within a gay sensibility; he constructs an all-gay world, a Genet prison without the guards. With the avidity of an anthropologist gone native, he inventories the rites and stations of banded gayness—the drug-saturated dance clubs and Dionysian raves, the porno houses and their muffled swift couplings, the public lavatories and secluded park thickets, the lingo, the jokes ("Do you know it, darling, it's a gay restaurant. It's called the Limp Ritz. It was the first restaurant in England to serve openly gay food").

A meticulous exterior eye surveys the particulars of gay life; our noses are rubbed, as it were, in the poetry of a love object's anus, "the hairs in his crack, which I oiled back with my tongue, and sniffed through the dry smell of the talc to his own rectal smell—a soft stench like stale flower-water. His asshole was a clean pale purple, and shone with my saliva." This evocation, as vivid as a fine verbal flair can make it, is from *The Swimming-Pool Library*; in *The Spell* we have the more twilit "grey-gold dusk of hair between his legs." Penile sizes, tilts, tints, and flavors are registered with a botanical precision; this reader was struck by how freely the particulars of a lover's parts are shared in the friendly equivalent of girl-

---

the sexy Mirabelle Turlough. There are Luc Altidore's mother, with her sad deserted air and proliferating needlework, and Luc's handsome sometime girlfriend Sybille de Taeye. Paul Echevin's late wife lives vividly in her son's recounting of her sudden death, and Paul's housekeeper, Lilli Vivier, casts a portentous shadow. In a bygone generation, the red-haired Scots actress Jane Byron cast a spell upon the Belgian Symbolist painter Edgard Orst which lasted to the end of his life, a spell transferred—after Jane vanished in the sea off Ostend—onto the local body of a physically similar prostitute called Marthe, of whom obscene photographs survive. Though Orst's passion is meant to serve as a parallel for Manners's erotic obsession for Luc, heterosexual love is seen through veils of distaste and puzzlement, as something perversely and tediously beside the point. Of a married school friend the narrator observes, "There was always something lacking in those men who had never had a queer phase as boys, it showed in a certain dryness of imagination, a bland tolerance uncoloured by any suppression of their own, a blindness to the spectrum's violet end." Nevertheless, *The Folding Star* is the Hollinghurst novel that, to date, most feelingly encompasses glimpses of the non-gay world.

talk—"What's his dick like?" is the standard question—and by how much can be seen through the restraining fabric of a trouser fly and by how readily erections spring up in passing contacts, without benefit of foreplay. Quarantined from female rhythms and scruples, the male sex drive functions at fever pitch.

And yet the mood within this bubble of hyperstimulation is rather lugubrious and disheartened. Boredom swoops in without hetero clutter to obstruct its advent. The romantic bliss of a new liaison—"A beautiful man was waiting for him and Robin glowed in the urgency and the lovely complacency of their wanting each other"—dissolves efficiently into disenchantment, especially among the needy and much-desired young. Danny (who, strange to say, is Robin's son) reflects on "how uncertain sex-magic was. It struck, and there was a tingle in the air around a man, and when you touched him it flowed round you too. Some people kept it for you for years. . . . And with others it faded, like a torch left on, or with the quick disillusion that followed a hit of coke."

The Spell is mostly about spells wearing off. The spellbound move, in the mid-Nineties, through London and the lovingly described countryside of Dorset. Partners change, and new loves shoot up in blasted hearts, but the usual "shake of the sex-dice" comes up snake eyes. *The Spell* suggests a *Midsummer Night's Dream* that ends when Titania awakes and announces, "Methought I was enamor'd of an ass." Robin, the leading man in the extensive all-male cast, comes to a realization about his shifting relationship with plump, playful, adorable, jobless Justin: "For the first time, it struck him as absurd to expect loyalty from someone he had met in a toilet." Nevertheless, the novel concludes, if not with Mendelssohn's Wedding March, with a brace of momentarily settled pairings, four men viewing together the sea's "curling . . . currents." Sentimentality and romanticism, those traditional vestments of the erotic impulse, are by no means shed in a same-sex idyll. Lust still seems a quest for beauty: "Lars's features had taken on a marvellous intensity, they seemed to have been cleansed to their essential beauty in a solution of desire." The quest, with no gender gap to clear, arrives non-stop at the mirror:

> As he peed he looked sideways into the mirror, and saw how terribly beautiful he was: the image itself was reflected again off some hard vain surface deep in his eye, and he thought, with easy pity, how little Alex would want to lose him.

Breakups come swiftly, too: "Well, I've changed, darling, people change. I'm sorry." The relationships that do survive enjoy the same intricacy of balanced imbalances—youth/age, wealth/poverty, taker/giver, top/bottom—as heterosexual matches. Robin, reconciled to Justin, is observed to be "lightly pussy-whipped, or botty-whipped was perhaps the word."

The observer is Robin's son, Danny. Paternity is an unsettling anomaly in this population. The novel begins in America, in the early Seventies, when Robin, who is in the Southwest investigating Frank Lloyd Wright's architecture, hears by transatlantic phone that his live-in girlfriend, Jane, is pregnant by him. This fruitful lapse is never explained, except as a by-product of Robin's "unrefusable sexual power." By the time the offspring is twenty-two, his mother, whom Robin has wed, betrayed with men, and divorced, lives fabulously far away, in San Diego, California. The complications of being a homosexual father are but lightly described, in a few rueful phrases. Danny's sense is that "his father's acceptance of him . . . was easier if he was uncommitted." Parents resist, whatever their gender preference, an attachment on a child's part that would supplant them. Danny has emerged from his fragmented, partly American upbringing as triumphantly, promiscuously gay; his "utopian policy was to have everyone once" and he "would be a great lover, that would be his career, though he knew next to nothing about love, just as some great musicians knew nothing about music, beyond their gift for making it." Those who know about love, like Alex, Danny's staid, older lover, must make their own arrangements with the inevitable let-down.

Alan Hollinghurst writes beautifully. His eye for nature is keen and tender; his sense of weather, both inner and outer, strong. He has an architect's feeling for décor and for the pathos of the sturdy buildings that our moods flit through. His rooms talk; of a Dorset husband and wife he writes that they "had renounced cigarettes, and the peculiar ashtrays mounted on stirruped thongs had gone from the arms of the sofa; but still the magnolia paintwork was dimly varnished with smoke and gave the room an atmosphere of terminated pleasures." Dawn and dusk come with an angelic delicacy to the long summer days:

Already the darkness was turning grainy and dimly translucent where a glass of water stood; the wardrobe mirror answered with the greyest gleam to the first hint of dawn at the window.

It was high summer, so the shift began in the refined late daylight and came to a close with the light strengthening again beyond the tinted plate-glass of the lobby. Around five their reflections began to dissolve and the narrow old street outside to redefine itself, remotely as though some trance-like stimulant were wearing off.

The psychologies of his numerous heroes are shrewdly traced, most revealingly in those intervals when each is alone.

And yet reading this relatively short novel is work. It lacks the campy excessiveness of *The Swimming-Pool Library*, with its la-di-da swell of a voracious narrator and its pitch-perfect invention of a Waugh-era aristocrat's journal, and also the engaging wry tone of *The Folding Star*, with its guidebook rendering of an ancient, ghostly, sweetly sinister Flemish city. Little momentum builds around *The Spell*'s intertwining affairs; nothing is at stake but self-gratification. Novels about heterosexual partnering, however frivolous and reducible to increments of selfishness, social accident, foolish overestimations, and inflamed physical detail, do involve the perpetuation of the species and the ancient, sacralized structures of the family. Hollinghurst's arresting voice, shimmering between rapture and lament, tells of a realm from which most human beings are excluded and whose inhabitants share a profound listlessness, as if the gravity there were stronger. There is something of Proust's grand sense of a Sodom in which aristocratic souls are condemned to absurd physical debasements. Except for the shadow of Robin's architectural vocation, none of the men in *The Spell* display any professional passion, nor, apart from Alex's fondness for music, is art a matter of much interest. A climactic party scene takes place while the village church bells are having the changes thunderously rung, and no one but the author and one negligible, unloved character listens. A classic Greek ideal of masculine fellowships disintegrates, before our eyes, into "sexual jostling and sarcasm," "thrilling squalor," and "miscellaneous fucks"; the spectacle is as melancholy as the book's lachrymose pink jacket. Perhaps the male homosexual, uncushioned as he is by society's circumambient encouragements to breed, feels the lonely human condition with a special bleakness: he must take it straight.

Fairy Tales and Paradigms

On Histories and Stories: *Selected Essays*, by A. S. Byatt. 196 pp. Harvard University Press, 2001.

The Biographer's Tale, by A. S. Byatt. 307 pp. Knopf, 2001.

In March of 1999, the English writer and critic A. S. Byatt, once best known as the sister of Margaret Drabble but now a formidable literary presence in her own right, gave the Richard Ellmann memorial lectures at Emory University, a series of three, and a week later hustled north to present the Finzi-Contini lecture at Yale. These four discourses, plus a paper delivered at Oxford in a series on the writing of history, and a contribution to an anthology in which women were invited to write about their favorite fairy tales, and an essay on the *Thousand and One Nights* for a *New York Times Magazine* millennial issue, constitute *On Histories and Stories: Selected Essays*. The seven pieces in sum offer the most spirited and knowledgeable discussion of fiction's basic questions that I have read for some time. These questions—the kind that surrounded the creation of the French *nouveau roman* and were reawakened a decade or so later by the magic realists of Latin America—are rarely raised in the United States, where discussions of how literature represents reality have been smothered beneath the arid fuss of politicized deconstruction. Our national notion of a hot literary topic is "Did Shakespeare favor the oppression of women?" or, more urgent yet, "Will the electronic revolution kill print?" But, meanwhile, works of imagination continue to be written, and no creative writer, at this late date, with all possible changes apparently rung on the century-old peal of modernism, can avoid asking to what purpose.

Byatt is a vigorous exponent of the view that there is nothing wrong with making books out of books—with admitting that the impulse to write stems from stimulating reading, and that literary adventure takes place in a mental world generated from existent texts. Her own recent works of fiction are furiously bookish, and her Ellmann lectures propose a look at "the sudden flowering of the historical novel in Britain," a flowering which defies a widespread critical view that (as she paraphrases her own sister's remarks, in a 1997 address to the American Academy of Arts and Letters) "it is the novelist's duty to write about the present, to confront an age which is 'ugly, incomprehensible, and subject to rapid mutations.'" This alleged duty to confront contemporary life has been urged lately upon Americans by the polemical journalist Tom Wolfe, and a hundred years ago was urged upon Sarah Orne Jewett by Henry James, who, in tactful chastisement of a work of hers titled *The Tory Lover*, wrote of "the 'historic' novel":

> . . . you have to think with your modern apparatus a man, a woman—or rather fifty—whose own thinking was intensely otherwise conditioned, you have to simplify back by an amazing tour de force—and even then it's all humbug.

Nevertheless, "historic" humbug continues to occupy not only the reprehensible "nostalgia/heritage/fancy dress/costume drama" (as Miss

Drabble put it) hacks but such distinguished and subtle contemporary
British writers as Julian Barnes, Peter Ackroyd, John Fowles, Pat Barker,
Graham Swift, Kazuo Ishiguro, and, of course, A. S. Byatt, whose monumental romance of literary detective work, *Possession* (1990), won the
Booker Prize. The beat goes on: the Australian Peter Carey and the
Americans Thomas Mallon and Toni Morrison favor historical venues
for their fiction; the Canadian *grandes dames* Alice Munro and Margaret
Atwood movingly explore female predicaments in past decades and centuries; and a charming, modest fictional reconstruction of Vermeer's
world, *Girl with a Pearl Earring*, by the young writer Tracy Chevalier
made a surprising foray onto last year's best-seller lists. The recently
deceased Penelope Fitzgerald is much cited by Byatt, as the author of a
rare kind of historical fiction (short, diffident, but rich in resonance), and
before her there was Anthony Burgess, who let his tremendous intellectual curiosity take him to the times of Shakespeare and Napoleon and
early Christianity, and William Golding, who ventured, one firm foot-
step after another, into Neanderthal prehistory and medieval cathedral-
building.

What led such an impressive crew to abandon what James called "the
palpable present *intimate* that throbs responsive" and submit to a precarious dependence upon, as he said, "the little facts that can be got from pictures and documents, relics and prints"? Byatt suggests a number of
answers: the wish to dramatize analogies with the present; the "political
desire to write the histories of the marginalized"; and, in this age of a dissolved sense of self, a liking for "historical persons because they are
unknowable, only partly available to the imagination, and we find this
occluded quality attractive." The question is, after all, less than absolute:
even a novel of contemporary life generally demands some reach of
research and fakery, since personal experience goes only so far; and, as an
author ages, personal reminiscences become ever more historical—
among the novels Byatt discusses are two, by Muriel Spark and Penelope
Fitzgerald, drawing, in 1963 and 1980 respectively, upon the authors'
memories of World War II.

A group of historical novelists, interviewed some ten years ago, came
up with a surprisingly uniform answer to this question of why they do it:
"They wanted to write in a more elaborate, more complex way, in longer
sentences, and with more figurative language." It is true that one of the
pleasures of contemporary imitations of the past lies in the language,
both in description and dialogue; though Hemingway, Henry Green,
Raymond Carver, and others made music of laconic, elliptical modern
idiom, people prior to 1920, rich and poor, do seem to have expressed

themselves better, with more cogency, pith, grace, mannerliness, and art-ful irony. As, in an increasingly visual and non-oral culture, linguistic ele-gance fades, its revival and preservation seem worth the effort, even at the cost of a certain campy, parodic note. Also, since World War II more and more writers have come up through graduate schools; they are not afraid of research, and trust it to contain life enough. And there is, I would suggest, an instinctive attraction to the time before "the religious sense was lost to the English novel"—a formulation by Graham Greene that Byatt quotes. "With the religious sense," Greene claimed, "went the sense of the importance of the human act." The novel as the West knows it was born of Christendom, and the possibilities of good and evil, hero-ism and villainy are crucial to it. George Eliot's *Middlemarch* is a far more intricate, organic, passionately mimetic construct than *The Pilgrim's Progress*, but both basically concern the protagonist's effort to save her or his soul. Without souls to save, are mundane lives worth writing about? The historical novel steals strength and drama from the era of disturbed but pervasive faith in which the genre's model classics were born.

Byatt, who is from an intellectual Yorkshire family, graduated from Cambridge University with first-class honors in 1957 and taught English and American literature full-time from 1972 to 1984, so she was not shel-tered from the winds of structuralist and deconstructionist theory that have dishevelled English departments since I was a student in one in the early Fifties. With calm assurance she slings terms like "closure" and "paradigm" and, better yet, "paradigmatic narratives." Her scope of ref-erence and the number of her plot summaries show a gluttonous appetite for reading. A multilingual Euro-era Brit, she is at home not only with the French theorists but with Italian philosophers of the tale such as Roberto Calasso and Italo Calvino; she responds to "a general European interest in storytelling, and in thinking about storytelling." She cites admiringly the Austrian Christoph Ransmayr, the Danish Karen Blixen, the Basque Bernardo Atxaga, the Dutch Cees Nooteboom, the German-writing, England-dwelling W. G. Sebald. Self-conscious, eclectic literari-ness is the hallmark of postmodernism, and she pays tribute to Calvino and Borges and to the icy, glassy fairy tales that entranced her girlhood. The texture of her own writing has the seraglio opulence—the feeling of a flat design luxuriantly filled—to be found at the opposite end of Europe, in the work of the Turkish Orhan Pamuk. Byatt is a writer actively searching for sources of energy outside the comfort zone of Brit-ish social fiction. "European storytelling," she writes, "derives great energy from artifice, constraints, and patterning." Of two works of her own, she allows:

I like the formal *energy* of the relations between Swedenborg's Divine Human and Hallam's insatiable love of God in *The Conjugial Angel*, and the personifications in *Morpho Eugenia*—Venus, Ant Queen, Dame Kind, Matilda.

The categorizations of pre-modern, pre-quantum science and religion excite her, and a reader of her fiction must be prepared to share this somewhat pedantic excitement.

Byatt's Oxford lecture, "True Stories and the Facts in Fiction," was delivered shortly after she completed her two dense and delicious novellas, *The Conjugial Angel* and *Morpho Eugenia* (published together, as *Angels and Insects*, in 1992), and tells us a good deal about her method of courting inspiration. Both novellas had their roots in courses she was teaching in the English department of University College London—the former in a lecture she "used to give on the presence of Arthur Henry Hallam in Tennyson's *In Memoriam*," and the latter in readings of Darwin "in connection with George Eliot's novels and essays." The notions involved, she admits, "could have turned into academic papers." Passages of both narratives have the exact texture of such papers, whether on insect societies or on *In Memoriam A.H.H.** Both stories began, she relates, with a footnote that piqued her curiosity and set her to dreaming, and reading. In the case of *The Conjugial Angel*, the footnote concerned the "occluded" historical figure of Emily Tennyson Jesse, the poet's sister and the fiancée of Arthur Hallam before his unexpected death, in Vienna, at the age of twenty-two. Byatt "immersed" herself, "over a period of years," in a

> disparate set of texts. Biographical texts about Hallams, Tennysons, and Swedenborg. Swedenborg's writings. Angels in dictionaries of angels, and the Book of Revelation. Victorian theories of the afterlife. *In Memoriam*, again and again. It is a process like trawling, or knitting, and recurring themes and patterns began to make themselves.

While exploring the key incident—in which Emily, after many years of marriage to a Captain Jesse, refused the proposal, offered in a séance, to

---

*Which she persistently, cavalierly quotes without the indented second and third lines intrinsic to Tennyson's stanzas. Also, in *Possession*, the poems she invents for R. H. Ash are more modernistically free and light in their punctuation than those of any English Victorian, including Gerard Manley Hopkins, would be. For the novel's other poet, Christabel LaMotte, she imports the impressionistic dashes of Emily Dickinson. Such liberties do not substantially detract from Byatt's achievement, that of making herself into a poet in order to write a novel.

be reunited with Hallam after death—Byatt read Alex[andra] Owen's *The Darkened Room*, "a gripping feminist account of nineteenth-century mediumship as one of the few professions open to women." To such readings Byatt brings not just her trawling or knitting compulsions but a brilliant creative humor: the séances that compose much of her novella's action are alarmingly, uproariously well imagined, with the psyches of the four attendees and two mediums all spinning away as automatic writing pours forth from the afterlife and uncannily realized angels and revenants come and go. (There is a séance in *Possession* as well, and Byatt has described how that novel's many fabricated nineteenth-century poems, undertaken with trepidation by a non-poet, "wrote themselves, hardly blotted"—"it was actually quite frightening.") If, in *The Conjugial Angel*, the frequent quotations from Victorian verse at times give us the classroom yawns, and Arthur Hallam's youthful effusions verge on the insufferable, it is all in the good if ghoulish cause of bringing dead voices back to life. Life is at stake, clayey death presses upon it; nothing less than our physical and spiritual natures are the topic, as they are of Tennyson's great graveside poem.

Byatt evidently walks toward her fictions in a daze of what Thomas Mann called "*directed* reading." Well after her composition has begun, she is open to fresh textual stimuli; while concluding *The Conjugial Angel*, she "found a wonderful piece of theology in Swedenborg for [the] final fictional séance." The very title of the companion novella, *Morpho Eugenia*, was encountered long after the author had named her heroine Eugenia. In a foreword to the Franklin Library signed edition of *Angels and Insects*, she writes:

> One thing that never ceases to surprise me is the way stories and ideas seem to attract discoveries like magnets—my heroine was called "Eugenia" (well-bred) from early on, but it was very late that I found in [W. H.] Bates a description of a real Amazonian butterfly, Morpho Eugenia, the shapely, the beautiful Eugenia—Morpho is one of the names of Aphrodite.

Making herself into a magnet, the author again plunged into reading matter: "Ants, bees, Amazon travels, Darwin, books about Victorian servant life, butterflies and moths—resisting, rather than searching out useful metaphors, but nevertheless finding certain recurring patterns." *Morpho Eugenia* soars a little less high out of its papery cocoon of erudition than the other, earlier novella; imagined passages of post-Darwin theology, of empirical ant-observation, of a philosophical fairy tale based on entomology go on at leisurely length while the country-house melodrama—sketched with a blithe flair and an ivory miniaturist's translucent touch—hangs suspended. The hero and the heroine (not Eugenia) write their way out of their poverty and subservient positions in the household, and this happy development puts the reader wistfully in mind of the immense appetite for the written word evinced by the Victorians and, still, by A. S. Byatt.

Her creative method—saturating herself in texts, counting on a flood of information to bring her what she needs—seems a hypertrophied form of normal authorial procedure. Her masses of borrowings and imitations are saved from inertia by an Iris Murdoch–esque belief in the momentousness of sexual attraction (usually described from the male point of view), and by a fine eye and ear for natural detail as well as for footnotes. What one takes away from *Morpho Eugenia* along with all the ant-lore and Darwin-darkened philosophizing are details such as the homely tendency of the beautiful but maturing Eugenia, when asleep, to make "a new, regular, comfortable sort of sound—Eugenia's recent snoring, a ruffling, like a wood-pigeon, a squeak like fingernails on silk, and then a snort like a hungry foal." That nasal squeak like fingernails on silk shows an avid realism. The whole elaborate, marvellous literary pastiche of *Possession* rests upon the drab "palpable present intimate" of late-1980s English academia—the London Library, the British Museum Reading Room, the cluttered warrens where scholarly passions are dourly pursued, the decaying tiled crispness of a new provincial university, the dismal Putney basement where the hero, Roland Michell, ekes out a marginal postgraduate career with his pallid, depressed girlfriend, Val, the two of them denied access to the house's back garden by an octogenarian landlady whose pet cats' piss odorously drips through the ceiling.

Relatively few such compellingly pungent particulars anchor the academic London of Byatt's new novel, *The Biographer's Tale*; its world is as fancy-tinged, hovering, and bubbly as that of the paired novellas. Its narrator, Phineas Gilbert Nanson, shares with Roland of *Possession* an epic monicker and small stature: "I should perhaps say, now, that I am a very small man. 'Small but perfectly formed' my father would say, several times a day, before his disappearance." Byatt's fascination with insect societies, where the fertilizing male is often smaller than the queen, may influence the unusual sizing of her heroes. Phineas's last name echoes that of Fridtjof Nansen (1861–1930), a great Norwegian Arctic explorer, scientist, statesman, and humanitarian. Nanson, like other Byatt heroes, re-enacts her own escape from academia into creativity; his adventures begin when he strikes out from the harbor of "postmodernist literary theory," with its monotonous revelation of "the same clefts and crevices, transgressions and disintegrations, lures and deceptions beneath, no matter what surface we were scrying." Amid the doctrinaire uncertainties and aporias of post-structuralist criticism he hankers for "*things*," and undertakes to research and write the biography of Scholes Destry-Scholes, the obscure author of a masterly three-volume biography of Sir Elmer Bole, a nineteenth-century traveller, consul, translator, and author, tirelessly prolific and polyglot in the superhuman Victorian manner of Sir Richard Burton.

Like Burton, Bole lived on the sexual frontier, marrying "a Turkish lady, Yildiz, the sister of a pasha," and his "childhood sweetheart, Evangeline Solway, daughter of an impoverished evangelical clergyman," in the same year, fathering three sons with the former and three daughters with the latter. His captain's paradise, an alternation between the "red apple" of the Turkish wife and the "green apple" of the English, finds a counterpart as Nanson's researches bring him into the arms of pale, slender, dark-haired Vera Alphage, the elusive Destry-Scholes's niece, and then those of Fulla Biefeld, a stocky Swedish pollination ecologist, with "gold and frizzy and springy" hair "so abundant and energetic that it was almost a separate life-form." To support himself during the search for Destry-Scholes, Nanson takes a "dogsbody" job with Puck's Girdle, a travel agency specializing in exotic, customized holiday trips and managed by two harmonious homosexuals, Erik and Christophe, Danish and French respectively; it suggests one of those airy enterprises in Anne Tyler novels, more redolent of authorial ingenuity than of practical viability. Puck's Girdle has an intricate paper Maelstrom in the window, and Destry-Scholes apparently disappeared into the actual Maelstrom off the coast of Norway. Scandinavia peeps in at numerous of this tale's loosely articulated junctures.

There is virtually no end to the amount of overlapping symbolification Byatt can generate. *The Biographer's Tale* takes its epigraph from Goethe: "These similitudes are charming and entertaining, and who does not enjoy playing with analogies?" Playful analogies and correspondences on the level of Phineas Nanson's quotidian adventures, with their sudden amorous rewards, pale beside those on the secondary level of quoted text, which occupies intimidatingly large chunks of the novel. One stretch of sixty-six pages, in a (very slightly) different typeface, reproduces Destry-Scholes's notes on aspects of the lives of "CL" (Carolus Linnaeus, the eighteenth-century botanist and taxonomist), "FG" (Sir Francis Galton, a cousin of Charles Darwin, a traveller in the Balkans and Africa, a scientist with an interest in anthropometry and eugenics, composite photographs and fingerprints), and "HI" (Henrik Ibsen, the Norwegian play-wright). The idea, as best I can grasp it, seems to be that Destry-Scholes was working toward a kind of composite photograph of the three men, a ghostly overlay of their travels, theories, and lies, which also might blur-rily be construed as the portrait of both biographers: "Was the composite portrait the face of Destry-Scholes? Was it, seen in some mad mirror, my own?"

Regardless, the patience of all but a reader superhumanly tolerant of extended digression will creak and snap under the load of near-random texts, assembled by an author whose love of collection, of assembling and ordering, in this case quite overpowers any urge to tell a smooth story. Her point might be that stories are not smooth, that the surface of things, like the textual surface that postmodern critics deconstruct, dissolves into "transgressions and disintegrations, lures and deceptions." Nanson tells Fulla, the personification of full nature, "I had come to the conclusion that literary scholarship was pointless, and so had embarked on biogra-phy . . . and now thought that was pointless, too." He discovers that "*all* writing has a tendency to flow like a river towards the writer's body and the writer's own experience." His account comes most alive when he describes, in generous olfactory detail, making love to Vera and Fulla, and Byatt's novel quickens with it. The rest is a kind of scrapbook, in which we keep encountering collections: shoeboxes of cryptic index cards; "tiny chocolate eggs, each wrapped in a different colour of silver paper"; Michel Foucault's book *Les Mots et les choses*, which comments on Linnaeus and taxonomy; the wildly assorted objects preserved in the London Linnaeus Society; the Vatican's "25,000 numbered trays or bins of coloured mosaic" which grows in a later accounting to "40,000 bins of mosaics [of which] 10,762 were classified." Reality's maddening approach to infinity—its defiance of final inventory—comes to Byatt by way of Borges, the father of postmodern fiction's ramifying, inescapable self-consciousness.

Among Destry-Scholes's baffling gifts to posterity is a bag of three hundred thirty-six glass marbles, "some obviously very old and beautiful, of many sizes, colours and patterns," along with a notebook recording, in a child's handwriting, mystical-sounding names and categories. Vera Alphage (an X-ray technician—alpha and omega, the truth of bones) obsessively attempts to match the marbles to the names, and to arrange them in a logical order, but this taxonomic exercise is in the end aban-doned: "We massed the marbles randomly in a great glass bowl I bought her for a present." Thus disarrayed, the marbles let her relax. Having fled systematic Derridean indeterminacy, Phineas Nanson arrives at appreciation of that near-chaotic thing of things the planet Earth. Reality eludes the nets that criticism and analysis lay "over the nature of things with different meshes and weaves." This seems to be Byatt's moral, crudely put. (One of the virtues of her thoughtful, many-layered fiction is to remind us of how crudely, how unprovisionally, most matters are put.) Although, in *The Biographer's Tale*, she takes the reader to the edge of exasperation and beyond, that reader must still be grateful to have the art of fiction reworked in such knowing hands, by one to whom the pleasures and rewards of reading are unquestionable.

Stonewalling Toffs

AIDING AND ABETTING, by Muriel Spark. 166 pp. Doubleday, 2001.

Dr. Hildegard Wolf, a contemporary, unlicensed Paris psychiatrist, who was formerly a fraudulent stigmatic and miracle healer in Bavaria called Beate Pappenheim, and whose unusual psychiatric method commences with her talking about herself while the patient patiently listens, counts among her loyal clientele not one but two gentlemen who both claim to be Lord Lucan, the fugitive English earl who disappeared from London on the night of November 7, 1974, having evidently battered to death a nanny whom he mistook for his wife. Upon this implausible—indeed, preposterous—premise, Muriel Spark builds a strangely gripping and gnomically illuminating short novel, *Aiding and Abetting*. Lord Lucan, a "Note to Readers" emphasizes, is or was an actual personage, who "has been 'sighted' in numerous parts of the world, predominantly central Africa." He was officially declared dead in 1999, though his body has never been found. In a sentence of typical aplomb, Spark assures the reader,

> What we know about "Lucky" Lucan, his words, his habits, his attitudes to people and to life, from his friends, photographs and police records, I have absorbed creatively, and metamorphosed into what I have written.

She additionally confides, "The parallel 'story' of a fake stigmatic woman is also based on fact."

Dame Muriel, it would seem, has been mulling the old scandal of Lord Lucan for some time. The need to consider a real event, with its much-reported facts and lingering mysteries, gives this novel a less peremptory texture than she has accustomed us to; the figure of Lord Lucan deepens and complicates, as does the nature of the evil credited to him. Spark focuses upon those who, in the immediate wake of the murder and for, possibly, decades thereafter, helped the murderer escape and supplied him with funds. After putting his inadvertent victim's bloody body in a mailsack, Lucan assaulted his intended victim, his wife, with the same "length of lead piping, specially prepared to deaden the thuds"; she escaped, with severe head wounds, to the shelter of a nearby pub. Why wasn't a criminal so blatant and clumsy in his crimes quickly apprehended? A slight acquaintance of Lucan's, Dr. Joseph Murray, expresses this view twenty-five years later:

> The police were slow. The friends who aided and abetted Lucan ran rings around the police. Those police were used to lowlife criminals from the streets and from the rooming houses of Mayfair and Soho. Clever sharpsters, they were unnerved by the stonewalling toffs; they were not exactly abject, not at all. But they were hesitant, out of their depth.

The aiders and abettors acted, Murray thinks, out of a class loyalty that has become obsolete: "We are not the same people as we were a quarter of a century ago. . . . We cannot afford to be snobs. Since Lucan's day, snobs have been greatly emarginated." Old-fashioned snobbery empowered Lucan in his ill-planned crime: "It was not only that he was a member of the aristocracy, a prominent upper-class fellow, it was that he had pitched his life and all his living arrangements to that proposition. His proposition was: I am a seventh Earl, I am an aristocrat, therefore I can do what I like, I am untouchable." Later in the novel, the author adds to this analysis the fatalist psychology of a compulsive, self-ruinous gambler:

> Lucky Lucan believed in destiny. By virtue of destiny he was an earl. His wife had been destined to die, according to his mad calculation. It was the madness of a gambler. . . . His sense of destiny obliterated the constant, well-known fact that the gambler loses and the bookie, the croupier or whoever, always wins in the end.

The novel's other characters, which proliferate as the plot develops ever newer kinks, are all in the grip of, if not murderous madness, obsessions and tics that snap them back and forth between Paris and London and Scotland and Mexico and darkest central Africa, where a fate as comically lurid as anything in Waugh (Evelyn) or Burroughs (William and Edgar Rice) puts the disturbances to rest, leaving the environment, in the book's chilly last words, "cleaner than usual." Ever since her first published, prize-winning short story, "The Seraph and the Zambesi," the dark magic of Africa has held for Spark an affinity with the dark magic of

Catholicism, to which she is an unabashed, if antinomian, convert. "Beliefs are essential," one character admits, having asserted that "witch men can cure." So can fake stigmatics, who smear their hands and feet with their own menstrual blood. "What else," it is asked, "should a woman of imagination do with her menstrual blood?" Blood is Spark's dominant metaphor in *Aiding and Abetting:* one pagan African explains, "Christians worship the Lamb, unlike the Hindus who worship the Cow. They wash in the blood of a lamb," and the other responds, "I don't know about that. I should think it was a sticky way to be washed."

Sex, too, can be sticky, and reeks of bewitchment. In this novel Dr. Murray and a young lady named Lacey repeatedly just miss the object of their concerted search, as if by design: "Even a simple manhunt had been so peripheral to their love affair that they had let him slip time and again, and enjoyed it." If the novel has a hero, it is Hildegard's burly lover Jean-Pierre Roget, a resourceful "metal- and wood-worker" equal to all repairs. He is impervious to the machinations of the two Lord Lucans and unperturbed by Hildegard's rebuffs—she is one of Spark's bedevilled heroines, too harried to be considerate. Many puzzle pieces breezily fly together to make the quick-moving plot, but they interlock snugly. In her ninth decade, Spark has produced one of the best of her sui-generis novels, to rank with *The Comforters, The Bachelors, Memento Mori, The Prime of Miss Jean Brodie, The Driver's Seat, The Abbess of Crewe,* and *Loitering with Intent.*

Her language deserves an admiring word. Never ornate, it grows simpler. Has any fiction writer since Hemingway placed more faith in the simple declarative sentence, the plain Anglo-Saxon noun? Hemingway's style sometimes gives the impression of striking a pose, whereas Spark's appears to be merely getting on with it, brushing aside everything she might say but doesn't care to. Decades of living in Italy may have rusted, or antiqued, her English idiom. We read that Lord Lucan "flourished a fly swat"; that "he stood up and out into the aisle to see them more clear"; that "DNA profiles and other new scientific perforations of bland surfaces were the enemy now." Of a minor character, as she picks up the telephone, we read, " 'Yes, speaking,' said the lady in the English tongue." The prose tends to be strict and briskly instructive. With Euclidean concision it delivers Hildegard's curious life story:

> She grew up on the pig farm. The sisters and brothers eventually married and went to live each in a house not far away. They continued in the pig business. Hildegard (then Beate) grew up, with all of them around, among the pigs. She went to school, was clever. She fought herself free from her home. She found Heinrich. She made blood-money.

Perhaps, as Spark ages, her gnarly Scots roots thrust up through the ground of her long Continental residence. Certainly her prose is lifted by a trip that her lovers, Joe and Lacey, take to Caithness, in northern Scotland:

> The great lovely steep hills were all around them. The feeling of northern nature, a whole geography minding very much its own business, cautious, alien, cold and haughty, began here. The sky rolled darkly amid patches of white light.

Unlike Ivy Compton-Burnett's clipped prose, which seemed fit only for cranky, quibbling people pent up indoors in Victorian parlors, Spark's can encompass, if curtly, whatever arises before it—the lightstruck landscape without, the bloody turns within.

Flesh on Flesh

ATONEMENT, by Ian McEwan. 302 pp. Doubleday, 2002.

Ian McEwan, whose previous novels have tended to be short, smart, and dark, has produced a beautiful and majestic fictional panorama, *Atonement*. The novel's first half takes place over two summer days in 1935, on a Surrey estate occupied by the Tallis family: Jack, the head of the household, whose work for the Ministry of Defence keeps him night after night in London; Emily, his wife, who is prone to migraines and long spells of daydreaming in her bed; Leon, the eldest child and only son, twenty-five and working in London in a modest position at a bank, though he has a law degree; his sister Cecilia, younger by two years, fresh from her finals at Cambridge, bored and at loose ends; and our heroine, thirteen-year-old Briony, given to posing philosophical questions and perusing the thesaurus, and for the last two years an increasingly active writer. She has just composed a play, *The Trials of Arabella*, to be performed in honor of her brother's homecoming. He is bringing a friend, Paul Marshall, the youthful owner of a candy factory, and there are three cousins just arrived from the north, the Quinceys—Lola, fifteen, and nine-year-old twins, Jackson and Pierrot—who are to act in Briony's play. The three are refugees from a broken household: Aunt Hermione, Emily Tallis's younger sister, has run off to Paris with "a man who worked in the wireless." To this cast of characters add some servants and the anomalous figure of Robbie Turner. Robbie is the son of the Tallises' former gardener; when the boy's father deserted him and his mother, they were charitably taken up by Jack Tallis, who gave Grace Turner the gardener's bungalow and has paid for Robbie's education, including three years at Cambridge. He has just passed his finals with a first in literature, while Cecilia earned only a third. Though at Cambridge simultaneously, they rarely met there, and are tense and awkward with each other this summer, in the domain where they grew up together. They, it is perhaps not too much to reveal, supply the novel's love interest.

McEwan's epigraph comes from Jane Austen, and promises a spacious family novel of humorous interplay, romantic intrigues, and near-tragic misunderstandings. The promise is to some extent kept; the homesick twins and the blossoming, manipulative Lola inject disturbance into the stagnant Tallis household. But in the warmth of these days, the year's hottest, a Virginia Woolf–ian shimmer overlays the Austenish plot, which keeps threatening to dissolve. The play, for example, does not go on (until sixty-four years later). Jack Tallis, the powerful absentee Old Man, an offstage deus ex machina, never descends. Instead, amid many images of water and vegetation and architectural heritage, various viewpoints backtrack and overlap, and certain scenes are replayed from widely different perspectives. The writing is conspicuously "good"; this goodness turns out to be, eventually, a subject of criticism—by Cyril Connolly, no less—in a droll show of artistic self-reference, although in the meantime it works an authentic spell. Picture after picture, in the haze of this midsummer, arises to challenge and flatter the reader's capacity for visualization. In a key moment, the lovers-to-be tussle over a precious vase, and a fragment breaks off and falls into a fountain:

> With a sound like a dry twig snapping, a section of the lip of the vase came away in his hand, and split into two triangular pieces which dropped into the water and tumbled to the bottom in a synchronous, see-sawing motion, and lay there, several inches apart, writhing in the broken light.

That see-sawing synchronicity, that writhing in the broken light show us more than we had expected to see. A seemingly half-baked comparison to a savannah writhes on, renews itself, and ends with a smiling metaphoric flourish:

> Then, nearer, the estate's open parkland which today had a dry and savage look, roasting like a savannah, where isolated trees threw harsh stumpy shadows and the long grass was already stalked by the leonine yellow of high summer.

The reader, seeing through Cecilia's languid eyes, is brought up short by virtually abstract images:

She lolled against the warm stone, lazily finishing her cigarette and contemplating the scene before her—the foreshortened slab of chlorinated water, the black inner tube of a tractor tyre propped against a deck chair, the two men in cream linen suits of infinitesimally different hues, bluish-grey smoke rising against the bamboo green.

"Infinitesimally different hues" signals the mode, as skyscapes, physiognomies, gestures ("She turned aside and made a steeple of her hands to enclose her nose and mouth and pressed her fingers into the corners of her eyes"), and scents ("the grasses giving off their sweet cattle smell, the hard-fired earth which still held the embers of the day's heat and exhaled the mineral odour of clay, and the faint breeze carrying from the lake a flavour of green and silver") are evoked with a refined care and verbal cunning. *This is written*, each page subliminally announces, and that undercurrent prepares the reader for the atonement of the title, in which Briony, the writer and the character becoming one, atones for a childish blunder with a mature woman's creative fiat. Even at the age of thirteen, she exults to herself, "There was nothing she could not describe."

The novel's second section transports us to another prose climate, as the terrors and confusions of the British retreat to Dunkirk in 1940 are harrowingly detailed. Some of the details are surprising and piquant—a caged parrot caught up in the chaotic scramble, a peasant with his collie plowing a field in intervals between bombing and strafing attacks, soldiers shooting their horses in the head and their motorized vehicles in the radiator. In the desperately crowded and underprovisioned conditions around Dunkirk, British soldiers threaten and assault one another while the enemy swoops overhead and the RAF and the Royal Navy fail to materialize. As a whole, the section is gripping, but it is not extraordinary, quite, like the novel's first half. The element of the marvellous—the latently menacing seethe of the everyday—has been replaced by the more vulgar excitement of overt peril. If we marvel, it is at the ability of contemporary English writers (McEwan was born in 1948) to capture the tastes and sights of a past they did not witness even as children. It is as if the earlier generation of writers—Waugh, Greene, Green, Golding, Powell, Orwell, Bowen, Spark, and dozens of lessers—has laid down, on this dense island soil, an accessible past, while Americans must reconstruct their more diffuse collective memory from barer hints. The imaginary writer of *Atonement* in her last pages expresses her debt to the research facilities at the Imperial War Museum, in Lambeth, and to an "old colonel" who has testily corrected her terminology and fine points. Her sixty pages of war's turmoil are followed by sixty of war's grisly wounds, which Briony, who has signed up as a probationer nurse, witnesses and learns to minister to. She extracts shrapnel, talks French to a young man who dies in her arms, removes the bandages from a blasted face:

> Using a pair of surgical tongs, she began carefully pulling away the sodden, congealed lengths of ribbon gauze from the cavity in the side of his face. When the last was out, the resemblance to the cutaway model they used in anatomy classes was only faint. This was all ruin, crimson and raw. She could see through his missing cheek to his upper and lower molars, and the tongue glistening, and hideously long.

The reader will possibly recall how the novel's lovers, in their moment of mutual possession, find their way to un-self-conscious passion through "the contact of tongues, alive and slippery muscle, moist flesh on flesh." Lust and disgust keep close company; in McEwan's hypnotic first novel, *The Cement Garden* (1978), another set of children left to their own devices, in another summer of unusual heat, experience the debility and putrescence of the body as well as its tabooed allure. *Atonement* concerns, among other historical phenomena, puritanism in 1935, when an impulsive four-letter word in a man's love letter could draw the attention of the authorities, with lasting consequences. The frail, moist flesh, mutilated in war, corseted and shamed in peacetime, and subject, in the long view, to swift decay, gives this intricately composed narrative its mournful, surging life. The poems of Auden and Housman are talismanic volumes within this novel about star-crossed literature majors, and *Clarissa* with its scribbling heroine; but equally prominent is *Gray's Anatomy*.

The novel's bloody illustrations of the horrors of war compel assent and pity, and yet, such is the novel-reader's romantic nature, it is the lovers that keep us turning the page; theirs is the consummation we devoutly wish. Our wish is granted, but with a duplicitous art. *Atonement*, in its tenderness and doubleness and final effect of height, in its postmodern concern with its own writing, and in its central topic of two upperclass sisters caught up in the period between the world wars, has a striking happenstance resemblance to Margaret Atwood's *The Blind Assassin*. Both revert, from the perspective of old women facing death near the bloated end of the twentieth century, to an era when a certain grandeur could attach to human decisions, made as they were under the looming shadow of global war and in living memory of the faded old virtues—loyalty and honesty and valor—that sought to soften what McEwan calls "the iron principle of self love." People could still dedicate a life, and gamble it on one throw. Compared with today's easy knowingness and self-protective irony, feelings then had a naïveté, a hearty force developed amid repression and scarcity and linked to a sense of transcendent adventure. Novels need this force, and must find it where they can, if only in the annals of the past.

Absent Presences

Spies, by Michael Frayn. 261 pp. Holt, 2002.

Bernard Shaw couldn't do it, Henry James couldn't do it, but the ingenious English author Michael Frayn does do it: write novels and plays with equal success. His most recent play, *Copenhagen*, about a problematical meeting in 1941 between the physicist Werner Heisenberg and his Danish mentor Niels Bohr, won three Tony Awards and ran on Broadway for more than nine months; his 1999 novel, *Headlong*, concerning the possible discovery of a lost painting by Bruegel, was listed among the Booker Prize finalists and the *New York Times Book Review*'s Editors' Choices. Frayn began light, writing topical and humorous columns for the *Manchester Guardian*, but has extended his reach and seriousness while keeping a sprightly intellectuality. A brilliant novella of a few years ago, *The Trick of It*, was comic in the obtuse maneuvering of its hero, a literal-minded young academic mismarried to a middle-aged novelist of the eccentric Spark/Murdoch/Rose Macaulay mold, but was profound in its grasp of the opposition between the creative spirit and the critical.

Frayn's new novel, *Spies*, drapes a valedictory sadness upon a mystery-story armature. Two boys—our unkempt, ductile hero, Stephen Wheatley, and his impeccable, domineering friend, Keith Hayward—set about investigating, in their little neighborhood of fourteen properties, Keith's abrupt declaration that his mother is a German spy. The boys live on a rather newly built dead-end street called the Close, between a small shopping district and, on the other side of the railroad tracks, rural dilapidation. World War II is in progress, and though neither the year nor the boys' ages are specified, later clues reveal that Stephen was two in 1935, which would give him Frayn's own birth-year, 1933, and make him ten in 1943 and eleven in 1944. The war feels well advanced—one house in the Close has been bombed, but no further air raids are mentioned in the summer of the novel's action—and Stephen, who, among other adventures, smokes cigarettes and kisses a girl, is advancing toward puberty. The neighborhood is carefully mapped, house by house, but only three homes are entered by Stephen and by the novelist's descriptive powers.

There is Stephen's own household, about which he seems remarkably incurious; it consists of his mother, a brother older by four years, and a gentle, conspicuously hairy father who was absent for a year on a secret project in the north and whose conversation is sprinkled with foreign expressions. There is the Haywards', consisting of Keith, his mother, and his father, an unfriendly constant presence who whistles tunelessly, busies himself with home improvements, and keeps sharp a bayonet with which he reportedly slew five Germans in the First World War. And, three houses down from the Haywards', there is Auntie Dee's: she is Mrs. Hayward's younger sister and the mother of a toddler, Milly, and the wife of the Close's war hero, Uncle Peter, a bomber pilot in the RAF. "His very absence was a kind of presence," we are told. "He was manifest in the little silver brooch that Auntie Dee always had pinned to her breast, that showed the three famous initials on a blue enamel background, with the famous wings outspread around them and the famous crown above."

The novel's gradual revelations cut on the bias through this human topography, described with a child's acuteness of sensation and innocence of perception. Stephen, now an elderly man living on the Continent, is stirred to revisit his old turf, after a half-century's absence, by a flowery scent in the air, "something quite harsh and coarse." The smell, which he cannot name, "has a kind of sexual urgency to it. And it unsettles me, as it always does. . . . I have a feeling that something, somewhere, has been left unresolved, that some secret thing in the air around me is still waiting to be discovered." Frayn asks a certain mental nimbleness from his readers; the secret thing emerges bit by bit, with no tidy summing-up. It is left to the adult reader, for example, to deduce that the mysterious markings the young sleuths find in Keith's mother's diary record her monthly periods (with tiny x's) and her occasions of intercourse (with exclamation points!), and that these and her frequent rests indicate a desire to conceive and give Keith a sibling. The boys never realize this, though they assign a pregnant fatality to the dark of the moon, which coincides with Mrs. Hayward's inscrutable x's. The additional hugger-mugger of her comings and goings on errands during which she briefly vanishes, and of the unsuburbanized rural area beyond the other end of the sinister railroad tunnel, an area full of barking dogs and ruined barns and unsavory rumors, is lifted into clarification but held there for only a moment, before dropping back into the other obscurities of childhood.

The ultimate conspiracy, sex, sends forth two agents to Stephen: intrusive, bothersomely knowing Barbara Berrill, a year older than he, and tall, brown-eyed, soft-voiced Mrs. Hayward herself, who as her private plot thickens needs to enlist the child in her errands and seductively invades his and Keith's sweet-smelling den of privet. Even a slow-witted reader will guess the heart of her predicament before Stephen, who, like the bookish, adult hero of *Headlong*, shows a formidable capacity for sustaining an obfuscation. Stephen does, however, deduce the reason for the scarves that Mrs. Hayward comes to wear at her throat—they conceal periodic wounds—and conclude that Keith, like his father, is a bullying sadist. Not all the Nazis are on the other side.

As in *Headlong*, slightly too much seems to happen toward the end, abetted by too many artfully delayed recognitions. The playwright in Frayn imposes the accelerating pace of farce on his ominous, tenderly evoked materials. A tangle of facial hair continues to hide an evident identity, a "terrible secret force" emerges from the railroad tracks, a small boy makes not one but several excursions into the dangerous night. And then the curtain quickly falls: Stephen never plays with Keith again, he never returns to their lair in the overgrown bushes of the bombed house, he never attempts to deliver a silk aviator's scarf entrusted to him, along with some words of undying love. Nor, to this reader's disappointment, does his tour of his boyhood turf encounter any human survivors of that remote time. Such tours, in my own experience, usually do, and in literature they are almost obliged to: Odysseus is recognized by the ancient dog, Argos, who was a puppy when he left; Captain Ryder discovers Nanny Hawkins still ensconced in her top-floor room at Brideshead; Mickey Sabbath, in Philip Roth's *Sabbath's Theater*, comes upon Cousin Fish still alive, though "a mere mist of a man." In *Spies*, a reunion seems prepared. Keith's old house, still named Chollerton, is kept up by someone's fanatic hands: "The mellow red brick is still well-pointed, the woodwork of the window frames and gables and garage doors as flawlessly white as when Mr. Hayward used to paint them himself, in white overalls as clean as the paintwork, whistling, whistling, from morning to night." Yet the proud owner, who could be Keith, carrying on his father's style, remains hidden. Stephen does not knock at the door, and when, farther along the street, he sees "a white-haired old lady" kneeling to weed what had been the Berrills' front garden, he fights a recognition:

> She glances up at me and I suddenly realize, with the most terrible jolt of recognition, of hope and dismay, that it's Barbara.
> She looks indifferently at me for a moment and then returns to her weeding. It's not Barbara. Of course it's not. I don't think it is.

Stephen is not seeking a companion survivor of time, to illuminate those distant events. He revolves them within himself, aided only by local geography, changed and unchanged. In this, *Spies* differs from Ian

McEwan's recent, in some ways similarly backward-looking novel, *Atonement*, and from Harry Mulisch's even more similar *The Assault* (1982), wherein subsequent revelations, over the years, change the meaning of a violent wartime night in a Dutch enclave of four houses. Stephen became, he tells us, a searcher after reality; his English marriage "was never quite a real marriage," and his job teaching engineering in the local polytechnic "never quite a real job." He found reality in another country, and now is brought back by what in German is called "*Fernweh*, which is in my case also *Heimweh*, a longing to be home," toward the end of life, to the Close and its "sweet, coarse, and intimately unsettling" scent of privet in bloom.

Aside from the understated tact and ingenuity of its mystery plot, Frayn's novel excels in its rendering of the power of early impressions, a power that fetishizes and eternalizes such modest phenomena as certain vague smells, certain details of dress coded with signs of class and origin, certain sounds betraying the life in other houses, certain coveted elegancies like the "jug covered by a lace weighted with four blue beads" in which Mrs. Hayward serves lemon barley water to her son and his friend in the garden of her polished, fascinatingly furnished house. Children are surrounded by clues, by elusive emanations from the opaque and impervious adult world, and thus are all spies, increasingly expert and secretive.

Mind/Body Problems—II

THE BODY, by Hanif Kureishi. 149 pp. Scribner, 2004.

Reversion to youth and a drastic mind/body disjunction are proposed by Hanif Kureishi in his short novel *The Body:* the hero, Adam, a playwright and writer in his wearying sixties, simply buys himself a new body, into which his brain is transplanted with no more trace than a small scar on the top of his head. The young surgeon cheerfully admits:

> "It takes time and great expertise. But so does cleaning a great painting. The right person has to do it. There are not many of those people yet. But it can be done. It is, of course, something that was always going to happen."

Kureishi, born in Bromley, Kent, in 1954, of a Pakistani-immigrant father and an English mother, has written some lauded screenplays (*My Beautiful Laundrette*, 1985; *Sammy and Rosie Get Laid*, 1987) and vivid, exuberant novels, of which the earlier (*The Buddha of Suburbia*, 1990; *The*

Black Album, 1995) show characters shedding their Asian, Islamic puritanism in favor of heady Occidental temptations, summed up by the first novel's teen-age narrator as "mysticism, alcohol, sexual promise, clever people and drugs." Bodies abound in Kureishi's fiction, and their doings are described with a lack of inhibition that distinguishes him from, say, V. S. Naipaul, who only in his latest novel, *Half a Life*, got down and dirty about the sexually seething immigrants' London he encountered in the 1950s. A generation later, Kureishi's easy frankness extends to the fraught psychological, conversational margins of sex acts, and such guilt-ridden works as the novella *Intimacy* and the short story "Strangers When We Meet" can be harrowing. But in *The Body* the hero, adrift both as a famous oldster in London cultural circles and as a beautiful youngster in the party scenes of Europe, is so assimilated, so denatured, so securely removed from the lively, home-based ethnic/ethical conflicts usually driving Kureishi's fiction that his sketchy adventures form less a novel than a parable.

As a parable, *The Body* has its telling moments, especially in the first half. The clinic, housed in "a run-down warehouse on a bleak, wind-blown industrial estate outside London," where Adam is persuaded to part with his body and his savings, is a slice of bland, upbeat bio-horror out of *Brave New World*. Having opted not for permanent occupation but for a six-month rental of a new body, Adam browses among the rows of suspended, refrigerated corpses ("once . . . there was culture, now there is shopping," he later reflects) and chooses an Adonis of color ("or rather, he had seemed to choose me"):

> Stocky and as classically handsome as any sculpture in the British Museum, he was neither white nor dark but lightly toasted, with a fine, thick penis and heavy balls. I would, at last, have the body of an Italian footballer: an aggressive, attacking midfielder.

Smoothly and painlessly transferred to this excellent vehicle, Adam takes the new name Leo Raphael Adams and doesn't quite know what to do with himself. He stands on his head, and he admires his new prowess at urination—"When I peed, the stream was full, clear, and what I must describe as 'decisive.' " (Contrariwise, the hero of Andrew Sean Greer's *Confessions of Max Tivoli*, on his backwards way to pre-puberty, laments that his penis has become "a sleek little snail . . . forever soft, rubbery, good only for peeing long distances on the side of the road.") Hanif Kureishi's Leo Adams, in his new housing, does get laid, as his mentor, Ralph, advises, but mostly lies low in hotel rooms and walks for miles, "as though I were at the wheel of a luxury car," relishing his smooth steady strides and the way he can "see over the heads of others on the street" (who said he was stocky?). He wanders from London to Europe; he enjoys a variety of casual conversations and employments—biographer's assistant, "picker" at the door of a club in Vienna, kept man of an American heiress in Perugia. He falls in with a fast film set, takes drugs, attends orgies.

Youth is wasted on the young, George Bernard Shaw once said; this seems true even the second time around. As Adam, our hero had been puny and shy of physical intimacy. "As a Newbody, however," Leo writes, "I began to like the pornographic circus of rough sex. . . . I begged to be turned into meat, held down, tied, blindfolded, slapped, pulled, and strangled, entirely merged in the physical, all my swirling selves sucked into orgasm." When such exertion palls, he stumbles upon a "spiritual center" on a Greek island, where he becomes an "oddjob," who lets the female clients and, eventually, the center's founder and directress adore him. Then, at a party on a yacht, he meets Matte, another Newbody and the yacht's owner; it develops that Matte wants Leo's body for his dying elderly brother, and Kureishi's parable closes with a chase, ending back at the brain-transplant clinic, where the electricity has been turned off and Adam's Oldbody has disappeared.

The Body has the clipped speed and casual logic of a screenplay and might make a good movie. Identity switch is easy to film; for example, *All of Me*, with Steve Martin and Lily Tomlin (1984), and *Freaky Friday*, with Jamie Lee Curtis and Lindsay Lohan, a recent remake of a 1977 movie with Barbara Harris and Jodie Foster. Intuitively, being in your own body seems easier to correct than the inexorable aging process. The hero of Hanif Kureishi's first novel says, of his mother, "I imagined that she considered her body to be an inconvenient object surrounding her, as if she were stranded on an unexplored desert island."* In fiction, we readily accept Gregor Samsa's awaking within the body of a gigantic insect and Dorian Gray's transfer of his body's ravages to a portrait. Yet in fact human consciousness is part and parcel of the body that holds it, and one regrets that Kureishi, in conducting his thought-experiment, didn't pursue some of his own hints. While Leo's body is still new to him, he tells Ralph:

---

*An image that uncannily anticipates a rude joke in the French novelist Michel Houellebecq's 2006 novel of mind/body readjustment, *The Possibility of an Island*:

"Do you know what they call the fat stuff around the vagina?"
"No."
"The woman."

"I can feel things, perhaps memories, of the man who was here first. Perhaps the physical body has a soul. There's a phrase of Freud's that might apply here: the bodily ego, he calls it, I think."

Leo's body belonged, Ralph tells him, to a Los Angeles homosexual who suffered from clinical depression and killed himself with carbon monoxide; but the fascinating idea of a haunted body, whose previous tenant makes himself felt throughout its nervous system and utmost cells, fades away as *la dolce vita*, still a heady topic for Kureishi, takes over the narrative. Leo's borrowed body becomes a mere commodity for which there exists a competing bidder.

Perhaps no novel can do justice to the ancient and still-popular concept of leaving our bodies, which are both our enablers and our prisons. Our relation to our bodies lies deeper than circumstance, undemonstrable and irrefutable, along with the sensation that there *is* a relation, of one thing to something else, though materialist science tells us that out of our bodies we are nothing. Kureishi, who studied philosophy at the University of London, glances at the ontology shivering in his ectoplasmic subject matter, but then turns away. When the playful, murderous Matte, who has been reading Nietzsche and Goethe, attempts to engage Leo in discussion, Leo retreats: "I didn't want to listen to him, or argue anymore. . . . I found the encounter disturbing. Matte and I were both mutants, freaks, human unhumans—a fact I could at least forget when I was with real people, those with death in them." Death equals real: that consoling notion lies near the heart of the confessions of both Leo Adams and Max Tivoli. When Matte, an enthusiast for the new brain-transplant technology, announces, "Death is dead," Leo responds, "Oh, no, everyone'll miss it so!" (Exclamation point mine.) He ends in sorry contemplation of his existence as a "stranger on the earth, a nobody with nothing," stuck in "the nightmare of eternal life." He seems to have forgotten that by trading his body in for a newer model he has postponed but not forever avoided the final breakdown.

Flashy to the Rescue

FLASHMAN ON THE MARCH, by George MacDonald Fraser. 335 pp. Knopf, 2005.

George MacDonald Fraser's twelfth book about the Victorian rogue and soldier Flashman finds both the author and the hero in dauntless fettle, the former as keen to invent perils and seducible women as the latter is, respectively, to survive and to seduce them. Fraser, an Englishman schooled in Scotland, served with the Highland Regiment in India, Africa, and the Middle East, before settling on the Isle of Man. He has written other fiction, plus history, autobiography, and film scripts, besides acting as Flashman's assiduous editor—the series is presented, under the overall title "The Flashman Papers," as its protagonist's memoirs, which need only a few footnotes and spelling corrections to become excellent entertainments. It was a brilliant stroke of Fraser's, in the first volume, *Flashman* (1969), to retrieve a minor figure in Thomas Hughes's greatly popular, intensely Christian best-seller *Tom Brown's School Days* (1857) and reanimate him as a lauded though inadvertent hero in the service of the British Empire. Hughes introduces Flashman simply as "Flashman the School-house bully," who likes to organize tossing the smaller boys at Rugby School in a blanket: "What your real bully likes in tossing, is when the boys kick and struggle, or hold on to one side of the blanket, and so get pitched bodily on to the floor; it's no fun to him when no one is hurt or frightened." Hughes is at pains to explain, "Bullies are cowards, and one coward makes many," but, beyond that, he is so little interested in Flashman that he dismisses him in a paragraph, halfway through the book, for getting "beastly drunk" on gin punch amply overlaid by beer. The famed headmaster, Thomas Arnold, "who had long had his eye on Flashman, arranged for his withdrawal next morning."

Thus rusticated, Flashman languished for more than a century, until he was reborn as Fraser's cavalryman. In *Flashman*, the former Rugby bully confesses his expulsion to his father and persuades this guardian, and his dead mother's brother, Uncle Bindley, to arrange and pay for his enlistment in the Eleventh Light Dragoons, Prince Albert's Hussars. The regiment has recently returned from India and is not apt, Flashman calculates, to be posted abroad again soon. But, under the war-loving, blockheaded Lord Cardigan, it swiftly resumes its quest for military glory, in the India and Afghanistan of 1839–42, taking Flashman with it. The great joke of his initial outing is that, though behaving with consistent selfishness and poltroonery, he not only emerges unscathed but is awarded a medal, with sentimental effusions, by the Queen. He is the anti-hero of Empire, the negative of the imperial virtues, developed as a positive in the muddle of battle. The irony weakens, though, in the course of the eleven sequels. To survive and triumph as he invariably does, Flashman must manifest at least two admirable traits: an almost supernatural gift for languages that carries him through many a covert operation, and a winning way with women that does much the same thing. Women get him out of as much trouble as they get him into, and the reader gathers an impression of a personal attractiveness and cool-headedness of which scarcely a hint existed in the craven bully of the relentlessly cautionary *Tom Brown's School Days*. Hughes's text allowed him only to be "big and strong" and to have "a bluff off-hand manner, which passed for heartiness, and considerable powers of being pleasant when he liked." The early Flashman of *Flashman* is thoroughly vicious, hitting out at women and hiding behind the battlefield heroics of braver men, and Fraser's tone is mordantly satiric at the expense of the Victorian upper classes. As the series proceeds, however, its anti-hero becomes a hero in spite of his own professions to the contrary.

Additionally to our hero's credit belongs the historical and ethno-graphic interest of the cumulative "Flashman Papers"; he is a keen observer and appreciator of the Empire's adversaries even as they strive to slay him. Of all his guises, none is more appealing than the ninety-year-old retiree who in the latest of his published papers ruminates:

> You can always tell when something is coming to an end. You know, by the way events are shaping, that it can't last much longer, but you think there are still a few days or weeks to go . . . and that's the moment when it fin-ishes with a sudden bang that you didn't expect. Come to think of it, that's probably true of life, or so it strikes me at the age of ninety—but I don't expect it to happen before tea. Yet one of these days the muffins will grow cold and the tea-cakes congeal as they summon the lads from belowstairs to cart the old cadaver up to the best bedroom. And if I've a moment before the light fades, I'll be able to cry, "Sold, Starnberg and Ignatieff and Iron Eyes and Gul Shah and Charity Spring and all the rest of you bastards who tried to do for old Flashy, 'cos he's going out on his own, and be damned to you!"

It may be Fraser himself, born in 1926, who is feeling valedictory. The Flashman of *Flashman on the March*, describing his intricate sub-rosa role in General Robert Napier's Abyssinian campaign of 1867–68, slips into nostalgic remembrance often enough to render an inventory of his previ-ous adventures. In recalling how he survived a plunge down the Blue Nile's Tisisat Falls, he evokes other near-drownings:

> I've known what it is to drown, on several occasions, most memorably in the Skrang river with a blowpipe dart in my ribs, and upside down in that infer-nal drain beneath Jotunberg Castle, and at the bottom of a bath in the amorous clutches of the demented Queen of Madagascar, but only in the maelstrom under the Blue Nile falls was I unable even to struggle feebly as I drifted upwards through that silvery radiance, the agony of suffocation gradually changing to a dreamy languor.

An encounter with the earthy Queen of the Wollo Galla revives memories of the Empress of China, the Maharani of the Punjab, the Rani of Jhansi, and Queen Victoria ("our own gracious monarch") herself. Twirling a revolver takes him back to the American Southwest; being tossed onto a roaring fire reminds him of how "during my service in the Punjab I had the misfortune to be basted on a gridiron"; being placed in chains evokes being caged in Russia, "and the Gwalior bottle dungeon, and China when the Imps collared me before Pekin." An atrocity perpetrated by Abyssinia's Emperor Theodore fetches to his mind's eye the "mass scalpings and blowing from guns and the knouting of a Russian peasant" that he witnessed in his adventure-laden years. Though Flashman has the resilience of a comic-book hero, his testimonies to nineteenth-century barbarities are not comic. Fraser's carefully documented slaughters weight these cheerful potboilers with history's grim ballast—at the risk, it might be said, of jaggedly dividing the reader's attention as he flips back and forth to the copious endnotes, a total of sixty-two in this novel, making nearly twenty distractingly informative extra pages.

Flashman's breezy language and assumptions reveal a good deal of the Empire's inner life. To its servants, at least on Flashman's level, it was a way out of foggy England, and a welcome sexual holiday. "One of the things that has always enchanted me about African women with an appetite," he confides, "is that they don't waste time before indulging it. Where their European sisters have to be jollied into the supine position . . . ladies of colour tend to make straight for the mutton." Illustrations follow:

A tall figure advanced silently into the shaft of moonlight from the high narrow window—a figure in a robe of saffron silk which slid to the floor without a sound, revealing a splendid golden body swaying slowly towards me, slim hands clasped over her breasts and then falling away to caress her hips as she passed from the moonbeam into the shadow.

In case we don't get the picture, Flashman explains, "It was being borne in on me that the moral climate of Abyssinia was not quite that of our own polite society." He becomes almost a bore on the topic:

In Ab society, which as I've told you is probably the most immoral on earth (Cheltenham ain't in it), rogering the hostess is almost obligatory, part of the etiquette, like leaving cards, and not at all out of the way in a country where it's considered a mortal insult to praise a woman's chastity, since it implies that she's not attractive enough to be galloped.

Boringness on the subject threatens his creator, too; to keep his pot boiling, Fraser keeps tossing fresh female bodies into it. No sooner is

Malee, with her above-mentioned splendid golden body and "long lovely Egyptian face and huge eyes" chalked up, than the formidable Uliba-Wark, her "proud Ethiopian head with its laughing eyes" and "voluptuous lower lip," her "lovely oiled limbs shining in the firelight," is wheeled into position, in turn to be supplanted by her plump but lusty half-sister, Masteeat, and the bare-breasted warrior Miriam, a "little satin stunner" with "blue eyes, bigod," for a change. She is later referred to as "a bonny bint"; Fraser eruditely sprinkles the narrative with Victorian slang omitted from most assigned texts. Flashman remembers Uliba-Wark to have been "as splendid a piece of bounce as I'd seen," advises the reader to "never miss the chance of a rattle," and apologizes for his failure to observe all the details of an Abyssinian feast served by girls wearing brass collars and tiny aprons: "You don't, when your *maise* is being poured by a lovely little Hebe who rests her bare poont on your shoulder as she stoops to your cup." The unspeakable "n" word is liberally bestowed upon anyone with a skin darker than English custard, though anthropological distinctions are not ignored: "I studied the escorts, and a formidable pair they were, tall, splendidly built, black as night but not negroid with their long heads and chins and straight noses."

What light does the old, politically incorrect Empire shed, as Britain celebrates the bicentennial of Nelson's victory at Trafalgar, on America's present efforts to bring order and democracy to the benighted? In an introductory "Explanatory Note," the author speaks in his own voice of the Abyssinian War of 1868:

> [It was] surely the strangest of all imperial campaigns, when a British Indian army invaded one of the least known and most dangerous countries on earth, and in the face of apparently insuperable hazards, and predictions of certain failure, marched and fought their way across a trackless wilderness of rocky chasm and jagged mountain to their goal, did what they had come to do, and marched out again with hardly a casualty. There has never perhaps been a success like it in the history of war. It took twelve thousand men, a mighty fleet, nine million pounds (a staggering sum at that time), a meticulous if extravagant organization, and a remarkable old soldier—and all to rescue a tiny group of British citizens held captive by a mad monster of an African king. Those were, to quote Flashman, the days.

Fraser returns in his endnotes to worry at the issues: "Should Britain have stayed, and pacified the country, assuming the white man's burden? There are those who think so. . . . Of one thing we can be sure: if Britain had stayed, revisionist historians would certainly have condemned it as another act of selfish imperialism." In the relaxed aftermath of victory,

General Napier applies to imperialism the old Scots adage "Ye canna dae right for daein' wrang!"

Advantageously, the Abyssinian campaign had a precisely defined objective, the rescue of the British prisoners, who included Her Majesty's envoy to the court of the Emperor Theodore, Captain Douglas Cameron. The indignant British public was for action, though it disliked the cost of "a penny or more on the income tax." The Empire was global, and it drew upon loyal Sikh and Indian armies for this African intervention. Western technology still had the edge: the Abyssinians, Flashman reports, were "shot flat, massacred if you like, by Messrs Snider and Enfield, gallant savages decimated by modern weapons." In the siege of his stronghold of Magdala, Theodore (who admired the British and wanted his son to go to school in England) committed suicide, relieving the Crown of the embarrassment of what to do with him. Napier exercised a conqueror's prerogatives by burning down Magdala and giving the territory to the Galla Queen Masteeat—a historical figure, unlike Flashman's slimmer bints. The British, though the Foreign Office helped precipitate the war by ignoring the Abyssinian monarch's letter to the Queen proposing a friendlier relationship, made shrewd use, once embarked upon their face-saving invasion, of local politics; Flashman's secret mission is to persuade, with a bribe of fifty thousand Maria Theresa dollars, the Galla Queen to encircle Magdala with her army and prevent Theodore's escape. Know your ground, spend what's needed for thorough preparation, quit while you're ahead, and leave nation-building to the natives, at each other's throats though they be: these would seem to be the lessons, possibly but not necessarily applicable to our second invasion of Iraq. History repeats, but always with differences. Abyssinia had no oil reserves worth securing, and its Coptic-flavored brand of Christianity wasn't inspiring terrorists in London.

Flashman's own conclusion proposes "suggesting to Her Majesty's ministers that next time they get a letter from a touchy barbarian despot, it might save 'em a great deal of trouble and expense if they sent him a civil reply by return of post." But, if they had placated Emperor Theodore, George MacDonald Fraser would have had one less historical imbroglio to convert into a postmodern penny dreadful, which treats us to, along with its hero's hairbreadth escapes and blithe lechery, a near-forgotten piece of history that once made headlines as gripping and as agitating as today's from the Middle East.

IN ENGLISH BUT NOT ENGLISH

Home Care

FAMILY MATTERS, by Rohinton Mistry. 439 pp. Knopf, 2002.

Whereas Salman Rushdie's celebrated *Midnight's Children* gave us Bombay with a headlong, fantastic, word-twirling magic realism, Rohinton Mistry, a Bombay-born Canadian, presents the same diverse, congested metropolis with a realism that, if too wry to be called sober, might be termed Tolstoyan. In a polished but economical and unobtrusive prose, he writes of household dramas, of plausibly confined, earthbound lives seeking to generate on their own a spark of relieving magic. Mistry harks back to the nineteenth-century novelists for whom every detail, every urban alley, every character however lowly added a vital piece to the full social picture, and for whom every incident illustrated the eventually crushing weight of the world. Liveliness, precision, weight: these old-fashioned mimetic virtues, and the broad sympathy that calls them into being, cannot be taken for granted during a time when the producers and consumers alike of fiction have had their sensibilities early deadened by an incessant barrage of visual entertainment as insubstantial as it is eye-catching. In a world of hurry and of quick artistic kills, Mistry has kept the patience to tease narrative and moral interest out of domestic life, in a subcontinent of more than a billion striving, often desperate souls. His new novel, *Family Matters*, announces its territory in the title; its plot concerns the disruptions and changes in an extended family when its patriarch, the retired professor Nariman Vakeel, at the age of seventy-nine, breaks his ankle and requires nursing care.

He has been living with his unmarried middle-aged stepchildren, Jal (male) and Coomy (female) Contractor [*sic*], in a spacious apartment in a building grandly called Château Felicity. Unable to cope with the hygienic needs of Nariman's body, which is afflicted with Parkinson's disease and osteoporosis as well as a ponderous thigh-to-foot plaster cast, the siblings foist the old man off on the lone child of his union with their dead mother, a daughter named Roxana. She and her husband, Yezad Chenoy, have an apartment barely big enough for them and their two young sons, Murad and Jehangir, in a building designated, modestly but optimistically, Pleasant Villa. As families do, they cope, thanks to Roxana's devoted energy and strength, Yezad's grudging acceptance of the situation, and the affectionate interest of the two boys. Though every viewpoint is animated by the author's omniscience, the younger son, Jehangir, receives the most fond and knowing attention, and writes a first-person epilogue, confirming our sense that the novel's emotional center is a boy's experience of his venerable, deteriorating grandfather. Senescence recapitulates existence: Nariman's dreams rehearse the tragedy of his life, a youthful love affair frustrated by his parents, while his elderly presence challenges the resources of each family member. As in Mistry's more grandly scaled, Commonwealth Writers Prize–winning magnum opus, *A Fine Balance* (1995), close quarters breed difficulty, ill temper, wisdom, and love. The physical care of the elderly is not sentimentalized; their odors and excretions are vividly rendered. Indeed, I have not encountered another novel, except the Marquis de Sade's *The 120 Days of Sodom*, in which excrement plays so prominent a role.

The Chenoys, the Contractors, and the Vakeels are Parsis, Zoroastrians whose religion enjoins an elaborate code of purity and purification. Yezad, though not at this point a believer, forbids his sons to touch their grandfather's bedpan and urine bottle, or to help the old man's eliminations in any way; this contaminating duty falls entirely on Roxana, who lifts her father's body at her strength's far reach. The doctrine of Parsi purity, fiercely expounded by Nariman's father, had doomed Nariman's long romance with Lucy, a Goan Catholic.

Coincidentally, Mistry writes about Parsis, a minority of less than a hundred thousand in India, while the novel out of India that has most recently met with great success in the West, Arundhati Roy's *The God of Small Things*, dealt with another dwindling Indian sect, Syrian Christians. The Parsis, the remnant of a migration from Persia around a thousand years ago, developed a flair for commerce under the British, and played a key part in the expansion and prosperity of Bombay under the East India Company. Need it surprise us if Anglophone Indian novelists tend to come from Westernized minorities, and if they tend to emigrate? Roy has stayed in New Delhi, a vociferous critic of the government and the West, but Mistry and Rushdie, a former Bombay Muslim, live in

North America, the latter in New York City and the former near Toronto. In this novel, Yezad's dreams of getting to Canada—"the land of milk and honey, also the land of deodorant and toiletry . . . of prosperity, house, car, CD player, computer, clean air, snow, lakes, mountains, abundance"—are wrecked, in a tragicomic scene, by a slovenly, churlish, condescending immigration officer, a Japanese-Canadian called Mazobashi, who flunks Yezad in a rapid-fire quiz on ice hockey. The melting pot holds many lumps. A sad and ominous irony of *Family Matters* is that Yezad, denied emigration and his just deserts as the manager of Bombay Sporting Goods, soothes his defeats in a re-embrace of Zoroastrianism that leaves him as tyrannically intolerant as his father-in-law's late father.

Family novels, accreted of small, walled-in events and mostly subdued emotions, work at the pace of entire lifetimes. As one sinks into them, their pulse becomes one's own. *Family Matters* has a nervous pulse; its Tolstoyan qualities, its ease and affections, are vitiated by a modernist jumpiness. Mistry writes in short paragraphs, and dashes from one viewpoint to another. The characters between Nariman and Jehangir in age could be fuller. Some, like Edul Munshi, the Contractors' downstairs neighbor in Château Felicity, are egregiously "flat," to use E. M. Forster's term. Munshi is built, albeit drolly, around one quality, a passion for home repair, which he performs ineptly. He is Chekhov's gun on the wall, destined to go off at the crucial moment. The Chenoys' Pleasant Villa neighbors, contrariwise, bring a nice excess of charm and suggestiveness to their functions in the plot: the concert violinist Daisy Ichhaporia, on the ground floor, lifts those who overhear her into a realm of impersonal beauty above family matters, and Villie Cardmaster, the nosy spinster next door to the Chenoys, entangles Yezad in playing Matka, Bombay's illegal lottery. She selects numbers through her dreams, which, as she gleefully describes them to Yezad, express erotic designs on him; though her yearnings fall on barren ground, her numbers, in the novelist's genial dispensations, do win. Yezad, even when not seen through the eyes of a son, has a bit of paternal aloofness. Understandable in his distaste for subway crowds and body odors, he baffles us with the force of his religious rebirth. Its understated key, presumably, is the guilty secret shared only with the reader: he has been party to the downfall of his Bombay Sporting Goods' Pickwickian proprietor, the antic, impulsive, fatherly Vikram Kapur. Mistry, though he has descriptive gifts, is sparing with them; Kapur's avaricious wife, for instance, is given no face or physical particulars at all, just a cool, brisk voice.

The novel, as it roams over many aspects of Indian life, portraying a land wherein privacy and honesty are subject to constant erosion, strikes a warm vein in the topic of the written word. Yezad's best friend, Vilas Rane, sells books at the Book Mart, a near neighbor of the sports shop, and as a sideline reads and writes letters for the illiterate. For his customers, watching him pen their dictation is "like the hungry [looking] on a feast to which they had no hope of being invited." For the letters' recipients, a new reality opens up. "It is like being with you in the city, sharing your life," comes the response through a village scribe. "We hear your voice in every line, so wonderful is the effect of the words." For the scribe, too, the effect approaches the miraculous:

> And Vilas, writing and reading the ongoing drama of family matters, the endless tragedy and comedy, realized that collectively, the letters formed a pattern only he was privileged to see. . . . If it were possible to read letters for all of humanity, compose an infinity of responses on their behalf, he would have a God's-eye view of the world, and be able to understand it.

Some such God's-eye view, of the world mapped in words, is an ambition possible, perhaps, only where literacy is still an adventure. Yezad is a novelist manqué. As he labors over his plea for admission to Canada, he tells himself, "Words had power to sway, words had accomplished mighty things, they had won wars. Surely the language of Churchill and Shakespeare and Milton, ignited with a careful mix of reason and passion, could win him a mere immigration visa." Inventing lies for Mr. Kapur, he discovers the art of fiction: "The deeper he went into the story, the more his characters acquired the solidity of flesh and blood. He recognized their potential instinctively, letting them grow was easy." And Jehangir, who hears his grandfather utter protests in his dreams, resolves to assemble some day the puzzle of family mysteries: "He turned the phrases over in his mind, storing them away with the other fragments he was saving. Some day, it would all fit together, and he would make sense of Grandpa's words." Such sense is the substance of the book we hold in our hands.

Jehangir's epilogue brings the action into the twenty-first century. Murad is turning eighteen, with a non-Parsi girlfriend, and Jehangir is fourteen, with his own sexual adventures beginning; their ages place the novel's main action in the mid-1990s. Nariman has moved back into his apartment, sharing it now with Roxana and her family and Jal. Domestic life is not always non-violent; five violent deaths have thinned the novel's cast of characters. The old man misses the crowded quarters at Pleasant Villa; his grandson writes, "I think it was very lonely for him to have his own room again." After a year of being cared for by hired attendants, Grandpa dies. His ceremonious dying—Daisy plays for him in full concert dress—is described, and then Murad's birthday, whose celebration temporarily overwhelms the furious father-son conflict. Rebellious Murad is embraced, prayed over, and allowed at last to wind the family clock. The reader is moved, even to tears, by these rites of passage among characters he has lived with long enough to feel as family.

Against the suspicion that the tears are too easily earned, it could be argued that family matters penetrate to our deepest level. They are the mill that grinds our flour, the daily chipping that gives us our shape. They are irresistibly momentous. Segmented by castes, creeds, and languages, beset by corruption and poverty, India has not, unlike some of its Asian neighbors (Pol Pot's Cambodia, China during the Cultural Revolution), attacked the family in a drive to improve mankind's lot. This lot, at bottom, may remain tragic; Nariman reflects at one point, "In the end all human beings become candidates for compassion, all of us, without exception." The exercise of compassion, by the writer and then by the reader, remains one of the novel's chief duties and complex pleasures.

Love and Loss on Zycron

THE BLIND ASSASSIN, by Margaret Atwood. 521 pp. Doubleday, 2000.

Margaret Atwood's new novel, opulent and tortuous, moves its narrative forward on five levels:

1. Iris Chase Griffen, born in 1916 and failing of a weak heart in the late 1990s, sets down an account of her present daily existence—the weather, the television, her short but adventurous walks in and around the small Canadian city of Port Ticonderoga, where the button factory founded by her grandfather now houses a set of shops and boutiques. She frequently walks there and has an unsatisfactory snack at the Cookie Gremlin, noting how a cookie is "huge, the size of a cow pat, the way they make them now—tasteless, crumbly, greasy," or at a doughnut shop where an orange cruller looms as "a great wodge of flour and fat, spreading out through my arteries like silt." Her appetite is lessening.

2. She also relates, from start to near-finish, her life, beginning as the elder of two granddaughters of the town's leading factory-owner, and spending a cloistered childhood in the rustic family mansion, Avilion. Her father, Norval Chase, is the eldest of three brothers, and the only one to survive the First World War, from which he returns with one eye and a bad leg and a habit of drink; her mother is a delicate do-gooder who

dies when Iris is nine, of a miscarriage. Iris and her younger (by three and a half years) sister, Laura, are basically raised by the housekeeper, Reenie, a woman who hails from "a row house on the southeast bank of the Jogues, where the factory workers lived." Reenie is full of tough-love down-to-earth sayings like "No flowers without shit." Tutors come and go in the house, and the father is distracted by business, philandering, and his memories of the war, which has left him an atheist. The girls grow up semi-wild. At the age of eighteen, Iris is consigned to marriage to the sleek, rising man Richard Griffen, who in the bargain takes over the button factory, which has been foundering in the Depression. Iris endures a loveless but posh marriage in Toronto up to and through the Second World War, bearing one child, Aimee. Laura, who has inherited her mother's idealism and has "a heightened capacity for belief" that beckons her to sainthood, is expelled from school and keeps disappearing into the sick wards and soup kitchens of the underprivileged until, in the novel's first paragraph, she drives her sister's car off a bridge into a ravine, where it bursts into flames. This catastrophe is the central event around which Iris's diaristic memoir circles.

3. A separate composition titled *The Blind Assassin* tells, in a tele-graphic, present-tense, quotation-mark-less style, of an affair between a nameless hero and heroine, she of the upper classes and he a scruffy, though educated and comely, man on the run, with Communist connec-tions. He bears a plain resemblance to a character in Iris's reminis-cences—Alex Thomas, a swarthy European orphan adopted by a Presbyterian minister, and a recent dropout from divinity school. The brief, Jean Rhys–ian novel was published in 1947, as a posthumous work by Laura Chase; Iris arranged its publication, an event with repercussions in her life story. It is published here, within the unbrief novel signed by Margaret Atwood, in clumps of short chapters alternating with Iris's autobiographical narrative.

4. As the two lovers meet in a succession of tawdry but fondly described borrowed rooms and apartments in Toronto, the hero, who is a science-fiction writer as well as a socialist fugitive, spins, to amuse and entrance his mistress, a tale of the planet Zycron, whose most glorious city is Sakiel-Norn. There, amid fountains and flowers and singing birds, the aristocrats, the Snilfards, wear masks of woven platinum and "a silk-like cloth made from the cocoon of the *chaz* moth," and prey on the Ygnirods, the "smallholders, serfs, and slaves." Sakiel-Norn is renowned for its fine carpets, which are fabricated by slave children who "go blind by the age of eight or nine." Once blind, they are compelled to be prosti-tutes, picklocks, or assassins. A blind assassin is hired to kill one of "the

Goddess's maidens"—nubile girls from Snilfard families who are ritually sacrificed every year. Since some of them, having lost faith in the presiding religion, have been shrieking or even trying to bite the King as he acts as High Priest in this throat-cutting ritual, the practice has grown up of cutting out their tongues well before the sacrifice. The blind assassin, when he caresses the mute prisoner, falls in love with her. Together they escape Sakiel-Norn, and are captured by hostile barbarians who call themselves the People of Joy and are called by their enemies the People of Desolation. This extraterrestrial fantasy parodies the lovers' social situation and, doubly nested in the novel within the novel, radiates outward through the book's realistic levels, making them glow. Atwood, as she showed in the futuristic *Handmaid's Tale*, is a dab hand at science fiction. Here, Zycron is out of this world's time but echoes, as the often interrupted narrator explains, ancient earthly history—the Hittites, the Babylonian Code of Hammurabi. Thus the tale extends the novel's general indictment of what (the novel reminds us) Maupassant called *l'histoire, cette vieille dame exaltée et menteuse*—that ancient dame exalted and false. History, embodying "the ill will of the universe," is the ultimate blind assassin, a vast repository of cruelties and annihilations.

5. Interspersed among chapters of the secondary *Blind Assassin* are press clippings, mostly from Toronto newspapers, detailing various Chase-family events: marriages, births, costume balls, speeches. Before the novel has gone twenty pages, three violent events are reported: in 1945, Laura's "accidental death" by automobile; in 1947, Richard Griffen's death, supposedly from a cerebral hemorrhage; in 1975, Aimee Griffen's death, from a broken neck suffered in a fall in her home, at the age of thirty-eight, after a "lengthy struggle with drug and alcohol addiction." These abrupt dispensations of fate create a mystery novel's suspense. The clippings, which arrive from thin air, generally run ahead of Iris's narrative, and we wait for over five hundred pages for her to catch up and explain everything.

Atwood's maze should be allowed its turns and surprises, which unfold cunningly, and at (too much?) leisure. The attentive reader may guess some secrets before they are revealed; other secrets are never revealed completely, as is the way with reality. A nagging sense of gimmickry, amid all these spinning wheels of plot, accompanies our awed and often delighted awareness of Atwood's mastery of period detail, of costume and setting, of landscape and sky, of odor and texture and mood and voice as this dwindling family floats down the twentieth century's dark river. Though North American in its gloomy ambition (saying No in Ontario thunder), the novel has a lively English talkiness and nimble ease with social nuance; the character of Reenie—her dour demotic idiom, her stubborn loyalty to her employers and the lonely Chase sisters—is given heroic lineaments. Two other female characters not yet mentioned make vivid impressions from their vanished time: Richard's sister Winifred Griffen Prior, a breezy young society matron, right-wing and, when Iris falls into her clutches, ruthless; and Callista Fitzsimmons, a left-wing artist who enters the Chases' lives as the sculptress of a World War I memorial that Norval Chase insists on imposing on Port Ticonderoga, though its figure of the Weary Soldier is thought to be too downbeat. She becomes her patron's mistress—taking him to roadhouses racily frequented by American rumrunners laying in supplies of legal Canadian liquor—and she introduces Alex Thomas into the Chase girls' lives. She is a vision of Twenties bohemian chic, striding about and shaking hands like a man, smoking cigarettes in a short black holder:

> She had pierced ears, and her red hair (done with henna, I now realize) was wound around with scarves. She wore flowing robe-like garments in bold swirling prints: fuchsia, heliotrope, and saffron were the names of the colours. She told me these designs were from Paris, and were inspired by White Russian émigrés.

Winifred, who takes over her teen-age sister-in-law's social education, favors green, wears shrimp-colored lipstick, has a low "whisky voice," and extends the lean flapper look into the next decade:

> I watched her move through the rippling pastel space of the Arcadian Court as if gliding, with little nods and tiny calibrated waves of the hand. The air parted before her like long grass; her legs did not appear to be attached to her hips, but directly to her waist; nothing joggled.

These zestful fashion notes are made by an author born in 1939: the bulk of this novel's realistic action occurs in what to her is history. The reader's last surprise is a Hydra-headed page of acknowledgments at the end, listing a formidable number of assistants and researchers, four editors, and three agents: minions of the Toronto-based Atwood industry.

In the book's spacious terrain of incidents, inventions, and moments, three areas stand out as heartfelt: the disconsolate solidarity of two sisters growing up in a big house with a dead mother and a non-communicative father; the wary, at times hostile dialogue of impassioned lovers hemmed into a narrow secret space and prevented from making full self-bestowals; and the brave, humorous tenacity of an elderly woman moving doggedly through her memories, the changing streets of her home town, and a suc-

cession of ironically beautiful, eternally youthful days, toward the imminent end. Atwood is a poet—thirteen collections' worth—as well as a
contriver of fiction, and scarcely a sentence of her quick, dry, yet avid
prose fails to do useful work, adding to a picture that becomes enormous.
Images on the edge of the fantastic vivify spiritual conditions. Returning
from a winter walk, the two girls "held hands and our mittens froze stuck
together, so that when we took them off there were two woollen hands
holding on to each other, empty and blue." Laura, after long absence,
looks translucent to Iris, "as if little spikes of light were being nailed out
through her skin from the inside, as if thorns of light were shooting out
from her in a prickly haze, like a thistle held up to the sun."

Anglophone Canada is blessed to have two such distinguished, large-
minded writers as Atwood and Alice Munro. Munro, though the less
ingenious and wittily cerebral of the two, and less prone to extensive constructions, gives the impression of being the more thoroughly invested in
her creations and the more open, in Chekhovian fashion, to unpredictable character developments. Some of the characters in *The Blind
Assassin*, such as the haunted war veteran and his wistfully fading wife,
have a faint dusty savor of the stockroom; they are animated, as E. M.
Forster said of Dickens's characters, by the author's own vitality, "so that
they borrow his life and appear to lead one of their own." The two Griffen siblings are absolute villains, right out of Dickensian melodrama. And
several minor aspects of the brilliant novel within the novel troubled me.
It is described as having been published in New York City in 1947, to
modest acclaim; yet, hard as it may be to believe now, no commercially
published novel of that time—not Erskine Caldwell, not Steinbeck, not
James M. Cain, not Edmund Wilson's officially banned *Memoirs of Hecate
County* (1946) could have contained the four-letter words with which
Laura Chase's supposed *Blind Assassin* is insouciantly sprinkled. "Nooky"
and "tits and ass" might have got by, and by 1951 Salinger's *The Catcher
in the Rye* was to transcribe "fuck you" from a graffito, but Norman
Mailer's *The Naked and the Dead* had to settle, in 1948, for "fug."
Obscene expressions coolly common now were then, in print, scandalously hot. Also, the little novel shines when cut up and snuggled into
Atwood's larger narrative, but I could not quite believe that it would
attract, by itself, the cult following, of Plathian intensity, ascribed to it:
phrases from it ("All Gods Are Carnivorous"—Laura Chase) appear in
the women's lavatory at the doughnut shop, and Iris cannot visit Laura's
grave without having to clear away flowers.

Atwood is commonly described as a feminist writer, and insofar as she
favors female heroines and shows her women at a societal disadvantage

this seems just; but her viewpoint has not been unilateral or cramped by doctrine. She aspires to see genderized humanity whole. *The Handmaid's Tale*, her portrait of a Taliban-style male tyranny, nevertheless manages to generate some sympathy for the heroine's personal oppressor, the Commander. Like a latter-day, fundamentalist Babbitt, he has a wistful, harried side, looking at moments "*sheepish* . . . the way men used to look." The Handmaid allows, "He is not a monster, I think." The men in *The Blind Assassin*, however, are pretty monstrous. Iris's father returns from the war dehumanized:

> He's in his uniform; his medals are like holes shot in the cloth, through which the dull gleam of his real, metal body can be seen. . . . My father is wearing a black patch over his right eye. His left eye glares balefully. Underneath the patch, not yet revealed, is a web of scarred flesh, his missing eye the spider.

Iris's next protector, her husband, is much worse—so coldly manipulative, so reflexively fascist in his politics, so brutal in his sexual behavior, so devoid of any attractive dimension, that she admits in her memoir, "I've failed to convey Richard, in any rounded sense. He remains a cardboard cutout." She evidently was never, not for a moment, responsive to him sexually, or interested in anything he said while they shared, night after night, "a drink or two before dinner, or three." Her indifference is almost an invitation to abuse. But even the unnamed hero of the novel within the novel, the unsleek, on-the-run chronicler of the planet Zycron, fails to emerge as lovable, though he is loved by the heroine. He feels alien, a more supple specimen of his invented invaders from space, the bare-chested Lizard Men of Xenor, "super-intelligent but super-cruel," with scaly vital parts "enormous . . . but at the same time vulnerable." The other side of the gender divide holds the Peach Women of Aa'A, luscious, compliant dream girls who grow on trees and whose perishability is announced by the appearance of fruit flies over their heads. When his Scheherazade mask slips, he is a male from Mars—curt, surly, ungrateful, remote. Here is a typical lovers' exchange:

> I worry about you, she says. I dream about it. I worry all the time.
> Don't worry, darling, he says. You'll get thin, and then your lovely tits and ass will waste away to nothing. You'll be no good to anybody then.
> She puts her hand up to her cheek as if he's slapped her. I wish you wouldn't talk like that.
> I know you do, he says. Girls with coats like yours do have those wishes.

Well, he is tense, an apologist might argue, and Iris's sexual largesse and his fugitive poverty embarrass him. But the novel is less moving than it might be if we could share the heroine's sense of his charm, his worth. She contemplates the single photograph of them together, taken at a picnic, and claims, "The picture is of happiness, the story not. Happiness is a garden walled with glass: there's no way in or out."

The reader cannot get through the glass wall either, which perhaps suits Atwood's message: the universe bears us ill will; love and justice are both blind idols; God is a ruin. "It's loss and regret and misery and yearning that drive the story forward, along its twisted road." The novel gets us in its grip and then loosens it and leaves us feeling lost. Love, throughout, is in insufficient supply, and when it exists is usually in the wrong place. The cosmos above us and underneath our feet is void; in our poor neediness we are as carnivorous and blind as the gods.

Dangerous into Beautiful

ANIL's GHOST, by Michael Ondaatje. 311 pp. Knopf, 2000.

Those of us who, baffled by some of the gaps and unlikelihoods of the dazzling movie *The English Patient*, turned to the novel, by Michael Ondaatje, for elucidation, discovered that in fact it was the movie that elucidated the novel and was the clearer, more unified work. The burned patient was allowed to elect his death rather than just fade away; Ondaatje's devious spy plot, involving the Italo-Canadian David Caravaggio, was subdued; and the romance between Hana and Kip, the war-worn nurse and the Sikh sapper, yielded pride of place to the pre-war adulterous affair between Count Lazlo de Almásy and Katharine Clifton, a romantic role that elicited from Kristin Scott Thomas one of the more dashing and affecting female screen performances of recent years. The novel's many admirers spoke of its "spooky ennui," its "dreamlike and enigmatic" qualities, its "poetry of smoke and mirrors." Ondaatje is a poet who has produced eleven books of verse since 1967 and one novel in each of the past three decades. Images are what interest him, and his fiction in that sense is already cinematic. In his new novel, *Anil's Ghost*, some of the ruling images are: the physical wounds inflicted by Sri Lankan civil strife as it raged from the mid-1980s to the early 1990s; a skeleton, tricksomely named Sailor, upon whose evidence our heroine, Anil Tissera, a thirty-three-year-old forensic anthropologist sent by the UN to investigate a number of murders on the island, hopes to incriminate the government itself; a man crucified on the tarmac of a highway, nails driven through his palms; swimming, a natural activity in this hot place and one in which Anil famously excelled at the age of sixteen, the fastest female in a two-mile race out to a buoy and back; the painting of the eyes of a statue of Buddha, which the painter must do in a mirror held by an assistant, since the eyes are the fuse that give the statue its life as a holy god. This last image should make an especially haunting cinematic moment, and ends the book with a wide panning shot, through the Buddha's freshly bestowed eyes.

Anil (a man's name, which she purchased from her brother in early adolescence with "one hundred saved rupees, a pen set he had been eyeing for some time, a tin of fifty Gold Leaf cigarettes she had found, and a sexual favour he had demanded") was born in Sri Lanka but for fifteen years has been away, studying medicine in London and then the United States, learning her forensic anthropology in Oklahoma and Arizona. Fond memories of her American years flicker through her head—the gallows humor in the lab, the after-hours bowling and visits to "wild suburban bars and clubs on the outskirts of Tulsa or Norman," the beauty of the desert, her friendship with a woman called Leaf Niedecker, and her affair with a science writer called Cullis Wright. Wright (not quite Mr. Right) is married and, after three years, Anil has left him; during a motel tryst, he tauntingly refused to release her, until she stabbed him in the arm with a little knife used to cut an avocado. After she left, summoning a taxi in the middle of the night, "he lay in the dark room, watching the twitch of his arm muscle flick the knife into movement," testing his powers of stoicism and our suspension of disbelief.

In Sri Lanka, Anil is assigned to work with an archeologist appointed by the government, Sarath Diyasena, "a broad-chested man in his late forties," and a whole new association develops from their joint investigations and travels with Sailor—an association but not physical intimacy or even much of a friendship. Ondaatje is better at showing withheld emotions than declared ones; like Joan Didion, another laconic, lapidary exponent of the higher hugger-mugger, he lets a glancing indirection convey the unseen weight of a cache of sinister secrets. He brings together strangers in fabulous settings—abandoned monasteries and tea plantations, Buddhist caves and hushed morgues—as if these conjunctions themselves constitute significance. Access to the characters' inner lives is restricted to trickles of flashback, and a jumpy multiplicity of chapters and abruptly introduced themes scatters the story to the winds of empty portent. *The English Patient* was praised as "an exquisite ballet that takes place in the dark." *Anil's Ghost* feels overchoreographed. It has a skeleton at its center, and there is something absurdist about the focus.

At one point a tape recorder is hidden in Sailor's ribs, and at another a drunk carries the skeleton in his arms—wouldn't it, un-wired-together, fall apart? Amid so much Ceylonese murder, so much explosion and torture and suicide, will one identification (which comes, at last, almost casually) make a novel's worth of difference? The main movement of the plot, Sarath's dangerous collusion with Anil, occurs beneath a surface etched with exotic detours, and at the end Anil's fate is merely implied. The warmest, most intelligible figure in the book is Sarath's younger brother, Gamini, a youthful carouser who becomes, as do most of his fellow doctors, a martyr to the overwhelming workload the national violence has thrust upon them.

This material is precious to Ondaatje, who, like his heroine, is a North American expatriate from Sri Lanka. Pages of acknowledgments testify to hours spent in researching such technical texts as "Injuries due to Anti-Personnel Landmines in Sri Lanka" by G. Goonetileke, and *Witnesses from the Grave: The Stories Bones Tell* by Christopher Joyce and Eric Stover, and in interviewing doctors and hospital staff in the author's afflicted homeland. For a harrowing two pages, we are inside the mind and loose, loaded shirt of a human bomb about to explode five yards from the Sri Lankan President. The horrific scenes of hospital care and the details of injury and atrocity and torture are the most vivid images the reader carries away, and should do much to make the remote, tangled, and prolonged civil wars in what was once Ceylon vivid to Americans. Ondaatje's willingness—nay, eagerness—to look human suffering in the face is one of his compelling virtues, and gives his dreamlike montages their stern depth. His first novel, an arty yet convincingly gritty meditation on the life of jazz's legendary first great horn-player, Buddy Bolden, was oddly titled *Coming Through Slaughter.* The phrase sets a tone for the fiction that follows, and harks back to *The Collected Works of Billy the Kid,* a 1970 cycle of murderous poems and prose passages centered upon another lower-class wild man from the southern United States.

Slaughter is part of life, and has its gory glamour. But it is not all of life. In *Anil's Ghost,* a dynamited Buddha is patiently reassembled; two estranged brothers are reunited in the civil disorder; a kidnapped doctor and a band of boyish Tamil guerrillas enjoy a birthday swim together; the constructive and merciful forces of the world continue to insist on exerting themselves. Artifice, present on every page of Ondaatje's delicate, mosaic prose, works on the side of the angels; Ananda, the painter of eyes, a despairing drunk whose young wife is among the victims of terrorism, "knew if he did not remain an artificer he would become a demon. The war around him was to do with demons, spectres of retaliation." Two pieces of wordplay in Sinhala, Sri Lanka's main language, frame the contrast. A flight of steps leading to a deserted temple was once marked with a sign that read WARNING: WHEN IT RAINS, THESE STEPS ARE DANGEROUS, but "someone had altered one Sinhala syllable on the sign, so it now read, WARNING: WHEN IT RAINS, THESE STEPS ARE BEAUTIFUL." And in a room in a tenantless plantation house someone has charcoaled on opposite walls the words MAKAMKRUKA and MADANARAGA, the first meaning a demon of agitation and upheaval and the second "with the speed of love."

If the Sri Lanka of this book, created by a writer who left it for England and Canada at the age of eleven, seems more a land of signs and ghosts than of intelligible human relationships, and its civil conflicts less palpable than *The English Patient*'s World War II, the very thinness carries its present truth, of a world being emptied of the traditional satisfactions of peace (family, procreation, veneration), a hyperactive and well-armed world where violence is too easy.

Both Rough and Tender

TRUE HISTORY OF THE KELLY GANG, by Peter Carey. 355 pp. Knopf, 2000.

Peter Carey, an Australian novelist now living in New York City, has turned his great talents to the historical figure of Ned Kelly (1855–80). Robert Hughes, in *The Fatal Shore: The Epic of Australia's Founding*, called Kelly "the last and greatest of the folk-hero bushrangers." Carey's *True History of the Kelly Gang* purports to transcribe documents, "thirteen parcels of stained and dog-eared papers," in which the celebrated outlaw, on the run, set down for the benefit of his daughter (whom he was destined never to see) a heartfelt account and justification of his short and violent life. The ingenuity, empathy, and poetic ear that the novelist brings to his feat of imposture cannot be rated too high; hardly a colloquialism feels turned wrong, hardly a homely phrase feels rote, patronizing, or quaint.

Kelly is allowed, in this work of imagined authorship, to spell correctly, even tricky words like "embarrassment" and "eucalyptus," though his writing preserves certain grammatical and orthographic peculiarities such as "were" for "was" and "v." for "very" and "wd." for "would" and "1/2" for "half," no matter what the context—"1/2 mad," "1/2 way along their length," "broke in 1/2," "her frightened 1/2 brother." He even writes of "a 1/4 horse." Profane language, deplorably common in Ned

Kelly's circle, is fastidiously handled with omitted letters ("b----r"), phonetic initials ("effing," "eff," "ess"), and the comically frequent epithet "adjectival" ("I'm Harry Power you adjectival fool"). The poetry that Carey can coax from this lightly educated ruffian's lightly punctuated prose gratifies us on every page.* A newborn sister viewed by candlelight is captured thus:

> My mother sat on the table holding your Aunty Grace to me. She were a little foal a calf her eyes were wide her newborn skin glistening white and bloody nothing bad had ever touched her.

A few pages farther on, Ned's sullen, strict father, John Kelly, is memorialized:

> We did not talk about our father knowing our very excitement were an insult against his memory and his soul were within each soul of ours and would be for every moment of our lives and there would never be a knot I tied or a rabbit I skun or a horse I rode that I did not see those small eyes watching to see I done it right.

When love comes, belatedly, into Ned's life, his prose rises to the occasion like the Song of Songs:

> Then we was playing what they call the game you never knew so many hooks and buttons and sweet smelling things we took them off her one by one until she lay across her bed there were no sin for so did God make her skin so white her hair as black as night her eyes green and her lips smiling.

That this paragon of family feeling and amorous tenderness is also a killer, horse thief, and rageful rebel against the legal government of Aus-

---

*The distance between Carey's prose and Ned Kelly's can be gauged by a reading of Kelly's so-called Jerilderie Letter, an eighty-three-hundred-word self-justification that the outlaw penned in 1879 in hope of publication in *The Jerilderie Gazette*, and which is preserved, along with his famous armor, in the State Library of Victoria. Writing in a careful, legible hand, Kelly does misspell occasionally—"postrate," "expence," "reconed," "massacreed," "buriel"—and uses numerals rather than spelling the word out, but there is no instance of the fractions that Carey employs so amusingly. Nor does Kelly confuse "was" and "were" as his invented voice consistently does. Kelly's narrative, even when recounting dramatic episodes like the slaying of the three policemen at Stringybark Creek, is confusingly compressed, where the novelist spins the same details into a gripping sequence of cause and effect, with dialogue and feeling and a strong sense of the natural setting. There is no obscenity in the Jerilderie Letter, but there is some impassioned invective, directed mostly at policemen: "a parcel of big ugly fat-necked wombat headed big bellied magpie legged narrow hipped splaw-footed sons of Irish Bailiffs or english landlords which is better known as Officers of Justice or Victorian Police."

tralia is explained, in part, by the fact that he is Irish, heir to the woe the English have visited upon Ireland for centuries and in latter times have inflicted upon the Irish convicts in Great Britain's continental penal colony. The outlaws of the American frontier also had their romantic appeal and symbolized for some the struggle of the poor against the mighty, but the situation was far more distinct in Australia, which England, under a policy of deportation that lasted from 1788 to 1868, used as a dumping ground for political prisoners and dissidents— Luddites, food rioters, Chartists, and, not least, agitators for Irish independence. By the early 1800s, twenty-five percent of the convicts in New South Wales were Irish, hauled there by transport ships that reported a death rate as high as thirty-seven percent. The colony's one convict rebellion—ill organized and quickly quashed—was perpetrated by "the Croppies" (Irish) at Castle Hill, outside Sydney, in 1804. The Irish in America faced prejudice and poverty, to be sure, but the United States had staged a successful rebellion against English rule and was founded on idealistic Enlightenment principles. In Australia, rough Georgian usages prevailed; the English were the warders of the Irish, their floggers, their executioners, and, under the system of convict slavery that existed, their economic masters.

The convict escapee, called a "bolter," became, in the great gray Australian bush, the bandit bushranger—in Hughes's rousing phrases, "that primal figure of popular Australian culture, the bushranger—enemy of flogger, trap [policeman] and magistrate, the poor man's violent friend, the emblem of freedom in a chained society." The American outlaw, as dramatized in a thousand Westerns, tends to be personally rather than politically aggrieved; though he can be an embittered ex–Confederate soldier or a victim of the big cattle or railroad interests, he symbolizes an antisocial extreme of individualism, freedom gone mad. Michael Ondaatje's book on Billy the Kid ends by portraying the outlaw as a juvenile madman. In contrast, the bushranger, according to Hughes, became an agent of national identity: "By taking to the bush, the convict left England and entered Australia. Popular sentiment would praise him for this transvaluation of the landscape . . . for another hundred and fifty years." In a populace seething with Irish grievances old and new, a bushranger like Ned Kelly or his mentor, Harry Power, could long elude the reach of the English authorities.

Kelly tastes the English yoke at the start of the novel. His first memory, acquired at the age of three, is of his mother baking a cake for her incarcerated brother. The child accompanies her to the jail: "We arrived at the Beveridge Police Camp drenched to the bone and doubtless stank of poverty a strong odour about us like wet dogs and for this or other reasons we was excluded from the Sergeant's room." The Sergeant proves to be "a huge red jowled creature the Englishman. . . . I knew not his name only that he were the most powerful man I ever saw and he might destroy my mother if he so desired." The officer tells her that "No cake shall go to the prisoner without me inspecting it 1st," and with his "big soft white" hands, "his fingernails so clean they looked like they was washed in lye," he digs in and breaks the cake into crumbs. At the lockup door, Kelly's mother must kneel in the mud and push the broken cake through a two-inch gap at the bottom:*

> Tears poured down her handsome face as she forced the muddy mess of cake and muslin underneath the door.
>
> She cried I would kill the b-----ds if I were a man God help me. She used many rough expressions I will not write them here. It were eff this and ess that and she would blow their adjectival brains out.

As the boy grows into his teens, brutalizing encounters with the authorities accumulate. The flavor of English-Irish relations is conveyed in a nuance when, greeted "Ned Kelly," our hero responds, "Edward Rogers," and observes Rogers to be "shocked that a mick had used his Christian name." Of another man of English blood, Ben Gould, Kelly writes that "though he were not Irish he carried the same sort of fire I mean that flame the government of England lights in a poor man's guts every time they make him wear the convict irons."

In his criminal adulthood, he believes that the Kelly gang's quasi-military exploits disprove the historic Australian taint: "We had showed the world what convict blood could do. We proved there were no taint we was of true bone blood and beauty born." Kelly becomes, as his mission evolves, a pamphleteer, in a neo-Jeffersonian style: "I wished only to be a citizen I had tried to speak but the mongrels stole my tongue when I asked for justice they gave me none." Yet the fugitive also, by the age of twenty-five, has developed a political realism: he comes to see that

> The bush protected no one. It had been men who protected Harry and it were a man who betrayed him in the end. Harry always knew he must feed the poor he must poddy & flatter them he would be Rob Roy or Robin Hood. . . . The sad truth is the poor people's love is cupboard love and all it took was £500 for the police to be led directly to his secret door.

---

*The image of a "muddy mess" returns, cosmically enlarged, at the end, when the besieged and outgunned hero realizes that all his causes are lost and "now the world was a filthy mire and mess."

Carey is not a pamphleteer; rebellion against an evil system is not the burden of his story, as it is, say, of Styron's *Confessions of Nat Turner* and Kleist's *Michael Kohlhaas*. The injustices and brutalities of nineteenth-century Australia are the novel's background rather than its topic; the foreground is occupied by the psychic evolution of Ned Kelly, from plucky oldest son struggling, with his feisty mother, to lift their fatherless family from the mire of poverty, into an increasingly canny and ambitious bushranger and from that into a dedicated autobiographer. His writing, carried to the verge of his last gun battle, forms his Achilles' heel. The chapters of his "true history" have become so important to him that he is flattered into his doom by a crippled schoolteacher, Thomas Curnow, a hostage who is released by Kelly when he promises to take the manu-script home and work some small improvements on its parsing. Like many another writer, Kelly is betrayed by his editor.

The person who has at last taken the original texts in hand and orga-nized this tidy book, with its scholarly chapter headnotes, is left mysteri-ous. The framework fails to tell us much that we would like to know. It is a matter of historical record that Kelly produced at least one extended document, the Jerilderie Letter; as with many historical novels, Carey's falls afoul of the reader's wish to consult that record unembroidered by fancy. *True History of the Kelly Gang* is most moving and persuasive where, presumably, little record exists—Ned Kelly's childhood and the strong impression his doughty, sexy, hard-riding mother made upon him.

Strong, but mixed. His Oedipal attachment is given a wry qualification on the first page:

> Ellen Quinn were 18 yr. old she were dark haired and slender the pretti-est figure on a horse he [John Kelly] ever saw but your grandma was like a snare laid out by God for Red Kelly. She were a Quinn and the police would never leave the Quinns alone.

The bibulous muddle of Quinn rascality never does permit Ned Kelly to follow his constructive and decent instincts; a series of shiftless lovers takes over the household, and when he is fourteen his mother pays her lover Harry Power fifteen pounds to take Ned on as an apprentice bushranger. There is a Beckett-like comedy to these scenes of the boy's initiation into crime, as Harry Power, "with his little speech about how he were forced to crime I will not trouble you with it here," pulls off one petty holdup after another, receiving only some odd change and disre-spectful banter from the victims. Ned tells his disappointed mother, "The bushranging aint as profitable as you'd expect." It is evidently a fact that Kelly at the height of his dangerous career offered to give himself up, to certain execution, if the authorities would release his mother from a three-year jail sentence. Carey fleshes out this filial love with many glimpses of a cabined intimacy in which "we was grown together like 2 branches of an old wisteria." At the age of eleven he assists his mother in a long night's childbirth; at thirteen, after his father's death frees her to claim some government land—to make what was called a "selection"— he sees her triumphantly mounted:

> She wore no hat but her black hair were braided and her face flushed and her black eyes bright and she sat astride her handsome chestnut mare with her skirts rucked up to show her smooth bare knees. Land ho she cried we got our land.

He writes, "In a settler's hut the smallest flutter of a mother's eyelids are like a tin sheet rattling in the wind."

Carey's conjuration of this maternal immensity, even as childbearing and fickle love wear her down to just her "dear familiar voice both rough and tender at its center," is matched by his evocation of the bush, the wilderness in its grandeur—"looking out across the mighty Great Divide I never seen this country before it were like a fairy story landscape the clear and windy skies was filled with diamonds the jagged black outlines of the ranges were a panorama"—and in its gloom, stained by human violence:

> On the ridges the mountain ash gleamed like saints against the massing clouds but down here the crows & currawongs was gloomy their cries dark with murder . . . on this day of horror when the shadows of the wattle was gluey with men's blood.

Even with an endpaper map, it is not easy to follow the plot through the geography of rugged Victoria Province, as Kelly gallops back and forth between Greta and Benalla and Wangaratta and Bullock Creek and Eleven Mile Creek. There are some intrusions of the supernatural—a banshee, prophetic dreams—that add to our disorientation. A theme of transvestism never quite earns the attention given to it; one edge of this curious territory touches homosexuality in the male world of bushranging and the other the old Irish custom of wearing women's dresses when committing acts of anti-English terrorism. Ned's mother and siblings come through clear enough, but his associates in the gang—Joe Byrne, Steve Hart, and Ned's younger brother Dan—remain a bit dim, for all the pages we spend in their company. Joe is an opium addict with a hare-lip and hard eyes who possibly has a homosexual relationship with the turncoat Aaron Sherritt, whom he assassinates; but the narrator's blind spots keep such interplay in low relief. Carey, with his resolute assumption of Ned's twangy, self-centered voice, has damped·one of his own strengths, a supple Dickensian gift for generating sharp-edged and colorful characters. His proclivity, in recent novels, for nineteenth-century settings is perhaps a way of gaining access to such characters; but they are gaudier by middle-class gaslight than by the smoky campfires of the Kelly gang. He confesses, in a postscript of acknowledgments, to fieldwork in North Eastern Victoria and to feeling, at times, "lost or bewildered or simply forgetful of the facts." Nothing gums up fiction like facts. Reality is rife with cameo characters, beclouded motives, circumstances too hedged and complicated to explain. Several ostensible clippings from Australian newspapers are included toward the end of the novel, along with extensive quotation from Henry V's inspirational "Saint Crispian" speech in Shakespeare's play; such textual nuggets fall like meteors from another planet, and pique our curiosity more than they satisfy it.

Nevertheless, *True History of the Kelly Gang* has a bold, warm generosity to it; Carey animates the hearts and energies of Australians thrust to the bottom of the social pile, and bestows upon his legendary outlaw Everyman's right to have his case heard.

Papery Passions

MY LIFE AS A FAKE, by Peter Carey. 274 pp. Knopf, 2003.

Peter Carey's new novel is so confidently brilliant, so economical yet lively in its writing, so tightly fitted and continuously startling in its plot, that something, we feel, must be wrong with it. It ends in a bit of a rush, and left several questions dangling in this reader's mind. Unfortunately, to spell out those questions would be to betray too much of an intricate fictional construct where little is as it first seems and fantastic developments unfold like scenes on a fragile paper fan. To be brief: the narrator and heroine is Sarah Elizabeth Jane Wode-Douglass, the spinster editor of the London avant-garde journal *The Modern Review*, who in August of 1985 sits down in Berkshire to recount an adventure which befell her thirteen years before, in Malaysia, when an old friend of her family's, the poet and novelist John Slater, twenty years her senior, persuaded her to accompany him to Kuala Lumpur for a week. Thus, she writes, she "entered that maze from which, thirteen years later, I have yet to escape."

At the center of the maze lies an old Australian literary scandal, the

McCorkle hoax, in which, purportedly in 1946, an obscure and, because obscure, bitter poet named Christopher Chubb passed off parodic verses of his own as the work of an authentic poet-of-the-people, the imaginary Bob McCorkle. McCorkle was supposedly dead, leaving his mighty works to be timidly brought forward by his unsophisticated sister. The rough-hewn opus was accepted and published with fanfare by the avant-garde journal *Personae*, whose editor was an enviably rich young Jew who had befriended Chubb, one David Weiss. When, on the strength of one punning line, Weiss was prosecuted for obscenity, Chubb exposed the hoax, humiliating Weiss further; in mid-trial Weiss died violently, apparently a suicide. Readers up on Australian artistic pranks—born, John Slater theorizes, of antipodean cultural insecurity—will recognize the lineaments of the real-life Ern Malley affair, which was perpetrated in 1944, by two skillful anti-modernists, Harold Stewart and James McAuley, victimizing a Melbourne magazine called, like it or not, *Angry Penguins*. The editor-victim was Max Harris, who did not die of the hoax but lived to write, in a recollection years later, "I still believe in Ern Malley. . . . I can still close my eyes and conjure up such a person in our streets." Carey quotes this article of strange faith in an afterword, and it, taken with the epigraph from Mary Shelley's *Frankenstein*, perhaps gives a sufficient hint of the novel's animating premise: Bob McCorkle lives.

A native Australian who has been resident for thirteen years in New York City, Carey has used the distance to contemplate and reshape some notable legends of his homeland: his previous novel, the epic, Booker Prize–winning *True History of the Kelly Gang*, retells the tale of Australia's most famous outlaw, Ned Kelly, in the hero's touchingly and comically ingenuous voice. The novel before that, *Jack Maggs* (1997), takes an Australian element from Dickens's *Great Expectations*, the transported convict Magwitch, and enlarges him into a pattern of adopted Australian nationhood. The Australian connection is understandably Carey's lifeblood, but his inspirations depend, in these instances, on other texts. He imposes personality upon paper rather than deriving, as novelists more customarily do, a paper work from personal sources. Novels of his that draw directly upon Australian reality, like *Bliss* (1981) and *Oscar and Lucinda* (1988), have a hectic fullness and fond cruelty reminiscent of Dawn Powell's novels of her native Ohio. Such brimming, jostling fullness thins a bit as Carey ventures, however nimbly, into the small continent's historic past. *My Life as a Fake* does more than take its start from a historical literary hoax; its central theme and its dominant metaphor are paper, its matted fibers pulled from the papery passions of the writers and editors who are the book's principal characters.

"The tropics are not kind to paper," Christopher Chubb observes, as the ulcerations of Malaysia eat away at his legs. His lowly position of bike-repairer on a "noisy street of Chinese shophouses with the unlikely name of Jalan Campbell" has been achieved at the end of a long chain of heated events having to do with printed words. In his dirty sarong and close-cropped hair, he makes our narrator think, in her first glance, "of both a prisoner and a monk." But, like him, Sarah is obsessed by literary greatness; neither money nor love much matters to her. John Slater has stooped to pursue both, and she rather despises him for it; in his worldliness he weighs upon her as "a large and meaty man." When Chubb calls her on the telephone, he has "a strange, papery voice," and she will end, despite Slater's emphatic advice to the contrary, by listening to that siren voice on and on, transcribing Chubb's tangled tale as he tells it. Chubb is easier to listen to than to conjure as a physical presence: the corners of his lips are shadowy, and his eyelids and hands are both "papery." Even his one suit, old and dirty, comes back from the cleaners paperized: "The process of cleaning had so shocked the fabric that it was now broken on the creases, papery and crumbling in his hand like the wing of a dead butterfly."

And yet books, at least the sacred volume of McCorkle's poetry, have an unexpectedly various, organic quality: "It was much heavier than I had expected, and very strange to touch—a peculiar texture, slightly oily in places, scaly in others." When this book is at last opened and read by our heroine, its contents are visceral: "Whoever he was or had been, Bob McCorkle was indeed a genius. He had ripped up history and nailed it back together with its viscera on the outside, all that glistening green truth showing in the rip marks." The great work puts her in mind of Ezra Pound, the ineffable, unfathomable Pound of the *Cantos*. She triumphantly claims, "This was worth being born for, this single giddy glimpse, on this high place, with the sound of my own blood singing in my ears." A book is not just paper but humanity, flesh and blood, as Chubb finds when he comes to nurse the dying master poet: "To be so intimate with Bob McCorkle was disgusting, as unnatural and frightening as holding one's own vital organs in one's hands."

Along with Pound, Milton, and the fictive Ern Malley, Joseph Conrad haunts *My Life as a Fake*. Teeming, torrid Malaysia is "*Lord Jim* or even worse," and Chubb, who talks "all day and almost half the night," resembles Conrad's dreamily long-winded narrator Marlow. And, indeed, now that the European colonization of Southeast Asia is a bittersweet memory, preserved in the words of Conrad and Orwell and Graham Greene, who will mediate this vast region for the Western imagination but the Australians? They seize it as their nearest escape from insularity, a vacationland and possible sphere of influence. As Malaysia ousts literature at the emotional center of the book, narratives within narratives uncoil. Chubb makes a new friend, the dark, wall-eyed Tamil Kanagaratnam Chomley, called Mulaha, who teaches school and makes a hobby of poisoning. Mulaha's tale of slaughter and vengeance under the Japanese occupation takes us far afield from the theme of literary fakery and from the pursuit of the white whale McCorkle, who has kidnapped what seems to be Chubb's infant daughter, sprung from a resourceful, shape-shifting beauty called, when Chubb first meets her, Noussette Markson.

Carey's prose is up to any task he sets it. His novel has many voices: Sarah's taut, blithe fluency, that of an upper-class intellectual; Slater's bluff, irresistibly British effrontery; Chubb's defensive meander, punctuated with Australian and Malay expressions; Mulaha's elaborate courtesies; a Chinese-Malaysian woman's aggressively fractured English—all without benefit of quotation marks. Usually I simply resent deprivation of these helpful, clarifying indicators, but Carey (who didn't use them in *True History of the Kelly Gang*, either) almost persuades me that human speech, thus unified with the narrative sentences, acquires a certain stateliness, as in the Bible. McCorkle, like the also heroic Ned Kelly, speaks in the near-Biblical accents of a common man whose dignity has been offended:

> I continued strolling until I found a caf run by a little reffo fellow in a dirty singlet. I got him to make me a chicken-and-lettuce sandwich and a chocolate malted milk. At dusk I returned to Birdsing's residence. . . . From the middle of his iris beds I could clearly see the accused through his window. He had a bottle of Victoria Bitter and a meat pie for his dinner. I also live alone and know what it is to spend these hours of solitude when I would rather have a wife and baby and the smell of stew bubbling in the pot. But what civilised person can sit down to a meal like this and not pick up a book to read?

Even Sarah, confessing to lesbianism, warms into an innocent lilt: "I shocked her often but delighted her all the more, and there was no part of her that was secret to me." Chubb, though demoralized by his experience of the word made flesh, brings the odd detail sharply to life:

> [Mulaha] was very fierce, very definite, like someone accustomed to giving orders, also like a small bird with fixed ideas. He took out a pen and rapped McCorkle's nose with it.

Carey's own voice breaks out in arrestingly apt similes: "McCorkle quickly made a bamboo frame on which to lash the naked, mud-caked woman. She was a tiny thing but dense as a bulldog."

Other reviewers of this folded and refolded tale of mental and physical adventure have claimed its message to reside in the fact that everyone depicted is a fake. I don't feel this; the characters are as genuine as their words permit them to be, though all, being characters, are caught up in the business of fiction, which is fakery.

Blood and Paint

THEFT: *A Love Story*, by Peter Carey. 272 pp. Knopf, 2006.

Why, I have sometimes wondered, has the very brilliant, very Australian novelist Peter Carey chosen to live, since 1990, in New York City? Perhaps, I reasoned, it was to gain the exile's significant artistic advantage of enhancement through distance, isolating his homeland from the eroding clutter of ongoing experience. Russia for Nabokov and Ireland for Joyce became luminous reconstructions, shimmering in every lost and recalled detail. But the answer may be simpler than that: if he is anything like the hero and heroine of his newest novel, *Theft: A Love Story*, Carey lives in New York to look at pictures. That he is something like his hero, the passionate but passé painter Michael Boone (or Butcher Bones, as he is called by his mentally handicapped younger brother, Hugh, known to his intimates as Slow Bones), seems beyond dispute: Carey and Michael Boone were born the same year, 1943, and in the same place, Bacchus Marsh, a town northwest of Melbourne. Butcher expresses, with fiction's inevitable hyperbole, an Australian cultural grievance he shares with the love of his life, Marlene Leibovitz, née Cook:

> We had been born walled out from art, had never guessed it might exist, until we slipped beneath the gate or burnt down the porter's house, or jemmied the bathroom window, and then we saw what had been kept from us, in our sleepouts, in our outside dunnies, our drafty beer-hoppy public bars, and then we went half mad with joy.

Half mad, too, with ambition and rapacious dreams of gaining attention and riches in the cultural centers—Paris and London, New York and Tokyo—far from Down Under's sea-girt isolation. Marlene, who comes from a town "not much bigger than Bacchus Marsh" called Benalla, where her mother ran a coffee shop, feels her cultural disadvantage even more viscerally than Butcher: confronting, in New York in 1974, the beautiful, decadent man who will become her husband, she thinks, "We Australians are really shit. We know nothing. We are so bloody ugly."

The beautiful decadent—a fraction more than half mad, as it turns out—is Olivier Leibovitz, the sole child of Jacques Leibovitz, an Estonia-born Cubist contemporary of Picasso. His major canvases, if authentic, are worth millions. Authentication is the powerful right of the possessor of the *droit moral*—"the one," according to Carey, "who gets to say if the work is real or fake." The right forms an entity under French law that can be inherited, just like a share of stock or a Limoges tureen. When Leibovitz died (at the age of eighty-one, in the sight of his five-year-old son, in a sudden collapse at the dinner table, face-down into a Picasso-designed cheese plate, which broke in two) the *droit moral* passed to his widow, Dominique, who swiftly appropriated fifty Liebovitzes, "many of them abandoned or incomplete," which she, in league with her lover and, subsequently, husband, Honoré Le Noël, the painter's attentive chronicler, doctored and signed and authenticated and sold over the years. The pair fell out, however, when Dominique discovered Honoré in bed with the English poet Roger Martin. In the divorce she won most of their remaining loot, but in 1969 she turned up strangled in a Nice (not nice) hotel. Though her ex-husband fought legally for the lucrative *droit moral*, the judge awarded it to Olivier, at this point a seventeen-year-old student at Saint Paul's in London. The boy knew little about art and, further, had come to hate his father's paintings so much that he couldn't bear to touch them; "These great works of art make him ill, really, physically ill," his wife, lovely Marlene from Benalla, confides to Butcher Bones. In New York, as a step in her seduction of Olivier, the young Aussie ignoramus had put herself to school under Milton Hesse, the author of a youthful monograph on Leibovitz, but now, nearing sixty, "in the process of becoming that creature we all fear the most—a bitter old painter whose friends are famous, whose own walls are now stacked with twenty-foot-long canvases no-one wants to buy." Marlene makes herself expert enough to become an authenticator, but it is her drug-raddled, art-averse husband who has the *droit moral*. She wants it, and Butcher Bones, after an impoverishing divorce and four years in jail for trying to steal his own paintings from his ex-wife, wants to recover his vocation and his fame. These two desires, and the mounting desire of the two Australians for each other, drive the plot of *Theft*.

The novel executes the plot conscientiously and cleverly, but seems frequently to look away from it, dwelling instead on softer, warmer issues such as loving Australia even as one leaves it, and the love the two brothers bear each other even as the elder regards the younger, defective one as a burdensome nuisance and is regarded in turn as an inconsiderate exploiter and a grotesque egotist. Butcher narrates most of the chapters, but Hugh breaks in for about a third of them. He is a magnificent creation, from the same family of lovable golems as Bob McCorkle in Carey's preceding novel, *My Life as a Fake*. His lightly punctuated ravings have the ingenuous poetry of the bandit narrator's voice in the novel before that, *True History of the Kelly Gang*. Hugh uses capital letters to fine rhetorical effect, as in this reflection on his brother's sudden enthusiasm for a show in Japan that Marlene promises him:

> It's a big bloody mystery to me that a man so dead set against QUEEN ELIZABETH OF ENGLAND could get himself so rigid about the crown princess of Japan, but soon he had a great STIFFY, THROBBING LIKE A SOCK FULL OF GRASSHOPPERS. And who am I to understand his secret squirming brain?

Even without capitals, Hugh in his spasmodic way can spin an eloquent meditation, as when he starts to brag of his useful services to Butcher's paintings, cutting the canvas along a specific thread and tweezing away the bodies of insects caught in the wet paint:

> I have been informed that there is no-one else on Earth who could part those threads for nine feet without an error. But then again I do not care, all is vanity, and many times I think I am nothing but a big swishing gurgling pumping clock, walking backwards and forwards along the road to Bellingen each day, spring, summer, flies, moths, dragonflies, all fluttering flittering tiny clocks, a mist of clocks, each moment closer to oblivion. Impediments to art. Who will remove us with the tweezers?

Exactly what is medically wrong with Hugh's head is never explained; all we know is that he neglects to wash and shave and likes sitting in a chair beside a sidewalk and was forbidden, by his fierce father, the butcher Blue Bones, to use the slaughtering knife, whereas his brother, "three inches shorter" and an aspiring painter, was allowed to. "I was not born slow, I know it," Hugh mysteriously claims, alluding to a violent upbringing in Bacchus Marsh. When agitated or offended, Hugh breaks the offender's little finger—a trick his older brother taught him—and under stress is aware of "sparks in my long muscles and a click in my head like a catching latch in need of oil." But he does not, like Lennie in Steinbeck's *Of Mice and Men*, squeeze to death what he likes to hold, or, like Benjy in Faulkner's *The Sound and the Fury*, need a constant attendant. He knows enough to spell "Filippino Lippi" and "myxomatosis," and to lyrically express the butcher's creed: "Never did a Bones take life lightly. If it was a fish or an ant, then possibly. But a beast's heart tips the scales at five pounds and no matter how many you slaughter you cannot do it without a thought."

The so-called Butcher, who refused to enter his father's profession, seems a slaughterer as he works, screwing and nailing Sheetrock and plywood onto hitherto ungouged floors, and rhapsodizing over paint like a vampire feasting on a vein:

> The undiluted greens I did not even bother with, but the others I was into like a snouty pig—huge luscious jars, greens so fucking dark, satanic, black holes that could suck your heart out of your chest.*

His every activity is brutal, strenuous, sucky: "I sucked love like phthalo green sucks light," he says of himself with Marlene, and Hugh reports, "Butcher bought a plastic wading pool and then constructed a metal crossbar and once this was bolted to the floor we would drag the canvas like a reluctant beast through a cattle dip of paint." Paint, to which Carey has evidently devoted considerable research, carries, like blood, life's essentials: "Green would not be my only colour, but rather my theorem, my argument, my family tree and soon I had all ten bloody power drills committed in one way or another, mixing my demon dark, with gesso, with safflower oil, kerosene, with cadmium yellow, with red madder; the names are pretty but beside the point—there is no name for either God or light."

At one point, Butcher describes himself as "running parallel with my huge demented brother, linked and mirrored like a double bloody helix." Siamese twins could scarcely be more connected. "If I lost my brother I was lost myself," Hugh writes. Butcher tells us, "He had my brawny sloping shoulder, my lower lip, my hairy back, my peasant calves." The two brothers, one a genius and the other a simpleton, generate in their streams of utterance a kindred prose, hectic and shambling and given to splashes of Biblical echo and pithy colloquialisms like "skip" (trash container), "ute" (utility vehicle), "skint" (broke), "dunny" (toilet), and "batty" (bottom). The DNA weave of fraternal kinship is so cunningly, affectionately worked that it overshadows the love between Butcher and Marlene. She is rendered as brisk, poised, resourceful, ruthless, and opaque in her worldly dealings but in intimacy magically weightless— "light and silky as a wish beside me"—and tender. Better yet, she thinks he is a great painter. She and Butcher, fools for art and for getting their way, are made for each other. We believe him when he avows:

---

*Cf. Bob McCorkle's prose in *My Life as a Fake:* "He had ripped up history and nailed it back together with its viscera on the outside, all that glistening green truth showing in the rip marks."

I was at home with her, with her light, slight body, her bottomless eyes. . . . The shape of her face, the bones, the slightly narrowed eyes, the taut lovely funny upper lip.

For all that, we tend to lose sight of her, amid the frolic of the Boone brothers' giddy, unbuttoned, reminiscing monologues. Peter Carey is a superb writer, whose prose is always vital and who infuses his characters, however eccentric, with a warmth that lets them live in our minds. But *Theft* is not a superb novel; there is something displaced at its heart. Its colorful means keep us at one remove from the central action, which, in retrospect, is perfidious and shocking. The homely idiom of *True History of the Kelly Gang* formed a running plea for the humanity of the murderous hero; here the unbridled egotism of the one narrator and the wistful confusions of the other prevent us from viewing developments clearly. We enter, perhaps, too late, when too much has already happened. We expect Butcher's divorced wife, called only "the plaintiff," and his prepubescent son, Billy, to take a bigger role, to figure in some final reckoning, but they hardly make an appearance. The former household is most vividly, if not very clearly, reflected in Hugh's erratic memories:

> They would not give me the knife and so I went to live with the so-called butcher and the darling boy, peaches in the grass, the sweet rotten aroma of his marriage, I knew it but could not name it as I circled round the boy, trying to keep him safe and then it was me that hurt him.

Hugh, the lumbering epitome of Australian backwardness, runs away with the novel, while the expertly researched and caricatured art scene hangs flat on a well-lit wall.

A Case of Deutschfeindlichkeit; *or, All About Abish*

DOUBLE VISION: *A Self-Portrait*, by Walter Abish. 220 pp. Knopf, 2004.

Walter Abish, though he has published relatively late and little, projects a distinct presence in contemporary letters, in part because of the black triangular eye-patch that distinguishes his photograph on book jackets. His three novels, three collections of short stories, and lone book of poems have won a number of grants and awards (a MacArthur Foundation grant, the PEN / Faulkner Award of 1980) and high praise from such disparate spirits as Harold Bloom, Richard Howard, and Wendy Lesser. A native of Vienna born in 1932, Abish, with his mother and father, fled Hitler's Europe in 1939 for Shanghai, and in 1948 left what was shortly to become Mao's China for Israel. He came to New York City in 1957, and by the early Seventies had begun to publish English-language short stories in cutting-edge magazines like *Confrontation*, *Extensions*, *Seems*, and *Statements: New Fiction*. These stories partook of American absurdism, à la Donald Barthelme, Guy Davenport, Robert Coover: effects of cryptic collage, hostile whimsy, and learned fancy are presented in a clipped, deadpan style. The tone served, it seemed, to insulate the writer from taking the events described too seriously. Popular culture, so amusingly appropriated in post-abstract painting, flavored the writer's vision; images filter in from the glamorous, trendy realms of film, television, photography. The papery realms of news items, maps, and classic literature are shuffled together. For instance, in Abish's first collection, *Minds Meet* (1975), the story "How the Comb Gives a Fresh Meaning to the Hair" conceives of Marcel Proust living in Albuquerque, where retarded children, cabbies, Pueblo Indians, and a young couple called Mr. and Mrs. Dip flit through short paragraphs bearing titles like "Fingernails" and "Marcel's Childhood." In Abish's second collection, *In the Future Perfect* (1977), some stories ("Ardor/Awe/Atrocity" and "In So Many Words") adorn narratives of a flat, American sordidness with alpha-numeric games, Teutonically rigorous in their ingenuity, that addle the reader's brain like the insistent chimes of a canzone or villanelle. What the New World means to Abish is restless sex wed to consumerist luxury—a quest for material perfection summed up in his aphorism "Above all America fears the limp prick."

Abish's first novel, *Alphabetical Africa* (1974), prankishly took the reader on an intricate trek through the alphabet, with the first and last chapters each confined to words beginning with "a" and the chapters in between accumulatingly using and then losing words beginning with the remaining twenty-five letters. Of this fiendishly demanding opus (akin to certain verbal experiments of Raymond Queneau and Georges Perec), Abish helpfully volunteered on the dust jacket:

> Feeling a distrust of the understanding that is intrinsic to any communication, I decided to write a book in which my distrust became a determining factor upon which the flow of the narrative was largely predicated.

Distrust—a dubeity of commitment and avowal—is his ground note. His masterpiece, the novel *How German Is It* (1980), harnessed postmodern verbal foolery to a thriller plot and a passionately distrustful concern with modern Germany. Written before his actual return to the German-speaking lands, which his immediate family (but not all his relatives) escaped in the late Thirties, the novel imagines an Americanized, prospering, democratic Germany sealed over the Nazi past like a deceptively smooth scab. The clean, chic, well-planned new community of Brumholdstein, named after a Heidegger-like philosopher called Ernst Brumhold, has been erected on the bulldozed site of a concentration camp in the town, formerly known as Durst. At one point, symbolically enough, a broken sewage pipe uncovers a mass grave, which emits a terrible stench and is finally cleared away by the federal government agency that deals with such remnants of the unsavory past. The characters, most of them too young to have participated in the Nazi regime, are nevertheless not at ease. The husbands are compulsively unfaithful and the women unnervingly compliant. The old class distinctions and snobberies still hold, beneath the surface of democracy. Urban terrorist groups recruited from the middle class nag the society with murders and explosions, and "Germany . . . its history, its achievements, its literature, its amazing economic recovery," has something inexpungeably suspect about it. Its very glossiness and timetable order and even the beauty of the summer in which most of the action takes place seem to mask something sinister.

The novel's main characters, the brothers Helmuth and Ulrich Hargenau, have many reasons for happiness, as a successful architect and novelist respectively. Further, they are (apparently) the sons of an anti-Nazi martyr; their father, Ulrich von Hargenau, participated in the 1944 plot to assassinate Hitler and was shot by a firing squad. But Helmuth, so handsome and efficient, has a manicky self-careless streak that produces too many affairs, too many tactless allusions to the Nazi past of respectable families, and too deep an association with a band of motorcycle-riding thugs. Ulrich, the writer, is more recessive and kindly, but he nurses a futile love for his wife, Paula, a terrorist whom he saved from prison by testifying against the eight other members of her gang. He receives threats in the mail and has gingerly returned to Germany after six months in France. A great range of plausible contemporary Germans—the plump, nimble-minded mayor of Brumholdstein; his lean and faithless wife, Vin; Helmuth's perfect wife, Maria, whom he abandons; their chatty and invincibly curious ten-year-old daughter, Gisela, named after her mother's close friend, who is half of a swish young couple identified only as Gisela and Egon; the attractive, insatiably intrusive photographer Rita Tropf-Ulmwehrt; the waiter Franz Metz, the Hargenaus' former servant and a traumatized Wehrmacht veteran who is building a matchstick model of the vanished concentration camp at Durst; his loutish son, Obbie; the not-so-prim unmarried schoolteacher Anna

Heller; the morose and churlish bookseller Jonke; and a number of others, all rooted in a highly circumstantial small-city landscape. Though the free-and-easy sexual interchanges seem borrowed from the swinging Manhattan of the Sixties and Seventies, and the mouth-wateringly specific German pastries may owe something to Abish's Viennese boyhood, the feat of imagination makes a persuasive match for the realistically transcribed Germanys of, say, Heinrich Böll and Martin Walser. The novel disdains to tie up all of its many threads, and has some of the improvisatory shagginess of Abish's shaggy-dog short stories, but it is given coherence and force by a real animus and a real question: How could the Germans have committed these unspeakable acts? How peculiarly German was the Holocaust?

Abish has been rather quiet in the quarter-century since this compelling, prize-winning, fully stocked novel: in 1990 he published a third short-story collection, *99: The New Meaning* (five collagist stories, in a limited edition), and in 1993 a short novel, *Eclipse Fever*, set mostly in Mexico, with Mexican characters. Now he has issued a wry, contemplative, and oblique experiment in autobiography, *Double Vision: A Self-Portrait*. In it, chapters of reminiscence headed "The Writer-To-Be" alternate with diaristic jottings from his contemporary self, "The Writer." He sketches his life as a boy in Austria and a young man in China but says little about his adult years in New York, or exactly when he arrived, or how he supported himself. He does not explain his eye-patch, leaving us to guess that it suppresses a painful double vision. The full-fledged "Writer" is mostly seen in terms of his visits, in the wake of *How German Is It*, to Germany and Europe. His parentage and early years are quickly disposed of, in a nervous style of existential notation:

> The oppressiveness of good manners. The emotional repression. My discontent. That's why my head is shaped the way it is. That's why my eyes are blue. We are talking about genes. About inherited traits. The way I smile— reluctantly . . . Is there no freedom at all from the family? The efficiently cool and remote mother and the energetic businessman father. Their distinctly separate worlds, their separate concerns collide uneasily in my brain.

He alludes, a few pages on, to his "incessant trigeminal headaches," as if his parents are still colliding in his head. They wound up, he reveals late in *Double Vision*, in Saint Petersburg, Florida—survivors who had the wit and the wherewithal to maneuver themselves and their only child out of Hitler's reach. Their virtues are acknowledged but a bit distantly. Abish alludes to rebellious behavior on his part without being specific; he confides that he provided his parents "far too little satisfaction, far too little pleasure," and that he suspected his mother of not finding her role "in any way pleasing or fulfilling." His father, he feels, loved him whole-heartedly, and, a perfume manufacturer, brought to the house the enchantment of "those tiny, elegantly shaped bottles snugly encased in their pale yellow boxes bearing the name Molinard as well as their poetic fragrances: Ambre, Iles d'Or, Habitana, Fleurettes, Orval. Whenever my father would pull out his handkerchief, the entire room, within seconds, was filled with the delicate fragrance of those evocative names."

So it was an unsatisfactory, scented childhood idyll that ended when, in March of 1938, Nazi Germany annexed Austria. Abish's recollections, diffident to this point, take on vigor:

> Soon after, the streets of Vienna took on the appearance of a staged spectacle—one of those beloved operettas that skirt reality—for the frenzied, flag-waving Viennese did not merely proclaim their solidarity with Germany and embrace their Austrian-born Hitler; rather, they embraced the Anschluss, seizing the opportunity to display those tantalizing new emblems, the paraphernalia of Nazism, and in a state of exuberance perform a celebratory dance.... A breathless encounter, as the Viennese—whose dialect, after all, is replete with double meanings—absorbed with a shudder of ecstasy the aesthetics of the swastika.

An oft-told historical tale takes on freshness through these six-year-old eyes. Abish's mother was thoroughly assimilated and had "sought, if not to disassociate, then to distance herself from the Jewish ceremonies," while the father's attempt to communicate their Jewishness to his son remained "ill defined" and "perplexing." The inevitable persecutions descended rather lightly at first: the day after Kristallnacht, Abish's father reported to work as usual. When arrested, he was vouched for by a businessman who owed him money and was released. The SA men who evicted them from their apartment were courteous and low-key, and Abish's mother packed with her usual calm and efficiency. Abish was permitted to carry away two small toys. That the Gentile society approvingly stood by while, elsewhere in Vienna, Jews were made, before approving onlookers, to scrub the sidewalk with toothbrushes is no mystery:

> I suspect the eventuality of a dividend, a payoff, as a result of this state-generated debasement wasn't lost on the gleeful spectators. How could the trickle-down rewards—in the form of academic advancement, the elimination of business competition, the forced sale of businesses, not to mention the vacated apartments, the auctions of the possessions the Viennese Jews were forced to leave behind—not animate the society?

Small wonder that a child exposed to such a turn of events would continue to distrust appearances, however apparently prosperous and benign. In *How German Is It*, the mayor of Brumholdstein, commenting upon a carpet that a guest has admired, idly brags, "My father acquired it before the war. Lots of things were quite reasonable before the war, I'm told." The carpet covers an abyss.

When, in the wake of publishing *How German Is It*, Abish meets real Germans and travels to Germany, distrust is the mood on both sides. *Double Vision* describes how, in New York, he meets, through friends, a visiting chemical-company executive, "the fixed smile on his sharp-featured face like an unaccustomed adornment," who soon tells him that Abish's novel infuriated him, exclaiming, "Alone, the incorrectly spelled German words!" He is interviewed by a female German, "trim, impeccably dressed, not a blond hair out of place," who, unable to get him to admit that his novel was "the Jew's revenge," has trouble finishing her article because, she says, "I suspect that deep inside your gut you harbor altogether different thoughts and emotions." Driven by another journalist from Amsterdam into Germany for the first time, Abish distrusts the scenery along the Rhine: "Everything on view seemed slightly exaggerated . . . almost staged—like a reproduction of the original." He asks himself, "At what stage in the reconstruction of Germany, at what point in this tremendous effort will the turbulent past fade, enabling the visitor to Germany to once again view the society with that credulous gaze of a nineteenth-century traveller?" Never, for this visitor. He sees tidy houses out of *How German Is It*, "so orderly, so clean, so characteristically German," though the border guard is less neatly dressed than he would have expected. The "Wagnerian Germany" of craggy castles and dark woods that his host appears to want to present fails to register with Abish, who discovers that the Pentax with which he had been "nailing [his] first impressions of Germany" was empty of film.

On a later excursion, as he employs his rusty German in dialogue with fellow-writers and cultural operatives, the empty-camera feeling persists. He doesn't like his editor, Gunther Maschke, a former left-winger turned right, and rejects the hotel that has been chosen for him; at a party he counterattacks the somewhat anti-Semitic prattle of an actor who petulantly asks, "Must we still feel guilt? Hasn't the time come when we are able to speak our minds?" Not infrequently the guest writer provokes "that by now familiar wisp of a smile I've noted on faces whenever a ticklish subject is brought up." Rarely does he hear "a welcome, unequivocal voice of condemnation," as he does from a schoolteacher leading his students through the camp at Dachau: "*Das war eine Todesfabrik!*—That was a death factory!" But at Dachau, too, Abish feels an "inexplicable detach-ment," a failure to feel, "even though, for all I knew, members of my own family were entombed here." He can't shake what others criticize as the "tendency to overinterpret everything German through the limited prism of the Hitler years." Waking each day to songbirds, he wonders if the concentration-camp inmates heard them, and finds, in the memoir of a Buchenwald inmate, that "the acrid, poisonous stench of burning corpses drove the birds away."

The two extended sections devoted to his years in China and in Israel have their interest, of course, as his evolving awareness prepares for his future as a writer. In China, at age sixteen, he enters "a mazelike building in which Chinese jugglers, puppeteers, actors, magicians, singsong girls, and storytellers in long gowns and carrying folding fans entertained the audience," and realizes he is the only non-Chinese in the crowd. His friends show no curiosity about this place of entertainment, and China itself, the vast country that is their host, is ignored in their school text-books. Shortly before Abish's departure, as the approach of Communist armies emboldens young Chinese, he is attacked on the street and chased by three of them. "I couldn't even bring myself to mention the assault to anyone—suddenly, to discover myself to be the enemy."

Several years earlier, when American servicemen ousted Shanghai's Japanese occupiers, he was enchanted by all things American—the brand names, the movies, the Hit Parade. American sailors, "mostly good natured if somewhat bored, still possessed the attractive shine of all things American." But they, too, suffered from a "total lack of curiosity." The writer-to-be is by nature curious, and in Israel he continues his self-education, both romantic and literary. He gets a part-time job with the USIA and prepares for a career as an architect. He finds, after many false starts, that he can read Proust with pleasure. He has a serious affair, and he gets married, but just so his bride, Bilha, can be spared the obligatory year's military service. The formality over, they soon divorce, and yet he visits her at her residence, "determined that nothing . . . spark a Proust-ian recollection." There is more here than is being said, and the Israel chapter is the vaguest and least memorable. His heart, at least for the length of this autobiography, is engaged by Germany, that deadly and dislikable land. In describing the Sabras, the native-born Israelis, whose famous directness and candor seem to him simply discourtesy, he cannot resist adding, "Ironically, it was in Germany, in the eighties—the last place in the world that I expected to be reminded of Israel—that I encountered a similar bluntness and lack of tact."

In 1987, Abish spent six months in Berlin, as a guest of the German

Academy Exchange Service. He confides, "I travelled blindly to the walled-in city, quite unprepared to dismantle the wall I had erected within myself." This final installment of "The Writer" chapters bristles with small, disagreeable encounters:

> A Berlin bus driver wordlessly indicated his displeasure with the way I positioned my ticket on the smallish metal tray by pointedly straightening it before he stamped it—all the while glaring furiously at me. What German lesson was being communicated?

When, pragmatically, he crosses a deserted street against the light, a motorist stops to upbraid him loudly; Abish, adopting local manners, shouts back, "What business is it of yours?" and is told, in an aggrieved tone, "You're wearing an eye patch . . . your eyesight is impaired. You might get hurt!" He finds that artists, critics, and writers he encounters "scarcely differ from the ones I know in New York" yet seem "weighed down by an incommunicable mental fatigue." The thriving, pre-Hitler German Jewish community has left in contemporary Germans "a diffuse and attenuated memory," although mansions and department stores once owned by Jews still stand. At parties he feels approached as a curiosity, "a Jew at the party," and a fellow-writer, Klaus Stiller, "cannot refer to Jews without an involuntary twinkle in his eyes. I can only conclude that for many people Jews must still be such an oddity." Though warned, "Don't go that way. It'll destroy you," Abish in Berlin accumulates a stack of books on Germany and genocide, including diaries kept during the Nazi era, which are generally devoid of any reference to the Jews and their doom. He exclaims of a Turkish waitress, "Her foreignness was such a welcome sight," and takes satisfaction in learning from an Ethiopian male nurse that among his patients "a majority of the elderly daydream of the Hitler days and still cast blame on the Jews for everything that has transpired." He observes police attacking protesters "with methodical rage." He notes how on the Berlin streets "the young appear laid-back," whereas a two-hour photographic session in his apartment becomes "an accurate assessment of my uptightness."

An American visitor to Germany does not have to be Jewish to feel there a *frisson*, a shudder of fascination at the abyss beneath the carpet. I was raised among the hard-working, pork-loving, *Heimat*-centered Pennsylvania Germans of eastern Pennsylvania and am altogether German on the maternal side of my ethnic heritage; visiting Germany, I expect to feel at home, and do, within the tourist's cosseted microcosm of hotel courtesy and efficiency, youthful and conscientious guides, and fluently spoken English. Yet I am wary, on this ground where a lethal madness ruled and commanded loyalty to the end. The extensive reconstructions in reunified Berlin have an uncanny suggestion of stating again, in boastfully huge Kaiseresque terms, an aesthetic that didn't bode well the first time. The tourist, between visits to Frederick the Great's elegant retreat Sans Souci and the world-class painterly treasures of the Gemäldegalerie, gets out of the bus and stands on the huge vacant lot, the Schlossplatz, where the palace of the Hohenzollerns, after extensive war damage in 1944–45, was razed by Walter Ulbricht's German Democratic Republic in 1950. Now that free-world wealth again controls all of Berlin, there is talk of rebuilding the *Schloss*—as the great Lutheran *Dom* nearby has been—though the expense will be titanic. Standing on the dusty Schlossplatz, beside the dilapidating Palast der Republik that the Communists erected, the tourist gazes across the Great Elector's Lustgarten at a building that looks familiar from old newsreels. It is the low white Altes Museum from 1830, with its eighteen Ionic columns and tasteful small rotunda, a masterpiece of the architect Karl Friedrich Schinkel. From a platform in front of it, Hitler used to address rallies massed on the acreage of the Lustgarten, cleared of flowers by the Nazis in 1935. For a moment the tourist feels, with a dark thrill, part of that saluting sea, with its huge throaty unison of "Heil Hitler"s. Schinkel's neoclassic architecture has a certain serene iciness, and as central Berlin fills in with reconstructions and new structures, one can't but think of the megalomaniacal architectural dreams that Albert Speer and his Führer projected for the capital of the thousand-year Third Reich.

Still, sixty years have passed; the surviving participants of World War II are fewer each year, and Germany is populated by people who had nothing to do with the Nazi regime. Millions of them are not even ethnically German. At times Abish, like Fassbinder in some of his films, implies something disgusting and scandalous in Germany's reconstituting itself as a viable capitalist democracy. Some young Germans have felt this also; the Baader-Mainhof gang, from an angle of leftist indignation, rephrased the insatiable shrill rage of Hitler and Goebbels. Whence this love of extremes, this intemperance? Thomas Mann, in a 1904 short story, "At the Prophet's," says of a young Nietzschean orator, "A fevered and frightfully irritable ego here expanded itself." The German tribes did not succumb to the Roman Empire, but remained outside its laws, and for all the achievements and decorum of contemporary Germans, a potential for lawlessness—for going beyond the tamely decent and workable—still hangs in the air. In *How German Is It*, Helmuth Hargenau, the model German gone awry, speaks eloquently of the link between

the passion for abstract thought that the philosopher Brumhold exemplified and the same philosopher's passion for "the thick forest, his beloved
forest, a forest . . . that is and remains spiritually close to us . . . the German forest in which dwells our spirit, our ideals, our cultural past, our
poetry, our truth." Earlier in the novel, Abish mentions "the innate German upper- and upper-middle-class instinct to combine what is essentially 'perfection' with the 'menacing.' " In registering the menace, and
reifying it with anecdotes and fiction, Abish is, in his own voice, giving
the news. One must accept this news with the reservation that, as history
has shown more than once, blanket distrust of any ethnic group is a
seedbed for massacre.

The Story of Himself

YOUTH: *Scenes from Provincial Life II*, by J. M. Coetzee. 169 pp. Viking, 2002.

The autobiographical impulse seizes some novelists, such as Henry
James, at the end of their creative labors; they relax at last from the trouble of disguise and manipulation and tell it like it was, as it is remembered, much as the host of a generous feast avails himself of his guests'
garnered good will by sleepily rambling on about himself. Others, like
Philip Roth in *The Facts*, take a mid-career opportunity to establish, amid
a dazzling crowd of fictions, some baseline data. And an increasing number of writers begin, as did Frank Conroy in *Stop-Time*, with autobiography, as if to get themselves out of the way before they settle to business.
J. M. Coetzee, the inventive, austere, and penetrating South African novelist and critic, has published, in his early sixties, the second installment
of what seems to be an ongoing memoirist project: *Youth: Scenes from
Provincial Life II*.

Its predecessor, *Boyhood: Scenes from Provincial Life*, appeared five years
ago, and perhaps better earned its subtitle: the hero, named John (as in
John Michael Coetzee) and rendered in the third person and the present
tense, is indeed a provincial boy, living, until a move late in the book, in a
bleak, new, but dusty housing estate outside the town of Worcester,
north of Cape Town. Dates and ages are left vague, but he seems about
eight and in what I took to be third grade when we meet him, and is thirteen when we leave him, back in Cape Town, where he and his family—
father, mother, younger brother—came from. "Scenes," rather than a
continuous history, are what we get, as the book's partial publication in

magazines like *Granta* and *Artes* suggests. The longest, least glum chapter depicts the family farm, which is run by John's father's brother Son and bears the pretty Afrikaans name Voëlfontein—"Bird-fountain." Excellent and deeply felt as the evocation is, it is something of what we expect from a memoir of a white southern African's childhood, as are Coetzee's accounts of his harsh schooling and his intimations of a precarious and unfair racial situation. Less usual is the dour flavor of the child's complex self-awareness. He has a "sense of himself as prince of the house" and dislikes both his parents for it—his father for failing to exert a father's leadership in the household, and his mother for loving him too much, making him fight for independence from her and turning him into "an irascible despot" at home and a physically timid overachiever at school. Coetzee declares, "Nothing he experiences in Worcester, at home or at school, leads him to think that childhood is anything but a time of gritting the teeth and enduring."

As John turns thirteen, he becomes "surly, scowling, dark. He does not like this new, ugly self, he wants to be drawn out of it, but that is something he cannot do by himself." His brilliance at school gives him little pleasure; it just breaks life into a relentless series of tests. (The test, which we pass or fail, is a recurring image in Coetzee.) John imagines no happy future that his cleverness may win for him, though he holds to "the idea of being a great man" and the conviction that "he is different, special." His state of mind, young as he is, is wintry: "His heart is old, it is dark and hard, a heart of stone." Writing tame exercises for his English class, he thinks:

> What he would write if he could . . . would be something darker, something that, once it began to flow from his pen, would spread across the page out of control, like spilt ink. Like spilt ink, like shadows racing across the face of still water, like lightning crackling across the sky.

This exactly captures the Gothic quality of an early Coetzee novel such as *In the Heart of the Country;* but John has years to wait till the writing of books. *Boyhood* ends with him at the funeral of his Aunt Annie, a schoolteacher who once said to him, "So young and yet you know so much. How are you ever going to keep it all in your head?" Aunt Annie had devoted herself to translating and publishing a religious book by her missionary father, a book that winds up as copies, bound and unbound, stacked in a closet. When the boy asks where the books have gone, no one knows: "He alone is left to do the thinking. How will he keep them all in his head, all the books, all the people, all the stories?"

Youth picks up John's story six years later, when he is nineteen and living alone in Cape Town, a university student surviving on academic odd jobs, and ends when he is twenty-four, residing in London as a friendless computer programmer and a frustrated poet. The second volume lacks the bucolic bright spots and familial furies of *Boyhood* but has an overriding, suspenseful issue: when and how will our hero find his vocation, evident to us readers if not yet to him, as a world-class novelist? In his account he is almost uniformly listless and miserable: "Misery is his element. He is at home in misery like a fish in water. If misery were to be abolished, he would not know what to do with himself." To the consoling argument that "misery is a school for the soul" and a necessary immersion for the would-be artist he counters, "Misery does not feel like a purifying bath. On the contrary, it feels like a pool of dirty water. From each new bout of misery he emerges not brighter and stronger but duller and flabbier."

At the age of twenty, in the wake of the 1960 Sharpeville Massacre and the formidable black reaction, as an increasingly repressive white government calls for more conscripts in its National Defence Force, he leaves South Africa for London, without completing his university degree. In London, he feels unwelcome, "a graceless colonial . . . and a Boer to boot." He is sex-starved. The beautiful English women he spies on in the streets, not to mention the "tall, honey-skinned Swedes" and the "almond-eyed and petite" Italians, seem impossible to meet, let alone impress; the lower-class English women among whom he works, though they have "a cosy sensuality . . . the sensuality of animals brought up together in the same steamy den," are even hard to understand, with their "triphthongs and glottal stops." The few conquests he does make, including a plump seventeen-year-old au pair from Austria, feel like mistakes. His only comfortable liaison is with an old South African girlfriend who arrives in London, sets herself up as a nightclub waitress, and with her fast and cheery ways has soon left him behind in the acclimation race. Meanwhile, his literary aspirations dwindle to picking through the literary magazines at Foyles and Dillons, wondering whether he should switch from poetry to prose and should imitate Henry James or D. H. Lawrence, and sitting in the Reading Room of the British Museum plowing through the many lesser novels of Ford Madox Ford, toward completion of a Master's degree *in absentia* from the University of Cape Town.

An optical defect, as it were, of autobiographical writing is that the narrator, relating the feelings and events that he has endured, appears more passive than he or she could have been; he is modestly blind to the impact he made on others, his own initiatives and aggression. Coetzee portrays himself as a lonely dunce at love, mooning over exotic movie stars like Monica Vitti and Anna Karina, yet by his own desultory count was a considerable seducer. At the tender age of nineteen, in Cape Town, he acquired a thirty-year-old live-in mistress, an attractive and somewhat disturbed nurse who showed him how sex, for a man, brings with it the whole woman, with her possibly inconvenient troubles, agenda, and ego. He acquired skill at dodging the consequences of involvements: still in Cape Town, he got a girl pregnant and let her cope with all the details of the abortion, and in London he allowed his docile little Austrian, after their last night together, to ease herself out the door in demure silence while he feigned sleep.

He writes of "London, the city on whose grim cogs he is being broken," while recording impressive survival skills. Jobless, he answers an IBM ad for computer programmers ("He has heard of computer programming but has no clear idea of what it is") and, after taking an IQ test ("He has always enjoyed IQ tests, always done well at them"), becomes a trainee and then a programmer. How many aspirants to literary greatness have enough incidental mathematical ability to succeed as computer programmers? True, Coetzee portrays the job as dreary, but he performs creditably; when he quits, after more than a year, to concentrate on becoming a poet, IBM resists his departure. Later, when his work permit needs renewal, he lands another computer job, in the Berkshire offices of International Computers, and rises to the point of installing a program of his devising in the Atlas computer "housed at the Ministry of Defence's atomic weapons research station outside Aldermaston." Though his Cold War sympathies are pro-Russian, he finds himself part of the free-world military effort, and in that uncomfortable position—"a twenty-four-year-old computer programmer in a world in which there are no thirty-year-old computer programmers," a would-be poet "well aware that his failure as a writer and his failure as a lover are so closely parallel that they might as well be the same thing"—his chronicler leaves him.

We know from other sources that Coetzee will go on to America, where he will earn a doctorate in linguistics at the University of Texas; the sequel concerning this step promises some relief from the climate of failure and balked ambition that pervades *Youth*.* Toward its end, there are a few hopeful developments: the hero acquires spectacles for his deteriorating eyesight; he discovers the highly congenial novels of Samuel

---

*A climate transferred to the allegorical landscape of his early novel *Waiting for the Barbarians*, whose protagonist, the elderly Magistrate, has a young man's air of being adrift, self-critical and self-indulgent in equal portions. The harrowing tortures that the shadowy Empire inflicts upon him might be construed as cousin to the torments of employment with the imperial International Business Machines.

Beckett; he generates, in recreational computer time, out of words from Pablo Neruda, some "pseudo-poems" that are published in a Cape Town magazine and make a small local sensation. He begins to realize that South Africa, "a wound within him," must be his subject. The eventual triple winner of the CNA Prize, South Africa's premier literary award, and double winner of the Booker Prize is struggling to be born. In the meantime, these recollections of a stymied, melancholy Afrikaner in London are more entertaining than is easily explained. We like the hero, for all his fecklessness and dogged self-denigration, much as we like the raving heroes of Hamsun's *Hunger* and Dostoevsky's *Notes from Underground:* naked honesty engages us. The brainy, taut prose speeds us along. True, vivifying details are sparse. A young colonial seeking a foothold in London is also the topic of V. S. Naipaul's most recent novel, *Half a Life*, and fiction's leeway allows him a satiric animation and a colorful particularity that are rare in *Youth*. There is nothing in the memoir, for example, like the comic dialogue of the West Indian hero's affair with his Panamanian mentor's coarse but luscious girlfriend, June, who works behind a perfume counter and exudes its aura along with blunt sexual advice, or of the lefter-than-thou snobbery of well-heeled bohemia. Coetzee's project does not permit him to linger at such scenes of metropolitan life; his characters are all incidental to "the story of his life that he tells himself," a concept expressed in *Boyhood* as "the only story he will admit, the story of himself." His setbacks and humiliations merely graze the inner core of self-regard where, in "depths of coldness, callousness, caddishness," he circles the riddle of becoming an artist: "Does giving rein to his penchants, his vices, and then afterwards gnawing at himself, as he is doing now, help to qualify him as an artist? He cannot, at this moment, see how."

And it cannot be easy, decades later, to take an accurate but aloof view of the youth one was. Coetzee's delicate self-mockery threatens to become condescending, and *Youth*'s repeated rhetorical questions verge on burlesque. "Will our solitariness lift, or is the life of the mind its own reward? . . . Does his first venture into prose herald a change of direction in his life? Is he about to renounce poetry? . . . Must he become miserable again in order to write?" Yet the suspense attached to this stalled life is real, at least for any reader who has himself sought to find his or her voice and material amid the crosscurrents of late modernism. Coetzee, with his unusual intelligence and deliberation, confronted problems many a writer, more ebulliently full of himself, rushes past without seeing. His eventual path, via Beckett and the purity of mathematics, was a kind of minimalism, a concision coaxed from what he felt as his innate coldness. "If he were a warmer person he would no doubt find it all easier: life, love, poetry. But warmth is not in his nature," he concludes. While he was still in Cape Town, his taste moved from Hopkins and Keats and Shakespeare to Pope, "the cruel precision of his phrasing," and, even better because crueller, Swift; he feels "fully in accord" with Pound's and Eliot's attempts to bring into English "the astringency of the French." In one of his courteous, admirably thorough reviews, Coetzee remarks that Doris Lessing "prunes too lightly" to be a great stylist, and his own paragraphs and plots feel sharply pruned, at times as brutally disciplined as Parisian lime trees. The academic hero of his novel *Disgrace*, hearing an African talk orotundly, reflects:

> The language he draws on with such aplomb is, if he only knew it, tired, friable, eaten from the inside as if by termites. Only the monosyllables can still be relied on, and not even all of them.

A delectable tension exists in this writer between a youthful wariness of tired, termite-ridden words and a childish desire to spill ink, out of control, and unload what is in his head. Even the low-energy years described in *Youth* take on, in the clipped telling, a curious electricity; its astringent pages leave us strangely keen to read on.

Pre-"Gay" Gray

THE MASTER, by Colm Tóibín. 339 pp. Scribner, 2004.

Fiction about actual historical persons, so intrinsically conflicted and impure, feels to be part of postmodernism's rampant eclecticism. True, examples exist before the twentieth century, in, say, Tolstoy's depiction of Napoleon and the Russian general Kutuzov in *War and Peace*, and in the portraits of the poet Petronius, the emperor Nero, and the saint Peter in Sienkiewicz's *Quo Vadis?* But until truth became thoroughly relative, and image seized priority over fact, and the historical past became an attic full of potentially entertaining trinkets, the famous dead were allowed to rest upon the record they left in their documents and documented deeds, in their letters and the accounts of their contemporaries. What could not be known was left unsaid. Henry James was especially fierce in guarding the sacred domain of fiction against profanation by the ungainly chimeras of historical fiction, which he resoundingly labelled "humbug." It is ironical, then, that he has himself become the hero of a historical novel, called, rather inevitably, *The Master*, by the gifted Irish writer Colm Tóibín.

The novel opens in January of 1895, in London, with the notorious failure of James's play *Guy Domville;* the première performance ended with the distinguished author's being showered with jeers from the exasperated audience as he mistakenly ventured onstage for a curtain call. The novel closes in October of 1899, as James, now established in the cozy safety of his newly purchased house, Lamb House, in the East Sussex borough of Rye, says goodbye to his brother William, William's wife, Alice, and their daughter, Peggy, after a long visit, and returns with satisfaction to sole possession of his quiet rooms. The years 1895–1901 were titled, in the fourth volume of Leon Edel's five-volume biography of James, *The Treacherous Years,* and as Tóibín imagines them they are not free of incident, though the public humiliation of the *Guy Domville* debacle, at their outset, is the most dramatic event. James visits and is visited; he remembers and ruminates. He reflects back upon his rootless childhood in Europe, his dear but vague mother, his less vague Aunt Kate, his vigorous, idealistic, and somewhat demented father; scenes of his youth include discovering Hawthorne's *Scarlet Letter* and witnessing the agony of his younger brother Wilky from the wounds of a civil war that Henry and his older brother, William, evaded within the scholarly shelter of Harvard. Two women important in his life, his cousin Minny Temple and his fellow-author Constance Fenimore Woolson, are mournfully, fondly conjured up, in flashbacks tinged with suggestions of their betrayal by James, who, with the selfishness of a committed artist and the obliviousness of a closeted homosexual, ignored their appeals for rescue. Two young men, the Irish manservant Tom Hammond and the Norwegian-American sculptor Hendrik Andersen, catch Henry's eye and occupy his daydreams, but nothing overt takes place, beyond some freighted gazing and hugging. The plots of his works during this period (summarized by Edel as dealing with "children and ghosts—with the phantasmagoric—and the ways in which the imagination endows reality with realities of its own") are skillfully woven into Tóibín's gossamer skein of implications. Henry, mentally masticating a troubling glimpse of sexual provocation,

> realized now that this was something he had described in his books over and over, figures seen from a window or a doorway, a small gesture standing for a much larger relationship, something hidden suddenly revealed. He had written it, but just now he had seen it come alive, and yet he was not sure what it meant.

Aside from the works themselves, the most important development from the standpoint of literary historians was a pain in James's writing hand so severe that he turned to dictating his texts, an emergency measure that proved, in partnership with the Scots stenographer William MacAlpine, congenial, expanding an already expansive style with a wealth of oral fillips.

It is hard to know, without mastering the copious biographical litera-ture that has grown up around the James family, what Tóibín has invented; my reading of the novel—not a fast read—was further slowed by frequent comparison of this fictional version with Edel's and Fred Kaplan's biographies. The fiction follows fact quite closely. For instance, James really did, in what seems a fantastic detail, hide himself in the audi-ence of an Oscar Wilde play while his own play was disastrously unfold-ing a few London streets away. He did spend the month of August 1865 in North Conway, New Hampshire, with his cousins, the Temples—a month that provided James with memories of the bright, brash Minny Temple that fed both *Daisy Miller* and *The Portrait of a Lady*. Also present during that summer idyll was Henry's friend Oliver Wendell Holmes, and, as Kaplan's biography puts it, "He and Holmes probably shared the one room in the crowded resort that Minny had been able to locate for them." To these facts Tóibín adds the supposition that James and Holmes for at least the first night shared the room's lone bed, in the nude; the handsome Holmes, fresh from soldiering in the Civil War, is at ease with the situation, but James sleeps badly. In Tóibín's anatomizing of the incident, after Holmes "turned and cupped him with his body and placed one hand against his back and the other on his shoulder," the young James "knew not to turn or move, but . . . subtly . . . eased himself more comfortably into the shape of Holmes, closing his eyes and allow-ing his breath to come as freely as it would." Even this conjectured inti-macy may have a source in research; in "Roaming the Greenwood," from Tóibín's *Love in a Dark Time*, a book of essays on homosexual writers, he mentions Sheldon Novick's "oddly convincing account of an affair that James may have had with Oliver Wendell Holmes, the future Supreme Court judge, in 1865 when he was twenty-two and Holmes twenty-four." Oddly convincing also, and highly circumstantial, is Tóibín's description of Henry James's servant problems: after his move to Rye, the couple who served him well in his London apartment, Mr. and Mrs. Smith, deterio-rate into drunkenness and dishevelment, respectively; the hypersensitive master's slow and pained recognition that they must be fired is one of the novel's livelier stretches of social comedy. The vivid Smiths don't make the index of any Edel volume, though there is a cursory mention or two; they do receive a paragraph in Kaplan's biography.

Tóibín's subject is the inward James, the master of literary creation and a vast hushed arena of dreams and memories and hoarded observations—a triumphantly inert protagonist. Outwardly, he is mute: "He was ready to begin again, to return to the old high art of fiction with ambitions now too deep and pure for any utterance." In exchange after exchange, our hero's telling contribution is silence: "He moved his lips, about to say something, and then stopped"; "He stared at her grimly and, he hoped, blankly and said nothing"; "He still did not speak"; "He said nothing"; "Because he did not reply, Hammond stopped and turned and they locked eyes"; "When he did not speak, she began again"; "Henry did not respond"; "He did not speak." The Master relishes silence not only in himself but in others: "He enjoyed how George Gammon let the silence linger"; "He admired her all the more for . . . how happy she seemed after a time to let silence reign between them." We sorely miss in the novel, and find abundantly in the biographies, the sound of James's voice, as it is heard in Edel's and Kaplan's frequent quotation of onrolling sentences and stabbing, mischievous phrases culled from his letters. Tóibín takes the divulgences and descriptions in these letters, and in those of James's correspondents, and turns them into a curious silent movie. In his telling, James's reticence extends to his letters home—

> He did not mention her in letters to his parents or his sister Alice or brother William. . . . He knew that every line of his letters was carefully analyzed in case some clue might be offered about where his heart lay. For his relatives in Boston, hungry for news, his heart remained as hard as he could make it

—and to his dinner-party conversation, which forms "a polite and polished blankness":

> He was ready to listen, always ready to do that, but not prepared to reveal the mind at work, the imagination, or the depth of feeling. At times, he knew, the blankness was much more than a mask. It made its way inwards as well as outwards.

Tóibín's Henry James, for all his powers of subtlety and observation, contains blankness and silence because he does not face or act upon his own homosexuality—a homosexuality apparent to almost every character in the novel except him. English hostesses provide attractive and receptive male servants for him; English conversational partners feed his fascination with overt homosexuals like Oscar Wilde and John Addington Symonds. But in the end James faithfully retreats into "the sad, helpless monotony of the self . . . the locked room of himself." In "Roaming the Greenwood," Tóibín blames James for this evasiveness: "It is astonishing how James managed to withhold his homosexuality from his work." Marcher, the hero of James's novella "The Beast in the Jungle," in Tóibín's reading doubles for the author:

Clearly, he has been unable to love May Bartram, as James was unable to love Constance Fenimore Woolson; and it is open to readers whether or not they believe that May has understood all along something Marcher cannot entertain. He may have failed to love her because he was gay. And because he could not deal with his own sexuality, he failed to love anybody.

Marcher and James had the misfortune of living before the cheerful, liberating word "gay" was appropriated; the gray areas which were James's métier for elaborately circumspect exploration are no place for the younger writer who has straightforwardly outed himself in Catholic Ireland. He does not entertain the possibility that James felt no need to be outed. The nineteenth century, hospitable to bachelor uncles and celibate scholar-saints, did not necessarily subscribe to the extremely high value the twentieth century assigned sex. The, to our sense, grotesque innocence of Ruskin did not prevent him from being a great aesthetic theorist; John Singer Sargent's apparent lack of a love life did not annul his vivacious art. A James contemporary as vital and assertive and pleased with himself as George Bernard Shaw was relieved of his virginity only by a forceful intervention from the widow Jenny Patterson on his twenty-ninth birthday. Sex was not yet considered the only game to be played.

A hypnotic attraction seems to have inspired Tóibín's extensive, misty, and intricate work of reconstruction, a marvel of lightly worn research and modulated tone. He is circumstantially precise about James's Florence; he details the bicycle ride from Lamb House to the beach. Having spent considerable time in this country, he is good on James as an American, nostalgic for "American voices, so filled with enthusiasm, [which] were not as original as they imagined, nor as uncomplicated by history as they supposed." As I was beginning to read *The Master,* I happened to tune in an often rerun PBS program on great modern pianists, in which one performer was described as drawing music from the piano without ever appearing to "do battle" with the instrument; Tóibín never appears to do battle with the English language, even to the extent of attempting a pastiche of James's ornate later style. The style of *The Master* flows transparently, though more primly articulated than that of Tóibín's previous novel, *The Blackwater Lightship.* In a suitable context, such as a tense lunch James provides for the distinguished Lily Norton, Tóibín can strike off sentences with a Jamesian (or Austenesque) edge of dry, world-weary precision:

He knew that Lily Norton would not be indelicate enough to mention the matter to anyone save her aunt Grace, who would be too interested in the news not to be fully deprived of it.

As he studied her across the table, it occurred to him that re-creation of herself, her deliberate broadening of her effect, could have atrophied other qualities more endearing to a potential suitor.

When the wandering plot touches an Irish topic or scene, an extra animation, conveying a hidden animus, enters in. James attempts to take refuge from the disgrace of *Guy Domville* in Dublin, accepting the hospitality of several members of the English governing, or, one might say, occupying, class. "The squalor of Ireland came right up to the castle gates and left him depressed and haunted," and he is maliciously teased, by another guest, about the James family's humble origins in rural Bailieborough. The Irish theme returns toward the novel's end, when one of James's Dublin hostesses, the irrepressible Lady Wolseley, shows up in Rye and enjoys an exchange of views with the visiting William James, who opines that "England has much to answer for in the way the country has been run." She serenely replies that she quite agrees, that her husband "spoke to the queen personally about the matter," and that "they both took the view that once Mr. Parnell was removed and not replaced, then all the Fenianism would die down." She cites the artistic Lady Gregory as her informant: "Her estates are in the very interior. She says that there is no social outrage of any sort in Ireland."

The arrival of William James and his family at Lamb House not only excites conversation on political topics; it activates, at last, scenes and dialogues in the living present, and shows in action the family dynamic that has been dolorously coloring Henry's recollections. In his older brother's presence, he takes on a new character and a new name—"Harry." He abandons his cagey silence and, in the face of William's eloquently expressed plea that the novelist return to America and its subject matter ("I believe that the English can never be your true subject. And I believe that your style has suffered from the strain of constantly dramatizing social insipidity"), fights back, in accents almost of rudeness:

"May I interrupt you?" Henry asked. "Or is this a lecture whose finish will be marked by the ringing of a bell?"

William wants him to write a novel about the Puritans; Harry, closely quoting a letter that the historical Henry James wrote to Sarah Orne Jewett, proposes to end the conversation "by stating clearly to you that I view the historical novel as tainted by a fatal cheapness." Not just literary matters but family matters—husbandly heart attacks, wifely confidences, adolescent Dickens-reading by Peggy James—spice up these last pages, before the not very revelatory dying fall of the novel's snug ending.

Henry has recovered his vocation; but we never see it as lost. From early youth, a highly intelligent man commits himself to becoming a writer, and he becomes just that, sacrificing any feeling or attachment that gets in his way: this is the basic plot. Tóibín's fictional Henry, when he is not writing, moseys through the Jamesian facts as they have emerged in biographies and published correspondence, but less experiences these facts than haunts them, with a luminous blur of a face. There is a soapstone quality to his bust as carved here.

Paradises Lost

SHALIMAR THE CLOWN, by Salman Rushdie. 398 pp. Random House, 2005.

Why, oh, why, did Salman Rushdie, in his new novel *Shalimar the Clown*, call one of his major characters Maximilian Ophuls? Max Ophuls is a highly distinctive name, well known to movie-lovers as that of a German-born actor and stage director who, beginning in 1930, directed films in Germany, France, Russia, Italy, the Netherlands, and, after 1946, the United States, from which he returned, in 1949, to France. His four final films, in French, are considered his masterpieces, but his American pictures, little appreciated at the time, have become influential, admired especially for their worldly air and their strikingly fluid camerawork. Readers of this review will be spared, as the reviewer was not, the maddening exercise of trying to overlay Rushdie's Ophuls with the historical one. The two have no connection save the name, and a peripatetic life including a period of Los Angeles residence, and a child who becomes a maker of documentary films—the real Ophuls's son, Marcel, made *The Sorrow and the Pity*, and the fictional Ophuls's daughter, first called India and then called Kashmira, is the auteur of *Camino Real*, a filmed trip up the West Coast along the mission-planting trail taken by Fray Junípero Serra in the 1770s. The real Ophuls was born in 1902 in Saarbrücken, near the French border in the Saar region of Germany, and died in Hamburg in 1957, after an adult life spent entirely in theatrical precincts; Rushdie's imaginary Ophuls is born around 1911 in the French city of Strasbourg and dies in Los Angeles in 1991, after distinguishing himself as the United States Ambassador to India from 1965 to 1967 and, after that, as the "U.S. counterterrorism chief." His daughter is told, "Your father served his country in some hot zones, he swam for America through some pretty muddy water."

Why has Rushdie attached a gaudy celebrity name to a different sort of celebrity, preventing the Ambassador from coming into sharp focus on his own? It is partly, perhaps, characteristic Rushdiean overflow; his novels pour by in a sparkling, voracious onrush, each wave topped with foam, each paragraph luxurious and delicious, but the net effect perilously close to stultification. His prose hops with dropped names, compulsive puns, learned allusions, winks at the reader, and repeated bows to popular culture. His plots proceed by verbal connection and elaboration as much as by character interaction. This story begins and ends in Los Angeles, so angels are on the author's mind, as two not unusually overloaded sentences demonstrate:

> He [Fray Juan Crespi, in 1769] named the Los Angeles River after the angels of Assisi and their holy mistress and twelve years later, when a new settlement was established here, it took its title from the river's full name, becoming El Pueblo de Nuestra Señora la Reina de los Angeles de Porciúncula, the Town of Our Lady the Queen of the Angels of the Very Small Plot of Land. But the City of Angels now stood on a Very Large Plot of Land Indeed, thought India Ophuls, and those who dwelt there needed mightier protectors than they had been given, A-list, A-team angels, angels familiar with the violence and disorder of giant cities, butt-kicking Angeleno angels, not the small-time, underpowered, effeminate, hello-birds-hello-sky, love-and-peace, sissy-Assisi kind.

Verbal hyperactivity of the sissy-Assisi kind nudges the hip reader on page after page: "appalled by his charm, by the erotic proximity of his snappy crackle of power"; "as graceful in his movement as the incomparable Max"; "The city was a cliff and they were its stampeding lemmings. At the foot of the cliff was the valley of the broken dolls"; "He went into his blighted apple orchard, seated himself cross-legged beneath a tree, closed his eyes, heard the verses of the Rig-Veda fill the world with beauty, and ceased upon the midnight with no pain." That last phrase is, of course, John Keats talking, in "Ode to a Nightingale." James Joyce and T. S. Eliot established brainy allusions as part of modernity's literary texture, but at the risk of making the author's brain the most vital presence on the page.

"A plague on both your houses" is one of the novel's two epigraphs. A studied duality gives structure to its teeming details. It sketches the ruination of two natural paradises, California and Kashmir—the former ruined by "human bloat" in the shape of trailer parks and "the new pleasantvilles being built in the firetrap canyons to house the middle-class arrivistes," as well as "the less-pleasantvilles in the thick of the urban sprawl . . . the dirty underbelly of paradise," and the latter by Islamic uprising and the matched savagery of the insurgency's attempted suppression by the government of India. Another doubling, posing the conflict of the extremes within human nature, is expressed in terms of ancient Asian myth:

> There were nine grabbers in the cosmos, Surya the Sun, Soma the Moon, Budha the Mercury, Mangal the Mars, Shukra the Venus, Brihaspati the Jupiter, Shani the Saturn, and Rahu and Ketu, the two shadow planets. The shadow planets actually existed without actually existing. They were heavenly bodies without bodies. . . . "The shadow planets act upon us from a distance and focus our minds upon our instincts. Rahu is the exaggerator the intensifier! Ketu is the blocker the suppressor! The dance of the shadow planets is the dance of the struggle within us."

The speaker in quotation marks is Pandit Pyarelal Kaul, a philosophy-minded Hindu widower, with a gift for cookery, who lives in the "second-best dwelling" in the Kashmiri village of Pachigam; at the opposite end of the village lives Abdullah Noman, the village's Muslim headman, "the *sarpanch*, who held them all in the palm of his hand." When, as in the Shakespeare play that calls down "a plague on both your houses," two offspring of the two families, not quite fourteen years of age, fall in love and make love, the village council, the five-man *panchayat*, unanimously comes to a surprising decision: let them marry. "The lovers were their children and must be supported. Their behavior was worthy of the strongest censure . . . but they were good children, as everybody knew." Abdullah invokes "*Kashmiriyat*, Kashmiriness, the belief that at the heart of Kashmiri culture there was a common bond that transcended all other differences." So beautiful Boonyi Kaul, "dark as a secret, bright as happiness," and Shalimar Noman, "the most beautiful boy in the world," who is called "the clown" because of the comic tightrope-walker's role he plays in "the traditional entertainments known as *bhand panther* or clown stories," marry in a blithely mixed Hindu-Muslim ceremony.

But at the time of this auspicious outcome, in the early Sixties, *Kashmiriyat* was already under siege. The subcontinental Partition of 1947 had left this northern princely state itself divided, between an Azad region controlled by Pakistan and a larger region uneasily under Delhi's rule. Kashmir had been the idyllic summer haven of the British colonials, who in 1846 installed a Hindu ruler over a population that after centuries of Mughal rule was predominantly Muslim. The village tolerance and Hindu-Muslim coexistence that Gandhi had hoped would prevail in postcolonial India gave way, in Kashmir, to sectarian battles, fitfully halted by UN-arranged cease-fires, and to terrorism aligned with global Islam.

The novel's knowledgeable details of military and political action, and its harrowing depictions of atrocity and counter-atrocity, are apt to be news to American readers, for whom, in six decades that headlined Eastern Europe, Berlin, Korea, Vietnam, and the Middle East, Kashmir has been off the front page. But to Rushdie it has been a grievous personal matter. *Shalimar the Clown* is dedicated "in loving memory of my Kashmiri grandparents." Pachigam and its elders, and their dynamic and dauntless wives, and the rich array of supporting performers, and the sensations of a childhood spent in the high meadows and narrow valleys, among clear lakes and rivers of snowmelt, under the aspect of shining glaciers and timeless traditions, are evoked with an affection bestowed on few other of the novel's venues. Rushdie feels the loss of the old Kashmir so keenly that he propels his ill-named Ambassador, the usually debonair and laconic Maximilian Ophuls, into uttering "a series of high-flown locutions" on a television interview, culminating in the *cri de coeur*, "In Kashmir it is paradise itself that is falling; heaven on earth is being transformed into a living hell."

Rushdie as a literary performer suffers, I think, from being not just an author but a *cause célèbre* and a free-speech martyr, thanks to the fatwa issued by Ayatollah Khomeini in the wake of *The Satanic Verses* (1988), a playful work that precipitated riots in India and Pakistan and gave American and English publishers and booksellers an early taste of heightened security. The fatwa, which invited any good Muslim to kill Rushdie, was withdrawn in 1998, but a decade of living in hiding deepened this previously gregarious author's expertise on two subjects: celebrity and human ruthlessness.

His fascination with fame and theatricality, movies and rock music, predated the fatwa, and gives his fiction a distracting glitter, like shaken tinsel. The reader squirms, a bit, at the movie-star trappings with which Rushdie cossets India Ophuls's fabulous long-legged beauty: a horde of unsatisfactory suitors, conditioning routines that include "weekly boxing sessions at Jimmy Fish's boxing club on Santa Monica and Vine where Tyson and Christy Martin were known to work out," her shooting practice "out in the desert at 29 Palms," her driving off to celebrate her birthday in her father's DeLorean, "a silver luxury speed-mobile with batwing doors." And does her father, in his farewell fling with the opposite sex, have to settle on an Indian woman, "the color of scorched earth," who turns out to be Zainab Azam, the subcontinent's "hottest box-office star . . . a sex goddess such as the Indian cinema had never seen"? Wouldn't the second-hottest box-office star have done as well, and been more plausible than such a lofty winner, in this poor world of losers stuck in less-pleasantvilles? Rushdie himself well knows, after all, what a cumbersome handicap celebrity can become, and his seeming insistence on extreme glamour for his characters limits his room for maneuver within fiction's curious democracy, wherein a cat can not only look at a king but outstare him.

The plot of *Shalimar the Clown*, beneath the tinsel and the outrage, the Hindu and Hollywood myth-making, the jittery verbal razzmatazz, is as simple as a legend. It hinges on an impetuous vow. On the first night Shalimar and Boonyi make love, Shalimar, "rolling over onto his back and panting for joy," says:

> "Don't you leave me now, or I'll never forgive you, and I'll have my revenge, I'll kill you and if you have any children by another man I'll kill the children also."

Boonyi takes the threat lightly:

> "What a romantic you are," she replied carelessly. "You say the sweetest things."

Eventually, become a young Asian wife, Boonyi attempts to break out of her confined and undereducated state. What she finds is another sort of confinement, whose freedoms enable her to indulge her most self-damaging proclivities. Her deserted husband, meanwhile, becomes in the service of Azad Kashmir an embodiment of Muslim fury and vengefulness, a monomaniacal killing machine. His first assassination is thrillingly anticipated: he has a gun, but opts for a knife, "because he wanted to know what it would feel like when he placed the blade of his knife against the man's skin, when he pushed the sharp and glistening horizon of the knife against the frontier of the skin, violating the sovereignty of another human soul, moving in beyond taboo, toward the blood."

The beyond-taboo moment has its counterpart in Rushdie's previous—and untidier and nakeder—novel, *Fury*, when the mild, scholarly Professor Malik Solanka, while consuming, alone in the kitchen, three bottles of wine, passes through self-pity and enters "a terrible, blaming anger"; he finds himself upstairs holding a carving knife over the sleeping bodies of his wife and his four-year-old son, "on his side, curled tightly into her, sleeping the pure deep sleep of innocence and trust." Solanka then and there decides to leave them and go to New York, where violence is commonplace. Fury, it turns out, is everywhere: in *Shalimar the Clown*, we read, "Everywhere was now a part of everywhere else. Russia, America, London, Kashmir. Our lives, our stories, flowed into one another's, were no longer our own, individual, discrete. . . . The world was no longer calm."

In his ten years under the fatwa, Rushdie experienced the vehemence of offended Islam, and, with an imaginative writer's impressionability, absorbed the experience and found vehemence within himself. His counterattack on his Islamic persecutors is under way in such broadsides as a recent Op-Ed piece in the *New York Times*, "India and Pakistan's Code of Dishonor," and in fiction that animates Islam's tenacious rage with faces and life stories. His invention, in *Shalimar the Clown*, of the "iron mullah," a zealot literally made of metal, is excellent hyperbole, and the mullah's speech inculcating warrior zealotry is awesome in its disconnection from anything the West calls civilization. Rushdie in his Manhattan retreat is no longer a third-world writer but a bard of the grim one world we all, in a state of some dread, inhabit. The novel's concluding pages conjure up the sensations of the hunter and the hunted wonderfully well, with uncharacteristic understatement, the mark of authority. The climactic ending, in one more cinematic allusion, suggests the most terrifying scene in *The Silence of the Lambs*. This time, though, the night-vision goggles are on the eyes of the Jodie Foster character. All is not lost, we are dared to believe.

IN OTHER TONGUES

Dying for Love

MEMORIES OF MY MELANCHOLY WHORES, by Gabriel García Márquez, translated from the Spanish by Edith Grossman. 115 pp. Knopf, 2005.

The works of Gabriel García Márquez contain a great deal of love, depicted as a doom, a demonic possession, a disease that, once contracted, cannot be easily cured. Not infrequently the afflicted are an older man and a younger woman, hardly more than a child. In *One Hundred Years of Solitude* (English translation 1970), Aureliano Buendía visits a very young whore:

> The adolescent mulatto girl, with her small bitch's teats, was naked on the bed. Before Aureliano sixty-three men had passed through the room that night. From being used so much, kneaded with sweat and sighs, the air in the room had begun to turn to mud. The girl took off the soaked sheet and asked Aureliano to hold it by one side. It was as heavy as a piece of canvas. They squeezed it, twisting it at the ends until it regained its natural weight. They turned over the mat and the sweat came out of the other side. Aureliano was anxious for that operation never to end.

Her condition is pitiable:

> Her back was raw. Her skin was stuck to her ribs and her breathing was forced because of an immeasurable exhaustion. Two years before, far away from here, she had fallen asleep without putting out the candle and had awakened surrounded by flames. The house where she lived with the grandmother who had raised her was reduced to ashes. Since then her grandmother carried her from town to town, putting her to bed for twenty cents in order to make up the value of the burned house. According to the girl's calculations, she still had ten years of seventy men per night, because she also had to pay the expenses of the trip and food for both of them.

Aureliano does not take advantage of her overexploited charms, and leaves the room "troubled by a desire to weep." He has—you guessed it—fallen in love:

> He felt an irresistible need to love her and protect her. At dawn, worn out by insomnia and fever, he made the calm decision to marry her in order to free her from the despotism of her grandmother and to enjoy all the nights of satisfaction that she would give the seventy men.

This curious blend of the squalid and the enchanted—perhaps not so curious in the social context of the author's native Colombia in the years of his youth—returns, five years later, in the long short story "The Incredible and Sad Tale of Innocent Eréndira and Her Heartless Grandmother" (translated 1978), which was made into a movie from a script by the author. The situation has become more fabulous, with its Catholic subtext—whoredom as the martyrdom of an innocent—underlined; Eréndira's would-be rescuer is Ulises, "a gilded adolescent with lonely maritime eyes and with the appearance of a furtive angel," and her grandmother fully demonic, huge in bulk, with "mercilessly tattooed" shoulders and, it turns out, green blood, "oily blood, shiny and green, just like mint honey."

Eréndira, when we first meet her, "has just turned fourteen," whereas Serva María de Todos los Ángeles, the heroine of García Márquez's uncanny short historical novel *Of Love and Other Demons* (1994; translated 1995), turns twelve as the book opens. Her mother is "an untamed mestiza of the so-called shopkeeper aristocracy: seductive, rapacious, brazen, with a hunger in her womb that could have satisfied an entire barracks." Her father, the second Marquis de Casalduero, is a "funereal, effeminate man, as pale as a lily because the bats drained his blood while he slept." Neither parent has any energy or affection to spare the child, so she is raised by the decaying household's contingent of slaves, and learns their languages, dances, religion, and diet—a goat's eyes and testicles are her favorite meal, "cooked in lard and seasoned with burning spices." Her most striking physical feature is her radiant copper hair, never cut and braided into loops so as not to interfere with her walking.

On her birthday, she is bitten by a rabid dog, and though she never develops the fatal symptoms, the medical precautions, and her own charisma, prove to be fatal. Her father, roused to notice her existence, falls in love with her, suddenly "knowing he loved her as he had never loved in this world," and so does the devout and learned thirty-six-year-old priest, Cayetano Delaura, who is placed in charge of the exorcism which the church has deemed necessary, in view of her willful and feral behavior. Delaura at last proclaims his love to her: "He confessed that every moment was filled with thoughts of her, that everything he ate and drank tasted of her, that she was his life, always and everywhere, as only God had the right and power to be, and that the supreme joy of his heart would be to die with her." Denis de Rougemont's analysis of romantic love as a Catholic heresy could scarcely find more vivid illustration. As García Márquez frames these cases, an element of whoredom is necessary to what Stendhal called the "crystallization" of love.

Sordid imputations swirl about the preteen Serva María. Condemned to a convent, she shows up in a hat, found in an old chest, gaily decorated with ribbons, and the abbess, in her perpetual puritan fury, calls it "the hat of a slut." Rumors of Delaura's attentions in her convent cell cause the child to be known as "his pregnant whore." The pair do embrace, and even begin to experience, through daily exposure, "the tedium of every-day love," but she remains a virgin, in hopes of an eventual marriage. Nevertheless, there is no doubt that she has the talent that the physician and seer Abrenuncio mentions when he says, "Sex is a talent, and I do not have it." For all of Delaura's vows, it is Serva María who stops eating and dies for love. Her hair tells the tale: the nuns shave it off, but when she is found dead, "strands of hair gushed like bubbles as they grew back on her shaved head," and two hundred years later "a stream of living hair the intense color of copper" flows from her crypt, to the length of twenty-two meters. The miracle was witnessed, it is explained in a foreword, by the twenty-one-year-old journalist Gabriel García Márquez.

His new novel—*Memories of My Melancholy Whores*, his first work of fiction in ten years, and a mere hundred fifteen pages long—revisits the figure of a young whore, "just turned fourteen," stretched naked on a soaked bed. The moisture, this time, is her own "phosphorescent perspiration," and her lover, our unnamed protagonist and narrator, is all of ninety years old. García Márquez, a master of the arresting first sentence, begins his little book, "The year I turned ninety, I wanted to give myself the gift of a night of wild love with an adolescent virgin." Though the author was born in 1927 and is thus still shy of eighty, many homey details seem lifted from within his own study. The hero is a writer, having for fifty years composed a column for the local newspaper, *El Diario de La Paz*; he reads and cites books, favoring the Roman classics, and keeps a collection of dictionaries; he listens carefully to classical music, and supplies the titles of his selections. The city he lives in is, as is he, unnamed, but its location "twenty leagues distant" from the estuary of the Great Magdalena River puts it in the neighborhood of García Márquez's native town of Aracataca, Colombia. As for the time of the action, the narrator gives his age as thirty-two when his father dies "on the day the treaty of Neerlandia was signed, putting an end to the War of the Thousand Days"; that would be 1902, so our hero would be born in 1870 and aged ninety in 1960. He tells us he is "ugly, shy, and anachronistic," and "has never gone to bed with a woman I didn't pay." A retired prostitute whom he meets on a bus refers to, perhaps in a reflex of professional flattery, "that burro's cock the devil gave you as a reward for cowardice and stinginess." He has never married and keeps no pets; a faithful servant, the "Indianlike, strong, rustic" Damiana, tends to his modest needs, moving about barefoot so as not to disturb his writing. Though impecunious, he attends many cultural events and knows the trials of fame: strangers approach him "with a frightening look of pitiless admiration." His prose displays, in Edith Grossman's expert translation, the chiselled stateliness and sudden, colorful felicities that distinguish everything García Márquez composes. *Memories of My Melancholy Whores*, reminiscent in its terseness of such stoic fellow-Latins as the Brazilian Machado de Assis and the Colombia-born Álvaro Mutis, is a velvety pleasure to read, though somewhat disagreeable to contemplate; it has the necrophiliac tendencies of the precocious short stories, obsessed with living death, that García Márquez published when still in his teens.

The virgin whom the veteran brothel madam Rosa Cabarcas provides for her old client is a poor girl who lives with her crippled mother and feeds her brothers and sisters by a daily stint of sewing on buttons in a clothing factory. She is, Rosa Cabarcas confides, "dying of fear" because a friend of hers bled to death in losing her virginity. To quiet her nerves she has been given a mixture of bromide and valerian that relaxes her so soundly that our hero's night with her consists of his watching her sleep:

> Her newborn breasts still seemed like a boy's, but they appeared full to bursting with a secret energy that was ready to explode. The best part of her body were her large, silent-stepping feet with toes as long and sensitive as fingers. . . . The adornments and cosmetics could not hide her character: the haughty nose, heavy eyebrows, intense lips. I thought: A tender young fighting bull.

His subsequent visits follow the same pattern: she, drugged and exhausted by overwork, sleeps while the ninety-year-old lies beside her, eavesdropping upon her breathing, at one point so faint that he takes her pulse to reassure himself that she is still alive. He imagines her blood as it circulates "through her veins with the fluidity of a song that branched off into the most hidden areas of her body and returned to her heart, purified by love." Whose love? Presumably his, directed toward an inert love object. He reads and sings to her, all in her sleep. Not once do we see her wake, or hear her talk, though the little novel's happy ending reports that she has feelings and awareness. The narrator's relationship, insofar as the action holds any, is with Rosa Cabarcas and those others who witnessed his whore-crazy prime, when he "was twice crowned client of the year." Sleeping Beauty needs only to keep sleeping; her beauty under the male gaze is her raison d'être, and what she does when kissed awake is off the written record, as is the cruelty of the economic system which turns poor girls, not yet women, into fair game for sexual predators. The narrator does not deplore the grim underpinnings of whoredom, or consider the atavistic barbarism of buying girls in order to crack their hymens. Such moral concerns are irrelevant to the rapture which is his basic subject— the rebirth of love and its torments in a body that he had thought was "free at last of a servitude that had kept me enslaved since the age of thirteen." He reassures the reader, "I would not have traded the delights of my suffering for anything in the world." He is, at ninety, alive, with love's pain to prove it.

Memories of My Melancholy Whores is less about love than about age and illness. Furtively vivid images give us whiffs of the underlying distress: "My heart filled with an acidic foam that interfered with my breathing"; "I'd rather die first, I said, my saliva icy." The narrator's asshole, we are told more than once, burns. His sense of reality keeps slipping, as it does with old people, sometimes into a startling loveliness: "The full moon was climbing to the middle of the sky and the world looked as if it were submerged in green water." Magic realism has always depended on the subaqueous refractions of memory. So does love: "From then on I had her in my memory with so much clarity that I could do what I wanted with her. . . . Incredible: seeing and touching her in the flesh, she seemed less real to me than in my memory." As both de Rougemont and Freud (in 1912's essay "The Most Prevalent Form of Degradation in Erotic Life") assert, the woman present in the flesh, the wife or surrogate mother with her complicated, obdurate reality and pressing needs, is less aphrodisiac than the woman, imagined or hired, whose will is our own. In *Of Love and Other Demons*, this phantom appears as a forlorn little princess, a wild and enigmatic waif. In *Memories of My Melancholy Whores*, she is a working-class cipher who surrenders in her sleep, and whose speechless body represents the marvel of life. The instinct to memorialize one's loves is not peculiar to nonagenarian rakes; in the slow ruin of life, such memory reverses the current for a moment and silences the voice that murmurs in our narrator's ear, "No matter what you do,

this year or in the next hundred, you will be dead forever." The septuagenarian Gabriel García Márquez, while he is still alive, has composed, with
his usual sensual gravity and Olympian humor, a love letter to the dying
light.

The Lone Sailor

THE ADVENTURES AND MISADVENTURES OF MAQROLL, by Álvaro Mutis, translated from the Spanish by Edith Grossman. 700 pp. New York Review Books,
2002.

A writer's time is hard to waste. The Bogotá-born, Brussels-reared,
Mexico City–dwelling poet and prose-writer Álvaro Mutis, obliged to
make a living, must have often rued the many hours he spent travelling to
drab ports and shaking strange hands when he was Standard Oil's head of
public relations in Colombia. Then, for twenty-three years in Mexico
City, after a scrape with the Colombian government that landed him in a
Mexican jail for fifteen months, he worked the media mills as sales manager for the television division of several Hollywood film companies. And
yet without this rambling career how could he have supplied the eerie
wealth of maritime and dockside details, the delirious abundance of geo-
graphic and culinary specifics, which give fascination and global resonance to his novella-length tales of Maqroll the Gaviero? These,
produced in a rush of deferred inspiration when Mutis was in his sixties,
have won him international recognition and, in 2002, the Neustadt Prize
for Literature. The seven separately published Maqroll books (Mutis,
now seventy-nine, is reported to be working on an eighth) were collected
in 1993 as *Empresas y tribulaciones de Maqroll el Gaviero*, and now have
been translated into English by the tireless, versatile Edith Grossman, as
The Adventures and Misadventures of Maqroll.

The tidy paperback volume, exactly seven hundred pages of smallish
Trump Mediaeval, with a warm and informative introduction by Francisco Goldman, has the supple heft of a newborn classic, a latter-day *Don
Quixote* whose central persona, both amusingly shadowy and adamantly
consistent, moves around the globe somewhat as the Knight of the
Mournful Countenance traversed the arid plains of Spain. Employing a
resourceful variety of narrative textures and strategies, Mutis follows his
hero through incidents of a Conradian exoticism; the narrative method,
like that of Conrad, picturesquely involves the assembly of a coherent
story from scattered documents, distant rumors, and elaborately couched

second-hand recountings on betranced tropical verandas. Yet Mutis denies any influence from Conrad, citing instead Proust and Dickens as prime inspirations: "A real influence," Goldman quotes him as saying, "is an author who communicates an energy and a great desire to tell a story. And it isn't that you want to write like Dickens, but rather that when you read Dickens, you feel an imaginative energy which you use to your own ends."

The problem of energy, in this enervated postmodern era, keeps arising in Mutis's pursuit of a footloose, offhandedly erudite, inexplicably attractive shady character. A lowly seaman with some high-flying acquaintances on land, Maqroll is a drifter who tends to lose interest in his adventures before the dénouement is reached. Readers even slightly acquainted with Latin American modernism will hear echoes of Borges's cosmic portentousness, of Julio Cortázar's fragmenting ingenuities, of Machado de Assis's crisp pessimism, and of the something perversely hearty in Mutis's fellow-Colombian and good friend Gabriel García Márquez—a sense of genial amplitude, as when a ceremonious host sits us down to a lunch provisioned to stretch into evening. Descriptions of food consumed and of drinks drunk, amid flourishes of cosmopolitan connoisseurship, are frequent in Mutis, even as the ascetic Maqroll goes hungry. North Americans may be reminded of Melville—more a matter, perhaps, of affinity than of influence. *Gaviero* in Spanish means "lookout"; Maqroll was one as a boy, in his first years at sea—"I had to climb to the top of the tallest mast and tell the crew what was on the horizon"—and Ishmael, too, was a top-man, feeling himself, "a hundred feet above the silent decks, striding along the deep, as if the masts were gigantic stilts," and revolving within himself "the problem of the universe." Both writers, through their wayfaring alter egos, stubbornly stare at a universe that, though apparently devoid of God, seems still to brim with obscure metaphysical import. "And some certain significance lurks in all things," Ishmael reasons, "else all things are little worth, and the round world itself but an empty cipher."

Mutis began as a poet, and until these Maqroll tales was best known as one, though in Mexico his voice was widely broadcast; he did the voiceover in the Spanish-language version of the television serial *The Untouchables*. Maqroll appeared as a character in Mutis's poems when the poet was a mere nineteen, and has been a frequent presence in his poems since. In 1986, according to Mutis, he realized, while editing the French translation of a prose-poem entitled "The Snow of the Admiral," that "it wasn't a poem but a piece of a novel," and, "with a great sense of fatigue," proceeded to write the novel, sending its three hundred manuscript pages to his agent in Barcelona along with the disclaimer, worthy of Maqroll's own diffidence, "I don't know what the devil this is." He was reassured that it was "quite simply a wonderful novel," and in five years he produced six more short books about Maqroll.

The Snow of the Admiral is indeed poemlike, and of these novellas the most intense and surreal in its atmospherics. The author begins with a solemnly circumstantial description of how, browsing in a second-hand bookstore in Barcelona, he picked up a beautiful edition of a nineteenth-century volume on the assassination of the Duke of Orléans, and found, in a pocket in the back intended for maps and genealogical tables, a quantity of pink, yellow, and blue commercial forms covered with tiny writing, "somewhat tremulous and feverish I thought," in a purple indelible pencil "occasionally darkened by the author's saliva." This shaky document proves to be a diary Maqroll kept while journeying up the (fictional) Xurandó River in a diesel-powered, flat-keeled barge. The captain of this quixotic craft, mourning a lost mistress, methodically keeps himself semi-inebriated; the boat's mechanic is a silent Indian; and the pilot's "features, gestures, voice, and other personal traits have been carried to so perfect a degree of nonexistence that they can never stay in our memories." The only other passenger is a "calm blond giant who chews a few words in an almost incomprehensible Slavic accent, and constantly smokes the foul tobacco that the pilot sells to him at an exorbitant price." Maqroll is headed for some rumored sawmills far upriver, beyond treacherous rapids, where he hopes to arrange for the transport and sale of lumber downriver. The project feels as futile as it is vague; he says to himself,

> these disasters, these decisions that are wrong from the start, these dead ends that constitute the story of my life, are repeated over and over again. A passionate vocation for happiness, always betrayed and misdirected, ends in a need for total defeat; it is completely foreign to what, in my heart of hearts, I've always known could be mine if it weren't for this constant desire to fail.

A family of four naked Indians comes aboard; he copulates with the woman, though she has "a rank smell of decomposing mud and rutting snake," and he thus contracts, it turns out, a nearly fatal fever, of which he is cured by the commander of a frontier military outpost. The sawmills turn out to be real, even majestic, but inoperative because of a government plot against their Finnish makers. Maqroll, narrowly rescued from this cul-de-sac, discovers in the uplands that an establishment called The Snow of the Admiral, where he had hoped to find a former, much-cherished mistress, Flor Estévez, is in ruins.

Yet the particulars of this useless voyage—the river currents, the encircling jungle, the stultifying heat, the grimy details of the barge's operation, the repulsive personality tics of those aboard—are rendered so vividly as to furnish a metaphor for life, as a colorful voyage to nowhere. Maqroll is in mid-life; his consciousness is a web of past adventures, of old loves and tortuously failed enterprises, and his dreams figure as importantly as his present perils. His next adventure, *Ilona Comes with the Rain* (a less melodious equivalent of *Ilona llega con la lluvia*), has a heroine, and the muddy Xurandó is replaced by the torpid urban landscape of Panama City, where Maqroll is deposited by the suicide of the captain of the bankrupt tramp steamer on which he has been serving. He is sinking into squalor and petty crime in Panama's constant downpours:

> A curtain of rain fell into the filthy waters of the Pacific, and from my window the city seemed to dissolve, before my indifferent eyes, into fierce whirlpools of mud, garbage, and dead leaves spinning around the sewer openings.

At this low point, good fortune strikes, as is its habit with Maqroll:

> A ritual was being enacted, one that occurs with such punctual fidelity in my life that I can attribute it only to the impenetrable will of those tutelary gods who lead me through the obscurity of their designs by invisible but obvious strings.

He meets up with Ilona Grabowska Rubenstein, a dynamic, leggy international con artist who in the past has shared her favors and her illegal schemes with Maqroll and his Lebanese soulmate and sometime partner, Abdul Bashur. Swiftly she takes Maqroll to bed, spruces him up, and appoints him her partner in an inspired venture, a whorehouse staffed with women dressed in the uniforms of airline stewardesses, thus catering to the fantasies of international travellers. The idea makes a fortune, but success bores both partners, and one of their *filles de joie*, who lives in a wrecked boat on the beach and imagines she has uniformed lovers from the time of Napoleon, fascinates Ilona fatally. This episode is less of a poem than the first, and more of a story, with the storyteller's vice of sentiment; the conclusion invites a donation of tears, of sympathetic sorrow.

Un Bel Morir appears to kill off Maqroll, after enlisting him, while he moldered in the seedy river town of La Plata (not the Argentine city), to run guns and explosives to rebels up in the cordillera. Both rebels and government eventually want to kill him, but he makes a getaway, albeit into the river's swampy estuary with a failing engine. Things look grim, yet we suspect that Maqroll, like the hero of a comic strip, leads a charmed life, with as many panels to come as his creator wishes to produce. Women—of whom a select few "filled his days with meaning and exorcised the demons of tedium and defeat whose attacks he feared as he feared death"—keep bestowing their magic potion. When Amparo María, a peasant girl, sleeps with him, we are told:

> The girl's feigned ecstasy became real, the result of her grateful admiration for the stranger who carried the burden of his years and the desolate, consuming experience of unknown lands and their intoxicating dangers and delights.

Possibly alert to the dangers of doting on his hero, Mutis next provides a tale in which Maqroll hardly appears, except as a cherished acquaintance of the principals. In *The Tramp Steamer's Last Port of Call*, the shortest of the lot and one of the best, the narrator relates an experience he himself has had, in a voice close to what we know of Mutis's own life: "I had to go to Helsinki to attend a meeting of directors of internal publications for various oil companies." In Helsinki, he asks to be driven to the point from which he can see across the Gulf of Finland to Saint Petersburg, a shimmering sight passingly eclipsed by the transit of a decrepit tramp steamer:

> The captain's bridge, and the row of cabins on the deck for crew members and occasional passengers, had been painted white a long time before. Now a coat of grime, oil, and urine gave them an indefinite color, the color of misery, of irreparable decadence, of desperate, incessant use. The chimerical freighter slipped through the water to the agonized gasp of its machinery and the irregular rhythm of driving rods that threatened at any moment to fall silent forever.

He sees the wretched, plucky ship, which fragmentary letters on its bow identify as the *Halcyon*, three more times, in Costa Rica, in Jamaica, and in the delta of the Orinoco River. Its apparition invades his dreams. While on another errand for the oil company, travelling downriver to a strike-threatened seaport refinery, he occupies one of the two cabins in a small tugboat; the other is occupied by a Basque sea-captain called Jon Iturri, who, it turns out, was the captain of the ghostly tramp steamer, which broke up and sank in the Orinoco. Its owner, Iturri relates, was a Lebanese woman, a younger sister of Abdul Bashur, named Warda. At their first meeting, he says, he was stunned by her "almost Hellenic" beauty:

> "Her blue-black hair was as dense as honey and fell to shoulders as straight as those of the kouros in the Athens Museum. Her narrow hips, curving

gently into long, somewhat full legs, recalled statues of Venus in the Vatican Museum and gave her erect body a definitive femininity that immediately dispelled a certain boyish air. Large, firm breasts completed the effect of her hips."

As he got to know her better, his admiration intensified: "Warda, when she was naked, acquired a kind of aura that emanated from the perfection of her body, the texture of her moist, elastic skin, and that face: seen from above, when we were in bed, it took on even more of the qualities of a Delphic vision." But the lovestruck captain was fifty, and a non-Muslim, and Warda was twenty-four and, the longer she lived in Europe, ever more approving of the conservative ways of her native Lebanon. The tramp steamer, which she inherited from an uncle, was financing her European sojourn with its profits; she flew to Iturri's ports of call and spent rapturous days in hotels with him, but their romance could last only as long as the fragile tramp steamer did. Warda's perfect, elastic, symmetrical beauty was one with the listing, disintegrating body of the ship as it conveyed her aging lover from port to port. The story, Mutis tells us at the outset, "has something of the eternal legends that have bewitched us over the centuries"; he ends by assuring us that "there has been only one love story since the beginning of time." Not a happy one.

The remaining three novellas—*Amirbar*, in which Maqroll mines gold and performs buggery on his slavish, infatuated digging partner, Antonia; *Abdul Bashur, Dreamer of Ships*, in which Maqroll's much-mentioned partner in skulduggery searches the world for a perfect steamer; and *Triptych on Sea and Land*, in which Maqroll's friendships with the fisherman Sverre Jensen, the painter Alejandro Obregón, and the child Jamil Vicente are described—all have their charms and excitements, and sustain the rueful mood, but we sense the author challenging his own ingenuity as he weaves cross-references and knits in dangling ends and patches some of the holes in the dreamily loose fabric of Maqroll's adventures. A stiff didactic brocade accumulates. These later tales expand the rolls of his acquaintanceship into, if not quite an Arthurian Round Table, a gallant brotherhood, "a small band . . . who have lived their lives under the sign of chance and adventure, and at the periphery of laws and codes created by men who, like Tartuffe, wish to justify their own paltry destinies." The brothers enjoy boozy reminiscences, hairbreadth escapes, and an amount of casual wenching that ill prepares us for the revelation that some of them, like Obregón and the narrator, are married. An elegant international machismo offers itself as a palliative for life's existential agony. Men with the right stuff can be recognized by their "inbred decency and . . . inflexible desire to respect the privacy of others," a "*gen-*

tillesse de coeur" built on a rich past: of a one-legged German sea-captain it is said, "His hard-won astuteness was concentrated in his eyes, where innumerable experiences, transgressions, compromises, things forgotten, and things remembered were carefully stored." The brotherhood includes not just Maqroll, Obregón, Abdul Bashur, and the narrator but the masculine-minded girl gangster Ilona, a lean tall waitress Maqroll calls the Governor, and a few actual persons, of whom Gabriel García Márquez appears at some length and Alastair Reid, the estimable Scots poet and translator from the Spanish, is mentioned once: a list of key nautical data includes "the speed at which you maintain the engines in order to enter the bay of Wigtown and anchor across from Withorn when you visit Alastair Reid." No doubt other real names and personal allusions are secreted in this increasingly chummy text.

Widening the circle has the final effect of narrowing it, of diluting the value of Maqroll the Gaviero as an isolated image of quintessential male experience. For what are these adventures and misadventures—gold strikes whose profits are squandered, voyages toward mirages, erotic conquests whose fruit is painful loss—but symbols of the chronic ventures and defeats of the restless, death-plagued male spirit? Like Hemingway's, Mutis's fiction advertises a lifestyle, a prescription for living. Part of the secret is travelling light; Maqroll has the "air of a sailor who's been thrown off his ship" and carries no more than his clothes and a few archly recondite books. What is it, in his minimal baggage, that keeps Maqroll rolling through the "network of itineraries," "the dark human labyrinth that leads to a small heap of gray ashes"? He and his creator worry alike at the problem, "Why live?" Maqroll explains that gold mines "interested me as a way to explore a world I did not know, the sort of challenge that allows me to go on living and not look for false escapes." A false escape, we gather, is one that spurns "the empty illusions of ambition and desire" and embraces "a destiny chosen and drained to the last drop of misfortune."

Misfortune is rarely so complete, however, as to lack the price of a good restaurant meal or of a night with a woman: "I embraced the Governor's firm body with the joyful despair of the vanquished who know that our only victory is the triumph of the senses on the ephemeral but true field of pleasure." The metaphysical joys of intercourse take the prose to pompous heights; we read that the Governor's legs "encircled my body with movements adapted to the rhythm of a pleasure that was postponed with Alexandrine wisdom," and a Canadian Indian lass "conscientiously controlled her sensuality, and this had the charm of an artful eroticism that concealed its simulations behind an exceptional aesthetic sense." But nothing distinguishes Maqroll's women so much as their willingness to knock themselves out for him, reaping misfortune and abandonment for their pains. His deepest relation is with his destiny, an obscure entity having less to do with God than with the gods, "the powers that move the strings." On the final page, Maqroll decrees, "If it exists at all, the pity of the gods is indecipherable or comes to us when we breathe our last." This could be from a story or poem by Borges; it is curious that poets from the most ostensibly Catholic of continents are drawn to the gloomy polytheism of pre-Christian paganism.

In the meantime, besides the consolations of sex and reading French books (*Mémoires du Cardinal de Retz*, Chateaubriand's *Mémoires d'outre-tombe*, Emile Gabory's study of the wars of the Vendée, the letters and memoirs of the Belgian Prince of Ligne, all listed in an appendix, "The Gaviero's Reading"), Maqroll experiences "confounding moments of incomprehensible joy." We don't hear much about them, moments like those that led C. S. Lewis, for example, to Christian faith, though a poem by Mutis, "A Street in Córdoba," describes (in Reid's translation) a "certainty that now sweeps over me like a sudden high temperature . . . / the certainty that in this street, in this city . . . / was the single, irreplaceable place where everything would come together for me / in this fullness that overcomes death and its devices." Maqroll usually distrusts happiness: "So many moments of irritating, wearisome disgust are returned to us years later by memory as splendidly happy episodes. Nostalgia is the lie that speeds our approach to death." The question "Why live?" is answered, if at all, by an implied harmony between the "sordid disasters" of the lived life and the abysmal negativity at the heart of the universe. Lone rangers, from Don Quixote to Sam Spade and James Bond, are customarily engaged in combat against bad guys; they afford themselves the escapism of a virtuous quest, a perpetual clean-up. Maqroll instead presents himself as one of the bad guys, "at the periphery of laws and codes," and proposes that bad guys aren't so bad, as they smuggle and pimp and deal their way through the world. They are good guys. Maybe so, but it leaves the reader with no one much to cheer for, in adventures that aspire to the epic.

Two's a Crowd

THE DOUBLE, by José Saramago, translated from the Portuguese by Margaret Jull Costa. 324 pp. Harcourt, 2004.

The Portuguese novelist José Saramago, born in 1922, has not let the Nobel Prize, which he received in 1998, slow him down. He was a late starter in the lists of fiction, having been a civil servant and sometime journalist to the age of fifty. He found his groove in the baroque magic-realist historical novel *Baltasar and Blimunda* (1982 in Portugal, when he turned sixty; 1987 in the U.S.), and combines, in the novels of his productive eighth decade—*Blindness* (1995; 1997), *All the Names* (1997; 1999), and *The Cave* (2000; 2002)—fantastic premises with a relaxed, disarmingly direct style and a quizzical, respectful interest in everyday life. His prose is open to philosophical and psychological speculation as well as to homely folk wisdom, and its flights into the impossible are balanced by a feeling for the daily routines and labors that compose, for most of humanity, the substance of existence. Saramago is, in the not uncommon fashion of Latin intellectuals, an avowed Communist; his sympathy for workers broadens and solidifies his fictional thought-experiments.

His new novel, *The Double*, deals with white-collar workers: the thirty-eight-year-old hero, the impressively named Tertuliano Máximo Afonso, teaches history in a secondary school; the divorced Tertuliano's present lady friend, Maria da Paz, works in a bank; Tertuliano's double, António Claro, acts in minor movie roles under the name of Daniel Santa-Clara; his wife, Helena, works in a travel agency. Their interactions and confusions, as intricate as those of a French bedroom farce, are scrupulously placed within the confines of working days and seasonal vacations, just as the waking nightmare, for Tertuliano and António, of confronting an exact physical duplicate is set in a sufficiently populous (though unnamed) metropolis of five million people, with their automobiles, their apartments, their anonymity. The wildly ramifying plot has an improvised air but proves to be tightly knit, constructed toward a stark dénouement. The tight construction floats, however, on a bubbling, uninhibited authorial voice of cheerful volatility, brimming with asides and self-corrections, such as "Well, that's not quite true," and "There are moments in a narrative, and this, as you will see, has been one of them, when any parallel manifestation of ideas and feelings on the part of the narrator with respect to what the characters themselves might be feeling or thinking at that point should be expressly forbidden by the laws of good writing."

Saramago has the gift of gab. Our impression is of a writer, like Faulkner, so confident of his resources and ultimate destination that he can bring any improbability to life by hurling words at it. Gabbiness is hard to illustrate in a concise review, but here is a relatively short example, working up to virtual impenetrability:

> Real life has always seemed to us more frugal in coincidences than the novel or other forms of fiction, unless we were to allow that the principle of coincidence is the one true ruler of the world, in which case, we should give as much value to the coincidence one actually experiences as to that which is written about, and vice versa.

And here is another, working up to a joke of sorts:

> If, as children used to be told, in order to illustrate the relationship between small causes and great effects, for want of a shoe the horse was lost, for want of a horse the battle was lost, the trajectory followed by the deductions and inductions that brought Tertuliano Máximo Afonso to the conclusion set out above seems to us no less dubious and problematic than that edifying episode from the history of wars whose first agent and ultimate culprit must have been, when all's said and done and with no room for objections, the professional incompetence of the vanquished army's farrier.

Of the book's two epigraphs, one is invented and the other comes from *Tristram Shandy*, Laurence Sterne's gabby proto-modernist masterpiece of self-inquisition, a work whose merry challenge to the conventions of the realistic novel has proved, after its initial London fame, more influential on the Continent than in England.

The traditional articulations of English fiction are dismissed in the very look of Saramago's prose, presented in paragraphs many of which are pages long. Direct speech is not marked even by dashes, let alone quotation marks; the utterances of a dialogue run together with only commas to separate them, plus the capitals that begin a sentence—a manner perhaps less confusing in Portuguese than in English, where the capitalized pronoun "I," following a comma, seems, falsely, to signal a different speaker. The reader must wonder what advantage of mimetic fidelity is gained in the author's mind: the long, unpunctuated paragraphs of Molly Bloom's stream of consciousness at the end of *Ulysses* declare a fresh, all-embracing, female point of view; the Austrian Thomas Bernhard's unrelieved blocks of type express his rageful contempt for the reader, Austria, and life in general. In Saramago's case, his embedding the dialogue almost invisibly in the expository prose must indicate a sense of his characters' speech merging with their thoughts and impressions, which in turn merge with the author's flowing voice, as overbearing and possessive, in its way, as that of a moralizing Victorian.

The Double gains in interest as the action moves from Tertuliano's distress and bafflement at his own duplication to his intervention in the life of his double, the double's retaliation, and the growing involvement of the two women, Maria da Paz and Helena. These women—like most of Saramago's—are sensible, warm, and alert, and their presence provides a civilized context, an index of peaceful possibility, for what becomes, between the two identical-looking men, a savage and vengeful war tinged with an atavistic horror of identity-theft and a belief in the triumphal value of seducing an enemy's woman. What tragedy resides in the outcome resides in the ill-used women's feelings; the men are less sympathetic. Tertuliano, that meek and lonely history teacher, is described at the beginning as suffering from depression; but, unlike Dostoevsky's "The Double" and Poe's "William Wilson," Saramago's *Double* does not wrap the perception of a double in the protagonist's delusional pathology or a suggestion of an inner self projected outward. The similarity objectively exists, down to the men's moles and fingerprints, and has the comedy of, in Henri Bergson's formulation, "something mechanical encrusted upon the organic." Cloning, one letter away from clowning, affords us a smile as well as a shudder. Tertuliano's double, unlike William Wilson's, is not a whispering voice of conscience; António Claro is a bit actor in movies turned into videos, a habitual seducer, a karate expert (he is stronger than Tertuliano, but not apparently more muscular), and a heel, who totes a gun—in short, a bad actor. The reader shares the hero's desire that he be erased. The novel, with its farcical elements, does not quite deepen into the dizzying vortex of identity issues that may have been intended; it remains more comic than not, and lacks the unforced momentum and resonance of *Blindness*, which, like Camus's *The Plague*, allegorizes societal breakdown and a basic fear. Most of us are afraid of going blind; being duplicated is a relatively minor worry.

Yet Saramago has a questing and well-stocked mind, amiably engaged in the patient investigation of human nature. To bulk out the lean diagrammatics of his plot, with its mere four principals, he ruminates on the vagaries of language and the difficulty of applying common sense to our actions. Both are aspects, perhaps, of the same problem, human irrationality. Human beings are too complex and conflicted for words. "All the dictionaries put together," Maria da Paz tells Tertuliano, "don't contain half the terms we would need in order for us to understand each other." A lack of words at the right time entangles Tertuliano in problems. He is unable, out of shame or caution, to tell Maria da Paz of the existence of his double, and his wordlessly mailing a false beard to

António Claro goads the other to plot revenge: "Good heavens, how ridiculous, where will it all end, cry those happy people who have never come face-to-face with a copy of themselves, who have never suffered the terrible affront of receiving in the post a false beard in a box, without even a pleasant, good-humored note to soften the blow." On the other hand, a letter to a film production company which Tertuliano forges in Maria da Paz's name provides a fatal link of evidence. A conversation with his inquisitive, solicitous mother leads him to think,

> Words can be the very devil, there we are thinking we allow out of our mouths only the words that suit us, and suddenly another word slips out, where it came from we don't know, we didn't ask for it to appear, and because of that word, which we often have difficulty remembering afterward, the whole conversation abruptly changes direction, and we find ourselves affirming what we denied before, or vice versa, what happened just now was a perfect example, I hadn't intended speaking to my mother so soon about this whole mad story.

Common sense actually figures in this mad story as a character, a voice that pops up in Tertuliano's head to complain about their relationship: "You and me, your common sense and you, we hardly ever meet to talk, only very occasionally, and, to be perfectly honest, it's hardly ever been worthwhile." The personification is less intrusive as the novel gathers steam, but near the end the author declares that, "with a little common sense, the matter could have ended there," and traces human problems to a verbal error:

> The proof that the universe was not as well-thought-out as it should have been lies in the fact that the Creator ordered the star that illumines us to be called the sun. Had the king of the stars borne the name Common Sense, imagine how enlightened the human spirit would be now.

One wonders. "Common sense" in Portuguese is surprisingly similar to the English: *comum senso* or *bom* [good] *senso*. Nevertheless, some spirit-altering connotations may be lost in translation. Is common sense really a cure-all? We are told of Tertuliano not only that he is depressed and bored but that, in his mother's words, "there's a part of you that has been asleep ever since you were born." Embracing double trouble is perhaps his way of waking up; the heart has its reasons that reason knows not of. The stagnating heart welcomes an irruption, even a harsh and dangerous one; the appeal of unreason cannot be legislated out of Utopia. To enthrone common sense as the king of the stars could spell the end of priests, magicians, beauticians, advertising executives, and novelists.

Mind/Body Problems—III

THE POSSIBILITY OF AN ISLAND, by Michel Houellebecq, translated from the French by Gavin Bowd. 341 pp. Knopf, 2006.

It is to the credit of the French novelist, poet, and provocateur Michel Houellebecq that, in his new novel *The Possibility of an Island*, he so boldly, with considerable energy and erudition, seeks to confront and encompass the fundamentals of the human condition—or, to quote his veiled reference to André Malraux, "what a pompous author of the twentieth century had felt fit to call 'the human condition.' " It is to Houellebecq's discredit, or at least to his novel's disadvantage, that his thoroughgoing contempt for, and strident impatience with, humanity in its traditional occupations and sentiments prevents him from creating characters whose conflicts and aspirations the reader can care about. The usual Houellebecq hero, exercising a monopoly on self-expression, presents himself in one of two guises: a desolate loner consumed by boredom and apathy, or a galvanized male porn star. In neither role does he ask for, nor does he receive, much sympathy.

Michel, the protagonist of Houellebecq's previous novel, *Platform*—the rather bleak and enigmatic English rendering of *Plateforme: Au milieu du monde*, possibly an allusion to global politics, or a pun for "flat style," a characterization most French critics find apt—helps promote, in conjunction with the ideally compliant and lewd travel agent Valérie, a momentarily booming chain of Asian vacation resorts for European sex tourists. In the new novel, a lengthy exercise in futuristic science fiction, the hero, named Daniel, involves himself in the founding stages of a worldwide cult, Elohimism, that delivers its adherents into practical immortality, achieved through replacement of the deceased individual by a DNA-derived duplicate possessed of not only the same bodily traits but the same memories. The original Daniel—Daniel1—lives more or less in the present era, in Paris and Andalusia, and his latest edition, Daniel25, lives two millennia hence, in a depopulated Spain. They and the intervening Daniels have become, thanks to the ingenious founders of Elohimism, what the novel calls neohumans, who reside in electrically fenced isolation, keeping in rather slack electronic touch with one another and waiting, with an indifference compounded of Buddhist detachment and genetic modification, to die and be replaced by eighteen-year-old clones. The Earth in these millennia has been beset by several disasters: first, a melting of the polar ice that reduced the planet's population from fourteen billion to seven hundred million, and then the Great

Drying Up, which reduced it further, to pathetic bands of savages who roam the blasted terrain outside the fenced islands of the neohumans, and who are killed if they come too close, as beseeching mothers with starving babies sometimes do. Daniel24 annihilates them with "the sensation of accomplishing a necessary and legitimate act."

Sound inviting? Want to go there? Curiously, of the novel's strictly alternating strands, the relatively laconic and sexually neutered commentary of the neohumans Daniel24 and 25 is the more interesting—more pregnant with suspense, more amusing to imagine in its technology and austerity, its attenuated eschatology. The far fuller autobiography of Daniel1, detailing Daniel's involvement with his wife, Isabelle, and a mid-life mistress, Esther, and relating his half-hearted participation in the hectic founding of the eventually triumphant Elohimite sect, seems by comparison an opinionated drone, an interminable blog from nowhere. Much of the fantasy feels warmed-over: the Canary Islands setting of the headquarters of the fledgling sect's leader suggests the opulent, fortified lair of a James Bond villain, and Daniel's two inamoratas, a loving wife who dislikes sex and a sexy twenty-two-year-old Spanish blonde who doesn't love him, both have the airbrushed unreality of Playmates of the Month. In fact, *The Possibility of an Island* has been excerpted by *Playboy*; Houellebecq and Hugh Hefner alike offer the ailing world a panacea of self-righteous hedonism. The twinkle in Hefner's eye becomes a furious glare in Houellebecq's. Their connoisseur's emphasis on the physical perfection of the naked young women whom they present as pieces of Utopia verges on pedophilia; Daniel1 writes, "The dream of all men is to meet little sluts who are innocent but ready for all forms of depravity—which is what, more or less, all teenage girls are." Houellebecq's spokesmen insist that sex is not merely an aspect of life, or merely one of its pleasures; it is everything: "All energy is of a sexual nature, not mainly, but exclusively, and when the animal is no longer good for reproducing, it is absolutely no longer good for anything." Of the beloved Esther we are assured,

> Like all very pretty young girls she was basically only good for fucking, and it would have been stupid to employ her for anything else, to see her as anything other than a luxury animal, pampered and spoiled, protected from all cares as from any difficult or painful task so as to be better able to devote herself to her exclusively sexual service.

Houellebecq's solemnly blunt descriptions of sex acts are notorious, or as notorious as such things can be in a sex-saturated age; but it is one thing to propagandize for sex and another to integrate it, as more than "naughty bits," into the conflict-ridden flow of incident and psychology that make up a novel. The reader has no trouble believing that Daniel1, over forty and physically no prize, sorely grieves when his pet slut Esther in her heedless youth tires of him; it is another thing for the reader to grieve along with him. This reader, actually, rejoiced when the breakup came, and wondered why Esther had been so slow about it.

Houellebecq does not attempt to portray his hero and his views as agreeable. Daniel1 made his fame and his fortune—forty-two million euros and growing—as a deliberately outrageous stand-up comedian and video artist, one of whose presentations is subtitled *100% Hateful*. Muslims and children are especially loathed targets. The show *We Prefer the Palestinian Orgy Sluts* was "undoubtedly the pinnacle of my career— from a media point of view, I mean," Daniel1 says, in a hard-to-miss allusion to the furor caused by the anti-Muslim views expressed in *Platform* and by Houellebecq's subsequent, unrepentant appearances in court and on television. Daniel1 produces a parody of a porn film titled *Munch on My Gaza Strip* (*My Huge Jewish Settler*), and a prospective script called *The Social Security Deficit* is summarized:

> The first fifteen minutes of the film consisted of the unremitting explosion of babies' skulls under the impact of shots from a high-caliber revolver—I had envisaged it in slow motion, then with slight accelerations—anyway, a whole choreography of brains, in the style of John Woo.

The film goes on to expose "the existence of a network of child killers, brilliantly organized and inspired by ideas rooted in Deep Ecology. The MED (Movement for the Extermination of Dwarves) called for the disappearance of the human race, which it judged irredeemably harmful to the balance of the biosphere." Tree huggers, get your guns. Daniel admits to "that legitimate disgust that seizes any normal man at the sight of a baby" and to a "solid conviction that a child is a sort of vicious dwarf, innately cruel, who combines the worst features of the species, and from whom domestic pets keep a wise distance." The despiser of dwarves doesn't love giants, either, at least literary ones: Shakespeare is a "sad fool," James Joyce "an insane Irishman" who wrote "ponderous prose," and Vladimir Nabokov a "mediocre and mannered pseudo-poet" whose style resembles a "collapsed pastry." Writers who get passing marks, sometimes grudgingly, are Balzac, Marcel Proust, Agatha Christie, Arthur Schopenhauer, and Heinrich von Kleist.

Daniel1 is not entirely hateful. He loves his dog, Fox, who through all his own replications is not only wholly affectionate but *happy:* "We sleep together, and every morning is a festival of licks and scratches from his little paws; it is an obvious joy for him to be reunited with life and daylight." The human difficulty in attaining and sustaining canine happiness arouses an emotion close to pity, described as "a horror, an authentic horror at the unending calvary that is man's existence." Nor is Houellebecq, shrill and even silly as he can be, entirely without strengths. His four novels—*Whatever* (1994), *The Elementary Particles* (1998), and *Platform* (2003) are the three others—display a grasp of science and mathematics beyond that of all but a few non-genre novelists. He is anthropologically alert to the deeper trends behind contemporary news, fashion, and mores; his macabre future takes off from such recent news items as the consensual cannibalism of two German men and the deaths of hundreds of neglected French elderly in a heat wave. His elaborate invention, in the latest novel, of a new religion stands on a foundation of present cultural facts: "Elohimism marched in many respects behind consumer capitalism—which, turning youth into the supremely desirable commodity, had little by little destroyed respect for tradition and the cult of the ancestors—inasmuch as it promised the indefinite preservation of this same youth, and the pleasures associated with it." His sociological/psychological/philosophical vocabulary opaquely thickens around his core topic—Pascal's, after all, and La Rochefoucauld's—of human isolation and unhappiness:

> The subject-object separation is triggered, in the course of cognitive processes, by a convergent mesh of failures. . . . It is in failure, and through failure, that the subject constitutes itself, and the passage of humans to neo-humans, with the disappearance of all physical contact that is its correlative, has in no way modified this basic ontological given. . . . It has, however, been shown countless times that the physical pain that accompanied the existence of humans was consubstantial with them, that it was the direct consequence of an inadequate organization of their nervous system, just as their inability to establish interindividual relations in a mode other than that of confrontation resulted from a relative insufficiency of their social instincts in relation to the complexity of the societies that their intellectual means enabled them to found.

Houellebecq's most ambitious scientific reach is to be found in *The Elementary Particles*, one of whose two protagonists, the biologist Michel Djerzinski, is introduced as among the "most clear-sighted and deliberate engineers" of the third "paradigm shift, which opened up a new era in world history"—the other shifts being the fall of the Roman Empire to Christianity and the post-medieval fall of Christianity to modern science. Djerzinski and his half-brother, Bruno Clément, split the customary Houellebecq protagonist into two: Michel (that name again!) is the near-autistic container of affective emptiness, while Bruno does duty, after some clumsy auditions, as the porn star. Their intertwined tale, which toward its end sings praises of the intricate Book of Kells, is knotty with words like "pubococcygeal," sentences like "According to Margenau's theory, human consciousness could be compared to a field of probabilities in a Fock space, defined as a direct sum of Hilbert spaces," and pages of tendentious analogy between quantum physics and biological processes. Djerzinski's theories end in the creation, as soon as the year 2029, of a race of new, immortal, non-violent, sex-free, egoless beings of whom the ostensible author is, to our surprise, one; he graciously dedicates his book to obsolete mankind. The paradigm-shift scenario approximates that of *The Possibility of an Island*, which, being more schematic and dogmatic, is the inferior novel.

But Houellebecq's best novel, the only one that is less idea-driven than experience-driven, is the first, a brief first-person narrative so shapeless and various that its English translator derived the title *Whatever* from the French *Extension du domaine de la lutte* (*Extension of the Field of Struggle*). Composed in short and jumpy chapters akin in tone to the amiable absurdism of Raymond Queneau and Robert Pinget, the novel begins like a Gallic version of Kingsley Amis's *Lucky Jim* or Jay McInerney's *Bright Lights, Big City*—an account of a young goof-off's embarrassments with liquor, women, and gainful employment. The unnamed narrator is, he tells us, an "analyst-programmer in a computer software company" with a salary "two and a half times the minimum wage." Houellebecq, after studying at the National Institute of Agronomy, spent eleven years debugging computers for the French government; he differs from most contemporary romancers in his extended acquaintance with office work, its applied technology and edgy relationships. His two most recent novels take an organization man's delight in diagramming the organization of, respectively, a more overtly sexual kind of Club Med and a clone-based global cult. The diffident but apparently competent software expert of *Whatever* addresses some specifically aesthetic questions: "The progressive effacement of human relationships is not without certain problems for the novel. . . . The novel form is not conceived for depicting indifference or nothingness; a flatter, more terse and dreary discourse would need to be invented." As he warms up, he formulates a distinctly Houellebecqian, furtively puritanical world-view:

> Love as a kind of innocence and as a capacity for illusion, as an aptitude for epitomizing the whole of the other sex in a single loved being, rarely resists a year of sexual immorality, and never two. In reality the successive sexual experiences accumulated during adolescence undermine and rapidly destroy all possibility of projection of an emotional and romantic sort; progressively, and in fact extremely quickly, one becomes as capable of love as an old slag. And so one leads, obviously, a slag's life; in ageing one becomes

less seductive, and on that account bitter. One is jealous of the young, and so one hates them. Condemned to remain unavowable, this hatred festers and becomes increasingly fervent; then it dies down and fades away, just as everything fades away. All that remains is resentment and disgust, sickness and the anticipation of death.

These stately pessimistic reflections, however, are overlaid with a personal development: in the wake of a professional colleague's sudden death in an auto accident, and under the strain of erotic frustration and alcohol, cigarette, and sedative abuse, the hero of *Whatever* suffers a breakdown; he abandons his job, consults a psychiatrist, and enters a hospital. A female psychologist takes him to task for "speaking in general, overly sociological terms"; he responds with the generalization that "this notion of ageing and death is insupportable for the individual human being," and invites her to sleep with him — the only palliative in sight. She prudently replaces her therapeutic presence with that of a male colleague, and he is eventually released: "I left the clinic on 26th of May; I recall the sunshine, the heat, the atmosphere of freedom in the streets. It was unbearable." The hero of Albert Camus's *The Stranger*, a classic repeatedly echoed in Houellebecq's oeuvre, found the harsh sun on an African beach unbearable; even the temperate French sun afflicts the tender mental skin of a stranger sixty years later. He cries a lot, and has volatile sensations, at one moment feeling, "with impressive violence, the possibility of joy," and at another sensing "my skin again as a frontier, and the external world as a crushing weight." Yet a recognizable everyday reality exists in *Whatever*, which is populated by characters who are not all either odious dolts or slavish sex-toys. We experience the hero's effort to rise into happiness ("It's not that I feel tremendously low; it's rather that the world around me appears high") as poignantly sincere, and his estrangement as a personal aberration rather than the universe's fault. Hereafter, in his novels, Houellebecq's will to generalize smothers the real world under a blanket condemnation, and his determination to invent a more congenial one grows.

In an epilogue of fewer than forty pages, *The Possibility of an Island* arrives at a tranquillized beauty that bears some relation to the concluding escape and convalescence of *Whatever*. Troubled by the departure of an e-mail communicant, Marie23, from her haven in New York City, Daniel25, as he is now numbered, puts on a light backpack and, with his beloved Fox, abandons his fenced individual preserve and his guaranteed immortality. He has only a vague plan: to walk southwest across the land that had been Spain to the Canary island of Lanzarote, where Elohimism started. Conveniently, the cult's scientific founders redesigned the neohuman body to survive on water, solar energy, and a small intake of mineral salts, eliminating the need to eat and to defecate. Fox, rapidly adjusting to the wild, catches rabbits and other small prey as master and dog traverse the bleak topography. Daniel25 in his improved body can walk for twenty hours at a time, and the human savages are more afraid of him than he of them. Houellebecq's idealization of sexual congress comes to a Swiftian halt when the timorous savages offer Daniel, as to a god, a human sacrifice, a terrified young female who opens her legs to him. Aware of "the procedures of human sexuality," though after two millennia of chastity the knowledge has become purely theoretical, the neohuman starts to oblige but is "overwhelmed by the pestilential odor that emanated from between her thighs . . . a mixture of the musty smell of shit and rotten fish." Rebuffed, she crawls toward him to commit fellatio—the gold standard of Houellebecq's erotic currency—but her mouth also stinks, and her teeth are rotten and black, and the neohuman "gently" sends her back untouched to her tribe.

Growing fainter, his faithful Fox slain with a bow and arrow by unreconstructed human beings, Daniel25 staggers across a featureless, ashy tract called the Great Gray Space, and reaches, two days after his supply of mineral salts has run out, "a string of puddles and ponds of almost still water" where once there had been ocean. The salty water revives his body and he prepares for, by his estimate, a sixty-year delay before death and irreversible dissolution claim him. He has twenty thousand identical days to live through: "I would avoid thought in the same way I would avoid suffering." In *The Elementary Particles*, it is said of Michel Djerzinski that "he'd always had a tendency to confuse happiness with coma." The love of his life, as she lies dying, "seemed to him completely happy." A fulfilled death-wish may be the best, all orgies past, that Houellebecq can offer. Daniel1, the performer of hateful sketches, boasts of being told by a friend:

> On the intellectual level I was in reality slightly above average, and on the moral level I was the same as everyone else: a bit sentimental, a bit cynical, like most men. I was just very honest, and therein lay my distinction; I was, in relation to the current norms of mankind, almost unbelievably honest.

But how honest, really, is a world-picture that excludes the pleasures of parenting, the comforts of communal belonging, the exercise of daily curiosity, and the moral responsibility, widely met, to make the best of each stage of life, including the last? The island possible to this airless, oppressive imagination has too few natural resources. The final edition of Daniel has sunk to the condition of a mollusk: "I bathed for a long time under the sun and the starlight, and I felt nothing other than a slightly obscure and nutritive sensation." The sensations Houellebecq gives us are not nutritive.

Suppressed Atrocities

CRABWALK, by Günter Grass, translated from the German by Krishna Winston. 234 pp. Harcourt, 2003.

Rumors from literary Germany this past year have had it that Günter Grass, in his mid-seventies and heavy with honors, has produced his best and best-selling novel in at least a decade. The grand old man of German criticism, Marcel Reich-Ranicki, no fan of Grass's later work, is reported to have said the new book—*Im Grebsgang*—moved him to tears. Now it has appeared in English, as *Crabwalk*. The book freewheels through a century of history and contains some fiction as well, but its central topic is the sinking of the refugee-laden German ship *Wilhelm Gustloff*, on January 30, 1945, by a Soviet submarine in the icy Baltic Sea, with the loss of more than nine thousand passengers and crew, making it the worst maritime disaster in history. The total exceeds by several multiples those of the *Titanic* (fifteen hundred) and the *Lusitania* (twelve hundred), though it was approached, we learn in *Crabwalk*, by the toll of two other German ships, the *Cap Arcona* and the *Goya;* seven thousand died in each when they were sunk by Allied forces in the chaotic last weeks of the Second World War in Europe.

As Russian troops invaded from the east, vengeful atrocities inspired panic in German nationals. The *Wilhelm Gustloff*, though it carried a thousand U-boat sailors on their way to Kiel to man submarines, plus three hundred seventy members of the naval women's auxiliary, some wounded fighters, and a few anti-aircraft guns, preponderantly held East Prussian non-combatants fleeing the Russian advance. Many were elderly; more were very young. They crowded aboard at Gotenhafen, several thousand on top of the sixty-six hundred the authorities counted, and included, according to *Crabwalk*, "close to four and a half thousand infants, children, and youths" of whom "not even a hundred survived." As with the *Lusitania* sinking thirty years before, the children—trampled, frozen, and drowned—most horrify the imagination. Grass's fictional survivor, Tulla Pokriefke, relates, "They all skidded off the ship the wrong way round, headfirst. So there they was, floating in them bulky life jackets, their little legs poking up in the air."

Like W. G. Sebald's sober contemplation—published last year in *The New Yorker*—of the Allied firebombing of German cities, *Crabwalk* serves the purpose of calling attention to assaults on the reeling Third Reich that neither the victors nor the defeated victims were motivated to publicize. As postwar revelations of the extermination camps stunned a world already well acquainted with Nazi ruthlessness, the Germans were in no position to ask for sympathy; they set about enduring occupation and picking up the rubble with a stoic silence that Sebald found uncanny. In regard to the *Wilhelm Gustloff*, the Soviet occupiers of what became East Germany did nothing to disturb the silence: the ship's sinking went unmentioned in the official bulletins of the Baltic Red Banner Fleet, and the sub's commander, Aleksandr Marinesko, a hard-drinking carouser from Odessa whose Romanian father spelled his name "Marinescu," was denied the recognition he had expected. Though he sank the twenty-five-thousand-ton *Gustloff* and another German vessel, the *General Von Steuben*, on the same trip, slaying more than twelve thousand of the enemy, he was not declared a Hero of the Soviet Union. Instead, after the war, he was relieved of his command, degraded to lieutenant, and finally discharged from the Soviet Navy, an "indifferent and negligent attitude toward his duties" being cited as the reason. Later, after accusing his superior in a supply depot of corruption, Marinesko was declared tainted himself and sentenced to three years in the Gulag Archipelago. Only in the early Sixties was he awarded a restoration of rank and a pension.

In the West, the *Wilhelm Gustloff* was not quite forgotten. One of the survivors, an eighteen-year-old purser's assistant when the ship went down, "began, when the war was over, to collect and write about everything connected with the *Gustloff*, in good times and bad." His books were published in West Germany but not in the German Democratic Republic. *Crabwalk* also alludes, without bibliographical niceties, to a "paperback book report by the Englishmen Dobson, Miller, and Payne." There was even a movie, *Night Fell over Gotenhafen*, a black-and-white made at the end of the Fifties by a German-American, Frank Wisbar, with German stars. Like the film *Titanic* forty years later, it used the disaster as the background for a romance, while conjuring up by studio arts the dreadful details. Grass writes:

> You see masses of people pushing, clogged corridors, the struggle for every step up the staircase; you see costumed extras imprisoned in the closed promenade deck, feel the ship listing, see the water rising, see people swimming inside the ship, see people drowning. And you see children in the film. Children separated from their mothers. Children holding dangling dolls.

Children wandering lost along corridors that have already been vacated . . . But the more than four thousand infants, children, and youths for whom no survival was possible . . . remained, and will remain, an abstract number, like all the other numbers in the thousands, hundred thousands, millions, that then as now could only be estimated.

The disaster, which Grass nowhere evokes more vividly than here in describing a movie, would seem to provide, in timely fashion, a way to think about collateral damage and war crimes. Can a nation war against a regime without warring against the people the regime rules? Is the very concept "war crime" tautological, given the context of determined violence? As Kofi Annan, the United Nations Secretary-General, said a few weeks ago, "War is always a catastrophe." Are discriminations possible between appropriate and excessive bombing, between legitimate and atrocious ship-sinkings, between proper combat of armed soldiers and such tactics as using civilians, including children, as human shields or disguising an ambush as a surrender? An American soldier recently wounded in such an ambush, when interviewed on television, shrugged and, with striking dispassion, conceded that, given the great imbalance of firepower between the Coalition and Saddam Hussein's Iraq, he could hardly blame his attackers for their murderous ruse.

Crabwalk does not extend blame, beyond suggesting that Marinesko was a lout looking to redeem his spotty service record with a dramatic strike. Germany in the first months of 1945 was down but far from out, as Hitler conscripted ever younger and older men to prolong the war's agony. The thousand young sailors were on their way to man "U-boats of the new, fabulously fast and almost silent XXIII Class." The book admits, "With its coat of gray paint, the *Gustloff* offered an ambiguous target." It was "neither a Red Cross transport nor a cargo ship . . . but an armed passenger liner under the command of the navy, into which the most varied freight had been packed."

The ship's brief career affords a look back into Nazism. The *Gustloff* was almost christened the *Adolf Hitler*, but instead acquired, at its launch in 1937, the name of the head of the Nazi Party in Switzerland, who, two years earlier, had been assassinated by a young Jewish medical student, David Frankfurter.* The sparkling-white one-class cruise ship, built for the Strength through Joy (*Kraft durch Freude*, the KDF) arm of Robert

---

*Frankfurter gave himself up and told the police, "I fired the shots because I am a Jew." He was sentenced to eighteen years by the Swiss court, immigrated to Palestine upon his release, found a position with the Israeli Ministry of Defense, and, although he had been a heavy smoker, lived to the age of seventy-two.

Ley's German Labor Front, carried selected workers on brief holidays to such scenic destinations as the Norwegian fjords, the Straits of Dover, and the island of Madeira; it also brought back the German volunteers of the Legion Condor from the Spanish Civil War. After 1939, it served as a barracks for sailors, and was tied up for years before its fatal last journey. As a by-product of its long docking and emergency activation, four captains competed on the bridge, of whom the most elderly, a sexagenarian called Petersen, tended to prevail; the result of their debates was that the ship sailed at a slow twelve knots, out in the unmined deep channel rather than close to the mined but submarine-proof shore, carrying lit running lights and, like the *Lusitania*, failing to take an evasive zigzag course. All four captains, remarkably, were among the few survivors. The date of the sinking—January 30th—we are more than once reminded, was the anniversary of Wilhelm Gustloff's birth, in 1895, and of Hitler's accession to power, in 1933.

These numerous facts, conveyed in crabwise stops and starts, are mixed or minced in with a fictional family drama. *Crabwalk*'s narrator is not Grass but Paul Pokriefke, a low-level journalist who was born during the sinking, his mother being conveyed in mid-parturition from the *Gustloff* to its lone escort vessel, the torpedo boat *Löwe*. Paul's mother, unwed and a mere seventeen at the time, is Tulla Pokriefke, a native Danziger who had minor roles in Grass's second novel, *Cat and Mouse*, and in his third, *Dog Years*. She settles, as it happens, in Gustloff's home town of Schwerin and switches her promiscuous loyalties from Hitler to Stalin while she labors in an East German furniture factory, following her father's trade. Even in *Cat and Mouse* she smelled of carpenter's glue; now she has snow-white hair incurred the night of the sinking.

Her son defects to West Germany at the age of fifteen, becomes a journalist, and marries a student, Gabi, ten years his junior; she gets pregnant, they have a son, Konrad, and divorce. When the Wall comes down, Konrad sees a lot more of his grandmother, who tells him her tales of the *Gustloff* and buys him a computer; he becomes an avid devotee of the Internet. Meanwhile, Paul, who despite his mother's urging has never written about his miraculous birth and the *Gustloff*, is employed to do so by a "person not to be confused with me," an "old man, who has worn himself out writing." Who might this person be but Günter Grass? In researching the *Gustloff*'s sinking, Paul finds a valuable cyberspace chat room operated, it turns out, by his son, who is now a Nazi apologist. Konrad engages there in fierce but half-playful debate with another teenager, a philo-Semite named David. Violence eventually ensues, followed by reflections on the effects of distracted parenting and a tormented national history. Pokriefke states, "The history we Germans have repeatedly mucked up is a clogged toilet. We flush and flush, but the shit keeps rising."

This moral is not new, nor is Grass's method of a crabwise narrative, revolving facts and incidents in a colloquial, sometimes humorous, somehow harried voice. The mix this time is especially potent, drawn from the Nazi depths and from the contemporary Babel of the Internet, which seethes like a global subconscious, spreading information and misinformation and what Nietzsche called *ressentiment*. The central characters— mother, son, grandson—are partially opaque, but so are we all, we are assured. Paul, the fatherless failed father, tells his many-sided story under the chastening direction of his ghostly employer, the *Überdichter*. "He, who claims to know me, contends that I don't know my own flesh and blood." He tells Paul to leave his son's thoughts out of the narrative: "No one knows what he was thinking and is thinking now. Every mind is sealed, not just his." The generations have their inexpressible secrets, as Nazi glamour calls to skinheads across a gulf of past atrocity and ruin. "Nothing absolves us," Paul concludes, with the earned weariness of old Europe.* We are not even absolved of the necessity to act, to go on.

Murder Among the Miniaturists

MY NAME IS RED, by Orhan Pamuk, translated from the Turkish by Erdağ M. Göknar. 421 pp. Knopf, 2001.

Orhan Pamuk is a fifty-year-old Turk frequently hailed as his country's best novelist. He is both avant-garde and best-selling. His eminence, like that of the Albanian Ismail Kadare, looms singularly; Western culture-consumers, it may be, don't expect Turkey and Albania to produce novelists at all—at least, novelists so wise in the ways of modernism and postmodernism. Pamuk, the grandson of a wealthy factory-owner and railroad-builder, has been privileged to write without needing to make a living by it. From a family of engineers, he studied engineering, architecture, and journalism, and practiced none of them. Until the age of thirty, he lived with his parents, writing novels that did not get published. When literary success dawned, he married, and now, living in Istanbul with his

---

*"Old Europe"—a phrase given passing notoriety by Secretary of Defense Donald Rumsfeld's dismissal of European objection to the 2003 American-British intervention in Iraq.

wife and daughter, he composes, according to an interview he gave *Publishers Weekly* in 1994, from eleven at night to four in the morning and then again, after arising at noon, from two in the afternoon to eight. The results have been prodigious: six novels which recapitulate in Turkish the twentieth-century novel's major modes. His first, *Cevdet Bey and Sons*, was likened to Thomas Mann's *Buddenbrooks;* his next, *The Silent House*, a multiply narrated week of family interaction, stirred mention of Virginia Woolf and William Faulkner; his third, *The White Castle*, a creepy seventeenth-century tale of double identity, evoked comparison to Borges and Calvino; the fourth, *The Black Book*, a missing-persons adventure saturated in details of Istanbul, was written, by Pamuk's own admission, with Joyce's *Ulysses* in mind; the fifth, *The New Life*, a dreamlike first-person contemporary tale, was called "Kafka with a light touch"; and the sixth, *My Name Is Red*, a murder mystery set in sixteenth-century Istanbul, uses the art of miniature illumination much as Mann's Doctor Faustus used music—to explore a nation's soul.

My Name Is Red weighs in, with its appended chronology, at more than four hundred big pages and belongs, in its high color and scholarly density, with other recent novels that load extensive book-learning onto a detective-story plot—e.g., A. S. Byatt's *Possession* and Umberto Eco's *The Name of the Rose* and *Foucault's Pendulum*. One worries, with such triumphally erudite and exhaustive postmodern novels, whether their rather ironically melodramatic story can carry its burden of pedantry and large import. Nineteenth-century novelists catered to a more generous, less nibbled attention span; they breathed with bigger lungs and naturally wrote long, deep, and wide. My impression of Pamuk is that, though he has the patience and constructive ability of the nineteenth-century fabricators and their heirs Proust and Mann, his instinctive affinity is with the relatively short-winded Calvino and Borges, philosophical artificers of boxes within boxes. Pamuk's boxes are bigger, but the feeling persists, of craftsmanship exulting in its powers, of giant gadgets like those with which the European powers used to woo Turkey's Sultan with evidence of Western technology.

Pamuk's ingenuity is yoked to a profound sense of enigma and doubleness. The doubleness, he has said, derives from that of Turkey itself, a nation straddling Asia and Europe and divided between the progressive "Kemalist" heritage of Kemal Atatürk's radical reforms of 1924—secularism in government, public education for all, voting rights for women, the replacement of the Arabic alphabet with the Roman one—and conservative Islam, now resurgent as a repressive, potentially violent fundamentalism from Morocco to Malaysia.

The ostensible topic of *My Name Is Red* is the threatened Westernization of Ottoman pictorial art, an offshoot, protected by the Sultan Murat III (r. 1574–95), of the Persian tradition of miniature painting. In honor of the thousandth anniversary (measured in lunar years) of the Hegira, which occurred in 622 A.D., an illustrated book is being prepared for the Sultan in the "Frankish" or "Venetian" style of receding perspective and recognizable individual portraiture. In the first chapter of *My Name Is Red*, a miniaturist named Elegant, a specialist in gilding, objects so strenuously to the blasphemy of this stylistic change that another miniaturist, unidentified, kills him and drops his body down a well. Later, the same assailant kills Enishte ("Uncle"), the organizer of this dangerous book. One of the three involved miniaturists—who are named, in picturesque Ottoman style, Butterfly, Olive, and Stork—must be the murderer. The detective, for want of another, is Enishte's nephew, Black, who has returned to Istanbul "like a sleepwalker" after twelve years away in Persia, "carrying letters and collecting taxes" and "working as a secretary in the service of pashas." In his youth he studied with the miniaturist apprentices but did not last the course; he exiled himself after Enishte rejected his suit for the hand of Enishte's daughter, Shekure. Now Black has been summoned back by his uncle to help him organize the book for the Sultan. When Enishte is slain, Shekure, whose first husband disappeared in battle four years earlier, hastily weds Black but will not let the marriage be consummated until he brings the murderer to justice.

This curious, sumptuous, protracted mystery novel consists of fifty-nine chapters told from a total of twelve viewpoints, including that of the murderer. The two slain characters address us from the afterlife, and we are even treated, at the end of the longest chapter, to the viewpoint of a severed head, whose eyes and brain for a while continue, in morose fashion, to function. The reader participates, wincingly, in two blindings by means of the very needle (a "turquoise- and mother-of-pearl–handled golden needle used to fasten plumes to turbans") with which the supreme master of Persian miniatures, Bizhad of Herat (c. 1460–1535), blinded himself, by one interpretation, "to make the statement that whosoever beheld the pages of this book"—the Mongol *Book of Kings*—"even once would no longer wish to see anything else in this world" or else, by another, more pragmatic theory, to avoid being forced to paint in an uncongenial way for the new conqueror of Herat.

Black, as he rushes about Istanbul trying to win Shekure's heart with feats of detection, relates the most chapters, twelve. Shekure relates eight chapters, and these speed by with the most ease and psychological interest; in her voice the novel becomes a romantic one, driven by emotion and intimate concerns. Preoccupied with her own feelings, her own survival, and the protection of her two young sons, she rarely lectures us on the nuances, stylistic and religious, of Persian-style miniatures. When other characters do, *My Name Is Red* acquires the brilliant stasis of the depictions themselves, and seems to go nearly nowhere. Esther, a Jewish clothes-peddler and matchmaker who furthers Shekure's romantic affairs, is another welcome female voice in this stifling male world. At the men-only coffeehouse behind the slave market, an unnamed storyteller—a "curtain-caller," in Persian terminology—performs nine impertinent, irreverent monologues based on rough drawings supplied by the miniaturists. After taking on the personae of a dog, a tree, a coin, Death, the color crimson, a horse, Satan, and two dervishes, he surpasses himself with his discourse on the topic of Woman. He realizes that in his society the topic is pretty well covered up:

> In the cities of the European Franks, women roam about exposing not only their faces, but also their brightly shining hair (after their necks, their most attractive aspect), their arms, their beautiful throats, and even, if what I've heard is true, a portion of their gorgeous legs: as a result, the men of those cities walk about with difficulty, embarrassed and in extreme pain, because, you see, their front-sides are always erect and this fact naturally leads to the paralysis of their society as a whole. Undoubtedly, this is why each day the Frank infidel surrenders another fortress to us Ottomans.

Though celibate, the storyteller as a youth had succumbed to his curiosity about this exotic other gender and tried on the clothes of his color and aunt; instantly he was invaded by sensations of sensitivity, along with "an irrepressible affection toward all children" and a desire "to nurse everybody and cook for the whole world." When he stuffed his aunt's pistachio-green silk with socks and cloths to simulate breasts, a rich range of contradictory feelings was enjoyed:

> I immediately understood that men, merely catching sight of the shadow of my overabundance, would chase after them and strive to take them into their mouths; I felt quite powerful, but is that what I wanted? I was befuddled: I wanted both to be powerful and to be the object of pity; I wanted a rich, powerful and intelligent man, whom I didn't know from Adam, to fall madly in love with me; yet I also feared such a man.

These androgynous intuitions lead the storyteller to sing of the doubleness that haunts the novel: "*My other parts insist I be a woman when I'm a man and a man when I'm a woman. / How difficult it is being human, even worse is living a human life. / I want to amuse myself frontside and backside, to be Eastern and Western both.*"

Shortly after this recitation, the storyteller is killed by a mob of the followers of the cleric Nusret of Erzurum, who preaches that the woes besetting Istanbul—fires, plagues, war casualties, counterfeit coins, decadent drugged behavior of dervishes and others—are laid "to our having strayed from the path of the Prophet, to disregard for the strictures of the Glorious Koran." Pamuk (who, in his interview with *Publishers Weekly*, pointed out that he was the first person in Turkey to defend Salman Rushdie and claimed that in his childhood "religion was something that belonged to the poor and the servants") makes us tremble for the fate of storytellers in a culture where, to quote him again, "the fundamentalist movement [is] the revenge of the poor against the educated, westernized Turks." The *New York Times* last June gave a grim report on the condition of books and fiction in Muslim lands. "In recent years in Egypt," said the *Times*, "mere questioning about a novel's content by any religious faction is usually sufficient grounds to get it banned." One wonders how religious factions in Turkey reacted to the Islamic content of *My Name Is Red*, which treats of the Islamic afterlife in deadpan detail, including "a portrayal of Our Exalted Prophet's bewilderment and ticklishness, as angels seized him by his underarms during his ascension to Heaven from the top of a minaret," and which investigates with what might seem blasphemous closeness the sacrilege lurking in pictorial representation.

"The maker of images or pictures is the enemy of God": thus Muhammad is alleged to have spoken in the collection of legends and sayings called the Hadith. Though the Koran contains no explicit prohibition of imagery, the Prophet, in the Hadith, says, "The angels will not enter a house in which there is a picture or a dog." Muhammadism's iconoclasm, born of the fledgling monotheism's rivalry with pagan idolatry, has been variously enforced, depending on the ruler, in Islam's far-flung domains. Persia and India were less strict than the Middle East. The Sultan Murat III, reigning in 1591, when most of this novel's events take place, was the Ottoman Sultan with the warmest interest in books and miniatures in the Persian style. The heyday of Ottoman court painting ended with him, and its justification was always tenuous, as Black describes it:

> Pictures are forbidden by our faith. Since the illustrations of the Persian master, even the masterpieces of the greatest masters of Herat, are ultimately seen as an extension of border ornamentation, no one would take issue with them, reasoning that they enhanced the beauty of writing and the magnificence of calligraphy.

The miniaturists themselves knew they were treading, as it were, a fine line, on the edge of Allah's creative prerogatives. The traits followed by the Persian masters—bright, unshaded colors; a high horizon; stylized faces, generally in profile; and little depth perspective—were designed to recall the world as Allah first saw it, freshly created. A traditionally depicted horse, say, shows Allah's idea of a horse, "the horse meticulously imagined by Allah." Human beings, too, are not meant "to resemble exactly those figures which we see around us. Quite to the contrary, they signify that they've emerged from Allah's memory. This is the reason why time has stopped for them within that picture." Miniatures depict this world "as if it were the Otherworld," which summons us, through its beauty, "toward life's abundance, toward compassion, toward respect for the colors of the realm which God created, and toward reflection and faith." As the miniaturist called Butterfly puts it: "Yes, God must have wanted the art of illumination to be ecstasy so He could demonstrate how the world itself is ecstasy to those who are able to see."

Yet seeing can become a temptation, and blindness—"a blessed darkness and the infinity of a blank page"—a virtuous renunciation. "Blindness is a realm of bliss from which the Devil and guilt are barred," the miniaturist called Olive asserts. In a realm so fraught with metaphysical nicety and deference, the inventions of European painting form a perilous irruption, bringing with them "the violence implicit in the desire to be one-of-a-kind, unique and exceptional." The traditional miniaturist masters often left their work unsigned, and suppressed the deviations that might have constituted a personal style. Individual portraits quicken the heretical desire to be "different from all others." The portraitists "dare to situate their subjects in the center of the page, as if man were meant to be worshipped"; however ordinary the subject, he is placed "in the center of this world, where Our Sultan should have been." And objects in European perspective, with distant ones smaller than those in the foreground, "weren't depicted according to their importance in Allah's mind, but as they appeared to the naked eye—the way the Franks painted." When it is pointed out that "exalted Allah certainly sees everything we see," the rejoinder states, "He doesn't perceive it the way we do. The confused battle scene that we perceive in our bewilderment, He perceives in His omniscience as two opposing armies in an orderly array." Heresy hovers on all sides of the issue: the coffeehouse storyteller impudently raises the possibility that the classical miniaturists, in attempting to show not what they see but what God imagines, are "committing the sin of competing with Allah." The trend, however, as of 1591, is clear: Frankish painting and the egotistic delights of individualization will prove irresistible, and Turkish artists, the murderer tells his confreres in one of his many concluding pronouncements, henceforth "can sit yourselves down and do nothing but ape the Europeans century after century! Proudly sign your names to your imitation paintings."

Pamuk's consciousness of Turkey's fate of imitation and inauthenticity prompts his characters' frequent feelings of detachment from their real selves. "I feel I'm living the present as if it were the past," the murderer says, and he watches his body commit a crime "as if it were a memory from long ago. You know how in dreams we shudder to see ourselves as if from the outside?" He warns that, if painters succumb to the Frankish manner, "we might resemble ourselves, but we won't be ourselves." Other selves haunt the innocent, too: Shekure says, "We re-entered that house in the dead of night, and it suddenly seemed that the elongated shadows we were casting by the light of the oil lamp belonged to others." Later, "as I cried it was as if I'd left myself and was becoming another, entirely separate woman. Like some reader troubled by a sad picture in the pages of a book, I saw my life from the outside and pitied what I saw." The author, the mysterious contriver of these dozen intertwining viewpoints, is both outside and inside this fiction. Shekure's younger son is called Orhan, and it turns out to be he who, with her coöperation, has written this novel. In the proud fashion of Joyce finishing *Ulysses*, Pamuk has dated *My Name Is Red* at the end: "1990–92, 1994–98." The novel bears traces of an interrupted composition, wherein the author had to get a fresh grip upon the many glittering threads of theory and incident. Orhan Pamuk's labor, in this otherworld of miniatures, was long, and the reader's labor at times feel long, between spells of being entranced and educated.

Translating from the Turkish, a non–Indo-European language with a grammar that puts the verb at the end of even the longest sentence, isn't a task for everybody; Erdağ Göknar deserves praise for the cool, smooth English in which he has rendered Pamuk's finespun sentences, passionate art appreciations, slyly pedantic debates, eerie urban scenes (it keeps snowing, which one doesn't think of as Istanbul weather), and exhaustive inventories. The inventory, Borges showed in his short story "The Aleph," evokes the terror of infinity; Pamuk gives us two pages listing miniatures through the ages, a paragraph crammed with the contents of the Sultan's Treasury, and a brisk itemization of Ottoman tortures. Göknar's English has such an air of classical timelessness that I was startled by the use, twice, of the word "ornery," with its flavor of American country dialect, and by the appearance, twice, of the phrase "could care less" when the opposite was meant. And I was unable to discover what the title referred to. Murat III, my independent researches discovered, had "a long red beard," but the most likely source within the novel is the coffee-house monologue delivered by the color crimson, a large pot of which is used to commit the second murder. The color of blood, it boasts, "As I bring my color to the page, it's as if I command the world to 'Be!' Yes, those who cannot see would deny it, but the truth is that I can be found everywhere." The world's name, in other words, is Red.

Arabesques of Ambivalence

SNOW, by Orhan Pamuk, translated from the Turkish by Maureen Freely. 428 pp. Knopf, 2004.

Orhan Pamuk's new novel abounds with modernist tracer genes. Like Proust's *Remembrance of Things Past*, it bares its inner gears of reconstituted memory and ends by promising its own composition. Its hero, a poet, goes by the name of Ka, a hard-to-miss allusion to Kafka's K., the hero of *The Castle*. Its setting, the forlorn provincial city of Kars—though *kar* means "snow," Kars is an actual place, in Turkey's northwestern corner, near Armenia; it was destroyed by Tamerlane in 1386 and occupied by Russia off and on in the nineteenth and early twentieth centuries—suggests, in four hectic days during which the city is snowbound, the mountainous, debate-prone microcosm of Thomas Mann's sanatorium in *The Magic Mountain*, with a lethal whiff of Dostoevsky's unnamed "our town" in *The Possessed*. The airy spirit of postmodernism also haunts the shadows and spiral staircases of Pamuk's intricate narrative. Like Italo Calvino, Pamuk has a passion for pattern-making; he maps Kars as obsessively as Joyce did Dublin and marshals the nineteen poems that Ka writes there into the form of a diagrammatic snowflake. Not that *Snow* doesn't flow, with suspense at every dimpled vortex. Pamuk is gifted with a light, absurdist touch, spinning out farcical plot developments to the point of implying that any plot, in this indifferent and chaotic universe, is farcical. He is attracted to the unreal reality, the false truth, of theatrical performance, and *Snow*, in its political aspect, pivots on two nights of performance at the Kars National Theatre, in which illusion and reality are confoundingly entwined.

The comedy of public events, where protest and proclamation rapidly age into melodramatic cliché, overlays certain tragic realities of contemporary Turkey: the poverty of opportunity that leads unemployed men to sit endlessly in teahouses watching television; the tension between the secularism established by Kemal Atatürk in the 1920s and the recent rise of political Islam; the burning issue of the *hijab*, the woman's head scarf; the cultural divide between a Westernized elite and the theistic masses. In its geography, Turkey straddles Europe and Asia; its history includes a triumphant imperial episode under the Ottoman sultans and, after long

decline, a secular, modernizing revolution under Atatürk. Tradition there
wears not only the fez and the turban but the uniform of the Islam-
resistant army.

Ka, a forty-two-year-old, unmarried Istanbul native who for twelve
years has lived as a political exile in Germany, comes to Kars, which he
briefly visited twenty years ago, in order to investigate and report on, for
a friend's newspaper, a local epidemic of suicide among young women.
He also wants to look up a university classmate, the beautiful İpek, who,
he has learned, is separated from her husband, Muhtar. Muhtar, another
old acquaintance, is running for mayor of Kars; this election is one of the
threads that are all but buried in the subsequent days beneath a veritable
blizzard of further complications and characters. The Anatolian venue,
its deteriorating architecture poetically redolent of former Armenian and
Russian inhabitants, is populated by Turks whose names have, to an
American reader, a fairy-tale strangeness: İpek, Kadife, Zahide, Sunay
Zaim, Funda Eser, Güner Bener, Hakan Özge, Mesut, Fazıl, Necip, Tes-
lime, Abdurraham Öz, Osman Nuri Çolak, Tarkut Ölçün, and (Ka's full
name, which he suppresses) Kerim Alakuşoğlu.

In his temporary role of journalist, Ka is given access to a succession of
local viewpoints, ranging from that of the deputy governor (who tells
him, "If unhappiness were a genuine reason for suicide, half the women in
Turkey would be killing themselves") and the police and the benign religious teacher Sheikh Saadettin Efendi to that of the outlaw terrorist Blue
and İpek's sister, the *hijab*-wearing Kadife, who in the end proposes that
women commit suicide to show their pride: "The moment of suicide is the
time when they understand best how lonely it is to be a woman, and what
being a woman really means." Early in his visit, İpek tersely sums up the
situation for him: "The men give themselves to religion, and the women
kill themselves." When he asks, "Why?" she responds with "a look that
told him he would get nowhere by pressing her for quick answers." But
the feminist question, in the course of over four hundred pages, pales
beside more vividly animated issues: Ka's revived ability to write poems;
his tortuous campaign to persuade İpek to marry him and join him in the
marginal existence of an exiled Turkish poet in Frankfurt; his debates with
several young students (Necip, Fazıl) at the Kars religious high school
over whether or not he and other Europeanized Turks are inevitably athe-
ists; and, in the most farcical-tragical twist of plot, a violent Kemalist
(pro-secular, anti–political-Islamist) coup in the snowbound municipality,
engineered from the stage by the veteran itinerant actor Sunay Zaim.

Ka, who on his first day in Kars witnesses the assassination of an education official who had forbidden head scarves, becomes increasingly
involved in many-sided intrigues and shuttles back and forth like the hero

of a thriller; but he is not believable as such, possessing, as he does, a pre-occupying ear for the poems being dictated to him by a higher power and entertaining a constant concern with his own uncertainties. Does he believe in God or not? Is happiness worth having? Ka decides, after an ecstatic interlude with İpek, that "the greatest happiness in life was to embrace a beautiful, intelligent girl and sit in a corner writing poetry." But even this unexceptional conclusion melts away under his doubts: he foresees that in Frankfurt a "crushing, soul-destroying pain would eat away at their happiness." And the handsome Blue, whose main terrorist activity seems to be seducing women, assures him, "People who seek only happiness never find it."

Dithering, reflective Ka, the embodiment of Turkish ambivalence, is, we learn, a Gemini. He acquires a near-twin (this author has a weakness for near-twins, for men who interpenetrate each other, like the seven-teenth-century Italian slave and his Muslim master in *The White Castle*, or like Necip and Fazıl in this novel) when "Orhan the novelist" takes on an increasingly voluble first-person voice and presence. Orhan, it turns out, has travelled to Kars to investigate the adventures of his friend Ka four years after they occurred. The narrative's subtext emerges as a sophisticated and esteemed writer's aporia—his bafflement—in the face of his nation's backwardness, superstition, and misery. What do Ka's inner states—the bliss of intermittent inspiration, the romantic dreams of erotic conquest, his intense nostalgia for a sheltered childhood, his flitting sense that Islam is correct and God does exist—have to do with the world's economic and political facts? His is the social class that left Islam to the servants and welcomed military coups, with their cozy curfews and stirring martial music broadcast over the radio. When Ka's friend and rival Muhtar is beaten by the police, "Ka imagined that Muhtar had found redemption in this beating; it might have released him from the guilt and spiritual agony he felt at the misery and stupidity of his country." The only lines that are quoted from Ka's nineteen suddenly inspired poems run:

> Even if your mother came down from heaven to take you into her arms,
> Even if your wicked father let her go without a beating for just one night,
> You'd still be penniless, your shit would still freeze, your soul would still
>   wither, there is no hope!
> If you're unlucky enough to live in Kars, you might as well flush yourself
>   down the toilet.

The unlucky, however, protest: during a political meeting that patheti-cally, comically, endearingly struggles to frame a statement for the

Frankfurter Rundschau, a passionate young Kurd cries, "We're not stupid, we're just poor!" He goes on, "When a Westerner meets someone from a poor country, he feels deep contempt. He assumes that the poor man's head must be full of all the nonsense that plunged his country into poverty and despair." The author himself, arriving at what he terms "perhaps . . . the heart of our story," asks,

> How much can we hope to understand those who have suffered deeper anguish, greater deprivation, and more crushing disappointments than we ourselves have known? Even if the world's rich and powerful were to put themselves in the shoes of the rest, how much would they really understand the wretched millions suffering around them? So it is when Orhan the novelist peers into the dark corners of his poet friend's difficult and painful life: How much can he really see?

Thus the aesthetic and private passions so crucial to Ka double back, in a way, upon politics. Empathy knits a society together and as well enables works of imagination. But do the rich and powerful, once having imagined their way into the shoes of the less fortunate, change course and renounce all they have, as both Buddha and Jesus advised? And would it do enough good if they did? Is not conflict, between classes and nations both, often between groups that understand each other all too well? They compete for the same goods, the same land, the same control of resources. Pamuk's conscience-ridden and carefully wrought novel, stirring in its scope, candor, and humor, does not incite us, even in our imaginations, to overthrow existing conditions in Turkey. When the Kars coup occurs, the enthusiasm among unemployed youths leads to the dry authorial comment "They seemed to think that last night's events marked the beginning of a new age in which immorality and unemployment would no longer be tolerated; it was as if they thought the army had stepped in expressly to find them jobs." Such realistic fatalism, and the poet's duty "to hear the hidden music that was the source of all art" and to believe that "life had a secret geometry," drains *Snow*'s ideological contests of blood. We *could* care less, but not much less. Ka has a drifting, ghostly presence that becomes exasperatingly mired in the role of negotiator, schemer, man of action; it wasn't clear, at least to this reader, what his decisive action, for which he suffers in the end, was. Nor is his love for İpek, beautiful and wise as she is conjured to be, very involving. Their exchanges have an enigmatic bleakness:

> "I learned everything they taught us about Islam, but then I forgot it. Now it's as if everything I know about Islam is from *The Message*—you know, that film starring Anthony Quinn." Ka smiled. "It was showing not

long ago on the Turkish channel in Germany—but, for some strange reason, in German. You're here this evening, aren't you?"

"Yes."

"Because I want to read you my poem again," said Ka, as he put his notebook into his pocket. "Do you think it's beautiful?"

"Yes, really, it's beautiful."

"What's beautiful about it?"

"I don't know, it's just beautiful," said İpek. She opened the door to leave. Ka threw his arms around her and kissed her on the mouth.

Perhaps—though Maureen Freely's translation is fluent and lucid throughout—it reads better in Turkish. If at times *Snow* seems attenuated and opaque, we should not forget that in Turkey, insofar as it partakes of the Islamic world's present murderous war of censorious fanaticism versus free speech and truth-seeking, to write with honest complexity about such matters as head scarves and religious belief takes courage. Pamuk, relatively young as he is at the age of fifty-two, qualifies as that country's most likely candidate for the Nobel Prize, and the near-assassination of Islam's last winner must cross his mind. To produce a major work so frankly troubled and provocatively bemused and, against the grain of the author's usual antiquarian bent, entirely contemporary in its setting and subjects, took the courage that art sometimes asks of even its most detached and private practitioners.

Extended Performance

WIZARD OF THE CROW, by Ngũgĩ wa Thiong'o, translated from the Gikuyu by the author. 768 pp. Pantheon, 2006.

The Kenyan novelist, playwright, journalist, and academic Ngũgĩ wa Thiong'o has written provocatively, in his book of essays *Penpoints, Gunpoints, and Dreams* (1998), about "performance"—not merely theatrical action, as in the performance of a play, but as "any action that assumes an audience during the actualization." He cites in illustration the exercise of political power, which involves "variations on the performance theme." A 1999 interview with Charles Cantalupo, a Penn State professor, elicited this elaboration:

So much in society depends on "performance." It provides new insights into certain behaviors. It is central to so many things. For example, you can't have religion without performance: performance, weekly, daily. . . .

Performance enables people to negotiate their way through the various realms of being. Performance is a means for people to realize their unknown, even if it's only in the imagination. Performance is a very important concept. I have learned from it, but also I have been involved in it.

In his crowded career and eventful life, Ngũgĩ has enacted, for all to see, the paradigmatic trials and quandaries of a contemporary African writer, caught in sometimes implacable political, social, racial, and linguistic currents.

Born in 1938, in the village of Kamiriithu, just north of Nairobi, in the so-called white highlands of colonial Kenya, Ngũgĩ was the fifth child of the third of his father's four wives; his father was a peasant farmer compelled to become a squatter after the British Imperial Act of 1915. Ngũgĩ attended mission-run and independent Gikuyu schools. He read Dickens and Robert Louis Stevenson, H. Rider Haggard and John Buchan. He was for a time a devout Christian, and at the age of twenty-three married his first wife, Nyambura, who was to bear six of his eventual nine children. In 1963, he received a bachelor's degree in English from Makerere University College in Kampala, Uganda, and practiced journalism in Nairobi. The previous year, his first play, *The Black Hermit*, had been produced in Kampala. In 1964, he left for England to pursue graduate studies at Leeds University; the same year, he published, under the name James Ngugi, *Weep Not, Child*, his first novel and among the first to be published in English by a black East African. *The River Between* (1965) and the classic *A Grain of Wheat* (1967) followed. Their success did not deter him, however, from questioning the importance granted in Kenyan education to the colonial language. At Leeds he had read, with revelatory effect, Marx, Fanon, and the Barbadian writer George Lamming, whom he credited with composing, in *In the Castle of My Skin*, "the first novel that painted a picture of myself in Africa." In 1968, Ngugi co-authored, with two others, an article entitled "On the Abolition of the English Department," asking, "If there is need for a 'study of the historic continuity of a single culture,' why can't this be African?"

Ngugi made headlines when, in 1969, he changed his name to Ngũgĩ wa Thiong'o, and when, in late 1977, Daniel arap Moi, Kenya's Vice-President, ordered him to be detained in Kamiti Maximum Security Prison for a year without trial. His offense had been involvement with a community theatre in his home village, and his co-authorship, with Ngũgĩ wa Mirii, of a play in the Gikuyu language, *Ngaahika Ndeenda* (*I Will Marry When I Want*). The play was banned; the theatre in Kamiriithu was razed. When the playwright emerged from prison, he announced that henceforth he would write in Gikuyu. His association with the theatre, he has explained, was a "homecoming: the only language I could use was my own." Prior to this decision, according to Maya Jaggi's recent profile in *The Guardian*, he had thought he must stop writing; "I knew about whom I was writing, but not for whom." His first novel in Gikuyu, *Caitgaani Muthara-ini* (*Devil on the Cross*, 1980), was written in prison, on toilet paper. His last novel in English, *Petals of Blood* (1978), tackled, from a distinctly leftist angle, contemporary corruption in Kenya and its government. Upon his release from prison, he was not reinstated in his position at Nairobi University, and in 1982 he left Kenya for London. His exile eventually took him to California, where he is a professor of English and comparative literature at the Irvine campus of the University of California and the head of its International Center for Writing and Translation; his second wife, Njeeri wa Thiong'o, directs the faculty-and-staff counseling center there. Ngũgĩ had vowed never to return to Kenya as long as Moi, who had become President, and his Kanu Party were in power; both were ousted in the elections of December 2002, and in 2004 Ngũgĩ returned, with Njeeri, to launch the first volume of a thousand-page novel, *Murogi wa Kagogo*, which he had been writing since 1997. Met by a crowd of well-wishers and press at Nairobi Airport, the author announced that he wanted to be "in touch with the everyday." Two weeks later, the everyday in Kenya arrived with a vengeance when the couple were attacked by four men in their high-security apartment complex. Ngũgĩ was beaten and his face burned with cigarettes; in another room, Njeeri was sexually assaulted. Jewelry, a laptop, and some cash were taken, but Ngũgĩ maintained to Maya Jaggi:

> "It wasn't a simple robbery. It was political—whether by remnants of the old regime or part of the new state outside the main current. They hung around as though waiting for something, and the whole thing was meant to humiliate, if not eliminate, us.... We think there's a bigger circle of forces—not just those who attacked us."

Three security guards and a nephew of Ngũgĩ's by marriage were apprehended; their trial is still going on. The frequency of violent crime in Nairobi is itself perhaps adverse comment enough upon the forces at work in post-colonial Africa. The forces ensconced in Ngũgĩ's imaginary Free Republic of Aburĩria, the venue of *Murogi wa Kagogo*, are demonically malign, and even the benign counterforces partake of magic and sorcery. English-language readers can now explore Aburĩria in an English translation by the author, under the title *Wizard of the Crow*. Such readers would do well to remember that it is a translation from a language whose narrative traditions are mostly oral and heavy on performance; the tale is fantastic and didactic, told in broad strokes of caricature. Its principal political actors wear physical distortions like large, firelit masks. Aburĩria's Minister of Foreign Affairs, Markus Machokali, had been an ordinary member of Parliament until he went to London for plastic surgery to enlarge his eyes, "to make them ferociously sharp, or as he put it in Kiswahili, *Yawe Macho Kali,* so that he would be able to spot the enemies of the Ruler no matter how far their hiding places. Enlarged to the size of electric bulbs, his eyes were now the most prominent feature of his face, dwarfing his nose, cheeks and forehead." A rival, Silver Sikiokuu, observing Machokali's subsequent promotion, flew to Paris and had his ears made "larger than a rabbit's and always primed to detect danger at any time and from any direction"; he is named Minister of State, "in charge of spying on the citizenry." A third aspirant to high office, Benjamin Mambo, had his tongue elongated in Paris, but "the tongue, like a dog's, now hung out way beyond his lips, rendering speech impossible," until a remedial operation in Germany extended his lips so "the tongue protruded just a little." A late entrant to the halls of power, John Kaniũrũ, is known as Johnny the Nose, John Nose, or "the nosy one."

As for the nameless Ruler, he gradually grows larger all over, through a mysterious complaint diagnosed as a full-body pregnancy, until his head scrapes the ceiling of even the grandest chamber of state. When he at last bursts, around page 700, he gives birth to an abortive Baby Democracy and a cloud of foul-smelling smog that permeates the capital, Eldares; from his ordeal the Ruler emerges slender as a snake, with a head "the size of a fist" and a flickering tongue observed by at least one keen-eyed witness to be forked. *Wizard of the Crow*'s fantasia of corruption and malformation is erratically filtered through the excited, drink-primed telling of an ordinary policeman, a delegate from the everyday—Constable Arigaigai Gathere, known as A.G. Any inconsistencies or vague spots in A.G.'s and Ngũgĩ wa Thiong'o's tangled tale can be passed off as an aspect of oral narrative, wherein auditors repeat to others what they hear and every listener thereby becomes "a teller of tales, insisting on his own authority."

The forces of evil in the seething dictatorship of Aburĩria are gamely resisted by a young couple, Kamĩtĩ, sometimes known as Comet Kamĩtĩ, and Grace Nyawĩra, who has her own gifts of shape-shifting and deception. The two meet in the office of Eldares Modern Construction and Real Estate, where Grace is the boss's secretary, and Kamĩtĩ applies for a job. Though the young man holds a B.A. in economics and an M.B.A. earned in India, the boss, Titus Tajirika—who turns out, in the many plot twists ahead, to embody the indestructible spirit of Aburīrian venality—denies him a job. The secretary, however, follows Kamītī when the office closes, and a beautiful liaison begins. They soon meet again, disguised as beggars, and take refuge in her room. There they talk and tussle; as their clothes slip off, he is transfixed by "her long gazelle neck, her shapely breasts so full, her nipples, the color of blackberry, so erect," but, since he fails to produce a condom, he wins only a stern lecture on AIDS and VD. Later, when she has pursued him across the plains to his mountain haven, he still hasn't learned his lesson. "I am sorry that I don't have any condoms," he sheepishly says, and again encounters contradiction:

> "No, no, don't stop," Nyawīra told him. "I brought some," she added as she unbuttoned his trousers.
>
> On the ground, in the cave, now wrapped in darkness, they found themselves airborne over hills and valleys, floating through blue clouds to the mountaintop of pure ecstasy, from where, suspended in space, they felt the world go round and round, before they descended, sliding down a rainbow, toward the earth, earth, where the grass, plants and animals seemed to be singing a lullaby of silence as Nyawīra and Kamītī, now locked in each other's arms, slept the sleep of babies, the dawn of a day awaiting.

O.K.—back to saving Aburīria. Kamītī when we first see him is airborne; light-headed from hunger, he collapses at the foot of a mountain of garbage where he is foraging, and sees himself from on high. His "bird self" hints at an unusual disposition, as does a preternatural sense of smell that nearly overwhelms him with a "stench blast" when he is near money or greedy people and that signals Nyawīra's proximity with a powerful smell of flowers. Fleeing the police in the wake of the political protest, he and Nyawīra improvise a fetish of bones and rags and he pens a warning, THIS PROPERTY BELONGS TO A WIZARD WHOSE POWER BRINGS DOWN HAWKS AND CROWS FROM THE SKY. TOUCH THIS HOUSE AT YOUR PERIL. SGD. WIZARD OF THE CROW. The highly suggestible Arigaigai Gathere reads the message and quickly propagates to the nation word of a wonderful wizard. Indeed, Kamītī, so unprepossessing that he has failed to find a job in three years of looking, does show a knack for consultation and healing. When, newly rich on consultation fees, he visits his home village, his father reveals that his grandfather Kamītī wa Kīenjeku was "a holy seer, a spiritual leader working with forces fighting the British in the war of independence." As if this genetic evidence needed cinching, his father explains, "With us, seers are born holding a seashell; and my son, you were born gripping a shell in your little fist." Kamītī's resourceful sessions with the disturbed and the possessed form some of the relatively few passages where the novel lifts free of performance into human exchange. His example spawns, in bedevilled Aburĩria, a plague of "afrochiatrists." When the Wizard, with his moral scruples and self-doubts, is not onstage, the novel becomes puppetry, a Punch-and-Judy show whose grotesque politicos keep whacking one another.

The political development worth protesting is, in a novel rife with Biblical allusions, the government's determination to build, as a birthday present to the Ruler, a kind of Tower of Babel—"a building to the very gates of Heaven so that the Ruler could call on God daily to say good morning or good evening or simply how was your day today, God?" The project, called "Heavenscrape or simply Marching to Heaven," overflows with opportunities for graft but needs the support of the Global Bank, whose representatives pay diplomatic visits without quite committing dollars. Against the giant boondoggle of Marching to Heaven stands the subversive but widespread, strongly feminist Movement for the Voice of the People, of which Nyawĩra is a leader. The members of the movement scatter plastic snakes and embarrass the government whenever they can, performing obscenely, for example, as dancers at a state ceremony.

The author of this bulky book offers more indignation than analysis in his portrait of post-colonial Africa. The days of the flamboyantly costumed independence leaders, with their theatrical fly whisks (like Kenya's founding father, Jomo Kenyatta) and "monkey skins, dashikis, or collarless shirts," are over; Aburĩria's Ruler is "always in Western-style suits," albeit "decorated with patches from the skins of the big cats." Like Zaïre's late, unlamented Mobutu Sese Seko, he wears a leopard-skin hat. His suits, tailored in Europe, have pinstripes "made of tiny letters that read MIGHT IS RIGHT." The passing of the Cold War is felt keenly by his ilk: "The Ruler . . . missed the cold war, when he could play one side against the other." Now "there was only one superpower and it knew only how to be wooed, not how to woo." The Global Bank is a cat's-paw of the United States, whose envoy, accompanied by Ambassador Gabriel Gemstone, tries to explain to the Ruler the new situation:

> "We are in the post–cold war era, and our calculations are affected by the laws and needs of globalization. The history of capital can be summed up in one phrase: *in search of freedom*. Freedom to expand, and now it has a chance at the entire globe for its theater. It needs a democratic space to move as its own logic demands. So I have been sent to urge you to start thinking about turning your country into a democracy. Who knows? Maybe with your blessings, some of your ministers might even want to form opposition parties."

The Ruler, however, prospering for so long under the rule of disorder ("for any attempt on the part of the people to organize themselves was deemed by the Ruler's government as a challenge to its authority"), cannot adjust to the new realism. His code, written out in his own testament, "Political Theory," asserts, "Real crooks are guided by realism." On this principle he promotes the thoroughly, helplessly venal Titus Tajirika, who has had his sympathetic moments and his momentary reversals, but keeps bouncing back. The Ruler "had started to think well of Tajirika the moment he realized that the man was a crook"; as such he could be entrusted "with any task that required bending or breaking the law under the guise of legality." Extreme crookedness ensures extreme loyalty to another crook, he reasons.

And where does all this—766 pages of fiction too aggrieved and grim to be called satire—leave Africa / Aburīria, "Aburīria of crooked roads, robberies, runaway viruses of death, hospitals without medicine, rampant unemployment without relief, daily insecurity, epidemic alcoholism"? Though there are some changes at the top, "shit is still shit, even by another name," feisty Nyawīra decrees. "The battle lines may be murky, but they have not changed." The Wizard, more ambivalently surveying all that has passed, reflects upon another sort of line, "the thinness of the line that divided the real and the unreal in human lives." The novel's frequent recourse to the unrealities of magic realism, in the course of what its own text admits may seem "too incredible a narrative of magic and greed," would seem appropriate to a culture so susceptible to the claims of the supernatural. Yet somehow magic realism still works best in the supple Latin hands of Gabriel García Márquez and José Saramago. In discussing *Wizard of the Crow* with Charles Cantalupo, when the novel was still in progress, Ngũgĩ declined detailed comment on its contents, saying,

> The characters are engaged in the constant performance of their own being for the narrative. You never quite know who they are. Often they reinvent themselves through performance. Even I, as their author, do not know where or how the whole novel is going to end except in the constant performance of their own being.

The narrative, then, is a journey without a destination, and its characters are improv artists. This ambitious, long-mulled attempt to sustain the spell of oral narrative in an era of electro-visual distractions leaves the Wizard where the reader finds him, up in the air.

Subconscious Tunnels

KAFKA ON THE SHORE, by Haruki Murakami, translated from the Japanese by Philip Gabriel. 426 pp. Knopf, 2005.

Haruki Murakami's new novel is a real page-turner, as well as an insistently metaphysical mind-bender. It seems more gripping than it has a right to be and less moving, perhaps, than the author wanted it to be. Murakami, born in 1949, ran a Tokyo jazz club before he became a published writer, with the novel *Hear the Wind Sing*, in 1979. Though his work abounds with references to contemporary American culture, especially its popular music, and though he details the banal quotidian with an amiable flatness reminiscent of minimalist fiction in the hungover 1970s, his narratives are dreamlike, closer to the viscid surrealism of Kobo Abe than to the superheated but generally solid realism of Mishima and Tanizaki. We often cannot imagine, while reading *Kafka on the Shore*, what will come next, and our suspicion—reinforced by Murakami's comments in interviews such as the one in last summer's *Paris Review*—is that the author did not always know either.

Yet *Kafka on the Shore* has a schematic rigor in its execution. Alternate chapters relate the stories of two disparate but slowly converging heroes. The odd-numbered chapters serve up the first-person narrative of a fifteen-year-old runaway from his affluent, motherless home in Tokyo; his father, Koichi Tamura, is a world-renowned sculptor, and the son has given himself the peculiar first name Kafka. He totes a carefully packed backpack and, in his head, talking in boldface, a scolding, exhorting alter ego called Crow—which is what Kafka means, or close to it, in Czech. The even-numbered chapters trace, beginning with a flurry of official documents, the life of a mentally defective sexagenarian, Satoru Nakata. He was one of sixteen fourth-graders who, in 1944, while on a mushroom-gathering walk with their teacher, fell into a coma, after an unexplained flash of silver in the sky. Nakata was the only one who didn't wake up, unharmed, within a few hours; when he did wake up, several weeks later in a military hospital, he had lost his entire memory and with it the ability to read. He doesn't know what Japan is or even recognize his parents' faces. He is able, however, to learn to work in a shop producing hand-crafted furniture, and when, upon the owner's death, the factory disbands, he supplements his government subsidy with a modest-paying sideline in finding lost cats, since along with his disabilities he has gained the enviable ability to converse with cats. (Cats frequently figure in

Murakami's fiction, as delegates from another world; his jazz club was called Peter Cat.) One cat search leads Nakata to a house—that of the sculptor Koichi Tamura, in fact—where he is compelled to stab to death a malevolent apparition in the form of Johnnie Walker, from the whiskey label. Fleeing the bloody crime scene, Nakata hitches truck rides south to Shikoku, the smallest of Japan's four major islands, where Kafka Tamura, as it happens, has recently arrived by bus.

Both the young man and the old, though independent and reclusive, have a knack of forming useful friendships. Kafka befriends Oshima, the androgynous, hemophiliac assistant at a small library where the boy can read all day and, eventually, bunk at night; Nakata in his winning simplicity finds a disciple in one of the truck drivers who gave him a ride, the lower-class, hitherto unenlightened Hoshino, "with a ponytail, a pierced ear, and a Chunichi Dragons baseball team cap." The double plot unfolds in cunningly but tenuously linked chapters. There is violence, comedy, sex—deep, transcendental, anatomically correct sex, oral and otherwise—and a bewildering overflow of possible meanings.

In a prefatory chapter, Crow promises Kafka a "violent, metaphysical, symbolic storm," with "hot, red blood." He assures him, and the expectant reader, "Once the storm is over you won't remember how you made it through. . . . But one thing is certain. When you come out of the storm you won't be the same person who walked in." At the center of this particular novelistic storm is the idea that our behavior in dreams can translate to live action; our dreams can be conduits back into waking reality. This notion, the learned Oshima tells Kafka, can be found in *The Tale of Genji*, the early-eleventh-century Japanese classic by Lady Murasaki. Oshima summarizes:

> "Lady Rokujo—she's one of Prince Genji's lovers—becomes so consumed with jealousy over Genji's main wife, Lady Aoi, that she turns into an evil spirit that possesses her. Night after night she attacks Lady Aoi in her bed until she finally kills her. . . . But the most interesting part of the story is that Lady Rokujo has no inkling that she'd become a living spirit. She'd have nightmares and wake up, only to discover that her long black hair smelled like smoke. Not having any idea what was going on, she was totally confused. In fact, this smoke came from the incense the priests lit as they prayed for Lady Aoi. Completely unaware of it, she'd been flying through space and passing down the tunnel of her subconscious into Aoi's bedroom."

Read in context, in the first section of Arthur Waley's translation of *Genji*, the episode borders on the naturalistic. Within the tight, constrained circles of the imperial court, emotional violence bursts its bonds. Both women are gravely sickened by the trespassing spirit of one of them;

Lady Rokujo, a beauty of great refinement, is horrified that her dreams about Lady Aoi are full of a "brutal fury such as in her waking life would have been utterly foreign to her." She reflects, "How terrible! It seemed then that it was really possible for one's spirit to leave the body and break out into emotions which the waking mind would not countenance."

From the inarguable truth of the second observation the possibility of one's spirit leaving one's body could be plausibly deduced in a prescientific, pre-electric age when, Oshima points out, "the physical darkness outside and the inner darkness of the soul were mixed together, with no boundary separating the two." In Murakami's vision of our materialist, garishly illuminated age, however, the boundary between inner and outer darkness is traversed by grotesque figments borrowed from the world of commercial imagery: Johnnie Walker, with boots and top hat, manifests himself to the cat-loving simpleton Nakata as a mass murderer of stray felines, jocularly cutting open their furry abdomens and popping their still-beating hearts into his mouth, and Colonel Sanders, in his white suit and string tie, appears to Nakata's companion, Hoshino, as a fast-talking pimp. The Colonel, questioned by the startled Hoshino about his nature, quotes another venerable text, Ueda Akinari's *Tales of Moonlight and Rain*:

> Shape I may take, converse I may, but neither god nor Buddha am I, rather an insensate being whose heart thus differs from that of man.

Later, with some exasperation, the Colonel tells Hoshino, "I'm a *concept*, get it? *Con-cept!*" Concept or whatever, he is a very adroit fixer when it comes to such supernatural hustles as handling the entrance stone to the spirit world, where the dead and the drastically detached live in the heart of the forest like writers at the MacDowell Colony—meals and housekeeping provided, and other residents discreetly out of sight.

This novel quotes Goethe as decreeing, "Everything's a metaphor." But a Western reader expects the metaphors, or symbolic realities, to be—as in *The Faerie Queene*, *The Pilgrim's Progress*, and Goethe's *Faust*—organized by certain polarities, in a magnetic field shaped by a central supernatural authority. No such authority controls the spooky carnival of *Kafka on the Shore*. To quote Colonel Sanders once more:

> "Listen—God only exists in people's minds. Especially in Japan, God's always been kind of a flexible concept. Look at what happened after the war. Douglas MacArthur ordered the divine emperor to quit being God, and he did, making a speech saying he was just an ordinary person."

In *Kafka on the Shore*, the skies unaccountably produce showers of sardines, mackerel, and leeches, and some unlucky people get stuck halfway in the spirit world and hence cast a faint shadow in this one. Japanese supernature, imported into contemporary America with animated cartoons, video games, and Yu-Gi-Oh cards, is luxuriant, light-hearted, and, by the stern standards of monotheism, undisciplined. The religious history of Japan since the introduction of Chinese culture in the fifth century A.D. and the arrival of Buddhism in the sixth has been a long lesson in the stubborn resilience and adaptability of the native cult of polytheistic nature worship called, to distinguish it from Buddhism, Shinto. Shinto, to quote the *Encyclopædia Britannica*, "has no founder, no official sacred scriptures, and no dogma." Nor does it offer, as atypically surviving kamikaze pilots have proudly pointed out, an afterlife. It is based on *kami*, a ubiquitous word sometimes translated as "gods" or "spirits" but meaning, finally, anything felt worthy of reverence. One of Shinto's belated systemizers, Motoori Norinaga (1730–1801), defined *kami* as "anything whatsoever which was out of the ordinary."

A tenacious adherence to Shinto in the Japanese countryside and among the masses has enabled it to coexist for a millennium and a half with Buddhism, Taoism, and Confucianism, and to be subject to repeated revivals, most recently, from 1871 to 1945, as the official national religion and a powerful spiritual weapon in Japan's imperialist wars. After Japan's defeat in the Second World War, Shinto, under the direction of the Allied occupation force, was disestablished, its holidays were curtailed, and the Emperor's divinity—based on the first Emperor's purported descent from the sun goddess—was renounced. But Shinto shrines remain, in the imperial precincts and in the countryside; its rites are performed, its paper wish-slips tied to bushes, its good-luck sachets sold to tourists Asian and Western. Shinto's strong aesthetic component, a reverence toward materials and processes, continues to permeate the crafts and the arts. *Kami* exists not only in heavenly and earthly forces but in animals, birds, plants, and stones. Nakata and Hoshino spend hours trying to learn how to converse with a stone—to divine what the stone, at times easily lifted and at others heavy to the limits of a man's strength, wants. *Kami* pervades Murakami's world, in which, therefore, many Western readers will feel, a bit queasily, at sea, however many fragments of globalized Western culture—Goethe, Beethoven, Eichmann, Hegel, Coltrane, Schubert, Napoleon—bob from paragraph to paragraph.

The novel's two heroes interact only in the realm of *kami*. Of their entwined narratives, the story of Kafka Tamura is more problematic, more curiously overloaded, than that of Nakata's holy fool, with its familiar elements of science fiction, quest, and ebullient heroics. As Hoshino remarks, "This is starting to feel like an Indiana Jones movie or something." Return and release to the underworld of his childhood coma are the old man's intelligible goals, for which he prepares with prodigious sessions of sleep. Less intelligibly, the "cool, tall, fifteen-year-old boy, lugging a backpack and a bunch of obsessions," labors under an ill-defined Oedipal curse. He hates his father enough to dream of killing him, and to feel small sorrow when he is killed, but we never see the father, unless it is in the bizarre guise of Johnnie Walker, and know only that he was a famous artist and, as such, probably pretty egocentric. Kafka's mother left home, with his older sister, when he was four years old, and when he encounters her in Shikoku it is in the form of a fifteen-year-old spirit projection of the library director, trim, prim, reserved Miss Saeki, who is over fifty. Miss Saeki and Kafka Tamura talk like this:

> "We're not metaphors."
> "I know," I say. "But metaphors help eliminate what separates you and me."
> A faint smile comes to her as she looks up at me. "That's the oddest pickup line I've ever heard."
> "There're a lot of odd things going on—but I feel like I'm slowly getting closer to the truth."
> "Actually getting closer to a metaphorical truth? Or metaphorically getting closer to an actual truth? Or maybe they supplement each other?"
> "Either way, I don't think I can stand the sadness I feel right now," I tell her.
> "I feel the same way."

Small wonder, as the teen-ager admits, that "the whole confused mess swirls around in [his] brain, and [his] head feels like it's about to burst." The Oedipus myth, shedding its fatal Greek gravity and the universality Freud gave it, just adds more vapor to the mist of fancy and strangeness through which the young hero moves toward the unexceptional goal of growing up.

In its last pages, the novel asks that it be taken as a happily ending saga of maturation, of "a brand-new world" for a purged Kafka. But beneath his feverish, symbolically fraught adventures lies a subconscious pull almost equal to the pull of sex and vital growth: that of nothingness, of emptiness, of blissful blankness. Murakami is a tender painter of negative spaces. After his coma, Nakata "returned to this world with his mind wiped clean. The proverbial blank slate." In his adulthood, "that bottomless world of darkness, that weighty silence and chaos, was an old friend, a part of him already." Throughout this chronicle, Murakami describes his characters falling asleep as lovingly as he itemizes what they cook and eat. Refrigerated cat heads, like the severed human heads of Tanizaki's tremendous novella *The Secret History of the Lord of Musashi*, have a lulling serenity, "staring out blankly at a point in space." Making love to a woman, "you listen as the blank within her is filled." Kafka Tamura says,

"There's a void inside me, a blank that is slowly expanding, devouring what's left of who I am. I can hear it happening." Heading into the forest, leaving all his backpacked defenses behind, he thinks triumphantly, "I head for the core of the labyrinth, giving myself up to the void." Existence as something half empty—a mere skin on the essential void, a transitory shore—needs, for its celebration, a Japanese spiritual tact.

Bitter Bamboo

MY LIFE AS EMPEROR, by Su Tong, translated from the Chinese by Howard Goldblatt. 270 pp. Hyperion East, 2005.

BIG BREASTS & WIDE HIPS, by Mo Yan, translated from the Chinese by Howard Goldblatt. 532 pp. Arcade, 2004.

China, we are told, is the nation of the future; its immense population, its acrobatic blend of totalitarian controls and booming free enterprise, and the commercial and intellectual success its emigrants have enjoyed in nations from Malaysia to the United States all augur impending global dominance. In literature, however, the Chinese mainland, as far as Western ears go, is pretty quiet. The one Chinese recipient of the Nobel Prize (if we don't count Pearl Buck) was an expatriate Parisian, Gao Xingjian. Mainland bookstores, the *New York Times* reports, are bustling, but nearly half the purchases consist of textbooks and half the translations are of American books. Meanwhile, American translation of contemporary Chinese fiction appears to be the lonely province of one man, Howard Goldblatt, the founding editor of *Modern Chinese Literature* and a professor presently at the University of Notre Dame. Goldblatt's midwifery has recently given us two novels by mainland authors: *My Life as Emperor,* by Su Tong, and *Big Breasts & Wide Hips,* by Mo Yan, whose *Red Sorghum,* which Goldblatt translated in 1993, won considerable notice and the hopeful remark from the Chinese-American author Amy Tan that "Mo Yan's voice will find its way into the heart of the American reader, just as Kundera and García Márquez have." Well, that's a tough old heart, and I'm not sure the Chinese are ready to crack it.

Su Tong was born in 1963, graduated from Beijing Normal University, and now lives in Nanjing. His novella *Raise the Red Lantern* was made into a film nominated for an Oscar. He is sufficiently at ease in his authorial persona to directly address the reader, explaining,

My Life as Emperor could be considered a pleasure cruise through my inner world. It has long been my wish to penetrate the millennia of China's history, to transform myself into an old customer at some teahouse on an ancient street in the midst of a kaleidoscopic world with its teeming masses, and soak up the passage of time with my eyes. I am fascinated by classical times. . . . I hope my readers do not approach *My Life as Emperor* with the idea that it is historical fiction; that is why I have set the novel in no particular time. Identifying allusions and determining the accuracy of events places too great a burden on you and on me. The world of women and the palace intrigues that you will encounter in this novel are but a scary dream on a rainy night; the suffering and slaughter reflect my worries and fears for all the people in all worlds, and nothing more.

The shrugging, dandyish tone is continued by the novel's hero and narrator, Duanbai, the fifth son of the deceased Emperor, who is unexpectedly named as the next Emperor: "Still a child at fourteen, I could not figure out why I had been chosen to continue the Imperial line." He had "despised" his father, and his succession is vigorously protested by the imperial concubine Madame Yang, who waves a testamentary edict naming her son, Duanwen, Duanbai's oldest brother, as emperor. She is bundled off, but declines to commit pro-forma suicide with the six other imperial concubines; retainers chase her down and throttle her with the traditional silk cord, but she hammers on her casket lid and sits up, still waving the edict. The casket is filled with dirt and nailed shut with "nineteen long nails." This is the first but not the last atrocious example of imperial administration.

Duanbai has been placed on the throne by his paternal grandmother, Madame Huangfu, and his mother, the Empress Dowager, Madame Meng; they sit beside him during his audiences with his ministers and tell him what to say. His own interest focuses mostly on his pet crickets in their cages. Gradually he realizes that he possesses the power to "obliterate" anything that annoys him. Near where he sleeps there is the Cold Palace, "in the grove of parasol trees," where concubines discarded by the former Emperor weep at night. Disturbed by the sound, Duanbai secretly instructs the Imperial Executioner to cut off their tongues; when these are brought to him in a "bloody paper packet," he is struck by their resemblance to "salted pigs' tongues, which were quite a delicacy." The crazed retainer who tends the palace's alchemy cauldron repeatedly says that "the fire is out, and calamity will soon befall the Xie Empire," and the reader does not doubt it. When General Zheng, "on the western front," sends an urgent communiqué, the adolescent Emperor tells the messenger, "You give me a headache the way you're always bringing me this and that. You say the barbarians have broken through our defenses? Well, drive them back to where they came from. How hard can that be?"

As Duanbai ages, he ventures into the lists of both love and war, but with a ruinous ineffectuality. In love with the birdlike Lady Hui, he lets her be persecuted by his mother and grandmother and by more earth-bound concubines; finally, Lady Hui is driven into prostitution, and when, his own fortunes having taken a downturn, he encounters her, he quickly grows disgusted with the "degraded body" of this "once lovely girl who had run beside the Imperial Stream flapping her arms like a bird." On the battlefield, he stays in bed, "warmed by woolen quilts," as his chief of staff, Yang Song, urges him to show himself to his troops. When the demoralized troops lose, he orders that the badly wounded Yang Song be killed rather than rescued. The sight of the wounded man, "his face a bloody mess" while his hands are occupied in "trying to keep a length of purple intestines from spilling out," makes Duanbai vomit. The Emperor is also nauseated by another sight as he ventures out into the troubled Xie Empire—that of a nearly naked boy eating insects in a tree. A guard explains to him:

> He's hungry. There is no more food at home, so he survives on insects. That is what many village people feed on during normal times. When natural dis- asters occur, after they have fought over insects, the people are forced to eat the bark of trees. . . . And when their hunger becomes intolerable on their way to somewhere, they dig up the clay roadway and use that to fill their bellies. That always kills them.

Theirs is a more merciful death, however, than that inflicted upon a defeated rebel leader, Li Yizhi, by eleven successive tortures ceremoni-ously titled Backward Disrobing Primate, Immortal Rides the Mist, Hol-low Out the Eggplant, and so on.

Su Tong's purpose in relating his combination "pleasure cruise" and "scary dream" must be, in part, an indictment of the imperial system, with its drastic inequities, its elaborate cruelties, its implacable protocols. But the Emperor's narrative has the shallow perspective of a Chinese scroll; it is hard to enter into it. Though the book is not long, the fall of the Xie Empire feels long in coming. Only when it has fallen, and Duan-bai is free to wander, in poverty and danger, in pursuit of his ambition to become a tightrope walker in a travelling circus, does the hero become a protagonist in the Western style, defined by aspirations, struggles, and discoveries. The novel turns companionably picaresque. Pushed off the throne after eight years there, Duanbai can suddenly see:

Everywhere I looked, the land was rich and fertile, and everywhere we stopped, we were surrounded by thatched huts lived in by men who farmed and women who weaved. Villages that spoked out in all directions were like a vast tapestry in yellows and greens that spread out ahead on my road to safety. A river, or a muddy road, or a few odd trees separated me from the lives of the common people, yet they were never far away.

My Life as Emperor culminates in its biggest bloodbath yet, and the cry of the bullfinch, "Die—Die—Die," might be its epigraph. Like Voltaire's *Candide*, this parade of misfortunes ends with a garden, "a weed-infested vegetable garden" in the deserted Bitter Bamboo Monastery on Bitter Bamboo Mountain, and with doubts cast on palliative human wisdom, represented in this case by Confucius's *Analects*. Su Tong's morbid fantasia wears an opaque lacquer of willful elegance. The reader suspects that exceptionally much is lost in translation. In sentences like "I knew then that I had truly fallen into the chrysalis of what transpires between a man and a woman" and "Her lips looked like a dead fish as they nibbled their way up my coiling dragon robe, producing a cheerless soughing sound," Professor Goldblatt is presumably pursuing the Mandarin text, ideogram by ideogram, but in one like "So it was a cinch that Duanwen was not licking his wounds in the residence of the Western Duke, having found safe haven at last," the English seems just plain tired.

But Goldblatt's exertions here are as nothing compared with those in translating Mo Yan. This author, born in 1955 into a peasant family in northern China, sets a groaning table of brutal incident, magic realism, woman-worship, nature description, and far-flung metaphor. The Chinese novel, perhaps, had no Victorian heyday to teach it decorum; certainly both Su Tong and Mo Yan are cheerfully liberal with the physical details that accompany sex, birth, illness, and violent death. Right at the start of *Big Breasts & Wide Hips*, we are witness to two difficult births, one by the very long-suffering heroine, Shangguan Lu, and the other by a donkey:

> The donkey struggled, yellow liquid shot out of its nostrils as its head jerked around and banged on the ground. Down at the other end, amniotic fluid and wet, sticky feces sprayed the area.

As to Mo Yan's metaphors, they are abundant and hyperactive:

> Sima Ting's persistent shouts floated in the air, like a fly in pursuit of rotting meat, sticking first to the wall, then buzzing over to the donkey's hide.

My thoughts leaped across and squirmed beneath the white cloud that had so gently covered her and Babbitt. . . . My eyes were like blood-sucking leeches, fastened to her chest.

Pastor Malory flung himself off the bell tower and plummeted like a gigantic bird with broken wings, splattering his brains like so much bird shit when he hit the street below.

The morning winds blew in from the fields, like a wet cat with a glistening carp in its mouth, prowling arrogantly on the sheet-metal roof.

A full-bodied girl to my right had a tender, yellow, budlike extra finger outside the thumb of each hand . . . and those darling little extra digits fluttered over her face like the curly tails of little piglets.

Such surplus energy of figuration attests to, if not greatness, a greatly ambitious reach. Mo Yan here seeks to accommodate in the story of one indestructible woman most of Chinese history from 1900, when Shangguan Lu, first called Lu Xuan'er, is six months old and is hidden in a flour vat while her parents are slain by German forces invading to suppress the Boxer Rebellion, to 1993, when she dies in the care of her only son, Shangguan Jintong, in church during a sermon preached, as it turns out, by the eldest son of her son's father, a Swedish missionary called Pastor Malory. The dauntless mother (the novel is dedicated to "the spirit of my mother," and Jintong is its narrator) survives these ninety-three years but is one of the few characters who do. Her eight daughters, the various men who have fathered them, her sterile husband, her ferocious mother-in-law, her fellow-villagers in Northeast Gaomi Township—all, with a few exceptions, perish in the waves of war, famine, and Communist enforcement that bathe this hapless land in suffering. So many die that individual deaths register with little more emotion than a hit in a shooting gallery. One piece of pain that does linger in the mind comes when five-year-old Xuan'er's feet are bound by her aunt:

> First she bent the toes back with bamboo strips and wrapped them tightly, wrenching loud squeals of protest from her niece. Then she wrapped the feet tightly with the alum-treated white cloth, one layer after another. Once that was done, she pounded the toes with her wooden mallet. Mother said the pain was like banging her head against the wall.
> "Please, not so tight," Mother beseeched her aunt.
> "It's tight because I love you," her aunt said with a piercing glare.

As her uncle tells her, "Girls who don't bind their feet grow up to be big-footed spinsters that nobody wants." But history undercuts this marital strategy when the Manchu dynasty falls and foot-binding is banned.

Xuan'er, sixteen and a beauty, is put on display; her "perfect lotus feet" are derided as "a poisonous legacy of a feudal system" while six young women with unbound feet sing and bounce around, "raising their feet high in the air to show their natural beauty," and an orthopedic surgeon demonstrates "how the broken bones of bound feet forever altered the shape of the foot." "A fallen phoenix," Xuan'er is humbly married off to the feckless son of a female blacksmith, and embarks on a strenuous life of domestic chores and wartime marches on crippled feet. At times Mo Yan, speaking through Jintong, seems to forget that his heroine is handicapped, so dynamic does he make her, but at others he remembers: "The deep footprints she made in the muddy road with her crippled, once-bound feet were still discernible months later."

Seven of her daughters are physically sound (the eighth, Shangguan Jintong's twin, is born blind) but meet unkind fates in the century's clashing currents. Eldest Sister, Laidi, is forced to marry a crippled mute soldier in the army of the People's Republic; Second Sister, Zhaodi, marries a local commander in the anti-Japanese forces who later becomes an anti-Communist rebel; Third Sister, Lingdi, daughter of a "peddler of ducklings," dies trying to fly; Fourth Sister, Xiangdi, becomes a prostitute in order to feed the others; Fifth Sister, Pandi, marries a commissar and, as Ma Ruilian, enjoys an active career in the Communist ranks; Sixth Sister, Niandi, marries an American pilot named Babbitt, who works with the eventually routed Kuomintang forces; and Seventh Sister, Qiudi, offspring of a rape by four soldiers, volunteers, along the self-sacrificial lines of Fourth Sister, to be sold to a Russian woman.

While growing up, however, the girls did not lack for appreciation by their little brother, who from infancy basks in the "glorious tradition of Shangguan women, with big breasts and wide hips." We don't hear much about the hips, but it's a rare page that fails to mention breasts: they smell of sulfur and lamb, and nipples are likened to dates, cherries, and button mushrooms. They drive the narrator to such verbal extravagances as "slightly upturned nipples as nimble as the mouth of a hedgehog" and "whenever her nipple was aroused, you could hang an oilcan from it." Jintong admires his mother's breasts from his little basket; they look to him "like a pair of happy white doves." He jealously wails at Malory's amorous attentions to them, until:

> She stuck the white doves up under my nose, and I urgently, cruelly grabbed one of their heads with my lips. Big as my mouth was, I wished it were bigger still. . . . I had one of them in my mouth and was grasping the other in my hands. It was a little red-eyed white rabbit, and when I pinched its ear, I felt its frantic heartbeat.

When his twin sister tries to nurse, he claws and kicks at her "until the poor blind thing cried her eyes out"; she survives on a thin gruel. Jintong refuses to be weaned at age seven, and a goat's teat is substituted, then goat's milk in a bottle:

> So I stuck the yolk-colored rubber nipple into my mouth. Naturally it couldn't compare with the real things on the tips of Mother's breasts—hers were love, hers were poetry, hers were the highest realm of heaven and the rich soil under golden waves of wheat.

So impressive and ardent are Jintong's evocations of nursing's primal pleasure that this reader was slow to realize that Mo Yan intended our hero to be not a typical healthy male but a case of arrested development. His mother strikes a rare note of maternal complaint when, being beaten by a Red Guard while an intimidated Jintong watches, she cries, "Stand up, my useless son!" Though he does in the end make the disgusting switch to solid food, he never quite makes the switch to real life, running afoul of Mao's revolution to the tune of fifteen years at a labor reform camp and emerging into post-Mao capitalism to waste several golden opportunities others have provided for him. His one consummated sexual relationship, arranged by his mother, is with Old Jin, the proprietess of a vast recycling station; she is much older than Jintong and has only one breast, but it is a big breast, and has some milk it. However, she wearies of babying him and decrees, "Shangguan Jintong, you're dog shit that won't stick to a wall, you're a dead cat that can't climb a tree. I want you to get your balls out of here!"

Professor Goldblatt, in his introduction, explains, "In a relentlessly unflattering portrait of his male protagonist, Mo Yan draws attention to what he sees as a regression of the human species and a dilution of the Chinese character." Amid so much slapstick mayhem and mammary lewdness, this moral drops out of sight. What does bear in upon the exhausted reader is China's crushing misery in the last century, which, beginning in the final years of imperial rule, neatly dovetails with the imperial misery portrayed, in a stylized but not implausible manner, in *My Life as Emperor*. Both worlds, ancient and twentieth-century, are stews of slaughter, torture, famine, flood, and, for the peasant masses, brutalizing overwork. The protagonists of both novels are immature weaklings. Nevertheless, unlike many braver and more engaged characters in these fictional annals, they survive to tell their tales. Their wanton weakness and self-absorption, and the natural poetry both are capable of, rebuke the societies that have made life on earth hellish. Bad societies offer no incentive to grow up.

Mo Yan's portrait of Chinese history has met ire on the mainland. Goldblatt quotes one critic as calling the novel "a sycophantic, shameless work that turns history upside down, fabricates lies, and glorifies the Japanese fascists and the Landlord Restoration Corps." The Japanese forces, whose invasion is the principal event of *Red Sorghum*, are relatively shadowy in this novel; but even a Western reader insensitive to the fine points of the civil conflict that placed Mao in power must notice that in this book Communist programs and propaganda are played mostly for laughs, and that the most praiseworthy men, the Sima brothers, are associated with the old, bourgeois regime and the Nationalist Army. Mo Yan's fate is to operate on the edge of official constraints; the novel, nearly a half-million words long as first published in 1996 in China, has undergone trimming and rearrangement right up to this translation, based upon "a further shortened, computer generated manuscript supplied by the author." Semi-capitalist China will not replay the censorship game by the same rules as were hammered out in the Soviet Union, but free spirits in China are still well short of enjoying free speech.

NON-FICTION

Groaning Shelves

THE BOOK ON THE BOOKSHELF, by Henry Petroski. 279 pp. Knopf, 1999.

Henry Petroski, a professor of civil engineering and history at Duke University, has developed a nice niche for himself as a popularizer of engineering and an expositor of manufactured things. The field is as vast as all human creation, and its details can be explained and followed without much of the specialized vocabulary that renders biology and physics semi-opaque to the uninitiated. *The Pencil* (1990) is his best-known work, an ingeniously designed volume of more than four hundred pages giving the surprisingly intricate history of this humble and ubiquitous artifact; *The Evolution of Useful Things* (1992) took us deeper than we would have thought possible into the ins and outs of paper clips, beer cans, forks, zippers, and such. His newest excursion into the commonplace, *The Book on the Bookshelf*, tills rather thin and overworked terrain. The evolution of the book from papyrus scroll to bound paper is an oft-told story, and for the history of book housing Petroski is noticeably dependent upon two turn-of-the-last-century works by John Willis Clark, *Libraries in the Medieval and Renaissance Periods* (1894) and *The Care of Books: An Essay on the Development of Libraries and Their Fittings, from the earliest Times to the end of the Eighteenth Century* (1901). To stretch his topic to more than two hundred and fifty pages Petroski resorts to much chat about the books and shelving in his own home, and tacks on a semi-facetious twenty-page appendix on possible ways to order a personal library, ranging from the obvious (by subject, by author's last name) to the whimsical (by color, by publisher, by author's first name, by opening sentence, by the Dewey decimal system). Engineering proceeds through patient considerations, but the actualities of shelf sag and window light begin to make sleepy reading, and matters of general literate knowledge are rather relentlessly spelled out:

> Jerome was famous for producing, among other significant works, the Latin translation of the Bible known as the Vulgate, so called because it was rendered in the common or "vulgar" Latin of the time and so was more generally accessible than the original Hebrew and Greek in which the Bible was written.

Nevertheless, we need to be reminded that people did not always live surrounded by books arranged on shelves, with their spines outward and stamped with the title, author, and publisher. (In truth, only in certain circles, smaller than academics like Petroski might imagine, could people be said to be surrounded; I am frequently struck by how many otherwise handsomely accoutered middle-class American homes have not a book in sight.) The first writing was on clay tablets or cylinders. The first approximations to books were Greek and Roman papyrus rolls as long as thirty feet, which generally carried their text in columns of lines parallel to the scroll's edges, much like pages. Called *volumina* in Latin, these rolled-up "volumes" were as a rule read from left to right, the read portion held in the left hand and the unread in the right, and had to be rerolled when read, like a videotape. They were tied with string, and for storage were sometimes kept in hatbox-shaped containers called *capsae*. Commonly, they were stored in divided shelves, and identified by tags attached to their ends. Seneca, the gloomy playwright and doomed adviser to Nero, described a rich man who "buys bookcases of expensive wood" and "goes yawning among his thousands of volumes . . . collected for mere show, to ornament the walls of the house." A library, the Stoic complained, has become "one of the essential fittings of a home, like a bathroom."

Early Christian times saw the spread of parchment (processed sheepskin) and vellum (related etymologically to "veal," though lambs and kids as well as calves were used). These thinned animal hides could be more securely stitched than brittle papyrus, promoting the codex, composed of sheets sewn together—originally in concertina style and then on one side, forming a spine—and protected by substantial covers, usually of wood and sometimes heavily decorated and bejewelled. Such early books, copied and illumined by hand, were rare and precious and mostly found in monasteries. The monks loaned them to one another with careful accountancy, to be perused and copied, and kept them in locked chests; a book chest surviving in Hereford Cathedral is six feet long and equipped with no fewer than three separate locks. When not stacked in such chests, books were propped on sharply tilted surfaces like modern music stands or lecterns. Woodcut representations of fifteenth-century scholars at work show random book dispersal over all available surfaces. Study carrels were built between the pillars of cloisters, and as literary activity increased and books multiplied, the bookshelf made a fitful appearance. An *armarium commune*—a wood-lined recess in a stone wall—that survives from the late twelfth century in the Cistercian abbey of Fossa Nuova, near Terracina, apparently had a single shelf, since removed. Book chests had begun to rise up, in the form of upright *armaria* fitted with doors where the lid had been and shelves in place of an undifferentiated interior. The shelves, however, in what representations survive, appear to have been slanted and held very few books apiece. Collections that numbered no longer in the tens but in the hundreds would require a crushing number of such *armaria;* a separate book room, a library, of about one hundred fifty square feet, appeared in the same abbey containing the *armarium commune.*

The early, late-medieval libraries took the form of long lecterns to which the books, freed from their locked chests, were chained, protecting them from theft, displacement, and perusal by unauthorized eyes. The chains were attached by rings to a rod, which was secured by a lock and key, below the lectern. The images of chained books are among the most haunting in *The Book on the Bookshelf,* since we do not intuitively recognize them as marking a forward stage in the liberation and dissemination of the written word. The stage lasted some centuries, well into the Gutenberg era. Petroski quotes Burnett Hillman Streeter's *The Chained Library: A Survey of Four Centuries in the Evolution of the English Library:*

> Fresh chains were being purchased at Chetham College, Manchester, in 1742, and at the Bodleian in 1751. At The Queen's College, Oxford, the chains were not taken from the books till 1780; at Merton not till 1792. Magdalen was the last college in Oxford to retain them; here they lasted till 1799.

Sixteenth-century examples of chained libraries are preserved at Hereford Cathedral and Florence's Laurentian Library; in both, primitive catalogues list at the end of each lectern the books on its long tilted shelf. Horizontal shelves appeared, above and below the lectern, as books relentlessly increased in number. Eliminating chains made possible the book press, or bookcase, and eventually walls of shelves, with detached benches and reading tables. As books were printed for a mass market, extensive private libraries arose. Samuel Pepys winnowed his hoard of books to stay at three thousand, so as not to overflow his thoughtfully designed, glass-fronted, made-to-order presses. He discovered that more books could be stored if they were arranged by size, with raised shelves holding a row of taller books behind a row of smaller ones; the effect, preserved in the twelve cases that Pepys left, with their contents, to Cambridge's Magdalen College, is impressively harmonious, though somewhat forbidding to a would-be browser.

Even after books came to rest on shelves, their spines were unlabelled and faced inward. Petroski explains:

> The exoskeletal spine, which holds up the innards of the book structurally in a fashion not unlike the way our own spines hold us up, was still the machinery of the book, however, and so it continued to be the part that was hidden as much as possible, pushed into the dark recesses of bookshelves, out of sight. Shelving books with their spines inward must have seemed as natural and appropriate a thing to do as to put the winding machinery of a clock toward the wall or behind a door, or both.

When books were few, they did not need to be labelled, any more than do familiar people. The fore edges, where schoolchildren still write their names, sometimes held painted decorations and identifying marks. But by the end of the sixteenth century, lettered spines had become the rule—except in the library of the Escorial, that bastion of Catholic conservatism, where into the twentieth century books were still shelved fore-edge out.

Mountains of books now exist on all sides, and institutional libraries have frequent recourse to the engineering sciences as they seek to house their treasure, which has been estimated to double every sixteen years. The British Museum's renovation of the 1850s surrounded the great domed Reading Room (a foot larger than the dome of Saint Peter's, two feet smaller than that of the Pantheon) with multilevel cast-iron book stacks; this advance was obsolete by 1920, when an attempt to add to the stacks strained the structure. By the end of 1999, twelve million volumes will be moved into the new British Library building, across from Saint Pancras Station. Rolling book presses, which enable aisle space to be conserved, were installed in the Toronto Central Circulating Library as early as 1930. Compact shelving on rails—bookcases packed like a deck of thick cards—can double capacity but would dangerously overload the upper floors of most existing structures. CD-ROMs take up little space, but the computer terminals to read them take up a great deal. Further, computers are vulnerable to hackers and electromagnetic catastrophes. Seldom-consulted books are finding their way into off-site computer-managed warehouses—neutron stars of printed matter, denser and denser.

Microfilm was once thought to be a panacea, but, according to a 1963 study, "experience began soon to show that there was great resistance from readers to the inconvenience of having to read through an apparatus." Now computer science promises us, via a research team at the Massachusetts Institute of Technology, the "Overbook," which

> would be printed in electronic ink known as e-ink, a concept in which page-like displays consist of microscopic spheres embedded within a matrix of extremely thin wires. The ink particles, which have one hemisphere black and one white, can be individually flipped by a current in the wire to form a "printed" page of any book which has been scanned into the system.

Who is to say, at the end of a century that brought us the movies, radio, radar, and the desktop ink-jet printer, that this cannot be? But the concept feels less than bookish. Our notion of a book is of a physical object, precious even if no longer hand-copied on sheepskin by carrel-bound monks, which we can hold, enter at random, shelve for future reference, and enjoy as a palpable piece of our environment, a material souvenir of the immaterial experience it gave us. That books endure suggests that we endure, our inner tale not writ in the water of an Overbook's e-ink.

Can Eve Be Reprieved?

THE WORD ACCORDING TO EVE: *Women and the Bible in Ancient Times and Our Own*, by Cullen Murphy. 302 pp. Houghton Mifflin, 1998.

Over a century ago, in 1895, Elizabeth Cady Stanton wrote, "The Bible teaches that woman brought sin and death into the world, that she precipitated the fall of the race, that she was arraigned before the judgement seat of Heaven, tried, condemned and sentenced. Marriage for her was to be a condition of bondage, maternity a period of suffering and anguish, and in silence and subjection, she was to play the role of a dependent on man's bounty for all her material wants. . . . Here is the Bible position of woman briefly summed up." Stanton, the co-founder, with Susan B. Anthony, of the National Woman Suffrage Association, was introducing the first volume of *The Woman's Bible*. The volume, a critique of the Pentateuch, went through seven printings in six months, and was condemned as Satan's work by a multitude of clergymen and editorial writers. The organization she had helped found, meeting in Washington a year later, voted to disown it: "This organization is non-sectarian . . . and has no connection with the so-called Women's Bible, or any theological publication." Nevertheless, the rebuked, bedridden, obese, and octogenarian Stanton carried through, in 1898, with the second volume, covering the rest of the Bible, from Joshua to Revelation, remarking in her introduction, "All through the centuries scholars and scientists have been imprisoned, tortured, and burned alive for some discovery which seemed to conflict with a petty text of Scripture." Her determination to arraign the Good Book cost her some public esteem; it was Susan B. Anthony who wound up, for what it was worth, on the dollar coin.

Discomfort with the way women figure in the Bible—in, say, the story of Adam and Eve in Genesis 2 and 3, and the strictures of Saint Paul in 1 Corinthians—was first voiced in English by the female mystic Julian of Norwich, who in her *Revelations of Divine Love* (c. 1393) cites the verse from the Pauline epistle to Timothy "But I suffer not a woman to teach, nor to usurp authority over the man, but to be in silence" and asks the reader, "Because I am a woman should I therefore believe that I ought not to tell you about the goodness of God?" The Quakers, founded in the seventeenth century, dispensed with some of the more egregiously patriarchal passages and imposed what is now called inclusive—genderless—language on translated Scripture. The nineteenth century saw in America the first ordination of a woman (Antoinette Brown, educated in theology at Oberlin and briefly installed as a pastor of a small Congregational church in South Butler, New York, before resigning) and some proto-feminist protest by the abolitionist Quakers Sarah and Angelina Grimké, whose *Letters on the Equality of the Sexes and the Condition of Women* (1838) entered spirited objections less to the Bible itself than to the male monopoly on its interpretation. But it was not until the early Sixties of the twentieth century that women entered the lists of Biblical scholarship, and it is with these women that Cullen Murphy, a practicing Catholic and the managing editor of *The Atlantic Monthly*, concerns himself in *The Word According to Eve: Women and the Bible in Ancient Times and Our Own*.

As the adroitly straddling subtitle suggests, this is a book with a forked topic: the ancient women in the Bible and the modern women who are trying to study them. A typical chapter begins with an evocation of a place (Union Theological Seminary in New York, the Jezreele Valley in Israel, the ruins of Nineveh in Iraq), goes on to present an interview or two with a female Biblical scholar, and ends on a quizzical, inconclusive note. "The Bible is often quite uninterested in, or unable to comprehend, the questions pressed upon the text from modern perspectives and experiences," the Biblical scholar Phyllis A. Bird is quoted as saying. Amy-Jill Levine, the Carpenter Professor of New Testament Studies at the Divinity School at Vanderbilt University, reports, "To go back to a Jewish woman's life in Judea before the destruction of the Second Temple—well, it's very hard to do." Bernadette Brooten, a professor at Brandeis University, whose doctoral dissertation became the book *Women Leaders in the Ancient Synagogue*, discusses the carved inscriptions that ascribe to Jewish women the titles of "priest" and "head of the synagogue" and ends by confessing, "I've often had this thought: that I'll die and go to heaven, and Rufina will meet me, and I'll greet her as *archisynagogos*. And she'll say, '*Archisynagogos?* Nah. That was just my husband's title.' " Murphy himself—a scrupulous and attentive but rather soft-spoken guide—concludes that "the actual lives of women in antiquity . . . remain dimly apprehended."

The contemporary women who bucked the "academic malestream" to become Biblical scholars are more vivid, even though their curriculae vitae tend to run together in the mind's eye. They were reared, by and large, in religious environments and in college showed an aptitude for the ancient languages and a passion for serious study that overcame the doubts of their male instructors. For example:

As a youth in Merced, California, Kathleen Corley was an evangelical Christian and a member of a charismatic movement. She used to distribute Bible tracts on streetcorners. . . . With some trepidation—the fear being that it might ruin her faith—she sought out higher education, enrolling at Westmont College, a highly regarded Christian school in Santa Barbara. . . . She took Greek, though her adviser tried to dissuade her from doing so, thinking it would be too hard. It turned out that she liked Greek and was good at it, and she sped right through it. In graduate school, at Fuller Theological Seminary, in Pasadena—another conservative institution—she continued with her Bible studies and picked up Hebrew and Coptic. Through a natural progression she became interested in the Nag Hammadi texts, a collection of early Christian documents discovered half a century ago in Egypt.

Tikva Frymer-Kensky, an Assyriologist and Sumerologist especially interested in questions of gender in Mesopotamia and the Hebrew Bible, "grew up in Forest Hills, in Queens, the daughter of Polish Jewish émigrés who were actively leftist in their politics and devoutly Conservative in their religion. . . . Her early ambition was to become a chemical engineer, but she found herself thwarted again and again by high school teachers—this was in the late 1950s—who turned her away from formative opportunities. 'It explains why, although I became and am a very strong feminist, I never had the rage against religion that many of my colleagues did, because I always suffered more out in the nonreligious world'—suffered more, that is to say, from the heirs of the Enlightenment, the modern men of science." At the Jewish Theological Seminary in New York, "she became the first woman ever to be accepted into the program for the teaching of Talmud."

A note of inadvertance, as well as of stubborn persistence, recurs in these personal histories:

> Karen King grew up in the ranching community of Sheridan, Montana, far away from this world [of Biblical scholarship]. She was drawn into it more or less by accident—"I stumble into things," she explains—when, as an undergraduate at the University of Montana, she happened to take a class from John D. Turner, a member of the *Nag Hammadi Library in English* project, who passed around copies of tentative translations of various Gnostic texts. . . . At Brown, King was for years the only female graduate student in the religion department. She was the only female graduate student anyone could clearly remember having been *in* the department.

King went on to study Gnostic texts, in the early 1980s, in what was then East Berlin, with the Koptische-Gnostische Arbeitsgruppe, in the Egyptian Museum. Back in the United States, she organized a conference on "Images of the Feminine in Gnosticism" and edited its papers into a book, which she gratefully sent her Berlin mentor, Hans-Martin Schenke. Murphy reports, "He told King some years later that he had given the book to his wife, thinking that she might have some use for it." Similarly, Karen Jo Torgeson, the Margo L. Goldsmith Professor of Women's Studies and Religion at Claremont College in California, sent *her* German mentor, Ekkehard Muhlenberg, a copy of her book *When Women Were Priests* and received a letter back saying, as she remembers it, "The cover is beautiful. The acknowledgments are deeply moving. But I'm afraid I cannot bring myself to read it." The German headwaters of theological scholarship are as yet but lightly tinctured by feminism.

And the feminist lessons of *The Word According to Eve* lie more in the biographies of its learned living females than in any dramatic reappraisal of women in the Bible. Murphy surveys a simmering field but offers no cooked dish, in the form of a proposition as memorable as, for instance, Harold Bloom's conclusion that one of the authors of Genesis was a woman. The possibility remains that the Bible has rather little to say to modern women: "At a symposium held at the Smithsonian Institution a few years ago, a member of the audience rose and remarked that after listening to all the things that feminist scholars had to say about women and the Bible, she wondered if she had any choice but to throw up her hands and forget about the whole thing." Tikva Frymer-Kensky, of the Conservative Jewish upbringing, responded, in part, "The Bible is an extremely complex document that revels in a multiplicity of choices, that is filled with gapped texts, that demands that the interpreter complete the text. . . . The Bible is a document of struggle, of God-wrestling." Cullen Murphy, with a (discreetly worn) Christian commitment, agrees: "The Bible remains an ageless provocation. . . . And is not provocation Eve's true vocation?"

One contemporary issue upon which Biblical study does bear directly is the struggle for female ordination, which the Roman Catholic Church, the Greek and Russian Orthodox churches, and the Seventh-Day Adventists still oppose. Saint Paul, the same who wrote that man is the head of woman and that women should be silent in church, also spoke, in his epistles, of a number of women as if they were leaders of Christian groups, at a time when there was no formally educated and ordained priesthood. In Romans 16:1–2, he wrote, "I commend to you our sister Phoebe, a deacon of the church at Cenchreae," applying to her the Greek word, *diakonos*, that he applies to himself and Timothy. The seventh verse of the same chapter salutes "Andronicus and Junia, my kinsmen, and my fellow prisoners, who are of note among the apostles, who also were in Christ before me." Scholarly violence has been committed to keep a woman from being hailed as an apostle; Martin Luther proposed that "Junia" was a mistake for "Junias," a presumed but non-existent diminutive for "Junianius." In Acts, Peter quotes the prophet Joel, "Your sons and daughters shall prophesy."

Outside of Scripture, the fifth-century tomb of a woman called Leta identifies her by the word *presbytera*, whose masculine form translates as "priest." In a ninth-century mosaic, the word *episcopa*, the feminine of "bishop," appears next to a woman named Theodora. A letter from Pope Gelasius I in 494 A.D. complains, "We have heard to our annoyance that divine affairs have come to such a low state that women are encouraged to officiate at the sacred altars." Pagan religion already possessed a strong tradition of women as prophets and seeresses. In general, the more intimately a religion is tied to household practices, the more important women will be in it; early Christianity was a house religion, whose first chapels were simple rooms set aside for worship.

Murphy quotes Amy-Jill Levine as wanting to ask Martha and Mary, "So what did you and Jesus talk about? What did you guys get out of this? What was in it for *you*?" One thing they got out of it was this charismatic young man's willingness to sit and talk with them, and his claiming (in

Luke 10:42) that Mary's education was more important than Martha's housework. In the Judaic culture of Jesus' time, women were not permitted to study Torah, did not join men for meals, had few legal rights, and were stigmatized as unclean after childbirth and during menstruation. Leonard Swidler, one of the few male Biblical scholars who figures in Murphy's survey, concludes in his *Women in Judaism: The Status of Women in Formative Judaism* that their status was of "severe inferiority" and that an "intense misogynism" surpassed the male bias of other contemporary cultures. By one rule, a male was forbidden to speak in public to a woman he did not know: Christ's disciples, in John 4, "marveled" that he had engaged a Samaritan woman in theological discussion beside a well. Again and again, his preaching and actions dismiss the taboos of a sexist and xenophobic Judaism; these liberating dismissals became one of the appeals emphasized by the Gospel-writers and Saint Paul. Paul, whose strictures on feminine silence and headdress have made him notorious among women, also wrote, "Husbands, love your wives" (Colossians 3:19) and "There is neither Jew nor Greek, there is neither bond nor free, there is neither male nor female: for ye are all one in Christ Jesus" (Galatians 3:28). Christianity, though not exempt from sexism, offered women spiritual equality and importance, and women, accepting the offer, played a major part in what Nietzsche scornfully called "the slave revolt of morality."

Women compose the majority of Christian congregations and in recent decades have made striking advances into the once all-male domains of leadership and scholarship. Female ministers, unthinkable in my boyhood, have become commonplace. Once installed, they make one wonder why it took so long, their gifts of nurture and communication so obviously suit the ministry. A third of all American divinity students, Murphy tells us, are female, and in a number of the most prestigious schools women constitute an absolute majority. How apologetic should Judaeo-Christianity be about its patriarchal history? The standards by which it is criticized—the ideas of equality, fairness, and freedom—are by and large of its own engendering. Nietzsche's alternative morality, that of the autocratic *Übermensch*, holds out no mercy to women and the weak. It is true, the story of the Fall, when taken as other than a poetic objectification of a perennial, prototypical event, can inspire such dire misogyny as that of Tertullian, who apostrophized Eve thus:

> You are the devil's gateway; you are the unsealer of that forbidden tree; you are the first deserter of the divine law; you are she who persuaded him whom the devil was not valiant enough to attack: you destroyed so easily

God's image, man. On account of your desert—that is, death, even the Son of Man had to die.

Murphy quotes this, and also Milton's lines, following his description of Adam's ruination, "Thus it shall befall / Him who to worth in women overtrusting / Lets her will rule." And I can recall hearing my grandfather read aloud with relish, to the females of his household, Saint Paul's assertion that the head of the woman is the man. The Bible, an accumulation whose most ancient elements are over three thousand years old, can be cited in support of male tyranny, of slavery, of homophobia, and of genocide.

Yet on the question of women—a question without an equivalent "question of men," whose greater physical strength and relatively unentangling role in the task of procreation have left them free to do the questioning—Judaeo-Christianity, as it has evolved in history, compares well with other cultural constructs. It was not Christianity that condoned, as late as 1910, foot-binding, a fashionable torture inflicted on female children, or the habit of female infanticide which skews China's gender balance even now. It is not Christianity that throughout Africa promotes clitorectomy as a means to properly shaped femininity. It is not Christianity that inflicts upon women, as in Iran and Afghanistan, hysterical restrictions that destroy their access to employment, education, social life, and even medical care.

Male attitudes toward women, mixed of the wish to draw close and the wish to flee, of resentment and adoration, of a child's dependence and a dominator's sadism, are bound to be somewhat unstable, fluctuating, and muddy. The whore/angel dichotomy occurs in the Bible and even approaches resolution there, in several-sided figures like Eve and Mary, a sinner and a virgin who are yet mothers. The strange figure of Mary Magdalene, concocted from several unrelated glimpses in the Gospels, has been the center of complex psychological activity which Marina Warner, in her *Alone of All Her Sex*, summarizes:

> The Magdalene, like Eve, was brought into existence by the powerful undertow of misogyny in Christianity, which associates women with the dangers and degradation of the flesh. For this reason, she became a prominent and beloved saint.

Ambivalence abounds. The contemporary women of *The Word According to Eve* are critical, in several senses, of the Bible, and yet are held to it by a powerful early attraction and dependence. The poet Alicia Ostriker, in a panel on the anthology *A Feminist Companion to Reading the Bible*, capped her "manifesto of complaint" by allowing that "the religion of the Bible is also the source of every value I hold precious." Were Elizabeth Cady Stanton alive now, she might feel *The Woman's Bible* is still being written, with a breadth and insight superior to her own and to that of her scholarly advisers, who were drawn from thin female ranks. She could not but rejoice at seeing women storm the bastion of Biblical scholarship, swarming in over the dusty ramparts of all those dead Middle Eastern languages and fragmentary parchments. Or she might, in one of her swerves of independent thought, decide that the Bible is an incorrigible document, set forever in its ways, beyond any doctoring with gender-sensitive rewordings, and that women had best hearken to what in it speaks to them and turn a deaf ear to the rest.

Was Sex Necessary?

MAKE LOVE, NOT WAR: *The Sexual Revolution: An Unfettered History*, by David Allyn. 366 pp. Little, Brown, 2000.

History begins where memory leaves off. Ever younger historians now tackle events still remembered by living participants—David Goldhagen on the Holocaust, Michael Lind on the Vietnam War—and bring sharp perspectives unclouded by personal involvement. David Allyn, a Princeton history instructor born in 1969, has composed a history of the sexual revolution, which by his chronology ended in the early Eighties, when he was barely adolescent. *Make Love, Not War*, subtitled *The Sexual Revolution: An Unfettered History*, comes with a prodigious bibliography and marches us through the revolution campaign by campaign.

The opening shot, in Allyn's account, was the publication, in 1962, of Helen Gurley Brown's *Sex and the Single Girl*, which proposed that single girls had a right to sex and urged its female readers to "accept all the parts of your body as worthy and lovable . . . your reproductive organs, your breasts, your alimentary tract." Brown, an Arkansas native with a lively sexual history before she married at the age of thirty-seven, had been persuaded to write the book by her husband, a movie producer, and she went on to edit *Cosmopolitan*, turning it into a monthly "self-help manual for the sexually active woman." Yet, Allyn tells us, she "never claimed to be a radical"; she denied advocating promiscuity, weakened her critique of the sexual double standard with an "enthusiasm for expensive cosmetics and plastic surgery," and allowed her publisher to delete from her book a section on birth control. Nor was Brown's battleground quite virgin soil; it had been softened up by such best-selling barrages as former zoologist Alfred Kinsey's *Sexual Behavior in the Human Female* (1953), which reported that roughly half of the 5,940 white American women Kinsey interviewed admitted to premarital sex and a quarter to extramarital affairs, and Grace Metalious's novel *Peyton Place* (1956), which dramatized females as both sexual victims and sexual aggressors.

Allyn's next chapter begins with Rudi Gernreich's perpetration, in 1964, of the "monokini," a gawkily strapped topless swimsuit that never caught on except in the publicity mills; more significant innovations surely were the first Playboy Club in 1960 and the first topless dancing, by Carol Doda at the Condor Club in San Francisco's North Beach district, in 1964. All could be grouped under the heading of commercial sexual display—not exactly revolutionary in themselves but made so by the vocabulary of civil rights with which they were, with frequent success, defended from the forces of censorship.

A few extra degrees of male titillation on beaches and in drinking clubs did not, however, transform the American bedroom; the middle-class masses were liberated by the Pill, an oral contraceptive developed around 1957 and licensed by the federal Food and Drug Administration in 1960. Allyn writes: "The pill, a synthetic estrogen taken once a day, at any time of the day, separated the act of intercourse from the use of birth control. With the pill, contraception became 'clean.' " He quotes the philosopher Ashley Montagu: "In its effects I believe that the pill ranks in importance with the discovery of fire." Montagu saw it as ending the male's "predatory exploitative attitude toward the female" and enabling the overall "rehumanization" of mankind. Montagu proved optimistic: the Pill turned out to have deleterious side effects for many women, as did the IUD, a squiggly-shaped intrauterine contraceptive device absent from Allyn's history. Both inventions, though, were unmitigated boons for men, relieving them of dependence on condoms and depriving women, whether wives or mistresses or fresh acquaintances, of one of the two time-honored reasons for saying No to sex, the threat of pregnancy. The other threat, venereal disease, had by the early Sixties been marginalized by cheap and effective antibiotic treatments for syphilis and gonorrhea. To glance ahead in our story, the revolution faltered when, in 1979, a viral disease, genital herpes, emerged to defy any antibiotic cure; it was followed by the realization, in the early Eighties, that a fatal virus, HIV, communicated from bloodstream to bloodstream through sex or intravenous injection, was killing tens of thousands, mostly men at that point, around the globe. The sexual revolution was an enchanted interval of

technological permission, in a country prosperous enough to give pleasure some major attention. At its peak, it was spurred, if spur were
needed, by the rebellious, reckless mood induced in young people by the
Vietnam War (1965–73). "Make love, not war" became a chant—as if
people hadn't, for millennia, been finding time for both.

Allyn's rather relentless, rat-a-tat survey leads us into a number of
semi-forgotten byways. Who but the most ardent social historian or revolutionary sentimentalist remembers Jefferson Poland, the founder of
the New York League for Sexual Freedom, later the national Sexual
Freedom League—one of the first men to wear flowers in his hair and
the organizer of a goosebumpy "nude 'wade-in'" at a San Francisco
beach in 1965? Or Craig Shoomaker, the founder of Homosexuals
Intransigent!, who in the organization's newsletter denounced bisexuals
as intolerably impure, proclaiming: "I hold it against a man's tongue that
it has slithered over a clitoris; I hold it against his penis that it has gotten
itself coated with the sebaceous lubricant of a vagina. . . . Just as I regard
a vagina as a thing I would not want to get near myself, I find revolting
the idea of vicarious heterosexual sex through a bisexual"? Or Dr. David
Reuben, the psychiatrist author of the best-selling *Everything You Always
Wanted to Know About Sex . . . but Were Afraid to Ask* (1970), which amid
much carefree misinformation recommended Coca-Cola as a contraceptive douche, hymning the spermicidal action of its carbonic acid without
mentioning the risk of peritonitis or a fatal gas embolism? And who
wants to remember the significant sexual component of the civil-rights
movement? Allyn asserts:

> As white female civil rights volunteers arrived in the South, they faced what
> was known as the "sexual test": repeated sexual propositions from black
> men in the movement. If women refused the propositions, they were
> "racist"; if they consented, they were labeled promiscuous, and they also
> invited the wrath of black women.

Stokely Carmichael, the Student Nonviolent Coördinating Committee
leader, is quoted as saying, "The only position for women in SNCC is
prone"; I remember it as "on their backs." The Sixties counterculture was
mostly a male trip. "Peace, Pussy, Pot" was a gender-biased slogan, and
one female hippie reminiscently complained in an interview, "The guys
fucked like rabbits—in, out, in, out. It was so boring you could die."

As well as collecting much piquant ephemera of the revolution, the
author details such lasting breakthroughs as the beautifully named legal
case, in 1967, of *Loving v. Virginia* (Richard Loving, a white brick-mason
who had married a black woman, against the state of Virginia) in which

the Supreme Court struck down the miscegenation laws still on the books of sixteen states. Then there were the Barnard College protests of 1968, after which colleges across the country relinquished restrictive parietal rules and the *in loco parentis* philosophy that lay behind them. Written and filmed pornography, stage nudity, communal cohabitation in the Sixties, group sex in the Seventies—each gets its chapter.

Allyn has been zealous in the pursuit of interviews; his bibliography lists eighty-three. One of the most vivid witnesses to bygone good times is Howard Bellin, a plastic surgeon who, along with his wife, Christina Paolozzi, an Italian countess and fashion model, explored Manhattan high society and the expanding sexual frontiers simultaneously. "Once I had six women in bed at the same time," he testified. "It was not wonderful. How do you keep six women focused on sex all at the same time? Maybe three at one time, but the other three would be talking." On another occasion, he was in bed with his wife when an emergency call came through: "I got a call from my friend Bob. It was two-thirty in the morning. He said he had two girls at his place and he was too tired but they wanted more." Bellin declined, but his wife overheard the conversation and said, "Don't be stupid. Go, have fun." Between fun and drudgery, the line could be fine. Bellin estimates that he had sex with over a thousand women. There is no testimony from those who went under his surgeon's knife the morning after an especially active night. But he himself—his wife, whom he divorced and then remarried, is now dead of a brain tumor—testifies: "The bottom line is, it didn't work. I never thought my kids knew, but they did and they resented it. In a way, I regret it. If we had really worked to stay together and not done all this craziness, it would have been better for the relationship."

But it is a rare penitent who would give back his or her sexual experiences. Amid all the damage to marital and social commitments, people felt happier for having more, and more various, sex. Mimi Lobell, a Manhattan architect and swinger, recalled her first threesome, with her husband and a female student of his: "It took forever and forever and forever for anything to happen. We were just too nervous; we didn't know how to break the ice. . . . Finally we did and it was wonderful and we felt fantastic and in love with the world." In a story by Alice Munro, "The Bear Came Over the Mountain," a male professor remembers the cultural moment when "Young girls with long hair and sandalled feet were coming into his office and all but declaring themselves ready for sex":

A whirlwind hit him, as it did many others. Scandals burst wide open, with high and painful drama all round but a feeling that somehow it was better so. . . . What he felt was mainly a gigantic increase in well-being. . . . He ran up steps two at a time. He appreciated as never before a pageant of torn clouds and winter sunsets seen from his office window, the charm of antique lamps glowing between his neighbors' living-room curtains, the cries of children in the park, at dusk, unwilling to leave the hill where they'd been tobogganing.

It was as Freud had said: happiness is sexual happiness. Allyn discusses spun-off Freudians like Wilhelm Reich and Norman O. Brown but has little to say about Freud himself. Yet it was Freud's blessing that drove and empowered the American sexual revolution. Everybody had heard of him; most everybody had been exposed to a smattering, enough to believe that sexual repression was bad. In his 1908 paper " 'Civilized' Sexual Morality and Modern Nervousness," Freud stated that psy-choneuroses "originate in the sexual needs of unsatisfied people." In 1909, delivering the third of his *Five Lectures on Psycho-Analysis* in Worcester, Massachusetts, he told his audience:

> First and foremost we have found out one thing. Psychoanalytic research traces back the symptoms of patients' illnesses with really surprising regularity to impressions from their *erotic life*. . . . It forces us to suppose that among the influences leading to the illness the predominant significance must be assigned to erotic disturbances, and that this is the case in both sexes.

In *Civilization and Its Discontents* (1930), the "pattern for our search for happiness" was defined as sexual love: "Happiness, in the reduced sense in which we recognize it as possible, is a problem of the economics of the individual's libido." These dicta, detached from Freud's wryly stoic pessimism and his careful tone of exploratory empiricism, flavored myriad sessions of psychotherapy and impromptu applications of what Hugh Hefner was proud to call "*Playboy* philosophy." Good sex became, in this puritan country, a new work ethic.

The righteous hunt for healthful satisfaction was on, and pity the child, parent, or marriage vow that got in its way. One didn't even need to be liberal to join in; a series of articles in the *Chicago Daily News* in 1967 exposed swingers as Midwestern squares. Allyn says, "Often very conservative in politics and dress, swingers tended to establish and follow strict rules in their sexual experimentation. . . . Suburban swingers, unlike their fellow hedonists the hippies, tended to be preoccupied with hygiene and cleanliness, scrubbing and polishing their homes to eliminate every possible germ before guests arrived for a sex party. They treated sex like any other form of suburban recreation." The American booboisie satirized by

Ring Lardner and Sinclair Lewis had found a pastime to replace Saturday-night bridge, but in other respects kept their meliorism. "Swinging," a contented Indiana housewife called Eunice told Allyn, "brought us all much closer together than we would have been otherwise."

On the other hand, sexual acting-up was one of the armaments with which the far left hoped to blow up American society. Bernardine Dohrn of the violent Weatherman faction wore a uniform that "consisted of a black miniskirt, leather boots, and a button reading 'Cunnilingus is Cool, Fellatio is Fun.'" Another collective, based in permissive Amsterdam, called itself Suck, and included for a time future cultural theorists Andrea Dworkin and Germaine Greer. Dworkin wrote that "sucking must be seen in and of itself as an act of political significance" and, later, having moved beyond sucking to "androgynous pansexuality," theorized that lifting all taboos, including those against pederasty and bestiality, would lead to "the development of a new kind of human being and a new kind of human community."

The envisioned Utopias tended to sour, as did the urban attempts to provide, for an admissions fee, sex-abundant zones. New Jersey investment banker Steve Ostrow created the Continental Baths in the basement of the West Side's Ansonia Hotel; for a time it became a fashionable night spot for gays and straights, and it gave Bette Midler her start as a cabaret entertainer. Ostrow rhapsodized, "The Continental has grown full with love, like my life! The world comes here now to feel the release of decades of pent-up sexuality, all those years of inhibition are splattered, if you will, against my walls!" But the gay men moved on—too many straight couples horning in—and the Baths were sold, to become the briefly successful Plato's Retreat, where the famous could be seen naked and partners could be randomized under strobe lights.

Sex has an exhibitionistic component, but more in this regard may amount to less. Isadora Wing, Erica Jong's faithfully libidinous heroine, in *Parachutes and Kisses* visits a "mattress club" called Eros Anonymous, and "her distinct impression was that religious orders ought to send monks there in order to help enforce their vows of chastity." Jong herself, in her memoir *Fear of Fifty*, visited Plato's Retreat with her then husband and found the layout grungy: "We wandered from the spa room (scummy water, pimply bodies) to the snack room (peanut butter and jelly, bologna and mustard—as at some very declassé kids' party), to the mat room (dentists from New Jersey hydraulically screwing their hygienists)." In one of *Make Love, Not War*'s sadder personal anecdotes, the pseudonymous Jody West relates how her liberated parents talked incessantly about sex and invited her to watch them have it (she refused). When she brought her first date home, her father "put condoms on every bed in the house. I was so embarrassed I wanted to cry." Allyn abandons his interviewer's role to confide that when he was twelve his father and stepmother recommended that he have sex with a prostitute: "I was left with the feeling that we would never be able to understand one another; that if I were going to talk to someone about my sexual feelings and experiences, it would never be with either of them." Freud pointed out, in his 1912 paper "The Most Prevalent Form of Degradation in Erotic Life," that sexual energy needs to be conserved:

> Some obstacle is necessary to swell the tide of the libido to its height. . . . In times during which no obstacles to sexual satisfaction existed, such as, may be, during the decline of the civilizations of antiquity, love became worthless, life became empty, and strong reaction-formations were necessary before the indispensable emotional value of love could be recovered.

Reactions to the sexual revolution arose in the Seventies from a resurgent evangelical Christianity (though a few evangels were caught with their pants down) and from anti-pornography feminists. The weakening, inflationary economy dampened the mood. Sexual liberation began to feel rotten from within. Larry Flynt's *Hustler* ran photos of naked prepubescents and a regular comic strip called *Chester the Molester*. Linda Lovelace, the child-faced heroine of the first great porn hit, *Deep Throat*, revealed in a 1980 autobiography that she had been beaten and threatened with a gun by her husband to compel her compliance while making indecent films. The law began to stir again: *Deep Throat*'s hero, the megaphallic Harry Reems, was arrested in his New York City apartment and extradited to Tennessee, where a Memphis jury in 1976 found him and eleven other defendants guilty of obscenity. (The conviction was overturned.) In 1974, the Supreme Court upheld the conviction of a San Diego publisher, William Hamling, who had brought out an edition, with hard-core illustrations, of the report of the Presidential Commission on Obscenity and Pornography. If the Court's 1973 *Roe v. Wade* decision, legalizing abortion, was, as Allyn writes, "the crowning achievement of the sexual revolution," the defeat of the Equal Rights Amendment, which ran out of time in 1982 with only three more states needed for ratification, was the legal triumph of the counter-revolution, led in this instance by Phyllis Schlafly. She claimed the amendment would "destroy the family, foster homosexuality, and hurt women." So, even without the emergence of herpes and AIDS, "by the early eighties, the sexual revolution was out of steam."

David Allyn likes the image of running out of steam enough to use it at

least three times. Though one must admire the wealth of detail and documented anecdote that fuels his steamy narrative, there is something
mechanical about his take on this, after all, intimate sea-change. The live
creature within the exoskeleton of headlines and communiqués remains
elusive. Allyn's skirmish-by-skirmish military approach does best with
those movements within the revolution which led a minority—gay men,
lesbians—to achieve, through organization, alliance, pronouncement,
and confrontation, some public acknowledgment of their equal rights.
The battle for legal recognition of same-sex couples, with all the benefits
society bestows on heterosexual couples, still goes on, but anyone alive in
the Forties and Fifties, when homosexuals of either gender were objects
of coarse fun and frank abhorrence, sees at the century's end an improved,
relatively tolerant situation, however marred by regressive incidents of
gay-bashing.

For the heterosexual mainstream, the main news is that the sky did not
fall in. Huge Technicolor genitals appeared on movie screens, Henry
Miller's *Tropic* novels freely circulated, young couples took to living in
what used to be called "sin," polymorphous perversity was preached and
practiced, and yet the society continued to function, and people in love
tended to create nuclear families. Grandmothers, when an adult grandchild brought a friend to visit, adjusted to letting them sleep in the same
bed—indeed, the grandmothers, if they had been flappers in the Twenties, or war brides in the Forties, had seen something like it before. Allyn
does not entertain much suspicion of a cyclical pattern in social mores,
each generation seeking to correct the perceived errors and excesses of
the preceding. To him, as in Philip Larkin's poem,

> Sexual intercourse began
> In nineteen sixty-three . . .
> Between the end of the *Chatterley* ban
> And the Beatles' first LP.

The decades of my own youth are in Allyn's terms flatly "the repressive
forties and fifties." His introduction states, "It is necessary to appreciate
that real sexual repression was always a threat in the 1940s and '50s. That
is to say, the state reserved the right to repress sexual deviance and dissent." Reserved it, yes, but exercised it with more caution and flexibility
than a child of the Sixties might think. Policing sexual behavior is a hopelessly huge task, and few organized societies are so ignorant of human
needs as not to build in some leeway for the sex drive. The Puritans had
their bundling; the most straitlaced rural communities had square dances
and haymows.

How repressed were we, back in those benighted Forties and Fifties? I do not recall feeling more repressed than was good for me. Even without reading Freud, one knew that civilization demanded some control of the libido. The extensive, elaborate "necking" and "petting" whereby adolescents kept their virginity but expressed their heat were what is now newly fashionable as "safe sex." My parents, who had courted and wed in the Roaring Twenties, sometimes offended my childish prudery by wandering around naked upstairs. They never, to my memory, made an admonitory remark (or any kind of remark) about masturbation, and, insofar as dating and late nights were discouraged, it was in the practical cause of preventing my premature marriage. The old repressions were occasioned by real threats and honest fears, which have been eased less than the revolutionaries expected. The enemy was not a set of aliens out there, denying and scolding; we were our own enemy, our inhibitions locked in for reasons of self-preservation. And these inhibitions, it might be said, generated a poetry of pervasive eroticism. The sideways glance, the glimpse of underwear, the whiff of perfume, the perhaps accidental touch, the intimacy achieved bit by bit, like a painstaking mapping of the heavens— all this would be forfeit in a Plato's Retreat of consummation on demand. We value what we need to fight for. Secrecy is a great aphrodisiac. The Victorians found excitement in an exposed ankle; the Japanese, in the nape of a woman's neck. If every beach becomes a meaty sprawl of near-nudity and every date a compulsory copulation, we risk allowing sex to seem paltry.

Chanel No. 1

CHANEL: *Her Style and Her Life*, by Janet Wallach. 180 pp. Doubleday, 1998.

Who is the greatest Frenchwoman of the century? Marie Curie's discoveries began in the nineteenth century and, anyway, she was born Polish. Brigitte Bardot, Catherine Deneuve, Simone Signoret, Jeanne Moreau—actresses all, images, in part the creation of others, including our fantasizing selves. Simone de Beauvoir, handmaiden of existentialism, inventor of feminism? But if we must name a writer, surely it should be Colette, who wrote as naturally as she slept, danced, or made love, who rendered the tangle of a modern woman's life with the casual calm of classic art. And if we think of Colette we come to Chanel, another tough, industrious child of the provinces who tapped into the realistic essence of

French style. Insofar as individual designers can be said to direct the vast, subconsciously swayed movements of fashion, it was she who brought sense and comfort to female clothes, shifting their control from the viewer to the wearer, from how clothes looked to men to how they felt to women. Breathtaking corsets, giant plumed hats, and floor-length skirts of cumbersome complexity and weight were the style in Gabrielle Chanel's girlhood, when women of means paraded as stiffly as manacled captives; in her long and steadily successful career as a designer, she first simplified the hat, then lightened and loosened the dress and lifted it to expose ever more of the ankle. Flapper minimalism was her meat. In the 1920s, she produced the first little black dress—in mousseline, chenille, satin, velvet; the Ford of fashion, the American *Vogue* called it—and the simple, snug suit, usually in lightweight wool jersey, that became her signature piece.

According to Janet Wallach's near-hagiographic picture-book *Chanel: Her Style and Her Life*, the birdy little gamine from Auvergne worked a miracle wherever one was needed: "Each new problem in life propelled her to new ideas. With women no longer able to order their drivers to take them shopping on rainy days [World War I was causing the inconvenience], Chanel invented a rubberized style based on the lines of a chauffeur's coat, with deep pockets and adjustable tabs at the cuffs." Walking on the hot sands of the Lido gave her "the idea to tie two straps around a sheet of cork and cut it into sandals, a style that became popular around the world." Her affair with the Duke of Westminster, the richest man in England, saw his country-weekend sweaters transformed into "snappy cardigans for women," the uniforms of his yacht crew adapted into sailor outfits and nautical chapeaux for milady, and the jewelry ("Indian bibs of rare diamonds and emeralds, matching bracelets of rubies, emeralds and sapphires, brilliant solitaires, strands of diamonds and emeralds, and ropes of pearls") that the besotted Duke bestowed upon her transmographied into gaudy costume ornaments—"she turned the snobbish realm of jewelry into the fantasy world of the fake." All this, and Chanel No. 5, too; the scent was named No. 5 without there having been a 1, 2, 3, or 4 and was marketed, in one of Chanel's brilliant adaptations of male accoutrements, in a bottle whose square solidity was "borrowed from the toiletry cases of her lovers." The elixir made her rich for life, a life, as Wallach tells it, that was one long romance and name drop.

Her own name, descended from a tribe of peasants who lived on the edge of a chestnut forest in the Cévennes and who were driven by the chestnut blight to become itinerant peddlers, was all she had to start with. Her parents married fifteen months after she was born. Her mother died when she was twelve, and her faithless, peripatetic father put

Gabrielle and her two sisters in an orphanage run by nuns at Aubazine; he was never to be seen by his daughters again. Though she did not elect, at seventeen, to become a nun, a chaste austerity, a quest for purity of purpose and line, remained at the heart of her flair. The nuns had taught her to sew. She took a job as a shopgirl in a lingerie-and-trousseau firm in Moulins, and worked extra hours for a tailor, mending the uniforms of the army officers garrisoned in the town. They noticed her, and made her a pet; she sang at a local cabaret. According to Wallach, she knew the words to only two songs: "Ko Ko Ri Ko" and "Qui qu'a vu Coco?" The soldiers would call out for Coco, and thus she acquired her nickname, although, a tireless obfuscator of her past, she would afterward claim that her father had called her that, in one of his rare visits home. She was not beautiful but had for assets a wide mouth, a long neck, an indomitable temperament. The Gaul rebel chieftain Vercingetorix had come from the volcanic hills of Auvergne, and Chanel spoke of herself as "the only crater of Auvergne that is not extinct."

By the age of twenty she had achieved the next social step up from shop-girl and amateur entertainer and become a kept woman. Her keeper was the infantry officer Etienne Balsan. His is the first name we encounter in her pilgrimage from man to man. A devoted horseman, an indifferent sol-dier, the good-humored heir of a textile fortune accumulated in Château-roux, he encouraged Chanel to pursue her possible stage career at Vichy, where her singing coach told her, "You've got a voice like a crow." His parents had recently died, and with his inheritance he purchased an estate called Royallieu, near Compiègne, and invited Chanel to join him there, among the horses and overdressed demimondaines who flocked to the place on the arms of Balsan's aristocratic friends. These women admired Chanel's manlike riding style and the simplified hats she had designed; they had her make hats for them, which they sometimes wore onto the stage. Photographs of Chanel modelling her sweeping creations appeared in a 1910 issue of the theatrical periodical *Comoedia Illustrée*. Her vocation as designer didn't take hold, however, until she met the Englishman Arthur "Boy" Capel, in a burst of Wallach's fulsome, you-are-there prose:

> She saw him first at Pau, a smart town for the racing set, and turned her charms on him at once. With coquettish technique she looked longingly into his eyes, fluttered her lashes, played her necklace to her lips and slith-ered her body closer to his. He was soon a regular guest at Royallieu.

For a time the two amiable playboys shared what she later called "my hot little body"; she got to Paris in 1913 by sharing Capel's apartment on the Avenue Gabriel and using Balsan's flat on the Boulevard Malesherbes for her first shop.

Fashion history is made in odd jumps. Boy Capel, supportive lover though he was, didn't take her out much; the scrawny crow-voiced milliner couldn't hold her own among the pneumatic courtesans who, gotten up in the ornate, high-waisted styles of Worth, Poiret, and Paquin, filled the cafés with their cultivated chatter. One time when he did take her to a restaurant, Wallach relates, "she ate too much and popped her stays. . . . Chanel swore she would never wear a tight corset again." Her lean styles, no longer confined to hats, became fashionable during the war; she opened shops in Deauville and Biarritz, and by 1919, she said, she "had woken up famous." She was the new woman:

> Slim, narrow-hipped and nearly breastless, she had shed her corsets, short-ened her skirts, cut her long hair and allowed her youthful face to tan in the sun. She lived openly with a man she loved but was not married to, and she enjoyed financial independence as an entrepreneur with a flourishing business.

Her lover, however, went back to England to find a wife and to father a daughter, while continuing to visit Chanel. It was after a visit to her, on his way to meet his wife in Cannes, that he died in a car crash. "She would never love another man as much as she had loved Capel," Wallach asserts; but it was not for lack of trying. She took up with the arty crowd, meeting Diaghilev and Cocteau, seducing Stravinsky, failing to seduce Picasso, and travelling to Venice with dear friends Misia and José-Maria Sert (the latter's murals can still be seen at the Waldorf-Astoria). Chanel was now rich enough to support in the style to which he was accustomed the Grand Duke Dmitri, dashingly exiled from Russia because of his part in the assassination of Rasputin. She always got something out of her lovers, though; Dmitri introduced her to Byzantine jewelry and to the Czar's former perfumer, the chemist Ernest Beaux, who in 1920 created Chanel No. 5. And then there was, after Dmitri, the surly, stocky poet Pierre Reverdy, Picasso's close friend, who shared with Chanel the knack of always being photographed with a cigarette.

Chanel's next lover, the Duke of Westminster, excites Wallach to her most breathless rhapsodies:

> Ruggedly good-looking with a large frame and handsome face, reddish blond hair and intense blue eyes, Westminster oozed elegance. . . . Loyal servants scurried to do whatever he asked, while high-society ladies scuffled to be at his beck and call.

Oozing while his lessers scurried and scuffled, the Duke nevertheless found Chanel resistant to his Channel-crossing courtship gifts of "out-of-season strawberries, peaches, nectarines and freshly caught Scottish salmon. . . . He even sent her a basket of fresh vegetables, and when her servant reached inside, he plucked out a giant emerald." How could the little orphan from Aubazine not succumb? He had houses everywhere, two great yachts, and in his fifty-four-bedroom main domicile, Eaton Hall, "the acres of walls were covered with paintings by Rubens and Raphael, Rembrandt and Hals, Velázquez and Goya." Chanel and the Duke were together for six years, sailing, hunting, consorting with the likes of Winston Churchill and the Prince of Wales. She even tried, in her mid-forties, to become pregnant with Westminster's heir, which would induce their marriage; she submitted, she later allowed, to surgery and "humiliating acrobatics." In vain: the Duke took to younger companions and married the deliciously named Loelia Ponsonby, half his age and "the well-bred daughter of the protocol chief to the king." Speaking of emeralds—late in their relationship, while cruising, Westminster tried to placate his French mistress with another giant; she tossed it over the side.

Chanel's next noteworthy lover was Paul Iribe, a chubby, complicated (Colette thought he was demonic) Basque cartoonist from Angoulême, who designed for her an array of antic, expensive jewelry. Hotheads the same age, they might have married, but in 1935 he collapsed before her eyes, on the tennis court of her Riviera villa, La Pausa, and died a few hours later. If Iribe had a touch of the demonic, Chanel's wartime affair nearly damned her with disgrace. When war was declared in 1939, she closed the House of Chanel for the duration; when the Germans invaded, she fled as far as Pau, but at the invitation of the new masters of Paris she returned to her rooms at the Ritz. She took a German lover, Baron Hans Gunther von Dincklage, called "Spatz"; a figure about Paris before the war, the son of an English mother, he was a Nazi intelligence officer with a taste for fine things and for staying away from Berlin. The lovers spoke to each other only in English, and were, it would seem, happy—"happy," in the words of Chanel's best biographer, Edmonde Charles-Roux, "in a world in which mountains of misfortune were rising around them." An obfuscation similar to that which hides her girlhood masks this period. After the war, Chanel joked, "At my age, when a man wants to sleep with you, you don't ask to see his passport." She and her German contacts concocted a scheme whereby Chanel would exploit her friendship with Churchill to arrange a conditional German surrender; she travelled to Spain with this purpose, taking with her Vera Bate, a pre-war English friend who had married an Italian colonel and was surviving the war in Rome until the Germans kidnapped her for Chanel's grandiose mission.

More damningly, Chanel attempted to use the Nazi anti-Semitic laws to wrest control of Chanel No. 5 from her old partner and backer Pierre Wertheimer, who was exiled in New York, supervising the perfume's successful American manufacture—it, too, had been kidnapped. (It was also manufactured in France, since Wertheimer had cannily put the company in the hands of an Aryan, and was therefore one of the few name products available to both Allied and Axis consumers.) Chanel's legal suit failed, and eventually she and Wertheimer settled to mutual advantage, but her attempted exploitation of the Holocaust was not becoming. According to another biographer, Pierre Galante, she enjoyed wartime favors because, "like her friend, Pierre Laval [the Premier of the puppet Vichy government], she was an Auvergnat." After the Liberation, it was said she was protected by her old shooting chum Churchill; she was briefly arrested but was spared public trial and a shaved head, unlike lesser women who had slept with the enemy. She exiled herself to Switzerland, where she continued living with and supporting Spatz.

Yet she was forgiven, because she was, in a way, France herself—the ubiquitous name of French chic, its subtle, rational, penetrating glamour. She returned to Paris at the age of seventy and, though her first showing, in 1954, drew mixed and even vicious reviews, the Americans continued to love her youthful little suits and dresses, and she enjoyed prosperity and acclaim until her death at the age of eighty-seven. Other designers, like Dior and Schiaparelli, could create sensations with their fanciful, overblown revivals of Belle Epoque femininity, but in the end no one designed for women as Chanel did. When *les grandes cocottes* came into her shop in 1913 wearing their immense hats, she asked, "How can the brain function in those things?" At the height of the miniskirt craze toward the end of her life, she insisted that the skirt should be one that—in the paraphrase of a third French biographer, Marcel Haedrich—"makes it possible to sit down decently." And skirts do return, after every fashion flurry, to the knee-grazing Chanel length.

She was forgiven because she was a genius with scissors in her hand and pins in her mouth, who even when she was the world's richest self-made woman continued to do the fittings herself, on her knees until they ached, ripping seams, resetting shoulders, lying flat on the floor to check hems and make sure "the underside is as perfect as the outside." Such perfection was felt. "Some women want to be gripped inside their clothes," she said. "Never. I want women to enter my dresses and to hell with everything else." Wallach ends her whirl through Chanel's fabulous life with a no-frills assessment of her couture: "All is practical, all is logical, all is done to make a woman feel good about herself."

The Poor Babies

LUSITANIA: *Saga and Myth*, by David Ramsay. 308 pp. Norton, 2002.

LUSITANIA: *An Epic Tragedy*, by Diana Preston. 532 pp. Walker, 2002.

The sinking of the Cunard liner *Lusitania*, on May 7, 1915, will always play second fiddle, in the ensemble of maritime disasters, to that of White Star's *Titanic* a little more than three years earlier. Of the two glamorous great ships, the *Lusitania* was the smaller by nearly a hundred feet of length and sixteen thousand gross tons; she had been in service for eight years and for exactly one hundred North Atlantic crossings before being torpedoed by a German *Unterseeboot* off the southern coast of Ireland, whereas the "unsinkable" *Titanic*, of course, epitomized human fallibility by rubbing up against an easily avoidable iceberg on her maiden voyage. Yet the scale of the *Lusitania* disaster, in terms of squandered treasure and lost life, was scarcely smaller—1,198 of the 1,962 on board died, as opposed to the *Titanic's* 1,523 out of 2,228—and its international repercussions were much graver. The ship had sailed from New York, and one hundred twenty-eight Americans, many of them women and children, died of drowning, injuries, or hypothermia in its sinking. Although the national indignation was not enough to pull the United States and the Wilson administration into a declaration of war against Germany, when the declaration did come, in April of 1917, recruitment posters urged, "Remember the *Lusitania!*" One poster simply showed a woman submerged in blue-green water with a baby clasped in her arms, above the single blood-red word "ENLIST."

Not one but two books have joined, this spring, the ranks of those already devoted to the disaster, its puzzles and its consequences. *Lusitania: Saga and Myth* was first published, last year, in England; its author, David Ramsay, a Scot transplanted to California, states in his acknowledgments that "the saga of the liner *Lusitania* has intrigued me for many years in the same way that others have been fascinated by the drama of the maiden voyage of *Titanic.*" Conversations with, among others, a former director of Cunard persuaded him that "the liner's history and the reasons behind her sinking had never been adequately told." His purpose has been "to examine and rebut the many myths of *Lusitania*," and his book has something of the close argumentation and carefully prepared ground of a legal proceeding, so that the disaster almost seems a mere prelude to its aftermath of hearings and evasive governmental maneuvers.

Diana Preston, an English writer of popular history whose previous books include *The Boxer Rebellion* and *The Road to Culloden Moor,* has produced *Lusitania: An Epic Tragedy.* Her creative impetus dates back to when she saw, outside the Merseyside Maritime Museum, one of the ship's recovered bronze propellers, "stark and huge as a dinosaur bone," and when she first examined the "yellowing, cracking photographs of the dead" to be found in the Cunard Company archives, at the University of Liverpool. Her telling excels in its reconstruction of the sailing and of the fatal day when, in eighteen chaotic minutes, *Lusitania* took its hit, listed, and sank. Preston, sifting the wealth of survivor interviews and court testimony, has a sharp eye for the animating, poignant touch and, once the human drama of the disaster subsides, deals with the subsequent "myths" and disputes in a relatively cursory fashion. Ramsay, whose direct description of the wreck concludes a third of the way through his book, quotes extensively from the two hearings—the inquiry under Lord Mersey in June of 1915, in London, and the trial for compensatory damages brought by American plaintiffs and tried under Judge Julius Mayer, in New York City, in April of 1918—and sets about debunking numerous rumors and theories of the time as vigorously and systematically as if they were current gossip. "Flogging a dead horse" was a non-nautical phrase that occurred to me during his thorough rehash. It must vex both authors that their ably written, devotedly researched volumes, so long in the making, should appear at the same time (and in the same year, for that matter, in which Günter Grass has published a novel on the Baltic sinking of the German ocean liner *Wilhelm Gustloff,* in January of 1945, by a Russian submarine, with the immense human toll of 9,343 dead). Of the *Lusitania* books, Preston's is the longer and, not only in its human particulars but in a certain nervy sweep to its conclusions, livelier; it is apt to be the more widely read, though I can picture maritime buffs happily settling, with their pipes and braided caps, to Ramsay's seamanlike knots.

Questions surrounded the *Lusitania*'s sinking. Why did the British Admiralty, which in the wartime emergency had ultimate control over Cunard liners, provide no escort in the Irish channel, though it was well aware, through broken codes, of U-boat activity? Was the *Lusitania*'s Captain Will Turner, who had recently taken command of the liner, remiss in following Admiralty precautions, notably their advocacy of zigzagging as a submarine-eluding maneuver? Was the ship carrying undeclared war munitions that exploded when the torpedo hit? If not, what did cause a second explosion, observed not only by passengers and crew but, through his periscope, by the captain of the submarine U-20, the intrepid and efficient Walther Schweiger? To what extent was Winston Churchill, First Lord of the Admiralty, distracted from his duties in the U-boat war by his cherished though ill-advised campaign to seize the Dardanelles? He was off in Paris, concluding an agreement on the use of the Italian navy in the Mediterranean, when the *Lusitania* sank, and the once-redoubtable John Arbuthnot "Jackie" Fisher, who had been brought from retirement to serve as First Sea Lord when Prince Louis of Battenberg was xenophobically driven from the post, was past his prime, if not somewhat demented. Churchill's commitment to the safety of non-combatant shipping appeared to be less than keen: three months before the *Lusitania* sinking, he wrote to the president of the English Board of Trade that it was "most important to attract neutral shipping to our shores, in the hope especially of embroiling the U.S.A. with Germany. . . . For our part, we want the traffic—the more the better and if some of it gets into trouble, better still." This pro-trouble position reappears in his 1937 pronouncement, in *News of the World:*

> In spite of all its horror, we must regard the sinking of the *Lusitania* as an event most important and favourable to the Allies. . . . The poor babies who perished in the ocean struck a blow at German power more deadly than could have been achieved by the sacrifice of a hundred thousand fighting men.

So, just as revisionist theories propose that Roosevelt lured the Japanese into attacking Pearl Harbor so that the United States would be brought into the war against the Axis, the *Lusitania* was possibly set up to be sunk. Certainly it was left to take its chances, with a new captain on board.

Captain Turner, a crusty salt of limited sociability, is presented more sympathetically by Ramsay than by Preston. Preston reports him saying, at the moment of his rescue from the wreck where over a thousand had perished, "What bad luck . . . What have I done to deserve this?" Ashore in Queenstown (now Cobh), he remarked, with chilling detachment, "Well, it is the fortune of war." Ramsay, who provides vivid portraits of the warring strong personalities within the Admiralty, shows them as initially determined to put the blame on Turner. The report of the canny officer responsible for liaison with merchant shipping, Captain Richard Webb, stated that "the Master . . . proceeded . . . at a speed three-quarters of what he was able to get out of his vessel. He thus kept his valuable vessel for an unnecessary length of time in the area where she was most liable to attack, inviting disaster." First Sea Lord Fisher explosively annotated this report, "As the Cunard company would not have employed an incompetent man, the certainty is absolute that Captain Turner is not a fool but a knave. I feel absolutely certain that Turner is a scoundrel and [has] been bribed. .... I hope that Captain Turner will be arrested *immediately* after the enquiry, *whatever* the verdict." Churchill, who did not return from Paris until three days after the sinking, was more politic, announcing in the House of Commons that Turner should not be prematurely blamed; but he privately confided, "We should pursue the Captain without check."

Turner, however, proved not easy to blame. At the June 1915 hearing headed by Lord Mersey, he made a gruff, monosyllabic witness but was skillfully represented as "an old-fashioned sailor man" by Cunard lawyers. His most debatable action prior to the torpedo strike was taking a "four-point bearing" from Irish headlands to fix his position, which involved changing course and then maintaining his direction and a moderate speed of eighteen knots for forty minutes. As it happened, this methodical maneuver headed the *Lusitania* right toward the enemy U-boat; Captain Schweiger later told a friend, fellow–U-boat captain Max Valentiner, "She could not have steered a more perfect course if she had deliberately tried to give us a dead shot." Schweiger had sighted the ship before the course change, and concluded that "I had no hope now, even if we hurried at our best speed, of getting near enough to attack her." A liner's best defense against a submarine was always its superior speed—over twenty knots against the nine a sub could make underwater. But Turner could not know the exact position of the submerged enemy, and his maneuver was defensible, even though one captain testified, at the liability trial held in New York in 1918 under Judge Julius Mayer, that a four-point bearing was unnecessary.

In the sharp light of hindsight, Turner might have held more boat drills, and made sure that the supplemental, collapsible lifeboats were better maintained (a number were hopelessly rusty, and painted fast to the deck), and been stricter about open portholes; but the quickness with which the boat sank, and the severe list that made lowering both port and starboard boats very difficult, and the damage that instantly rendered the great ship impossible to steer and even to halt in the water, and the diminished quality of the crew in this period of wartime conscription, and the grim fact that many crewmen were trapped belowdecks by the failure of the electric elevators, all contributed to a disaster beyond the captain's control. Both hearings cleared Cunard of negligence, and the American plaintiffs were advised to seek restitution from imperial Germany. Turner went on to command other boats, and indeed was torpedoed once again, and again survived, retiring in 1919 to a village near Dartmoor. There, journalists so harassed him that he returned to Liverpool, to die in seclusion at the age of seventy-six. He found the *Lusitania*, not surprisingly, a painful subject to discuss. Toward his end he was heard to complain that he had never received Admiralty instructions to zigzag and had been denied "a fair deal."

"The poor babies"—they became the symbol of the ambushed ship. "There were in fact an unusually large number of children on board," Preston says—fifty-one boys, thirty-nine girls, and thirty-nine infants. They had been, a passenger recalled, "the life and charm of the voyage." Of the one hundred twenty-nine, ninety-four died, including thirty-five of the babies. Drawing upon tearjerking contemporary accounts, Preston makes sickeningly real the confusion and terror of the wreck and its aftermath in the fifty-two-degree North Atlantic. In the flooding corridors and cabins, on the heeling decks, children lost track of their parents and siblings; infants were handed to strangers and tossed into lifeboats. Desperate attempts were made to keep them alive in the ocean, though the young were especially vulnerable to hypothermia; babies were hoisted onto wreckage and even a bobbing steamer chair, and a survivor reported seeing "a man pathetically pushing a dying child along on a folded life jacket." Mothers struggled for hours in the water to hold up their infants only to discover, when lifted into lifeboats, that the children were already dead. A witness reported:

> Just as we got her to the raft . . . her baby girl closed its tiny eyes in her arms. Almost overcome with exhaustion the mother caught hold of the side of our boat, the lifeless mite still close to her heart, and when we got her into the boat she could hardly speak. . . . Then, lifting the little one in her arms, she turned to those in the boat, and in a tearful voice simply said, "Let me bury my baby." Within a few seconds the almost naked body of the child floated peacefully on the sea.

One survivor recalled "the bodies of infants laid in life jackets, and floating around with their dead innocent faces looking towards the sky." There were so many that, as he swam, he pushed them aside "like lily pads on a pond."

Among many false reports of German atrocities—rapes and crucifixions in Belgium that did not, amid much actual brutality, occur—this was the real thing, irrefutable proof of German "frightfulness," to use a favorite word of Allied headline-writers. Preston's conclusion is that the sinking of the *Lusitania* did Germany "far more harm than good." The autocratic German authorities, "wrapped up in a sense of grievance," kept handing propaganda victories to their foes. Kaiser Wilhelm II, Queen Victoria's eldest grandchild, was weakened in his belligerence by admiration of the English, distrust of his fiercest military advisers, and recoil from the global outcry. He was "shocked by the extent to which he was being demonized." Yet he himself had bestowed the epithet "Hun" upon his tribe:

> In a notorious speech to German troops departing for China in 1900, he had urged them to "give no quarter! Take no prisoners! . . . Even as, a thousand years ago, the Huns under their leader Attila gained such a name for themselves as still resounds in terror . . . so may the name of Germany resound!"

Captain Schweiger's feat—downing a seven-deck liner with a single torpedo—was hailed by the German press, but the Kaiser and the diplomats seeking to keep America neutral were less pleased. Schweiger was ordered to report to Berlin, where, according to Admiral Tirpitz, the foremost advocate of unrestricted submarine warfare, he was "treated very ungraciously." The captain's diary account of the torpedoing was doctored to include humane scruples and to heighten suggestions of British incompetence; this "official" version was never signed by Schweiger. He went to his own watery death in 1917, while commanding another submarine, having lost the U-20 on the Danish coast. After the war, his fiancée told an interviewer that when he visited her in the period following the *Lusitania*'s sinking he was "haggard and so silent and so different"; nine months before his death, he wrote a comrade of his that he longed for the end of "this very sad time."

Faint heart never won fair lady or victory in war, Preston assures us: "Germany's great mistake, having sunk the *Lusitania*, was to edge slowly away from unrestricted submarine warfare." Only a ruthless exploitation of its submarine advantage, she says, might have produced, after the bloody stalemates of Verdun and the Somme, a brokered peace. By 1917, when the Kaiser's qualms had been dismissed, it was too late. In an extraordinary wartime communication, the erratic Admiral Fisher, now relieved of First Sea Lord duties, wrote Admiral Tirpitz, who had been forced by imperial doves to resign in 1916, a chummy letter beginning "Dear Old Tirps" and ending:

> Cheer up, old chap! Say "Resurgam"! You're the one German sailor who understands War! Kill your enemy without being killed yourself. I don't blame you for the submarine business, I'd have done the same myself.

Preston asserts, "A quarter century later, all nations practiced unrestricted submarine warfare." The old Cruiser Rules, which called for a sub to sink a merchant ship only after stopping her and allowing the crew to disembark, were as dead as the protocols of medieval chivalry. The distinction between civilian innocents and combatants who are fair game for annihilation vanishes as war becomes a contest between the entire resources of nations. In the same spring the *Lusitania* was sunk, Germany introduced poison gas into the Western front and with a solitary zeppelin launched the first air raid on the civilian population of London. These events, according to Preston, "were signposts on the path to Guernica, Hiroshima, and beyond. . . . The new barbarism of total war had begun."

Yet poison gas, one wants to protest, was not used, between armies, in any subsequent European war, and since Hiroshima and Nagasaki atomic weapons have never, through a host of armed conflicts, been employed. Humankind does try to avoid repeating its atrocities. As civilization struggles to subdue barbarism, signal disasters have their uses, as boundary markers on the outer limits of the possible. They make us grateful to be on the safe side of them. They argue for the high value of ordinary existence, with its mixed motives and resistance to simplification.

It is useful to see, in David Ramsay's careful survey of the *Lusitania*'s economic and political context, how pre-war Germany expressed its growing aspirations in building great ships for the transatlantic run, and to have an admiring portrait of Albert Ballin, the German Jew who led the Hamburg-Amerika Line to dominance in German shipping. It is useful to see Woodrow Wilson, like the Kaiser on his side, entertain ambivalence and doubts. As a Southerner, Wilson dreaded war and its ruinous aftermath; as a devout Presbyterian, he could be rigid in his righteousness; as a widower, he was susceptible to romance, and was distracted at the height of the *Lusitania* crisis by his courtship of Edith Mary Galt. We are surprised to learn that William Jennings Bryan, now best remembered as the blustering butt of the Scopes Trial in 1925, took, as Wilson's Secretary of State, what might now be called a liberal and fair-minded stand against jingoist warmongering and the steep pro-British tilt of American neutrality.

Diana Preston's panorama of the "epic tragedy" of the *Lusitania* is enlarged by her picture of life aboard the bustling liner before it sank, and by her following pages on the hard, wet, crowded, dangerous existence within a German submarine, where a man off duty was expected to sleep in order to conserve the common oxygen. Her eye for the piquant detail generates a glittering web of trivia. We learn of Admiral Lord Charles Beresford, "He was rumored to have been the lover of the murdered Empress Elizabeth of Austria. He shared her passion for riding to hounds, surpassing it to the extent of having a hunting scene tattooed across his buttocks with the fox disappearing into the cleft." We are told that Jennie Jerome, Churchill's American mother, "discreetly took lovers" and was a neglectful mother until her son showed signs of journalistic prowess. We learn that one proposed British stratagem for combatting submarines was to train seagulls to defecate on the periscopes. During the *Lusitania*'s sea trials, not only was there excessive vibration but steam escaped from the third-class drinking fountains. Under way, the liner consumed a thousand tons of coal a day. Its firemen worked in shifts of exactly twenty-one minutes. Second-class passage for its last voyage had been reduced from seventy to fifty dollars. Card sharks plied the great passenger liners, back and forth.

The reader's heart races, the ship moving toward its doom is so laden with the stuff of life. Preston compulsively notes gaudy costumes in her large cast of characters: the codebreaker Sir Alfred Ewing had "a predilection for mauve shirts and dark blue bow ties with white polka dots"; the lawyer Sir Frederick E. Smith was "tall and vain" and "habitually wore a red flower in his buttonhole"; a grand-jury witness, Gustav Stahl, appeared "wearing his finest clothes—a dark suit, new straw hat, green tie with a stickpin bearing a porcelain dog's head, polished tan shoes, and lavender socks with scarlet-embroidered flowers." Such details pertain, we can say, to the great denuding that a luxury vessel occasions when it sinks—though in fact those passengers who tore off their clothes did worse in the cold water than those who stayed dressed. Bodies damaged beyond recognition by the sea and its fish were sometimes tagged with small scraps of fabric snipped from their clothes, for identification. So nothing is irrelevant, and Preston's farraginous method accumulates a fitting monument to a multitudinous loss. One lays down these two volumes, which utilize the yellowing records as well as the fresh data gleanable from underwater dives and German archives, trusting that they will be, well into this century, the last word on the subject.

Drawn to Gypsies

LITTLE MONEY STREET: *In Search of Gypsies and Their Music in the South of France*, by Fernanda Eberstadt. 242 pp. Knopf, 2006.

Fernanda Eberstadt, an ambitious, resourceful novelist with a lush style and a Manhattan background, has written, in *Little Money Street*, a piquant non-fictional account of her successful attempt to penetrate the Gypsy enclave of Perpignan, France. This city, at the eastern end of the

Pyrenees, holds five thousand Gypsies in an urban center of around a hundred thousand souls. Eberstadt and her husband, Alastair Bruton, and their two small children found themselves living in a rented house outside Perpignan because Bruton, we are told a bit abruptly, "was writing a book about the decline of religion in modern Europe, and was looking for somewhere half to hole up in, half to base it on." Why this obscure, unprosperous, and atypical region of France—the province of Roussillon, ceded by Spain as late as 1659 and still regarded by many of its natives as "Northern Catalonia"—should serve his investigative purpose is left mysterious, but its usefulness to his wife is made clear. In the course of a cosmopolitan life she has always, she tells us, "been drawn to Gypsies": after a childhood glimpse of a trio begging at an outdoor café in Paris, she has "sought out Gypsies—Gypsies who run traveling circuses in Ireland, or sleep in the ruined Byzantine city walls in Istanbul, or camp on the beach in Palermo, or even live in a brownstone basement on the Upper West Side of Manhattan." Though her six years of living in Roussillon may have left her with "the same attraction to their intractable difference," readers of her account, if this reviewer is an example, will be cured of whatever faint desire they may ever have entertained to live like a Gypsy.

It's a miserable life, for the shiftless, jobless, largely illiterate men and twice as bad for the home-bound women, generally married in their teens to other teens who will bully, betray, tyrannize, and most likely beat them. As to their children, they stay up so late watching television and hanging out on the street that they are usually too sleepy to go to school; Gypsies must be the only significant ethnic group in France that actively discourages literacy and encourages truancy. Compared with them, the embattled immigrants from the Muslim world are models of aspiration to bourgeois order and enlightenment. One of Eberstadt's more *hallucinante* chapters describes a conference on education held at Collège Jean Moulin, a junior-high school for preponderantly Gypsy students. "The occasion is pretty merry," she writes. "People who work with Gypsies tend to laugh a lot. It's a laughter of hysterical exasperation, because if you didn't laugh, you'd hang yourself or quit." The school's principal, a "barrel-chested, crew-cutted Catalan" named Paul Landric, is quoted:

> "If an Arab kid cuts school, he stays in the street so his parents don't find out. If a Gypsy plays hookey, it's *in order* to stay home. Here, it's the parents who are the disruptive influence, mothers who want to coddle their sons, fathers who don't want their daughters to be seen hanging with boys at school. The girl is a commodity, and they don't want her to lose her market value."

Her value, as a virgin, is ascertained not by the young groom on the wedding night but, according to archaic folk custom, by the probing finger of a tribal crone: Eberstadt's partially renegade Gypsy friend Linda explains, "For Gypsies, it's a nasty old woman who is paid to penetrate the girl, like a gynecologist but with dirty hands, in front of all the husband's family. It's terrifying, it's inhuman." Landric sums up: "People talk about preserving Gypsy culture. But what am I as an educator supposed to do when the comportment of my students is frankly pathological?" Eberstadt, liberal enough to doubt liberal pieties, complains that "if these pedagogues were nineteenth-century missionaries to a cannibal island, they could not be more convinced that the belief system they wished to impose upon the Gypsy savages—in this case, egalitarian secularism— was as unequivocal a good as clean water." Yet she comes down, finally, on the side of clean water, asserting that the French authorities are "using their utmost powers of imagination and sympathy to devise ways of freeing a community that was clearly stuck and unhappy."

Gypsies were not always so stuck; their nomadism, now legally discouraged by most European governments, excused their educational recalcitrance, and they maintained "a seventeenth-century agrarian culture designed for seasonal pickers, small artisans, blacksmiths, market sellers." They used to be "horse-breeders, blacksmiths, basket-weavers," trades which became obsolete in the Sixties. But Eberstadt is not offering to solve "the Gypsy problem," or to give a history of this curious people, which, linguistic evidence indicates, originated in India, and which has endured centuries of disapproval and persecution throughout Europe, including decimation* in the Holocaust.

She engages with Gypsies as a small set of local friends, and came to them via a CD put out by Sony in 1999, *Ida y Vuelta*, featuring a mostly Gypsy band called Tekameli. The CD, she tells us, is "supremely cultic . . . veiled, hermetic . . . arcane": "The musicians are Frenchmen singing Pentecostalist hymns in a language—Gypsy Catalan—that very few people know exists. It brings news from a place no one's heard of, and the news is at once too close and too distant to be intelligible." Any of us, to be sure, would be fascinated by music so hard to describe or pigeonhole, but perhaps only a New York writer, marooned with her family in a "fairly desolate," "half-savage," and "malnourished" backwater of Europe would have undertaken a vigorous pursuit of the members of the elusive band:

---

*Literally: an estimated one-tenth of the world's Gypsy population, five hundred thousand out of a total five million, perished in gas chambers and concentration camps.

For months, I listened hypnotically to *Ida y Vuelta*, while pursuing Tekameli leads and Gypsy research on the side. I left phone messages on dead voice mails. I spoke to musicians' daughters, nephews, cousins-in-law, who told me to call back later, by which time the telephone had been cut off. In a perfect emblem of futility, I sent letters composed in painstaking schoolgirl French to men I later discovered were illiterate. . . . I moped, I fretted, I sulked.

She was advised by a Catalan disk jockey to attend an *assemblée*—a church of the Protestant Pentecostalism that since the 1960s has exerted a dominating influence on France's Gypsy population. She found the church packed with gender-segregated Gypsies, singing and testifying in Gitan, the gruff Catalan dialect tongue used in Saint-Jacques, a former Jewish ghetto in Perpignan settled by Gypsies when the Vichy government cleared out the Jews. In the *assemblée*, a young man, entering late, took the chair beside her, and, seeing her, "started back in involuntary fright, the appalled recoil of a toddler who's just realized that the adult whose knees he's reaching for isn't his mother." She declares, "It was then that I understood something of the reality behind Gypsy defiance, Gypsy insults, Gypsy leers. St. Jacques Gypsies are in fact far more scared of non-Gypsies than even the timidest non-Gypsy is of them."

A resolutely non-timid non-Gypsy, Eberstadt finds her way in, eventually, via the discontented wives and female consorts of the Tekameli musicians. Two, especially, allow themselves to be befriended and seen close-up: Linda, "thirty years old, tall and beautiful, with a dimpled white smile, hair done in a headdress of African braids, good make-up, and charm like a Mickey Finn," and her sister, "small, bedraggled" Diane, her "sheepish grin" marred by brown or missing teeth. It is runty, scatter-brained Diane, and not handsome, efficient Linda, who is the common-law wife of Moïse Espinas, the lead Tekameli singer and "possessor of the greatest voice north of Barcelona." Moïse, who is twenty-eight when Eberstadt meets him and already growing plump, has "a complicated atti-tude toward music, as if his own gift lies in a state of untaught purity that might be defiled either by too much use or by exposure to other people's music." He and his colleagues would rather play cards than rehearse. Guy Bertrand, a musical Frenchman who gives himself credit for developing Roussillon Gypsy music into commercial viability, sees little future for it:

"It's not easy to work with Gypsies. . . . They have no structure in their lives, no discipline, no vision, and hence they can't critique themselves, they can't develop. Musically, they are as good at fourteen as they ever will be. . . . In all the years I've known him, Moïse has never done a single thing to deepen or improve or develop his music. All he's done is strut around for journalists, blowing his money, and making babies all over the world."

In Eberstadt's reckoning, Gypsy values amount to a disabling intensification of "family values": a good wife, in her obligatory ankle-length black skirts, can't leave the house without a husband's permission, and men would rather laze around "at home, *tranquille,*" than work. It is "a culture in which girls are best off brain-dead." Eberstadt indignantly concludes, "What differentiates '*la loi gitane*' "—Gypsy law—"from Judaism or Islam or more fundamentalist brands of Christianity is 'that there is no corresponding code of male probity, nor is there any sense of divine will behind the prohibitions. Gypsy laws, it seems, are made not to glorify God but merely to spite women!"

Nevertheless, the transplanted New Yorker has some good times with her new friends. She develops a kind of crush on Linda—"a gorgeous woman in full command of her own sexuality"—and in girlish mall outings and reckless car rides with Diane she experiences the "kind of wild abandoned fun I haven't known since I was seventeen." She even gets taken by Moïse himself to a cockfight—indeed, the Perpignan championship, twenty-five bouts held in a nameless settlement of Andalusian Gypsies—and is the only woman in the crowd. Her description of the bouts and their promoters is as gaudy and appalling as the cockfight scene in Nathanael West's *The Day of the Locust.* This chapter and her succeeding one, describing the laughter-filled education conference, constitute the book's most vivid reportage and together cinch its apparent point that the Gypsies are a hopeless case, their recreations as vicious and vacuous as their traditional defense mechanisms are self-ruinous:

> They forget their French and keep their children out of school and marry them to their first cousins aged fourteen. They accept bribes to vote for Mayor Alduy. They lose their teeth and are too frightened to go to the dentist. They die of minor diseases against which other French people—people who go to school—are inoculated. And they don't leave a trace.

As writing, *Little Money Street* is lively and varied, moving proficiently between statistics and anecdote, warm sympathy and cold condemnation. As narrative, *Little Money Street* has a distracting double focus; trying to see the Gypsies, we keep seeing the hip, assertive, irresistible journalist. She is more than marginally visible, imparting confidences like "I think, This place is godforsaken, but its broken beauties are in my bloodstream." The reader is flattered to share the other worlds of sophisticated experience that she brings to bear upon her sorry Gypsy slum. A visit to a Perpignan community center begins with this riff:

It is a concrete building painted in one of those schoolchildren's murals of happy faces and sunflowers that tend to embellish neighborhoods where drive-by shootings are a common occurrence and life expectancy for young males is a whole lot lower than the national average.

A gang of young Gypsy men slinking on the street, "cigarettes dripping from downy lips," wins a burst of global allusions: "They are often heart-breakingly beautiful, these boys, sometimes astonishingly debauched-looking, in a manner recalling Caravaggio ephebes, Pasolini's *ragazzi di vita*, and they dress in a bygone style of gangster dandyism." Allusiveness so generous has the effect of taking our minds down side roads, wondering what *un*astonishing debauched looks the witness has seen, and exactly *when* a bygone gangster style *was* chic, and whose heart is breaking.

Eberstadt's vocabulary sometimes shows an impatient petulance, as when the Gypsies' aged Mercedeses are reported to have "engines canni-balized from crappier cars," the earthy adjective returning in a heated lament over the consumerism "in which people are persuaded to express their love for their children through the acquisition of crappy goods they can't afford." Her assimilation of the Gypsy point of view becomes per-haps too thorough when she tells of a flagrant case of shoplifting—over eight hundred dollars' worth of goods—thwarted by "a fellow-customer, an unidentified toady who should rot in hell." A female small-town mayor, an innocent bystander in the narrative, gets nailed as "a porky blonde." The author's relative youth seems vaunted in so florid a display of pop-musical lingo as

> The blend of loony upbeat Afro-Caribbean bounce and hoarse flamenco-style yowls of brokenhearted prayer—an effect as schizophrenically origi-nal as R & B—created a music that seemed to express the perverse vagaries of a soul yearning for union with God.

Such verbal largesse foments a somewhat *en haut* tone; we are led to reflect that the author was possibly welcomed into the company of Gypsy women not only for her charm and flattering curiosity but because, in her past advantages and present freedoms and—a significant attraction—command of her own car, she loomed in their restricted, impecunious world as a phenomenon and even as a deliverer. Near the end of her long stay, a drug-addict's husband makes begging motions: "But the funny thing is, in six years of hanging around St. Jacques Gypsies, this is the first time anybody's ever hit me up for money. I figure I've got off lightly, so I head for the nearest cash machine."

We are not surprised when, late in *Little Money Street*, its author con-fesses, "Writers—most writers—are opportunists: I had got my material, more than I could possibly use, and now . . . I needed not to see Diane in order to be able to 'see' her better." As the writer's children age, the culture gap widens; and months go by without her phoning her Gypsy friends. Yet—to end on a happy note—when, "after a long absence," she does "ring Diane's doorbell," she receives "a prodigal welcome." Old times are remembered, old friends revisited, new developments registered. Moïse has become a grandfather at thirty-one and has "been in mysteriously bad health." At the farewell party that Eberstadt and her family give before they move to a bigger house, a four-hour train ride away, in central France, Moïse sings, but still as "a great singer who hates to sing . . . for whom his 'gift' is something that at times he's seen as an easy way of making money or getting girls, but that more often is awkward, shaming, even anguishing." After a few songs, the chatter of the non-Gypsy guests, "as if we were in a restaurant and he were hustling for spare change," offends him and he stalks off. Later, he is coaxed to sing again, in a "voice waning from neglect." Soon he will be baptized and sing only canticles, reducing his family to living on welfare and handouts from relatives. Eberstadt's mildly melancholy coda to her dire portrait of contemporary European Gypsies leaves us with the mollifying impression that all parties end untidily, all lives are more or less muddles, and we all are, as the French officially term nomadic minorities, "*gens du voyage*."

Survivor / Believer

To Begin Where I Am: *Selected Essays*, by Czeslaw Milosz, edited and with an introduction by Bogdana Carpenter and Madeline G. Levine, translated from the Polish by Levine, Richard Lourie, Louis Iribarne, Catherine S. Leach, Lillian Vallee, Jane Zielonko, Robert Hass, and the author. 462 pp. Farrar, Straus and Giroux, 2001.

Of the eleven U.S. citizens who have been awarded the Nobel Prize for Literature since 1930, when Sinclair Lewis became the first, Czeslaw Milosz, the 1980 winner, is the least well known to the American public. Lewis, Pearl Buck, Ernest Hemingway, and John Steinbeck were bestselling novelists, as have been, on occasion, Saul Bellow and Toni Morrison. William Faulkner's modernist intransigence may have repelled middlebrow readers but fed into his eventually immense reputation; Eugene O'Neill dominated American drama as no playwright has before or since. Isaac Bashevis Singer wrote in Yiddish but was much published in English translation, and the Russian poet Joseph Brodsky brought to this continent the fame of defiant anti-Soviet dissidence and a nervy willingness to write both prose and verse in English. Milosz, a friend and admirer of Brodsky's, has continued to write in Polish, although his education in the tongue of his adopted land includes four and a half years, following World War II, in the Washington diplomatic community. His permanent American residence dates from 1960, when he accepted a post in the Slavic department of the University of California at Berkeley. To the American literary establishment, the West Coast is out of sight and mind, and Milosz's low visibility was reinforced when, with the collapse of the Iron Curtain, he could reforge his native connection with Eastern Europe; he now, at the age of ninety,* divides his residence between Berkeley and Kraków, Poland.

And yet this strange migratory bird nested within our republic has flourished here. In the handsome and substantial *New and Collected Poems 1931–2001* recently published by Ecco Press, four-fifths of the pages were written after 1960, and, remarkably, nearly a third after 1991, in Milosz's eighties. This decade saw the appearance, first in Polish and then in English, of four collections of new poetry. In the year 2001 there has been a cascade of publications in addition to the collected poems: the reissue in a separate volume, as freshly translated by the author and Robert Hass, of Milosz's long poem of 1957, *A Treatise on Poetry; Milosz's ABC's*, an alphabetically listed array of short essays, erudite, diverse, and autobiographical; and *To Begin Where I Am*, a selection of prose pieces edited and with an introduction by Bogdana Carpenter and Madeline G. Levine, and translated from the Polish by many hands, including that of the author. The earliest piece was written in 1942, in the form of a letter, in dire wartime circumstances, and the latest, "Happiness," in the late 1990s, during the mellow sunset years of California exile and sentimental return to native soil. Written in English, first published in 1998 in *Architectural Digest*, "Happiness" describes a visit to the Lithuanian valley where Milosz lived on his grandparents' farm for a period of childhood:

> I was looking at a meadow. Suddenly the realization came that during my years of wandering I had searched in vain for such a combination of leaves and flowers as was here and that I have been always yearning to return. Or, to be precise, I understood this after a huge wave of emotion had overwhelmed me, and the only name I can give it now would be—bliss.

---

*Milosz died in August 2004. Asked for the cause, his assistant told the Associated Press, "It's death, simply death. It was his time—he was ninety-three."

One is reminded of another Slavic celebrant of bliss, bliss tinted and twisted by the losses of exile, Vladimir Nabokov, who left America's haven just as Milosz arrived. In *To Begin Where I Am*, the author's brief opening statement, "My Intention," expresses the lifelong priority Milosz has given to subjective specifics over abstract conceptions: "I have read many books, but to place all those volumes on top of one another and stand on them would not add a cubit to my stature. Their learned terms are of little use when I attempt to seize naked experience, which eludes all accepted ideas." He has striven to remain "free to be suspicious and to ask naïve questions"; his "certainty of having something important to say to the world, something no one else will be called to say," is weakened by "the thought of all the people who ever were, are, and ever will be" and the likelihood that "our books in their brightly colored jackets will be added to the mass of things in which names and titles sink and vanish." Still, he keeps writing, in accents simultaneously lofty and intimate.

Neither his essays nor his poetry venture far from the substance of his life: his birth, to ethnically Polish parents, in Lithuania, which was part of the Russian Empire up to 1918, so that children in school were forbidden to speak any other language; his years attending high school in Vilnius, the ancient Lithuanian capital (Wilno in Polish); his move in 1937 to Warsaw, where he endured World War II, writing "idyllic verses" and taking an active part in the anti-Nazi underground; his postwar diplomatic service on behalf of Communist Poland (though he was never himself a Party member); his defection to Paris in 1951 and his eventual United States residence and citizenship. Such a life—unlike, say, those of Wordsworth or Wallace Stevens—cannot be imported into poetry without threatening to steal the show from the reflections and expressions it engenders. The footnote to the poem "With Her," for example, written in Berkeley in 1985, consists of this glimpse into the agonized muddle of a ravaged Europe, with its paradoxes:

> In 1945, during the big resettlements of population at the end of World War II, my family left Lithuania and was assigned quarters near Danzig (Gdansk) in a house belonging to a German peasant family. Only one old German woman remained in the house. She fell ill with typhus and there was nobody to take care of her. In spite of admonitions motivated partly by universal hatred for the Germans, my mother nursed her, became ill herself, and died.

It is with a survivor's authority of witness that Milosz disputes, in an essay on Boris Pasternak, the critics of *Doctor Zhivago* who objected to the novel's wealth of coincidental meetings: "Anyone who has lived through wars and revolutions knows that in a human anthill on fire the number of extraordinary meetings, unbelievable coincidences, multiplies tremendously in comparison with periods of peace and everyday routine."

His experience of the anthill on fire is not pressed upon the reader; rather, it emerges indirectly, often, in prose, by way of biographies of friends and fellow-poets who did not survive, whose fates landed them among the enforcers of fascist or Communist ideology. Milosz's poetry touches on the war years in a guarded, reticent voice of glancing memory and veiled allusion. But in a long and eventually published letter to his fellow-writer Jerzy Andrzejewski, one of a series composed in 1942 and 1943, he speaks in a sterner, more immediate voice, that of a Roman Catholic intellectual surrounded by horror, in occupied Poland, which the Germans themselves called "the cloaca of the world." It is not given to every writer to be present at the collapse of civilization. Milosz writes, "The habits of civilization have a certain enduring quality and the Germans in occupied Western Europe were obviously embarrassed and concealed their aims, where in Poland they acted completely openly." In another essay he declares, "What we beheld surpassed the most daring and the most macabre imagination." To Andrzejewski he reports, in a tone of anthropological detachment, the disappearance around him of "a ceremonious attitude toward death":

> It is a different matter when, as today, new ideas are being born—for example, the idea of the mass extermination of people, akin to the extermination of bedbugs or flies. . . . A certain insectivity of life and death, as I'd like to call it, is created. I suspect that we are beginning to look at man partly as a living piece of meat with tufts of hair on his head and his sexual organs, partly as an amusing toy that speaks, moves—but all one has to do is raise one's hand and squeeze the trigger and an ordinary object is lying in the same place, as inert as wood and stone. Who knows, perhaps this is the path to absolute indifference, including indifference to one's own death. It may happen that with good training and appropriate schooling people will die easily, from a lack of desire; they will treat dying as almost an everyday activity, between two shots of vodka and a cigarette that they won't get to smoke.

He seeks, amid the orgy of sadism and sudden death in Poland, "a reliable foundation apart from any faith," and comes up with humanity's "ethical instinct," while admitting the plasticity of ethical schemes: "A German, a model son, husband, loving father of a family, will torment a subhuman, a Jew or a Soviet soldier, because he is obsessed with his vision of duty and justice, which commands him to cleanse Europe of simple vermin." Concluding his debate with Andrzejewski (whose replies, in an exchange of nine letters, have been published in Polish but not English), Milosz takes his own ethical stand within the Catholic Church, apart from "the path of Humanism and the Reformation." All too smoothly he traces a progression from Luther to Rousseau and Nietzsche and thence to the Nazi "worshippers of the magnificent beast in man" and Alfred Rosenberg, the infamous minister of the German-occupied Eastern territories and the author of racist theories that radicalized the young Hitler.

Milosz, remaining true to the teachings of his childhood's priestly instructors, is still a practicing Catholic. This fact seems to leave him, as much as anything, bemused. The poem "Helene's Religion," from the 1998 collection *Road-Side Dog*, might well describe his own:

> On Sundays I go to church and pray with all the others.
> Who am I to think I am different?
> —Enough that I don't listen to what the priests blabber in their sermons.
> Otherwise, I would have to concede that I reject common sense.

It goes on to express a credo, a quasi-Thomist proof:

> It's not up to me to know anything about Heaven or Hell.
> But in this world there is too much ugliness and horror.
> So there must be, somewhere, goodness and truth.
> And that means somewhere God must be.

In his essay "If Only This Could Be Said" (1991), he attempts to tackle his religion frontally: "Ought I to try to explain 'why I believe'? I don't think so. It should suffice if I attempt to convey the coloring or tone. If I believed that man can do good with his own powers, I would have no interest in Christianity. But he cannot, because he is enslaved to his own predatory, domineering instincts, which we may call *proprium*, or self-love." He writes as one on the settled far shore of the struggle to believe, but evidence of his struggle comes in two essays, written in English, on two theologians who impressed and moved him during the Fifties: Simone Weil and Lev Shestov.

While not tempted to imitate Weil's suicidally ascetic lifestyle, he admires the severe purity of her solution to the problems of evil, of suffering, and of God's apparent abdication from the affairs of the world. Weil affirms the earthly domination of *la pesanteur*—gravity, and its laws, which she calls necessity: "The absence of God is the most perfect testimony of perfect love, and that is why pure necessity, necessity which is manifestly different from the good, is so beautiful." In other words: "Creation is an abdication. But [God] is omnipotent in the sense that his abdication is voluntary." Our task is "to love God through and across the destruction of Troy and Carthage, and without consolation. Love is not consolation, it is light." God does grant, amid the universal determinism, grace, an emanation from a realm beyond the range of mechanical necessity: "Impossibility is the door of the supernatural. We can only knock at it. Someone else opens it." With a certain mathematical rigor (Weil, originally a teacher of philosophy, was well versed in mathematics and physics) she travels a sweeping *via negativa* to arrive back at traditional Christian assertions.

Shestov, a Ukrainian born in 1866, debated with the once-famous Christian apologist Nikolai Berdyaev, and was listed by Camus as one of the spokesmen for the new "man of the absurd." As paraphrased by Milosz, Shestov, following Dostoevsky's *Notes from Underground*, was what Plato called a *misologos*, a hater of reason; rather than play the game of chess proposed by the philosophers of reason, which is stoic acquiescence, Shestov "overturns the table with a kick," asking, "Why should the 'I' accept 'wisdom,' which obviously violates its most intense desire? Why respect 'the immutable laws'?" Overturning the table with a kick is a gesture that would appeal to Milosz's natural gaiety, his "despairing cheerfulness," though perhaps it makes light of the materialist table's real *pesanteur.* But the ultimate measure of gravity is each person's death, and to one who lived through a time of "dying as almost an everyday activity" lightness may enter in. Milosz is one of the last of the literary believers who were conspicuous in the Fifties; he translated Weil and T. S. Eliot into Polish, and it was thanks to his reading of Shestov that he and Joseph Brodsky "were able to understand each other intellectually."

To Begin Where I Am, which its American editors have aimed away from the Polish arcana abundant in *Milosz's ABC's*, contains essays on Brodsky, and on Pasternak, Eliot, Robert Frost, and Robinson Jeffers, but none of these poets excite the detailed, vivifying explication awarded the two theological thinkers. Copiously well read, at home in a fistful of languages, and a boyhood naturalist as well, Milosz gives the impression of a man rooted in his own existence, which theology and history have penetrated more deeply than have other people's attempts at literature. A self acquires its substance early, and such essays of youthful experience as "Dictionary of Wilno Streets" and "Journey to the West" are the most full-blooded. The latter, recounting a hiking-and-paddling trip he and two friends, called Elephant and Robespierre, took to Paris in 1931, is idyllic yet ominous; the many German juveniles they meet on the road and in youth hostels are polite but repel all attempts by the Slavic boys to make contact. Remembering the dormitories they shared, Milosz writes, "The future was already there, among those beds. Today I sometimes think that Elephant's closest neighbor could have been the Gestapo officer who later tortured him during questioning." The jovial, gentle Elephant, whose mind was "liberal and skeptical, resistant to the temptations of heroism," jumped from a window to his death after being tortured. A different fate awaited the severe, bony Robespierre, the trio's leader. His shrill voice was broadcast on the Moscow radio, and by 1950 he had become portly and a "high-ranking Stalinist bureaucrat" in Warsaw.

Other essays use old friends to illumine, like phosphorous flares, the violence that beset Poland. In 1943, Warsaw's Jewish ghetto rebelled and its residents were butchered in reprisal; in 1944, the Polish underground, activated by a command order from the London government in exile, staged an uprising which the Germans quelled in a two-month battle while the Russian army, just across the Vistula River, halted its advance and let the insurgents, who would have obstructed the Communists' intended reordering of Poland, be wiped out. Many young people known to Milosz died in "these frenzies of voluntary self-sacrifice"; the Germans deported the remaining population and razed the city, before retreating west to their own doom. But Milosz does not remember only the victims of violence. He recalls his cousin the French poet Oscar Milosz; a Polish actress who murdered her lover at his own request and became a nun after being pronounced not guilty. In "Miss Anna and Miss Dora," he brings again to life a pair of "old, poor, and helpless" spinsters, for little more reason than that "no one but me remembers their names anymore." For an exile, no remembered face or scene is too incidental to clarify the basic mystery of being.

Milosz's poetic project, like Whitman's, is to sing the man, the whole man, not the partial man of the modern avant-garde, which has "created out of the poet a creature with a head covered with mathematical lumps, with exceptionally large lenses for its eyes, and suffering from atrophy of the heart and liver." He would counter such "narrowing and desiccation" with a broad realism: "I seek in poems a revelation of reality, of what is known in Greek as *epifaneia*." Again: "Language must name reality, which exists objectively, massive, tangible, and terrifying in its concreteness." Yet traumatic reality requires "the distance necessary to transform this material artistically." In "Ruins and Poetry," one of the Norton Lectures Milosz gave in 1981–82 at Harvard, he states, "The reality of the war years is a great subject, but a great subject is not enough and it even makes inadequacies in workmanship all the more visible." The "many terrifying poems" born of the Holocaust as it was happening last less well than poems more elliptical and plain, even rudimentary, in diction: transcribing the breakdown of civilization, "man constructs poetry out of the remnants found in ruins."

Many sorts of poet leave Milosz dissatisfied: the "Communist orators"

Eluard and Aragon; the reflexive pessimists Frost and Larkin; and those who, like Francis Ponge and Wallace Stevens, replace the " 'suchness' of things" with "purely intellectual deconstruction into their component parts." He confesses, "Often these are dazzlingly intelligent constructions, but I find very little in them for myself." For himself, he likes in poetry "the tension that derives from contradictions." He praises Eliot for his "almost unbelievable undertaking: he built out of impossibility, absence, ruins." Cultural confusion and fragmentation have occurred before: "Renaissance man lamented the chaos that surrounded and inhabited him, but that is precisely what led to the greatness of Marlowe and Shakespeare." The situation of Renaissance man, torn between the wisdom of the church and the wisdom of the rediscovered ancients, between faith and reason, between, like Hamlet, the sins of action and those of inaction, remains modern man's situation, and Milosz urges resistance to the "nihilizing pressures" of such monisms as materialism and Buddhism:

> Alas, our fundamental experience is duality: mind and body, freedom and necessity, evil and good, and certainly world and God. It is the same with our protest against pain and death. In the poetry I select [in his anthology *A Book of Luminous Things*] I am not seeking an escape from dread but rather proof that dread and reverence can exist within us simultaneously.

A believer full of reasonable doubts, an American with his heart in Lithuania and his mind in a vanished Warsaw and a persistent Paris ("the most amazing thing about Paris for me is that it still exists"), an essayist distrustful of engagement in the European sense but by no means disengaged, a Californian fond of our nature but cool toward our culture, Milosz declines to be typecast, a giant hiding in our midst.

Twice Collected

COLLECTED POEMS, by Philip Larkin, edited by Anthony Thwaite. 330 pp. Farrar, Straus and Giroux, 1989.

COLLECTED POEMS, by Philip Larkin, edited by Anthony Thwaite. 218 pp. Farrar, Straus and Giroux, 2004.

American poetry-lovers of late have been treated to two one-thousand-page volumes of collected poems—those of James Merrill, edited by J. D. McClatchy and Stephen Yenser, and those of Robert Lowell, edited by Frank Bidart and David Gewanter. The more slender oeuvre of the British poet Philip Larkin (1922–1985) has been posthumously honored in another style of lavishness: not one but two *Collected Poems* have appeared, the earlier one edited by Anthony Thwaite and published here by Farrar, Straus and Giroux in 1989, and now a second one, a hundred pages shorter, also edited by Thwaite and published by Farrar, Straus and Giroux. This singular double homage came about not through any carelessness but from an abundance of the caring that Larkin's work arouses in its admirers.

Thwaite, a distinguished poet and critic and a long-time friend of Larkin's, was delighted to discover, as he undertook, in 1986, the duties of a literary executor, that the deceased poet had been a methodical preserver of his own drafts and copious youthful efforts. In a 1959 essay, "Not the Place's Fault," on his boyhood in Coventry, Larkin remembered, "I wrote ceaselessly . . . : now verse, which I sewed up into little books, now prose, a thousand words a night after homework." Seven of the little books were among his effects, four dating from September of 1939 to August of 1940, and three produced in 1941 and 1942, when he was at Oxford. From 1944 on, Larkin, setting up shop as a postgraduate writer, preserved and dated his handwritten drafts, as they moved toward typed, corrected, and final versions. He had become, after his graphomaniacal boyhood, a scrupulously slow and patient reviser. Thwaite cites the eight-line poem "Take One Home for the Kiddies," which was begun in April of 1954 and completed in August of 1960. Less prolonged but effortfully fitful was the creation of two of Larkin's finest longer poems. Thwaite reports:

> 'Church Going', begun on 24 April 1954, went through twenty-one pages of drafts, was 'abandoned 24.5.54', and then resumed and completed in July of that year. 'The Whitsun Weddings', begun in May 1957 with its first stanza complete, was then dropped, resumed in July 1958, reworked from twenty-three pages until 6 September, picked up again on 19 September and completed after eight further pages of drafts on 18 October.

Given this unlooked-for wealth of creative specifics, Thwaite and his fellow-executors decided to produce a chronological arrangement that ignored the order Larkin himself had used in his four commercially published collections—*The North Ship* (1945), *The Less Deceived* (1955), *The Whitsun Weddings* (1964), and *High Windows* (1974). The first *Collected* opens not with the poems of *The North Ship* but with the oldest poem, "Going," that Larkin chose to publish ten years later in *The Less Deceived*. Thwaite's introduction calls it "the first poem of his maturity." "Going" is followed, however, by a number of poems not included in *The Less Deceived* but in the unpublished collection *In the Grip of Night* (1947) or the self-published *XX Poems* (1951), which Larkin had pulled together after *The North Ship*, published by the raffish Reginald Caton's small Fortune Press, sank with scarcely a trace.

In addition, Thwaite incorporated, in the 1989 *Collected*, a number of poems never published by Larkin in any form and in some cases left unfinished. Some of the unfinished poems, like "Negative Indicative" and the one-hundred-thirty-two-line "The Dance," come from Larkin's prime and evince his characteristic virtues. Some finished poems that Thwaite includes, such as "The March Past" and "The Winter Palace," were excluded by Larkin from his own collections. To the main selection, titled "Poems 1946–83," Thwaite appended a second section, "Early Poems 1938–45," containing seventy adolescent, collegiate, and post-collegiate poems (including the entire contents of *The North Ship*) that the author had long abandoned in his wake. More than one critic protested the editorial discourtesy of running the good and the indifferent, the aborted and the canonical all together, and in an order not of the poet's choosing.

The first *Collected Poems* has the undoubted interest of a chronological arrangement: the successive items flicker in and out of focus as they lose and recover one sensibility's peculiar genius. In their recurrent obsessions and tone, the stronger poems reach backward and forward to their equally achieved kindred while the weaker sisters meekly duck their heads. The reader sees, as Thwaite promises, "the growth of a major poet, testing, filtering, rejecting, modulating, achieving." And he sees not just growth but sclerosis, as Larkin's production all but ceased in his last decade—one of the more striking poetic abnegations since Rimbaud's. There was one soaring exception to his painful silence: "Aubade," of 1977, the last and bluntest and stateliest expression of his lifelong dread of death:

> the total emptiness forever,
> The sure extinction that we travel to
> And shall be lost in always. Not to be here,
> Not to be anywhere,
> And soon; nothing more terrible, nothing more true.

Larkin was a mere fifty-five when he wrote those lines. How interesting it is to see the unblinking honesty, the quiet wit, the easy metrical intricacy in gear once more, and then, but for a few personal or official verses, shut down for good.

There is interest, too, in the pre-1946 poems, wherein Auden's jaunty knowing and Yeats's vatic largeness and Eliot's dour, mocking music conspire with a faux-rural imagery of wind and sea and sun and trees and heart and blood to enwrap the young Larkin in a fog of abstraction and myth that delay his arrival at the mundane realism, vivid in each wistful, shabby detail, which we know will become his. His early poems are frustratingly obscure, addressed to vague nymphs by a speaker entranced by his own coldness. Usually brief, they end with empty flourishes: "I take you now and for always, / For always is always now"; "Pour away that youth / That overflows the heart . . . walk with the dead / For fear of death"; "And grief stirs, and the deft / Heart lies impotent"; "No gale-driven bird / Nor frost-encircled root / As cold as my heart." These sentiments, inverted valentines, as yet lack their objective correlatives in workaday England. They strike poses in a humorless vacuum.

The second, present version of *Collected Poems* constitutes Thwaite's reply to complaints about the first. A terse introduction describes the earlier chronological ordering and explains that the new edition is "partly a considered response to suggestions that what was needed, too, was a book that followed Larkin's own deliberate ordering of his poems in each successive book . . . with perhaps an appendix taking in earlier published strays and also a handful of poems after *High Windows* had gone to press." Unfinished poems and poems never published by Larkin in any venue are omitted. Of the copious juvenilia, only a poem printed in *The Listener* when Larkin was eighteen and seven poems from Oxford publications are included, with none from the secondary-school *Coventrian*.

Having patiently read both versions of *Collected Poems*, this reviewer believes that the second, chastened version, confining itself to the four trade volumes Larkin supervised and the uncollected poems "published in other places," does give the verse itself a better shake. The type is slightly smaller, producing fewer runover lines. Without the date and bibliographical ascription accompanying each poem on the page, as in the first volume, there is a space in which the practicing poet "testing, filtering," etc., yields to the presence the poet was seeking to create in the texts. *The North Ship*, for instance, with most of its thirty-two poems titled simply, as originally, with Roman numerals instead of, as in the first *Collected*, an empty iteration, in bigger type, of the first line, acquires a collective personality, that of a palely loitering pre-war knight seeking to work out a murky relationship—though it seems to be he, and not the belle dame, who lacks mercy. There is something courtly and metaphysically intricate here reminiscent of those amorous sonnets, by Wyatt and

Surrey and Spenser and Shakespeare, that marked the renascence of English poetry. A conflicted sensibility is seeking its terms. Yeats's magical world, with its emblematic winds and streams and ships and gold, here and there blends with a world of gritty experience:

> The bottle is drunk out by one;
> At two, the book is shut;
> At three, the lovers lie apart . . .
> I lie and wait for morning, and the birds,
> The first steps going down the unswept street,
> Voices of girls with scarves around their heads.

The order in which the items of a collection are arranged may seem a negligible detail, but for the writer or the editor to whom the duty of arrangement falls it matters greatly. Thwaite quotes Larkin's jocular explanation "I treat them like a music-hall bill: you know, contrast, difference in length, the comic, the Irish tenor, bring on the girls." The orderer, generally, wishes to begin and end on a high, defining note; to mix weak with strong, shorter with longer, formal with free; and to lead the ideal reader along a certain contour of implied argument. *The Less Deceived*, the collection which followed, after ten years, the youthful *North Ship*, opens with the full-throated "Lines on a Young Lady's Photograph Album," in nine strictly rhymed *abbab* stanzas—Larkin's development, curiously, combined a more elaborate metrical formality with a more relaxed, plainer voice. Here, in an affectionate but astringent meditation on a female friend's photographed past, the playful poet earnestly explores how the images lacerate him "simply by being over." His exclusion from the past that "holds you like a heaven" has positive consequences: "It leaves us free to cry" and flatters the subject, who in these frozen images is "invariably lovely . . . Smaller and clearer as the years go by." The next poem, "Wedding-Wind," dates back to 1946, and reverts to Yeatsian exaltation. The heroine, like the photographed young lady, feels herself redeemed from inexorable time, symbolized here by the wind's incessant blowing. A bride's joy defies change:

> Shall I be let to sleep
> Now this perpetual morning shares my bed?
> Can even death dry up
> These new delighted lakes?

The poet speaks directly in the next poem, "Places, Loved Ones." The rootless, self-deprived Larkin persona proclaims his failure to find "the place where I could say / *This is my proper ground, / Here I shall stay*" and to meet "that special one / Who has an instant claim / On everything I own / Down to my name." The theme of a puzzled yet irremediable and somewhat satisfactory isolation continues to preside in "Coming" ("I, whose childhood / Is a forgotten boredom") and "Reasons for Attendance" and "Dry-Point," both about pulling back from sex. In the first, he watches through a window young dancers "Shifting intently, face to flushed face, / Solemnly on the beat of happiness," while he stands outside, nursing his artistic vocation:

> Surely, to think the lion's share
> Of happiness is found by couples—sheer
>
> Inaccuracy, as far as I'm concerned.
> What calls me is that lifted, rough-tongued bell
> (Art, if you like) whose individual sound
> Insists I too am individual.

In "Dry-Point," the poet has experienced sex—"Bestial, intent, real"— but mourns the "sad scapes" and "salted, shrunken lakes" (lakes again!) that ensue; yet he also, if I read the lines aright, dislikes "the bare and sunscrubbed room . . . that padlocked cube of light" where sex obtains no entry. "Next, Please" carries the poet's disappointed hopes into the brilliant extended metaphor of a sighted "armada of promises" that draw near but never land. Although "We think each one will heave to and unload / All good into our lives," only one ship seeks us, "black-sailed" death, "towing at her back / A huge and birdless silence." Death, then, joins sex and singleness as an underlying topic. The next, and oldest, poem, "Going," begins, eerily, "There is an evening coming in / Across the fields, one never seen before, / That lights no lamps," and ends by entering into the consciousness of a corpse: "What is under my hands, / That I cannot feel? / What loads my hands down?" The succeeding "Wants" awards death a certificate of approval, declaring, in its two refrains, that there are two wants—"Beyond all this, the wish to be alone" and "Beneath it all, desire of oblivion." The tenth poem, "Maiden Name," returns to the mode of apostrophe, addressing in courtly fashion a woman who could be the object of the first poem; she is charged this time with abandoning her maiden name, which still "shelters our faithfulness, / Instead of losing shape and meaning less / With your depreciating luggage laden."

These ten poems compose a suite, leading the reader through variations on themes—aging, marriage, the pursuit of happiness, the certainty of death—that circumscribe a personality and a much-mulled personal situation related to the chronic coldness of the less resolute, less objective voice of *The North Ship*. The matured voice both questions and confirms the morose celibacy of a temperamental loner dedicated to his art. He views the active, hopeful, mating world now with a wry love, now with a sharp exasperation, but always through death's dark glass. There is a certain Byronic pride in the poet's inconsolability. Celebrating, in "No Road," a broken-off affair, Larkin concludes:

> To watch the world come up like a cold sun,
> Rewarding others, is my liberty.
> Not to prevent it is my will's fulfillment.
> Willing it, my ailment.

The collection's masterpiece, "Church Going," views an empty church, visited by the poet on a bicycle, from an archeological distance; he observes its wilting Sunday flowers, hears its "tense, musty, unignorable silence, / Brewed God knows how long," and wonders

> When churches fall completely out of use
> What we shall turn them into . . .
> Power of some sort or other will go on
> In games, in riddles, seemingly at random;
> But superstition, like belief, must die,
> And what remains when disbelief has gone?
> Grass, weedy pavement, brambles, buttress, sky . . .

His ruminations drift effortlessly down the intricate *ababcadcd* rhyme pattern of the seven stanzas to the faint but sweet faith that a church will always attract the visit of someone who "will forever be surprising / A hunger in himself to be more serious, / And gravitating with it to this ground." The solitary atheist breaks through to identification with the masses of past worshippers ("so many dead lie around"), much as, in a later, even more epiphanic poem, "The Whitsun Weddings," the bachelor poet eventually, along with the holy-day newlyweds who have boarded his London-bound train, partakes of "all the power / That being changed can give." Though he is held back from change, from the risky and foolish plunge of marriage, he sympathetically participates; it was Larkin's capacity, for all his caustic reserve, to identify with the common experience of a depleted, post-imperial England that made his poetry beloved. The dislikable crustiness displayed in passages of his letters, also edited by Thwaite, and in Andrew Motion's biography should have come as no surprise, since the drama of his greatest poems hinges on the breaking of his personal crust and attaining a generous, deep-breathing self-transcendence. Later poems achieve identification with the poor women, "mustached in flowered frocks," who submit to the ministrations of an American faith healer ("Faith Healing"), and with the wives of men killed in a mine explosion ("The Explosion"):

> for a second
> Wives saw men of the explosion
>
> Larger than in life they managed—
> Gold as on a coin, or walking
> Somehow from the sun towards them. . . .

In *The Less Deceived*, the poems that follow "Church Going" ring changes on the tune of stoic depression, of life being (in "Age") a "tall game I tired myself with joining" and (in "Triple Time") "Threadbare perspectives, seasonal decrease." Employed for five years as a sub-librarian in the Queen's University Library in Belfast, and about to become the head of the library at the University of Hull, he addresses "the toad *work*" ("Toads") and accepts its lifelong companionship, "For something sufficiently toad-like / Squats in me, too." In an especially curious twist of identification, a young woman's rape recorded in Henry Mayhew's *London Labour and the London Poor* imposes Larkin's own post-coital disappointment, confessed in other poems, upon the rape's anonymous perpetrator, "stumbling up the breathless stair / To burst into fulfilment's desolate attic" ("Deceptions"). The image of a desolate attic recurs in "Absences," one of Larkin's brief, painterly landscape studies; a crashing sea is evoked, and above it, the cloud-filled sky:

> Above the sea, the yet more shoreless day,
> Riddled by wind, trails lit-up galleries:
> They shift to giant ribbing, sift away.
>
> Such attics cleared of me! Such absences!

The suddenly personal image is surreal, as is, two poems later ("If, My Darling"), the premise that his darling has leapt into his head, to "find herself looped with the creep of varying light, / Monkey-brown, fish-grey, a string of infected circles / Looking like bullies, about to coagulate." A grotesque and rueful physicality persists: "Skin" addresses his integument as "an old bag / Carrying a soiled name," and begs its pardon for not finding, "when you were new, / No brash festivity / To wear you at." But life is not entirely composed of missed opportunities; the last poem in *The Less Deceived*, like the first, looks back upon an active past, in this case ("At Grass") the triumphs—"The starting-gates, the crowds and cries"—of pastured racehorses quietly "at grass" fifteen years later. They have lived, as do poets in their moments of accelerated inspiration.

A quite random or a strictly chronological ordering of this collection might also achieve some harmonies and happy juxtapositions, but only the poet's own arrangement carries the sense of a conversation with him, as he proposes and rethinks and offers yet another concretion of his private reality, "each one," as he says in another context, "double-yolked with meaning and meaning's rebuttal." In the parlance of sound engineers there is something called "room tone"—the auditory impression of silence in a certain recording chamber. Recording some of it, while performers are present though holding their breath, is essential to the editing process. A poet's own arrangement has his private room tone, and with a technician as skillful and perfectionist as Larkin this delicate quality is not negligible. For this reason the second *Collected*, holding the four slim collections as he fine-tuned them, should take priority on the poetry-lover's shelf over the first.

The first is so close to an edition for scholars that pedantic concern intrudes upon aesthetic pleasure; we come to miss the fragments that Thwaite mentions but leaves out. His earlier introduction fascinatingly specified "When I see Literature," from 1950, "addressed to a personified figure called 'Literature' "; "extensive drafts of a poem on the dates of coins and their significance to him . . . written in the summer of 1954"; "attempts at four poems on the seasons, written at about the same time"; "a long poem, called 'The Duration', beginning 'It was like a war', which takes up fifteen pages of drafts between April and June 1969; and what was apparently his final struggle with a substantial poem, 'Letters to my mind', drafted in October and November 1979."

Larkin, though modest in manner and volume of production, achieved major eloquence and formal perfection, and was esteemed in the world of general readers to a degree that, among poets, only John Betjeman and Dylan Thomas matched in postwar Great Britain. The weight of depression he carried endures as a severe purity in his poems. It would seem that, at some point early in his development, Larkin retracted any large hopes for human interaction. In *A Girl in Winter*, the second of his two novels (and why only two, when they are so good?), his heroine, Katherine Lind, foresees:

Life would be happy insofar as she was happy, sad insofar as she was sad. The happiness would depend on her youth and health, and would help no-one. When she was ill, it would drop away, like the flame of a wick being turned down; when she grew old, it would be thin and infrequent. And in these times no other thing or person would be able to help her, though they might try sincerely, and she might try equally sincerely to be helped. But they would not be able to touch any more than people standing ten yards apart can take each other's hands.

Yet his poems, though cramped by pessimism and self-distrust, do reach out. He wrote two kinds of masterpiece. There are the short, chiming summations of life's meagre prospects; they begin "They fuck you up, your mum and dad. / They may not mean to, but they do" ("This Be the Verse") and "Sexual intercourse began / In nineteen sixty-three / (Which was rather late for me)" ("Annus Mirabilis") and "Home is so sad. It stays as it was left, / Shaped to the comfort of the last to go / As if to win them back" ("Home Is So Sad"). Such lapidary compression recalls Ben Jonson and Robert Herrick and returned in the twentieth century with A. E. Housman and Yeats's more songlike verses.

Then there are Larkin's great longer poems—"Church Going," "The Whitsun Weddings," "The Old Fools," "Dockery and Son," "Aubade." Their voice—ruminative, frank, levelly idiomatic, and seemingly unconscious of itself as poetic—extends the voice of Wordsworth's self-explorations, his voice of cogitation and confession, grown loose and prosy in *The Prelude* and at its most thrilling in "Tintern Abbey," as his eye processes the scene before it:

> These hedge-rows, hardly hedge-rows, little lines
> Of sportive wood run wild: these pastoral farms,
> Green to the very door . . .

Wordsworth's prescription for poetry, stated in the 1800 introduction to *Lyrical Ballads*—"fitting to metrical arrangement a selection of the real language of men in a state of vivid sensation"—still applies to this modern case. Both poets began with the same ingredients: self-preoccupation and an instinctive response to nature. Larkin's early poems, forced and contorted as they seem, did not falsify; wind and sea and sun and green growth spoke to him. His human sadness measured itself against nature, setting (in "The Trees") our mortality against the tireless green cycles ("Yet still the unresisting castles thresh / In fullgrown thickness every May. / Last year is dead, they seem to say, / Begin afresh, afresh, afresh"). A few years from his own end, the poet knelt down to extract a dead hedgehog from a mower's blades ("The Mower") and drew the elemental moral

> we should be careful
> Of each other, we should be kind
> While there is still time.

LITERARY BIOGRAPHY

Mud and Flames

BYRON: *Child of Passion, Fool of Fame*, by Benita Eisler. 837 pp. Knopf, 1999.

Benita Eisler's impressive, if somewhat overwrought, biography, *Byron: Child of Passion, Fool of Fame*, begins with a description of the burning of the poet's memoirs, a month after his death, in the London offices of his publisher, John Murray. Of the six men present, one was Murray, in this case an anti-publisher consigning a source of mighty profits to the flames; another was his sixteen-year-old son, invited to witness this epochal event; two represented the separate interests of Byron's estranged wife, Annabella, and his half-sister, Augusta Leigh; another, John Cam Hobhouse, was Byron's oldest friend and a faithful fellow-traveller but also a Whig MP and a considerable prig. Only the sixth, the Dublin-born poet Thomas Moore, wanted to save the memoirs; they had been given to him by Byron, and he, with Byron's approval, had sold the copyright to Murray. He nearly came to blows with Hobhouse, but the memoirs, bound in two volumes, were fed piecemeal to the fireplace. One wonders if their rescue and eventual publication would have significantly enlarged our already copious knowledge of the profligate poet's crowded thirty-six years and reduced the torrent of biographical writings that began when his fever-ridden corpse had scarcely cooled.

Eisler's hefty tome follows by two years *Byron: The Flawed Angel*, by Phyllis Grosskurth, which in turn bobs in the wide wake of Leslie A. Marchand's three-volume biography (1957) and his thirteen-volume edition of *Byron's Letters and Journals* (1973–94). Byron's fame and charisma were such that his correspondents almost all* saved every letter they received, and Byron freely confided his most intimate feelings and expe-

---

*An exception was John Fitzgibbon Clare, a Harrow schoolmate whose name, accord-

riences. The details of his sex life—a remarkably varied one, including homosexuality at school and after, much whoring and tupping of servant girls, an orgiastic interlude in Venice, incest with his half-sister, and numerous seductions and liaisons within his own social class—have gradually emerged, and the graphic details and four-letter words in his letters to male friends can now be printed. So his memoirs (from which he had, he wrote, "omitted *all* the really *consequential* and *important* parts") might have added little to the picture created by the surviving documents and the autobiographical elements of his generally self-dramatizing poetry; nevertheless, their deliberate destruction, especially by his close friends Hobhouse and Murray, affronts us with its high-handed, irreversible violence. Its paradoxical effect was to enhance by one more flamboyant stroke the diabolical Byron legend.

Eisler, whose books prior to this seven years' labor include *Class Act: America's Last Dirty Secret* and a study of the relationship between Georgia O'Keeffe and Alfred Stieglitz, gives us a Byron who, up to his second and final departure from England in 1816, was a monster of vanity and appetite, with one possibly redeeming quality: he could write. The Byrons were a wild noble line. The first lord, John Byron of Colewyke, bought from Henry VIII a newly dissolved monastery, Newstead Abbey, in Nottinghamshire, and converted it to baronial use as a picturesque ruin, incorporating the southern wall of the church nave into his own residence. He passed his holdings down to a son begotten on a neighbor's wife, having legitimized his heir by marrying the lady. The heir, called "Little Sir John of the Great Beard," was knighted by Queen Elizabeth. The poet's grand-uncle, the fifth lord, was known as the Wicked Lord; under his tenure the property became "the scene of licentious *fêtes champêtres.*" In 1765, in the course of a dispute at a tavern in Pall Mall, this Byron ran his opponent through with a sword and killed him. Later, "from a brooding sense of guilt and grievance," Eisler suggests, he descended into periodic madness: "Dark tales were told in Nottinghamshire" of how he "shot his coachman dead over a trifle" and "when displeased, he would throw Lady Byron into the pond."

His nephew, the poet's father, was a chip off the old unstable block. "Heartless and swaggeringly handsome," John Byron, called "Mad Jack," was a devoted seducer and gambler who as a twenty-two-year-old Guardsman made a fine catch of another man's wife: the Marchioness of

---

ing to Grosskurth, Byron "never heard without a wild beating of the heart," but who told Thomas Moore that he had destroyed all Byron's letters. Nevertheless, several survive; three are quoted in Eisler.

Carmarthen, born Amelia d'Arcy, Baroness Conyers, and Countess of Mertola, ran off with Mad Jack at first sight, causing her husband, later the Duke of Leeds, to lock her out of their house. She brought with her, however, an annual income of four thousand pounds. She married her lover, lived with him in Paris and Chantilly, bore him three children (of whom only Augusta, the youngest, survived infancy), and died mysteriously at the age of twenty-nine. Her death deprived Jack of four thousand quid a year; his search for the next heiress took him to the favorite resort of fortune hunters, Bath, and landed him the thirteenth Laird of Gight, Catherine Gordon—the last of her family, sketchily educated, hot-tempered, and even at the age of twenty distinctly overweight. But she owned a castle, lands, and thousands in Aberdeen bank shares. A curiosity of their union was that, by her parents' wills, a female inheriting the Gight estates had to marry a Gordon or her husband had to take the Gordon name; Jack became John Byron Gordon.

The bride's assets were no match for the bridegroom's debts. He was clapped into prison as soon as he surfaced in London, and upon his release "kept moving to stay ahead of the bailiffs." He was still on the lam when his son, baptized George Gordon, was born in London, on January 22, 1788, after a long and difficult labor, with "a caul and a malformed right foot." This foot—the most famous extremity in English literature, not excepting Shakespeare's "dyer's hand"—Byron tended to blame his mother for, citing her "excess of delicacy" in the period before delivery, referring to either her tight corsets or an undue modesty during obstetrical examinations. Catherine in turn, a doting and self-sacrificing but sharp-tongued parent, was not above taunting her son about his deformity, confounding it with the moral malformation inherited from his scapegrace father. Byron related how, before he departed for his first European trip, in 1809, his mother (who was to die while he was away) had, "in one of her fits of passion, uttered an imprecation upon me, praying that I might prove as ill-formed in mind as I am in body." His foot, which pained him when young and humiliated him as an adolescent, was, in Eisler's reading, the key to his reckless, ruthless personality:

> Byron's deformity would cause him emotional injury beyond any other psychic wound he would ever sustain. Turned inward, his rage became depression, but also something more insidious: the sense that he had a special dispensation from the moral sanctions imposed upon others and a lifelong entitlement to the forbidden.

Literal entitlement fell to him at the age of nine, when his grand-uncle the Wicked Lord died, making the boy, who had been living with his mother in shabby rooms above shops in Aberdeen, the sixth Baron Byron of Rochdale. His father had died seven years before, in France, of tuberculosis and alcoholism, at the age of thirty-six—the same age, oddly, at which both the poet and his only legitimate child, Ada, were to die. Though there were some lands and properties in the inheritance, the estate was so cash-poor that the Wicked Lord's body had to wait nearly a month while credit was arranged to cover the costs; Catherine sold her Aberdeen furniture to meet the bills, and not enough was left for coach fare to Newstead Abbey. Finally, at summer's end, mother and son went south for good. Byron became an Englishman; he spoke always with a trace of Scots burr, though he vehemently denied it, such an accent being as much an embarrassment to him as his clubfoot and his obese, coarse mother. He also brought from the country of his childhood a love of wild and mountainous landscapes, his mother's republican sympathies, and a dose of Calvinist Puritanism that colors his works with gloom and damnation—he referred to himself as *le diable boiteux*, the lame devil. By the age of eleven, he was suffering painful quack treatments of his foot and sexual abuse at the hands of his nursemaid, May Gray, a hard-drinking young Scotswoman who taught him Scripture as well as masturbating him. He confided to his journal:

> My passions were developed very early—so early—that few would believe me—if I were to state the period—and the facts which accompanied it— Perhaps this was one of the reasons which caused the anticipated melancholy of my thoughts—having anticipated life.

The young Byron's principal acquisition in becoming a peer of the realm was the obligation to live like a lord, which brought with it a habit of mortgaging the future to maintain a baronial present. Both he and his mother, Grosskurth states in a happy phrase, "were victims of institutionalized extravagance." Catherine lived frugally so that young Lord Byron could go to Harrow and "enjoy a generous allowance, which included outfitting him at his father's fashionable tailor." At Cambridge he wore the gold-embroidered gown a noble was entitled to, furnished his rooms elaborately, ordered bottles of wine by the dozen, and kept a carriage and three horses, with liveried footmen. On departing the university, he refurbished Newstead Abbey expensively and entertained there scandalously, dressing his male guests as monks and providing "Paphian girls" for their delectation. Leaving behind an ailing mother and more than fourteen thousand pounds in debt, he embarked with his Cambridge friend Francis Hobhouse for Lisbon and points east—travels that would become the basis of *Childe Harold's Pilgrimage*. When, in 1816, he left

England a second time, self-exiled to escape the scandals loosed by his separation from his wife of one year, he equipped himself with a splendid coach that was a replica of Napoleon's.

More than once in his life, military grandeur beckoned: in 1813, contemplating a Greek journey, he bought uniforms, swords, "shoes and inexpressibles without number," five bedsteads, five saddles, camp kettles, rifles, pistols, powder flasks, six portable three-foot telescopes, and for himself, on this expedition that never took place, a set of new luggage and "a portable writing desk of heavy wood, with a secret drawer." When, in 1823, he actually did equip a military expedition to help free Greece from the Turks, he designed picturesque uniforms for himself and his personal staff, including "helmets worthy of Homeric heroes, with plumes waving above the Byron crest and motto, 'Crede Byron,' the whole secured by a wide chin strap that clearly meant business." His second-in-command, Edward Trelawny, was another romantic adventurer but "found the uniforms and helmets so ridiculous he refused even to try his on. . . . The helmets went back into their pink boxes."

Byron's financial extravagances were matched by his erotic investments. In the period leading up to his marriage to Annabella Milbanke early in 1815, he was (1) in love with and sleeping with and at times living with his half-sister, Augusta Leigh, (2) attempting to disentangle himself from his romance with the love-crazed Caroline Lamb, (3) using in this attempt the sexagenarian Lady Melbourne as a confidante to whom he entrusted the erotic details of his life and the letters from his smitten correspondents, (4) paying ardent though not quite consummated court to Lady Frances Webster, the wife of an old Harrow chum, (5) enjoying an affair with the coolly promiscuous, forty-year-old militant Whig Lady Oxford, in the course of which he sexually molested her eleven-year-old daughter, Lady Charlotte Harley, to whom, under the name of "Ianthe," he dedicated the seventh printing of *Childe Harold*, with attendant high-flown verses.

As the carriage pulled away from his wedding to Annabella, "Byron began singing and ranting," reviling her family, bemoaning her meagre dowry, and pitying her "that she had not married a better man." Samuel Rogers, one of the readers of Byron's destroyed memoirs, remembered the poet's recording that on his wedding night he awoke and, surrounded by crimson bed curtains, cried out, "Good God, I am surely in hell!" He proceeded to make his bride's life hellish, harping on the insanity in his family, retreating into black moods, dragging her on a visit to Augusta in which he ordered "both of them to take turns embracing him," and threatening to commit suicide with pistols he always kept loaded.

Though the marriage had its tranquil interludes, and Annabella proved, as the proficient rake had predicted, "an eager acolyte and passionate lover," the trend was sharply downward; by the end of the year, Byron, faced with the impending seizure of his possessions by bailiffs and deranged by nights of brandy drinking, was threatening his now pregnant wife with loaded pistols, and taunting her about his affair with a Drury Lane actress.

Annabella, early in her dreadful year of wedlock, had turned to Byron's sister as the person she knew to be closest to him, ignoring evidence of their incest. For the last weeks of Lady Byron's pregnancy, Augusta came to London and stayed at the Byrons' rented mansion at 13 Piccadilly Terrace. There, while Byron drank and raved and smashed furniture and fired pistols, she maintained what fragile order the household had. When she pointed out to her brother that he was destroying them all, he said, "I am determined to fling Misery around me & upon all those with whom I am concerned." Viewing his infant daughter—Ada, the future pioneer of computer science—for the first time, he reportedly exclaimed, "Oh! What an implement of torture I have acquired in you." Servants had to restrain him from raping his newly delivered wife. He took to reading the Marquis de Sade. Fearful for his sanity, Annabella wrote to Dr. Baillie, who had treated Byron's foot when he was at Harrow, "Undoubtedly I am more than anyone the subject of his irritation, because he deems himself (as he has said) a villain for marrying me . . . adding that the more I love him, & the better I am, the more accursed he is."

Early in 1816, less than a month after their daughter was born, an unsigned note from Byron ordered Annabella from his house. She fled in the dead of winter with Ada to the Leicestershire home of her parents; they, as the story of her year gradually emerged, reacted with horror and proposed that the couple separate. Annabella agreed and, in the face of pleading, apologetic letters from her husband ("Dearest Pip, I wish you would make it up—for I am dreadfully sick of all this. . . . If you will—I am ready to make any penitential speech or speeches you please—& will be very good & tractable for the rest of my days—& very sorry for all that have gone before"), remained implacable. The reader feels a weight roll from him: after a callously outrageous life of being indulged and excused, Byron at last encounters a definite refusal. Rather than face the disclosures of adultery, incest, pederasty, and sodomy that might have arisen from a public trial, he agreed to legal separation. Divorce in that age was prohibitively complicated and expensive, involving the Ecclesiastic Court, an Act of Parliament (never obtainable by a woman), and, if the father's custody was challenged, Chancery Court. After much obstruction and protestation of his innocence, and after portraying himself as a martyr in the poem "Fare Thee Well!," Byron signed the papers and left England. In Europe he became the Byron cherished by posterity—the carefree great poet of *Don Juan*, the close friend of Shelley and the patron of that poet's heterodox circle, the husbandly lover of the Countess Teresa Guiccioli, and the would-be savior of Greece. England had been poisonous for the poor lame bookish boy from Aberdeen.

Richard Ashley Rice, introducing his 1933 selection *The Best of Byron*, wonderfully says of John Drinkwater's 1925 biography, "It does not lose sight of Byron's essentially clear poetical mind in the analysis of his essentially muddy behavior." The clarity to some extent grew from the mud. When Byron's friend Douglas Kinnaird questioned the cynical frankness of *Don Juan*, Byron wrote back in his most flashing, irresistible epistolary style:

> As to "Don Juan"—confess—confess you dog—and be candid—that it is the sublime of *that there* sort of writing—it may be bawdy—but is it not good English—it may be profligate—but is it not *life*, is it not *the thing*?—Could any man have written it—who has not lived in the world? and tooled in a post-chaise? in a hackney coach? in a Gondola? against a Wall? in a court carriage? in a vis-à-vis?—on a table? and under it?

His poetry forms a counterpoint of honest endeavor to his dissipations and aristocratic pretensions. He began writing poems in early adolescence, and was encouraged by the Pigot family, who lived across the green from his mother's rented house in Southwell, a Nottingham village not far from Newstead Abbey. At the instigation especially of Elizabeth Pigot, who was five years older than the eighteen-year-old Byron, he assembled and had privately printed his first volume, the modestly titled *Fugitive Pieces*. Not content merely to have his juvenile poems see print, he revised and added to them industriously. Some early readers in Southwell were shocked by a series of verses "To Mary," a young London doxy with whom he had enjoyed the ups and downs of love. While pleading in defense, "My Lyre, the Heart;—my Muse, the simple Truth," he called in all the copies of his first book and burned them; only four survive. He hastened, however, to salvage some of the contents and augmented these verses to create *Poems on Various Occasions*, printed in January of 1807 in a private edition of some hundred copies; with more revisions and additions, this by June had become *Hours of Idleness*, the first book of Byron's to be issued to the public. It was described on its title page as by "George Gordon, Lord Byron, a Minor."

By now Byron was enrolled at Cambridge, where his desultory studies barely interrupted his "continued routine of Dissipation" and his frequent trips to the pleasure spots of London. He was additionally preoccupied by a strenuous regimen of weight loss; five feet eight inches tall, he weighed at his plumpest more than fourteen stone, about two hundred pounds. The budded poet saw the book's pleasant initial reception spoiled by some vitriolic reviews, mocking his nobility and his minority. Worst was one in the *Edinburgh Review* by Henry Brougham, who concluded unpresciently, "We must take these poems as we find them, and be content, for they are the last we shall ever have from him." Byron was already hard at work on his extensive counterattack, the satiric *English Bards and Scotch Reviewers*. Having coaxed a degree from Cambridge, he retired to Newstead Abbey and honed this new, sensational work as his twenty-first birthday approached. "I am a mighty scribbler," he proudly wrote Augusta.

Byron's literary fluency is phenomenal, like Goethe's or Bernard Shaw's. Hungover, ailing, on the move, frantic with debt, besieged by scandal and women, and aristocratically scornful of the rhymer's trade ("No one should be a rhymer who could do anything better," he confided to his journal), he nevertheless managed to find time, often late at night, in which to write. After the first two cantos of *Childe Harold* made him famous in 1812, he wrote with a popular success no poet since has matched. *The Corsair*, composed at the rate of nearly two hundred lines a day while Byron was staying with Augusta in Cambridgeshire, sold out its first printing of ten thousand in a single day in 1814, a record for poetry that still stands. *The Giaour* sold out seven editions in 1813 and was in its fourteenth by 1815. As he settled into Italian residence, Byron shifted from aristocratically refusing his royalties from Murray to bargaining hard: "You offer 1,500 guineas for the new canto—I won't take it. I ask 2,500 guineas for it—which you will either give or not as you think proper." He made light of his publisher's demand for more best-selling verse—

> My dear Mr. Murray,
> You're in a damned hurry
>   To set up this ultimate Canto—

but wrote rapidly to meet it. In two days he wrote the eighty-eight stanzas of the first draft of *Beppo*, the transitional work in which he first employed ottava rima, the stanza form that would give *Don Juan* its impudent music—"the rolling ottava rima," Eisler says, "with its bullet shot of a last line."

The Oriental tales, with their smoldering passions and rebel cries, which galvanized his contemporary public, and the lyrics, which were given so many musical settings in the nineteenth century, have faded, but *Don Juan* shines undimmed, an oddly contemporary masterpiece, shamelessly personal and rambling yet kept in proportion by an ironic humor and authentic wisdom. Byron had worked everything through, we feel, although his behavior was still muddy. The metrical cleverness of *Don Juan* alone is captivating. The rigorous ottava rima becomes a garment of breezy looseness as Byron slips and trips through triple rhymes, often trickily feminine, to arrive at the frequently risible couplet, of which the best-remembered is:

> But—Oh! ye lords of ladies intellectual,
> Inform us truly, have they not hen-peck'd you all?

No other romantic poet took Pope and Dryden as models; the disorderly life found refuge in dispassionate comedy and verbal agility. In words and in water, Byron shed his limp. Lady Byron, whom Grosskurth in her biography accuses of literary ambition for herself and of a vindictive envy of her husband's success, nevertheless, after reading Canto III of *Childe Harold*, wrote a friend, "He is the absolute monarch of words. . . . It is not my duty to give way to hopeless and wholly unrequited affection; but so long as I live, my chief struggle will probably be not to remember him too kindly."

Annabella was one of the "ladies intellectual." Her fondness for mathematics led Byron to dub her "my Princess of Parallelograms," and in time led her to give their daughter, Ada, an education that fitted her to become a knowing handmaiden of Charles Babbage and his mechanical computer, the Analytical Engine. Annabella was an intelligent observer of her difficult husband. Eight months pregnant and being psychologically tortured in his grandest, maddest style, she noted in her journal "the instinctive goodness of his heart" and said that his imagination was "too exalted—and when he cannot do good on the vast scale which it presents, he does not descend to perceive the lesser opportunities of common existence." To him, as he begged her to return, she wrote, "It is unhappily your disposition to consider what you *have* as worthless—what you have *lost* as invaluable. But remember that you declared yourself *most miserable* when I was yours." Benita Eisler, with such acute and not unloving analyses as part of the rich record she is examining, might have spared us a few of such shrink-wrapped dicta as "Yoked to a deep emotional hunger, his urgent sexuality required an exclusive object." She leaves us little to like about Byron except his written works, exposing his ingratitude, mendacity, manipulativeness, arrogant improvidence, sentimental conceit, apparent pedophilia, sexual predations upon the less well born of many climes (Shelley when he visited Byron in Venice was shocked that "he allows fathers & mothers to bargain with him for their daughters"), and casual cruelties directed at women, ranging from his devoted mother to his helpless natural daughter Allegra, whom he consigned when she was only four to an insalubrious convent wherein she died without a single visit from him.

Through these eight hundred big pages Eisler writes well, of Byron's poetry as well as of the complications of his life, but she developed, during her long literary journey, a curious tic of waving goodbye: "He would never see his 'unrepentant Magdalen' [Lady Oxford] again, nor would he ever again risk loving so dazzling and demanding a woman"; "In the ten days between their departure and Augusta's arrival in London he was 'kinder' to her, Annabella recalled, than he had ever been—or ever would be again"; "Byron would never see his wife or their child again"; "Byron would never see England, his wife, daughter, or sister again"; "But events now conspired to ensure that . . . he never set foot there again"; "But he did not mention a dark foreboding; he would never see his friend [Hobhouse] again."

Nor is poetry likely to see another Lord Byron again. The explosive kind of fame which he enjoyed stems from repression and its relief in a mass medium—e.g., the Fifties sexual puritanism that Elvis Presley and James Dean undermined with their surly looks, and the stifling Soviet atmosphere in which poets like Yevgeny Yevtushenko and Andrei Voznesensky could pack stadiums with the merest hint of political deinhibition. Most of Byron's short life was lived in the more than twenty years of England's war with France. Terror of an English counterpart to the French Revolution had produced, Eisler points out, governmental curtailment of English rights: "The political reality that permitted the Regency to waltz on unafraid was that England had become a police state." It was less the sexual content of Byron's poems than the open political attacks on the Tories and royalty that infuriated his critics and made his publishers quake. In his journal he wrote, "I have simplified my politics into an utter detestation of all existing governments. . . . The fact is, riches is power, and poverty is slavery all over the earth, and one sort of establishment is no better nor worse for a *people* than another." Antiestablishment radicalism and anarchy, many of us may still recall from the Sixties, are sexy. It is essential, for the sexual subtext, that the spokespersons be young. Byron in his twenties, through the persona of Childe Harold and the erotically charged exoticism of the Eastern tales, insinuated a dark subversiveness that made thousands of female readers want to sleep with him, to experience liberty in their loins. Narrative verse, exemplified by Milton and popularized by Sir Walter Scott, was still a mass medium. Though Wordsworth and Rousseau had turned their selves into their main subjects, Byron in his newsworthy scandals as well as in his poetry projected a *personality*, a personality Napoleonic in its insatiability and capacity for ruinous defeat. *Don Juan*, now considered his masterpiece, is less mythic—indeed, it is anti-mythic, a long, good-humored, Italianate shrug—and had to wait for its modernist renown to rise from the ashes of the Byronic furor.

Incommensurability

SØREN KIERKEGAARD: *A Biography*, by Joakim Garff, translated from the Danish by Bruce H. Kirmmse. 867 pp. Princeton, 2005.

Joakim Garff, an associate professor at the Søren Kierkegaard Research Center at the University of Copenhagen, in a brief preface to his giant *Søren Kierkegaard: A Biography*, states that "the Danish biographies of Kierkegaard that have appeared since George Brandes's critical portrait was published in 1877 can easily be counted on the fingers of one hand, and Johannes Hohlenberg's biography from 1940 is the most recent original work in the field." Garff's compendious yet lively work is undeniably a *Danish* biography; it assumes on the part of its readers a prior acquaintance with, say, the poetry of Adam Oehlenschläger and the intellectuality of King Christian VIII, a firm sense of what the rix-dollar could buy in the 1840s, and a Copenhagener's natural familiarity with the saga of his world-famous, locally notorious fellow-townsman Magister Søren Aabye Kierkegaard.

The Kierkegaardian tempest needed Copenhagen's teapot. In the years of the great Dane's short and not entirely unhappy life, from 1813 to 1855, Copenhagen still had its medieval walls and numbered fewer than one hundred twenty five thousand residents—one resident for every three of this exhaustive tome's nearly four hundred thousand words. Kierkegaard was born in the little city and died there, and left Denmark only five times, once on a day trip to Sweden and repeatedly to Berlin, where, after an initial sojourn spent attending lectures, he usually holed up in rented rooms and relentlessly wrote. Though he complained of "the costly amusement . . . of being an author in Denmark," he left a rapturous page of praise for the Danish language, "a language that understands jest fully as well as earnestness; a mother tongue that captivates its children with a chain that 'is easy to bear, yes, but hard to break.' " What he wrote about, in a dozen hectic years, under his own name and a welter of pseudonyms, was himself, a singular being tricked up in many alter egos and attacked from many angles, not only examined but cross-examined, an intricately guilty defendant on trial. One wonders if Kierkegaard could have found his own existence so absorbingly important if he had been born into a larger city, where the edges of his ego might have frayed into the wider fabric of urban indifference. A satirical caricature in the Copenhagen magazine *The Corsair*, published at the height of his local celebrity, shows him standing at the center of a revolving belt of stars, everyday objects, prominent Copenhagen structures, and the sun itself. The caption reads:

> There are moments when one's ideas become confused and one thinks that Nicolas Copernicus was a fool when he maintained that the earth revolved around the sun. On the contrary, the heavens, the sun, the planets, the earth, Europe, and Copenhagen revolve around Søren Kierkegaard, who stands silently in the center and does not even remove his hat for the honor being shown him.

This was no joke; Kierkegaard's great contribution to Western philosophy was to assert, or to reassert with Romantic urgency, that, subjectively speaking, each existence is the center of the universe. He offered himself as a corrective to idealism, from Plato to Hegel:

> Now if we assume that abstract thought is the highest manifestation of human activity, it follows that philosophy and the philosophers proudly desert existence, leaving the rest of us to face the worst. . . . The difficulty inherent in existence constitutes the interest of the existing individual, who is infinitely interested in existing. Abstract thought thus helps me with respect to my immortality by first annihilating me as a particular existing individual and then making me immortal.

Garff's "labor of love," as he calls it, not only describes the coziness of Kierkegaard's milieu but partakes of it. Though assiduous in setting forth, year by year, in many short chapters, the facts, from the philosopher's Jutland ancestors and the variant spellings of his family name to the forlorn auction inventory of his bachelor estate, Garff has a voice of his own—an "informal style and conversational tone," to quote his translator.* Garff's informal voice enlists us in the village gossip of Kierke-

---

*Professor Bruce Kirmmse is himself a distinguished Kierkegaardian, the author of several books on the subject and the editor of the valuable *Encounters with Kierkegaard: A Life Seen by His Contemporaries*. He is also chairman of the editorial board for Kierkegaard's

gaard's time. Of his subject at the age of twenty-two, he tells us, "Everyone could see that Søren Aabye needed a change of atmosphere both mentally and physically. He had to get out of town." Johanne Luise Pätges, the wife of the influential littérateur and tastemaker Johan Ludvig Heiberg, is cattily described as "a goddess sprung from the proletariat, who at the age of thirteen had become the object of his distinguished erotic lust and who was now indisputably the leading lady of the Danish stage, the dazzling, bespangled muse of the age." When Kierkegaard as a young divinity student is introduced into the Heibergs' circle, we are assured that "the contrast between the pietistic Moravian moderation and simplicity of his family home and the delicate, crystalline sociability of the Heibergs must have been so glaring that it would have required an unusual effort for him merely to stay on his feet." Venturing deeper into Kierkegaard's head, Garff characterizes the writer's older and more conventional brother Peter Christian as "Goody-goody Peter, Pusillanimous Peter, that conscientious and self-sacrificing person, who, however, was fundamentally a complete neurotic and unfit for life." Energetic metaphors animate disputes and rivalries among the long-dead: "While Møller"—Peder Ludvig Møller—"had wasted his substance on the many bedsheets of Copenhagen, Kierkegaard gathered his own into his trusty silver pen, which released its contents with bold virtuosity onto sheets of paper that will survive even the forgetfulness of history." Or, in an even more aggressive metaphor, "Kierkegaard's critique of cultivation . . . has here been transformed into a theological torpedo that was guaranteed to collide with the monuments and shrines of cultural Protestantism."

Though some of Garff's metaphors and friendly interjections ("Hallo, Copenhagen!" he exclaims at one point) savor of warm words exchanged around a porcelain stove, his tone helps create a sense of excitement, of

---

journals and notebooks, in an edition forthcoming from the Princeton University Press. It was this press that, mostly in the 1940s, and in translations mostly by the Episcopal clergyman Walter Lowrie and the bilingual couple David and Lillian Swenson, performed the heroic task of bringing the voluminous works of the then outré Danish philosopher into English, and it is reassuring that, sixty years later, Princeton is still on the job.

Garff's assidthe, it might be mentioned, was not matched by his indexer, who confounds and conflates Peder Ludvig Møller, a journalist and libertine who was one of Kierkegaard's principal tormentors in the *Corsair* affair, with Poul Martin Møller, a professor of whom his student Kierkegaard always spoke with "the most profound devotion." Worse, the index lumps as "Schlegel, Friedrich ('Fritz')" Kierkegaard's fiancée's eventual husband, Frederik (Fritz) Schlegel, with the German author and critic Friedrich von Schlegel (1772–1829). Nietzsche, who is mentioned at least twice, is absent from the index, as are Jesus and Saint Paul and Berlin and such central Kierkegaardian concepts as the leap and repetition.

caring, of importance, of—locally and cosmically—scandal. The word "scandal" derives from the Greek *skándalon*, originally having the meaning of "trap" but coming in the New Testament to mean "cause of offense," and translated in the King James Version as "stumblingblock," as in Saint Paul's first letter to the Corinthians: "But we preach Christ crucified, unto the Jews a stumblingblock, and unto the Greeks foolishness." To Paul's contemporaries and to Kierkegaard's, the scandal of Christian dogma (God incarnate crucified and risen from the dead) was something to be gotten around and built in, a stumbling-block converted into the cornerstone of Christianity's humane, worldly-wise church. After Kierkegaard, to thinking Christians the scandal was of the essence—a confrontation, for "crisis theology," with the drastic otherness and unaccountability of God, on the far side of a leap of faith unaided by reason and propelled by human dread and despair. *Either/Or*, the title of Kierkegaard's most popular work, posed, in two volumes, the situation: either the aesthetic, hedonistic, amorous life or the ethical, religious life. It was a bourgeois illusion, a blasphemy, to think that they were not incommensurable.

Kierkegaard's quiet life, occupied primarily in study and writing, was marked by four scandals. The first was not his own, though he made it his own. In February of 1846, he wrote in his journal:

> How terrible for the man who once, as a little boy watching sheep on the moors of Jutland, suffering terribly, hungry and weak from the cold, had stood atop a hill and had cursed God—and the man was unable to forget it when he was eighty-two years old.

Hans Peter Barfod, the devoted but somewhat cavalier editor of a multivolume set of selections titled *From Søren Kierkegaard's Posthumous Papers*, in 1865 called this striking passage to the attention of Peter Christian Kierkegaard, by then a bishop in the Danish church. Peter exclaimed, "That is my father's story—and *ours*, too," and, according to Barfod, he "recounted the details of the matter, which I ought not repeat here." Barfod never did confide the details to print, and, out of respect for the surviving brother's feelings, "couldn't find it in his heart" to include the passage in his edition of Søren Kierkegaard's papers. These writings, in notebooks and on stray scraps of paper, were often Kierkegaard's way of jotting down ideas for his unique mixture of philosophy, confession, and fiction; they should not be taken as literal autobiography. Yet it seems to be a fact that he and his father, who for all their differences "had important common ground in a few strange ideas," had discussed this shepherd boy's curse and deduced from it a divine curse that condemned the father to outlive all seven of his children. They were all, supposedly, destined to die before their thirty-fourth birthdays, so as not to outlive Christ. Five—two brothers, three sisters—did so, but Peter surprised Søren by surviving his thirty-fourth birthday, and then the younger brother surprised himself by following suit, living to the age of forty-two. Peter lived too long; besieged by illness and religious scruples, he resigned his bishopric and gave up his legal majority, assuming the legal status of a child, and eventually died at his father's age of eighty-two.

Other calculations show that the father, Michael Pedersen Kierkegaard—who fled the hardships of Jutland at the age of eleven and, apprenticed in Copenhagen in his mother's brother's dry-goods shop, eventually became one of the city's wealthier merchants—impregnated his serving maid, Ane Sørensdatter Lund, well within the conventional year of mourning for his first wife, Kirstine, and married Ane less than five months before the birth of their first child, Maren Kristine. Two more daughters and three sons followed, and finally Søren Aabye in 1813, when his father was fifty-six and his mother forty-five. Søren was thus living proof of an incorrigible concupiscence and, as such, an embarrassment to himself.

An undated and physically separate journal entry speaks of a "great earthquake" that led Søren to believe that his "father's advanced age was not a divine blessing, but rather a curse." An early reader of Georg Brandes's biography asked Peter Christian outright if the father's revelation was sexual, having to do with "unfaithfulness to a spouse"; the idea was indignantly dismissed. Garff, following up some shadowy hints in Søren's references to leprosy, speculates that the earthquake had to do with syphilis, a fatal taint passed on to the children. The Danish word for "original sin," Professor Kirmmse tells us in brackets, is *Arvesynden*, "inherited sin." This much seems clear: Michael Pedersen was a lusty youth and man, whereas Søren had a significant aversion to the physical side of sex; it is not clear whether or not he died a virgin. Some commentators have taken a mangled (by Barfod) journal entry, "My God, my God . . . The bestial sniggering," as evidence of a disastrous experience in a brothel; Garff rather doubts it.

The second scandal in Kierkegaard's life was his brusquely breaking off, in August of 1841, an eleven-month engagement to the eminently marriageable Regine Olsen. Like Kierkegaard, nine years her senior, she was the last of seven children of excellent family: her father, Terkild Olsen, was Councillor of State and a director in the Finance Ministry.

The family was cultured—Regine painted miniatures—and religious, attending, like the Kierkegaards, meetings of the Moravian Congregation of Brethren. She was, by the slender testimony before Kierkegaard made her a figure in world literature, pretty and cheerful; there was nothing wrong with her. Garff says, almost impatiently, "She was just a lovely girl of the upper bourgeoisie who wanted to be happy, like everybody." In the version of Kierkegaard's farewell letter to her that has come down to us (in his book *Stages on Life's Way*), the key sentence to her reads, "Above all, forget the person who writes this; forgive a person who, whatever he might have been capable of, was incapable of making a girl happy."

Why was he incapable? For nearly a year he had been going through the motions, dining with her and her parents, arranging meetings and outings, sending letters and gifts. His executors returned her letters, which she burned; but twenty-six of his, of some length, survive. These letters, according to Garff, show a marked improvement in Kierkegaard's literary art—too much so: "For by virtue of their indisputably aesthetic qualities, the letters make it clear that their author was to become not a husband but a writer." At the same time, he was busy in the pastoral seminary, judging the sermons of others, delivering his own, appearing to prepare, as his recently dead father had wished, for a respectable career in the ministry. His father's death, in 1838, had made him and Peter Christian, the only surviving children, heirs to a large estate of one hundred twenty-five thousand rix-dollars. Each received a quarter outright; the rest was placed in stocks and bonds generating income. Whatever his source of value in Regine's eyes, the jilted nineteen-year-old, in the words of the jilter, "fought like a lioness" to keep him, breaching decorum by invading his rooms upon receipt of his letter and, in his absence, leaving a "note of utter despair" that pleaded with him, for the sake of Jesus and the memory of his father, not to leave her. It was only two months later, in a face-to-face confrontation, that she accepted his defection: in Kierkegaard's version of the encounter, she removed from her bosom "a little note on which were some words from me" and slowly tore it to pieces, afterwards stating quietly, "You have played a terrible game with me." Garff underlines the symbolism: "This little gesture was a decisive act: Regine freed herself from the writing; she had given up being a Regine of words on paper and had returned to reality."

Two years later, returned to reality, she became engaged to Frederik Johan Schlegel, her girlhood tutor, whose courtship had been interrupted by Kierkegaard's entry into her life. As a lawyer rising in government service, Schlegel was a very suitable husband: "practically the exact opposite of Kierkegaard: stable, harmonious, healthy, un-ironic, and patient."

Kierkegaard continued to live in the world of words, pouring out convoluted, philosophically erudite, stylistically scintillating apologies and homages to Regine, their romance first transfigured in "The Seducer's Diary" portion of *Either/Or*. The publication, in 1843, of this novelistic bundle of discourses, subtitled "A Fragment of Life" and pseudonymously signed "Victor Eremita," made a sensation in Copenhagen. An already established literary Dane, Hans Christian Andersen, who was in Paris at the time, was informed in a letter from Signe Læssøe, "A new literary comet . . . has soared in the heavens here. . . . It is so demonic that one reads and reads it. . . . I think that no book has caused such a stir with the reading public since Rousseau placed his *Confessions* on the altar."

"If you marry, you will regret it; if you do not marry, you will also regret it," says *Either/Or*. In his religious masterpiece *Fear and Trembling*, a passionate retelling of the Biblical story of Abraham and Isaac, Kierkegaard has Abraham seize Isaac by the throat and tell him, "Stupid boy, dost thou then suppose that I am thy father? I am an idolater. Dost thou suppose that this is God's bidding? No, it is my desire." To himself he says, "After all it is better for him to believe that I am a monster, rather than that he should lose faith in Thee." This accords with the view that Kierkegaard came to take of his rejection of Regine—it was for her own good that he acted the villain, performing a "blackening of the breast" to wean her from him with her spirit unbroken. As late as the writing of *Repetition* in 1843, he was toying with the idea of reuniting with her; the announcement of her engagement to Schlegel caused him to revise the text, adding a pinch of misogyny. Yet the moment of their parting ("a very young girl, almost a mere child—the lovable tears of her misunderstanding") haunted his journals, and at his death he left the remnants of his drastically depleted fortune to her. Mrs. Schlegel, whose husband had become the governor of the Danish West Indies, rejected the bequest but, when a widow in Copenhagen, as the nineteenth century wound down, she voiced reminiscences that, Garff tells us, "always began with Schlegel, whose excellent qualities she praised to the skies, but . . . always ended with—Kierkegaard." Neither she nor all of Kierkegaard's torrential comments, direct and indirect, upon the matter ever quite explained the breakup, which had outraged her family and titillated local society.

There had been signs during the engagement: he was fitfully neglectful, winning kittenish rebukes. According to Garff, at some point she "had been too erotically straightforward" and was primly reproached by the pious seminarian in a later letter of which a surviving draft reads, "I intend to give you a serious dressing-down because in your passion you once went beyond a certain boundary." He had confided enough unease to his brother so that Peter Christian noted in his journal that "after a long period of struggle and dejection, Søren broke off his connection with Miss Olsen." As Søren lay dying in Royal Frederik's Hospital, he talked to his disciple and confidant Emil Boesen, who faithfully visited and, ten years later, was persuaded to write an account of their conversations. One passage has Kierkegaard saying:

> "It's death. Pray for me that it comes quickly and easily. I am depressed. I have my thorn in the flesh, as did Saint Paul, so I was unable to enter into ordinary relationships. I therefore concluded that it was my task to be extraordinary, which I then sought to carry out as best I could. I was a plaything of Governance, which cast me into play, and I was to be used. . . . And that was also what was wrong with my relationship to Regine. I had thought that it could be changed, but it couldn't, so I dissolved the relationship."

He spoke fondly of her to Boesen, and was not beyond making a pun: "I was afraid that she would have to become a governess. She didn't, however, but now she is Governess in the West Indies."

What was this "thorn in the flesh" to which Kierkegaard often alludes? The phrase is Saint Paul's, in 2 Corinthians 12:7: "And lest I should be exalted above measure through the abundance of the revelations, there was given a thorn in the flesh, the messenger of Satan to buffet me." Because his conversion experience on the road to Damascus, according to the description in Acts, threw him to the ground, it has been conjectured that Paul was an epileptic. Garff does some fascinating detective work in investigating the possibility of the "falling sickness" as Kierkegaard's shameful infirmity and the cause, as with Dostoevsky, of his fits of exaltation and of his graphomania. A contemporary, Professor Frederik Christian Sibbern, recorded rumors of epilepsy, and in one known instance Kierkegaard abruptly fell down, but the most provocative clue is the hospital notation that the patient used *valeriane officinalis*. Kierkegaard's physician, Oluf Lundt Bang, in his *Handbook for Therapy* wrote that "marriage must be discouraged" for persons suffering from a host of diseases, including epilepsy, and for that complaint prescribed "large doses of *rad. valerianæ*," valerian root. But in the thorough records that Royal Frederik's Hospital kept during Kierkegaard's last forty-one days, no epileptic attack was mentioned. Garff spends less time on the possibility, raised in the far reaches of Kierkegaard studies, "that he might have been equipped with a curved penis, whose vaginal maneuverability would in all probability have been somewhat limited."

From the third besetting scandal, the assault of ridicule launched by the scurrilous journal *The Corsair* against not only Kierkegaard's ideas but his physical person, has descended to posterity the impression that the philosopher was conspicuously deformed. A series of caricatures in *The Corsair* by Peter Klæstrup show a swaybacked, even hunchbacked, figure with a sharp nose, tall hat, stick cane, and comically thin legs, whose trousers, more comically still, are of unequal length. It was this last oddity that the populace of Copenhagen fastened upon as the subject of jibes and taunts, making Kierkegaard's cherished daily perambulations in the streets a torment; he spoke of "that slow death, being trampled to death by a flock of geese." The characterization was witty, but the experience was painful, remembered in his journals long after it had subsided as analogous "to the gladiatorial animal combat of pagan times." If Christ were to return to the world, he wrote, "he would perhaps not be put to death, but would be ridiculed. This is martyrdom in the age of reason." Things got so bad that, in 1846, the martyr's tailor, C. M. Künitzer, claimed that his reputation was enough besmirched by the fuss that Kierkegaard had better go elsewhere to have his trousers made. Detached observers felt that Kierkegaard—who had dared *The Corsair* to single him out—overreacted, compulsively talking of little else: a letter to Hans Christian Andersen reported that "the poor victim is not enough of a philosopher to ignore this annoyance, but is preoccupied with it day and night and talks about it with everyone." He had imagined himself a friend of the people, an aristocratic dandy engaging even the lowliest Copenhagener in conversation during his strolls. Now every schoolboy and ruffian called insults after him. His own nephew, Troels Frederik Lund, spotted his uncle on the street and was about to greet him when, as he remembered it,

> at that moment I heard some passersby say something mocking about him and saw a couple of people on the other side of the street stop, turn around to look at him, and laugh. His one trouser leg really was shorter than the other, and I could now see for myself that he was odd-looking. I instinctively stopped, was embarrassed, and suddenly remembered that I had to go down another street.

It was as if the crowd had sniffed out Kierkegaard's own poor opinion of his body. By the 1840s he suffered from hemorrhoids and constipation, insomnia and dizziness, urinary difficulties and abdominal pains, and occasionally spat blood. His journal of 1845 exclaims, " 'A new horse!'— oh, would that the victorious health of my spirit might dare to cry out, 'A new horse, a new body!' " In the margin beside this notation he disdainfully clarified: "this sweat-soaked, stifling cloak of mush that is the body and the body's fatigue." In 1848 he noted, "In my youth my agony was frightful." He was given a physician's discharge from the Royal Life Guard after three days' service. He would not ride horses, fence, or dance.

Yet two drawings of his head by his distant cousin Niels Christian Kierkegaard when Søren was in his late twenties show a romantically handsome youth. Regine found little fault with him; she recalled, "Yes, he was somewhat high-shouldered and his head tilted forward a bit, probably from all that reading and writing at his desk." (In curiously bitter retrospect, her ex-fiancé confided to his journal, "She did not love my well-formed nose, nor my fine eyes, nor my small feet—nor my clever head—she just loved me, and yet she did not understand me.") The reminiscences of others mention Kierkegaard's "high shoulders, the restless, somewhat hopping gait," whose zigzags made him difficult to walk beside, and claim that his back was "a bit curved." The hospital examination soon after he was admitted recorded nothing abnormal about his spine. His enemy and admirer, Aron Goldschmidt, the editor of *The Corsair*, left the most sensitive impressions of Kierkegaard's physical aspect:

> The shape of his body was striking, not really ugly, certainly not repulsive, but with something disharmonious, rather slight, and yet also weighty. . . . He went about like a thought that had got distracted at the very moment at which it was formed.

Goldschmidt remembered a friendly conversation, before the *Corsair* affair, in which Kierkegaard seemed to grow larger as he talked. The observer reported:

> There was a long pause, and he suddenly took a little hop and struck himself on the leg with his thin cane. . . . The movement was peculiar and seemed almost painful. . . . I am sure there was something painful in it, something of the following sort: It was the fact that this learned, thin man wanted to be a part of the joys of life, but felt himself either unable or not permitted to do so.

No autopsy was performed on Kierkegaard's body, presumably by his own wish. This disappointed some medical students, who wanted to study his brain. The fact that he died at the age of forty-two would appear to substantiate some "thorn in the flesh," but Garff rules out tuberculosis and syphilis, two common killers of the era, and other diagnoses cannot be confirmed. "And when you get right down to it, what do the physiologist and the physician really know, then?" Kierkegaard had asked in his journals. The thorn in the flesh, one concludes by default, was a complaint of the spirit. The humiliating *Corsair* affair, from this distance a tawdry and typical instance of provincial malice cutting a local eminence down to size, worked in Kierkegaard like a vision-inducing poison. In 1848 he wrote, "Truly, I would never have succeeded in illuminating Christianity in the way that has been granted me, had all this not happened to me." A little later: "It has permitted me to experience the sort of isolation without which one does not discover Christianity. . . . No, no, one must in fact be acquainted with it from the ground up, one must be educated in the school of abuse." He spoke of his trials as "Christian experiences." By the mid-1850s his understanding of Christianity had been so radicalized that he proposed, "Christianity is the invention of Satan, calculated to make human beings unhappy."

The man once "incapable of making a girl happy" sees human unhappiness as intrinsic to traffic with God:

> What is absolutely the decisive factor is that Christianity is a heterogeneity, an incommensurability with the world, that it is irrational with respect to the world and with respect to being a human being in a straightforward sense. From my early years, I have winced at a thorn in the flesh, and to this was also connected a consciousness of guilt and sin. I have felt myself to be heterogeneous. This pain, my heterogeneity, I have understood as my relation to God.

His journals repeatedly cite the early pagan characterization of Christianity as *odium generis humani*, a hatred of everything human. Early in his development, at the age of twenty-two, he had already noted "the strange, suffocating atmosphere we encounter in Christianity," and that "in comparison to the pagans [Christians] are like a gelding compared to a stallion." He wrote that "becoming a Christian is like every radical cure: One puts it off as long as possible." Now he was ready, but at the price of loudly insisting on incommensurability and denouncing every worldly aspect of the Danish state church—its pomp and its bishops and the comfort it offered the comfortable bourgeoisie. He launched upon the fourth scandal of his life, the so-called attack on Christendom.

The attack was a counterattack, upon the geese. "The simple class of people . . . have been taught to laugh at me, thereby cutting themselves off from the one person in this country who has loved them most sincerely." The common man is told in a storm of articles and privately financed pamphlets that he should shun church and the pastors, "these abominable people whose way of making a living is to prevent you from even becoming aware of what true Christianity is." And what are the rewards of becoming aware? "To become a Christian in the New Testament sense is such a radical transformation that, from a purely human perspective, one would have to say that it is the greatest tragedy for a family if one of its members becomes a Christian." This enemy of organized Christianity, who as late as 1847 had thought of becoming a country pastor, sought, and found, a kind of martyrdom. Hearing of his hospitalization, one citizen of Copenhagen speculated, "Most likely illness, nervous stress, and a sort of convulsive irritability have played a large role in his bitter and negative activities, during which he displayed to the entire world his face, marked as it was by hatred of humanity." The prominent church leader Nikolai Grundtvig denounced Kierkegaard as "the Father of Lies . . . who confuses his adherents with the appearance of clarity and with all sorts of brilliant delusions, but nevertheless kills everything human in them, leading them to the outer darkness."

Kierkegaard's father had been a follower of Grundtvig. Of the two Lutheran bishops that bore the brunt of Søren's assault, one, Jakob Peter Mynster, had been the father's confessor and the other, Hans Lassen Martensen, had been young Søren's tutor. The attack was a father-son affair, a repetition, in a sense, of the curse by the Jutland shepherd boy. It was a vomiting-up of the gloomy religiosity that the father had worked upon the son:

> Oh, how frightful it is when I think for even a moment of the dark background of my life, right from the earliest days. The anxiety with which my father filled my soul, his own frightful melancholia, of many things in this connection that I cannot even write down. I acquired such anxiety about Christianity, and yet I felt myself strongly drawn toward it.

This was confided to his journals; in public writings, he advised Christians, "Take an emetic. Come out of this halfway condition." A generation before Nietzsche, God was pronounced dead as a practical matter; theism so severely preached was hard to distinguish from atheism. The outer darkness that Grundtvig had evoked stood ready for Kierkegaard. The last entry in his journal reads in part:

> I came into existence through a crime. I came into existence against God's will. The crime—which in a sense is not my crime, even though it makes me guilty in God's eyes—is to give life. The punishment fits the crime: to be deprived of all lust for life.

Human life itself is a *skándalon*. There was sophistry in Kierkegaard's attack, but also the powerful, nay-saying passion of Paul and Augustine: life and the world are the enemy. Garff's concretely local biography, big as it is, does not find space to speak of Kierkegaard in the world at large, after his death—his reputation's slow creep out of Denmark, by way of

Germany; his influence on Kafka and Karl Barth and Unamuno and Sartre and Auden; his paternity of existentialism and Protestant neo-orthodoxy; the breath of new life he gave, however little he would have wished it, twentieth-century Christianity. Dying, having excoriated the established church and adamantly refused to take communion from an ordained clergyman, he nevertheless reassured his comforter, the pious Emil Boesen, who had asked him if he believed in Christ and took refuge in him. "Yes, of course, what else?" Either, by one of his formulations, a person was lost in the "dizziness of abstract infinity" or was saved "infinitely in the essentiality of the religious."

The Man in Bed

MARCEL PROUST: *A Life*, by William C. Carter. 946 pp. Yale University Press, 2000.

Proust is now as far from us in time as the early Romantics were from the generation of Shaw and Wells. Yet he continues to be loved; his work has not petrified into the intimidating mesas, the scarcely scalable formerly volcanic cones, that time and lessening literacy have made of Joyce, Musil, Mann, and even Kafka, who left his more ambitious works uncompleted. These vintage modernists, so bold and fresh in their lifetimes, have taken on the nature of assignments, to be worked through as the classic Greek and Latin texts were for earlier generations of the educated. But Proust remains as light and inviting as a feather bed, a nearly infinite mass of prose gently sighing up and down like a calm sea glinting with myriad coins of moonlight. A young correspondent of mine wrote that he had just begun to read Proust; he likened it to a first date, and said it made him feel shy. The novelist Mary Gordon, I recently learned, begins her writing day by reading ten pages of Proust, somewhat the way Karl Barth used to play a Mozart recording before settling to theology. Though we may have trouble remembering where we were when we first opened *Ulysses* or *The Castle*, most of us can remember when we began to read *Remembrance of Things Past*.

The title, lifted from a Shakespeare sonnet and bestowed upon *À la recherche du temps perdu* by Proust's first English translator, C. K. Scott Moncrieff, met protest at the outset and is under definitive attack now; the 1993 Modern Library translation—Scott Moncrieff's as amended by first Terence Kilmartin and then D. J. Enright—is bluntly titled *In Search of Lost Time*. The Proust-lover quails; Scott Moncrieff's ornate and sinuous English prose, based upon the first, highly faulty French texts, was for many of us the gate that opened into Proust's incomparable gardens, and one resents any alteration to sites of enchantment. After years of rumors that poet Richard Howard would be doing a retranslation, word arrives that a new translation is in the works for Penguin Books,* a committee job under the editorship of Christopher Prendergast; may it be less wooden, less purged of period flavor and what we might call "swing," than are the modern replacements of Constance Garnett's translations from the Russian. Scott Moncrieff's was a labor of love, and Proust has attracted other such labors, in the form of precious small books of devotion (by Samuel Beckett, François Mauriac, Roger Shattuck, Howard Moss, Alain de Botton) and a splendidly Proustian two-volume biography by the English scholar George D. Painter. Now a new biography, *Marcel Proust: A Life*, by an American professor of French at the University of Alabama at Birmingham, William C. Carter, has been published by Yale University Press—a formidable volume of over nine hundred pages, adorned by two generous sheafs of photographs and a striking jacket featuring the rather Draculaesque oil portrait by Jacques-Emile Blanche of the young Proust dressed to kill.

Carter explains in a preface why a new biography is "overdue": a "wealth of fresh material" has become available since the publication of Painter's second volume in 1965. More than five thousand letters have been published in Philip Kolb's twenty-one-volume edition of Proust's correspondence; seventy-five of the notebooks in which Proust composed are available in the Bibliothèque Nationale; a number of sketches and poems by the adolescent author have turned up; and French editors have busily re-edited and annotated, for the 1989 four-volume Pléiade edition, the notoriously dishevelled, compulsively revised text of *À la recherche du temps perdu*, the last third of which was posthumously printed. There is no doubting that some new material exists; but also there is no gainsaying that Carter is not the writer Painter was. Painter's pages are saturated with the Proustian perfumes; his factual account—a pioneering work in that, he claimed, "the subject has never yet been treated with anything approaching scholarly method"—follows the mythologizing scheme of Proust's fictional opus to the point where both the biography and the novel end with the word "Time." Painter's text abounds with beautifully phrased metaphors, epigrams, and psychologizing. For instance, the moot matter of Proust's asthma:

---

*Published in 2002, in six volumes by seven different translators, to mixed reviews.

In his attacks of asthma the same causes were at work as in his childhood fits of hysterical weeping; his unconscious mind was asking for his father's pity and his mother's love; and his breathlessness reproduced, perhaps, the moment of suffocation which comes equally from tears or from sexual pleasure. He sinned through his lungs, and in the end his lungs were to kill him. Other great writers, Flaubert and Dostoevsky, suffered from epilepsy, which stood in an inseparable and partly causal relation to their art. Asthma was Proust's epilepsy. In early years it was the marking of his difference from others, his appeal for love, his refuge from duties which were foreign to his still unconscious purpose; and in later life it helped him to withdraw from the world and to produce a work "de si longue haleine." Meanwhile, however, he was only a little boy choking and writhing in the scented air under the green leaves, in the deadly garden of spring.

Carter, on the other hand, writes with little flair and occasional lameness. On Proust's boyhood he writes as if for children:

> To show their displeasure and to indicate to Marcel that he was unwanted, [his schoolmates] would speak to him sharply or feign a shove, dismissing him rudely with a wave of the arm, causing his large, dark eyes to fill with sadness.

Without any source citation, we are told, "Sometimes he felt so lonely and desperate when his mother left him at night that he identified himself with the wretched man abandoned by his own father and nailed to the cross." When Proust ventures out into high society, Carter writes as if for the society page:

> Many of the ladies carried parasols to shield their delicate, ivory skin from the sun, while the gentlemen wore their best top hats. There were titled ladies and gentlemen galore, including the countesses Greffuhle, Fitz-James, Pourtalès, and Potocka, the princesses de Brancovan and de Chimay, and Comte Boni de Castellane. The poet José-Maria de Heredia and his three ravishing daughters were there. . . .

Painter refers to the great novel as *À la recherche*, where Carter favors *Search*, which suggests a computer command. Though Painter's biography feels more spacious and leisurely, it is in fact shorter, its two volumes totalling, without end matter, seven hundred pages as against Carter's eight hundred ten bigger pages of text.

Carter gives us a solid Proust—a man who stood five foot six, not only endured but enjoyed his year in the military, fought a duel (showing, a friend noted, "a sangfroid and firmness that appear incompatible with his nerves"), played tennis and the piano, passed his law exams, and earned an advanced degree in philosophy. This new biography gains interest and density as it follows the delicate child, carried in his mother's womb during the hardships and hazards of the 1870–71 Prussian siege of Paris, through a pampered childhood and self-indulgent youth into the bedridden, drug-raddled adulthood that produced a heroically long and intricate masterpiece. It is an inspiring story—a life justified in the majestic retelling of that life, in a novel whose climax is the vision of itself, as its hero arrives at the blessed condition of an author. If Carter's method is pedestrian, his mighty subject flies high: the life ends with a quote (from *Search*, if you must) evoking those fictional artists (Elstir, Vinteuil) in whose company we "do really fly from star to star."

Though Painter by no means neglected the evolution of *À la recherche du temps perdu*, I don't remember from his pages quite the sense of possessed, self-destructive authorial activity that Carter's last chapters describe. The typesetting of the vast novel in its successive volumes was, like that of Joyce's *Ulysses*, a printer's nightmare—"one of the most demanding productions in the history of publishing." Huge amounts of lead involved in the setting were immobilized while the author and publisher fumed and quarrelled. The workers, who composed on monotype, began to "refuse copy that was too difficult to read because they were paid per thousand letters. The time they spent trying to decipher Proust's handwriting lowered their wages considerably." Employing a method invented by his beloved housekeeper Céleste Albaret, Proust amended and augmented his manuscripts and proofs with scribbled "paste-ons," or *paperoles*, of which one, when unfolded, "measured one and a half meters." As he wrote into dawn by the light of his green-shaded bedside lamp, his eyes began to ache and weaken. His solution to the problem was typically impractical and extravagant: rather than undertake a daylight visit to an optometrist, he had Céleste go out and buy him a dozen pairs of steel-rimmed spectacles, then he "chose a few that improved his vision and told Céleste to keep them all." In the fall of 1922, as he was dying of pneumonia, refusing the treatments urged by his doctors (which included his younger brother, Robert) and starving himself on a self-imposed diet of fruit, ice cream, and cold beer brought from the Ritz, Proust labored with his last strength on the typescript of *The Captive*, at one point suggesting a cut of two hundred fifty pages which was not made, and at another demanding that the presses be stopped, at his expense, so that he could change the ending of an excerpt, "Albertine Sleeping," in the magazine *Nouvelle Revue Française*. On the last night of his life, according to Painter, he wrote insertions in a quavering, scarcely legible hand and called Céleste in to take dictation—he had some refinements to add to the dying of his fictional character Bergotte, "Now I'm in the same condition myself."

These feverish revisions carried to the edge of the grave the expansion that Proust imposed on his chef d'oeuvre, as if determined to get everything he knew and felt into it. The work grew from what was to be an essay arguing against the critic Sainte-Beuve; it took novelistic form in Proust's mind around 1908 and was offered to a prospective publisher, Alfred Vallette, as a book of about four hundred pages, ready to appear by January or February 1910. It was bipartite in structure—time lost and time regained. The two ways of the narrator's childhood walks, called Swann's Way and the Guermantes Way, were to be shown, at the end, to join, just as Swann's daughter Gilberte marries the Marquis Robert de Saint-Loup, one of the Guermantes. Involuntary memory, whether worked by a madeleine dipped in tea or by uneven paving stones underfoot, recaptured lost time and revealed to the narrator his vocation as a writer.

Thus, in the original scheme Sainte-Beuve's confusion of the creative self and the social self would be banished. In his 1908 notebook Proust had written that Sainte-Beuve erred in not viewing "literature as a thing apart, or at least detachable, from the rest of the man and his nature" and in ignoring "what a very slight degree of self-acquaintance teaches us: that a book is the product of a different self from the self we manifest in our habits, in our social life, in our vices." Proust, unhappy with his outer self, which had disappointed his parents and accomplished little in the world, insisted on the existence of a better, creative, hidden self. Homosexuality had been from the start part of Proust's narrative, even when its provisional title was *Contre Sainte-Beuve*—"a genuine novel," he wrote Vallette in 1909, "and an extremely indecent one in places." As he worked, the project grew under him. By 1912, *Swann's Way*, the first installment, would make "a single volume of 800 or 900 pages," he wrote a friend and early consultant, Georges de Lauris. On Christmas Eve of that year, two publishers simultaneously rejected *Swann's Way*, including the *Nouvelle Revue Française*, on the advice of André Gide. Proust, whose fortune after his parents' deaths totalled the equivalent of four and a half million dollars, decided to publish the book at his own expense. Once *Swann's Way* appeared, on November 14, 1913, under the imprint of Bernard Grasset, "Proust would never again," as Carter ringingly puts it, "have to justify his enterprise or go begging for a publisher." He prepared the typescript of what he imagined as the second volume, *The Guermantes Way*, and began to receive proofs from his new publisher, the *NRF*, where Gide had performed a penitent about-face.

Two misfortunes intervened: in August of 1914, World War I commenced, and a few months earlier, Alfred Agostinelli, a twenty-five-year-old Monacan chauffeur and secretary of Proust's, drowned off Antibes in the course of flying lessons. Proust had loved Agostinelli (who had a common-law wife), and he lavished his grief on a monstrous expansion of the sections of the novel concerning Albertine, a love of the narrator's for whom Proust already had a plan: "In the second part of the novel the girl will be financially ruined and I will support her without attempting to possess her because I am incapable of happiness." In the revised novel, Albertine, after being, like Agostinelli with Proust, a captive of and then a fugitive from the narrator, dies. The war having halted publication, Proust had the time as well as the passion to expand his novel from a half-million words to more than a million and a quarter between the years 1914 and 1922.

Whether or not the total work, thus inflated, should be considered a casualty of the war depends on the reader's appetite for Proust's inimitable delicacies. Another early reader and adviser, Louis de Robert, privy to Grasset's worries over the first volume's length, told the author, "Don't cut anything—it would be a crime. Everything must be kept; everything is rare, subtle, profound, true, right, precious, incomparable." When Proust was still an obscure sometime columnist and parodist, the poet Anna de Noailles captured in a phrase the intoxicating compound of his sensibility, the "marvelous mixture of irony and sweetness, like two opposing rivers gliding close to one another." Yet even earnest devotees may feel that, after *The Guermantes Way*, the rivers have forgotten how to stop flowing—that a machine at the bottom of the sea keeps grinding out the remorseless news that love is both obsessive and futile, and oblivion is its destination. Carter's biography makes clear upon how narrow a basis of experience Proust's pronouncements on love rested. That he had a keenly affectionate nature is shown by his towering portraits of the narrator's mother and grandmother in his novel, as well as by his avidly flirtatious and rather cloying letters to his friends both male and female. But if he, who told Gide late in his life that he "had never liked women except platonically," ever found a man who loved him in return, the fact has eluded biographers. His friends, when he was still healthy enough for peer friendship, tended to put him off and get married; his beloved pet Agostinelli fled him, while trying to maintain a mercenary connection; some of the waiters Proust so lavishly tipped may have come back to his apartment with him, but his main physical gratification, found in Albert Le Cuziat's male brothel, seems to have been masturbation while watching a hireling of the place masturbate, or, if that failed, after watching famished rats attack one another. This magnificent sensibility dwelt in a toxic desert. As François Mauriac, in his *Proust's Way*, put it:

The corruption of a life, stagnant though remarkably attentive, defenseless against the outer world, given over entirely to swarming sensations, besieges, penetrates, gnaws and destroys the human beings to whom the novelist had given existence. . . . It remains for us to find ourselves to-day more sensitive than we were in the dazzlement of first reading, to that contamination of a whole romantic world by that morbid creator who bore it too long mingled with his own life, mixed with his deep murkiness, and who communicated to it the germs with which he found himself infected.

Fortunately, the last, relatively short installment, *Time Regained*, was conceived along with the rhapsodic opening chapters, "Overture" and "Combray." Versions of the beginning and end were completed as early as 1909. The expanded manuscript, according to testimony from Céleste Albaret and letters to Gaston Gallimard, was apparently complete in 1916. Proust did not live to revise the last sections in proof. His final letter to Gallimard said, in deathbed surrender, "I think now the most urgent action is to deliver all my books to you. The sort of tenacious work that I have done for *The Captive* . . . forced me to set aside the following volumes." *Le Temps retrouvé*, deciphered by the *NRF* editors from Proust's notebooks, was published in 1927; a Pléiade edition of 1954 contains emendations on almost every page. But, even in its mangled and problematical form, the last volume ends the great novel in the same crisp, giddy, and mesmeric key in which it began.

Proust's life, unlike that of many writers, makes a good story, none the worse for the subject's having already told it, in his own way, in his masterwork. There is a great deal we do not know about "Marcel"—as the narrator is tentatively named late in the course of *À la recherche**—that we do know about Proust: his messy finances, his penchant for gambling, his homosexuality (Marcel is neither Jewish nor homosexual, though intensely observant of both minorities), and his literary endeavors. Marcel's father, the novel tells us, has shown a prose-poem by his young son to Monsieur de Norpois, who is not impressed, and, volumes later, Marcel sends an article to *Le Figaro*, which, in a still later volume, publishes it; but there is little sense of the continual literary ambition which Proust in fact displayed. It was a blessing in disguise that his early efforts met with small success. *Pleasures and Days*, a collection of youthful stories and

---

*The passage comes early in *The Captive;* Albertine does it. "The uncertainty of awakening revealed by her silence was not at all revealed in her eyes. As soon as she was able to speak she said, 'My———' or 'My dearest———' followed by my Christian name, which, if we give the narrator the same name as the author of this book, would be 'My Marcel,' or 'My dearest Marcel.' "

poems, was much delayed in its publication and, expensively priced, sold a bit more than three hundred copies; he accumulated, between 1895 and 1899, close to a thousand pages of a novel, *Jean Santeuil*, which he set aside, for the next five years, to work on translating, with the help of his mother and others who knew English, John Ruskin's *Bible of Amiens* and *Sesame and Lilies;* he published, in various Paris magazines, reviews and pastiches and parodies which attracted considerable favorable attention. His extraordinary gifts were recognized by some, such as Anna de Noailles, Madame Emile Straus, and *Figaro* editor Gaston Calmette, but in general he was so firmly regarded by the intelligentsia as "the epitome of a bourgeois snob and a dilettante" that Gide rejected the manuscript of *Swann's Way*, he confessed, with barely a glance.

Proust was fortunate that when, approaching the age of forty, he came into his voice and the fullness of his material—the events of his life, regained through the miracle of involuntary memory—the material was virtually untouched by previous exposure. *Jean Santeuil* and *Contre Sainte-Beuve* were unpublished, and all their anticipations of *À la recherche du temps perdu* were, like half-forgotten first drafts, available for a truly masterly reworking. It all came down to one book. No wonder it had to be vast. Posterity tends to give novelists a longer ride on one or two big books than on a raft of smaller ones. As Proust, dying at fifty-one, approached the end of his curious martyrdom—an adult life spent mostly in bed, seeing, he complained in a letter, "only the awful walls* of this room, never illuminated by daylight"—he divined, let us hope, how long a ride lay ahead.

Poet on the Fault Line

ROBERT FROST: *A Life*, by Jay Parini. 487 pp. Holt, 1999.

From one perspective, the life of Robert Frost (1874–1963) was a triumph. His childhood impoverished and rather rootless, his education intermittent, his temperament depressive and combative, he did not see his first book of poems published until he was nearly forty; yet he lived to become the most popular and honored American poet of the century—as William H. Pritchard dryly put it, "he became the goodest greyest poet

---

*And these, after 1919, were not even the famous cork-lined walls, which he left behind when circumstances compelled him to move from 102, boulevard Hausmann.

since Walt Whitman." But Whitman never read at a Presidential inauguration, or earned a handsome living giving public readings, or won the equivalent of Frost's four Pulitzer Prizes for Poetry.

From another perspective, Frost's life was a Job-like series of intimate disasters, which helped produce, for his eighty-eight years, chronic psychosomatic complaints and alienating compulsions. His parents, who met as schoolteachers and shared an interest in literature, were mismatched, though their familiar names, Will and Belle, nicely chimed. His father, William Prescott Frost, Jr.—the only child of a New Hampshire farm family, a Harvard Phi Beta Kappa, a San Francisco journalist with political ambitions, a drinker, a professing atheist, a gun-lover, a sometimes abusive husband and parent—died when Robert was eleven, leaving the family with eight dollars. Robert's mother, born Isabelle Moodie in Leith, near Edinburgh, was the child of a sea captain who drowned soon after her birth and "a hussy who ran away from the arduous duties of motherhood"; Belle's parents shipped her off to Ohio at the age of eleven. Six years older than her husband, Belle was a mystical Swedenborgian who published religious poetry and whose brave attempts to support her family with schoolteaching in New England sometimes led to Robert's being called into class to maintain discipline. He later spoke of her "incipient insanity"; a friend called her "a queer woman." When Robert, at the age of seven, began to hear voices, this was congruent with his mother's mystical bent. She died of cancer in 1900. That same year, Frost's first child, Elliott, who was three, died of typhoid fever; Frost blamed himself for not getting better medical care, and later said that it was "like murdering his own child." Elinor, his wife, went into a steep depression, and though she bore him four more children (a daughter, Lesley, had been born the previous year; another daughter, Elinor Bettina, died soon after she was born, in 1907), their relations were never the same. The children gave him much eventual grief: Marjorie, the youngest and Frost's pet, died in 1934 of a post-partum infection; Frost's son, Carol, killed himself with a deer rifle at the age of thirty-eight, in 1940, two years after his mother had died of a heart attack; and Irma, the second daughter, after a long history of mental illness and an unhappy marriage, was committed to an insane asylum, where she lived, supported by Frost and his legacy, until 1981. Frost's only sibling, Jeannie, also ended in a mental institution, from which she wrote her brother, "I am very peculiar and did not start right. If I ever was well and natural it was before I can remember." She died in 1929.

No one could take such an avalanche of family woe lightly; Frost tended to take it all upon himself. As his adult children's marital woes and hospital bills mounted, he wrote to Louis Untermeyer, "All this sickness and scatteration of the family is our fault and not our misfortune or I wouldn't admit it. It's a result and a judgment on us." He thus echoes his dying mother, who, in a hectic household scene, had pronounced that little Elliott's death was "God's judgment." There was no lack of blaming in the Frost family. Immediately after Elinor's death, Frost asked Lesley, the child who had inherited the most of his tough and enduring spirit, if he might now live with her. She responded with a flat No and, according to Lawrance Thompson's three-volume biography, an outburst of accusation:

> She said she had seen him cause so much injury to the lives of his own children—particularly to Irma, Carol, and Marjorie—that she would not permit him to move into her home, where he might also injure the lives of her two daughters. Her rage increased as she went on to insist, through her tears, that she could not forgive him for his having ruined her mother's life. It was his fault, she said, that her mother was dead, for it was his own selfishness which had forced her mother to climb those stairs to the upper quarters, repeatedly. . . . Then she hurt him most by concluding that he was the kind of artist who never should have married, or at least never should have had a family.

These must have been bitter words for a man to hear who, whatever his lapses of paternal attention, and however much oxygen his own ego sucked out of the household atmosphere, had spent countless bucolic hours in his children's company, entering into their games and sharing with them his love of nature and his sense of fun. The four growing children were an intrinsic part of the years spent on a thirty-acre farm in Derry, New Hampshire, from 1900 to 1911, where he found his voice as a poet and his most treasured and characteristic images. Years later, in "Directive," he returns in his mind to the ruined site of this idyll:

> First there's the children's house of make believe,
> Some shattered dishes underneath a pine,
> The playthings in the playhouse of the children.
> Weep for what little things could make them glad.

Frost was first a poet but a family man close second, and perhaps his crowning domestic grief was that, after Elinor's death, he fell in love with a married woman, Kathleen Morrison, who declined to divorce her husband and marry Frost, though she served him, for an undetermined period, as a mistress and, for his last twenty-five years, as a proprietorial secretary and manager. But there was a terrible loneliness to him, as he reaped the rewards of those last years, an endless rambling quest for reassurance, speaking and reading and reciting and collecting prizes and honorary degrees and, afraid since childhood of the dark, sitting up past midnight with anyone who would listen to him talk.

The many Frost biographies, the first of which dates back to 1927, have a troubled history of their own. The early portraits, from Gorham B. Munson's initial biography up to Elizabeth Shepley Sergeant's and Sidney Cox's books of 1960 and 1961, respectively, tend to depict Frost as a wise farmer-poet embodying, in Sergeant's phrases, "the stability and optimism of the Victorian age" and "a positive view of life"; he is anointed an "endearing personality" and "one of the most beloved poets and sages of our mid-twentieth century." A tart and bulky corrective to these adoring views arrived in 1966, with the first volume of Lawrance Thompson's two-thousand-page biography, which was to go to three volumes, the last composed by the dying author with the collaboration of R. H. Winnick. Thompson, a New Hampshire native born in 1906, first enters the picture as an organizer of a Frost exhibit at Wesleyan in 1936. Frost invited him to be his official biographer in 1939, the year when Robert Newdick, who had been doing research and having conversations with the simultaneously wary and attention-seeking poet, unexpectedly died during an operation for appendicitis. Employed at this time as curator of rare books at Princeton, Thompson at first suggested Frost's friends Louis Untermeyer and Bernard De Voto as better candidates to do the job, but finally acceded; he was thirty-three and Frost sixty-five, and neither could have foreseen that more than twenty years of uncomfortably close association would go by before Frost died in 1963. As Archibald MacLeish perceived, "Thompson saw too much of him— learned to dislike him very heartily."

The relations between Frost and his young biographer were further strained by Thompson's becoming, as we read in Jeffrey Meyers's 1996 *Robert Frost*, Kathleen Morrison's lover. Meyers is the first biographer to tell us much about Morrison. Like Frost's mother, oddly, she came to this country from Scotland when she was eleven. She had been born in Nova Scotia, the daughter of a Scottish Episcopal clergyman who, after serving several parishes in Scotland, accepted a call from a fashionable Philadelphia church. She graduated from Bryn Mawr in 1921, and in 1927 married Theodore Morrison, a Harvard lecturer in English whom she had met while both were working at *The Atlantic Monthly*. Though frequently described as "cold," calm, and intensely conventional in outward deportment, Kay Morrison in her prime evidently maintained a male harem that included Frost, De Voto, her stoical husband, and—the newest member of Frost's court, and eight years younger than she—his official biographer. Thompson, who privately called Frost and Elinor "good examples of psychotics," foretold his animus in a 1964 introduction to Frost's letters, which he says reveal "periods of gloom, jealousies, obsessive resentments, sulking displays of temper, nervous rages, and vindictive retaliations." Thompson's introductions to the two biographical volumes he completed argue a psychohistory of early wounds: Frost's disorderly and reckless father; his mother's humiliating failures at teaching school; Elinor's early rejections of her passionate suitor; and the flinty manner of William Frost, Sr., even as the old man, a Lawrence, Massachusetts, mill manager, generously helped support his son's and then his grandson's family. Frost reacted to these reality checks with shame, mendacity, and an exaltation of the "form-giving" of poetry as "a means of defense against the threat of psychological chaos or insanity." Sampling Thompson's massive work after reading accounts of it, one is struck by its overall judiciousness and sympathy as it seeks to understand Frost's less attractive traits in terms of his inner struggles. And at the least Thompson provides an unsurpassable wealth of detail and lets Frost, a pungent, uninhibited letter-writer and interview-giver, speak for himself through abundant quotations.

Nevertheless, Thompson's biography provoked a reaction, most notably Pritchard's *Robert Frost: A Literary Life Reconsidered* (1984), in which the author, after cross-examining the case Thompson made, with great subtlety and good temper interrogates Frost's work, making the best of the "playful, complicated, devious Frost" present in the poems. After all, the fact that Frost had a gloomy, fearful, and malicious side had been proclaimed by such critics as Lionel Trilling and often acknowledged by Frost himself: "I have been one acquainted with the night," one famous poem begins. John Walsh's book on Frost's English years, *Into My Own* (1988), quotes him as saying, "Evil clings so in all our acts that even when we not only mean but achieve our prettiest, bravest, noblest, best, we are often a scourge even to those we do not hate." And after Elinor's death, he wrote to a friend, "God damn me when he gets around to it."

Jeffrey Meyers's biography, in counter-reaction, insists on the more sensational data. His second sentence lets us know that one American ancestor of Frost's "was banished from Kittery, Maine, for intimacy with an Indian girl and not allowed to return until he had married an English wife." Meyers outs the Morrison affair—both the Morrisons vetted the third Thompson volume, covering the years 1938–63, and suppressed any whisper of physical impropriety—and, though critics found Meyers's readings of some poems crude and of some situations melodramatic, he lays down a thick and vivid barrage of brisk, persuasive assertions.

Into this welter Jay Parini has dropped his *Robert Frost: A Life*. It is hard to see what it adds. Parini himself, in an afterword, provides a history of the biographies, upon which the above account draws, and he admits, "The reader must . . . wonder why another biography of Frost is necessary." For exegesis of the poetry, Pritchard's and a number of other closely argued volumes exist. On the life, Thompson and Meyers are more animated and concrete. Is it enough that Parini is very fond of Frost? His preface begins by claiming that Frost has been his "favorite poet ever since the ninth grade" and ends by calling the book, whose inception dates back to 1975, "a labor of love" that he was reluctant to complete. His intention, he says, was not "to supplant or overtake previous biographers and critics but merely to add a significant layer"—the significance inhering in a relatively few highlighted poems, discussed as "feat[s] of rescued sanity" in "the complex circumstances" of Frost's life. His tone places his work in the earlier, near-hagiographic tradition of Frost biography: "Each class brilliantly taught, each vivid public reading, each child comforted or cared for, each tender moment with his wife was accomplished by steadiness of vision and hard spiritual work."

A poet and fiction writer as well as literary scholar, Parini strikes some nice phrases: Dutch elms were "long-necked, elegant trees," and of the revised poem "Fire and Ice" he writes, "Frost pulled it together, lacing the rhymes as tightly as a boot." His readings of the poems gravitate toward their religious implications: "As usual in Frost, the poem moves subtly beyond the physical circumstances of the poem, reaching toward a level that could be called metaphysical." Frost, loyal to both his parents, remained of two minds about religion. He remembered his mother's devoutness as "beautiful," and theistic issues frequently frame the inner debate of his poems and plays; musing on his poem "Kitty Hawk" at the Bread Loaf conference in 1959, he said, "The whole, the great enterprise of life, of the world, the great enterprise of our race, is our penetration into matter, deeper and deeper; carrying the spirit deeper into matter." On the other hand, he claimed no religious affiliation, and in his last interview, before entering the hospital for the final time, he told the reporter:

I don't take life very seriously. It's hard to get into this world and hard to get out of it. And what's in between doesn't make much sense. If that sounds pessimistic, let it stand.

Parini coins an apt phrase when he writes that Frost's poems "live on that perilous fault line between skepticism and faith." The peculiar standoff within Frost's ambivalent cosmos wins this poetic insight: "Frost's characters, literally and figuratively, seem endlessly forced to calculate the costs of movement."

But a certain blandness, even lameness, of style suggests that Parini wearied more than once during his long traverse across the wide scree of accumulated Frost data. His subject's complicated psyche receives injections of healthful simplicity: "He had come to England to make his name as a poet, and he would not give up until he had done so"; "With a quiet sense of triumph, Frost made his way northward." There is insufficient resistance, in a book about a poet, to the trite: "This is called having your cake and eating it, too"; "Like Dylan Thomas after him, Frost was prepared to 'rage against the dying of the light' "; "Deep inside, he would never get over it." As honors pile upon the aging hero, the acknowledgments become feebly dutiful: "Frost was profoundly moved by this gesture." And the concluding peroration goes into adjectival shock: "America had lost a poet of astounding grace and wisdom"; "The poetry itself is marked by an unbelievable, even visionary, clarity"; "Frost explored the theology of doubt with astounding honesty and passion"; "The contradictions of his life and work remain stunning." Amid such ineffectual homage, the dry, precise, low-pitched quotes from Frost ("My poems are all set to trip the reader head foremost into the boundless") sing.

Still, for those who are strangers to Frost's life and works, Parini is a benign guide, who never wanders far from the texts—so smoothly gnarled, so deftly deep—into rancorous psychologizing and gossip. He makes clear what a well-stocked mind Frost had, despite his fondness for playing the Yankee bumpkin. I. A. Richards, who knew him late in life, said that Frost "had an unusually theoretical mind, and liked to talk about language and meaning. . . . He knew vast stretches of English and American poetry by heart, and reached easily for examples in his conversation. I was always startled by his verbatim recall of poets from Shakespeare through Tennyson." To a degree matched only by Auden among major twentieth-century poets, Frost took clues from science—botany and astronomy principally. His knowledge of Greek and Latin probably surpassed that of Pound and Eliot, who flaunted their erudition more. He studied the classic languages at Lawrence High School (where he and Elinor had been co-valedictorians) and at Harvard (where he and Wallace Stevens were classmates, though neither graduated). The chiselled quatrains of his first collection, *A Boy's Will*, suggest those of the professional Latinist A. E. Housman and testify to the curious connection between classical studies and a lean, honed English. Frost's general knowledge of history and philosophy enabled him to ramble winningly through commencement speeches like that at Oberlin in 1937. Frost believed in the speaking voice—in yielding to his "voices"—and his theoretical bent led him to concoct his cherished theory of "the sound of sense," defined in the preface to his *Collected Poems* of 1939 as "the dramatic tones of meaning struck across the rigidity of a limited meter." This remarkably dense yet colloquial preface is one of the finest modern statements on poetry, with its parallel between the shape of love and "the figure a poem makes":

> It begins in delight, it inclines to the impulse, it assumes direction with the first line laid down, it runs a course of lucky events, and ends in a clarification of life—not necessarily a great clarification, such as sects and cults are founded on, but in a momentary stay against confusion.

This formulation is rephrased a few paragraphs on as the famous simile "Like a piece of ice on a hot stove the poem must ride on its own melting." We are reminded of the image, in his late poem "A Considerable Speck," of the tiny "living mite" he observes moving on a sheet of paper:

> No one can know how glad I am to find
> On any sheet the least display of mind.

He can be brilliantly open to digression—for example, the splendid seventeen lines in "Birches" describing the pliable trees after an ice storm, a self-interruption which he wraps up with

> But I was going to say when Truth broke in
> With all her matter-of-fact about the ice storm . . .

Poetry is discourse and process. "Poetry is the renewal of words forever and ever," he wrote Robert P. Tristram Coffin. "Poetry is that by which we live forever and ever unjaded. Poetry is that by which the world is never old."

Many who never met Frost nevertheless gathered a personal impression. He was, as no less a successor bard than Allen Ginsberg put it, "relentless" in the number of public readings he gave. In Ginsberg's words: "He created an audience for poetry readings. . . . He was the first voyager, a kind of pioneer, the original entrepreneur of poetry." It would have taken an effort of avoidance to have been at Harvard in the early Fifties and not to have heard Frost read; he lived over on Brewster Street for much of the academic year, though his relations with the university were informal. A reading that I (fallibly) remember was given in Sanders Theatre, that rather Elizabethan auditorium within the Victorian immensity of Memorial Hall. Frost shambled about on the stage as if he had been prodded from a sound winter's sleep; he "said"—as he put it— his poems rather rapidly, minimizing their music in his haste to get on with his spoken commentary on whatever came to his mind. In the front rows sat the flower of the English faculty, most conspicuously Archibald MacLeish, the Boylston Professor of Rhetoric and Oratory and our lead- ing poet in residence. Compared with these examplars of civilized letters Frost was an untamed beast, a man who had wriggled or quarrelled his way out of every academic post he had held, though his appetite for instructing others was powerful. As a literary artist, he was, we all knew, the real thing, the one man in the hall—and, for that matter, in all of safe, sane Cambridge—who had staked his whole soul on poetry and had gained the prize, the prize as he had defined it when he wrote of Edward Arlington Robinson, "The utmost of ambition is to lodge a few poems where they will be hard to get rid of."

Suddenly, abruptly, he shuffled a few steps to the edge of the stage, bent over, and attacked Archibald MacLeish, whose handsome big head—the head of a tall man, though MacLeish was not tall—happened to be in profile from my angle. MacLeish had recently issued a radio play, *The Trojan Horse*, whose message in that heyday of McCarthyism was that the United States should not take into itself the Trojan horse of totalitarian tactics. Who could dispute so unexceptionable a message and the agitated liberalism that had given rise to it? Well, Frost could. "You know," he told his old friend and admirer in the astonished hearing of us worshipfully assembled undergraduates, "if you're going to beat a fella, you got to get to be like him." He may have said "sort of like him" or some such qualification, and I believe he continued a while on this theme, long enough for its anti-anti-McCarthyite drift to register. It was Frost in action, cruelly playful, a cat reaching out from the stage to tease its mouse, an eminent mouse who had been faithful in the hospitality, cor- diality, and homage he had granted, over the years, to the greater poet. Yet Frost, his biographies tell us, found MacLeish irritating, in both his shortcomings and his successes. Frost's version of the Job legend, *A Masque of Reason*, had been panned by left-wing critics, whereas MacLeish's later *J.B.* had been a Broadway success. Of *J.B.*'s moral, which MacLeish's preface spelled out as "Our labor . . . is to learn through suffering to love," Frost had snorted, "People think everything is solved by love. Maybe just as many things are solved by hate."

And so on this occasion. As I remember it, Frost didn't raise his voice, and spoke as if helpfully, to an obtuse student. MacLeish smiled, slightly, through the assault; he knew his man, and perhaps had heard it all before. But we of the young audience had not, and this flash of bullying rather soured, for me, the charm of hearing "Stopping by Woods on a Snowy Evening" and "The Gift Outright" in the voice of their maker. In long retrospect, I think there was something salutary in seeing a revered man break loose from our consensual politics and raise the possibility that life, between great powers and old friends, is combat, and not clean combat at that. The pugnacious refusal to let MacLeish's easy metaphor pass stemmed from the same independent, unaccountable, self-created, precariously maintained vigor ("There's a vigorous devil in me," he once wrote Untermeyer) that had lodged his best poems where they could not be got rid of.

No Brakes

SINCLAIR LEWIS: *Rebel from Main Street*, by Richard Lingeman. 659 pp. Random House, 2002.

What has Sinclair Lewis done lately to deserve a new, 554-page (plus notes and index) biography? Mark Schorer's even bigger biography of forty years ago, *Sinclair Lewis: An American Life*, would seem to have closed the case, at least until Lewis's reputation—stuck in a slot below that of Theodore Dreiser, whose clumsy naturalism attained in at least two novels a tender, awed sense of tragedy Lewis's satires never mustered, and above that of Upton Sinclair, the remorselessly prolific idealist with whom Lewis was frequently, to his disadvantage, confused—emerges from its doldrums. Lewis's pair of breakthrough novels, *Main Street* (1920) and *Babbitt* (1922), both of which contributed new terms to the American vocabulary of self-comprehension, compose a volume of the Library of America, and the Library plans to include in another volume *Arrowsmith* (1925), *Elmer Gantry* (1927), and *Dodsworth* (1929), the other major novels of Lewis's prodigious decade. *Main Street* made a publishing sensation the likes of which hadn't been seen since *Uncle Tom's Cabin* (1852) or at least *Ben-Hur* (1880); the full-price edition, by the fledgling firm of Harcourt, Brace, and a cheaper edition, by Grosset and Dunlap, together sold over two million copies. Best-selling does not a classic make; *Babbitt* eventually outsold *Main Street* and comes closer to being a contemporary classroom standard, though far surpassed in that regard by a modestly successful short novel of 1925, F. Scott Fitzgerald's *The Great Gatsby*.

The writers slightly younger than Lewis—Hemingway, Faulkner, Fitzgerald—have remained more interesting than he to the critics and academics who perpetuate literary reputations. "Sinclair Lewis is nothing," Hemingway pronounced in his testamental *The Green Hills of Africa*, and a certain attic dust of datedness, as on quickly obsolete gadgetry, began to gather on Lewis's sensational novels as early as 1930, when he became the first American to win the Nobel Prize in Literature. It turns out that the choice, that year, had come down to Lewis and Dreiser, and the three-man committee went for Lewis, two to one, because he embodied "a vigorous trend in modern literature—high-class American humor." Lewis himself, forty-five at the time, was overheard (by Lillian Gish) to say, "This is the end of me. This is fatal. I cannot live up to it." It was not soon fatal, but things were never the same for him, and the rest of his life, while he continued famous and rich, is the tale of a losing struggle against alcoholism, loneliness, restlessness, and depleted, scattered creativity.

No doubt it is to blow the dust off the oeuvre that Lingeman has undertaken to tell the author's tale again, but it is hard to know from what angle he is blowing. His acknowledgments claim, "I am critical of the late Mark Schorer's monumental 1961 biography," yet no criticisms emerge until the very end, when an epilogue states that the monumental biography (earlier cited as "an indispensable resource") is "pervaded by such a tone of disapproval that it left the impression with many readers that Schorer disdained both Lewis himself and his work. . . . Schorer's book gave academics and general readers a license not to read Sinclair Lewis, if they needed one." Such a license is generally issued at desks broader than a biographer's, and this peruser of Schorer's ten-year labor of research and criticism felt less disdain than impatience bred of overlong immersion in a character almost everyone found exasperating. Schorer writes in the lofty, sometimes sardonic voice of Fifties mandarinism ("Perhaps it is futile," he gloomily muses, "to approach any Lewis novel as a work of art"), but his biography is at most junctures more energetic, more circumstantial, more engaging, and more earnestly analytical than Lingeman's.

Lingeman, who earlier devoted two excellent volumes to Dreiser, here seems hurried, and given to summation. He doesn't show Schorer's hospitality to direct quotation—Lewis, after all, crossed the path of almost every literary American of the half-century—and many brisk assertions must be taken on faith. "He took the Yale entrance examinations in June, and while browsing in a Saint Paul bookstore met the owner, Arthur Wheelock Upson, a published poet who impressed him vastly." Who says Upson did? "It was not that he didn't want to be like the other boys; he wanted very much to belong, but on his terms." How do we know this? The critical first seventeen years of Lewis's life, spent in Sauk Centre, Minnesota, get thirteen pages; Schorer gave them forty-one, more richly exploiting the not inconsiderable record of small-town news clippings, Lewis's adolescent diary, and his abundant later reflections upon his roots. A portion of what Lingeman offers might be true of almost any boy: "Sometimes, he had to hold in his anger and became moody and withdrawn. This made him wary, touchy, and thin-skinned, lashing out at rejection yet needing acceptance, wanting to belong."

The prose can be untidy to the point of vagueness: "In her memoir, Gracie gives her wedding night the faint virtue of having avoided the Victorian bride's trauma in the hands of a clumsy husband." Some sentences are hastily overloaded: "Jimmy Sheean, to whom Dorothy had been a rock in Moscow when his woman friend had tragically died, and who had returned to the States, joined them at Dorothy's invitation." There is a curious chumminess of diction: we find the phrase "baching it" (making do as a bachelor) and the word "rock" jauntily employed above and then in "Flanagan, a rock in a crisis." A manuscript is called a "script," Hemingway's prose described as "carefully beveled" (chiseled?), and the word "dope" used, by my count, six times to mean "information," only once with quotation marks to indicate slang. To be fair, Lingeman can write wittily, as in calling the Lincoln Highway in the Twenties "a notional rather than national road," and in saying of Lewis in Minneapolis society that "his impersonations, raucous speech, love of disputation, and unconventional manners soon mobilized tribal antibodies." But too often he writes like someone with his attention slightly elsewhere, and being editorially advised to get on with it. His biography of Dreiser gave the reader an impression of a basic nobility in the subject, amid considerable muddle and folly. Lewis's foremost virtue comes across as his brute industry: he was heroically able, in whatever unhomey shelter his wanderlust had brought him to, to rise, through whatever grisly thickness of hangover, and go to his typewriter and pound out his daily five thousand words.

Lewis typed with his two forefingers, which as he aged became so sensitive from hard use that he taped them. He produced the lesser novel *The Prodigal Parents* (1938) by writing from five in the morning to seven at night for two months. He composed the 221,000 words of *Main Street* in fourteen weeks, and the four hundred fifty-eight pages of *It Can't Happen Here* (1935) in four months. He did not, like many speed merchants both modern and Victorian, submit first drafts to the printer; he told James Branch Cabell that he had "destroyed all but a few pages" of the first thirty thousand words of *Main Street*, and the editor of his first novel, *Our Mr. Wrenn* (1914), marvelled at the ease and good humor with which he executed suggested revisions. John Hersey, who acted as Lewis's secretary for a summer, was horrified, as he "endlessly" retyped drafts, "to see thousands upon thousands of words—not scattered words and phrases but long passages, whole scenes—ruthlessly slashed out." In England in 1923, Lewis and Arnold Bennett showed each other their manuscripts: Bennett's, of the masterly *Old Wives' Tale*, was, in Lewis's eyes, "a strange MS, handwritten, in the most delicate script, legible as typing, with almost no changes in it, and decorated with colored initials by him, so that it's like a monkish scroll," whereas the first typescript of Lewis's "new novel," presumably *Arrowsmith*, struck Bennett as "all blue and red with millions of alterations,—a terrible sight." Writing was for Lewis an industrial process, of which the first stage was gathering raw material—interviewing specialists such as clergymen and Realtors and occupying relevant terrains (Kansas City for *Elmer Gantry*, Duluth for *Cass Timberlane*). The second stage was turning his notes, outlines, detailed character sketches, careful maps, and extensive synopses (sixty thousand words in *Babbitt*'s case!) into fiction.

The one place he did not scour for dope was within himself. The women and the venues of his life left traces in his imagination, and certain characters speak his mind more than others, but his novels took their inspiration from a sociological topic rather than a confessional or self-exploratory impulse. While drawing on Sauk Centre memories all his life, Lewis never, Schorer points out, wrote the "Moon-Calf" novel so frequent in American literature—the autobiographical account of a "sensitive and misunderstood adolescent" in an unsympathetic environment. Yet young Hal Lewis certainly was a Moon-Calf, spindly, pimply, ill-coördinated, unpopular, romantically book-obsessed. And a Moon-Calf he remained, while acquiring wealth enough to wear London suits, travel through Europe, buy big houses, divorce two women, and get radium treatments for his face, which ravaged it further. I would have welcomed from Lingeman a more detailed medical account of his subject's red, riddled face, for which acne and sun damage seem inadequate diagnoses. Hemingway viciously harped on Lewis's ugliness, even putting it into the novel *Across the River and into the Trees*, though it was Mary Hemingway who, after an encounter with the elderly Lewis in Venice, penned the horrific image "His face was a piece of old liver, shot squarely with a #7 shot at twenty yards."

One wonders how his facial appearance, which might have made many men wish to be inconspicuous, consorted with his insatiable desire to show off and dominate a room. He was compulsively theatrical; as his affair with the young actress Marcella Powers intensified his interest in the stage, he wrote numerous plays and ebulliently acted in other people's, taking such roles as that of the Stage Manager in Thornton Wilder's *Our Town* and, in Paul Vincent Carroll's *Shadow and Substance*, that of a priest opposite Powers's girlish aspirant to sainthood. "The theatre fascinated him," the playwright Marc Connelly later wrote, "but I do not think he ever had any comprehension of its technical demands." Amateur performance was his métier. Bennett, the most sympathetic and patient of Lewis's British observers, noted in his journals:

> Lewis has a habit of breaking into a discussion with long pieces of imaginary conversation between imaginary or real people of the place and period under discussion. Goodish, but too long, with accent, manner, and all complete. He will do this in any discussion; he will drag in a performance, usually full of oaths and blasphemy.

Schorer, finding boyhood acquaintances still alive in Sauk Centre, reported that two of them concurred in remembering Lewis as "a show-off and something of a bore." Corroborative testimony abounds. William E. Woodward, in a 1934 *New Yorker* Profile, allowed, "Even his pleasing talent for impersonation dazes people unless they know him well." Rebecca West, an astute and initially enthusiastic critic of his work, said that his torrent of talk "was wonderful, but after five solid hours of it I ceased to look upon him as a human being." A Minneapolis journalist, William McNally, watching Lewis paralyze local society with "impersonations that went on for hours," concluded, "He cannot travel other than 'on high' and has no brakes." In the aftermath of *Babbitt* he continually talked Babbittese, and when his second wife, the long-suffering Dorothy Thompson, was ushering him, straitjacketed, into an ambulance during an attack of the DTs, he forestalled her reproaches by expertly mimicking her: "You've ruined your life, you're ruining mine! You've ruined your sons, you miserable creature. You're sick, sick."

Mimickry is, of course, a way of avoiding conversation, of drowning out interchange. Lewis, Lingeman says, "had a phobia about being alone," but he contrived to be alone when surrounded by people, deafened by his own "endlessly narratory" voice. One of the few friends who stayed the route with him, Carl Van Doren, said, "What Red doesn't realize is that in order to have friends, one must be willing to suffer a little boredom, and Red has never learned that, and he has almost no friends left." His personal qualities carried into the fiction: it tends to be, aside from some of its well-felt domestic moments, loud and blatant, more performance than picture. Everything illustrates his point. George Babbitt reads the newspaper, with comments to his wife:

> "Lots of news. Terrible big tornado in the South. Hard luck, all right. But this, say, this is corking! Beginning of the end of those fellows! New York Assembly has passed some bills that ought to completely outlaw the socialists! And there's an elevator-runners' strike in New York and a lot of college boys are taking their places. That's the stuff! And a mass-meeting in Birmingham's demanded that this Mick agitator, this fellow De Valera, be deported. Dead right, by golly! All these agitators paid with German gold anyway. And we got no business interfering with the Irish or any other foreign government. Keep our hands strictly off. And there's another well-authenticated rumor from Russia that Lenin is dead. That's fine. It's beyond me why we don't just step in there and kick those Bolshevik cusses out."

Further, his satire, as more politically committed critics pointed out, ends up in a kind of hopeless surrender to the values satirized. No wonder he could never make headway on the big labor novel that he contemplated for decades; his sympathies were thoroughly bourgeois, and his knowingness had to do with the maneuvers whereby the bourgeoisie regroups after a setback and carries on. His novels have happy endings, and when something tragic happened to him, like the death of his elder son, Wells, in World War II, he turned from it. The boy, the product of Lewis's marriage to Grace Hegger, was better than his disrupted upbringing warranted—a graduate of Harvard *magna cum laude*, the promising author of a novel, and such a spit-and-polish aide-de-camp that a German sniper may have shot him under the impression that Wells himself was the general whom he was accompanying in a jeep in Italy. Lewis's reaction was to rebuff expressions of sympathy and treat the grieving mother with what she called an "abominable" coolness.

And yet the single photograph in the bedroom of his Duluth mansion was of Wells. When all complaints about Lewis's rude, skittish, impossible social behavior are registered, there remained something goodhearted about him, as we can read in "First Job," Hersey's account of his pleasant summer with Lewis, a summer when Lewis was not drinking. In a more bluntly rivalrous literary atmosphere than obtains now, he was generous in praise of other writers, even those, like Dreiser and Hemingway, who quarrelled with him. His yen to perform in the theatre and the

lecture hall had its self-abnegating, modest side, and there was a generosity, too, in the topics he chose to address, with his ebbing novelistic
powers, after the war: feminist issues in *Cass Timberlane* (1945) and *World
So Wide* (1951), racism in *Kingsblood Royal* (1947), a melodramatic, slash-
ing book that blacks liked more than whites. Paul Robeson's wife,
Eslanda, wrote him that "It is a beautiful job, and one which Negroes
could not have done, because it just isn't our side of the medal." "Main
Street" and "Babbitt" became glib tags only after he had exercised the
social vision to uncover and name them. John O'Hara—who extended
middle-class realism into a sexual frankness that offended Lewis himself—said, "All the other novelists and journalists and Babbitt himself
were equally blind to Babbitt and Zenith and the United States of
America until 1922." Who in the last century more manfully and systematically attempted to fill the demand, in recent times voiced by Tom
Wolfe and Jonathan Franzen, that American novelists cast off solipsism
and introverted subtlety and embrace the nation as it exists, in its striving
variety and dynamism?

Sauk Centre now holds a Sinclair Lewis Avenue, and boasts on signs of
being "The Original Main Street"—it has enlisted Lewis in the booster-
ism that he mocked. The town is the occasional site of the annual meeting of the Sinclair Lewis Society, which issues, Lingeman says in his
acknowledgments, a "lively newsletter." I have scanned Lingeman's seventy pages of notes and seven pages of bibliography hoping to snag my
eyes on publications since 1961 that might urge an updating of Schorer's
biography, and noticed few. In these forty years a new sexual frankness
has become permitted, if not compulsory, in biography, and Schorer's
explanation of why Michael Lewis, Sinclair's younger son, was forty-five
minutes late for dinner with his father in Rome—"He had been enjoying
Rome during the afternoon and arrived about forty-five minutes late"—
can, with a puzzling change of meal, be amplified by Lingeman to:
"When Michael Lewis arrived at Christmastime, he committed the faux
pas of spending the night with a prostitute he picked up on Via Veneto.
This escapade caused him to arrive late for Lewis's rigidly planned
lunch." Sexual specifics that Thompson confided by letter to Schorer's
discretion can now be broadcast:

> She summed up Lewis's problem as premature ejaculation due to nervous-
> ness: "He could be tender, playful, delightful with women *except* in the
> sexual relationship." She told Schorer that Lewis would "fuck her quick and
> then abuse her verbally."
>
>   Later, Lewis's inadequacies as a lover would drive Dorothy to others for
> affection. As she told Schorer: "All his wives, even when they stuck to him,
> had affairs."

Well, who ever said alcoholic Moon-Calves made great lovers? As for his "alcoholism," the word has taken on, thanks to the helpful credo of Alcoholics Anonymous, the dignity of a disease, whose victims are mired beyond their own willpower. But Lewis could quit, when he wanted to, and the fact that he didn't want to more often suggests a character trait, not a physiological one. The invaluable Thompson (always marry a writer if you want your underside in black and white) recorded in her diary a night when instead of taking her to a full-dress ball as he had promised he called up, said, "I'm shot. . . . Come here, darling," passed out in her arms, woke up enough to make love and buy sausages, in that order, while the "alcohol odor oozing from his pores was 'like rank weeds.' " Next morning, shaky but articulate, he explained that he knew he must choose between spirits and her and he could not give up spirits. From her diary:

> "A man takes a drink," he said, "the drink takes another, and the drink takes the man. And it's got me. I don't know how it began. It was my father and Gracie. They both hated me—and you will hate me too. I am a rotter, but I won't go like Verlaine—like Oscar Wilde. I'll take care not to get that far."

He did get that far, but, dying at the age of sixty-five, took longer than it took Verlaine and Wilde, and longer than his fellow–Midwestern topers Scott Fitzgerald and Ring Lardner. He shared with Thompson that night a no-win/no-lose formulation which left room for doing his work but not any for family life or reflective leisure. His frenetic activity—all those books, all those addresses, all those binges—seems in the retelling one long escape, an anesthetic administered to a peculiarly American pain just before the last screw of his talent could be turned. Rebecca West sagely complained as early as 1927, "If he would sit still so that life could make any deep impression on him, if he would attach himself to the human tradition by occasionally reading a book which would set him a standard of profundity, he could give his genius a chance."

It is the conflicting fate of an American artist to long for profundity while suspecting that, most profoundly, none exists; all is surface, and rather flimsy surface at that. Lewis admired Thoreau, and made fitful retreats into the North American wilderness to regroup his resources, only to fill the tent with the fumes of Scotch and the rattle of his impersonations. Three quotations from Lewis come to mind as epitaphs, two of them cited by Lingeman: "I love America, but I don't like it," and "Everyone ought to have a home to get away from." The third is reported by Schorer, who has the everlasting advantage over his successor biographers of having entered the field when it still held living witnesses: "Once, to the Leonard Bacons, whose very nuzzling dog was giving him a good deal of attention, Lewis said, 'I'm just like this dog. All I want is affection.' " Affection may be what he wanted, but attention is what he got.

A Natural Writer

THE ART OF BURNING BRIDGES: *A Life of John O'Hara*, by Geoffrey Wolff. 373 pp. Knopf, 2003.

What has moved Geoffrey Wolff, author of six novels and two previous biographies, to write a life of John O'Hara? Though O'Hara while he was alive felt, for all the fame and wealth his writings earned him, relatively slighted by critics and prize-givers, he became in the decade after his death, in 1970, the subject of three separate biographies: *O'Hara*, by his friend Finis Farr (1973); *The O'Hara Concern*, a "laborious excavation" (in Wolff's phrase) by that tireless excavator of twentieth-century American literary leavings, Matthew J. Bruccoli (1975); and Frank Mac-Shane's efficient, judicious *Life of John O'Hara* (1980). Also, in 1971 and 1972 the *Pottsville Republican* ran a series of articles on O'Hara's early life by Charles W. Bassett, and in 1977 Bruccoli edited and published a collection of O'Hara's writings on writing, off-puttingly titled (with quotation marks) "*An Artist Is His Own Fault*." The next year, the great excavator came up with a valuable selection of O'Hara's letters, along with *John O'Hara: A Descriptive Bibliography*, which includes even the blurbs wrung from the famous author on behalf of other people's books. Decades after this flurry of posthumous attention, Wolff has evidently judged O'Hara ripe for a more personal treatment, a kind of interactive biography, in which his own voice and opinions freely vie, like a post-Freudian psychiatrist's, with those of his subject.

As a biographer, Wolff has been drawn to mismanaged lives: *Black Sun* (1976), subtitled *The Brief Transit and Violent Eclipse of Harry Crosby*, told of a self-dramatizing Boston Brahmin who figured as a poet and publisher in Paris literary circles before committing suicide in 1929, at the age of thirty-one; *The Duke of Deception* described, as best it could, Wolff's father, an elusive, dandified, debt-ridden con man. With his father, the personal tone was unavoidable. With O'Hara, it sometimes comes off as pushy and presumptuous:

Oh, was Dr. O'Hara cross when his son came home with his skeptical airs and a pink slip! Well, if Fordham wasn't a sufficient social and intellectual challenge for his exacting Johnny-boy, how about Keystone Normal School (say what?) in Kutztown, midway between Allentown and Reading in Mennonite country, where the flappers and philosophers journeyed downtown by horse and buggy, wearing black suits and ankle-length bulletproof skirts.

When O'Hara, late in a well-lubricated evening with the Brendan Gills, emerged from his bedroom wearing full cowboy regalia, the Gills laughed, but Wolff fumes, " 'Cowboy-crazy' after all! And how predictably silly was O'Hara's bristling fury! So why is it that my sympathy—indeed a feeling of full-hearted fraternity—is drawn to the ridiculous yob with the big, boozy face?" The trouble with such generously bestowed fraternity is that O'Hara wasn't only, or even primarily, a ridiculous yob; he was a sensitive and productive literary artist, with some alcohol and anger problems. Unlike Harry Crosby and Duke Wolff, he did not ruinously mismanage his life. He was too cantankerous and late-rising to hold a job for long, but this was a mercy in disguise; it kept him at what he did best, free-lance fiction writing. He flirted with but never succumbed to professional disaster, producing his pages through many a hangover and giving up alcohol at the point where continuing to drink might have killed him.

He did not win the Nobel Prize he hankered for, but he was not a loser. He was an Irish-Catholic prep-school dropout from the Pennsylvania coal regions; cast as a teen-ager from the comfortable middle class by the death of his father, an admired doctor, at the age of fifty-seven, he became one of the best and richest writers of his time, a time overshadowed by Hemingway, Faulkner, and Fitzgerald. Amid the appurtenances of financial success (tweed suits, memberships, Rolls-Royces, interviews), he kept an artist's embattled integrity and an artist's renewable freshness. His last short story for The New Yorker, titled "How Old, How Young" (1967), was one of his best. It is true that, especially before his second marriage, in 1937, to Belle Wylie, O'Hara acquired the reputation, through numerous accumulated anecdotes, of a very nasty drunk, capable of physically assaulting not only women ("Although I may often have felt like belting a woman," he pleaded in extenuation, "I have never actually taken a poke at one except in anger") but a dwarf, in a well-witnessed incident at "21." In Hollywood, just before falling in love with Belle, O'Hara behaved badly enough at a party to call Robert Benchley, whom he had taken a swing at, the next morning to apologize. The mild-mannered Benchley responded, "For what, John? . . . You're a shit and everybody knows you're a shit, and people ask you out in spite of it. It's nothing to apologize about." But to this same untethered, roistering period belong his first and best novel, *Appointment in Samarra*, and many of his finest stories, nurtured on the very binges and grudges that fuelled his misbehavior. Bars were a venue of research for him, and resentment an instrument of social analysis.

Wolff as a biographer is drawn to personality puzzles: his father and Harry Crosby were gifted men who went bad; O'Hara poses a reverse puzzle. How did a man so coarse and dislikable and, in social matters, so self-defeatingly defensive and overeager manage to write so well, with such empathy and tact? Specifically, how did O'Hara, despite Harold Ross's personal dislike of him, manage to sell so many stories (a record number, in the end) to *The New Yorker*? His contributions appeared early in the magazine's existence and were copiously revived in 1960, after an eleven-year break wrought by O'Hara in the wake of Brendan Gill's sardonic review of *A Rage to Live*. Wolff does not, it seemed to me, get *The New Yorker* exactly right. It is not true, as he asserts, that John Cheever's "The Swimmer" was "so abundant in its deliberate improbabilities and dislocations that it had to be published by *Playboy*." *The New Yorker* published it, in the issue of July 18, 1964. Nor is it the case that "very short pieces" were "what the magazine called 'casuals.'" Strange to say, *any* piece of fiction, however extended and ambitious, was called a casual. More important, Wolff, drawing upon *New Yorker* archives deposited in the New York Public Library, accuses O'Hara's long-time editorial champion, Katharine White, of condescension, nitpicking, prudery, and even of wanting to knock his word-rate, elevated by Ross to a dime, down to nine cents. An editor and a writer will have differences, but I think Wolff, borrowing prickliness from his subject, reads too much into Mrs. White's polite cavils and "long-faced" rejections "expressed with regretful and self-justifying delicacy." He finds that a sketch of O'Hara she wrote for her archive at Bryn Mawr (oh, those poisonous archives!) reveals an "essential disdain" achieved from a "vantage . . . always from on high, looking down." Against her claim that she and Ross "coddled" O'Hara, Wolff argues that "the record" shows the writer "dismissed, mocked, scolded, and almost always patronized." Well, the record also shows that *The New Yorker* published most of the O'Hara still worth rereading, and that up to his break with it in 1949 he repeatedly took refuge in its pages, after bruising encounters with the Hollywood script mills and the reviewers of his novels.

Anyone who reads, in O'Hara's *Selected Letters*, the run beginning "Dear Mrs. Angell" and mounting to such friendly salutations as "Dear Katharine" and even "Dear Kate," gets a different impression, of a brisk and hopeful editorial relationship, long on business and short on extraneous courtesies. Bruccoli's biography reports, "Mrs. Angell regarded O'Hara as a lovable man"; in an interview with Bruccoli she declared, "John O'Hara cared about people and was essentially a kind man and a real friend, which few egotists are." Any healthy relationship is based on mutual advantage; in this case, the editor needs something to publish and the writer needs a buyer. O'Hara needed *The New Yorker*, for its prestige as much as for its modest pay, enough to ride out editorial friction; Wolff rather ingenuously marvels that O'Hara "never seemed fully to recognize [Ross's] antipathy." To have recognized the antipathy would not have served his literary purpose. He had to overlook and persevere, instead. Wolff acknowledges that "it was no small thanks to Katharine Angell and others with influence that he surmounted the high barrier of the boss editor's distaste."

Mrs. White once confided to this reviewer a sidelight on the famous break of 1949, which she claimed had less to do with Gill's panning than with O'Hara's demand, as Wolff describes it, that the magazine pay him a $250 kill fee for each story submitted and returned. This impossible demand had reasoning behind it: O'Hara felt that *New Yorker* short stories were so specialized, so subtle and slight, that a writer could not sell elsewhere a story written with its pages in mind. (In a letter to his other editor, William Maxwell, in 1939, he said, "I write it so that The New Yorker will buy it. It won't go anywhere else.") It seems undeniable that his penchant for brand-name-dropping and for run-on dialogue was beneficially curbed by this one magazine's scope; the small bottle improved the wine. Perhaps only an editorial policy determined to capture "the real thing" (a phrase of William Shawn's as well as of Henry James's) with "casuals" light on contrivance and melodrama would have embraced stories as wryly minimal, as poemlike in their deceptively uninflected realism, as O'Hara's.

In the course of tracing his subject's fortunes, Geoffrey Wolff imparts plenty of his own views on writing. Frequently, he resorts to an expansive first-person singular; e.g., "Writing these words, I feel more than a little discomfort about subverting my conviction that a novelist is bound to honor only what provokes his or her interest. To hold that a writer owes the reader a damned thing (and vice versa) . . . is to traffic in Hallmark sentiment, to make a plea for moral fiction, for allegory, for vulgarity." Literary matters excite him to some fearful syntactical contortions:

What happened to O'Hara in Pottsville during those dark months in 1930 of soul-scouring can't be specified, but it's reasonable to guess that he sounded a kind of abyss. Writers—or anyone who has suffered the flu—will recognize that odd state he must have entered, a numb reverie not unlike the fevered sweats Keats endured from consumption, and an extraordinary out-of-himself (gussied up in Keats's case as selfless "poetical character . . . not itself, everything and nothing," having "no Identity," continually "filling some other Body")* physiologically congruent with the creative state.

The asterisk directs us to the footnote "To Richard Woodhouse, October 27, 1818." Wolff's other biographies were composed with a certain taut incisiveness; this one, especially in the second half, relaxes into colloquial asides, parentheses, and proliferating footnotes. Like a writing instructor with the end of term in sight, dishevelled and chatty, he confidentially shares insider information. Of rejection: "Writers never forget that particular pain, a stab of shame that something tended and tendered has been repulsed." Of finishing up: "It is difficult to overstate the retrospective euphoria that coherent work, however painful or shaming the story being told, can confer on a writer." Of revision: "There's always in the writing of a novel the difficulty of ongoing revision, of amending on page two hundred of a manuscript a detail that creates a trickle-back adjustment to myriad tributary passages upstream." Of submission: "This is not an unusual response—postcoital tristesse, postpartum blues—for the surrender of a book to an editor." Of ruthless ego: "Whatever decency a writer salvages from his personal history, moral punctilio, bushido, or common consideration is incidental to a writer's essential selfishness." Of characters: "Fiction writers are in the business of cornering their characters. Their work lives by the principle of obstacle and resistance, its heat issuing from friction." These aperçus are nicely turned and keenly felt, but the reader suspects they tell us more about the cogitations and travails of Geoffrey Wolff than those of "a natural writer," as O'Hara described himself in his exuberant foreword to his 1961 collection, *Assembly*. William Shawn, no gossip, once allowed to me, in his murmurous but definitive way, that O'Hara was "not very self-critical."

His long novels were typeset from first drafts belted out on his typewriter in the wee hours of the morning. He bragged to Lucius Beebe that his short stories for *The New Yorker* never took him more than two hours to write. Mrs. White winced when the hurry showed, lamenting, "I really do think you are a first-rate writer and only suffer from haste or something." She took a stab at the "something" by saying, of a rejected story, "It now seems as if the writer didn't care, had no emotion about the whole thing." But O'Hara was a reluctant reviser, unable to enrich material that already seemed to him self-evidently rich. The *premier coup*

speed and flatness, of course, are what makes the best of O'Hara so unnerving: the stories, so lightly, declaratively engraved on their plain surfaces, open on depths that swallow us. Wolff may be right in suggesting that the formative minds of *The New Yorker* could not quite place O'Hara. Wolcott Gibbs, a fellow-drinker who managed the difficult trick of a long friendship with the pugnacious author, in his introduction to O'Hara's collection *Pipe Night* wrote that "his range of subject and treatment is too great for an editorial mind accustomed to writers, generally speaking, as rigidly typed as the seals in the circus." O'Hara's being "equally at home in all these worlds" is an "inexplicable gift" to "a man [Gibbs] who has never really grasped any social system more intricate than the one obtaining at the Riverdale Country School."

The New Yorker of those years, jealously staking out its turf in the morass of American culture, did not encourage its contributors to venture beyond the magazine; O'Hara's raw and roaming ambition, as well as his gruff manners, lifted Eustace Tilley's eyebrow. Gibbs's collection *A Season in the Sun* (1946), dedicated to O'Hara and almost entirely pre-published in *The New Yorker*, depicts the lazy, boozy, sun-soaked Long Island beach life both men enjoyed; one story, "Love, Love, Love," contains a character, the autobiographical protagonist George Crane's friend Mark Anderson, whom I take to be, in part, O'Hara. My suspicions are strengthened by a hidden clue: Gibbs's story alludes to a malapropism, "crypty" (for "cryptic"), that O'Hara coined as the climax of his story "I Could Have Had a Yacht." Anderson is described as amiable, with a reservation:

> Lately, however, there had been a distinct feeling of strain and a kind of spiritual absence, as if he were turning weighty problems over in his mind. At first, Mr. Crane had put this down to literary abstraction, for Mr. Anderson was a writer, the author of two novels having to do with mild sexual confusion in fashionable circles. . . . At the moment, he was living on the proceeds from his second book, *Penelope*, the story of a constant but relentlessly talkative wife, which had been sold to the movies. Mr. Crane now decided that there was nothing in his friend's career that could warrant the deep and apparently permanent depression into which he seemed plunged. Even if he was planning a sequel to *Penelope*, his writing required no dark and anxious searching of the soul; all it needed was a typewriter and sufficient energy to manipulate it.

This is fiction, but it has, for me, the clang of truth, one worldly writer's sneer at another, a typist with energy. The conundrum "How did this rough beast, at his best, write so well?" remains. "A Respectable Place," the final story in the Modern Library *Selected Short Stories of John*

O'Hara, to which Lionel Trilling wrote the eloquent introduction, never fails to stun me as it briskly shows how a neighborhood bar, maintained by its owner, Matty Wall, as "a respectable place," is destroyed by a corrupt civic establishment, chiefly the police force, because a drunken cop once shot up the place and Matty accepted the offered restitution. The little conversational steps whereby unanswerable injustice is achieved have the beauty of a dance, down to the last pirouette, in which Matty Wall stands all drinks on the house: "This was strictly against the law, but Matty knew he wasn't going to open up again." In the introduction, published in 1956, before O'Hara had befouled his reputation with too many sprawling, best-selling novels, Trilling likens him to Kafka, in his "imagination of society as some strange sentient organism which acts by laws of its own being which are not to be understood; one does not know what will set into motion its dull implacable hostility, some small thing, not very wrong, not wrong at all; once it begins to move, no one can stand against it." The comparison might be extended to the observation that, though Hermann Kafka and Dr. Patrick O'Hara were impressive in different ways, both left haunting, unappeasable images in their sons' imaginations.

And yet the ultimate units of society, the human individuals lost within the crushing agglomeration of hostility, rivalry, snobbery, exclusion, and defeat that O'Hara felt in his bones, have hopes and passions, and can be regarded with tenderness by a writer whose bleak style seems at first not to care. A small story from *Files on Parade* (1939) titled "By Way of Yonkers" sticks in my mind as especially moving. Its two principals, the young woman unnamed and the man named only in the last sentence, exist on the lower levels of Depression survival. She, with her gunmetal stockings and Cossack hat and "neat, short nose with jigsaw nostrils," seems to be a hooker. She arrives at the man's shabby apartment so late that he tells her she must have come by way of Yonkers, and when he asks "How'd you do?" of the engagement that delayed her she not quite evades the question:

> "Oh—" she said it very high. Then: "All right. Financially. But do we have to talk about it? You and me?"

She talks instead about her fading appetite for liquor, and the expense of dental care. He, lying inert and fully dressed on his bed, talks of being broke, of not wanting to take money from her, of how he can't seem "to make a connection in this town." The town is New York, and he is a minor gangster thrown out of work by the repeal of Prohibition. But he has met a man who offered him a connection in Milwaukee, and he is going to go there for a long time. The concluding words are unspectacular and unexpectedly sweeping:

> [She asks,] "Any chance you being back in town soon?"
> "Well, not right away, honey. First I have to build up my connection again."
> "Well, I don't have to tell you, I'm glad for you. It's about time you got a good break." She resumed rubbing his ankle. He put his hand on the top of her head.
> "Yeah? You're as good a break as I ever got."
> "Ah, Christ, Bill," she said, and fell face down in tears.

We are moved not only by their plight of presumably eternal separation but by the dignity that O'Hara, in a literary era of programmatic proletarian advocacy (Odets and Steinbeck and Mike Gold), instinctively brings to his two specimens of lowlife. He does not view them politically, from above; he is there in the room with them; we feel the unspoken presence of an author so knowing, so unjudgmental, so nearly an outcast himself.

Wolff, unlike O'Hara's other biographers, shortcuts the four exhaustingly circumstantial, commercially successful, and sometimes prize-winning later novels in one chapter, "The Tomes." He complains of their prolixity, their reliance on characters' suicides, their "leering tropism for the border dividing sex from violence," their tendency "to dash expository cold water on a character's fevered exclamations from narrative ambush," and their breakdown "in voice, pacing, proportion, energy of character, psychological credibility, and moral vision." He even quotes again, approvingly this time around, from Gill's *Rage to Live* review— which ends, we should remember, with the inverted compliment "It is because of O'Hara's distinction that his failure here seems in the same nature of a catastrophe."

Wolff's first chapter, "The Region," interestingly dwells on the advantages of Pottsville for a would-be writer. A shadow of itself now—"sooty, grim, and used-up," Wolff writes, and quotes a 1984 article in the *Philadelphia Inquirer* that quipped, "Even the parking meters look cold and penniless"—Pottsville still teemed during O'Hara's youth. With an ethnic diversity including Pennsylvania Dutch farmers, Irish and Welsh coal miners, Lithuanians, Hungarians, Swedes, and the predominantly Anglo-Saxon, Protestant aristocracy of bankers and managers thriving on the anthracite industry, the town was a treasury of class distinctions and yet small enough, at around twenty-five thousand, so that all its elements rubbed elbows. A doctor and his eldest son sampled this society at every stratum, and the particular democracy of Prohibition mingled gangsters and molls with the country-club set, of which the O'Haras, though Irish, were dancing, horse-riding members. Dr. O'Hara's early death and unthrifty estate management, it might be said, extended John's social education, through his jobs in local journalism, to much more eventual profit than admission to the young man's envisioned paradise of Yale and its clubs would have.

Even in the bitter taste that its provincial meanness left in his mouth, Pottsville—where some remembered John O'Hara as "a bum" who "told a lot of lies about this town"—was a good environment for a writer to come from, which is not to say that a writer had to emerge. There are many more places than writers to immortalize them, and other national literary figures that hail from the Schuylkill Valley, such as Conrad Richter and Wallace Stevens, sublimated their experience of these gritty environs into a much hazier lyricism. A talent like O'Hara's is multiply determined, and jiggling the multiples will be an attractive challenge as long as a writer has readers. We want to revisit and understand the pleasure we have been given. "Good writers deserve to be remembered," Wolff was told by William Maxwell, who of *New Yorker* personnel receives the biographer's best review, for editing O'Hara for years without undue contention and for responding to Wolff's inquiries by typing his cogent answers on the spot. In *The Art of Burning Bridges* (a title, like much of the text, a touch over the top), a biography is imbued with not just curiosity and memorial admiration but an invigorating sense of rivalry and, across the years, comradeship.

Young Iris

IRIS MURDOCH: *A Life*, by Peter J. Conradi. 658 pp. Norton, 2001.

There would be no need to complain of literary biographies—so often superfluous, bloated, and carping—if they were all as good as Peter J. Conradi's life of Iris Murdoch. Conradi offers a real expansion of our sense of the pre-eminent English novelist of the second half of the twentieth century; he brings to the table personal and literary intimacy with his subject, and a treasure lode of hitherto unpublished journals that she kept (with some post-factum excisions) since her college days, plus caches of her letters retained by their recipients. A professor emeritus of English at Kingston University, he had been acquainted with Murdoch and her husband, John Bayley, since 1981, and was especially friendly in the last decade of the century, as Murdoch, from about 1994 on, slowly sank into the fog of Alzheimer's disease. Upon her death in 1999, Conradi was named her co-executor. The matter of his writing her biography came up while she was still alive, and, though self-effacing and considerably secretive, she gave him her blessing in 1997, saying simply, "You're a good friend." In her remaining few years, to the extent she was able, she collaborated with him by providing interviews and suggesting contacts. Conradi had, in 1986, written a book-length study of her work (*Iris Murdoch: The Saint and the Artist*) and, in 1997, collected her essays, under the title *Existentialists and Mystics*. He is fond but not infatuated: he strives to see, with an occasional touch of irritation, into the sometimes murky psychology of his voluble, seductive subject. On the second page of *The Saint and the Artist*, he provides as brisk a summary of her artistic failings as an adverse critic could desire:

> She can be uneven, over-intellectual or romantic. There is some unfinished and repetitive writing. The books can seem contrived or over-plotted, the characters sometimes insufficiently imagined. Her social range is not huge, she says little about work and often appears to take money for granted. She can seem to be playing a complex game with the reader. There is, as early reviewers noted, "too much" in the books.

His biography, his introduction says, "might have been entitled 'Young Iris' "; it is preponderantly concerned with the relatively obscure years between Murdoch's birth in 1919 and the mid-Fifties, when, with the publication of her first novel in 1954 and her marriage to John Bayley in 1956, her restless questings—intellectual, religious, and amorous—arrived at a settled vocation and permanent relationship. But Conradi's critical acumen and literary learning also illuminate Old Iris as he surveys a massive oeuvre and an increasingly public existence. For example: "Her best fiction is part-fed by a species of cool rage which may relate to a radical *contemptus mundi et vitae*, but is sufficiently rooted in the world for it to live in the imagination of the reader." With delicacy and a finely apt quotation, he measures out judgment on the propriety of Bayley's loving yet ruthlessly exposing memoir *Elegy for Iris*, which, published while Murdoch was still alive, brought letters of gratitude from other caretakers of Alzheimer's victims but also protests from those who, Conradi writes,

> felt Iris was cast in this very public role of quixotic benefactress without her consent. Like the gentleman witnessing Lear's madness, it was a "sight most pitiful in the meanest wretch / Past speaking of in a king!"

The biographer relays Francis Wyndham's comically majestic picture of Murdoch at her desk: "Like a Henry Moore statue seated between two massive piles of manuscript, moving only to write, one pile of empty paper, the other full, her industry phenomenal." Of the not infrequent carelessness of her writing, and her spurning of editorial advice (most persistently offered by her American publisher, Viking), he cites Plato's "emphasis on the provisionality of all imagery" and her own remark, in a review of a book by her acolyte A. S. Byatt, that the novel is "the most imperfect of art-forms"; we are led to the conclusion that a spiritual virtue of sorts, a way "to escape definition," lay behind "the wilful obstinacy of her imperfection—as in her refusal to be edited."

Along with its felicities of perception, its warm sympathy with its subject, and its wealth of fresh material, Conradi's book has a few imperfections of its own, including some woolly sentences and misattached modifiers surprising in an English professor, e.g., "Like William Golding, and perhaps Muriel Spark, the Second World War made Iris think anew about human wickedness and irrationality," and the sentence quoting Shakespeare above: *what* is "like the gentleman witnessing," etc.? And there are oddities of format. The ample, sprightly notes in the back are difficult to consult, since they are headed only by chapter numbers while the chapter running heads give only the titles. Divisions within the chapters are marked by spelled-out numbers in capital letters, a distractingly obtrusive device that possibly, in its extra distinctness, has the advantage of enabling Conradi to cover a large territory in swift strides: the chapter titled "Discontinuities" takes up, in sections of a thousand or two words, Murdoch's dim sense of personal identity, her fitful artistic connection with the theatre, her disappointments with film adaptations of her novels, her happy marriage (she called her husband "Puss" and signed her checks "Iris Bayley"), her love of urban anonymity, her Buddhism and Platonism, learning languages as her "only recreation," and "four lesser novels from the 1970s."

John Bayley's memoir and Conradi's life both emphasize Murdoch's selflessness. "Nobody less narcissistic than Iris can well be imagined," Bayley writes, and observes that, as Alzheimer's closed in, "Iris's own lack of a sense of identity seemed to float her more gently into its world of preoccupied emptiness." Conradi, a practicing Buddhist who rejoiced with Murdoch in the possibility of a Godless religion, approvingly writes that "Both the saint and the true artist were equally, in her coinage, 'unpersons.' " And yet the young Iris abounded with a good firm sense of herself, enough so that as a schoolgirl "she *didn't care much what people thought*. . . . She was there to get on with things and enjoy them." The cherished only child of a Protestant Irish couple transplanted to England, she remembered her isolated little family as "a perfect trinity of love." (She made much of her Irishness in interviews, and, indeed, was born in Dublin and spoke with a brogue. Yet at the time of her birth, Conradi shows, her father, a civil servant from Belfast who had served as an officer in the British army for three years of the First World War, had moved to London and was working there. The baby and her mother, a gifted singer from a colorful family of faded Dublin gentry, the Richardsons, followed within a year.) Iris had an English upbringing, enlivened by summer visits to her many Irish relatives. The Chapmans of Portrush remembered her childhood personality as one of "goodness, kind-heartedness, strangeness, strong will and shyness"; a friend from Oxford recalled "something 'aboriginal' in Iris—'simplicity, naiveté, power, and space.' "

Her father, a gentle, bookish, and modestly paid clerk in the Ministry of Health, scrimped and borrowed to send her to expensive progressive schools. At the age of five, she was enrolled at the Froebel Demonstration School, near their home in London's West End; the Scots headmistress, Ethel M. Bain, led her charges in elaborate chivalric rites that included jousting with "King Bain" and eating a boar's head concocted of sponge cake. At the age of thirteen, Iris went away to Badminton School, in a suburb of Bristol, on a scholarship, which gave rise to the taunt, in a letter from her fellow-writer Brigid Brophy, that she had been a "poor girl who only just made it into a rich girls' school." The headmistress, the formidable Beatrice May Baker—who until her death at ninety-seven remained a friend of Murdoch's—exposed her rich girls to a regimen of cold baths in the morning, serious academic studies, and, as fascism took hold on the Continent, left-wing idealism. A teacher recalled Iris as "a good hockey player, interested in and gifted at art (painting), not particularly musical, though she 'had a go,' but excelling at classics and English." Conradi adds, "It would not be surprising if Iris's omnicompetence aroused dislike or envy; none has stepped forward to say it did." By her senior year she was head girl and translating Sophocles, praising the Soviet Union, meeting W. H. Auden, winning prizes, editing a collection of poems by Bristol schoolchildren, and conducting her first romance, initially an epistolary one, with James Henderson Scott, a poetry-writing Belfast dentistry student and a convert from Methodism to Catholicism. After they met, she cooled the romance, though they did sail to Belfast together and "climbed the tower of Queen's University, tying a friend's pyjamas to the flagpost." Scott recovered enough from Iris's rejection to fall in love elsewhere and to give his inaugural lecture as professor of dental anatomy at Queen's in blank verse. When he died, she wrote his widow that he had been to her a "great awakener."

There was much awakening to come. She won a stipend of forty pounds a year for three years at Somerville College at Oxford. Women were still, the acting dean warned the new students, "very much on probation in this University. You may think that it doesn't matter if you do something a little wild, but I can tell you that it will." Wild Iris took root; while remaining a virgin, she fended off as many as six proposals of marriage in one term. Michael Foot, a fellow-Oxonian who was to be one of her conquests, recalled that "practically everyone who was up with Iris fell for her. She had personality and that wonderful Irish voice." She also had a stocky figure and an arguably plain face, but it was left to her prospective mother-in-law to remark, in 1954, "She's like a little bull!" Of her Oxford years, Iris later wrote, "My God, that was a golden time." Many of her college friends remained so for the rest of her life. Conradi explains, "Friendships formed just before the war partook of the same intensity as did politics and love; no one, after all, knew who would survive the coming onslaught." Murdoch had intended to study English but switched to classics—"Mods and Greats"—a degree that took four years instead of three. She joined the Communist Party, probably in 1938, and spent two August weeks in 1939, the last days of peace, touring with the Magpie Players, singing and "enacting the roles of 'care-free students.' " Among the men who engaged her interest at Oxford were Frank Thompson, a poet and Wykehamist who spoke six languages, enlisted in 1939, and eloquently corresponded with Iris until his death in Bulgaria in 1944; Eduard Fraenkel, a refugee Jewish classical scholar, physically deformed and intellectually intimidating, who taught her in his *Agamemnon* seminar; and Donald MacKinnon, another instructor, a High Anglo-Catholic who taught philosophy and was, according to George Steiner, "that most searching of modern British moral philosophers." Her involvement with all three was chaste but passionate; they enamored her mind and haunt her fiction.

In 1942 she graduated from Oxford with a first and, having registered as "willing to carry out war work in the short-staffed civil service," was assigned to the Treasury and moved to London. She resigned from the Communist Party, possibly on the Party's advice, and omnicompetently became expert in the details and mathematics of government bureaucracy. She found a quaint flat, 5 Seaforth Place, in a tiny alley off Buckingham Gate, and shared it with Philippa Bosanquet, a lifelong Oxford friend and an eventual philosopher of note. Early in 1943, with typical honesty and dispassion, Iris wrote to Frank Thompson some personal news:

I should tell you that I have parted company with my virginity. This I regard as in every way a good thing. I feel calmer & freer—relieved from something which was obsessing me, & made free of a new field of experience. There have been two men. I don't think I love either of them—but I like them. . . . I am not just going wild. In spite of a certain amount of wild talk I still live my life with deliberation.

In 1944 she applied to join the United Nations Relief and Rehabilitation Association. She worked in the London office for fifteen months, acting as a secretary and calculating postwar salaries for civil servants drafted into war work. After a stint in Brussels, she was posted to Innsbruck, the headquarters of the French zone of Austria, to Puch, in the American zone and, finally, to Klagenfurt and Graz, in the British zone. This Continental tour, which ended in July of 1946, reinforced her cosmopolitan tendencies; she met Sartre and Raymond Queneau, read Rilke and Simone de Beauvoir, and imbibed the astringent but intoxicating liqueurs of existentialism. She was also exposed, close at hand, to the misery of war and its aftermath, which had created millions of displaced persons, many of whom were repatriated to certain death in Stalin's Russia or Tito's Yugoslavia. Refugees and exiles henceforth figured heavily in her personal acquaintance and in her literary imagination. She herself became, once she returned to England, a sort of displaced person, academic but not quickly assimilated by academe. She won a Commonwealth Scholarship to Vassar, but admitted on the visa application form that she had been a member of the Communist Party, and was denied entry under the McCarran-Walter Act. (Hence the United States, though she did eventually visit a few times with her husband, is a distant, fabulous, forbidding realm in her fiction; she has no American novel like Muriel Spark's *The Hothouse by the East River* or Martin Amis's *Money*.) Conradi marks this postwar period as her low point:

> The failure of her attempt to get to Vassar left her depressed, lost, lacking the sense of a future. She was unemployed from July 1946 until she went up to Cambridge in October 1947, and her financial situation was dire. Under a photograph of herself taken that bitter winter of 1946–47, in a cold and snowy London, she wrote in her photograph album a single, expressive word: "Nadir."

It was in this desolate time, when neither her romances nor her attempted novels were working out, that she drew closest to Anglo-Catholicism, befriending clerics and converts, drawing too close to Donald MacKinnon for his wife's comfort, and reading the writers made fashionable by Christian existentialism—Unamuno, Heidegger, Berdyaev, Kierkegaard, Simone Weil, Gabriel Marcel. At Cambridge, where she had been granted a studentship in philosophy, she met

Wittgenstein, but did not quite fall under his spell; she seemed, according to the writer Elizabeth Sewell, "really a stranger," who "never fit in." However, her faithful friend Philippa, now Philippa Foot, told her of a philosophy tutorship at Saint Anne's College, Oxford, and when Murdoch won the job in July of 1948 her life got back on track, a track it never left: Oxford became her professional and imaginative base of operations—a sheltered theatre of philosophical and erotic venturing, an island of dreaming towers wherein men and women flitted and form-shifted with the freedom of bodiless spirits, in an ether of intelligent self-regard and benign androgyny, Prospero and Ariel intertwined and not even Caliban denied his portion of love.

After parting company with her virginity, young Iris had become a bold and busy sexual adventuress. The loved child had grown to be a love addict. Her entanglements have the prolixity more of the Sixties and Seventies than of the Forties and Fifties. Looking back, in 1968, on her journals from 1945 onward, she noted, "That business of falling in love with A, then with B, then with C (all madly) seems a bit sickening." In medias res, however, in 1952, she pleaded in her journal, "I mustn't live in this torment of emotion," and then parenthetically added, "(Empty words—I shall always live so)." In 1948 she wrote, "One of my fundamental assumptions is that I have the power to seduce anyone." The main men, after the mysterious two in 1943, were Michael Foot (Iris was his first lover, and, when rejected by her, he was accepted by her flatmate Philippa); Tommy Balogh (a "brilliant but abrasive" Oxford tutor, he had been Philippa's lover and, fickle as he was, gave Iris much grief); David Hicks (he was the first man to kiss her, in 1938, and in 1946 jilted her after a whirlwind engagement); Franz Steiner (a frail, polymathic Czech-German Jewish anthropologist and religious poet styled by Iris "the most beloved" of "my Jewish teachers," he had a heart condition that made physical intimacy perilous and brought about his death at the age of forty-three); Arnoldo Momigliano (this Jewish Italian scholar came up to Oxford from London on weekends, read Dante with Iris in her flat, and travelled with her several times in Italy); and, making the biggest impact of all, Elias Canetti. A Sephardic Jew born in Bulgaria, Canetti lived in England for most of his life but composed his sinister, Nobel Prize–winning works in German. Introduced to Iris by Franz Steiner, he ensnared her in his tyrannical London ménage, which included his one-armed wife, Veza, and his slavish mistress, Friedl; he became the archetype of all the domineering monster-masters in her fiction. With uncharacteristic explicitness she described their lovemaking in her journals:

[He] held me savagely between his knees & grasps my hair and forces my head back. His power. He subjugates me completely. Only such a complete intellectual & moral ascendancy could hold me.

Canetti's fierce spell was incongruously broken by the advent of mild, innocent, stammering, hyper-English John Bayley. From 1953 to 1956, the two men warred in her affections, which were not confined to the list above, or altogether to men. The triumphant Bayley was awarded with a solemnly confessed roll call of his predecessors, as we read in his *Elegy for Iris*:

Had I not heard all about them, the people of her past and present, at one time or another during the period of our own intimacy?

It appeared that I had not. Unknown figures arose before me like the procession of kings in *Macbeth*, seeming to regard me with grave curiosity as they passed by. There was so-and-so with whom she had first been to bed, and so-and-so and so-and-so who had wanted to marry her. . . . There seemed so many of them, these fortunate persons, and to my amazement, I had just learned that some quite ordinary people, as I thought of them, acquaintances and even colleagues of my own, had at some time or other in the past been recipients of Iris's kindness. They had desired her, and not been rejected.

At the age of thirty-seven, Murdoch married a man six years younger and lived with him, in Oxfordshire houses famous for their messiness, like a (Bayley's word) "co-child." She had cleared the decks for what her journal a couple of years earlier announced: "My task after all to write—thank God for this much of a solution." Her tumultuous love life had been a long tutorial in suffering, power, treachery, and bliss; the romantic seethe was for her, like the sea for Conrad and war for Hemingway, a treasury of essential impression. Her promiscuity, if we call it that, manifested the openness of which other aspects were her avid intellectual appetite, the empathy with others that made her a famously kind and attentive friend, and the "Negative Capability" that Keats named as Shakespeare's creative secret. When we read Murdoch we feel the ideas and images and imagined personalities pouring through her, unobstructed, cumulative, complicating, gaining power over her mind "without," as Keats said, "any irritable reaching after fact and reason."

Her published novels began sharp, terse, angular, and blithely enigmatic, on the French model of Queneau, and she ended as one of the most expansive and leisurely expositors since the Victorians. Her early mode achieved its masterpiece in *A Severed Head*, a glittering *ronde* of pairings among the London elegant, capped by a gender inversion of the author's harsh and magical affair with Canetti, whose Jewish sorcery was transposed onto the idol-like figure of Honor Klein. I remember that book being passed around among young suburban couples in the early Sixties as a species of *news*. This news—that love is everywhere, violent, protean, consuming, comical, cruel—never grew stale for her, though for the reader the filaments she spun from this centrifuge could feel, even in the best of her late books like *The Sea, The Sea* and *The Philosopher's Pupil*, a bit like cotton candy. We bite down on air, on life as all illusion. Her characters make an exclusive diet of one another; she once defined happiness as "to be utterly absorbed in at least six other human beings." Utter absorption can cloy. Murdoch gives her characters the full benefit of her past emotional tumult but sometimes denies them what Conradi calls "her own native good sense, that of a cheerful, prudent Ulsterwoman." The philosophical problem she insistently poses—can the Good survive the death of God?—pales to abstraction amid the demonic mischief and moral anarchy of her plots. Indubitably concrete and alive are her world's details, human, animal, mineral, behavioral, and atmospheric. The descriptions of nature, dashed down in commaless strings of adjectives like those of Saul Bellow, phrase the *gloria mundi*. She possessed the quality she missed in Sartre, as she noted in her calmly brilliant first book, *Sartre: Romantic Rationalist:* "Sartre has an impatience, which is fatal to a novelist proper, with the *stuff* of human life." Murdoch was beautifully patient with stuff, putting it all down in a steady harvest: a student of philosophy and the classics alert to every ripple and quirk of contemporary life, a word child who, confident of being loved, could afford to lavish herself on everything around her.

ART

One Obstinate Survivor on Another

GOYA, by Robert Hughes. 429 pp. Knopf, 2003.

Spain may have lost her American empire, but dead Spanish painters lately rule the hemisphere of art: Picasso going *mano a mano* with Matisse at MoMA Queens; Velázquez and Zurbarán up at the Met this spring, soberly showing Manet the way to modernity; this fall at the Met, the Heaven-oriented El Greco megashow; and now a thick, lovingly produced book, *Goya*, by Robert Hughes. Hughes, a native Australian who moved to the United States in 1970 and was, until 2001, the chief art critic for *Time*, has been a robust, even rambunctious writer, unabashedly opinionated and flamboyantly metaphorical and aphoristic: I have seen his prose characterized as of the Muscle Beach school, which, transposed to the higher cultural tone of Sydney's Bondi Beach, seems fair enough. He has done the workouts to get himself into shape, and if he turned a few handstands and kicked sand at a few ninety-pound weaklings, his pleasure in his own strength and suppleness of mind and pen has been infectious.

Goya begins, however, with two pages of acknowledgments startlingly different from the customary bows to sources and editorial helpmeets. First off, he thanks his wife for giving him the strength to do the book at all, "after a near-fatal car crash on a desert highway in Western Australia in 1999." The crash received ample publicity at the time, and again when Hughes appeared in court in Western Australia, charged with "dangerous driving causing grievous bodily harm." The charge was dismissed, then reinstated on appeal; Hughes entered a guilty plea and paid a twenty-five-hundred-dollar fine. Testimony indicated that he was driving on the wrong side of the road and ignored flashing headlights and honks of the horn from the oncoming vehicle. The head-on collision left many of his bones pulverized; he underwent a dozen operations and a total of six months of hospitalization. "Three and a half years after the accident," the acknowledgments tell us, "I am almost back on my feet," and he offers himself this consolation:

> Perhaps, if life is fully experienced, there is no waste. It was through the accident that I came to know extreme pain, fear, and despair; and it may be that the writer who does not know fear, despair, and pain cannot fully know Goya.

So it is a wounded critic who portrays an artist wounded, in 1792, by an illness that left him stone-deaf and, in 1808, by Napoleon's conquest of Spain. Hughes has been interested in Goya, he writes, ever since his adolescence, when he purchased a copy of the print *El sueño de la razón produce monstruos* ("The sleep of reason brings forth monsters"), studied other such reproductions in books, and "realized to [his] astonishment

Goya, Los caprichos, *plate 43*, El sueño de la razón produce monstruos *("The sleep of reason brings forth monsters"), 1796–97. Etching and aquatint.*

what extremity of the tragic sense the man could put onto little sheets of paper."

Among pre-modern artists whose reputations flourish in the present day, Goya is unusual in that his content matters more than his painterly technique. His cycle of etchings *Los desastres de la guerra* is still viewed as an effectively shocking depiction of war's horrors; the etchings called *Caprichos* and the late "black" paintings done on the walls of his farmhouse outside Madrid win admiration as uncanny incursions, with their witches and murky combats, into the subconscious, anticipating Surrealism. Goya emits, nearly two centuries after his death, a whiff of scandal, of potent mystery. Yet for all of his long life he was a workmanlike practitioner, performing whatever commissions were available—portraits, religious subjects, benign and colorful panoramas to be turned into tapestries.

The son of a gilder in the Aragonese capital of Zaragoza, Francisco José de Goya attended the Escuelas Pías de San Antón, a church school that offered free education to children of the poor. Goya was not notably poor; his father was a craftsman employed on the decoration of Zaragoza's grand new basilica to the Virgin, and his mother belonged to the *hidalguía*, the lowest order of Spain's proliferating aristocracy, *hidalgo* being a contraction of the noncommittal phrase *hijo de algo*—"son of somebody."* At the age of thirteen the boy was apprenticed to a painter, José Luzán, whose brothers were gilders and knew Goya's father. Goya recalled simply that, in four years, Luzán taught him the rudiments of design and made him copy the best prints he possessed. Hughes writes, "He seems to have taken, as one essayist rather harshly put it, no more interest than a carpenter in philosophical or theological matters, and his views on painting . . . were very down-to-earth: Goya was no theoretician." His early works show common life as sunny, and his passions were those of an average male Spaniard—hunting and the bullfight. It was, we are left to feel, a blunt, unappeasable sense of truth that led Goya to shed conventional decorum and to become the most expressionistic, daring, abstractifying visual artist prior to Impressionism, with the exception of the Englishman J. M. W. Turner.

Of Goya's life, there is not much to know aside from the work. His wife, Josefa, was the sister of a young Zaragoza artist, Francisco Bayeu, originally thought to be far more promising than Goya, who flunked an

---

*According to Hughes. The former Spanish bullfighter Barnaby Conrad informed me, however, that "son of someone" would be *hijo de alguien*. *Algo* means "something"—therefore "of some substance." The difference is noteworthy but not, perhaps, crucial.

attempt to win a scholarship to the Royal Academy of Fine Arts. The struggling painter married Josefa in 1773, when he was twenty-seven. Out of as many as twenty pregnancies she bore him seven children whose baptisms are recorded, but of these only one, Francisco Javier, survived. She herself died in 1812, making room for a housekeeper, Leocadia Zorrilla de Weiss, who brought her own two children into the aging artist's household. Leocadia has come down to posterity as handsome and shrewish—a good combination for a deaf painter. She followed Goya in his elderly relocation to Bordeaux in 1824 but received nothing in his will. The bulk of his estate went to Javier, his only surviving legitimate descendant. Goya was fond of Javier, but Hughes pronounces him "a flop of a son, lazy and just short of a wastrel. He made no career for himself [and] died at the age of sixty-nine, having done very little with his life." So much for family attachments. Goya admired the glamorous Duchess of Alba, as did many others. Hughes breathes hot, then cold, on the relationship:

> That he desired her, with the passionate and rather hopeless possessiveness men in their fifties and sixties can feel for much younger women, there can be little doubt. . . . She, in turn, was flattered by the attentions of the most fashionable artist in Spain. They were friends. But that, in broad outline, is all we know about Goya's relationship to the duchess of Alba.

She did *not* pose, as has been conjectured, for *The Naked Maja* (1797–1800) and her clad twin of some five years later, *La maja vestida*. That distinction belongs, it would seem, to one of the young mistresses of Manuel de Godoy, Spain's Prime Minister under Carlos IV, before Napoleon's intervention. Godoy's notorious womanizing extended to Queen Louisa herself, and "most probably" *The Naked Maja*, showing (according to Hughes) "what are certainly the first curls of female pubic hair in Western art," represented "the great love of Godoy's life, a spectacularly pretty and sexy Málagan girl named Pepita Tudo." After thirty years, the exiled Godoy's neglected wife died back in Madrid, and he made the curly-haired Pepita an honest woman by marrying her.

Hughes at times appears conscientiously methodical as he moves through the art, but he is lively on the wan comedy of Spanish history during Goya's life span. A lukewarmedly reform-minded monarch, Carlos III, yielded to a weak-minded son, Carlos IV, who hunted his days away while revolution beheaded his cousin in Paris, and who allowed himself, with his court, to be kidnapped by Napoleon; after six years during which Napoleon's brother Joseph Bonaparte officially ruled Spain as José I, the Bourbon monarchy was restored by Carlos IV's ultraconservative son, Fernando VII. Goya had been employed by Carlos *père* and was greatly appreciated by Carlos *fils*, who made him *primer pintor del rey*—"first painter to the King." Though he accepted no salary from José I, *el rey intruso*, he did accept commissions: he included the King's profile in his *Allegory of Madrid*, and executed a few portraits of the King's mistress, the King's Secretary of State, and the King's aide-de-camp and the aide-de-camp's little son. Goya also served on a commission to select fifty Spanish paintings as a gift to Napoleon, and accepted, in 1811, a royal decoration scornfully known as *la berenjena*, "the eggplant." He was thus exposed, after 1814, to charges of collaboration, which eventually faded away. But Fernando's government, welcomed back with such enthusiastic verses as "*Vivan las cadenas, Viva la opresión*" ("Long live our chains, Long live oppression"), was ruthless in hunting down French sympathizers (*afrancesados*), who tended to belong to Spain's minority of Enlightenment intellectuals (*ilustrados*). Goya, investigated not only by the new court but by the Inquisition, eventually sought exile. Occupiers, as we know, do not come without what they regard as benefits; José I brought with him a liberal constitution and incipient relief from the grip of the church and the aristocracy upon the Spanish land. But the people, like the Irish and Iranians, rallied to their native institutions, however benighted; they extolled the absentee monarch as *el deseado* ("the desired one"). The emphatic Robert Hughes terms him a "detestable archreactionary," a "tyrannous weasel," and "the royal toad."

The dreadful accident in Western Australia has not extinguished this author's old habits of incidental invective and capsule tirade. In a passing put-down of *Death in the Afternoon* as "unreadable today," he describes Hemingway as "sounding like such a lady" because of "what his style owed to an American lesbian, Gertrude Stein"; in a reinforcing connection with Queen Louisa's reported sexual misbehavior, Hughes cites "that saint of kitsch sentiment Princess Di" and, without particulars, uxorious Prince Philip; of Andy Warhol, that saint of American openness, we are told that, "given the chance, [he] would probably have served the Nazis with enthusiasm"; Velázquez is sideswiped as "one of the most dedicated snobs that ever touched a brush"; and the scornful epithet "chinless" attaches to two villains in a mere seven pages: "Generalissimo Franco, that stumpy tyrant whose narcissism knew no bounds," is alleged, by the photogenically strong-chinned author, to have had a "chinless profile," and we are invited to remember, apropos of war crimes, "the chinless police chief blowing out the brains of a plaid-shirted suspect at point-blank range with his kicking .38 on a Saigon street." The learned prose is peppered with slangy expressions from below the salt: the elderly John Ruskin was "cuckoo"; "right-wing loonies" used to oppose fluoride in drinking water; Goya painted "things that went bump in the night"; and "Licht is certainly right on the beam about the essential *marcialidad* and modernity of Goya's challenging cutie."

A compulsive social critic and free-swinging historian, Hughes performs in *Goya* primarily as an art critic, and he labors considerably to dispel the reader's suspicion that Goya doesn't give the eye quite enough to do. Hughes more than once notes that, however violent or fantastic the subject of a print, an underlying "geometrical severity" makes it "as Neoclassical as a David":

> We do not habitually think of Goya as a Neoclassical artist: his work is too disturbing. . . . But in truth, the signs of what he shared with men like Piranesi, Jacques-Louis David, the architect John Soane, and even that singular didactic fantasist Etienne-Louis Boullée are written all over the *Caprichos*. The most obvious of these are the compositional structures he uses, which tend to be very explicit and readily reduced to geometrical formulas. . . . He loves the diagonal and constantly uses it as the basis of his groups and figures. . . . Goya enjoyed the contrast between the abstract severity of some compositions and their intense human emotions.

Goya's artistic education, devoted to copying prints, fitted him for black-and-white etchings, to which he skillfully added the novel tool of aquatint, a method of inducing an even halftone on the plate with a dusting of fine particles of resin. As a handler of pigment, Goya strikes the viewer more with his increasing freedom of brushwork than with any coloristic brilliance; his palette is customarily brownish and subdued, clayey and parched, showing what Hughes calls "dun-colored tact." However, the canvas of which this is said, the large *Family of Carlos IV,* often taken as Goya's riposte to Velázquez's great *Las meninas,* stirs him to this fervent praise: "The surface is Goya at his most energetic, a free, spotted, impasted crust of pigment that keeps breaking into light, full of vitality with never a dull touch." Of Goya's possible limitations—the milky vapidity of his allegorical and religious figures, a button-eyed cartoonishness that thins the human presence of some portraits, an insecurity with anatomy very noticeable in *The Naked Maja*—Hughes says little. For him, Goya has few faults that are not by-products of his virtues: the courage, the fury, the "obstinately realistic" drive to express the unspeakable in foreboding, enigmatic images ultimate in their honesty.

Goya's fascination with life's extremes of torment and emergency and broken-down order suits our modern sense that these extremes, and not the mild quotidian middle ground of experience, hold the real truth about human existence. Goya's work, long before the *desastres de la guerra* prints and the *Walpurgisnacht* of the Black Paintings, sought out this truth in representations of cannibals, insane-asylum inmates, witches, bullring gorings, crimes of passion, and bandits—not the amusing ban-

Goya, Los desastres de la guerra, *plate 37*, Esto es peor *("This is worse"), etched 1810–13, printed 1863. Etching and aquatint.*

Goya, Los desastres de la guerra, *plate 39*, ¡Grande hazaña! ¡Con muertos! *("Great feat! With dead men!"), etched 1810–13, printed 1863. Etching and aquatint.*

dits of folk ballad but merciless killers inhabiting Spain's waste spaces, visiting theft, rape, and murder on those who have ventured, in carriages, from their havens of safety. The 1793 oil *Attack on a Coach* prefigures the *Asalto de bandidos* series of 1808–12, which take rape from the playful realm of classical mythology to that of contemporary atrocity: the tall woman, seen by firelight, being stripped of her clothes preparatory to being raped and stabbed to death is a more disturbing, moving nude than *The Naked Maja*. Yet even the *maja*, little minx that she is, has a touch of nervous vulnerability in her frontal pose; she is a realistic remove from Titian's imperturbable Venus or Velázquez's Rokeby Venus, who turns her magnificent back on us while gazing into a mirror. For Goya, a naked woman is no goddess; she can be hurt.

To bring human pain into depiction was a mighty deed, for which Goya, who painted for four kings, received small reward in his lifetime. Instead, he receives recognition from the bloodied generations since, and this thorough, profusely argued and illustrated homage from Robert Hughes. The author's own ordeal gives force to his haunting phrasing of Goya's "fear of being no longer able to impose himself upon the world, brought to the surface in an acute form in his deafness." The desire to impose oneself upon the world is a rarely expressed motive for art, yet it can be felt in Goya, as he relentlessly bared the nightmare beneath the world's surface, and was felt by the artist himself. Approaching eighty, still working, he declared in a letter to a friend, "I've no more sight, no hand, nor pen, nor inkwell, I lack everything—all I've got left is will."

Metropolitan Art

NEW ART CITY: *Manhattan at Mid-Century*, by Jed Perl. 642 pp. Knopf, 2005.

A hundred pages shorter than André Malraux's *The Voices of Silence*, which surveyed art from its first traces in caves up to the present as of 1953, and a hundred pages longer than Robert Hughes's *The Shock of the New*, which in 1980 took on modern art from Cézanne to Pop, Op, Happenings, and Earthworks, Jed Perl's *New Art City* claims in its subtitle to cover only *Manhattan at Mid-Century*. This is not a coffee-table art book; its illustrations, though numerous, are all small and black-and-white. A dense text rules the textbook-size pages—557 of them, not counting notes, acknowledgments, and index. Can there be that much to say about so concentrated a space and span of time? Have no fear: Perl, the art critic for *The New Republic*, is a fiercely fluent word-spinner, and he comes laden with a staggering knowledge of American artists and their critics from, say, 1948, when Willem de Kooning had his first one-man show and Jackson Pollock began to drip in earnest, down to 1982, when Donald Judd started to colonize the flat wilderness of Marfa, Texas, with a hundred same-sized aluminum boxes.

The book could have been called *Abstract Expressionism and Its Aftermath*, except that the Abstract Expressionists themselves are given relatively curt treatment, as if the author doesn't dare look at the sun too long. Perl devotes the bulk of his philosophically intricate and aesthetically subtle considerations to the second-generation "colonizers rather than explorers" (in B. H. Friedman's paraphrase of W. H. Auden) whose fate it was "to live in an Age of Silver, or maybe of Lead." *New Art City*'s roll call tends to proceed two by two; it opens with de Kooning and Hans Hofmann, a pair of mature immigrants with an Old World passion for brushed paint, and ends with Fairfield Porter and Donald Judd, an unlikely duo of Silver Age "empiricists"—that is, in Perl's terms, practitioners more concerned with the reality before them than with any romantic role in the historical progression of art styles.

The thesis of the book, to be brief about it, is that art in Manhattan passed in mid-century and beyond from the nighttime creations of existential, heroic, romantic, art-history-minded revolutionaries hardened in the depressed Thirties to the daytime works of empirical, eclectic, unheroic, relatively theory-free individualists who had ripened in the afterglow of the Action Painting giants. These giants are evoked here and there in the book—Mark Rothko and Barnett Newman toward the end—and not always in worshipful terms. Pollock, Perl tells us, "was an artist with a fine-tuned, rather small lyric gift" graced by a big support system and a ton of publicity; by the end of the Forties, "the technique of dripping or flinging the paint, which Pollock originally borrowed from the Surrealists . . . soon became repetitive, a maze of lines that lock up the canvas all too efficiently." Concerning another paint-flinging giant, Franz Kline, Perl admires his famous personal charm and the "buoyant, open-ended, angst-less void" expressed by his white spaces but complains that "Kline's swaggering black-and-white abstractions can have a perfunctory look—they suggest a too easily existentialized romanticism." Perl's least qualified and most strenuous praise is for such relatively undersung achievements as Joan Mitchell's scrubbily brushed abstractions, Nell Blaine's quasi-naïve still lifes, Leland Bell's heavily simplified nudes, and the obscure Earl Kerkam's worried, often incomplete nudes and self-portraits, expressing "a quieter kind of yearning" as opposed to de Kooning's "gonzo, exhibitionistic romanticism."

Well, in our anarchic post–Silver Age, we are all free to like what we like, and patience with the lesser lights is what an art critic is paid for. Perl's long trek, however, through the Silver Age galleries is a wearying one. His pace enthusiastically picks up with such distinctive artists as David Smith, Joseph Cornell, Alex Katz, and the abstract, pre-cartoony Philip Guston, but our overall impression of being buried in an avalanche of reworked art reviews is reinforced by the inclusion of more and more quotation of other critics, at greatest length Harold Rosenberg and Clement Greenberg. Perl prefers the more doctrinaire Greenberg. He accuses Rosenberg of seeming to be "riffing on Greenberg's ideas, giving his formalist sense of tradition an existentialist zing" and of composing an essay that is "all glittering bits—a hot-air construction."

While one would not mistake Perl's hip, allusion-rich prose for hot air, it does, in its schematizing ease and eager phrasemaking, exude some warmth. As warm air will, it can induce a certain grogginess. "If oil paint was tradition, collage was revolution, but of course the kind of painting that was done on Tenth Street was very much related to the revolution of Cubist collage, and so the connection between painting and collage was complicated, part of the loopy history of modern art": a sentence like this leads us perilously close to nowhere. Complication goes without saying; we wait for the illuminating generalization. The words "existential" and "empirical" remain hazy, as much as Perl loves them and uses them. The verb "existentialize" doesn't exist in my dictionary, and I groped to attach meanings to such nuanced variations of the concept as "in their wackily existentialist way" and the report that some Buckminster Fuller domes were sent out "in the world in a pure, almost existentialized form." *Almost* existentialized—an unlucky near-miss!

In his commendable desire to stretch the language of visual perception and philosophical understanding, Perl coins compound adjectives as if hyphens were snowing upon his word processor. He gives us: "an individual's at-an-angle relationship with society," "go-with-the-flow neighbors," "an increasingly knit-together, everything-is-one-thing, homogenous character," "knock-you-in-your-teeth actualities," "the wacky-bleak fascination of a play by Samuel Beckett," "this everything-becoming-something-else moment," "more-than-material yet grounded in the materials of art," "the whatever-happens-happens nihilism," "Ashbery's go-with-what-amuses-you attitude," and "the stark, nobody-knows-you-when-you're-down-and-out decrepitude." Some of these Germanic compounds, like "at-an-angle" and "go-with-the-flow," are handy enough to be used more than once, but they are, along with stretch adverbs like "amazingly," "infinitely," and "immensely," and such tenuous concepts as "everydayness," "brownishness," and "ordinariness [that] melts into the silveriness of the images," symptomatic of the stresses placed on the vocabulary of those who would write about art.

And write about art modern man evidently must. The belief that, as the premises of religion and patriotism suffer discredit, an inspiring humanism survives in the production of paintings and sculpture afflicts us all. Volumes of commentary both precede and follow creative acts. The masters of Impressionism and Cézanne were relatively inarticulate—their theories spoke in their praxis—but since then every movement has had its manifestos, and some of the announced programs, as with the Italian Futurists and English Vorticists, proved more vivid than their visual byproducts. And some, as with Dada, made the denial of art their program. Of the Abstract Expressionists, Pollock and Kline wrote little, but Motherwell and Newman and, most grandiosely, Clyfford Still wrote and opined much. It is the nature of twentieth-century art to cast a dense literary shadow. When one reads, in Perl's last two chapters, of the pungent and aggressive reviews of contemporary shows that Judd and Porter produced for art journals, one wonders if proving themselves as art critics wasn't a way of lending credibility to their own works—what Perl might describe as the in-your-face-affectless constructions of Judd and the I-paint-what-I-see-and-so-what canvases of Porter.

If one of *New Art City*'s underlying messages is that heroic "existential" Abstract Expressionism was something to get over, and another is that an "empirical" Silver Age mixed of representational and abstract private styles shouldn't be sniffed at, it takes a dim view of the mighty movement that came in between, beloved of collectors and of the non-buying public alike. Perl sees Pop as the return of Dada, which didn't deserve an encore. Marcel Duchamp—with Piet Mondrian, Manhattan's most dramatic elder-in-exile—strikes Perl as a sinister *éminence grise*. He quotes an article composed by gallery-owners Sidney and Harriet Janis in 1945; it explains of the Frenchman, whose American career amounted to little more than a few arresting stunts, that "he has worked out a system that has produced a new atmosphere in which irony functions like an activating element, causing a pendulum-like oscillation between acceptance and rejection, affirmation and negation, and rendering them both dynamic and productive." Perl's comment is uncharacteristically sharp: "Here, in some carefully chosen words about Duchamp published at the end of World War II, we are face-to-face with a vision of artistic development as amusingly slippery or ironically aimless that would become commonplace a little more than a decade later. It's a poisonous attitude, so I believe."

When, in 1958, Dada's deadpan irony was reborn in Jasper Johns's first show, Perl gets personal and nearly nasty:

> Johns liked to give his surfaces a beguiling complexity, often with glued-on layers of newspaper. The surfaces were worked over—worried over. In all of these paintings, there was a suggestion of the collage or the readymade, for Johns' sensitized surfaces became a mocking echo of the pancake-flat object—a flag or a target or a map—that he has taken as his subject. He used his slurpy encaustic paint to make painterly love to his quotidian subjects. He was slumming—oh so elegantly.

Irony, mockery—these are poisonous, damaging the health of the humanistic enterprise, diminishing "the grandeur of art" so that it "was no longer a force that by pushing artists forward granted them their freedom." Johns's painstaking technique of encaustic over collage is "slurpy," an image that becomes, in "painterly love," curiously sexual. The critic tells us what Johns likes, and when he is slumming. He does not entertain the possibility that the famous flags and targets and maps were a way of coping with the chronic modernist issues of representation and reality, central to the surreal puns of Max Ernst and Magritte and Dalí. And yet in other instances Perl grants artists the freedom to do what feels right, to let each work be "an attempt to give form a shape that matched the artist's emotions." The concomitant obligation is to avoid doing what *doesn't* feel right, and Johns, with many in his generation, avoided trying to redo the great deeds of Western art, including the flamboyant gestures of the Abstract Expressionists. An image that is also a thing—a flag or target or map—is one way to subdue expressionism while keeping painterliness.

Pop was a counter-revolution that made art experts feel, as Leo Steinberg admitted, like philistines. Perl quotes with zesty approval Fairfield Porter's disparaging review of a Johns retrospective in 1964, as displaying "the course of an education that has been carried out in public." Porter went on, "It shows the reaction to his education of an individual intelligent enough at first to take in all that he is being taught while giving it only part of his attention." Perl adds, "And so Jasper Johns went straight to the top of the class." Usually non-combative, Perl on Pop takes sides all over the place; Leo Steinberg, quoted on Johns as an ally, is guilty of "an avant-garde soft-headedness" when he tries to find something good to say about Robert Rauschenberg's enigmatic combines: "What he liked about Rauschenberg's work was the mushy meanderings that the combines kicked off in *his* mind."

As for Roy Lichtenstein and Andy Warhol, they are understood as deft perpetrators of implicitly fraudulent effects: Lichtenstein's blown-up comic strips won acceptance because "they were susceptible to a kind of formalist, Bauhaus-inspired analysis that had been familiar at least since the 1940s," and Warhol, who left doing shoe advertisements to imitate Lichtenstein's big cartoons, happened, in his factory of duplication, on "one Pop subject that had an immediate, visceral appeal for a sophisticated (and even for an intellectual) audience: the movies." Cleverly concentrating on stars associated with intellectuals like Arthur Miller and Richard Burton, he "presented gallerygoers with a Hollywood universe in which just about everybody had at one time or another found a fantasy of romantic involvement. The whole arrangement worked beautifully for the part of the audience that wasn't interested in heterosexual sex." The little sting in this last phrase brings us to the matter of "sophisticated campy taste" that flavors the Pop movement; many if not most of the name artists were homosexual, and an "at-an-angle" derision of the straight world blinds Perl, it seems to me, to the innocence of Pop's basic appeal; as with Norman Rockwell's *Post* covers, the public recognized elements of the world it lived in. Claes Oldenburg, who wound up designing drolly huge public monuments, began, in 1961, with The Store, a mock-emporium located in a working-class district where the East Village met the Lower East Side, stocked with grungy, brightly and messily enamelled plaster replicas of merchandise—candy bars, men's shirts, pastries, corsets—redolent of the 1940s. Perl offers a sour epigram: "An art without a will of its own was an art drifting into nostalgia—that was always the condition of Pop."

The Pop episode prompts the sole deviation from Perl's "what-happens-happens," "go-with-what-amuses-you" survey. He is as fondly respectful of Cornell's fey little boxes of assemblage as he is affronted by Rauschenberg's *brut* combines, and Judd's artifacts, which might seem as impudently blank as Johns's flags, are cherished for the aesthetic values they bring over from the industrial world: his plywood boxes "were about the beauty of plywood, its color, its patterning, its edges with their sandwiched layers." No Dada urinals, snow shovels, and bottle racks need apply, without those buzz-sawed, sandwiched layers.

The book's title and subtitle lead a reader to expect more concrete speculation as to why New York, which after all didn't lack bohemian strivers prior to 1945, replaced Paris as the world's art capital. One reason is perhaps too obvious for Perl to dwell on: the city was the economic capital of the only major combatant nation to emerge from World War II with its infrastructure intact and its civilian population unharmed. The private wealth of the postwar boom was a more flexible and lavish patron

than the government's Depression mural projects could be. The expanding size of the Abstract Expressionist canvases, an index of their ambition
and their strategy of engulfing the viewer, related to the size of the cheap
lofts being vacated by downtown Manhattan's declining industries. The
bold splashes found receptive pale walls in the skyscraper city rising to
the north, its desert-pure midtown apartments and its newly fashionable
museums. Downtown abounded in cheap living, found art, permissive
cafeterias, and jazzed-up friends. An Englishman, Cyril Connolly, in
Horizon in 1947, said it best: New York presented "an unforgettable picture of what a city ought to be: that is, continuously insolent and alive, a
place where one can buy a book or meet a friend at any hour of the day or
night." He promised, "Something important is about to happen." Who
feels that now?

Deceptively Conceptual

BY ITS COVER: *Modern American Book Cover Design*, by Ned Drew and Paul
Sternberger. 192 pp. Princeton Architectural Press, 2005.

Book covers and jackets might seem to hover beneath serious critical
notice, but nothing human is alien to the academic discipline called "cultural studies," be it baseball cards or vampire movies or female footgear.
All such devices open inward into the secrets of Everyman's psyche and of
capitalism's perfidious designs upon Everyman's pocketbook. The first
line of mass-market paperbacks in this country, in fact, was called Pocket
Books, produced in 1938, soon after the success, in England, of Penguin
Books. The English-speaking countries were slower than those on the
Continent to eliminate the huge fraction—around forty percent—of
book production costs invested in the many-layered hard cover itself.
The year 1929 had seen, in the United States, the birth of Charles Boni
Paper Books, but these were marketed by subscription to the Rockwell
Kent–fancying carriage trade and did not long outlast the stock-market
boom. I remember as a boy the dramatic arrival, in the town variety store,
of a rack of Pocket Books, mostly mysteries, whose discreetly lurid covers
were covered by a thin sheet of cellophane that tended to curl at the corners and could be peeled entirely off by persistent little fingers. They cost
a quarter, compared with a dime for a comic book, and had much more
text, as well as sexier covers. The two such covers reproduced in *By Its
Cover: Modern American Book Cover Design*, by Ned Drew and Paul

Sternberger, date from 1948 and 1958. *The Case of the Fiery Fingers*, a Perry Mason mystery by Erle Stanley Gardner, shows a leggy lady in a very see-through nightie; Columbia professor John Erskine's wry *The Private Life of Helen of Troy* is fronted, under the Popular Library imprint, by a pneumatic Helen in a clinging chiton and the rather sensationalist headline HER LUST CAUSED THE TROJAN WAR.

From such two-bit cheesecake it was, we learn in *By Its Cover*, an elevating leap into the postwar, upscale modernist designs of New Directions hardcovers and the new quality-paperback lines. Drew and Sternberger, both Newark-based associate professors of art and graphic design, lump dust jackets with paperback covers and trace their intertwined development in terms of modernism and postmodernism. Modernism in book form is exemplified by Joyce's *Ulysses*, and *By Its Cover* begins with Ernst Reichl's striking but almost illegible jacket for the first American edition of that work in 1934; the title's seven letters, in elongated and squared-off form, take up the entire front surface, echoing the mazelike course the characters pursue through a June day in Dublin. For the 1949 Random House edition, E. McKnight Kauffer's jacket keeps large letters as the only decorative element but in a more playful and easily deciphered manner. We are told that the 1986 version by Carin Goldberg "once again incorporated the language of modernism, but now as a self-conscious act of historical quotation." Goldberg's colorful simplification of Reichl's august maze is bold and festive compared with the Modern Library's placid 1940 jacket by an unknown designer, though the exaggerated "U" remains, this time in a hand-lettered script. The newest Random House edition, of 2002, restores the 1934 original, as itself a classic—a respectfully preserved artifact from the storied age of modernism.

"Modernism," like "pornography" and "literary fiction," is a term hard to define, though we all feel we know what it means—Apollinaire and Gertrude Stein, Bauhaus workers' housing, the enigmatic and erudite complexity of *Ulysses* and *The Waste Land*, the defiant distortions of Picasso's *Les Demoiselles d'Avignon*. Book covers, however, with their ineluctable role as advertisements for the contents of the book, can scarcely attain the proud *non serviam* of high modernism—art for its own willful, bourgeois-baiting sake. Alvin Lustig's abstract or biomorphic patterns for New Directions editions of Kafka, Henry Miller, and Djuna Barnes in the Forties do not seem much more modernist than Arthur Hawkins's sanserif, Art Deco–ish designs for Shaw and W. Olaf Stapledon in the Thirties, though there is a certain intransigent aloofness in the modest size of Lustig's title typefaces. At the same time that he was pre-

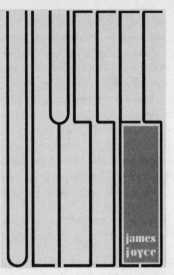

Ernst Reichl, book jacket for the Random House Ulysses, *1934, reprinted 2002*

senting Henry James novels in an ultra-cool linear design laid over brown and gray rectangles, Lustig was perpetrating, for Lorca and Italo Svevo, crowded collages anticipating postmodernism's eclectic clutter. In different covers he echoes the high art of Miró, Arp, and Clyfford Still. Designing primarily for James Laughlin's idealistic New Directions, Lustig was freer from the crasser commercial pressures, but his pronouncements, as teacher and design guru, on the book designer's social mission seem precariously lofty. *By Its Cover* claims, "For him, like his European predecessors, modernism reflected larger social goals of integrating art and life, blurring the boundaries that had separated high art and utilitarian object." Lustig, before his early death in 1955, put it more grandly yet:

> If I seem to place a heavy mantle of responsibility on the shoulders of those who are really only expected to make nice shapes and colors, it is because history demands it. Every act that allows productive facilities to serve only itself [sic], contributes inevitably to the threat of destruction that already looms on the horizon.

So, far from *non serviam*, book design serves unnamed masters whose selflessness forestalls atomic war. Lustig's contemporary Paul Rand took a more playful approach to the craft, as shown in the curly, spindly handwriting in which he lettered his covers. His artistic signature was distinctly whimsical, though he is, according to Drew and Sternberger, "best remembered for his corporate trademarks." His earlier book covers are his most radical, as illustrated by the jumpy redoubled letters "DADA" for *The Dada Painters and Poets* (1951) and by the torn theatre ticket, on a black ground, that wrapped reviewer Harold Clurman's *The Fervent Years* (1950). Unillustrated but cited are "his 1938–45 covers for *Direction*, a small anti-fascist magazine of art and culture whose modest budget and political stance lent themselves to bold simplified forms in limited colors." Pro-fascist magazines (how many were there in the U.S.?) presumably had bigger budgets. The authors' insistent politicization of design aesthetics has a musty and wordy Marxist tone:

> Perhaps this tension between the demands of commerce and the possibility for conceptual depth made modernism attractive to so many American designers: it offered an interweaving of rigorous formal aesthetics and potential for creative expression with an ultimate goal of social and economic utility.

Economic utility to whom? To book manufacturers, basically. Publishing forms a minor branch of the entertainment industry, and book design is increasingly a matter of fashion—that is, of attention-getting. In the visual clamor of a bookstore, the important thing is to be different; a whisper amid loud competition becomes a piercing cry, and the ugly becomes beautiful if it attracts attention. Yet an utter flaunting of conventional expectations may baffle and repel the public; when the title and the author's name are left off the front of the book, as in three examples taken from the early 2000s, it sends a subliminal message of contempt for the written word, the product being packaged. Even a clever conceit like Paul Sahre's spelling out in Morse code the title of *Hello World: A Life in Ham Radio* risks turning buyers off.

The postwar book designer has two audiences—that of other designers, who applaud daring, witty "creative expression," and the bookstore browser, whose supposed interests are ever more zealously safeguarded in "a corporate environment where marketing analysts, editorial boards, and authors insist on significant participation in the design process." In this board of overseers, authors have the disadvantage of an intimate and proprietorial acquaintance with the text, while the marketing analysts have only a record of previous flops and successes to go by, and no way of producing that impression of *something new* which is one ingredient of a commercial success in the creative arts. In the end, nobody buys a book jacket, though sometimes a jacket—like Robert Scudellari's inviting, bright-red wrapper for the very successful *Stories of John Cheever* (1978), with its huge silver "C"—does cheer on searchers for a Christmas present to bestow. Books, like boxes of chocolate, are in large part bought to be given away.

Paul Bacon, described by Drew and Sternberger as "one of the most remarkable designers to adapt to the needs of the corporate publishing world of the 1970s," had talent, they admit, but only when "blended with a humble attitude" did it enable him to make the leap from small jazz magazines and record sleeves to hardbound best-sellers, offered up to the public "with the austerity of corporate design." Bacon's jackets for *Compulsion* (1956) and *Catch-22* (1961) are humble indeed, combining clear type, generous areas of blank color, and very small and not especially indicative figures that leave the book's contents up to the peruser's imagination. The designs do not get between the customer and the book, whereas his jackets for *The Most of S. J. Perelman* (1958) and *One Flew over the Cuckoo's Nest* (1962) do—at least, they breed expectations of the antic and the psychedelic, respectively, that might be disappointed. Bacon's jackets for the historical novels *Confessions of Nat Turner* (1967) and *Ragtime* (1975) play with type that gives a less obtrusive foretaste of the text. About half, I would say, of the covers and jacket fronts reproduced in *By Its Cover* try too hard—they come forward, as it were, pre-emptively, including two that mimic, with disconcerting accuracy, cigar boxes. A good cover should be a bit recessive in its art, leading us past the cover into the book itself. In the postwar battle (as *By Its Cover* sees it) between modernism and Mammon, seduction is a more successful tactic than aggression.

We look to books not only for stimulation but for reassurance. There is no mention in *By Its Cover* of Edward Gorey and the hand-lettered, gently scratchy covers he executed in the Fifties for Doubleday Anchor books, but they spoke reassuringly, in the fledgling days of the paperback revolution, of dependability. A wealth of previously hard-to-find treasures, from Melville's *Redburn* and Gogol's tales to Kierkegaard's *Fear and Trembling* and Stendhal's long essay on love, were poured into the same staid yet impish mold, the Gorey style of cover. Milton Glaser, the most distinctive and prolific artist at Push Pin Studios, did something of the same in the Sixties, for a number of Vintage titles and the Signet edition of Shakespeare's plays. People like sets of things, as signs of ultimate order. Though the heyday of the uniform bound edition passed with the Victorians, modern bibliophiles can take pleasure in paperbacks whose consistent appearance implies a congenially shared sensibility. The slightly larger and unabashedly "progressive" (one of Drew and Sternberger's favorite accolades) format of Grove Press's Evergreen series offered a spread of sometimes spicy titles as aspects of one big feast of outré masterworks. Readers in those early postwar decades had a sudden, bountiful alternative to the bulky fare found on the hardcover best-seller list, and the relatively adventurous covers were part of the intellectual romance.

As assayed by *By Its Cover,* the next three decades of design, the final three of the century, were characterized by the advent, triumph, and refinement of postmodern eclecticism, whose hallmark is "not only an awareness and understanding of the past, but a willingness to quote from it unapologetically." Modernism, in its Bauhausian, Utopian aspirations, looked to the future; postmodernism to the past. Instead of streamlining and "Less is more" we get knobby, collaged "appropriation" of pre-existing images, either photographic or culled from the world's vast archives of type fonts and pre-photographic engravings. Put bluntly, the designers of covers and jackets ceased to draw. Pen and brush yielded to the ever-more-capable computer as the graphics tool of choice. Rather than generate images, designers manipulated them. Of the illustrated examples of dazzlingly inventive recent work by Carol Devine Carson, Chip Kidd, and John Gall—all part of the admired in-house design team at Alfred A. Knopf—few bear any trace of the designer's own hand. One exception, piquantly, is Chip Kidd's own novel, *The Cheese Monkeys,* for which Kidd provided an "unfinished comp," an inked-in cover sketch with visible pencilled guidelines; it provides an ironic tribute, perhaps, to the lost tradition of hand-lettered jackets, elegantly upheld by English publishers and, until the irresistible onslaught of computer fonts, by American designers like Neil Fujita and Muriel Nasser. In a discussion of some third-millennium jackets devoid (except, presumably, on the spine) of lettering entirely, *By Its Cover* speaks of a "sort of broader engagement in which the designers consider their viewers to be participants in the construction of meaning," and of the design "not as an isolated creative act, but as an activity of integrating object, means of reproduction, and audience."

Well, when hasn't it been ever such? A book is an object, a work of manufacture whose many elements, from type and binding to quality of paper, are susceptible to aesthetic criticism—has print, for example, ever been as sharp and clear as it was in the vanished days of letterpress?—but whose meaning has always had to be constructed, as the writer and a reader collaborate in imagining a series of scenes and events. Any artistic creation collaborates with the viewer, reader, or listener, and the present-day designer of books appeals to a sensibility very differently stocked—

digitally stocked, as it were—from that of the young book-fancier of fifty years ago. To me as a consumer, the computer-generated jackets and covers have a certain hard-edged coldness and clutter; to me as a book producer the digital-graphics revolution has the virtue of removing a contemporary illustrator from the equation. Appropriating a Blake watercolor, say, or a Dürer etching or an Ingres painting for the cover's pictorial element puts the text in excellent company without diluting the text's descriptive authority. Nobody confuses these artists' representations with the author's, but their validated excellence may rub off. There is also a convenience of speed; I once watched over a designer's shoulder while she cropped and enlarged an appropriated painting until it perfectly balanced and fit with the lettering. It was like arriving at "Bingo!" Bingo is still the goal, though the path to it now snakes through a maze of technology and warehoused historical styles and images.

One designer is described as having "combed French and Italian flea markets for ephemera with inspirational typefaces"; a flea-market, rummage-sale sort of aesthetic, traceable to Pop Art and especially to Robert Rauschenberg, can be, in the words of the design critic Steven Heller, "deceptively conceptual, giving the impression that a statement exists, when in reality the pseudo-poetic imagery camouflages the fact of a nonexistent point of view." Drew and Sternberger quickly propose that "a 'nonexistent point of view' might have significance in and of itself." Zero is also a number. You can, possibly, tell a book by its cover, but the cover still isn't the contents.

Dürer's Passions

DAUMIER AND REDON have their lithographs, and Picasso his etchings, but no major artistic reputation owes more to prints than Dürer's. His woodcuts, propagated by the relatively new power of the printing press, circulated through Europe and made his fame; they combined the sturdy starkness of folk art with the elaboration and expressiveness of Renaissance painting. To this day, for all the brilliance of his oil paintings, including the first European series of self-portraits, and the tender precision of his watercolors and drawings, and his importance as the German artist who, with both written theory and exemplary practice, brought the lessons of the Italian Renaissance north, his name likely conjures up a black-and-white image—one of the set of surreal, majestic woodcut illustrations to the *Apocalypse* (c. 1497–98), say, or his copperplate engraving *Adam and Eve* (1504) or *Knight, Death, and the Devil* (1513). Since Dürer prints are in the collections of most museums, exhibitions are relatively easy to assemble; in 1971, the five hundredth anniversary of the artist's birth in Nuremberg, the Boston Museum of Fine Arts drew exclusively upon its own collection to mount the extensive *Albrecht Dürer: Master Printmaker.* Now, in the fall of 2000, Harvard's Fogg Museum, having assimilated the old Germanic Busch-Reisinger Museum that once stood on the other side of Memorial Hall, has supplemented its own considerable holdings with some loaned prints to give us, in ninety-three works, the full array of Dürer's six versions of Christ's Passion—the successive events, from the Last Supper to the Crucifixion, of Christ's week of redemptive suffering.

The works are handsomely displayed in one large, irregular room painted a deep maroon on the lower half of the walls and a dark green on the upper. The earliest passion, called the *Albertina Passion* (1494–1500), and the latest, the *Oblong Passion* (1520–24), are both fragmentary, containing respectively four and ten images. *The Green Passion* (1504) consists of eleven drawings in pen and brush on green paper, heightened with white gouache; the originals are in the collection of the Graphische Sammlung Albertina in Vienna and are represented at the Fogg by reproductions two-thirds the size of the originals. Finely limned, their dark ground spotted with chalky white, they are probably hard to look at even in the original; yet, moving from Christ's arrest in the Garden to his entombment, the cycle seems planned and is minutely executed, possibly toward some painted version to adorn a noble's chapel. *The Nailing to the Cross* and the *Descent from the Cross* are notably lucid, dramatic, and moving.

But it is the *Engraved Passion* of 1508–12 and the two woodcut series the *Large Passion* (1497–1510) and the *Small Passion* (1508–10) that make the show worth a museum's space and a museumgoer's time. They date, roughly, from the same period of Dürer's life, and were moved forward more or less simultaneously, in one wave of interest. It is hard to imagine this narrative, the center of the Christian story and a topic of depiction from Romanesque capitals to Rouault canvases, ever being more earnestly, searchingly, and, as it were, introspectively illustrated. This is an exhibition with a thesis, put forward a few years ago by a young man who at the time was not even a graduate student. James Cuno, the director of the Fogg, in a brief foreword to the exhibition catalogue describes the event:

Jordan Kantor had just received his B.A. from Stanford when he showed up at the office door of the Fogg Museum's print curator, Marjorie Cohn. He said he had an idea for an exhibition about Dürer's Passion prints. Jerry [Marjorie] listened politely, and the more Jordan explained his thesis, the more she thought there was something to what he was saying. Finally, she said she would think about it.

After she thought, and Kantor exercised his gift for salesmanship on Harvard's Professor Joseph Koerner, Kantor was enrolled in the Ph.D. program in the history of art and architecture and, six years or so later, the Passions are up on the walls. In an essay of thirty-three pages, Kantor puts forward his notion, which is perhaps less than revolutionary:

> Dürer's Passions reveal the artist's own struggle to distill a personal vision of what a Passion should be. . . . Dürer did not just want to depict the Passion; he wanted to do it in a way that demonstrated his God-given genius. He wanted to create *Dürer's* Passions. Dürer's desire to create a personalized version of the Passion story was also certainly connected to his close identification with Christ. . . . This collapse of boundaries between artist and subject also parallels the strategy Dürer developed throughout his career to knit his viewer into the image. . . . As a young artist, Dürer imagines Christ as highly emotional, resisting his inevitable suffering and death. Late in his career, Dürer pictures his protagonist as calmer and more resigned to his fate. Halfway between these, as in the 1505 drawing, he pictured Christ as an impotent object.

It is no secret that Dürer depicted himself as Christ, or read Christ into his self-portraits: there are the beautiful chalk drawing *Self-Portrait as Man of Sorrows* (1522) and the iconlike oil self-portrait of 1500, among other evidences. Both covers of this strangely subdivided catalogue (splitting the reproductions from their titles and dates) carry Dürer's dramatic charcoal *Head of Dead Christ* (1503); the artist and viewer draw morbidly close to the dead Saviour's gaping mouth and shuttered eyes. But close identification with the suffering and humiliated Christ was a Christian's duty, urged with especial fervor as the pomp and show of medieval piety turned toward the private exertions of the soul that foreshadowed Protestantism. Ecclesiastical authority faltered and monks and popes became scandals, but the psychological and physical reality of the Gospel drama offered devotion a perennial basis. Dürer aimed, like a modern newscaster, to put himself—faithfully represented by his prominent monogram—and the viewer *there*. In the repellently well-observed charcoal head, we sense with a physical chill the rigidity and rot of death beginning. This death will some day be ours.

But what struck this viewer, perambulating the maroon walls, was the multiplicity and variety of other presences than Christ's in these scenes. The world is much with the Incarnate Deity. The figure of Jesus is in fre-

Dürer, Head of Dead Christ, *1503. Charcoal.*

quent danger of being lost in the crowd; the animation and variety of incident within the crowd disperse attention from the sacred action at the center. This is most true of the *Large Passion*, seven of whose sixteen panels were executed in the last years of the fifteenth century, and then rounded out with a second installment in 1510. In its *Flagellation* (1497), no fewer than sixteen subsidiary figures taunt, whip, stare, blow horns, and, in one arresting visage, finger-whistle at the central figure; in the *Bearing of the Cross* (1498–99), an astonishing linear congestion of figures and draperies press down on top of the diagonal arm of the cross, whose weight has brought Christ to his knees; in the *Crucifixion* (1497), the area not covered with figures on the ground is filled with angels catching Christ's blood in chalices; in the *Deposition* (1497), Christ is more than half eclipsed by mourning handlers of his body, beneath a furiously detailed thicket with its roots.

Scrutinizing such details in the half-size reproductions on the catalogue's shiny coated paper approaches the painful; one revelation of the exhibition is the relative comfort of viewing the woodcuts at their actual fifteen by eleven inches, printed on the soft, matte, pure rag paper of the fifteenth century. Seen as Dürer meant them to be seen, the visages of his minor actors and bystanders lose some of their knitted, snarling look, and a few of them—like the vivid, not quite malevolent face at the back of the *Deposition*'s crowd—gaze right back at us. In this series' *Last Supper*

Dürer, Flagellation, *from the* Large Passion, *1497. Woodcut.*

(1510), we can follow the expressions into the darkest depths of the heavily crosshatched shadows (is that Judas scowling?) and, in the *Harrowing of Hell* (1510), examine the somewhat wistful and shy expressions of the bizarre, beaked, horned, and scaly devils in residence as they contemplate their gracious visitor. These prints were designed to be bound into a book as large and gorgeous as the *Apocalypse* encased in the center of the room at the Fogg.

The *Small Passion*, thirty-seven woodcuts and an alternative block, which generally measure less than five by four inches, was designed for a mass audience. Extending the Passion into its full cosmic significance, the prints compose the most readily intelligible and vivid sequence, beginning with *Adam and Eve Eating the Forbidden Fruit* and their *Expulsion from Paradise* and moving into the life history that will redeem the Fall, from the *Annunciation* to the *Ascension*, the *Descent of the Holy Ghost*, and the *Last Judgment*, in which the damned are swallowed by a large-mouthed Satan and the saved move toward an ineffable light. Published as a book in 1511, the prints date at the earliest to 1508, and show little of the sometimes awkward congestion of the *Large Passion*. Consciousness of producing a handy popular work has led Dürer to a dramatic simplicity and a music of recurring imagery. The sword with which the angel of the *Expulsion* banishes the sinners returns suspended near Christ's head as he judges Mankind; the flailing motion with which Christ ousts the moneylenders from the Temple returns as he is dragged before Annas and scourged in the *Flagellation*; Mary kneeling at her lectern in the *Annunciation* is still kneeling there when the risen Christ appears to announce his Resurrection; long handles, breaking up the eddying of hatching, appear in connection with crucifers, spears, halberds, and, in the most arrestingly secular image, a shovel, as Christ in a rakishly brimmed sunhat appears as a gardener to Mary Magdalene and tells her, "*Noli me tangere.*"

A number of these small woodcuts achieve a classic expression of their well-worn subject matter: the *Expulsion* with its magnificently clothed angel, touchingly steatopygous naked pair of sinners, and mournful backward glance from Adam; the *Annunciation* astir with an excitement that ruffles even the feathers of the descending Dove of the impregnating Holy Spirit; the wonderfully airy and architectural *Nativity*; the grave and beautifully lit *Christ Washing the Feet of Saint Peter*; the agonized *Bearing of the Cross* (a considerable improvement over the *Large Passion* version); the understated, modestly populated *Crucifixion*; the eloquent *Descent from the Cross*. In this last, the face of Christ is quite hidden; he is visible only as a head of hair, as he is in *Christ Before Annas*; in several others his face is deeply shadowed, or sharply averted. One wonders how new to iconography was this subjection of the God-Man to the laws of perspective and group action; certainly no Byzantine artist, or Sienese, would have let Christ's face be eclipsed in a process of representational realism. Medieval Christian art was in that sense as aspective as Egyptian; the artist shows us not what he sees but what he knows. Dürer dares submerge God in the human tumble, omitting his halo in all but the *Last Supper* and the post-Resurrection appearances. If the *Large Passion* impresses us with its masses of witnesses, the *Small Passion* shows the action they are witnessing, felt as if from within—an ordeal coming ever faster. As Kantor points out, the pictoral composition, "even the direction of the crosshatching," enforces the momentum and turns, as it were, the page. The visual stream, like a stream in nature, ripples and dimples into whirlpools; some of the most dynamic images—the *Mocking of Christ, Christ Nailed to the Cross*, the *Lamentation*, the near-comic *Ascension*—have a circular motion that floods the frame.

All this is presented with a linear clarity that leaves no detail fudged or vague. A word of praise should be reserved for the anonymous woodcutters, who with such remarkable patience and skill and keen eyesight translated Dürer's drawings to raised ridges of wood. A crudely made woodcut, like those of the early, abortive *Albertina Passion*, reads in its

Dürer, Noli me tangere (Christ Appearing to Mary Magdalen as a Gardener), *from the* Small Passion, *c. 1510. Woodcut.*

Dürer, Christ Washing the Feet of Saint Peter, *from the* Small Passion, *c. 1510. Woodcut.*

halftones as white scooped from black; but even in its finest, closest cross-hatching the *Small Passion*, on a scale little bigger than that of playing cards, reads as black on white, each tiny rhomboid of white left by the artist's pen lifted out by the woodcutter's chisel.

The woodcuts are, then, a collaboration, whose final texture and definition are supplied by an artisan. But an engraving or etching is from the hand of the artist, who often supervises the inking of the intaglio plate as well. The fifteen plates of the *Engraved Passion* are marvellously fine; into rectangles slightly smaller than those of the *Small Passion*, Dürer scratched details that for comfortable appreciation need a blow-up to twice the real size. My impression was of a greasy darkness in which only a few passages have the breathing room, the daylight tonality, common in the woodcuts. Though executed in the same rough period as the *Small Passion* and the second installment of the *Large*, the *Engraved* was the last to be completed, and has a tang of decadence. Familiarity with the Gospel tableaux has bred something like contempt. The costumes, however common in Dürer's Nuremberg, strike a twentieth-century viewer as bizarre and even clownish—e.g., the double-crowned hat of Caiaphas in *Christ Before Caiaphas*, the petal-fringed cap of the most prominent spectator in *Ecce Homo*, the furry top hat in the *Entombment*, and the towering construction, crumpled like an animal's snout, worn on the head of

Dürer, Deposition (Descent from the Cross), *from the* Small Passion, *c. 1509–10. Woodcut.*

the pug-faced attendant kneeling to hold the basin in *Pilate Washing His Hands*. Under the witchery of the graver's needle, a strange lightness possesses the figures: Christ and his two tormentors in this *Flagellation* appear to be doing a stately dance; the lead lamenter in *Lamentation* is gesturing over her head as if with castanets; and the lissome Christ in *Resurrection* is doing a graceful two-step on the lid of his tomb. The details of armor, of creased faces, of distant villages are rendered with fanatic intensity, but the clear didactic thread has been lost. Virtuosity has replaced exemplification of virtue. Dürer's monogram is always prominent, and is manifested through a number of ingenious conceits—in plaques and tablets and stone slabs, and carved flat into flooring, obedient to the picture's perspective. The Passion has become, in part, self-advertisement.

Dürer did not soon return to the Passion after 1512, but in the 1520s, after Luther had nailed up his theses and altered northern Christendom forever, a number of pen-and-ink drawings, and one completed woodcut, pick up the Passion again, in the so-called *Oblong Passion*. Some of the drawings, especially the crowd scene of the *Bearing of the Cross*, are superb; the lateral format gives Dürer space to animate a pedestrian throng. Jordan Kantor proposes that in this last Passion the artist tends

Dürer, Resurrection, *from the* Engraved Passion, *1512. Engraving.*

to marginalize and dematerialize the physical presence of Christ. A 1523 *Last Supper* has Jesus at the end of the table, at the extreme left of the picture. Several sketches of the *Agony in the Garden* show the agonist facedown and, as it were, levitating. An engraving for a *Crucifixion* was left in outline on Dürer's death, and looks bloodless and schematic. At a far cry from Grünewald's twisted, skeletal Christ of ten years earlier, Dürer's final version shows him standing firmly on a ledge on the Cross, his arms stretched out more in command than in torment. Crucifixion has become an abstract idea; passion, at least in this engraved outline, has fled. Dürer's personal involvement has faded, and the work was left unfinished. It seems true that as the impulses of Protestantism—and, to come, Pietism—were felt in art, holy subjects could not be tackled without personal, even egoistic, feeling. To project the story of the Incarnation, one had to put oneself into it.

The Thing Itself

IT FELT NOT TOO STRANGE, flying down from Boston a month to the day after the World Trade Center disaster, braving the bristling beefed-up security in the city's disgraced Logan Airport—tall state troopers in blue jodhpurs and diagonal belts, pink-cheeked boys in Reserve camouflage outfits, grizzled cops squinting at a long day of light duty, the same old security personnel galvanized by a new sense of mission as they waved their peepy wands—and gazing down on the widespread loveliness of a Connecticut whose trees were glowing with autumnal red as we approached New York by a wary new route well away from the Hudson and wounded Manhattan, coming in to La Guardia over more golf courses than I had ever known existed in Westchester County, and taking a taxi (the driver bitterly complained of his month of diminished fares) to the fine little Bruegel show, in this mournful fall of 2001, at the Metropolitan—fifty-four of his sixty-one surviving drawings, sixty prints based on his drawings, and another twenty drawings imitating his or long thought to be by him.

Bruegel's world, like ours, showed a gaping divide between the monstrous and the magnificent, between freaks and demons and hellish fantasies out of Hieronymus Bosch and landscapes near paradisal in their impervious splendor. Like ours, his was an age rent by religion: his increasingly Protestant Netherlands was a province of Catholic Spain, and toward the end of Bruegel's short life (he died in 1569, probably in his early forties) Philip II of Spain sent the Duke of Alva and twenty thousand troops to administer a reign of terror and chastise the infidels. Scholars have pored over the meagre record of the artist's life and over his enigmatic art for clues as to where Bruegel himself stood. Some of his best patrons belonged to the Catholic establishment, yet his paintings democratically vote for the peasantry as it tried, beneath the clash of creeds and principalities, to do its work and have a little fun.

Bruegel painted peasants with such lively sympathy that his first biographer, Karel van Mander, supposed him to have been one. Yet only one drawing at the Met, *The Bagpipe Player*, dated in the mid-1560s, presents the kind of figure study that must have fed into his monumental rural folk, folk who grow in size and expressiveness on the painter's later canvases. A number of eminently Bruegelian sketches of such figures, complete with color notations as if for paintings, turn out, two scholars independently demonstrated in the late 1960s, to be by Roelandt Savery (1556–1639). The Savery brothers appear to have made an unsavory business of aping Bruegel; Jacob Savery (1565–1603) produced twenty-five pen landscapes signed with Bruegel's name and considered authentic until well into the twentieth century. The temptation to forgery and close imitation—some of it long considered authentic Bruegel and indeed of authentically high quality—arose from Bruegel's great popularity, which underwent no eclipse after his death, and from the scarcity of his sketches.* Martin Royalton-Kisch, in a catalogue essay on Bruegel as a draftsman, bemoans, "The sixty-one surviving drawings (and the six copies of lost ones) can only be a pitiful fragment of a much larger corpus." Teasingly, van Mander's brief biography claims that on his deathbed Bruegel directed his wife to burn a number of drawings "because . . . he was afraid that on their account she would get into trouble or she might have to answer for them." That his were parlous times had not escaped him.

The bulk of drawings that did survive are detailed, carefully limned scenes, in shades of brown ink, meant to be engraved and offered for sale by the pre-eminent Antwerp print publisher, Aux Quatre Vents (To the Four Winds), headed by Hieronymus Cock. Exceptions in the exhibit include: the well-known presumed self-portrait, *The Painter and the Connoisseur* (mid-1560s); a looser-than-usual drawing called *The Rabbit Hunt*, for which Bruegel himself did the etching (1560); an even sketchier image,

---

*His paintings, too, are scarce enough to be, like Vermeer's, virtually priceless. Michael Frayn's antic, instructive novel *Headlong* (1999), in positing the modern discovery of a maddeningly valuable lost painting, imagines the missing sixth of Bruegel's 1565 *Labors of the Months* series, of which three exist in Vienna, one in Prague, and one in New York, at the Metropolitan.

Pieter Bruegel the Elder, The Bagpipe Player, *c. 1600. Pen and brown ink.*

from around the same time as *The Rabbit Hunt*, of Christ's journey to Emmaus, of which no engraving exists; and seventeen landscape drawings executed during Bruegel's youthful trip across the Alps to Italy and back from 1552 to 1554, possibly on a commission from Cock to gather material for scenic prints. These landscapes are astonishing in their breadth and intensity; though the wall commentary and the catalogue speak of Northern traditions of landscape versus Southern traditions, the viewer feels confronted with the thing itself, the Alpine landscapes first beheld, in their airy vastness and elevation of view, by a visitor from the Lowlands.

The earliest, *Southern Cloister in a Valley* (dated 1552 in Bruegel's hand), is naïvely frontal; bushy growth on a hill across a lake becomes a fuzz of dots and tiny loops. The cloister at the foot of the hill and its adjacent gardens are rendered with a dainty literalism; only the trees and figures in the foreground loosen up the young artist's pen. This is thought to be one of the few landscapes he drew directly from nature. Whatever his purpose in making so meticulous a record, a later owner cared enough to enhance the drawing with colored washes. The foreground tree of *Wooded Landscape with Mills*, the next in chronological order, combines Dutch mills (wind-, water-) and gabled houses with a tree that is not only, from its hilly setting, Italian but, in its dramatic, muscular rendering, Italianate, uncannily resembling a tree in a Titianesque woodcut of a decade later.

What Bruegel learned, and how, concerning the technique of representation during his visit to Italy remains a conjectural matter. Thanks to the spread of engraved prints, Florentine and Venetian masters could be studied in Antwerp. Of the many drawings of Roman structures and ruins that Bruegel presumably made, only a modest study from across the Tiber of the marine customs house remains. But in the course of his two years' wandering (he got as far south as Sicily), his landscapes gained dash and depth, diagonal thrust and chiaroscuro. Two arboreal studies late in his trip (c. 1554) show a sweeping and confident hand. Trunks, foliage, ground, clouds, animals are skimmed together, in *Landscape with a Group of Trees and a Mule*, into one speckled element; it is, as the commentary has it, "an accomplished whirlwind of a sketch." The other, *Stream with an Angler*, is more studied and solid, yet here, too, the penstrokes serve as a unifying atmosphere, permeating every interval. Bruegel in his sketches is a more nervous and fiery draftsman than is apparent in his somewhat stolid, though crowded, paintings.

Landscape with Fortified City conjures up a towered, walled hillside city in such vivacious detail that it was thought to be Avignon, but it is imaginary, possibly a vision of Jerusalem. *Alpine Landscape* (c. 1553) lifts us dizzily above a cultivated plain at the foot of a tumultuously craggy, but populated, mountain; such paeans to geology (and to mankind's antlike place within it) were to form the gist of the twelve ambitious etchings known as the Large Landscapes (c. 1555–56). In them, the effect of surging rock becomes explosive and volcanic. The religious figures sometimes tucked in the foregrounds—Saint Jerome, Mary Magdalene, even Christ and two apostles, in peaked hats, in *The Way to Emmaus* (c. 1555–56)—are so incidental they suggest a drastic if not blasphemous de-emphasis. The drawing for the Emmaus print, in fact, is titled *Landscape with Three Pilgrims*, and the central pilgrim, Christ himself, seen from behind, lacks the easily overlooked halo supplied in the etching; perhaps it was added by the engraver at the publisher's request, to improve the print's saleability. Bruegel consistently downplays the figures that give his scenes their ostensible raison d'être; they are lost in the dynamic expanse of nature. W. H. Auden admired this trait, writing of Bruegel's *Fall of Icarus*, whose titular hero is represented by a single, easily overlooked white leg disappearing into the sea in the lower right corner,

> That even the dreadful martyrdom must run its course
> Anyhow in a corner, some untidy spot
> Where the dogs go on with their doggy life and the torturer's horse
> Scratches its innocent behind on a tree.

Pieter Bruegel the Elder, Alpine Landscape, *c. 1553. Pen and brown ink.*

There are a great many innocent behinds in Bruegel, and little religious drama. His largest surviving painting, *Christ Carrying the Cross* (1564), has Christ at the geometric center of the teemingly populated panel, but he is virtually hidden beneath the T-shaped cross and amid a crowd of nine jeering, tugging tormentors. He is a challenge to find, and so is Saint Paul in *The Conversion of Saul* (1567), and perhaps this is the point. God's eyes see what ours cannot. Three centuries after Byzantine and high-medieval art presented iconic portraits with a minimum of natural or architectural context, artists increasingly suggested that all we see on earth *is* natural context—houses and mountains, crowds of trees and people—and that God, we must presume, invisibly inhabits these vistas. Romantic theology began in the Renaissance.

Because they lack a center of religious feeling, Bruegel's didactic and allegorical prints are hard to love, and not easy to study, compared with his landscapes and portraits of ordinary life. His compositions have a checkerboard quality that lets us look where we will. It was very late in his abbreviated career as a painter that Bruegel began, in his splendid series *The Labors of the Months*, to explore ways to distinguish foreground and background and to organize the pictorial space into an integrated, receding unity. Until then his approach leaned toward inventory—assembling illustrations of children's games or proverbs or, in *Dulle Griet* (c. 1562), female insubordination on a plane that is seen from above, like a stage from a balcony. In his elaborate representations of the seven vices (1556–57), the inventories are highly antic—fanciful architecture looms behind multiple scenes of allegorical grotesquerie; human figures in various sizes vie with chimeras compounded of fish and reptiles and human heads. Houses have faces and imitate the bulbous, sharp-edged tropical vegetation beginning to enter the European imagination. Everything means something, though it takes the midnight oil of modern scholars to decipher rebuslike riddles that Bruegel's contemporaries no doubt deciphered at a glance and with a smile, as we used to decipher the drawings of Saul Steinberg.

Bruegel was hailed as the new Bosch. Hieronymus Bosch (c. 1450–1516) was a lifelong resident of s' Hertogenbosch, a Brabant city, forty miles northeast of Antwerp, from which Bosch took his name. Like Bruegel, he is an artist with virtually no biography, but, closer by three generations to the Middle Ages, he is the more deeply sunk into impersonality. Not a single work can be attributed to him with certainty; he was basically a workshop of genius. One feels, comparing his phantasmagoria with Bruegel's, that it is spikier and closer to the hell of the Middle Ages, to the cathedral gargoyles and the flitting sprites and imps of superstitious folktales. Aux Quatre Vents did a good trade in prints fashioned after Bosch and paid Bruegel for work in the same popular manner; why it was popular remains, to a modern sensibility, as mysterious as our own fads and tastes may be to cultural historians of the future. Bosch's vision, most famously bodied forth in the great triptych at the Prado, *The Garden of Earthly Delights* (1480–90), has been described by the scholar Paul Vandenbroeck as one of Nature dangerously permeated by sex, a universal eroticism to be found in Bosch's recurrent forms of flower and seedpod. This cosmogony well conforms with the book of Genesis and could play a subliminal role in Bosch's imagery's lasting appeal. Insofar as his paintings can be compared with Bruegel's prints, Bosch is airier, needling and penetrating and hair-raisingly supernatural where Bruegel is earthy, blocky, humorous, and humanistic. Bosch makes us think of dragonflies; Bruegel of toads. Bruegel's monsters—drawn from the level of reality where fools, cripples, and beggars overlap with creatures of fur and fin— have active, productive anuses and rueful, semi-aggressive expressions like those of the man next door. The modern viewer wonders if anyone was ever turned away from sin by the carnival of these cautionary prints. At this remove of time and piety, *The Temptation of Saint Anthony* (1556) shows nothing tempting: a funhouse hodgepodge, rather, featuring a huge hollow head with a lozenge-paned window for an eye, a plume of

Pieter Bruegel the Elder, Summer, 1568. Pen and brown ink.

smoke for a tongue, and for a hat a fish big enough to contain a wrestling match. The vase on legs in the foreground looks like a delightful house pet, if he can be housetrained. No wonder Saint Anthony turns his back; allegory strains the eyes.

What we treasure in Bruegel is his realism—the sense we get that through him we are looking into the sixteenth century more clearly than through any other artist of the time. The taste of actual atmosphere, of a bygone Europe's climate, in the winter paintings *Hunters in the Snow* (1565) and *Census at Bethlehem* (1566) and *Adoration of the Magi in the Snow* (1567); the heavy, itchy heat of summer captured in the drawing *Summer* (1568), its two principal figures clothed in such respectful detail that peasant costumes could be reconstructed on their model; the moment of Halloween shock preserved in the one surviving woodcut based on a Bruegel drawing, *The Wild Man* or *The Masquerade of Orson and Valentine* (1566), a token of the widespread pagan remainders, the bizarre festivals and costumes which enlivened quotidian existence in Europe much as electrically promulgated entertainment does now; the surreal reality of the basket-headed *Beekeepers* (c. 1567–68); the imposing, intricately rigged ships, some of them with sails filled to bursting, presented in etchings based on vanished Bruegel drawings: of such is Bruegel's gift to us, the life of his time seized at a coarser, more mundane level than the myth-minded artists of Italy descended to. His drawings are not the main part of this gift, but they are the basis of it, where his eye and hand began, and where they laid claim, through the medium of his prints peddled to an anonymous public, to a new form of patronage.

With prints, it should be noted, the hand and eye of the engraver become an important adjunct to those of the artist. Bruegel's drawings for mechanical reproduction have a careful, easily traced clarity that precludes the dashing atmospheric effects of some of the landscape drawings. Nor are all engravers the same: Joannes and Lucas van Doetecum show great delicacy in producing a slightly pallid impression; Pieter van der Hayden, the engraver of the seven sins and most of the elaborate, symbol-laden designs, scrupulously follows Bruegel's lines while losing some animation and halftones; Philips Galle, who did the seven virtues, produces a greasier, darker effect, with noticeably blacker hatching and more three-dimensional shadows; Frans Huys, who did the ships and a few others, is perhaps the best of the lot, in a painstaking, subservient craft. If Bruegel's prints do not quite seem, like Dürer's or Rembrandt's, an oeuvre unto themselves, they compress much energy into their spaces and expand our appreciation of a great painter.

The Imaginary Builder

GIOVANNI BATTISTA PIRANESI was a frustrated architect, whose one commission was for the restoration of the Church of Santa Maria Priorato in Rome. Born in Venice in 1720, he moved to Rome at the age of twenty and turned to the production of souvenir views, or *vedute*, of the city. Until his death in 1778, he remained a celebrant of Rome's massive buildings and ruins, depicting them in an outpouring of etchings that, according to as impassive an authority as the *Encyclopædia Britannica*, are "the most original and impressive representations of architecture to be found in western art." His first volume of representations, *Architecture and Perspectives, Invented and Etched by Gio. Batt.a Piranesi, Venetian Architect*, appeared in 1743 and consisted of twelve prints presenting idealized reconstructions of "an ancient capitol," "a magnificent bridge," "an ancient temple," "an ancient mausoleum," and so forth—Roman ruins extrapolated into a pristine, elaborately decorated timelessness.

Since Rome with its vast ruins, pompous post-medieval churches, and heroic hilltop vistas presented a medley already bordering on the fantastic, and since Piranesi was an aspiring architect bent on showing what his imagination could do, the visionary quality of these early prints does not seem incongruous; their surprising extension into a fantastic underworld followed in 1749, in a set of fourteen plates titled, in Italian, *Invenzioni capric. di carceri (Fanciful Images of Prisons)*. These imaginary *carceri*, inspired in part by the architect's acquaintance with the immense Roman sewers, were to become Piranesi's best-known works. After producing many superb etchings of actual Roman ruins in all their majestic dilapidation, Piranesi in 1761—the year in which he set up his own printmaking business—reissued the *Carceri*, heavily reworking the fourteen plates and adding two new ones. It has been the happy inspiration of the Boston Museum of Fine Art, drawing solely from its own collections, to present the engravings of 1749 and of 1761 in juxtaposition, in a show titled *Piranesi and Architectural Fantasy*, running from April to September of the year 2001. The large prints, roughly twenty-four by twenty inches, take up one room; a second room exhibits the work of artists contemporary with Piranesi or influenced by him, along with some pen-and-wash sketches by the artist himself, showing his "fiery brushwork" and thoroughly practiced eye for the anatomy of buildings.

But the *Carceri* are the main attraction, and this viewer was struck by their extraordinary freedom and even fury of execution. Piranesi etched on large copper plates as freely as most artists use pencil and paper. He went, especially in the 1761 reworking phase, for the impressionistic effect, shading not only with parallel gouges of the graver but with an evolved scribble like that which can be seen these days in the cartoons of Edward Sorel. The result is as dashing and headlong as the music manuscripts of Johann Sebastian Bach. The meticulousness of his usual engravings—especially meticulous in his utilitarian albums of architectural ornaments (1769) and of "vases, candelabras, grave stones, sarcophagi, tripods, lamps, and ornaments" (1778)—has been ousted by a personal urgency. He is working, one feels, not to win rich customers but to unburden his soul.

The 1749 originals, initiated during a return to Venice in 1745–47, are personal and bizarre enough: high-roofed interiors hold a multitude of arches, stairways, catwalks, ladders, drawbridges, columns, projecting beams, dangling chains, and various gloomy apparatuses suitable for dungeons. Shadowy figures, stooped and dwarfed, move about in a many-storied maze like dazed members of the damned. A semblance of sunlight falls wanly down into some of the perspectives, and clouds are seen in *The Grand Piazza* and *The Giant Wheel* (really a round window, the wall cap-

Piranesi, The Pier with a Lamp, *from the* Carceri, *1749 version. Engraving.*

Piranesi, The Pier with a Lamp, *from the* Carceri, *1761 version. Engraving.*

tion explains), but the feeling overall is of hopeless, albeit palatial, enclosure. The details come from the streets of Rome, but are here disposed in giant punitive crypts. A kind of communal subconscious, the dank and menacing underside of European polity, is revealed.

When Piranesi returned to these dire visions over a decade later, he darkened the plates dramatically, crosshatching the foregrounds and loading fresh detail into the background recessions. He added catwalks and archways and crossbeams to the point where, as in *The Gothic Arch*, the perspective no longer reads, and instead frustrates the eye, like a tricky Escher print. Escher, that compulsive twentieth-century engraver of impossible patterns, of visual twist and transformation, comes to mind more than once as one's eyes roam through Piranesi's tangled castles. Impalpable space is here so subdivided and crisscrossed as to become, by visual calculus, palpable. Some grim work of construction appears to be in progress; we can almost hear the echoing clangor. The plates take their titles, often, from rough artifacts that loom in the foreground as threateningly as guards or arresting officers—*The Well*, with its hanging bucket and loose, lianalike rope; *The Sawhorse*, its spread-legged form almost swallowed in the darkness of the later version and surrounded by cruel spikes, silhouetted; *The Pier with a Lamp*, its lamp less striking than the three sculptured heads holding heavy tethering rings in their mouths; and *The Pier with Chains*, the massive pier squared since its first version and a viciously toothed drawbridge added, along with a trio of Latin slogans promising terror and infamy to treachery and evil conduct.

The engraver's alterations, imposed over a resmoothed section of plate or else scratched into place with an effect of hasty transparency, are not all improvements: *The Arch with a Shell Ornament*, one of the most reproduced of the *Carceri*, was more intelligible and eloquent in its simpler 1749 version; *The Round Tower* lost its sure, swift sketchiness. But the general intensification of shadow and detail is a gain, making the vistas more theatrical and more hellish. This venture of Piranesi's into theatricality has two recognized parents: the Arcadian fantasies of the Venetian Marco Ricci, and the Baroque stage designs of the Galli-Bibiena family. Piranesi himself briefly studied stage design under the Valeriani brothers. Theatricality was the Baroque version of spirituality; the rococo aftermath of the eighteenth century minimized the spirituality, as the power of spectacle ousted human scale from official architecture and the theatre itself. Once the neoclassical alexandrines of Racine and Molière died away, the human voice counted for less and less in drama, and only operatic voices adequately filled the giant painted shells of aristocratic entertainment. Piranesi's *Carceri* seem shaped for the shout of the costumed male chorus, the piercing high note of the betrayed heroine, and the sobbing tenor farewell from the hero.

What did Piranesi consciously intend with these fantastic vistas, which were dear enough to him, and evidently to a buying public, that he reissued them, strenuously revised? He was demonstrating, perhaps, his architectural virtuosity to the clients whose commissions never came— or came once, late, in his mid-forties. And he was offering to the public, with his unprecedentedly refined and confident etching technique, vicarious realities not so different from actual buildings. Prints were the photographs, the pictorial bulletins, of their day. In a Europe debating the relative sublimity of Greek and Roman architecture, and where the fresh discoveries of archeology were turned into eclectic contemporary design, views of buildings had news value and even polemical content.

But why *carceri*? It is easy for the modern mind, accustomed to the totalitarian atrocities and Orwellian dystopias of the twentieth century, to read political protest into these images of dungeons. As the Enlightenment drained away the theistic justification for monarchy, the burdens of taxation and penal punishment were felt as increasingly intolerable—a crushing oppression without earthly reason or heavenly reward. Society for a few was aristocratic play, amid music and mirrors, and for the many others an endless, laborious captivity. The paved city itself—and no city loomed as more stonily imperious than Rome—had the hardness and compression of a prison, walled with the imposing façades of wealth and power. De Chirico's empty piazzas and Richard Estes's photorealistic representations of the unpeopled streets of New York and Tokyo revive the nightmare note that Piranesi struck.

He himself, however, may have seen his gloomy chambers more brightly than we, as imaginary spaces carved and subdivided with an exultant ingenuity—grottoes in the public gardens of graphic art. The second room of the MFA's exhibition shows, via such artists as Ricci and Lajoue, Cuvilliés and Blondel, that the eighteenth century did not lack for florid visual fancies. Apparitions escaped from the medieval world of fairies and the classical world of nymphs and satyrs formed an Arcadian froth on the crumbling castle of Christian supernature much as grass, flowers, and bushes flourished on the tops of Roman ruins. Europe's ruins posed in the midst of its population the problem of time, the shudder of the grave. Piranesi's descendants led art into Romanticism, which relocated God from Heaven and the cathedral sanctuary to the glories of Nature and the urges of the human heart. These *Carceri* could be taken to symbolize our own depths, majestically projected by the power of perspective—cavernous ripostes to the monuments decaying in the air

above. There is something exhilarating about them, as the artist feverishly loads more structural features upon their unfolding archways and
squeezes further chambers and stairways, fine as postage stamps, out of
relatively underdeveloped spots in the first etchings. The will to construct pushes deeper and deeper into formlessness; *Homo faber* receives in
these imaginary vaults a reverberating homage.

Personal Considerations

A TRIBUTE *to Saul Steinberg, composed after his death in May of 1999, for* The New York Review of Books.

The *New York Times* obituary quoted a fellow-cartoonist as saying, "Steinberg was not a warm man. He was chilly and Olympian with a somewhat hauteur tone [sic]," but in my slight acquaintance with him he consistently appeared gracious and kind. Our acquaintance was slight but long: in 1945 I wrote him from my small town in Pennsylvania asking that he send me, for no reason except that I wanted it, the original of a drawing I had seen in *The New Yorker*, of one man tipping his hat and another tipping back his hat with his head still in it. At this time I was an avariciously hopeful would-be cartoonist of twelve or thirteen and Steinberg a thirty-one-year-old Romanian Jew whose long American sojourn had begun but four years before. Perhaps he thought that his new citizenship entailed responding to importunities from unknown American adolescents. He sent me not the original but a duplicate he had considerately made, with his unhesitating pen, and inscribed it, in impeccable New World fashion, "To John Updike with best wishes." Nearly fifty years later, when I turned sixty, he sent me a pencil drawing of a rabbit on a fragmentary table drawing a Steinbergian scroll, with the inscription "John Up. 60! Love from Saul ST."

He would not, perhaps, like having these small personal generosities broadcast in this telling; his sensibility was fertile but fastidious, expressed in the polish of his tailoring and the soft but distinct phrasing of his speech, as if he were translating, with a barely perceptible hesitation, out of an arcane, possibly wordless inner language. He spoke not exactly with an accent but with an un-American tendency toward epigrammatic precision. He made little of his Romanian origins; "pure Dada," he called his native land. Yet if one thinks of the Romanians, all

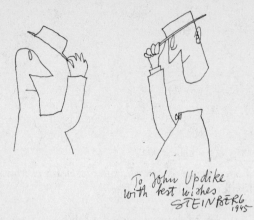

To John Updike
with best wishes
STEINBERG
1945

exiles, that have figured prominently in the culture of the twentieth century—Brancusi, Ionesco, Tristan Tzara, the aphorist E. M. Cioran—one glimpses a shared economy, a willingness to invent visionary forms and to seek a comprehensive simplicity. Ambitions so innocently sweeping might have less easily arisen among natives of a less marginal European country, one with enough gravity of tradition to hold its creative spirits in orbit.

Steinberg studied and made his artistic beginnings in that lightest-hearted of major nations, Italy, receiving in 1940 a doctoral degree in an architecture that he never practiced but whose linear elevations and visual shortcuts infused his innovations in cartooning. His father was a printer and bookbinder who became a manufacturer of cardboard boxes, preparing the way for his son's mature romance with paper, with alphabets, with trademarks and documents and maps and fingerprints and rubber stamps and all such variegated fauna of the two-dimensional, man-created world. Hilton Kramer, one of the many art critics provoked to wit by Steinberg's own, wrote, "There is a kind of primitivism in all this, an animism, for everything in Steinberg—even the most inanimate object or abstract thought—is teeming with aspiration, ambition and portents." The power to generate images was never merely a means to an end for Steinberg; imagery was, itself, a matter for celebration. Those deadpan postcard-shaped images he produced in the Seventies of middling American post offices and banks and motels and Main Streets carried his joy in the joke of image to a delicate extreme—like those sometimes three-dimensional tabletops and desktops he rendered in the

same period, rectilinear homage to what simply is, things here and there and the ominous blankness of the table or the prairie pressing through in the spaces between.

Like Nabokov and Milos Forman, to name just two other affectionate adult immigrants, Steinberg saw America afresh, with details to which natives had grown blind or numb. American parades, American cowboys, American mountains of Art Deco, New York taxis in their screaming, bulbous décor, the quaint gingerbread pomp of suburban mansions and railroad stations—these visual events were mixed, not so paradoxically, with the emblems of the intended Utopia, the Latinate slogans involving Lex and Lux and Pax and Tax and Vox Populi, the Statue of Liberty enjoying her middle-class marriage with Uncle Sam, the practical partnership of S. Freud and S. Claus. When, from the window of his studio on Union Square, Steinberg saw the great American city descending into a sump of whoredom and homelessness and what he called "Mickey Mouse brutality," he sought for the visual vocabulary to render it and came up with roachlike pedestrians scrabbling along amid giant congealed automobiles, and implacable Amazons whose high-heeled boots ended at their necks, and tall Mickey Mouses blandly toting machine guns. Steinberg's fine doodling pen line—a handwriting of the mind, a punning seismograph—turned to relatively coarse and indefinite pencil and crayon, deployed in clashing, scrawled mimesis of a perceived ugliness; his art became ever more a gallery art, aimed at collectors and couched in a private symbology. *The New Yorker* of this time, so liberally race-blind that blacks had not appeared in its cartoons for decades, could not have found it easy to accommodate a vision so culturally diverse and unwinsomely grotesque, so macabre and grim; but in fact the magazine did salvage a few covers from Steinberg's Boschian visions.

He and William Shawn shared some points of sensibility—laconic, quietly erudite men with a taste for the quizzically existential. If the *pièce de résistance* of an issue of Harold Ross's magazine was a lusty Peter Arno cartoon, that of one of Shawn's was a Steinberg spread, often some delicious example of synesthesia such as the sounds of different musical instruments seen as clouds and swirls of abstraction or a page of "Country Noises" heard as typographical borders and ornaments. A reader could study it lovingly, as the joke unfolded its several levels. Steinberg came to English late (while waiting to be admitted to this country in Santo Domingo, he read *Huckleberry Finn* for practice), and its basic vocabulary kept a primal kinesis for him: one *New Yorker* cover shows "Today" blasting off from a crumbling "Yesterday" on a route plotted "Breakfast Lunch Dinner Tomorrow." On another, "I HAVE" hangs like dirty wash on the terra firma of "I AM" while the "O" in "I DO" shines above with solar effulgence. On others, an army of "WE ARE"s being led by "I SHALL" carries the banner "ARE WE?"; the "M" and "W" of "MYTH" and "HOW" are the mouths of fish about to eat up "WHY?" and "TRUTH"; and the letter "E" wistfully dreams of "É."

Within the magazine, until Steinberg's ambitions overflowed the spot cartoon, one encountered people with zigzag faces who seemed to be both coming and going, and a man shooting an apple off his own head, and a woman with a vase for a head, with the flower of a thought in it. A businessman talks a torrent of scribbled words inside a speech balloon shaped grandly "NO." Speech balloons, those indispensable aerial platters in comic strips, show up sideways in the mouths of alligators, and tucked under people's arms like baguettes, and mimicking a street map of Paris or (a competing vacation in a luncheon chat) the island of Sardinia. And so abundantly on. Such an inventory dulls, perhaps, the surprise with which one encountered a Steinberg, in pages where—the half-blind scrawls of Thurber aside—the cartoons, whether by Arno or Whitney Darrow or Garrett Price, showed a solid representational technique. One did not open *The New Yorker* then prepared to find a nude photograph or a headline-making exposé; a spiky Steinberg conceit was as exciting an ornament as one might encounter on those good gray lawns of carefully weeded prose.

As the Abstract Expressionists forced us to know that we were looking at paint, Steinberg compelled us to realize we were looking at ink. His drawings turned a corner in mental space and left the looker disoriented;

in his ceaseless effort to explore the spaces of transformation, Steinberg resorted to three dimensions, painting imaginary women seated on the edge of real bathtubs, and men sedately folding themselves into card-board boxes. He worked in wood, creating unopenable books with invit-ing titles—equivalents of his elegantly penned documents that cannot be read. He drew on photographs of junk-store furniture, of crumpled paper, and of New York rooftops. He drew awninged front entrances on sheets of graph paper, turning them into skyscrapers. To call these inven-tions "visual puns" is to make them sound slighter than they are; they are wormholes between different universes that are simultaneously contig-uous and parsecs apart. He created for himself a unique niche between high art and commercial cartooning—a niche in which he, perhaps, was not always comfortable. The *Times* quoted him as saying, "The art world doesn't quite know where to place me."

But in his restlessness he resisted being placed. The huge and legal-headache-making celebrity of his image of the world as seen looking west from Ninth Avenue—the typical New Yorker's dismissively foreshort-ened perspective, *The New Yorker*'s cover for March 29, 1976—may mark a moment after which his work became less ingratiating and more rest-less. A great deal of his later oeuvre is scattered in gallery catalogues. One would be happy now for a retrospective album that would reach back, if possible, to the cartoons he published as a student in Milan, and the propaganda drawings he did for the OSS as an American soldier, to be dropped behind enemy lines to encourage anti-German resistance. Something subversive remained in his art, undermining the intuitive connection between what we see and what we know, calling into ques-tion, like a good metaphysician, the bases of our experience. He was a comedian of epistemology, whose problematics engaged him; Descartes's formula "*Cogito, ergo sum*" more than once recurred among his verbal reifications. His cartoons, even the apparently simplest Möbius strip of a doodle, occur in a realm of thought, where style is substance and double takes are the least we owe the artist. "Drawing is a way of reasoning on paper," he said. Steinberg never, even in his most extended illegible flour-ish, seemed other than reasonable, nor did we ever doubt that his was, with unusual precision, a representation of the world we live in.

Introduction *to* The World of William Steig, *edited by Lee Lorenz (Artisan, 1998).*

I own a Steig. This one. It hangs in a room where I work, and every time I look at it it makes me happy. The homely woman rocks far back in a chair with thick rockers shaped like the crescent moon, laughing while the crescent moon, posed points down above her face, laughs back. Or maybe she is laughing back at the moon. The heavenly presence seems male, so there is a sexual current as well as a cosmic one. I saw the drawing—too small and sly to be a full-fledged cartoon, too big and suggestive to be a mere decorative "spot"—in a 1976 issue of *The New Yorker*, loved it, wrote to the artist, and received an arrangement to buy, at a discount, the original from his gallery. It thus joined my tiny collection of talismanic drawings:

· a head of a dog that James Thurber, in a Connecticut hospital and nearly totally blind, drew for me when at the age of twelve I wrote him a fan letter;

· an *Esquire* Petty girl that George Petty signed for me, calling me, though I had thought my request was maturely phrased, "Johnny";

· three originals by Saul Steinberg, the first sent to me in 1945, and the last a published cartoon of a man shooting an apple on his head, marked up with Scotch tape and printer's thumbprints;

· the originals of the watercolors Arnold Roth painted for the jackets of my three books about Henry Bech, also three terrific ink sketches of Bech that Roth just jotted down, the way you and I would make a quick grocery list;

· and a number of caricatures of me by David Levine, Paul Szep, and some others.

And, oh yes, a black-and-white illustration Warren Chappell did for a children's book of mine based on *Die Zauberflöte*, and the original of a *New Yorker* cover by Arnold Getz showing a Manhattan street—probably Fifty-second—in a snowstorm: a doorman shovels, a passing man leans into the wind, and a poster outside a bar displays a leggy female attraction nearly nude in the teeth of the blizzard. I admired the cover at the time, and when it showed up at an exhibit at the New York Public Library I managed to buy it from the great Getz.

All these artworks cheer me up. My psyche is such that looking at most graphic art makes me happy, especially art that has been reproduced or intended for reproduction. My tiny gallery is a concentrate of happiness. Chappell's Papagena and Papageno are dancing; Steinberg's William Tell suicide will not hurt himself; Steig's rocking woman is jubilant, and the moon jubilates with her.

Steig belongs with Thurber and Steinberg in that his cartoons do not only deliver a joke but make us reflect upon the nature of reality. There is a psychological and philosophical resonance in Steig that has long set him apart in *The New Yorker*. His ideas are all his own; his drawings are extensions of his life. That life, as you will read in the text of this album, was nurtured in an emotional, demonstrative, and creative family and has been sustained in a succession of creative domestic settings. His siblings, wives, and offspring have almost without exception been creative artists of some sort, and Steig, for all his insight into stunted and inhibited children, seems to be one of those adults in whom the creative child has never met discouragement. He has the dauntless energy of prelapsarian innocence. An Edenic nudity romps through his inner landscape.

His art has moved from more or less commercial cartoons into symbolic and expressionistic realms ever closer to the wellsprings of experience, such as his late-starting but fast-accumulating shelf of children's books, and those recent *New Yorker* spreads in which he depicts, in a childish style of unnerving directness, such elemental narratives as those of Genesis and Exodus, Greek mythology, fairy tales, and our legendary American beginnings. There is no overt satire in these depictions, but, rather, a bliss of simple belief, a seeing as if for the first time the narrative images with which children, at least in Steig's childhood, were primed for existence in Western culture. The daydreams of small fry, their dreams of glory, were what made his name as a cartoonist, and the surreal drawings of *The Agony in the Kindergarten* were perhaps his most brilliant breakthrough into a purer kind of cartoon. His representations of childhood have always implied a continuity with adult experience: children are not a zoo of entertainingly exotic creatures but an array of mirrors held up to the quintessentially human.

In this of course he is a Freudian, though without the Viennese physician's pessimism. Freud thought that normal human unhappiness was the best that psychotherapy could bring us to, whereas Steig, the child of socialists, has wider and higher hopes: "I believe that people are basically good and beautiful, and that neurosis is the biggest obstacle to peace and happiness. In my symbolical drawings I try to make neurotic behavior more manifest. . . . I am essentially identified with nature's point of view, as against civilization's." Thus he wrote in introducing *Dreams of Glory*— perhaps the most idealistic and thoughtful preface a cartoonist ever addressed to his public. "We should all be busier removing the obstacles to the decent and joyous life we could be living. . . . I want you to know that I mean you well and that I work for you as well as for myself." He describes his own dream of glory, which is to be "such a completely mobile being that I can do and feel whatever the human body and spirit are capable of."

Glory, not attained only in dreams but accessible to clear eyes and a susceptible heart, is the essence of his later *New Yorker* covers, colored with glorious freshness and drawn as if with the unpremeditated certainty of a child's crayoning. A creative man is an optimistic man, and small wonder that Steig was attracted to one of the few gurus of psychology, Wilhelm Reich, who offered a practical device with which to secure happiness. Steig must be among the last users of Reich's orgone box, and, since he has remained vigorous and productive to the age of ninety,* who is to scoff?

He has become, with the death of George Price, the last of that marvellous crew of artists who filled *The New Yorker*'s pages with comic art that was art. His first contribution came in 1930, and Lee Lorenz's biographical account makes it clear that the long association was not free of conflict. Steig's uninhibited thrust and concern with profound humanistic issues more than once overflowed Ross's somewhat narrow and prudish conception of what his magazine should publish. At one point Steig felt threatened and affronted, in his terrain of earthy city life, by the relatively one-note proletarian cartoons of Syd Hoff. However strained, the

---

*Steig died in 2003, at the age of ninety-five.

New Yorker ties held, and then strengthened under the editorship of William Shawn and Robert Gottlieb. Steig—unlike Arno, Price, and Addams, to name three—found venues and creative satisfaction outside the magazine, notably in his children's books and the books of expressively surreal drawings. (Lest we forget, there were others working this vein in the Forties and Fifties, such as Abner Dean and Robert Osborne.) But it is hard to imagine *The New Yorker* without Steig's sly glimpses into the subconscious, whether through the eyes of a child or through winsome permutations—like my rocking woman and laughing moon—of sexual relations. He gave the cartoon chorus a baritone of seriousness, of hard-won life-wisdom, and in recent decades has struck a purely lyric note like the warble of a panpipe. He was, in those citified, civilized pages, something of a wild man, but one who knew things better not forgotten, and whose freedom all could envy.

For years, Steig has drawn directly in ink on paper, without a preliminary pencil sketch. He professes his favorite artist to be Picasso, a model of confidence, abundance, and rude health. The aspiration to health disposes Steig to the organic. His appetite for love and admiration shapes his figures like flowers yearning in sunlight. It has been pointed out that there is little modern machinery in his world, but as in a magnified garden there are bugs—giant bugs—and monsters of many sorts, some of which can be tamed.

Lee Lorenz, in assembling an album covering all of Steig's oeuvre, faced an embarrassment of riches; he has moved through it with the sure eye and hand of a *New Yorker* art editor, which he was, along with being a cartoonist of explosive verve. Such a compilation serves to celebrate an original who has endured, who has taken his talent in one direction after another and found new territory deep in his old age. Steig's art is not just testimony to his love of life but robust evidence of the necessary interaction between art and life, reality and fantasy. Blake is another touchstone for him, Blake the singer of satisfied desire and the prophet of man unshackled. Children in their dreams of glory are free, free to create omnipotent selves, and my laughing, rocking woman, even with her unfortunately warty nose, is satisfied, free to flirt with the moon.

INTRODUCTION *to a section of* The Complete Cartoons of The New Yorker *(Black Dog & Leventhal, 2004)*.

The decade 1955–64 did not think of itself as a halcyon time, but in retrospect it seems so. Between the Korean police action and the Vietnam involvement, it saw the Cold War in its purest form, as a show of global threats and feints, brinkmanship brought to a terrifying but casualty-free climax in the Cuban crisis of 1962. The vast Communist world and the embattled legions of capitalism somehow agreed to avoid World War III, while at home in America consumerism and industrial production struck a balance which produced, for masses, a greater ease of living. As one of these captions has it: "You know how it is. You have a little more, you live a little better."

The suburbs were the arena of the new plenty, at the expense of cities and farms. Not that the men in gray flannel suits were altogether happy with their split-level lives. One child says to another, "I don't know what my father does all day. All I know is it makes him sick at his stomach." There were rebellious stirrings, even under the anodyne Eisenhower. In popular culture, early rock drowned out the mellow remnants of the big bands; in painting, the stern and heroic canvases of Abstract Expression morphed into the cheerful junk art of Pop and the deadpan quiddity of Minimalism; in writing, baroque mandarins such as Bellow and Nabokov added new, lighter notes to the sonorities of our native naturalism. A certain lightness and gaiety, indeed, permeated the décor and mind-set of a hard-working land.

The microcosm of *New Yorker* cartoons reflects the cultural macrocosm spottily, with a time lag. The foremost domestic issue of the time was the struggle of the black minority for civil rights, yet people of color are almost totally absent from these cartoons, except for a joke showing an anxious drugstore clerk facing a diverse mob of customers and calling out, "Joe, these people say they want flesh-colored Band-Aids." This joke, in fact, was no joke, as the Johnson & Johnson marketeers discovered. Though Peter Arno's sculpturally solid brushstrokes and exclamatory visages still appeared in this decade, his world of tuxedoed elderly rich and impossibly busty and wide-eyed nymphs (who never think of bringing charges of sexual harassment) belonged to a bygone era of metropolitan stylization. So, too, Syd Hoff's plump tenement-dwellers, in their slips and sleeveless undershirts, and George Price's hatchet-faced inhabitants of decaying, lovingly detailed interiors furnished entirely, it appears, with hasty purchases at garage sales. These lively types represented old economic divisions and old apportionments of the national esprit. One graphic artist of genius, Charles Saxon, emerged to depict, in unfailingly beautiful and dashing charcoal renderings, *Homo suburbianis*—middle-aged, modestly prosperous, suffering somewhat the same discontents of civilization and its repressions as Thurber's less dapper citizens of earlier decades.

Harold Ross had died abruptly in 1951, and the presence of the more introspective William Shawn at the helm is reflected in the deepening intellectual adventuring of Saul Steinberg and William Steig into, respectively, the epistemology and the psychology of the Zeitgeist. Both men pushed *The New Yorker*'s envelope into new, profounder, captionless realms of cartooning. In the meantime, there was topical news. Cars grew fins; space travel by terrestrials and extraterrestrials grabbed the imagination. A Luddite revolt against the computer, still in a massive box, was envisioned. The razing of Penn Station and the erection of the Guggenheim Museum were noted. Dining al fresco became a Manhattan possibility ("Please hurry, Hilary. Your soup's getting dirty"). Anatol Kovarsky and others reached across the millennia toward ancient worlds, where Trojan horses treacherously loomed and Egyptian slaves hauling rocks for the Pyramids loyally claimed, "It's an honor to be associated with an enterprise of this magnitude."

The magnitude of free-world leadership weighed on the collective mind: "The Russians have the International Ballistic Missile, and we have the Edsel." There was the nagging threat of nuclear war ("Do you hear something ticking?") and the global ingratitude of the less fortunate: as embassy windows crash, huddled diplomats observe, "It's ironical. Our Peace Corps built their brickyard." At home, feminine dissent reared up: a well-heeled woman asks her scowling, cigar-chomping mate, "Darling, would it upset you terribly if I came out for peace?" The daughters of the bourgeoisie donned sandals and black pants and let their hair grow long, occasioning one matron to sniff to another, "Thank God I'm not an individual." In an elegant Saxon cartoon six months later, a well-padded matron tells another, of a young woman who has come to a cocktail party in a poncho, "They sent her to Bennington to lose her southern accent, and then she turned her back on everything."

Everything, the new possibility has become, doesn't work. Toward the end of 1964, a salesman gives an ominous pitch to a customer: "This toy is designed to hasten the child's adjustment to the world around him. No matter how carefully he puts it together, it doesn't work." By 1964, sex, so cheerfully conspicuous in the Ross-era cartoons of Arno and Cobean, was making a comeback, though couched in careful euphemism. One wife to another, of a husband chasing butterflies: "It could be worse. He could be out chasing you know what." In this period, the parodist, humorist, and novelist Peter De Vries took a hand in polishing the captions to a high degree of risibility. The drawings, relatively, lost polish. Few were, as many had once been, fun just to look at. Certain deliberately hasty and sketchy renderings by Bruce Petty, Dana Fradon, and Al Ross outdid even Thurber in their reductiveness. Postmodern, post-art-school cartooning had arrived.

THE WOULD-BE ANIMATOR: *A reminiscence for Herb Yellin's album of homage to cinema,* Lord John Film Festival *(2006).*

The process of cartoon animation was made vivid early in my childhood. The Disney Company told America all about it, via the silver screen. Even before the self-explanatory sections of *Fantasia* (1940) there was at least one "short subject," as brief films preceding the "featured attraction" were called, that led moviegoers through the Disney studio, revealing animators at work in their cubbyholes. These men (no women) turned out sheaves of sketches that, when ruffled at the right speed, produced an illusion of motion. On celluloid, lines in motion, fourteen (or was it sixteen?) positions a second, limned a kinetic world livelier than ours; our flesh and blood, both ponderous and fragile, were transmuted into rubbery, indestructible energy. While that peculiar barking documentary voice of the Thirties—a baritone pregnant with ominous emergency—accompanied Disney's visual tour, we saw painted "cels," arty backgrounds, multi-plane camera set-ups, head animators like Ub Iwerks and Ward Kimball, and the anonymous "in-betweeners" who drew the intermediate positions between graphic high points sketched by their superiors. I wanted to be an animator—to live in Hollywood and make imaginary mice and crickets and crows and dwarfs and big-eared elephants come to life. Had I been informed that the Disney studio was a sweatshop, and the products of its golden age—*Snow White, Pinocchio, Fantasia, Bambi,* and *Dumbo*—were made possible in all their splendidly worked-out detail by masses on low Depression wages, I still would have been pleased to be part of a machine that generated such spectacular and mirth-giving illusions. "Life's really worth living," a contemporary popular song asserted, "when you are mirth-giving."

There was a springiness, a raffish bounce, to the early animated cartoons. Mickey Mouse was still a rodent and something of a rascal, improvising his way through a ratty world, and the flowers shimmying in unison on their flexible stems had the eerie sex appeal of the female chorus chirpily chiming on the sound track. Vaudeville was not yet dead, nor the stage magic show. Those early animators had the opportunity to remake the world from scratch, along lines of surreal lightness and polymorphous animism. It has been lamented that Disney led the new medium down a stodgy, literalist path, re-creating gravity, as it were, on a planet where it did not naturally occur. The animation of an adult human being, presented without caricature, was an avoidable problem that Disney was determined to meet. Snow White has a porcelain stiffness to her movements, and the Prince is so woodenly unconvincing that he was edited almost entirely out of the story whose hero he is. They both were traced from live-action films, instead of being built up in forms a cartoonist could manipulate on a sketch pad.

And yet, to the five-year-old child who saw *Snow White* when it came out in 1937, realism was intrinsic to the wonder of it—the ambitious handling of the third dimension, the mock–boom shots that lowered the viewer's eye through the woods, the exuberant thoroughness with which the dwarfs' cottage furnishings were constructed and carved, the metamorphosis of the woodland wildlife into the heroine's ingenious assistants and would-be protectors, the whole host of loving little animations to entertain the quick-eyed children who might have gotten lost in the harrowing tale of adult jealousy, attempted murder, and, for the ultimately pitiful witch, mob vengeance. The dwarfs themselves are successfully animated human flesh, in all its resilient floppiness, but child-sized. If Disney never quite managed to animate a realistic adult, he did manage, in *Pinocchio*, a caricatured boy, rounded out of puppethood. Conscientious anatomical studies yielded, in *Bambi*, deer real enough to range from coltish clumsiness to regal power. These triumphs of simulation succeeded one another in a mere five years—*Pinocchio* and *Fantasia* came out in 1940, *Dumbo* and *The Reluctant Dragon* in 1941, *Bambi* in 1942. War put a crimp in Disney's animation factory from which it never quite recovered; even this adolescent devotee winced at the impure marriage of live-action and cartoon figures (dancing cacti!) in *The Three Caballeros* and *Saludos Amigos*. Art for art's sake was no longer the credo. For the war effort Disney designed countless squadron and division insignias and produced a film I have no recollection of seeing: *Victory Through Air Power*.

Like many a veteran, the studio found the postwar world changed; this audience of one, too, had changed, his family moving him out of the small town whose movie theatre was a cozy two blocks away. The older I got, the more awkward it became for me to indulge my passion for animated cartoons. I persuaded a high-school classmate, another would-be artist, to go with me, home from college, to see *Alice in Wonderland* in 1951; I had something in my eye that night, and the hectic animation of Lewis Carroll's Victorian fantasy added to my corneal irritation and sense of being a touch old for this. *Cinderella* of the year before had possessed much of the old Disney charm, with two squeaky mice of a post-Mickey species, but even it, in its shrillness and forced pace, showed that the luxurious realistic detailing of the pre-war films was past; we had entered a Silver Age of animation. Then, suddenly, seven-minute cartoons faded from the standard two-hour movie bill of fare, and the Disney Company was devoting itself to corny real-actor "family" movies, to its Anaheim amusement park, and to its weekly television show. The exigencies of television, I noticed when I watched Saturday-morning kiddie programs with my children, had set animation way back, to stylized simplifications that needed only to make a mouth move or an arm shoot up to further the action. Pop-up books were as intricate. Some of this cut-rate animation, fuzzily dependent on the new technique of photocopying, served witty scripts—*Rocky and His Friends* comes to mind—but there was little to enrapture the eye. I was something of a snob, it might be said, who never believed that the headlong postwar cartoons produced by M-G-M and Warner Brothers, with Bugs Bunny, Yosemite Sam, Daffy Duck, Tweety, Wile E. Coyote, Tom and Jerry, *et alii*, were as enchanting as the pre-war Disney shorts, in which Mickey yielded his starring role to Donald Duck and my exact age-mate (born in 1932) Goofy. But, then, maybe I was easier to enchant at ten than at fifteen.

In adulthood I was driven by my appetite for animation to dragoon my children, then stepchildren, and finally grandchildren to help me keep up with animated features. The Beatles' hallucinogenic *Yellow Submarine* (1968) and Ralph Bakshi's X-rated counterculture *Fritz the Cat* (1972) needed no child escort to view. *Who Framed Roger Rabbit?* (1988) was both a tribute to cartoon animation, mixing copyrighted characters never previously allowed on the same screen, and a demonstration of the computer-aided technical overkill that allows present-day animators to do too much, too fast. MTVs don't need to make sense, any more than dreams do, and thirty-second TV commercials must punch up the pace to keep our attention riveted. The discontinuities and jitters of television have conditioned today's young eyes; they look for a video game on every screen.

It seemed to me that with *The Little Mermaid* (1989) and *Beauty and the Beast* (1991), Disney got some of its groove back, but *The Lion King* (1994) threatened to wear the groove into a rut, and *Pocahontas* (1995) and *Mulan* (1998) campaigned too hard for the preteen-feminism vote. The computer *Toy Story*, both the first and the second, and Spielberg's two *Shrek* features bring me into a brave new world where I long in vain for the homely bliss of singing flowers and skeletons playing the xylophone on one another's ribs. In the *Shrek*s, Eddie Murphy's frantically chattering donkey challenges Donald Duck for unintelligibility (though the youngsters around me seem to get it), and Princess Fiona, the unflappable, belching martial-arts ogress, brings to a plucky conclusion the search since *Snow White* for a cartoon *jeune fille* a real man could love. It is hard to watch these ever more subtly shaded and elasticized representations, built all of algorithms, without being distracted by the old childish question, *How do they do it?* Marshall McLuhan said the medium is the message; here the process is the product.

And me, what of that five-year-old would-be animator? I never found the road to Hollywood that wound through Shillington, Pennsylvania. I went to Harvard instead, whence all roads led to Oxford or Somerville. Now, it turns out, there is a road in the sky whereon jet planes carry fresh-graduated young *Harvard Lampoon* editors out to the scriptorium for *The Simpsons* and its imitators. Still, I never wanted to *write* for cartoons, I wanted to *draw* for them. What I really wanted, I now think, was to *act* in them—to be myself a set of dancing lines, indestructible and jivey.

INTRODUCTION *to* Poor Arnold's Almanac *(Fantagraphics Books, 1998).*

All cartoonists are geniuses, but Arnold Roth especially so. The first time I saw a Roth drawing, I was zapped. Those shaggy zigzag lines! Those pointy noses! Those infinitely rubbery limbs! Those big, big eyes with every eyelash in place! And amid the linear hyperactivity lurks a curious clarity—every detail "reads," there is no fudging. A superabundant creative spirit surges through a Roth drawing like electricity; the lines sizzle.

Consider the sheaf of strips done for the New York Herald-Tribune Syndicate, Sundays only, between May of 1959 and May of 1961, and revived for a bit in 1989. Originally titled *Poor Richard's Encyclopedia*, it shows an encyclopedic scope: Roth was game to produce a dozen panels, ten or so separate gags, on topics ranging from Dogs to Sleep, Alaska to Lions. Though he has described in interviews how the strip was untimely dropped by the syndicate, it is hard to believe he could have indefinitely maintained the stream of ideas. The strips are drawn in a relatively tight, early Roth style—notice the exquisitely neat lettering—but in specimens like "Gardening" and "Books" we can see traces of the fearless exaggerations of the mature, full-feathered Roth.

Born in 1929, he comes from Philadelphia, a city with a long, proud tradition of art and illustration. He graduated from Central High and was expelled from the Philadelphia College of Art; he kept leaving class to have a smoke, and he was late in the morning from staying up all night playing alto sax in jazz bands. Though his main ambition was always to be a cartoonist, the jazzman in him can be detected in the lyrical visual swoops and his preference for improvisation with the pen, as opposed to careful preliminary drawings in pencil. On his way to commercial success, he worked in a picture factory painting tree foliage with a sponge and in a toy factory painting eyes on ducks. He also executed little Pennsylvania Dutch lampshades for Woolworth's. Like most of his ilk, he wanted to be a *New Yorker* cartoonist; but when an interview showed him the extent of control the art department expected to have over its artists, Roth walked away. He has been free-lancing on the wild side ever since. He is allergic to editorial interference; it takes away from the jazz. He has worked for *Playboy*, and for a magazine called *Trump* that Hefner founded and folded, and for one called *Humbug* that lasted a year. For a time he lived in England and was a steady contributor to *Punch*. These days he appears most everywhere, from *Esquire* to *Time*—wherever the paper is glossy. To my lasting delight, he has done three beautiful book jackets for me, at my invitation. He is not only a linear wizard but a fine colorist, in the delicate English style. English artists—Gilray, Rowlandson, Cruikshank—have meant a lot to him; he reminds us, a bit, of Searle and Scarfe. Nevertheless, he is an American original, irreverent, tireless, manicky, and secretly efficient. He can *draw*, is what it comes down to, and his work jumps with joy.

INTRODUCTION *to* Chip Kidd: Book One: Work: 1986–2006 *(Rizzoli, 2006)*.

For a few years in the mid-1940s, between the ages of eleven and thirteen, I used to deliver movie circulars for the local cinema. My pay was a week's movie pass. Wartime taxes had put the ticket price up to eleven cents, and to buy into all three of the features that the Shillington (as it was flatly called) projected each week, at seven and nine p.m. Mondays through Saturdays, would have taken too huge a bite from my thirty-five-cent allowance, leaving only two cents for the Sunday-school collection. A bunch of us boys gathered at the theatre on Saturday mornings, and each team of two was given its sheaf of circulars and its territory. Shillington, a town of nearly five thousand, was divided into several sections, and then there were outlying districts like Mohnton, Pennwyn, and Lincoln Park. Some were a trolley-car ride away, and others a bike ride. Lincoln Park I remember as being just a little beyond the old quarry on the

Shillington boundary, a no-man's-land of no-nonsense middle-class brick homes whose offspring wound up in the Shillington public schools. Imagine my sense of eternal return, of geographical ambush, when, decades after leaving the area, I learned that Chip Kidd, my publisher's dashing young virtuoso of book-jacket design, came from Lincoln Park.

Bucks County, on the Delaware, was in those distant days a weekend resort for New York writers and theatre types, and Chester County a playground for the Philadelphia horsy set, but Berks County was a work-ingman's county, divided between farmers plowing its loamy fields and millworkers crammed into the rowhouses of Reading, the county's per-petually depressed and crime-friendly metropolis. Yet the region was not unfriendly to popular culture. Radios babbled their daily soap operas in every dentist's office; every town of any size had its little movie palace, and Reading had five (Loew's, the Warner, the Astor, the Embassy, the Ritz) along Penn Street alone; art and music still rode high in public-school curricula; and shops carrying craft and art supplies were easy to find. Art, of the practical, sign-painting, enroll-in-our-course-and-become-a-well-paid-cartoonist sort, had its place in the local industries. We wallowed in kitsch—even the Amish had their hex signs—and relied, pre-television, pre-computer, on the print medium to bring us imagery from the metropolitan centers of entertainment. It was a golden age of comic strips, animated cartoons, movie fan magazines, comic books; we would all be a little richer had we kept the primordial *Super-man* and *Batman* comics we bought for a nickel and saved until the next paper drive. The sensory and romantic deprivations of provincial exis-tence call for avid consumption of the news from fantasylands.

Though the cultural climate of southeastern Pennsylvania has surely changed in the two-and-thirty years between my boyhood and Chip Kidd's, the soil must still be fertile for the young homebody and media-maven—"for all of us," as Kidd wrote in his epic album *Peanuts: The Art of Charles M. Schulz* (Pantheon, 2001), "who ate our school lunches alone and didn't have any hope of sitting anywhere near the little red-haired girl and never got any valentines and struck out every single time we were shoved to the plate for Little League." Véronique Vienne, in introducing her monograph *Chip Kidd* (Yale University Press, 2003), claims on doubtless good authority that his greatest design influence was daytime television; that at age two he was already a *Batman* fan, complete with mask, cape, and gloves; and that "he developed a love of graphic design by staring in supermarkets at the packaging of Batman playthings." He majored in graphic design at Penn State, studying under Lanny Sommese (an experience with some relation to the antic events of Kidd's one novel,

The Cheese Monkeys), and at the tender age of twenty-two was hired by Knopf as a junior assistant to Sara Eisenman.

The rest is, so to speak, graphic history. In a field, book-jacket design, where edge, zip, and instant impact are *sine qua non*, Kidd is second to none, and singular in the complexity of the comment his book jackets sometimes deliver upon the text they enwrap. His jackets, for example, for the novels *My Name Is Red*, by Orhan Pamuk, and *Was*, by Geoff Ryman, suggest with their dizzyingly variegated panels the vertiginous, layered contents within. On the biographies of William Blake by Peter Ackroyd and of Jim Thompson by Robert Polito, Kidd's tightly tiled imagery fairly shouts with the pain of a life. His series of jackets for Elmore Leonard form a suite of photographic motifs from the nation's psychic underworld.

In the intensity of his wish to use a jacket's few square inches to arrest and intrigue the bookstore browser, he exploits every resource of modern printing. On Richard North Patterson's *Silent Witness*, embossing uncannily duplicates the feel of crinkled and stretched police tape; on Haruki Murakami's *The Wind-Up Bird Chronicle*, a semi-visible diagram concocted by Chris Ware (a cartoonist frequently employed by Kidd) underlays a partially blurred photo of a mechanical bird taken by Geoff Spear, another favorite collaborator; on Kurt Andersen's *Turn of the Century* not only is the cover image of New York mirrored in the lower half but the word CENTURY is inverted also. Not that Kidd's jackets are always complicated. Katharine Hepburn's autobiography *Me* was done with simple typography; a tyrannosaur silhouette starkly adorned Michael Crichton's *Jurassic Park;* and rather famously (in the whispering galleries of jacket design) a stuffed bunny on its head presented an enigmatic, vaguely horrific image for Paul Golding's *The Abomination*. Ditto an enlarged doll's head on Donna Tartt's *The Little Friend*. Kidd reads the books he designs for, and locates a disquieting image close to the narrative's dark, beating heart. The sideways eyes on his jacket for Richmond Lattimore's translation of the New Testament may have bombed with booksellers but in two seconds achieved what Mel Gibson tried to do in two hours: make Christ's death real.

Can Kidd draw? Presumably, yet the mark of his pen or pencil rarely figures in his work. His tool is the digital computer, with its ever more ingenious graphics programs. In the expanding electronic archives of scannable photographic imagery, he is a hunter-gatherer. His jackets for books of poetry, exempt from any demand for mass-market appeal, show him at his freest and—see the snuggled spoon and fork of Vikram Seth's *All You Who Sleep Tonight*—wittiest. There is a playful thinginess and concreteness to Kidd's designs: Robert Hughes's essays on art are fronted by the back of a canvas, a Cuban novel by Cristina Garcia is wrapped in cigar-box imagery. A book on Samuel Beckett, stunningly, floats the subject's miniaturized head in a sea of black. And so on, idea after idea.

What remains to be said is that Chip Kidd, my fellow–Berks Countian, is wonderfully easy to work with—open and adaptable and unflappable when confronted with authors who have ideas of their own. I had the notion, on my novel *Seek My Face*, of an abstract-looking mess of brush-strokes that would resolve at a distance into a face. Kidd actually went down to Washington Square, bought an inexpensive, broadly worked portrait, and had the face photographed under a raking light, to bring up the shadows of the impasto. He has the good humor and spendthrift resourcefulness of an artist who trusts the depth of his own creativity. In an edgy field, he is not only edgy but deep.

FOREWORD *to the catalogue of* My Father's House, *an exhibit of works on paper and canvas by Will Barnet at the Montserrat College of Art in Beverly, Massachusetts, in 2004.*

Among the larger towns of the North Shore, Beverly lacks neighboring Salem's rich history and stately Federalist architecture, and Gloucester's raffish, picturesque glamour. Instead, it has a pretty coastline and did have the United Shoe factory, an immense conglomeration—not shoes but machinery for making shoes was the product—now refurbished as the Cumming Center. Will Barnet's father worked at the United Shoe as a machinist, and Will, his youngest child and younger son, grew up amid the trappings of what he remembered as "a model of a New England town," with its sparkling sea, its elm-shaded streets, its aura, now faint and now strong, of the Puritan past. On a street not far from the tilting slate headstones of Beverly's old cemetery, Will helped his father build a spacious house in which the family's two sisters lived to the ends of their lives, and to which Will, after moving to New York in the early 1930s, often returned, a loyal son of the household and of the region.

The region's cultural resources permitted this son of an immigrant millworker to conceive and nurture the desire to become a creative artist—in his words, "to liberate oneself by enveloping one's feelings into some kind of creative form." The boy's own father told him that factory work "destroyed a man's soul"; his introspective mother, Sarahdina, and her Boston-based brother, Harry, encouraged Will to pursue his dreams. The nearby public library—to which Barnet as an adult has been a generous patron—fuelled that pursuit. From the age of six or seven he read adventure tales, some of them illustrated by Howard Pyle and N. C. Wyeth; the public schools of the time offered an education stronger in history and art than is customary now. In an upstairs Art Room of the Beverly Library, with the indulgence of the head librarian, Will discovered and explored the Old Masters of Europe. As he aged, the fledgling artist gained access to the collections of museums in Salem and Boston, and by 1928 had enrolled at the Boston Museum School. Three years later, in 1931, he had progressed to the Art Students League of New York, and by 1935 he had become the League's professional printer, received his first one-man exhibition, and married his first wife.

Summed up so briefly, Barnet's is a classic and common story of a determined talent's emergence from a far from entirely barren and unsympathetic provincial environment. Unique to Barnet, of course, are the predilections that shaped his individual style. The formal balance and simplifying tendency so striking in his mature work were presaged, we can speculate, by a Japanese play for which he designed the sets in high school, by his boyhood absorption in the classical art of Greece, and by the wealth of carved figureheads and highly stylized objects from Asia and Polynesia that he saw in Salem's Peabody Museum. Even as he became increasingly knowledgeable about European masters, and was selecting his own favorites (Rembrandt, Daumier, Vermeer, Modigliani), he maintained his youthful interest in Native American art, with its earthen colors and bold abstraction. And yet are we wrong to sense in his work a specifically New England quality, derived from the chaste and elegant severity of its tombstones, its saltbox houses, its plain wooden furniture, its clean cold light? Though his direct heritage did not include Puritanism, the hymnlike metrics and slant metaphysics of Emily Dickinson's poetry have repeatedly served him as an overt inspiration. His style, like hers, seeks the bone of things.

The works assembled here as *My Father's House* come from the full extent of his artistic life, beginning when his mother and father were available to the teen-age artist as models. Visits home by the successful cosmopolitan artist yielded in the early Sixties a number of graphite studies of his two sisters, and thirty years later he returned to them as they dwelt in the solitude of their father's house at 11 Pierce Street. One plump, one lean, they not so much inhabit as haunt the geometries of the oversize windows and stark furnishings. This is the spacious house that the boy had had a hand in building. Here, in the basement, at the age of twelve, he had set up his first studio. Here he had observed the activity of five other human beings and a pet parrot, and here he had often returned, as a relief and refreshment amid the distractions of a metropolitan career. Now time has nearly emptied it, reducing its reality to the spareness of his own art. The four large paintings, all from 1992, at the heart of this exhibition, their color subdued and their details minimal, reveal, in Blake's phrase, a "fearful symmetry." Barnet's formality had always something about it of a child's careful, enumerating vision. Home, where we first learn to see, is not just where we come to birth, but where we reckon with death.

A REMINISCENCE *of Hyman Bloom, produced for the Spring 2002 issue of* Harvard Review.

Of my instructors at Harvard, Hyman Bloom was far and away the quietest. His utterances were few, he murmured when he emitted them, and he moved about the classroom on shoes notable for the thickness and the silence of their soles. The sound of one hand clapping was the Zen subtext of his instruction in drawing—"Advanced Composition," taken by me in the spring of my sophomore year, in 1952. We were, fifteen or twenty of us, enrolled in one of the scant two courses in the practice of art (as opposed to its appreciation) that Harvard in that era offered. I was pursuing a Radcliffe girl who had already taken the other course, in painting, under Patrick Morgan. Bloom was of course himself a painter, whose moldering rabbis and corpses were notable more for their lurid coloring than their linear draftsmanship, and I do not recall that we were invited to emulate the master. Instead, we were offered as model a painting by one of the Bellinis, Giovanni I think; the painting showed Saint Francis receiving the stigmata, but Bloom directed our attention to the wiry, serrated vegetation in the foreground and the scrupulously rendered rocks and pebbles. He had us hold our pencils lightly, resting on our palms and the inside of our fingers as if we were receiving a baton in a race, as in a sense we were. He was there in our midst not primarily as an instructor but as a living exemplar, a local artist who, like his fellow-Bostonian Jack Levine, had achieved national reputation. The electricity that haloed his stealthy-footed presence was generated by recognized achievement rather than inspired pedagogy, though I did take away a lesson: art was a job you did on your own, holding the implements with a certain lightness and with a humble certainty of employing them fallibly. I don't recall that Bloom, in his murmured comments on the work on our drawing boards as he moved about the room, ever emphatically praised or criticized any drawing. Rather, by small indications he implied that we could do better, that the goal was not yet achieved, the race not yet run, and this implication, as I try to recall his visage from nearly fifty years ago, was accompanied by not exactly a smile but by the lightest, most tentative beginning sketch of a smile.

INTRODUCTION *to* Wolf Kahn's America: An Artist's Travels, Paintings, Pastels, and Text *by Wolf Kahn (Harry N. Abrams, 2003)*.

Humanity needs to travel—in search of food, of safety, of mates, of better land. Modern man has it easy in terms of miles traversed; more than once I have flown across the country in five or six hours and reflected that the vast living map unscrolling five or six miles beneath the airplane window took several centuries to settle, from coast to coast, when white settlers travelled on foot and in wagons pulled by quadrupeds. In the last century mankind learned to see from altitudes that dwarfed those attained from treetops and mountainsides, while railroads, steamships, and automobiles accustomed us to superhuman speeds.

Yet this is not to say that we traveled more; a man who is on foot or on horseback experiences, it may be, more of his environment as it slowly changes around him than a passenger encapsulated in a rushing vehicle. On the so-called bullet trains common in Europe and Japan, any but the most distant view hurtles by too quickly to be relished, and trying to focus induces a headache. The modern motorist, at least in the American Northeast and the major cities elsewhere, has little to admire but an asphalt chute lined with the clamorous signs of the nationwide franchises.

An artist in paints and pastels like Wolf Kahn still sees on his travels. It is good to have here his genial written record of how he sees—of how he arrives, in various settings, at his subject, and how he meets, with his box of pastels and his conveniently low stool, the visible challenge. His writing, like his luminous art, holds a core of happiness; he is glad to be where he is, and reluctant but eventually glad to venture elsewhere. Art is a sedentary occupation, yet the observing eye feeds on motion, and fresh vision on an occasional change of scene. Wolf Kahn brings the hot pure color of Abstract Expressionism to an idea of landscape that is tranquil, reflective, and (as his titles tell us) witty. He scans what is before him for patterns, for broad and sometimes astonishing contrasts. He brings back from his survey of nature colors—magentas, purples, orange-pinks—that must be seen to be believed. We do believe them; his images keep a sense of place and moment, though what strikes us first is their abstract gorgeousness. Gorgeous, but they do not leave the earth. In this book we are tied more securely to the earth by Kahn's modest, practical accounts of where he was and how he got there.

These images, he declares in his first essay, are mementos of his life's travels, which otherwise he can hardly remember. Art for the artist has personal resonances viewers can only sense dimly, as an intenser vibration; Kahn is unusual among painters in his willingness to describe those resonances. The art, of course, must finally lift free of the personal, enjoying the enigma of its own being, without the artist as commentator. But when comment is granted in so carefree and factual a voice, we welcome it and the opportunity to understand works of art as instances of geography and of personal history. *I was here:* the impulse to send postcards is widespread, as is the desire to make a record of one's transient life. Art builds upon such common impulses a structure of exceptional skill and, we might say, informed wonder—the celebrative instinct informed by tradition and the innovations that bestow continuing vitality on an art form. In Wolf Kahn, the wonder is close beneath the skin of both his dashing, vibrant pictures and his amiable prose.

SAINT NICK: *Essay for the catalog of* George Nick: A Retrospective *(Boston, 1993).*

In a letter to his wife (October 13, 1907), Rilke wrote of Cézanne's work, which he had just seen in the memorial exhibition at the Salon d'Automne, "The good conscience of these reds, these blues, their simple truthfulness, it educates you; and if you stand beneath them as acceptingly as possible, it's as if they were doing something for you. You also notice, a little more clearly each time, how necessary it was to go beyond love, too; it's natural, after all, to love each of these things as one makes it: but if one shows this, one makes it less well; one *judges* it instead of *saying* it." Lesser, more sentimental painters, he goes on to say, "paint: I love this here; instead of painting: here it is."

One thinks naturally of George Nick's painting in terms of good conscience and simple truthfulness, of saying instead of judging. The occasions of some of the loveliest of his paintings are homely ones: plain houses in Chelsea and Charlestown, rusting old locomotives and the shadow-striped undersides of overpasses. Yet, as if not wishing to typecast himself as a celebrant of the run-down and the grittily urban, Nick has in recent years turned to more upscale subjects—the sandstone façades of Newbury Street and Commonwealth Avenue, and pleasant enough bucolic glimpses in Vermont and North Carolina.

Any subject will do, as long as the subject is not exploited for its anecdotal or picturesque qualities but is taken in good conscience as an occasion for pure painting. The bleak industrial forms of the power plant at Bellingham are invited, quite without condescension or moralistic socialism, to yield up their visual pleasures. Have any self-portraits been more devoid of vanity or of egotistic showmanship than Nick's—his mouth ajar in concentration, his hair neither combed nor deliberately left uncombed? When, as in some of his venerable European vistas, the architecture is theatrical, theatricality is underplayed, as if we are examining a stage set between the acts, with the lights down. His exceptional fidelity to visual appearance is itself left unemphasized, rather than, as in photorealism and in meticulous literalists like Philip Pearlstein and William Bailey, presented as something to marvel at.

Nick's refusal to develop a manner, even to the extent that Neil Welliver and Alex Katz have manners, has cost him ready identification in the art annals, perhaps, but it has also left him free to keep searching for ever more pristine contact with the scenes before him. Since the Seventies, when his renditions of suburban houses reached a crisp and luminous peak, he paints more expressively, on larger canvases, with wetter pigments; he has abandoned the pleasures of a dry precision and seems to have moved closer to his subjects, accepting the bulging perspective of a camera eye. Whatever direction he takes, however, he remains armed in innocence and an energy that arises not from a set interior angle but from a vast exterior world almost uniformly endowed with visual excitement.

His response to this excitement—his counterattack, as it were—has broadened so that the viewer needs to take a step or two farther back to appreciate his truthfulness. The quiet bliss of resolution—of fragments, stabs, and smears of paint resolving, back from the moonscape of the dabbled canvas, into a simulacrum of what daylight displays to us in three dimensions—is not the only pleasure painting affords, but it is the pleasure we experience first, in our first infantile recognitions of image, and one for which even the most resolute abstraction suppresses a certain nostalgia. It was the Impressionists who in their broadening, loosening brushwork not only reaffirmed this primal bliss but revealed it in older artists (Vermeer, Velázquez) whose details could now be seen to be impressionistic. A certain speed, as distinguished from haste, has more and more characterized George Nick's attempt to capture the shimmering world. Yet, though his brushwork is more agitated, his color and composition remain calm. An integrity of drawing (his translucent outlines in blue wash are paintings in themselves, which it seems a pity to cover) underlies the solid justice of his colors, and an integrity of faith beneath that—a faith that a painting does not have to be forced upon reality, through some trick of exaggeration or other, but can be drawn forth by a simple attentiveness, a patient scanning. He omits without giving an effect of omission. His attention, like a quietly singing shuttle, collects harmonious patches of surprisingly pure color—color with a clear conscience.

The aesthetic and the ethical are no great distance apart, as Rilke's tenderly phrased appreciation of Cézanne suggests. Those of us lucky enough to know George in the flesh must sometimes shield our eyes against his core of blazing dedication, and smile at the elaborate apparatus of his sainthood—the highly recognizable picture-window truck, almost a Magritte fantasy in its placement of a miniature studio on wheels, once painted bright orange and now a more camouflaging green, ornamented with a martyr's wreath of parking tickets. Cézanne and Monet, trudging out into the heat and rain with their three-legged easels, have nothing on this daily pilgrim. Rising at dawn to arrive miles distant as a certain slant of morning light befalls a chosen railroad bridge or storefront, he is Nature's acolyte; no mere coincidence has brought him to dwell in Emerson's and Thoreau's town of Concord. Dedicating himself to representation in the heyday of Abstract Expressionism, he has Fairfield Porter's stubbornness without Porter's family fortune.

Both the serenity and harshness of the independent spirit speak in his canvases, in a mood of morning light, with most of the day still to come. The "here it is" of his paintings does not need to advertise love; love exists here not as a sentiment but as an assumed condition of being.

FOREWORD *to the MFA Publications Reprint of* Just Looking *in 2001.*

Just Looking was originally published by Alfred A. Knopf, Inc., in 1989. Although my childhood passion was graphic art, my exposure to high art, as the first essay in this volume states, was slight. I became an art critic so casually, with so just a diffidence as to my competence, that the collection of these incidental pieces had to be prompted by the suggestion of someone else. Judith Jones, my long-time editor at Knopf, made the suggestion; her then assistant Kathy Zuckerman labored patiently at securing the many required permissions and transparencies; and Peter Andersen, the volume's designer, meticulously and inventively arranged each page. The publication of such a book is a far more elaborate and coöperative venture than that of a sheaf of poetry or prose; its republication, re-engaging the old problems of permission fees and faithful reproduction, is scarcely to be thought of. Imagine my surprise and pleasure, then, when I was informed that a publishing house newly created under the auspices of Boston's Museum of Fine Arts wished to reissue this, my lone art book, in the new century.

Manufactured in Italy, the Knopf edition had enjoyed an optimistically large printing that generated, for a time, an excess of copies. But those copies gradually disappeared, and I have more than once had to resort to my own dwindling stock to supply the occasional seeker of this title. For me, *Just Looking* retains the value of a scrapbook, a souvenir of happy hours spent in contemplation of art, whether hanging in museums or, as with the shorter pieces commissioned by the short-lived American version of *Réalités*, clipped from magazines. Assembling so various a scrapbook had its challenges. Ralph Barton's lovely black-and-white wash illustrations for the 1928 Boni & Liveright edition of Balzac's *Droll Stories* had to have their touch of magenta filled in by Peter Andersen's own hand, and searching for photographs of Jean Ipoustéguy's sculpture took me deep into the Fogg Museum's basement archives. These two essays, on Barton and Ipoustéguy, were my original, unsolicited ideas—my most arduous ventures into research and appraisal. Though Barton was a keen Francophile, and these illustrations constituted an act of homage, the Barton pages were eliminated from *Un Simple Regard: Essais sur l'art* (Horay, 1990), the only edition in a foreign language with which *Just Looking* was favored. *Le Monde*'s reviewer (under the heading "Le Regard froid du dilettante") said testily, of the twenty pages I devoted to France's own Ipoustéguy, "*C'est trop.*"

A by no means unfriendly American notice in the *New York Times Book Review* by the esteemed art critic and philosopher Arthur C. Danto chastised me for including a few of my own youthful drawings and characterized many of the pieces as "ekphrasis"—that is, not criticism at all, yielding "but enhanced understanding of the writer, and his or her preoccupations." Danto also noted (again, in friendly fashion) that my essays would not "hold great urgency for those whose concerns with art connect with the great critical issues of today." What those issues, now the issues of yesterday, or the day before, were, he did not have space to spell out—but it is true that I penned my impressions from well outside the art establishment and the New York "scene." For me, regressively enough, something broadly called "beauty" must attach to art, along with an aspiration to permanence. The deliberately ugly and impermanent make me look away. Such an attitude may be outmodedly dandyish, given the industrial heat and machinations within the mills of the art business, including the art-crit business, but to Danto's gentle charge of being "an artistic *flâneur*" I can only plead the examples of Baudelaire and Henry James, who both published frequent observations about the visual arts near the outset of this long period in which these arts have led the way— have been the most spectacular and fresh of human expressions, have most popularly sought the tune for modernity to dance to.

Looking at pictures takes less time than reading a book or listening to music; it tells us something even at a glance. These pages preserve a succession of glances and, in their unsteady wake, reflections. It was to the MFA that, nearly fifty years ago, I travelled from across the Charles in company with a Radcliffe student, a fine-arts major, and watched her circle and ponder, notebook in hand, a little, well-lit, headless Attic sphinx. Fitting it is, then, that this same museum should undertake this reissue of my encounters with a parade of glowing sphinxes.

FOREWORD *to the Stackpole Books edition of* Buchanan Dying *(2000)*.

The original edition of *Buchanan Dying*, in 1974, carried as preface this brief "Note":

> Even the writer of a closet drama imagines himself the first and lowliest laborer at a glittering edifice of collaboration. Were this play to be produced, care should be taken with the lighting and the accents. The one-room set should be simple but solid; darkness will transform it into a forest, a cabin, or an inner arena. A few changes of furniture make Wheatland the White House. Spotlighting must be used to permit actors to withdraw, where exits are not specified. Contrariwise, when the political speeches are given, the entire audience might be illuminated, as part of the scene. As to the accents: the utterances that have descended to us in historical records and memoirs, which I have tried to blend with utterances imagined, are couched in the rounded and scarcely idiomatic public language of the nineteenth century. But the geographical breadth of this cast of characters, and the conflicts among them, can live in their accents; the Southern accent, especially, must be heard by the audience, as it was by Buchanan, as an insistent, melodious tugging.

These blithe and grandly simple directives were put to the test in two subsequent productions. First, the play was performed, with all the trimmings of costume and stagecraft, at Franklin and Marshall College in Buchanan's own town of Lancaster, Pennsylvania, from April 29 to May 8, 1976, in the Green Room Theatre. Edward S. Brubaker directed the production and cut the text to bring it within a playable time. Peter Vogt played the protagonist, Leslie Stainton (who has recently come forth with a biography of the Spanish poet Lorca) was Harriet Lane, and She-vaun Keogh took the alluring triple role of Anne Coleman, Susan Sparks Keitt, and the Czarina of Russia, in which latter persona she displayed a sparkling French accent and a wealth of glittering jewels. The next year, in March of 1977, six performances were mounted by the Institute for Readers Theatre at San Diego State University, thanks in large part to the personal enthusiasm and energy of Robert McCoy, an associate professor of English there. McCoy directed, and the demanding part of Buchanan was enacted by Sheldon Gero; Pam Adams played Harriet Lane, and Lenetta Kidd performed as Anne Coleman and her avatars. The full text was also shortened for this production, in which the uncostumed actors read—with animation, of course—from unmemorized scripts.

Both brave, dutiful versions have faded in my mind, these twenty-some years later, but for a few details such as Miss Keogh's fine accent and Mr. Gero's evident restless agony as he lay immobilized within Buchanan's long and wordy dying. It is a cruel play to inflict on a performing company, it occurred to me as I sat in the audience. No further productions have been proposed. (One nibble from public television came with the sharp hook that it all would have to be revised, along sensible lines proposed by sensibilities other than the author's.) As I watched, on these two occasions, brightly lit stage actors moving through my basically verbal and inward drama, I wondered if a motion picture, with its fluid scene-shifts and facial close-ups, was not what I had written. Playwrights tell of their rapture in seeing their words recited on the stage; my own sensations were discomfiture and pity for these pretty flies trapped in my sticky amber. Trying to remember the play in performance, I come up with backstage irrelevancies: my mother attended the Lancaster performance and looked regal—every inch a first-nighter—wearing a gray fox fur I had given her from a trip to Russia twelve years before, and my wife-to-be went with me to San Diego, which we had expected to be summery in March and where we nearly froze in our thin clothes as we hurried across the great paved spaces of the campus. Both female companions, needless to say, were loyal to the playwright and his play, but I could not help suspecting that the event they graced had been at bottom disappointing: a full-length portrait of political impotence and private timidity may be better suited to a book read in solitude than to the social festivity of the theatre, with its ancient roots in proclamatory rite and religion.

Yet the book itself, falling so curiously between several stools, was lightly reviewed—at most thoughtful length by the historian Arthur Schlesinger, Jr., in *The Atlantic Monthly*, and not at all in the *New York Times*, which has a policy against reviewing published plays—and sold proportionately, though it did creep into a small second edition. Over the years Alfred A. Knopf, Inc., allowed its handsomely designed and typeset volume to drift out of print. Now we have this new printing* by Stackpole Books, which differs from the Knopf text only by a score of small corrections and the addition of this foreword. I had long harbored a hope of revising the play, cutting it down to two practicable, symmetrical, rather Beckettian acts—first, Buchanan, yielding to blandishments to be more dynamic, slowly gets out of bed; second, Buchanan is beaten back to bed, where he completes his dying. Two rereadings persuaded me that less might be, after all, merely less. Willfully wandering as the drama is, it does hold most of what I wanted to say about the fifteenth President, in his long and various career. Exhaustiveness is a novelist's method, and what we have here is a kind of novel, conceived in the form of a play, with an ample afterword composed of leftovers.

Readers now might have to be reminded, as readers in 1974 did not, of the national protest over Vietnam, which at its height prevented President Johnson from publicly speaking in any venue less sheltered than a television studio or a military installation. Had any President been so vilified—the play *MacBird* marking a low point in the slander and venom—since Buchanan himself? A President, unlike the leader of a parliamentary system, cannot ask for a vote of confidence and resign if none forthcomes; he is stuck with his elected term and his chosen policies, even when strident popular opposition arises. The questions raised in the crisis years 1965–73 find echo in the pre–Civil War crisis, when a peaceable, compromising, legalistic President presided over a widening split no compromise or legalisms could bridge. Harriet Lane, faced with the indignant grief of an old friend turned war protester, asks, "Does power only contaminate? If public office become perforce vile, then none but villains will choose to serve." Buchanan puts it, "Society for its manifold blessings asks in exchange sacrifice and compromise. Concession is the world's walking gait. . . . Government is either organized benevolence or organized madness; its peculiar magnitude permits no shadings." He himself is something of a peacenik, dreading the men of violent action of whom Andrew Jackson is his chief exemplar; the Reverend Paxton tells him, "In truth you disdain these heroes as brutes of delusion and spendthrifts of blood." And the dying Buchanan cringes from the smell of blood emanating from the apparition of Lincoln.

Leadership of any country save one in a comic operetta involves some

---

*Itself, as of 2006, out of print.

decisions whose consequences are bloody. The problem is not as simple as the chant "Hey, hey, LBJ, how many kids did you kill today?" By pursuing a tactical conflict on the other side of the world, LBJ, rightly or wrongly, thought he was saving kids from worse, nearer wars. True, he had a streak of the bully and did escalate a war, whereas Buchanan evaded beginning one, leaving his successor an unlit powder keg. Still, my attempt was to extend sympathy to politicians, as they make their way among imperfect alternatives toward a hidden future. To phrase this sympathy in terms of the overheated years leading up to the Civil War, deploying much mid-nineteenth-century rhetoric and some generally forgotten political issues of the time, was to ask a good deal of my audience. We can absorb historical details as they foreshadow a national icon's triumph, as in such plays as *Sunrise at Campobello* and *Abe Lincoln in Illinois*. But when they are called in to illuminate a figure as obscure, calumniated, and problematical as Buchanan, and are used to illustrate my thesis that the pattern of his Presidency was established in an unfortunate broken romance occurring in his young manhood, and to further propose that a dark thread in his life ran from his stern father through a number of personal and political enemies right up to God Himself—well, the attention of even an ideal audience, iron-bottomed and rabbit-eared, might be strained.

So with this newly reissued book in your hands you are in the best position to share my one excursion into American history. The stage, my original "Note" might have said, is your head; the actors and actresses and their costumes and gestures are yours for the conjuring. Cursory stage directions like "(*gasps and hubbub*)" might have been multiplied without easing the reader's task. I still suspect that my initial conception of a small novel, of four alliterative chapters, with dates running down the outside margin, was the correct one, had I had the wit and confidence to execute it.

I did return to the Buchanan matter in a 1992 novel, *Memories of the Ford Administration*, the purported narrative of a historian, Alfred L. Clayton, living in New Hampshire and working on a biography not, as you might suspect, of Franklin Pierce but of Pierce's successor, the fifteenth President. In scenes of historical fiction alternating with Clayton's memories from the frisky mid-Seventies I drew closely upon some of the play's scenes (tea with the Hubley sisters, the walk with Andrew Jackson, the 1860 Cabinet meetings) and made up others, such as a diplomatic conversation with Hawthorne in England in 1855 and a kind of love song to fellow-Senator W. R. D. King in the form of a congressional speech that Buchanan delivered early in 1838. By interposing a fallible narrator, who openly writes of the difficulties of achieving historical precision, and even accurate personal memory, I hoped to maneuver access to my elusive hero. But the effort to delve into history left me convinced of the unconscionable amount of bluff, fraud, and elision that any allegedly historical account, labelled fiction or not, entails. It is alarming to me that historical novelists openly brag that they have knowingly distorted the record, transposing dates and fudging conversations in the name of some supposed higher truth. But what truth can be higher than what actually did happen, moment by moment, incident by incident?

To be sure, total consecutive truth is lost to time, along with most of the artifacts of our daily life, and all but a scattered few of our spoken words, and all of our precious feelings. Time's grinding chews it all up. What remains even of twentieth-century events is an approximation and stylization, born of hasty records and rough-hewn news reports. Nevertheless, I felt that my sense of American reality was enhanced by my dip into nineteenth-century records and reports. To read of how the republic struggled to keep slavery even as that institution's barbarism became unignorable, and of how an elected government desperately sought the glue to hold opposed sections together under the sacred Constitution, and of how personal exchanges in Washington influenced vast public issues, and of how private psychology was translated into national policy; and above all to read historians—to relax into the humane, tolerant, encompassing voice of an Allan Nevins or a Roy Nichols, and to marvel at how they shape a coherent story out of a million happenstances—all this benefited my ongoing education, adding a bit to my credentials as an American writer.

A writer educates himself in order to educate others, and the mixed, even jagged texture of this particular work testifies how far from smooth the transfer can be. But that some transfer takes place here, not just of information but of the affection behind my initial and enduring interest in the eminent Pennsylvanian James Buchanan, I dare to hope, and this new edition seems to confirm.

A "SPECIAL MESSAGE" *for the Franklin Library's Signed First Edition Society edition of* Gertrude and Claudius *(2000).*

Claudius and Gertrude are the villains of *Hamlet:* Claudius the fratricide and usurper, and Gertrude his consort, who married him within a month of her former husband's sudden death. In feverish indignation her son exclaims:

> A little month, or ere those shoes were old
> With which she followed my poor father's body,
> Like Niobe, all tears; why she, even she—
> (O God! a beast that wants discourse of reason
> Would have mourn'd longer) married with my uncle.   (I.ii.147–51)

But she is not a partner in murder and intended murder. Shakespeare clearly shelters her from knowledge of Claudius's sinister machinations; she attends the duel between Laertes and Hamlet as an innocent spectator, and is fatally ignorant of the poisoned drink which Claudius has arranged for Hamlet as a back-up scheme.

How did she come to marry with such unseemly haste? Lust, Shakespeare appears to answer, in the same mood of revulsion in which he wrote some of the sonnets and *Troilus and Cressida*, a play composed a year after *Hamlet*. But, then, he was stuck with the barbaric plot he inherited from Danish legend, and perhaps that of the so-called Ur-*Hamlet*, which had been acquired by his theatrical company. Gertrude as he presents her appears poised, kindly, moderate, and coolly clear-sighted. Concerning what she herself calls her "o'er-hasty marriage" (II.ii.57), she keeps her own counsel. When asked how she likes the play within the play, she famously responds, "The lady doth protest too much, methinks" (III.ii.236). Her own nature, we gather, is not of a protesting, explanatory, or apologetic sort. Harrowed, in the turbulent interview of III.iv, by her son's lurid portrayal of her second marriage, she professes that he has showed her "black and grainèd spots" within her soul and has cleft her heart in twain; nevertheless, she continues to display no lack of marital harmony in her subsequent appearances with Claudius. Right after Claudius has confided to his "dear Gertrude" a litany of his reign's woes, a pro-Laertes mob breaks into Elsinore; with fierce loyalty she tells the mob, "O, this is counter, you false Danish dogs" (IV.v.110), and, a few lines farther, is quick, facing Laertes himself, to exonerate her husband of Polonius's death.

She has relatively few lines in the play but they are among the best-phrased and most-remembered: "The lady doth protest too much" to Hamlet; "More matter, with less art" to Polonius; and, to Hamlet again, some parental counseling on death:

> Thou know'st 'tis common; all that lives must die,
> Passing through nature to eternity.   (I.ii.72–73)

On the occasion of Ophelia's burial, having eloquently reported her death in IV.vii, she scatters flowers with this memorable eulogy:

Sweets to the sweet! Farewell.
I hop'd thou shouldst have been my Hamlet's wife.
I thought thy bride-bed to have deck'd, sweet maid,
And not have strew'd thy grave.　　(V.i.245–248)

It is hard for the viewer not to love Gertrude, whether she is played by Glenn Close in the Mel Gibson movie or by Julie Christie in the Kenneth Branagh version. One of only two female characters in the play, she embodies the mature womanly qualities that cruel circumstances prevent Ophelia from attaining: queenly dignity, wifely loyalty, motherly concern. Claudius explains to Laertes why he has not brought Hamlet to justice:

The Queen his mother
Lives almost by his looks; and for myself—
My virtue or my plague, be it either which—
She's so conjunctive to my life and soul
That, as the star moves not but in his sphere,
I could not but by her.　　(IV.vii.11–16)

His love for the Queen is the King's noblest feature, and her love for him her only fault; for years it seemed to me that, amid all the other marginal ornamentation that this most performed and pondered of Shakespeare's plays has attracted, a case for Claudius and Gertrude should be made.

Making the case necessitated consulting the Scandinavian sources of the story, including the speculative origin of the curious name Amleth/Hamlet. The old legends are blunt, and the only additional facts of much import are found in the first pages of Saxo Grammaticus's *Historia Danica*, which tell us that Horwendil (Hamlet *père*) and Feng (Claudius) were the sons of the governor of Jutland, Gerwindil, and Gerutha was the daughter of a king, Rorik, whom they served. So she was of royal blood and a considerable political prize to the man who won her hand. A trace of this emerges in the Shakespearean scene with which my novel concludes: Claudius speaks of Gertrude as "Th' imperial jointress to this warlike state" (I.ii.9). So in my imagination she became, like many another well-born maiden, a pawn in the hands of ambitious men. My other principal inventions were Claudius's European travels, which help explain why Shakespeare's plot finds him and his brother already well advanced in middle age (Gertrude, if we accept, as we must, the gravedigger's assertion, in V.i, that Hamlet is thirty, can't be much younger than forty-eight), and Polonius's collaboration in the Queen's adultery, which helps account for the effusive warmth with which the King treats him and for the animus the Prince consistently expresses.

My aim was to invent, after Saxo Grammaticus and François de Belle-forrest, a telling which would dovetail without contradiction into Shake-speare's play, insofar as its abundant internal contradictions and hiatuses admitted. I embroidered, yes, but meant my threads to knit seamlessly into the action of *Hamlet*. Shakespeare conceived his Danish court in terms of Elizabethan manners and conventions, though he did insert, albeit in the last scene (V.ii), the curious fact that Danish kings were, from among the nobility, elected—a provision that encourages a struggle over the succession. The story of the Prince who feigns madness to escape being killed by his usurping uncle arises in a Scandinavian antiq-uity impossible to date. Yet Hamlet's Elsinore is a real European site, and the events more nearly contemporary than those in *Lear* and *Macbeth*. One Shakespeare commentator dates the time of the action at around 1250, and it is to a mid-thirteenth-century ambience that I tried to be faithful, though some of the details of costume may have arisen later in the Middle Ages. Hamlet is not one of Shakespeare's history plays, nor is my novel historical in the way of, say, Sigrid Undset's majestic *Kristin Lavransdatter* trilogy. I hoped to keep the texture light, like that of a printed play, and to move from the mists of Scandinavian legend into the daylight atmosphere of the Globe, where under the sun, with minimal scenery, the actors wove a reality of rhythmic words. I sought to narrate the romance that preceded the tragedy.

PREFACIO *to* Poemas 1953–1999 *(Pre-Textos, 2002).*

I was greatly pleased to be told, some years ago, by José María Moreno Carrascal, that out of his disinterested liking for some of my poems he was translating a selection of them into a volume of Spanish. Several aspects of the honor pleased me. Spanish is, among European languages, second only to English in the extent of its conquests and the number of its speakers. More important, from some of its writers—Cervantes, Una-muno, Ortega y Gasset, Salvador de Madariaga, Neruda, Borges (a few of whose poems I presumed, with assistance, to translate), Camilo José Cela, Gabriel García Márquez, Mario Vargas Llosa—I have taken plea-sure, terror, and courage over the years.

On a personal note: my mother was a Hispanophile, who longed to write a novel about the conquistador Ponce de León, the discoverer, in 1513, of Florida; he was, the legend goes, in search of the rumored Foun-tain of Youth. His band of men became the first Europeans since the Vikings to set foot on the North American continent. Thus, for a time, the entire continent was named Florida, and world history might have a milder flavor if the name had stuck. My mother extended her novelistic researches three times to Spain itself, the third time in 1977, accompanied by me and my younger daughter, who was sixteen at the time. I was the driver and the guide, and my heavy responsibilities prevented me each night from falling asleep easily; I improved those insomniac hours by writing sonnets, one per day, and together the eight "Spanish Sonnets" make up, in my view, one of my finer poetic flights.

The poems herein have been chosen by the translator. What poetic effect "carries" into another language and what does not is bound to remain a mystery to a monolingual speaker. Surely the "light verse" with which I was so much occupied in my early years as a writer is almost indissolubly wedded to the tricks of the original language and to topical references scarcely worth explaining these decades later. I began as a "rhymester," a more or less expert juggler of metrics and rhyme, and as I aged have less and less depended upon these devices. Poetry even at its barest and sparest is not prose—the mere breakage into lines compels a closer look, a sharper ear—but it should among its virtues possess the prosaic ones of clarity and flow. To the virtues of denotation poetry adds something extra. Certain subtle properties of the language, be it English or Spanish or Russian, must be brought into play; in its own language the poem is drawn like a magnet through a whispering force-field of latent allusion and connotation. With grateful confidence I entrust these properties to Señor Carrascal's affectionate and conscientious care. Just as a traveller can be better treated in a strange inn than in his own castle, so may these poems fare with Spanish hospitality.

FOREWORD *to* Humor in Fiction, *a limited edition by the Lord John Press, 2000.*

Thirty years ago I was asked to attend, and be a speaker at, a week-long international PEN conference in Seoul, South Korea. The dates were June 28 to July 3, 1970; the topic of this ambitious gathering, involving two hundred foreign delegates and seventy Korean participants, was "Humor in Literature East and West." Among the topics discussed, as session after session reeled by in a cascade of simultaneously translated ethnic jokes, were "Characteristics of Vietnamese Humor," "Humor and Satire in Persian Literature," "A Few Words on Turkish Humor," and "Humor in Sanskrit Drama." My assigned title was "Humor in Fiction," and I sought to tame my potentially infinite topic by discussing, in the manner of Erich Auerbach's masterful critical survey, *Mimesis*, one long quotation each from four Western classics all of which could be broadly termed humorous: *Don Quixote, Candide, Huckleberry Finn*, and *A Handful of Dust*. That talk, delivered on July 1st, was reprinted entire in the bulky conference proceedings and *The American PEN* magazine (vol. 2, no. 3), and in part in my collection *Picked-Up Pieces* (1975), but this publication marks its first complete reprinting in hard covers.

Humor in Fiction remains one of my most ambitious flights of criticism, on a topic dear to me. Dear, too, has become that week in Korea, with its lamplit dinners in summer gardens, its visits to temples and the 38th parallel, its glimpses from the embattled Korean edge of the Asian vastness, its many gracious Korean hosts and hostesses, its camaraderie with my fellow-delegates John Cheever, Donald Keene, John Oliver Killens, and our delegation head, Charles Flood, who had been a few years ahead of me at the *Harvard Lampoon* and who impressed me with his command of French as he subdued an insurrection by an indignant Paris intellectual. My daughter Elizabeth, then fifteen, accompanied me, and her long blond hair was much admired. John Cheever, with his wife, Mary, and his son Frederick, made another family unit, and much inimitable, unrecapturable Cheever merriment underlined the humor of the occasion.

FOREWORD *to the Easton Press limited edition of* Licks of Love *(2000)*.

I used to turn out short stories like a blueberry bush producing berries. Financial need was the fertilizer, and a ready market was the sunshine. Since the happy year of 1954, when a story of mine first appeared in a national magazine, many magazines eager for short stories have withered away, and my pen has reluctantly migrated to greener genres. Still, it is hard to believe that in the six years since my last short-story collection, *The Afterlife and Other Stories* (1994), only twelve stories, and one of these a much-revised piece dating from the late 1950s, presented themselves for muster. True, some are on the long side ("The Cats," "Licks of Love in the Heart of the Cold War"), and the five loosely linked constituents of the "quasi-novel" *Bech at Bay* (1998) could be said to be short stories; still, it seems clear to me that the brief fiction that once constituted most of my livelihood and my main claim to the proud title of author has been eased aside by the pushy demands of novels and, oddly, of book reviews. These reviews tend to be the length of short stories and to appear in the same journal, *The New Yorker*, where my stories once often appeared; they demand a kindred spurt of energy and strive for somewhat similar harmonies and resolutions, so that I may be fooled into thinking a short story is what I have written. But only I am fooled. Reviews, even the most earnest of them, are contingent and dispensable, whereas short stories, even the slightest of them, aspire to be timeless and self-contained—human matters crisply packaged and preserved for keeps.

Women, in most but not all of these dozen, are the inspirations and, if all went well in the writing, the objects preserved for contemplation: a bevy of them in the first story and "His Oeuvre"; single instances, loved and lost, in "New York Girl" and "Natural Color" and the title story; peripheral acquaintances, nonetheless adored, in "Lunch Hour" and "Metamorphosis." For my susceptible heroes, no acquaintance, where the opposite sex is concerned, can be too glancing to strike a spark and kindle some excitement. Love makes the world go around, and its licks can be feathery but keenly felt. Filial love moves some of the longest and most confessional of these tales, and parental love shadows the shortest, "Oliver's Evolution." "Scenes from the Fifties," the oldest story here, waited close to forty years for its thwarted cathexes to find their natural discharge.

"Rabbit Remembered," a novella-length story of sibling affection, goes back as far—to *Rabbit, Run*, written in 1959 and published in 1960. The idea of tucking this sequel into a book of my recent short stories occurred to me in 1999, the year in which the bulky non-fiction collection *More Matter* was published and the short novel *Gertrude and Claudius*, a prequel to Shakespeare's *Hamlet*, was composed. Rounding off Rabbit Angstrom's saga and tying up its most conspicuous loose ends appealed to me only if it did not violate the integrity of the tetralogy which has him as its ever-present hero, from the moment when he comes upon a pickup basketball game among boys to that in which he tries to console his only son from his Florida deathbed. A new novel would have been a violation, a contradiction of *Rabbit at Rest*'s final, promissory word, "Enough." It would have been the unwarranted extension of an implicit contract, a jimmying-open of a closed box, and furthermore I did not have a novel's worth to say about Nelson and Annabelle. Their coming together belonged in its matter to the sequence of novels but in its form to the short story—to the realm of the single, swiftly concluded action. The reader of the novels, of course, had to be considered: some of this novella's pleasures lie in sharing with the author his own pleasure in having assembled a coherent imaginary world. Episodes echo other, distant ones; Billy Fosnacht and the Harrison boys emerge from the margins of earlier installments; and Rabbit's ghost presides, not quite palpably, over this long-deferred meeting of his children. But only the sketchiest prior knowledge of Rabbit's earthly adventures is essential, I would like to think, to following their sequel.

A prequel, a sequel—thus have I marked the year 2000, which hung on the farthest rim of my possible future when I was a child. Now I am sixty-eight, an age at which most of my age-peers have retired and a few have already died. I am packing my bag, it may be; at least my desk, as I write these words, is otherwise ominously clean.

NOTE *on "Bech Noir" for* The Best American Mystery Stories 1999, *edited by Ed McBain.*

Henry Bech has been a character of mine since 1964, when he appeared in a short story called "The Bulgarian Poetess." Like me he is a writer, but in other respects he lives a life I envy but have not attempted to live. While looking through the two Library of America volumes of crime novels from the Thirties, Forties, and Fifties, I got the idea of Bech as a noir hero. Murdering critics is something most writers, I suspect, have wanted to do. The device of poisoning an envelope flap was used, I discovered later, in an episode of *Seinfeld*, but by then it was too late, my die was cast. The computer details, accurate enough at the time, are probably obsolete by now. As a boy and young man, I read a great deal of mystery fiction—Ellery Queen, Agatha Christie, Dorothy Sayers, John Dickson Carr and his pseudonyms. As an adult writer, I have always been leery of violence and character assassination; but I found that, once you get going, there is an intoxicating pleasure to it. Evildoers, beware!

NOTE *on "Personal Archeology" for* The Best American Short Stories 2001, *edited by Barbara Kingsolver.*

My hero's inexplicably Germanic name, "Fritz," holds the "F" that, some time ago, in a lazy code, I began to foist upon short-story heroes who were conspicuously alter-egoistic. The device created a sort of brother, not a twin but close in age and outlook to me and, though freed from any obligation to plead my case, able to shoulder, with brotherly good humor, some of my circumstances. A certain Frankness, we could say, was thus attained. I do in fact live on New England land that holds buried clues to its past owners, a class of predecessor whom Americans, ever since the Puritans took title from the Indians, have regarded with scant sentimentality. We move, we buy, we move again. Only retirement offers the leisure to consider where, exactly, we are, and who was here before us. The motorcycle parts and white plastic litter are real; I made up the teacup.

From such buried physical treasure it is not a long leap to Freud and those other archeologists of the mind who attempt to explicate and order the results of those hectic nightly digs, our dreams. A life is composed of strata; dreams and waking guilt-pangs unearth a scattered, dirty number of clues—to what? To the mystery, the evolving majesty even, of each existence. Proust speaks of deciphering underwater hieroglyphs as the writer's essential task. He also speaks of changing perspectives, as time's railroad journey rounds a curve. An aging writer cannot but notice how the events he keeps remembering change over time, generating new stories, for which he is grateful.

NOTE *on "The Walk with Elizanne" for* The Best American Short Stories 2004, *edited by Lorrie Moore.*

I never miss a high-school class reunion, and never come away without a story. Not all of them I write, but this one I did, soon after my fiftieth. It has two heroines—three, counting Betty Lou, who did the work of this particular get-together. But Mamie, being the gracious, thoughtful hostess as she lies in the hospital bed with her bones disintegrating, is the presiding spirit, the class pep girl, the embodiment of sentimental loyalty to that accident which places a group of assorted young Americans in heated daily proximity for a number of years. Her attempt to make sense of her coming death prepares the hero for the reunion non-attender, Elizanne, who brings from afar, from fifty years away, a breath of that old heat, when their lives lay all before them, and death was an unreal possibility. In villages of old, people watched each other age day by day, year by year; in modern America, where leaving home is virtually a duty, fitful illuminations show us the distances we have traversed since those moist, anxious first contacts in a world that, as Prospero says to Miranda, "'tis new to thee." What a wonder it is to see peeping out, from the crumpled face of a fellow-septuagenarian, unmistakable evidence of a human identity first met in kindergarten! It is a miracle. All our lives, older people around us bore us with the telling of stories in which nothing is extraordinary except that they are *their* stories; they were *there*. And the faces from kindergarten have not changed, not really. Yet the great stilts of time that Proust evokes at the end of *Remembrance of Things Past* are undeniably there, too, under our feet. We have grown impossibly tall in a dimension we never believed in. "The Walk with Elizanne" is a religious story, of course—at least it tries to evoke that ineluctable strangeness of human existence in which religion takes root.

A COMMENT *on a story, "Your Lover Just Called," chosen by me for the anthology* This Is My Best *(Bookspan, 2004).*

What could be more confining and depleting than this exercise—a popular favorite with questioners in a lecture audience—of asking an author to pick his "best"? If he succumbs, he in an instant relegates all the considerable rest of his work to the status of second-best. If he resists, he implies that he has no best, no standards. I cope with it by trying to pick a different specimen every time I am asked. This time let me name "Your Lover Just Called," a short story about a recurrent fictional couple of mine, Joan and Richard Maple. Over a dozen stories involving them exist, most of them collected in a paperback volume called, in the United States, *Too Far to Go* and, in England, *Your Lover Just Called*. This particular story was written in late July 1966 and has a high-summer feel to it, of heightened physical activity and loosened inhibitions. The story flowed easily; the Maples usually had no trouble talking to each other and generating action of a fraught domestic sort. I enjoyed having a ringing telephone as a subsidiary character, along with the sentimental Mack Dennis, but the image that sticks pleasurably in my mind, as something precious saved from the flux of American middle-class errands and yearning, was the double view that Richard enjoys from the dark backyard, of his older daughter in her lemon-colored nightie fiddling with her dolls and scratching an armpit in her well-lit bedroom while below, stereoptically, her mother tilts her head flirtatiously and with a gracefully extended arm holds a drink safe from being spilled by a kiss. To me the double sight, and the hero with his cigarettes and scratchy throat halted in amazement on the grass, have something in them of the magic and mournful secrecy of family life, as we each revolve with our separate needs in the transient, loving shelter of the house we all share.

RECURRENT CHARACTERS: *An essay done for* Inside Borders *in November of 1998, in tune with the publication of* Bech at Bay.

As with old friends, it is pleasant to deal with recurrent characters. They are already named, and their salient traits are established. They have eye color, hair color, and pasts, if the author can remember them or has the patience to look them up. In the course of putting my four novels about Rabbit Angstrom into a single Everyman's volume, I had the pleasure of smoothing over the several inner contradictions that had cropped up over the more than thirty years of their composition. Harry has a son, Nelson, who is two in the first novel, *Rabbit, Run*, and then in the sequels is twelve, twenty-two, and thirty-two, roughly speaking. But the successor novels take place in different times of the year, and some deviate from my basic arrangement of returning in the ninth year of each decade, so it becomes important to know when Nelson's birthday is, a fact I failed to establish at the outset. Indeed, fictional characters generally don't have birthdays, but it became important to me that Nelson—especially at the moment he becomes a teen-ager—have one, which I placed, after much calculation, on October 22, 1956. To celebrate, I inserted a sliver of a birthday party into the adult mischief of *Rabbit Redux*, courtesy of Nelson's Aunt Mim.

It is a pleasure, even a wonder, to watch recurrent characters develop and change in the course of time. Janice Angstrom's mother, Bessie Springer, was a plump, pinch-mouthed peripheral character, overshadowed by Rabbit's parents and her husband, until the third novel, *Rabbit Is Rich*, where she emerges as a survivor and the custodian of what family fortune still remains in this dysfunctional kinship set. She moved onto center stage and I had to love her. Jack Eccles, a major agonist in the first novel, shrinks to a cameo in the second, and Cindy Murkett, the voluptuous young object of Harry's obsessive desire in the third, briefly shows up, overweight and forlorn, in the fourth. Time does weird things to us, and the ten-year intervals between the Rabbit novels made a number of startling reappearances possible; the characters, in my conception, were rarely where the reader of the previous novel might expect them to be. Janice, whom we first meet as the woefully insignificant spouse of a Harry still trailing clouds of athletic glory, gains strength and assets in the course of the saga; it takes her most of her lifetime, but she comes into her own, as Harry, despite an occasional surge of energy, slowly sinks. The ideological trend of the decades acts to strengthen her, whereas time brings him little wisdom and reassurance, just an inexorable recession of his youth.

There is a pleasure, too, in the miraculous fiat of resurrection. Joan and Richard Maple, first sighted in a 1956 short story, "Snowing in Greenwich Village," were rediscovered six years later, as a suburban couple, in "Giving Blood" and in more than a dozen stories thereafter, up to "Here Come the Maples" in 1976. The story of their marriage was made into a television play, *Too Far to Go*, and bound into a paperback of the same name, and that would seem to have been the end of them; but then they reappeared as newly born grandparents in "Grandparenting" in 1994. One revives characters because one can't bear to say goodbye forever. They still have life in them, and that life is part of the author's own. Joan and Richard Maple perform a duet whose basic pattern survives nearly forty years; the duet usually ends on a suspended note, of unfulfillment amid a kind of pale beauty, a hovering grace note faithful to the wry Fifties romanticism that set their tone.

Sometimes one revives a character to do him better justice. James Buchanan, the fifteenth President of the United States, was treated by me in a play, *Buchanan Dying*, written in lieu of a balked novel, and then, eighteen years later, in a novel whose hero, Alf Clayton, is balked in the course of writing Buchanan as history. The challenge presented by this relatively obscure and yet many-sided President, a fellow-Pennsylvanian whose failures seemed more sympathetic and human than the successes of less conflicted and less peaceable men, was thus discharged in a reprise which I do not expect to repeat. Buchanan's life, unlike that of a fictional character, does not ramify indefinitely; it is made up of historical data which refuse to budge. One's only excuse for writing fiction about a historical figure is to fill in the blanks—in Buchanan's case a youthful betrothal that blew up in his face and left him forever timid. He became President by the politic stratagems of caution and temporizing, and yet in 1860 the Union blew up in his face. It is a great story, but two attempts to tell it are enough.

It would have seemed, too, that there had been enough of my Jewish American writer Henry Bech: two slim and jaunty collections of seven stories each, with the symmetrical titles *Bech: A Book* and *Bech Is Back*, the second title echoing that of the third Rabbit installment, *Rabbit Is Rich*. The two characters are American males but have little else in common; they are slices from opposite sides of my pie. The first story about Bech, like my first novel about Rabbit and my first story about the Maples, held no intention of a sequel; but certain assays ("The Bulgarian Poetess" won the O. Henry First Prize for its year, 1965) suggested that a vein was there to be mined. Bech offered himself as a vehicle for experiences only a literary man could have, and for the city man I had once hoped to be. A single long story, "Bech in Czech," came to me in 1987, five years after *Bech Is Back* had closed the book on this character. The only way to get that lone straggler into hardcovers seemed to be to write a third Bech book, which I sat down to do, letting the stories run longer than saleable length, though one of them, "Bech Noir," appeared in a cut version in *The New Yorker*. Bech, who was born in 1923, is into his seventies now, but defies death in a way Harry Angstrom could not. Harry lived through his senses, his intuitions, and his body; Bech lives for words, which suffer neglect and misprision but not certifiable death. In *Bech at Bay*, the author's past, very sketchy at first, takes on (I hope) substance—a dislocated, dreaming youth, an annealing experience of war, a Greenwich Village apprenticeship, a disabling initial success. He is the writer in me, creaking but lusty, battered but undiscourageable, fed on the blood of ink and the bread of white paper. The pleasure of dealing with him again, and having Arnold Roth create another frisky book jacket, could not be resisted, so here he is again, Bech at bay, even *passé*, seventy-five if a day, but my heart's irrepressible darling.

An INTERVIEW *conducted by Henry Bech, apropos of* Bech at Bay, *for the* New York Times, *March 1, 1999.*

One—not the only one—of the spiritual burdens of being a New Yorker is an undue reverence for the *New York Times;* when a minion of that sacrosanct rag approached this above-signed ancient penman and asked him to interview, not for the first time, a writer a tad less ancient than he but inconveniently resident hundreds of miles up the Atlantic seaboard, I could not find it in my heart to say no. John Updike was the name of my designated victim, on the slender but penetrating excuse that he had chosen to perpetrate, in his impudence and ignorance, a book titled *Bech at Bay*, five tales full of fantastic details concerning the latter-day life of a Jewish American prosist bearing my once-good name.

My traducer's lonely aerie was not easy to locate, though I had been there once before, on a similar journalistic errand. North of Boston, the landscape becomes a drab pudding of rocks and conifers, of abandoned factories and clapboarded shacks boasting (the houses wear wooden badges, with names and dates) of pre-Revolutionary origins. The nondescript burg that gives Updike refuge lies, along the tattered coast, one urban notch north of the old China-trade port where Hawthorne once spun his dismal witcheries. Even in 1835, as I recall, Hawthorne felt that the good times, the majestic times of tall ships and tall Puritan hats, had gone by. And indeed today's autumnal air, with its dutiful postcard splash of flaming maples, savored of the mellowly bygone, of once-vital cultural impulses now subsided into the wide spatter of mock-Georgian educational institutions and reflexive liberal impulses which gives Massachusetts its all-Democrat representation in Congress.

Along a winding road that bisects a girls' college, past an iron fence that once stood guard before the summer residence of Henry Clay Frick, my nervous limo driver and I went; we travelled (if I may, in so self-reflective a piece, quote from my earlier account) "across some railroad tracks to what I presumed was the wrong side, where, after a few divagations into the driveways of indignant gentry, we eventually came upon the author, looking as elderly and vexed as his neighbors." Not quite "vexed" this time, perhaps—his step more hesitant, his white hair skimpier, Updike greeted me with a fraternal cordiality that I found, frankly, offensive. Though he lives, in the manner of suburban princelings, surrounded by foliating excrescences, this reporter did not beat about the bush. Pulling out my Zippo-sized tape recorder, I interrogated him as follows.

Q: How could you have done this to me?
A: This further book of your uproarious adventures? I love you, Henry—isn't that reason enough? You are the person I, once a woeful country boy, wanted to be: a New York writer, up to his ears in toxic fumes. But I came to the metropolis, inhaled, and fled. What remain of that ignominious episode are the words "New York" on my elder son's birth certificate, and you. You have stayed the course. I envy you. I envy you your city banter, your wised-up women, your dignified ennui, your underground ability to tell uptown from downtown and the express from the local. Me, aboard the subway, I find myself hurtling toward Harlem when I was aiming at Little Italy.
Q: John, you aren't trying. You're taking a disingenuous delight in this pose you have of being a hick. It excuses you from shouldering the discontents of civilization, from delivering, if I may say, the authentic depleted fin-de-siècle goods. Look at this so-called *Bech at Bay*. You really think I go about *mur*dering people? You really think I could sleep with the Latina paralegal assistant of my attorney in Los Angeles when I was being sued by some quite implausibly loathsome talent agent? You think I go about jumping on women like that?
A: (*ominously*): People do.
Q: (*brushing past the obvious hot topic*): And this Jewishness you give me. What do you know about being Jewish? *Très peu*, I venture to estimate. As much as you learned listening to the Jack Benny program back in Shillington, P-A. Ask Cynthia Ozick. Ask Leon Wieseltier. Ask Orlando Cohen.
A: Cohen is my invention. Don't internalize your critics, Henry. It's death to the creative spirit. It breeds fictional tirades.
Q: You're no more Jewish than Henry Adams, and not near as funny about it.

A: It is my American right to give it a try, even in today's strident climate of defensive diversity. To be a writer at all, it seemed to me, is to be to some extent Jewish—outsiderish but chosen, condemned to live not by your inherited property but by your wits. Anyway, Henry, I don't see you as a *Jewish* writer. I see you as a Jewish *writer,* all but overwhelmed by the awesome possibilities of our oft-trivialized profession. Like the whiskey priest in *The Power and the Glory*—no matter how bad it gets, he can still put God in men's mouths. We can still put truth in men's heads. We share that—yes?—that boyish awe?

Q: I'll ask the questions, thanks. What I got out of your five tales, skimming through the galleys on the Shuttle—a bumpy flight, by the way, especially over Providence—wasn't so much awe as terminal discouragement. If this is the literary life, give me *le silence éternel de ces espaces infinis* anytime.

A: It's true, the life isn't what it seemed in the tweedy days of Thornton Wilder and Bennett Cerf. And you reach an age when every sentence you write bumps into one you wrote thirty years ago. Each hard memory has only so many bits. The enterprise has ever been thin, a mere dusting of words on the surface of the unsaid. That silence you mention always hangs on the other side of the paper. Still, in my limited experience, the barrel bottom remains moist; there has invariably been one more thing to say. Last summer, for me, you were it. I missed you. I missed New York. I had one leftover story, about Czechoslovakia, that came too late for *Bech Is Back*, and wrote some to go with it, to make a book, a quasi-novel. You were my one more thing, and now here we are; I am yours.

Q: (*grudgingly*): That's cute, I guess.

A: (*discourteously*): Excuse me now, but I must trim these here goldanged bushes.

FOREWORD *to my own bibliography, as compiled by Jack De Bellis and Michael Broomfield (Oak Knoll Press, 2007).*

Somewhere (was it in *Time* magazine?) the great Calvinist theologian Karl Barth said of the afterlife that he thought of it as *this* life, viewed under the aspect of eternity. If so, it seemed to me a rather comfortless recycling; but now that I have, in this huge and fanatically detailed bibliography, something of the sort—my life in print viewed under the aspect of definitive inventory—I acknowledge some comfort. It comforts me to see that even those shreds of praise called blurbs, gouged out of a published book review or dragged from a weak-willed writer by the claims of friendship, did not die with the jackets they momentarily adorned but are lifted into the Paradise of scholarly record by the angelic De Bellis and Broomfield. The same vigilant guardians, with their flaming swords and twittering computers, have also assembled, of a size (but not, I hope, a worth) virtually equal to that of the fruit of my own purgatorial labors, an Inferno of reviews by other pens; within these everlasting covers I am forever joined with my critics, however harshly dismissive and blithely inaccurate many of them may have been. My consolation is that their scribbled notices are available only within the crumbling archives of, in many cases, remote and ephemeral journals, whereas the wise and kind firm of Alfred A. Knopf, Inc., which first published me in 1959 and has gamely continued ever since, maintains a generous number of my titles in print. Knopf has further indulged my own compulsive bibliographical bent by letting me re-collect my poetry and early short stories, with dates of composition (as opposed to the sometimes delayed and wayward dates of publication) painstakingly compiled by me from manuscripts held in Harvard's Houghton Library, in the two volumes *Collected Poetry 1953–1993* and *The Early Stories 1953–1975*.

My instinct of self-preservation is strong; Knopf has also allowed me, beginning with *Assorted Prose* in 1965, five increasingly, embarrassingly bulky collections of non-fictional prose—articles, speeches, book reviews, humorous essays, introductions to myself and others, brief squibs in response to editors' demands and then "tweezered," to quote one sardonic reviewer of such a collection, "into immortality"—not to mention a book of pieces on golf and two of art reviews. May every author be as thoroughly published, and as conscientiously bibliographed, as I have been. In my most far-reaching flights of boyhood daydreaming I never imagined a book such as this, which leaves almost no word I put into print, or on tape, or videotape, unaccounted for.

Professor De Bellis, author of an earlier bibliography and of *The*, yes, *John Updike Encyclopedia* (2000), has been with me more years than I can count, providing me with the sometimes eerie though flattering sensation of being observed as scrupulously as, if the Gospels are to be believed, the fall of a sparrow. De Bellis is not merely a fellow-Pennsylvanian: he is an adopted son of Allentown, a city always regarded with envy by those of us born in the locale of Reading, a larger but less snappy and prosperous burg. Michael Broomfield, a resident of another heartland of mine, New York City, is the most zealous, I think, of my collectors—he is certainly the one most frequently in touch with me, to explore some nuance of my assorted oeuvre.

And why, the reader is entitled to ask, has this oeuvre been so copious and various? In my own impression of my work habits, I am more steady than speedy. I could not afford to be especially sensitive to the fluctuations of inspiration, since I had early thrown myself into the role of free-lance writer, with no other professional duties, including the deceptively congenial ones of a teacher, to excuse me from my desk and a daily production. My initial ambition, as I have said in all too many of the interviews dutifully listed within these covers, was to be a cartoonist, a limner in ink on Bristol board. At college my yearnings turned somewhat literary, but in the direction, still, of magazines—their glossy covers, their fleeting but flashy life on the drugstore racks. The aloofer aspirations of the committed novelist and the career poet were beyond me even after I began, in the years after college, to break into print. To this day I remain highly susceptible to the siren call of periodical publication; it pays, and seems real to me—a participation in the nation's flow of discourse and entertainment, though the number of magazines where I want to appear, and that want me, has dwindled sharply since the 1950s. At the same time, beginning with my exposure to the Linotype presses of the *Reading Eagle*, where I worked for some summers, and to the then-busy binderies of that city, I have admired the physical operations of the print industry, and have thus happily participated in the production of the limited editions and broadsides that lengthen this bibliography and keep my little band of faithful collectors on their toes. This bibliography, even so, is not a closed book, though the closing can't be far off.

I could have helped a little more, I now realize with a guilty pang. My own archives consist of shelves of my books, foreign and domestic, in my home, particularly two shelves that hold often-handled first editions of my fifty-odd volumes marked up with corrections that have been made in later printings or that I hope will some day be made. Upstairs, in a storage room, four cardboard boxes contain over fifty years of tearsheets from magazines. I could, for the benefit of my bibliographers, have delved more deeply into these brittle, slippery, yellowing stacks, which contain many an oddment and all my unsigned contributions, mostly from 1955 to 1968, to *The New Yorker*'s Talk of the Town section. The worthiest of these last, in my judgment, have been salvaged in my books—chiefly *Assorted Prose* and the limited but handsome *Talk from the Fifties*—and the rest can be forgotten. Something, after all, must be forgotten, or nothing can be remembered; forgetfulness is the writer's great internal editor. I have given De Bellis and Broomfield information when I could easily produce it, and even when it was not so easy, but this bibliography is their creation, not mine. The satisfactions of creating a bibliography surely include those of independent research and discovery, while the sulky, distracted author tries to put everything he has already written behind him. My old friend John Cheever once shocked me by declaring that he didn't have a single copy of his books in his house; he had given them away. I, less pure and resolute in disdaining the vain backward glance, confess to being secretly fortified, in forging ahead, by the remarkable gift of attention bestowed by the patient compilers of this inventory.

THREE BRITS: *Fond tributes, the one to Tina Brown written on the occasion of her abruptly leaving* The New Yorker *in July of 1998 and never before published; the one to Frank Kermode contributed to a "liber amicorum" for him, published under the title* There Are Kermodians *by Everyman in 1999; and the one to André Deutsch read by Diana Athill at his memorial service in July of the year 2000.*

A magazine draws its vitality from its editor's, and for these six years of Tina there has been no lack of life at the top. She came in with a mandate—indeed, a responsibility—to shake things up, and shake she did; the bigger type, the photographs, the topical covers, the shuffled and reshuffled Talk of the Town were all shocks which an elderly contributor and faithful reader could only hope were, like electroconvulsive therapy and cold baths, ultimately beneficial. She, a petite female of the type the British call "sparky," fielded the flak with a smile and radiated faith that the cure would take. Many of her innovations will certainly take; there is no going back: *The New Yorker* will remain leaner, franker, hipper, saucier, gutsier than she found it. She made it more woman-friendly and celebrity-friendly. She upped its beat; she tried to bring a stately old galleon to the responsive sleekness of a racing sloop. The captain wore a little black dress, and when you saw her flitting through the shining pale halls of the magazine's new offices you marvelled at all those directives and renovating energy flowing from a figure so personally unassuming, disarmingly direct, and readily amused. She was warm, quick, and alert in a way no male American could have managed; her warmth was the source of a hopefulness and esprit de corps new to a magazine traditionally produced by morose, reclusive wordsmiths tapping behind closed doors in a mood of wry disgruntlement. The final weekly product of all that murky solitude was, among other things, fun; Tina brought the fun into the production process, into the publicity process, and decreed a party atmosphere. Her party in these offices is over, but its brave vibrations linger into the new dawn.

* * *

To an American author, English reviews arrive after the fact, when the book's native fate has been decided and more than enough critical discourse on its merits and defects has been absorbed; nevertheless, even tardy bees can sting or make honey. For years I was aware of Frank Kermode as the best of English book reviewers—one who never fell into the cozy vice of cattiness or the shrillness that comes too easily to clever people dealing, in the British fashion, with half a dozen titles for an allotted eight hundred words and even fewer pounds sterling, and one who seemed purposed neither to inflate the author nor to cut him down to a predetermined size. A bibliophiliac geniality tempered his complaints, and a professorial solemnity tempered his enthusiasm. In the vanity fair of literary journalism he played the just, calm, omniscient man. And so it was that, during one of Kermode's fits of teaching in our Cambridge, the one in Massachusetts, I grilled a friend who had had him to dinner about the attributes of this paragon, and was astonished to be told that he appeared to be "perfectly nice," "rather quiet," and even (the sense if not the phrase was here) "cheerfully ordinary."

Years later, in London in the late Sixties, I was personally to experience this phenomenon, of great erudition and cerebral flair carried modestly, even meekly. In his autobiographical writings he dwells upon his origins outside the English isle as a Manxman, and his murmurous social diffidence, his gentle lightness of manner, and the ruthless sharpness of his mind all derive, one guesses, in some way, from that small outlying home, that fragment of old Viking empire east of Northern Ireland. He is, for all his decorum, an invader, a rogue, marking his career with a certain restlessness and moments of rebellion. With admirable extracurricular energy he has persisted in keeping one voice active in the popular press and another actively enunciating scholarly discriminations of a fine abstruseness, arriving at conclusions that seem unarguable—indeed, just what we would have concluded, had we troubled to know all that, or goaded ourselves to read this closely.

His sympathetic temperament, with its subversive undertow, declares itself in his love of the poets of the English Renaissance and in his concern, not quite loving, with the wrinkled, wormholed texture of the Bible, a text whose traditional claims upon close human study are quite obsolete for him, though for over two thousand years they generated a wealth of glosses that suit his intricate investigative purposes. He has the ability, anachronistic in an age of a haughty, dismissive criticism that lords it over authors as the unwitting tools of past oppressions and misconceptions, to confess puzzlement, and to make his puzzling fruitful for the reader. I think, offhand, of his close focus, in his consideration of *King Lear*, upon the brief exchange between Edgar and Gloucester whose most famous phrase, "Ripeness is all," takes a flicker of possible intonations from its Shakespeareanly crammed context: "Perhaps the lesson," Kermode speculates, "isn't that 'ripeness is all,' but only that as long as you can still say that (or anything else), you have to hurry along, get on with life." With a naïveté beyond wisdom, Kermode wonders, in one of his guarded but charming pieces of self-description, why George Herbert hit upon a certain word, this inscrutable but successful choice containing the secret of poetry. The concepts of secrecy and error occur in his titles and recur in his works; the something finally unfathomable and indeterminate in Shakespeare constitutes, in Kermode's attentive readings, the mark of the playwright's inexhaustible (from the standpoint of critics) genius.

In his autobiography *Not Entitled*, Kermode describes his inability to write a novel (a deficiency of presumption, I would say, rather than of any other qualities), but the openness, the questingness, the several-sidedness of his criticism approach the courage and joy of creativity. His analyses enlarge rather than diminish, and heal rather than dissect. One of the first critics in the English-speaking world to grasp the import and worth of structuralism and its successor French modes of thought, he found himself compelled, in his long prologue to *An Appetite for Poetry*, to defend the continuing humanistic value of the canonical classics and literary studies against deconstruction's radical devaluations and the absurd curricula that politically hip faculties offer the student body instead. Even in defense of what is most precious to him, however, so surprisingly and drastically undermined in recent decades by those ostensibly enlisted to preserve and expound it, Kermode's tone is level, respectful of the need for theory and renovation, and only incidentally wry.

Sharing on a few extended occasions proximate localities, and second wives who had much to say to each other, Kermode (accented on the first syllable, I learned) and I found ourselves with opportunities to make mutual observations if not confessions. Men with access to other means of self-expression tend to hold their tongues. Most of what I know about him I learned from reading his written words. As one who perpetually feels guilty at not serving in our century's central crusade, which ended when I was thirteen, I am always aware of Frank's five years of wartime service, sailing seas shared with "people ruthlessly dedicated to the idea of ripping you apart or drowning you." Yet he is a funny man. A sudden slant smile seems to announce the realization that he is standing on a tipping deck. The years have translated the uncertainties of his provincial childhood and imperilled young manhood into a graceful diffidence, a mannerly light armor proof against the shocks and deficits of old age.

As long as he can write for print, a high standard is being upheld in at least his instance. Decent devotion to literary merit and a humble and tenacious will to understand and explicate the best examples of it would not seem to be unattainable virtues, but this babbling, dumbed-down age makes them harder to attain than formerly, and their exponents rarer, with a touch now of the embattled heroic. Frank Kermode, for many of us, is a hero.

My first meeting with André Deutsch was under circumstances that he considered, I know from having heard him tell the story, dramatic. We met, back in 1960, in his hotel room in the Boston Ritz while we waited for my then wife to telephone word from our suburban home as to whether or not Victor Gollancz would publish, uncensored, a novel of mine called *Rabbit, Run*. André had read the American proofs on a plane to Istanbul and knew that Gollancz was balking at what would now seem quite innocuous sexually explicit bits. André was rather bafflingly but ingratiatingly enthusiastic about my book and greatly pleased when word came through that he was, as far as Victor Gollancz was concerned, welcome to it. He described himself later as immensely nervous during our suspenseful hour together, but I remember him as smooth, affable, amusing, and youthful. My American publisher, Alfred A. Knopf, had described André to me as a promising young fellow on the British publishing scene, and in all our years of association he remained young in my mind—energetic, buoyant, impulsive, overcommitted, and prepared to take the world as a festival open for business all days of the year.

I remember once in New York, having given me dinner, he insisted on propelling me into the bright hazard of Times Square, so he could inspect some electronic, digital watches that were a novelty on the market and on sale on Broadway at midnight. As I recall, I was the one who ended up buying one, not he. In London, lording it over his domain in its several adjacent, charmingly cramped buildings on Great Russell Street, he presented another face of enterprise, André Deutsch Ltd., where minions at his bidding sped and books piled up in the corners. His was a tasteful, high-minded, but thrifty operation, and of the many Americans that he published in the Fifties and Sixties I was one of the few who stuck with him to the end. And why not? His editions were handsome, with sometimes wildly inventive jackets, and he brought out what I wrote, not just the novels but poems and material as outré as a long play, heavy with appended apparatus, about an American President obscure even to

Americans. As with *Rabbit, Run*, he didn't blink. In addition, he was a friend, a fellow-Londoner for a year, a not infrequent American visitor, and a skilled photographer who for years used on his jackets a photo he had snapped of me with my face swollen from my first tooth implant.

He combined, in unpredictable proportions, a cheerful heedlessness with a truly tender, protective side. In my last glimpse of him, he and his lovely Gwen had taken me out to dinner in one of their haunts and, on returning to the parking garage, he realized that he had quite forgotten where he had parked the car. Parking cars was one of André's enterprises; during a visit to Florence that had me along, he spent most of his time ingeniously stashing his little rented Fiat in nooks and crannies where the Florentine police would not, he felt, find it. There he and Gwen stood, as I remember the moment, looking a bit like children dressed up for a party but lost amid the dripping concrete layers of the parking garage, she calm and radiant in her confidence that André would think his way out of this fix. And, of course, he did. Bless you, André, for all your clever kindness.

AN ACCOUNT *of my childhood reading composed for the* New York Times, *and appearing in print there on July 4, 1965. It reappeared on the* Times Internet Web site *in 1997; I had quite forgotten it, but it rings truer than any of the too-numerous later attempts of mine to describe my childhood reading, no doubt because the memories were fresher, and at age thirty-three I was fresher altogether.*

My reading as a child was lazy and cowardly, as it is yet. I was afraid of encountering, in a book, something I didn't want to know. Perhaps my earliest literary memory is my fear of the spidery, shadowy, monstrous illustrations in a large deluxe edition of *Alice in Wonderland* that we owned. A little later, I recall being appalled, to the point of tears, by a children's version of the Peer Gynt legend in an infernal set of volumes designed for the young, called *The Book House*. I also remember, from the same set, a similar impression of pain, futility, and crabbed antiquity conveyed by an account of Shelley's boyhood. I read both these things when I was sick in bed, a usually cheerful time for me.

Still later, in the fifth or sixth grade, I was enticed into reading, for my own good, *The Adventures of Tom Sawyer*. The adventure in the cave with Injun Joe chasing Tom and Becky gave me lasting claustrophobia and a dread of Mark Twain, beside whom Poe and Melville seem good-humored optimists. O. Henry was the only recommended author unreal enough for me to read with pleasure. Having deduced that "good" books depict a world in which horror may intrude, I read all through my adolescence for escape. From the age of twelve I had my own user's card to the Reading (Pennsylvania) Public Library, a beautiful, palatial haven; for don't misunderstand me, I loved books—their bindings, their order, their fragrance. I read all the books the library had by Erle Stanley Gardner, Ellery Queen, Agatha Christie, and John Dickson Carr, in that order. Also humorists: Benchley, Thurber, Stephen Leacock, Perelman. Fifty books by P. G. Wodehouse I must have consumed; when I go back to Reading I sometimes visit the library and marvel at the shelf. Science fiction just barely escaped being too alarming; I read of it copiously until its implications—of time and space so vast that the individual life is as nothing—began to sink in.

With such books, and with streams of magazines, I dissipated my youth, while my contemporaries were feasting on classics. I could hear them gnawing joyfully all around me. But I, I had a narcotic need for newness, modernity, in books; dead authors threatened to drag me down with them. Oh, I tried to break my bad habits. Once I borrowed *The Waste Land*, having seen it mentioned in *The New Yorker* as a modern classic, and found its opacity pleasingly crisp, though my greatest pleasure may have been the feeling of me, a mere fourteen-year-old, checking it out of the library.

My last vivid boyhood fright from books came when I was fifteen: I was visiting my uncle and aunt in Greenwich, Connecticut, and, emboldened by my success with *The Waste Land*, I opened their copy of *Ulysses*. The whiff of death, of God's death, that came off those remorseless, closely written pages overwhelmed me. So: back to soluble mysteries, as in mystery novels, and to jokes that were not cosmic. My inability to read bravely as a boy had this advantage: when I went to college, I was a true *tabula rasa*, and received gratefully the imprint of my instructors' opinions, and got good marks.

Now I find my greatest reading luxury is a small book, between one and two hundred pages, which treats, in moderately technical language, a subject of which I was previously ignorant. I think of, with great pleasure, the Pelican book by Sir Leonard Woolley on his Sumerian excavations, and a treatise, in the same series, on the English badger. Lately I have enjoyed an exhilarating study of suicide in Scandinavia.

A RESPONSE *to the question "Who have been your Masters?" from* The Yale Literary Magazine, *in February 2000.*

I am at the point where I have answered some standard questions so often I have come to doubt the truth of my answers. I read James Thurber, Robert Benchley, Agatha Christie, Ellery Queen, and John Dickson Carr as a boy with great happiness and total immersion in the text: does this make them Masters? At college—another than Yale—I majored in English and specialized in the poetry of the English Renaissance, including of course the plays of Shakespeare, but also was grateful for courses in the Romantic poets, the modern poets, George Bernard Shaw, and Tolstoy and Dostoevsky: does that make these masters my (your cap) Masters? To this day I don't read a book without finding something in it to admire and covet. (While James Joyce was going blind, I remember reading somewhere, he read *Gentlemen Prefer Blondes,* by Anita Loos.) But, when asked such a question, I generally name two writers I took to after college—Henry Green, whom my then wife and I discovered in our year at Oxford (1954–55), and Marcel Proust, whom I began to read, in my wife's sun-lotion-spotted copy of *Swann's Way,* in New York City in 1955. Both quite bowled me over, showing me what words could do, in bringing reality up tight against the skin of the paper, and I credit their examples with a considerable expansion of my literary ambitions. But in fact I had become a published writer (in *The New Yorker*) before I read either, so it wasn't as if I were totally comatose while waiting for the kiss of Mastery. As to their styles creeping into mine, I would welcome it, and indeed did welcome it. My homely American material was so different from their milieux that I felt no danger of duplication.

A RESPONSE *to the request of Michael Dirda, of* Book World, *for books that serve as comfort—especially needed, it was suggested, in the wake of September 11, 2001.*

For comfort and for energization when spirits drift low I turn to Shakespeare, less often in the portly blue double-column *Complete Works* edited by George Lyman Kittredge, acquired by me as textbook for the invaluable Harvard course taught by Harry Levin in the early 1950s, than in individual paperbacks, light in the hand and as easy to pack as a pillbox. Each play can be read in a handful of hours; the oeuvre as a whole always holds a play never before read or a favorite half forgotten. Recently I read *Titus Andronicus* for the first time and reread *As You Like It*, the first so repellently violent and rough-hewn, the second such a fine-spun, high-flying piece of poetry and feminism. How could I have forgotten how it is Touchstone who says, of his future wife, "a poor . . . thing, but mine own" and how the wronged Duke decrees that "Sweet are the uses of adversity"? Or never before noticed marvellous lines like Jacques's "Motley's the only wear" and Rosalind's "Do you not know I am a woman? When I think, I must speak"? Four centuries later, Shakespeare is still our literature's master entertainer, truth-teller, surpriser, and consoler.

A RESPONSE *to* GQ*'s request, in 1999, to select my favorite year of the disappearing century.*

Nothing much happened in 1946, which was the beauty and wonder of it. For years, the newspaper headlines had been screaming of defeats and victories, of Pacific islands and European cities that most Americans had never heard of but which were suddenly way stations in a life-and-death struggle. I remember, that year, surprise at the look of newspapers with only one or two column heads—the look of peacetime, with its minor bickering and local catastrophes. Oh, of course there was still news; things still happened. Civil war raged in China; Trygve Lie was elected Secretary-General of the United Nations; twelve top Nazis were sentenced to death in the war-crimes trials at Nuremberg—serve the bastards right. Winston Churchill announced in Missouri that an iron curtain had fallen across Europe, and on this side of it the Communist Party won a plurality in French elections. With wartime freezes lifted, American workers went on strike—two hundred thousand at General Electric, seven hundred fifty thousand in the steel industry, four hundred thousand coalworkers. Truman seized the coal mines and threatened to seize the railroads.

Crises real enough, but modest when measured against World War II and almost overlookable in the euphoria of the first full postwar year. The armed forces went from eleven million to one million in strength, the birth rate jumped twenty percent, the cost of living was up thirty-three percent over 1941. But the physical look of the country had scarcely changed since the Depression took hold around 1930. The cities had stolid downtowns built of brick and granite, with trolley cars and movie palaces; the small towns had family grocery stores and Main Streets shaded by elms. Outside the towns, farmland stretched darkling under a light skein of railroad tracks and two-lane roads. Hope and Crosby were still stars of screen and radio; Ingrid Bergman and Betty Grable and Greer Garson triangulated the possibilities of femininity; *The Best Years of Our Lives* dominated the Academy Awards. The Dow-Jones had a high of 212 and a low of 165. It was a world of backyard gardens, of men wearing sweat-stained fedoras and suspenders, of Flag Day and give-away cigarettes and Dish Night at the movies. The GIs had fought to keep this world intact.

But postwar would not be pre-war. In 1946, RCA began to sell television sets, with ten-inch screens. United Airlines announced the purchase of jets for commercial use. At Harvard, a giant electronic computer, ENIAC, computed a thousand times faster than humans could. In Paris, a bathing suit called the bikini debuted. In Las Vegas, Bugsy Siegel opened the Flamingo. Big bands broke up. Skirts went down. *The Outlaw*, starring Jane Russell in a Howard Hughes–designed uplift bra, was released in defiance of the production code. In Mississippi, blacks for the first time voted in the Democratic primary. As to me, I was all of fourteen, and my family for the first time since my early childhood owned an automobile. There were brand-new cars on the road, with wooden sides and Jeeplike frames. Butter and sugar were back on the shelves; ration tokens and coupons were gone. Nineteen forty-six was a year after everything had happened, and also the year before everything that would follow. It felt triumphant, to be an American.

SUMMER LOVE: *A brief meditation on this familiar topic for the chronically revived* Life *magazine, in July 2005.*

The heart melts in the heat and everything seems lovable. From the ages of five to thirteen, in Shillington, Pennsylvania (pop. 4,900), I spent my summers at a playground a few steps from the bottom of our backyard. You came out through our big privet hedge and crossed a little unpaved alley topped in small gray stones to a narrow cornfield with paths worn through it; on the other side of the corn rows you came to the town's school property, acres of it, enough to hold a football gridiron with a cinder track around it, a softball field, and, to the right, with bigger bleachers and a grassier outfield, a hardball field. The diamond had been excavated from a small hill, with steep banks on both the first- and third-base sides, and on top of the first-base slope stood the playground, on a kind of mesa, with an open-sided pavilion, a basketball stanchion, two slides, a set of three swings, a roundabout that you pushed and could make you sick with dizziness, a sandbox, a box for box hockey, and, off to the side toward another, bigger cornfield, two wooden outhouses, one for girls and one for boys.

Every morning, having eaten my Rice Krispies—which in those impressionable years almost deafened me with their snap, crackle, and pop—I set off down through our yard, past the long grape arbor with its angrily buzzing traps for Japanese beetles, toward the playground, my heart beating as fast as a lover's. You saw pretty much the same children at the playground day after day, and half of them were girls. They had sun-browned legs and wiry bodies; in the winter I walked to school with these same girls through the fallen leaves and horse-chestnut pods, the winter snows, the spring mud and showers. But they bewitched me most in summer, when they wore least clothes, and were the most idle and lackadaisical—partners in the mild crime of killing time, amid the squeak of swing chains and the click of Chinese checkers in the pavilion's shade. Now some are dead and some are sick and some have moved out of Pennsylvania, but they are with me still, the pre-pubescent nymphs of romantic summertime.

In that latitude the temperature flirted with a hundred degrees for a few of the dog days, but to a child it can hardly ever be too hot. I liked the sun licking the backs of my legs, and the sweat between my shoulder blades, and the violet evenings, with ice cream and fireflies, wherein the long day slowly cooled. I liked the ants piling up chewed dirt like coffee grounds between the bricks of our walk, and the milkweed spittle in the vacant lot next door. I liked the freedom of shorts, sneakers, and striped T-shirt, and I liked the way I looked in the mirror, with freckles and a short hot-weather haircut. We love easily in summer, perhaps, because we love our summer selves.

THE BEAUTIFUL: *Words on the topic extracted from me by* Allure.

The beautiful is, from one perspective, simply what we need—a meal to the hungry, a bed to the weary, another body to the lusty. From a different perspective, appreciation of beauty is empathy with a creator. Vermeer's little *Young Woman Standing at a Virginal*, for instance, in London's National Gallery, is a cool and muted work of minimal dramatic content, and yet, the last time I saw it, it seemed to me very possibly the most beautiful painting in the world, in the way the painter's brush evenly masters every surface (silk dress, pearl necklace, velvet chair seat, red ribbons, marbled virginal sides, plaster wall, baseboard tiles, paintings within paintings, gleaming nubbled gold frame, alert and enigmatic face with greenish skin) and provides, without any virtuosic fuss, the illusion of atmosphere. The young woman stands in a space that receives light and cushions it. This is the ordinary world re-created by a human hand and eye, and our sense of the beautiful becomes a kind of awed applause at another human being's extreme and tender skill.

A RESPONSE *to a request, from a Miss Gordon, in May of 1997, for a kiss from my work. I never heard from Miss Gordon again. My ardor may have frightened her off.*

Dear Ms. Gordon:
  Here is a kiss from a short story called "Flight," written in 1959:

> On the upstairs landing, as I went to turn into my room, Molly came forward with a prim look and kissed me. With clumsy force I entered the negative space that had been waiting. Her lipstick smeared in little unflattering flecks into the skin around her mouth; it was as if I had been given a face to eat, and the presence of bone—skull under skin, teeth behind lips—impeded me. We stood for a long time under the burning hall light, until my neck began to ache from bowing. My legs were trembling when we finally parted and sneaked into our rooms.

The protagonists are teen-agers, and the boy at least is sexually pretty innocent. While not his first kiss, it is perhaps the first passionately felt one, which begins his first passionate relationship. The image "as if I had been given a face to eat" has stuck in my mind, as an expression of the cannibalistic strangeness of kissing—this avid pressing upon another of the organ whereby we eat, talk, cough, and spit, as if the mouth is an essence of ourselves. Later in the story the narrator lovingly mentions "the way her lower lip was like a curved pillow of two cloths, the dusty red outer and wet pink inner." In love we fetishize the other's lips, feet, eyes, hair, seeking for a condensation of what we might call his or her soul. The kiss here is clumsy, and perhaps all acts of love are just stabs at saying what we mean. This kiss goes on and on, however, being not only a metaphor for sexual possession but delicious (as well as grotesque) in itself.

EARLY EMPLOYMENTS AND INKLINGS: *My first job.*

"You're hired": sweet words, in this world of getting and spending. I have heard them rather rarely; my last regular paycheck was issued when I was twenty-five and poised to anoint myself a self-employed writer. My first paying job that I can recall was swatting flies ten for a penny on my family's side porch. The pay rate, considering the number and sluggishness of Pennsylvania flies, seems high; perhaps I broke my employers' bank. Though I was keen and eager, at the age of six or so, the job did not open out into a career.

Next, at the age of twelve, I worked for a weekly pass to the local movie theatre. I and some six or eight other boys would gather at the Shillington, with its triangular marquee and slanting lobby, on Saturday mornings, and be entrusted with bundles of little tinted leaflets, folded once like a minimal book, advertising the week's coming attractions. Shows, some of them double features, changed every other day, and took Sundays off. Gangster films, musicals, Disney cartoons, romantic comedies, Abbott and Costello, Biblical epics—all offered a war-beset, Depression-minded America ninety minutes of distraction from its troubles. We boys were dispatched in pairs, some of us to territories as remote as Mohnton and Sinking Spring, and scampered up and down the concrete steps of hilly Pennsylvania to leave our slithering beguilements on expectant porches where tin boxes held empty milk bottles and rubber mats said in raised letters WELCOME. When the leaflets were gone—some very bad boys, it was rumored, would dump theirs down a storm drain—we returned to the theatre for our magic pass. More than once, to save the seven cents the movie-house proprietor had given us for the trolley car, my partner and I would saunter the several miles back to Shillington, between the gleaming tracks.

Next, a dark chapter. I must have been sixteen when I was deemed eligible to work in a lens factory in the gritty city of Reading. They were sunglass lenses, at least in our end of the plant—they came mounted on hemispheres fitted, in turn, onto upright hubs that held them under rotating caps in a long trough full of a red liquid abrasive called "mud." They had to be changed every twenty minutes, as I remember; I was always falling behind, and a foreman kept coming around to chalk rejection marks—white "X"s—on my overcooked hemispheres, with their blank and slippery eyes. The red sludge got all over you, inexpungeably, into hair, ears, and fingernails. A wan, Dickensian boy about my age tried to teach me the ropes, but my only prowess emerged at the brief lunch break, when a country skill at quoits enabled me to outscore my malnourished, city-dwelling co-workers.

On the vast factory floor, various machines mercilessly thrummed around me, and my stomach churned. In my nervous moments of repose I smoked cigarettes, flipping the butts right onto the scarred old floor. I could smoke all I wanted; the jaded adults around me didn't care. But such compensation fell short: if this thrumming, churning misery marked the entrance to adulthood, childhood wasn't so bad. I quit after three days, promising my parents to work profitably instead at my strawberry patch on the farm to which we had moved. Agricultural labor is as mirthless as industrial, but the strawberry season lasted only three June weeks of straddling the wide rows, as the sun baked your bare back and daddy longlegses waltzed up your arms. For the rest of the summer I tried to write a mystery novel.

When I was eighteen, between high school and college, the editor of the *Reading Eagle* told me I was hired, as a summer copyboy. This was even better than swatting flies. It paid a bit better, too—thirty-four dollars and change in a small brown envelope every Friday. My duties were to hang around the editorial room, doing a breakfast run for the doughnut-prone, coffee-addicted staff and carrying copy into the Linotype room, where men in green eyeshades tickled the keyboards of the towering Mergenthaler Linotype machines. Their activity was noisily industrial, and smelled of hot lead and human confinement, but its product made sense to me. A copyboy's last duty of the day was to bring up a stack of fresh, warm newspapers (the *Eagle* was an afternoon paper) from the roaring pressroom and distribute them, with a touch of ceremony, to the editors, the reporters, and even the paper's owner, a local magnate who sat waiting in his grand front office. He always thanked me. I felt as much as he part of a meaningful process—a daily distillation, one more installment of life's ceaseless serial. This was my element, ink on paper.

MY PHILADELPHIA: *In response to a 1998 request for my impressions of the metropolis from a magazine called, not surprisingly,* Philadelphia.

To a child from the hills of Berks County in the 1930s and '40s, Philadelphia was an ominous blob on the horizon. It was highly dangerous there, the local rumors went, and even the water was bad. Philadelphia water was pure poison, we were told, and indeed from the look of the Schuylkill as it percolated through Reading upstream we could believe it. The Schuylkill was black with coal dust, great black dunes of which glistened in its center while it sluggishly moved under the Bingaman Street Bridge on its way to the City of Brotherly Love.

Contact with the poisoned metropolis was not entirely possible to avoid, however; for several summers my father commuted to Penn to get his master's degree, and, every summer, radio broadcasts of major-league baseball emanated from Shibe Park, where two last-place teams, the Phillies and the Athletics, alternated series before meagre crowds of what were widely agreed to be the rudest, loudest fans in the sport. Nevertheless, I listened, even keeping the box score as I stubbornly crouched, many a muggy afternoon, in the armchair next to our little Philco. We had moved, in the fall of 1945, from a small town three miles outside Reading to a farmhouse eleven miles south of it, and my most intense fanship fell in those first lonely years, before a driver's license gave me some freedom to seek out companionship off the airwaves. I rooted for Elmer Valo and Del Ennis, and in 1946 signed up for a midsummer bus trip to see the Athletics host the league-leading Boston Red Sox in a Sunday doubleheader. Ted Williams hit several home runs, one of which cleared the stands on a rising trajectory, but—such is the problematical nature of individual baseball contests—the Sox lost both games, and had their march to cinching the American League pennant (and eventually losing the World Series to the Cardinals) delayed by a day.

This happened *in* Philadelphia, but was it *of* Philadelphia? My parents had one Philadelphia friend; my mother's roommate at Ursinus had married a contractor who built houses block by block, adding his mite to the infinity of row houses in the north of the city. "Friends from Philadelphia" became the title of the first short story I sold to *The New Yorker*—a sense of sacred visitation gave the tale its excitement, for, as I say, Philadelphia was to us mostly a rumor from beyond the horizon. It was not until the advent of television that Philadelphia invaded, as it were, the rural innocence west of King of Prussia, and its news became our news, its crimes our crimes, its entertainments ours. For the first thirteen years of my life I lived on Philadelphia Avenue, in Shillington, without its ever occurring to me that the street, followed far enough—past the poorhouse, past the Jewish cemetery, through Gibraltar and Birdsboro— might actually lead, in the guise of Route 724, to Philadelphia.

My adult life has taken me there, now and then. Coming back by train from college in Massachusetts, I would have to kill a few hours on the city's sidewalks, sometimes well after midnight, before catching the Reading Railroad home. Flying south to visit my mother in her long widowhood, I would drive up the Schuylkill Expressway and observe how the city, in towers of greenish glass, was mounting ever higher above the once-sacrosanct altitude of William Penn's hat. Doing research on James Buchanan, Pennsylvania's lamented only President, I was entrusted with crucial documents from the secession crisis of 1860–61, in the reading room of the Historical Society of Pennsylvania, while modern Philadelphia seethed and honked below the windows. I have spoken at its Museum of Art, and been interviewed on WHYY, and seen my stepson graduate from Penn. But the visit most crucial to my development remains, I suppose, one in 1949 or 1950, when the old downtown Wanamaker's used to host an annual competition of high-school art, and some cartoons of mine won a blue ribbon. It was a sign of approval pinned in the heart of the metropolis. The exhibit of my contemporaries' work, as I remember it, was vast on that departed department-store floor, and proclaimed a precious secret: the blob on the horizon was art-friendly.

A RESPONSE *to the question of why do I live in New England, posed in this case by a fledgling journal called* The Improper Bostonian, *in 1999.*

Like many another auslander, I came here to college (Harvard) and, after testing the climate elsewhere, returned and stayed. I had married a Radcliffe girl, when there still *were* Radcliffe girls, and I thought she as well as I might prosper in the salt air and the cultural aftermath of Hawthorne and Whittier, Thoreau and Oliver Wendell Holmes. Foreign art movies were showing in Harvard Square back then, Ted Williams played left field for the Red Sox, and Cardinal Cushing ripped through the radio rosary like a buzz saw quartering a cedar of Lebanon. My objective was to see if, away from the energy-wasting, ego-eroding literary hustle of New York City, I could make my modest way as a free-lance writer, and it turned out, one year at a time, that I could. Also one year at a time, my children grew into New Englanders, and now have produced seven New England grandchildren, so that moving elsewhere, to fashionable venues like Florida or Montana, gets harder instead of easier.

When William Dean Howells left Boston for Manhattan in the 1890s, he took the last slant ray of the Emersonian heyday with him, but, in the century since, Boston has retained the aura of a place where civilization, if not dynamically generated, is affectionately regarded. Its brick raggletaggle bespeaks a horse-drawn past; its vast student population keeps even the mustiest neighborhoods young. Tucked in its northern suburbs, I have remained something of a Harvard boy, handing in term papers, but by mail to editors in New York. Boston's distance to New York seemed about right forty years ago and, though it has grown less, as a fifty-minute shuttle flight has replaced a five-hour train ride, still seems about right—within easy reach but beyond instant intimidation. New England is one of the oldest areas on the American map, yet, perhaps because so many have left it for flatter farmland and broader avenues, it still has space within it, where a man can breathe and a writer can write.

A RESPONSE *to a request from Weston M. Hill, Harvard '94, who in 2002 was putting together "a celebration and history of Harvard Dorm Life" and asked for "a story or poem (or even a photo) about [my] experience of living in Lowell House and/or in Hollis in the Yard."*

It was on the top floor of Lowell House, E-entry. My freshman roommate and I, juniors by now, had taken in a senior and a sophomore. The four of us lived in five rooms in a row, two tiny ones (the sophomore and I), then a living room, then two more bedrooms. The senior had a girlfriend, a serious red-haired girlfriend, and when he was in bed with her, the resident of the fourth room had to get into it by means of a usually locked door from the next suite. One day, our mole in the next suite was not there to effect the discreet detour, and, after much stewing and consulting with the sophomore and me, the resident of the far room knocked sharply on the door of the intervening *chambre du plaisir* and forced its inhabitant, clad in a white towel and a dark scowl, to open the door and let the excluded roommate pass through, skirting the bed where only some tousled red hair peeped above the covers.

Believe it or not, subsequent generations, this was pretty stirring stuff in 1953, worth days of discussion and reflection, days of sulking and reproach. But what strikes me now about this memory is that the three male principals—the lover, the adjacent roommate, and the adjacent-suite dweller—are all now dead, dead before seventy, after careers as, respectively, a CIA operative, a history professor/cultural critic, and an English instructor/poet. Only the sophomore, who became a potter in Rockport, Massachusetts, and I are left. The redhead lives on, in the dimension of a myth.

STATEMENT *for* Ethics, Literature, & Theory: An Introductory Reader, *edited by Stephen K. George (2005).*

It occurred to me, as a small child, that the artist adds something to the world and does no harm. A fiction writer's duty is to deliver reality as it has come to him—to describe the details, conflicts, and puzzles of being a live human being. Such a description not only entertains him (though it does do that) but broadens the sympathies and understanding of his or her readers. His "responsibilities to the work of art" are those of any craftsman to his product, polishing and shaping it to the point where it gives aesthetic delight. Such an endeavor is, to me, so self-evidently moral that posing the author as a preacher or his work as preachment fatally sullies something intrinsically pure. The author is a citizen and a social creature, and undoubtedly social impulses will figure in his fiction or poetry; the very act of self-expression indicates a wish to communicate, to share, to please, to influence. But his raison d'être is religious—homage to what is and gratitude for being alive, offered up with the directness and innocence of a child's crayon drawing.

MY CONTRIBUTION *to a series of brief statements on National Public Radio called* This I Believe. *So naked a topic made me shy, and I kept ignoring it, until a panicky call from NPR drove me to write this out in longhand on March 18, 2005, which happened to be my birthday.*

At the age of seventy-three I seem most heartily to believe in the human value of creative writing, whether in the form of verse or fiction, as a mode of truth-telling, self-expression, and homage to the twin miracles of creation and consciousness. The special value of these indirect methods of communication, as opposed to the value of factual reporting and analysis, is one of precision, oddly enough: the story or poem brings us closer to the intricate texture of experience. Imaginary people become realer to us than any named celebrity; celebrities are glimpsed in a series of rumored events whose causes and subtler ramifications must remain in the dark. An invented figure like Anna Karenina or Emma Bovary emerges fully into the light of our understanding, which brings with it identification, sympathy, and pity. Creative writing tests me to the limits of what I know and what I feel.

I also believe, instinctively if not very cogently, in the American political experiment, which I take to be at bottom a matter of trusting the citizens to know their own minds and vote their own interests. To govern with the consent of the governed—this spells the ideal, and though a totalitarian or oligarchic government can obtain some swift successes, in the end only a democracy can enlist a people's energy on a sustained and renewable basis. To guarantee the individual maximum freedom within a social frame of minimal laws ensures, if not happiness, its hopeful pursuit.

Cosmically, I seem to be of two minds. The power of materialist science to explain everything, from the behavior of the galaxies to that of molecules, atoms, and their submicroscopic components, can scarcely be doubted. Such science forms the principal achievement of the modern mind; its manifold technical and medical benefits are ours to enjoy. On the other hand, subjective sensations, desires, and, may we even say, illusions compose the substance of our daily existence, and religion alone, in its many forms, attempts to address and placate these. We are part of nature, and natural necessity compels and in the end dissolves us; yet to renounce all and any supernature, any appeal or judgment beyond the claims of matter and private appetite, leaves in the dust too much of our humanity, as through the millennia it has manifested itself in art and altruism, idealism and *joie de vivre*.

Index

Note: Italicized numerals indicate pages with illustrations. Boldface numerals indicate pages where the author and/or work is specifically the subject of a review or prose piece.

Illustration Credits

A Note About the Author

John Updike was born in 1932, in Shillington, Pennsylvania. He graduated from Harvard College in 1954, and spent a year in Oxford, England, at the Ruskin School of Drawing and Fine Art. From 1955 to 1957 he was a member of the staff of *The New Yorker,* and since 1957 has lived in Massachusetts. He is the father of four children and the author of sixty books, including collections of short stories, poems, essays, and criticism. His novels have won the Pulitzer Prize, the National Book Award, the American Book Award, and the National Book Critics Circle Award, the Rosenthal Award, and the Howells Medal. A previous collection of essays and reviews, *Hugging the Shore,* received the 1983 National Book Critics Circle Award for criticism.

A Note on the Type

The text of this book was set in a digitized version of Janson, a typeface long thought to have been made by the Dutchman Anton Janson, who was a practicing type founder in Leipzig during the years 1668–1687. However, it has been conclusively demonstrated that these types are actually the work of Nicholas Kis (1650–1702), a Hungarian, who most probably learned his trade from the master Dutch type founder Dirk Voskens. The type is an excellent example of the influential and sturdy Dutch types that prevailed in England up to the time William Caslon developed his own incomparable designs from them.

Composed by North Market Street Graphics,
Lancaster, Pennsylvania
Printed and bound by R. R. Donnelley,
Crawfordsville, Indiana